PEAK:

Introduction to Criminal Justice: Practice & Process

With this comprehensive and reader-friendly text by acclaimed author Kenneth J. Peak, students learn about core topics in criminal justice and how to solve problems they are likely to face on a variety of criminal justice career paths.

Peak: Introduction to Criminal Justice: Practice and Process PREPARES with Practical Career Coverage

When it comes to textbook content, career coverage ranks high in importance in our instructor and student surveys. Peak covers careers in both the printed textbook and online, and is the most comprehensive coverage available today!

In addition to career coverage throughout the text, "Practitioner's Perspectives" allow students to "hear" from professionals in the police, courts, and corrections discuss the nature of their work, academic preparation, and decisions they make every day.

PRACTITIONER'S PERSPECTIVE

FORENSIC SCIENTIST (CRIMINALIST)

Name: Renee Romero
Current position: Director, Forensic Science Division, Washoe County Sheriff's Office
City, state: Reno, Nevada
College attended/ academic major: Michigan State University/BA, chemistry, forensic science; University of Nevada, Reno/ MS, cell and molecular biology

How long have you been a practitioner in this criminal justice position? Since 1989—24 years

My primary duties and responsibilities as a practitioner in this position are:

Being responsible for the management of the Forensic Science Division at the Sheriff's Office. This entails managing budgets, planning for future forensic technology changes, and ensuring we are meeting our accreditation standards. Prior to becoming the director in 2008, I was a practicing forensic scientist (criminalist). While I have limited controlled substances experience, the majority of my experience is in the DNA field. The primary duty of a forensic scientist is to examine evidence from criminal cases. This evidence can range from drugs, firearms, toxicology, and DNA to shoe prints, tire tracks impressions, and latent fingerprints. A forensic scientist usually specializes in one specific discipline. After examining the evidence the forensic scientist must issue the findings to the investigating agency and then work with the district attorney's office to prepare for expert testimony when the cases go to trial.

The qualities/characteristics that are most helpful for one in this career are: Attention to detail, organization, and excellent communication skills.

In general, a *typical day* for a practitioner in this career would include:

Spending time in the laboratory examining evidence, reviewing findings, and writing reports. The day may be interrupted with changing priorities based on the investigative needs of new cases as they arise.

My advice to someone either wishing to study, or now studying, criminal justice to become a practitioner in this career field would be:

To obtain a scientific degree. If you believe you are interested in toxicology or controlled substances, then work toward a chemistry degree. If you think you are interested in the DNA field, then work toward a molecular biology degree—and you must also earn college credits in genetics, molecular biology, and biochemistry. The field of forensic science is getting more competitive, so obtaining a master's degree would be beneficial as well.

Computer technologies now assist police in investigating traffic crashes; this officer is using collision reconstruction software.

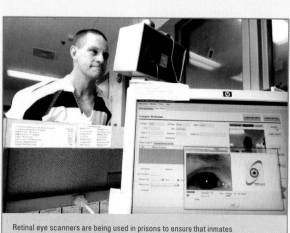

Retinal eye scanners are being used in prisons to ensure that inmates do not swap identities in order to escape.

Peak: Introduction to Criminal Justice: Practice and Process
PROVIDES Comprehensive Coverage with an Applied Focus

Comprehensive coverage stemming from author experience provides students with important trends, historical backgrounds, and practical lessons needed for a strong foundation to apply to future careers. Peak bridges the academic and practitioner perspectives with features that resonate with students.

> *"These features are very important in facilitating critical thinking among students. It helps them understand and apply the knowledge they have learned rather than simply memorizing material."*
>
> **—Richard Stringer,**
> *Old Dominion University*

Peak: Introduction to Criminal Justice: Practice and Process
CHALLENGES Student Misconceptions

ASSESS YOUR AWARENESS:

Test your knowledge of criminal justice fundamentals by first reading and responding to the following seven true-false items; check your answers after reading this chapter's materials.

1. Under the U.S. system of justice, people basically join together, form governments (thus surrendering their rights of self-protection), and receive governmental protection in return.

2. Very little if any political or discretionary behavior or authority exists in the field of criminal justice; its fixed laws and procedures prevent such influences.

3. "Three-strikes laws" basically refer to state statutes sentencing offenders with three qualifying felonies to a minimum of 25 years in prison.

4. All prosecutions for crimes begin with a grand jury indictment.

5. Police make the final decisions concerning the actual crimes with which a suspect will be charged.

6. *Parolee* is the term used to describe one who has served time in prison.

7. The U.S. system of criminal justice is intended to function, and indeed does function in all respects, like a "well-oiled machine."

Answers can be found on page 401.

Assess Your Awareness features begin each chapter

This text addresses student misconceptions with features such as Assess Your Awareness, which provides students accurate explanations of concepts and key terms.

"I really like the Assess Your Awareness in the beginning of each chapter. I think this section allows students to think about their own beliefs and see if their beliefs are rooted in fact. Additionally, this serves as a great assessment of understanding."

—Patrick Cundiff, *East Carolina University*

you be the... DETECTIVE

SUICIDE OR MURDER?

As the coach opened the door to the locker room, the only light that shone was from the players' large shower area. Upon flipping the light switch, he saw the body of his once "ace" pitcher, Hines, lying on the floor in the shower. In his pale left hand he held a gun. There was a bullet wound in his left temple. Under his tanned right hand was a note saying "My pitching days are gone, my debts and humiliation more than I can bear. Sorry." His nearby locker contained a half-empty bottle of beer, his uniform, an uneaten stadium hot dog, a picture of his two children, and his Acme-brand ball glove with "RH" stamped in the webbing. Wet footprints were observed walking in and out of the shower. Upon surveying the scene, the responding detective said "I do not believe this was a suicide."

1. What fact(s) led to this conclusion?

"I love the fact that in multiple places throughout the text the author works to dispel the myths of criminal justice system."

—Jon Maskaly, *East Carolina University*

Peak: Introduction to Criminal Justice: Practice and Process EMPHASIZES Ethics

Peak devotes an entire chapter to ethics, one of the fundamental issues in today's introductory criminal justice course. This text encourages students to think critically about ethics by examining policy issues in the news.

"The ethics chapter is not covered in my current text and this coverage is key to criminal justice."

—Jon Maskaly,
East Carolina University

"The bell, the book, and the candle" test can be used as a guide against making unethical decisions.

ETHICS TESTS FOR THE CRIMINAL JUSTICE STUDENT

Following are some tests to help guide you, the criminal justice student, to decide what is and is not ethical behavior[57]:

- *Test of common sense.* Does the act make sense, or would someone look askance at it?
- *Test of publicity.* Would you be willing to see what you did highlighted on the front page of the local newspaper?
- *Test of one's best self.* Will the act fit the concept of oneself at one's best?
- *Test of one's most admired personality.* What would one's parents or minister do in this situation?
- *Test of hurting someone else.* Will it cause pain for someone?
- *Test of foresight.* What is the long-term likely result?

Other questions that the officer might ask are "Is it worth my job and career?" and "Is my decision legal?"

Another tool is that of "the bell, the book, and the candle": Do bells or warning buzzers go off as I consider my choice of actions? Does it violate any laws or codes in the statute or ordinance books? Will my decision withstand the light of day or spotlight of publicity (the candle)?[58]

MEXICO: WHERE POLICE "ETHICS" MATTERS LITTLE

Mexico has long been involved in fighting an epidemic of corruption as drug cartels bribe poorly paid police officers and state officials.

Massive firings of police for corruption is not uncommon: In mid-2010 more than 3,200 Mexican federal police were fired for failing to do their work or being linked to corruption; of those, 465 were charged with crimes, and more than 1,000 officers faced disciplinary proceedings for failing confidence exams.[19] Another 500 officers were dismissed in late 2012 after failing tests specifically targeted at weeding out corrupt officials.[20]

The problem is real and goes beyond involvement in drug crime: Municipal officers have killed their own mayors, state jailers have assisted inmates who escape, federal agents are forced to rise up against corrupt commanders, and officers themselves have been murdered because they work for gangster rivals.[21]

Nor have substantial amounts of U.S. aid and training under the Mérida Initiative (a cooperative agreement between the governments of the United States and Mexico to combat drug trafficking,

Mexican police have long been known to engage in graft and corruption, as drug cartels have bribed and exploited many of the poorly paid officers.

organized crime, and money laundering) worked; Mexico's 32,000 federal police remain understaffed and replete with graft.

Peak: Introduction to Criminal Justice: Practice and Process ENCOURAGES Critical Thinking

Critical thinking is key to nearly every instructor's CJ course. Peak's features push students to fully engage while reading the text by presenting a number of student-centered scenarios. These activities demonstrate the application of concepts to a variety of policing situations to get students thinking critically.

> "I am particularly impressed with the coverage of the search-and-seizure concept and probable cause. The 'You be the ___' section does a fantastic job in explaining the often argued abstract concept that is probable cause."
>
> —**Jerry L. Stinson II,**
> *Southwest Virginia Community College*

LEARN BY DOING

1. You are a patrol sergeant lecturing to your agency's Citizens' Police Academy about the patrol function. Someone asks: "Sergeant, your officers obviously can't enforce all of the laws all of the time. Which laws are always enforced, and which ones are not?" How do you respond to her (without saying something absurd like "We enforce all of the laws, all of the time," which of course would be untrue)? How would you fully explain police discretion to the group?

2. The "Crime & Investigation Network," based in the United Kingdom, advertises on its website that it "investigates the darker corners of human life" and "offers viewers stories of real life crime" that "open the door to real crime labs, police archives and courtrooms, allowing

viewers to join detectives as they examine evidence and piece together clues." You can access and participate in solving a number of different crimes at http://www.crimeandinvestigation.co.uk/games/solve-the-murder.html.

3. For a practical view of traffic problems and solutions, go to http://www.popcenter.org/problems/street_racing/ and/or go to http://www.popcenter.org/problems/drunk_driving/. These are guides published by the federal Center for Problem-Oriented Policing. Read and describe the kinds of problems that are caused by illegal street racing and/or drunk driving. As importantly, consider what efforts are described in the guides that police are using to successfully address these problems.

Peak: Introduction to Criminal Justice: Practice and Process OFFERS a Broad, Contemporary Focus

Key trends, emerging issues, historical backgrounds, and practical lessons are provided for students to apply in their future careers.

FOCUS ON "STAND YOUR GROUND" LAWS

The fatal shooting of Trayvon Martin by George Zimmerman in Sanford, Florida, generated tremendous controversy because of its racial overtones and the state's "stand your ground" law; Zimmerman was acquitted in July 2013 for the shooting.

The killing in Florida of Trayvon Martin by George Zimmerman in February 2012 caused a major controversy that, by its nature, implicates the entire criminal justice system and binds the police and prosecutors under a controversial statute known as the "stand your ground" law, which essentially

expands the common law "castle doctrine" that allows a homeowner to use deadly force against an intruder. "Stand your ground" became law in Florida in 2005; at least 25 states have since enacted some version, extending the common law to the outside of one's home and to any other place where he or she has a right to be. Under the law, when killers state they acted in self-defense, they cannot be convicted of homicide unless it can be proven *beyond a reasonable doubt* (the highest legal standard) that the victim did not attack the killer. The laws were originally intended to give citizens a presumption of innocence when defending themselves, while also generally banning police from detaining someone if they have evidence that the shooter was attacked "in a place he had a right to be." Prosecutors largely despise the law because of the aforementioned burden of proof, while defense attorneys have found it to be a means of defending people who claim they had a right to meet force with force.

Source: John Arnold, "The Law Heard Round the World," *Time,* April 9, 2012, http://www.time.com/time/magazine/article/0,9171,2110471,00.html (accessed March 9, 2013); also see "Trayvon Martin Case (George Zimmerman)," *New York Times,* July 19, 2012, http://topics.nytimes.com/top/reference/timestopics/people/m/trayvon_martin/index.html (accessed March 9, 2013).

Peak: Introduction to Criminal Justice: Practice and Process
SUPPORTS

Comprehensive Instructor Resources

- **Test banks** provide a diverse range of pre-written options as well as the opportunity to edit any question and/or insert personalized questions to effectively assess students' progress and understanding

- **Sample course syllabi** for semester and quarter courses provide suggested models for structuring one's course

- Editable, chapter-specific **PowerPoint®️ slides** offer complete flexibility for creating a multimedia presentation for the course

- EXCLUSIVE! Access to full-text **SAGE journal articles** have been carefully selected to support and expand on the concepts presented in each chapter

- **Lecture notes** summarize key concepts by chapter to ease preparation for lectures and class discussions

- Lively and stimulating **ideas for class activities** that can be used in class to reinforce active learning. The activities apply to individual or group projects.

- **Chapter-specific discussion questions** help launch classroom interaction by prompting students to engage with the material and by reinforcing important content.

- A **Course cartridge** including exclusive video cases and short-answer assessment quizzes provides easy LMS integration

- **Multimedia content** includes audio resources, web resources, reference links, court case links, CJ in the News links, and original SAGE videos that appeal to students with different learning styles

"I would strongly advise students to utilize the study resources and encourage them to explore the current events. I typically incorporate videos into my lectures, so having a selection of videos already accumulated would be helpful."

—**Patrick Cundiff,** *East Carolina University*

Peak: Introduction to Criminal Justice: Practice and Process IMPROVES Performance

SAGE edge for Students provides a personalized approach to help students accomplish their coursework goals in an easy-to-use learning environment.

SAGE provides students comprehensive multimedia online resources at **edge.sagepub.com/peak**

Comprehensive Student Resources

- Students benefit from the NO PASSCODE REQUIRED, NO ADDITIONAL COST **open-access SAGE edge site**, which provides valuable resources to enhance learning.

- Mobile-friendly **eFlashcards** strengthen understanding of key terms and concepts

- Mobile-friendly practice **quizzes** allow for independent assessment by students of their mastery of course material

- A customized online **action plan** includes tips and feedback on progress through the course and materials, which allows students to individualize their learning experience

- **Chapter summaries** with **learning objectives** reinforce the most important material

- <u>EXCLUSIVE!</u> Access to full-text **SAGE journal articles** that have been carefully selected to support and expand on the concepts presented in each chapter

- **Multimedia content** includes audio resources, web resources, reference links, court case links, CJ in the News links, and original SAGE videos that appeal to students with different learning styles

SAGE edge

Sharpen your skills with **SAGE edge** at **edge.sagepub.com/peak**. **SAGE edge for students** provides a personalized approach to help you accomplish your coursework goals in an easy-to-use learning environment. Access the videos, audio clips, quizzes, cases and SAGE journal and reference articles that are noted in this chapter.

"A free and open-access study site is key as I would definitely use the flashcards and study questions to prepare."

—Student quote

Peak: Introduction to Criminal Justice: Practice and Process
ENGAGES

Multimedia-rich INTERACTIVE eBook

The dynamic **Interactive eBook** is ideal for students in online and traditional courses who prefer a more contemporary, multimedia-integrated presentation for learning. It is fully searchable and provides students with integrated links to engaging video and audio as well as access to complete academic and professional articles, all from the same pages found in the printed text. Students will also have immediate access to study tools such as highlighting, bookmarking, note-taking, and more!

"If a fully searchable interactive eBook with embedded video and audio were available at no extra charge, I would be likely to adopt the book."

—Dianne Berger-Hill, *Old Dominion University*

Video icon: Links to original video interviews with the author and Los Angeles County Lieutenant Brian D. Fitch as well as carefully selected, web-based video resources for use in independent or classroom-based explorations of key topics.

 The Hiring Process

Crime and media

Reference icon: Links to recent, relevant full-text articles from SAGE's leading research journals, encyclopedias and handbooks support and expand on the concepts presented in the chapter.

Audio icon: Links to podcasts and audio resources cover important topics and are designed to supplement key points within the text.

 Evidence

Mid-Chapter Quiz: Police at Work

Quiz icon: Links to mid-chapter and end-of-chapter quizzes for independent assessment of progress made in learning course material

Case icon: Links to in-depth information about the court cases that are discussed throughout the text

 Miranda v. Arizona

Peak: Introduction to Criminal Justice: Practice and Process
SAVES

SAGE Price ADVANTAGE

SAGE provides students a great value and is priced 30-50% less than the average competing text price.

"The SAGE value price is a huge benefit and not having to worry about passwords is priceless."

—Students everywhere responding to SAGE's value and password-free study site

INTRODUCTION TO CRIMINAL JUSTICE

INTRODUCTION TO CRIMINAL JUSTICE

PRACTICE AND PROCESS

Kenneth J. Peak

University of Nevada, Reno

Los Angeles | London | New Delhi
Singapore | Washington DC

Los Angeles | London | New Delhi
Singapore | Washington DC

FOR INFORMATION:

SAGE Publications, Inc.
2455 Teller Road
Thousand Oaks, California 91320
E-mail: order@sagepub.com

SAGE Publications Ltd.
1 Oliver's Yard
55 City Road
London EC1Y 1SP
United Kingdom

SAGE Publications India Pvt. Ltd.
B 1/I 1 Mohan Cooperative Industrial Area
Mathura Road, New Delhi 110 044
India

SAGE Publications Asia-Pacific Pte. Ltd.
3 Church Street
#10-04 Samsung Hub
Singapore 049483

Acquisitions Editor: Jerry Westby
Associate Editor: Theresa Accomazzo
Publishing Associate: MaryAnn Vail
Associate Digital Content Editor: Rachael Leblond
Production Editor: Olivia Weber-Stenis
Copy Editor: Melinda Masson
Typesetter: C&M Digitals (P) Ltd.
Proofreader: Kate Peterson
Indexer: J. Naomi Linzer
Cover Designer: Gail Buschman
Marketing Manager: Terra Schultz

Printed in the United States of America.

Library of Congress Cataloging-in-Publication Data

Peak, Kenneth J., 1947–
Introduction to criminal justice : practice and process / Kenneth J. Peak, University of Nevada, Reno.

pages cm
Includes bibliographical references and index.

ISBN 978-1-4833-0735-0 (alk. paper)

1. Criminal justice, Administration of—United States.
2. Crime—United States. 3. Criminal law—United States.
I. Title.

HV9950.P4293 2014
364.973—dc23   2013033340

This book is printed on acid-free paper.

14 15 16 17 18 10 9 8 7 6 5 4 3 2 1

BRIEF CONTENTS

TABLE OF CONTENTS

Part I: Criminal Justice as a System: The Basics   1

3. THEORIES OF CRIME AND MEASURING VICTIMIZATION 48

4. ETHICAL ESSENTIALS: "Doing Right When No One Is Watching" 78

Part I I: The Police   103

5. POLICE ORGANIZATION: Structure and Functions   104

6. POLICE AT WORK: Patrolling and Investigating   130

Part III: The Courts 201

9. COURT ORGANIZATION: Structure, Functions, and the Trial Process 202

Part IV: Corrections 281

12. PRISONS AND JAILS: Structure and Function 282

13. THE INMATES' WORLD: The "Keepers" and the "Kept" 306

Part V: Spanning the System: Methods and Issues   357

To Emma O., Oliver K., Dominic W., and Ava D. Love, Deedo

PREFACE

*Themes and
Organization of the Book*

A UNIQUE APPROACH

Famed educator John Dewey advocated the "learning by doing" approach to education, or problem-based learning. This book is written, from start to finish, with that philosophy in mind. Its approach also comports with the popular learning method espoused by Benjamin Bloom, known as "Bloom's Taxonomy," in which he called for "higher-order thinking skills"—critical and creative thinking that involves analysis, synthesis, and evaluation.

This book also benefits from the author's having more than 35 years of combined practitioner's and academic experience, including several positions as a criminal justice administrator and working in both policing and corrections. Therefore, its chapters contain a palpable, real-world flavor that is typically missing for college and university criminal justice students. The book's subtitle—*Practice and Process*—reflects this pervasive applied emphasis.

Hopefully readers will put into use the several features of the book that are included toward accomplishing this overall goal: in addition to chapter opening questions (which will allow students to assess their knowledge of the chapter materials), learning objectives, and a chapter summary, each chapter also contains a number of boxed features such as case studies, "Focus On," "Learn by Doing," "You Be the Judge" (or prosecutor, defense attorney, and so on, as the case may require), and "Going Global" exhibits and exercises. Also provided are "Practitioner's Perspectives" (with people in the field describing their criminal justice occupation) as well as brief glimpses into comparative criminal justice systems, law, and practice in selected foreign venues. Taken together, these supplemental materials should also greatly enhance the reader's critical analysis, problem-solving, and communication capabilities, and allow you to experience the kind of decisions that must be made in the field.

In today's competitive job market, students who possess these kinds of knowledge, skills, and abilities will have better opportunities for obtaining employment as a criminal justice practitioner and succeeding therein. While the book will certainly delve into some theoretical, political, and sociological subject matter, it attempts to remain true to this *practical*, applied focus throughout and to the extent possible.

Distinctive Chapter Contents

This book also contains chapters that are devoted to topics not normally found in introductory criminal justice textbooks. For example, Chapter 4 is devoted to criminal justice ethics. These are certainly challenging times in terms of crime and corruption in our society, and perhaps nowhere is there a need for accountability and transparent ethical behavior than among those who work within our criminal justice system. For that reason, a complete chapter on ethical issues and challenges is warranted. Chapter 16 also describes three unique and contemporary issues that are demanding serious consideration on the U.S. criminal justice policy-making agenda: terrorism, gun control, and marijuana laws. Finally, several chapters also include technologies that are employed in the system.

In sum, this book will introduce the student to the primary individuals, theorists, practitioners, processes, concepts, technologies, and terminologies as they work within or are applied to our criminal justice system. Furthermore, the concepts and terms learned in this introductory textbook will serve as the basis for more complex criminal justice studies of police, courts, and corrections in later course work.

Chapter Organization

To facilitate the above goals, we first need to place the study of criminal justice within the big picture, which is accomplished in the four chapters composing Part I. **Chapter 1** generally discusses the major theme and organization of this book, foundations and politics of criminal justice, an overview of the criminal justice process and the offender's flow through the system, and how discretion and ethics apply to the field. **Chapter 2** generally defines many legal terms and concepts as they apply to crime, and includes the sources and nature of law (including substantive and procedural law, common law, and criminal and civil law), the elements of criminal acts, felonies and misdemeanors, offense definitions and categories, and legal defenses that are allowed under the law. **Chapter 3** reviews some of the prevailing explanations concerning why people commit crimes, and the three methods now used for trying to measure how many crimes are committed in the United States. **Chapter 4** concerns ethics and includes definitions and problems, with emphases on the kinds of ethical problems that confront the police, the courtroom work group, and corrections staff. Included are legislative enactments and judicial decisions involving ethics at the federal, state, and local levels.

Part II consists of four chapters that address federal law enforcement and state and local policing in the United States. **Chapter 5** discusses the organization and operation of law enforcement agencies at the local, state, and federal levels; included are discussions of their English and colonial roots, the three eras of U.S. policing, and local (municipal police and sheriff's offices), state, and selected federal law enforcement agencies. Also included are brief considerations of Interpol and the field of private security. **Chapter 6** focuses on the kinds of work that police do, particularly with respect to the broad areas of patrolling and investigating; after beginning with their recruitment and training (including the need for more women and minorities in the field), we then look generally at the patrol function, including the dangers of the job, the traffic function, the use of police discretion, community policing, and the work of criminal investigators. **Chapter 7** broadly examines several policing issues that exist today: use of force, corruption, civil liability, and selected technologies. **Chapter 8** examines the constitutional rights of the accused (as per U.S. Supreme Court decisions) as well as limitations placed on the police under the Fourth, Fifth, and Sixth Amendments; the focus is on arrest, search and seizure, the right to remain silent, and the right to counsel.

Part III consists of three chapters that generally examine the courts. **Chapter 9** generally looks at court organization and functions at the local trial court, state court, and federal court systems. Included in the chapter are discussions of the courts as hallowed places in our society, their use of the adversarial process, the trial process (including pretrial motions and activities), and the jury system. **Chapter 10** considers the roles and functions of those persons who compose the courtroom work group: judges, prosecutors, and defense attorneys. Finally, **Chapter 11** discusses sentencing, punishment, and appeals. Included are the types and purposes of punishment, types of sentences convicted persons may receive, federal sentencing guidelines, victim impact statements, capital punishment, and selected technologies in the courts.

Part IV includes three chapters and examines many aspects of correctional organizations and operations. **Chapter 12** examines federal and state prisons and jails generally, in terms of their mission, evolution, and organization; included are general discussions of prison life, to include inmate classification, supermax prisons, and selected technologies. **Chapter 13** considers generally the lives led and challenges faced by both corrections personnel and the inmates; included are selected court decisions concerning inmates' legal rights; administrative challenges with overseeing executions, inmate litigation, drugs, and gangs; and the work of personnel in local jails. **Chapter 14** reviews community corrections and alternatives to incarceration: probation, parole, and several other diversionary approaches. Included are discussions of the origins of probation and parole, functions of probation and parole offices, several intermediate sanctions (e.g., house arrest, electronic monitoring), and community corrections at the federal level.

Finally, Part V contains two chapters that consider methods and issues that span the criminal justice system. **Chapter 15** examines juvenile justice—an area where the treatment of offenders is quite different in terms of its overall philosophy, legal bases, and judicial process. Included are the history and extent of juvenile crime, the case flow of juvenile courts, and juvenile rights. **Chapter 16** provides an in-depth view of several particularly challenging and problematical problems and policy issues confronting today's criminal justice system: terrorism (including a companion issue: government use of unmanned aerial vehicles), gun control, and legalization of marijuana.

ABOUT THE AUTHOR

Kenneth J. Peak is professor and former chairman of the Department of Criminal Justice, University of Nevada, Reno, where he was named "Teacher of the Year" by the university's Honor Society. Following four years as a municipal police officer in Kansas, he subsequently held positions as a nine-county criminal justice planner for southeast Kansas; director of a four-state technical assistance institute for the Law Enforcement Assistance Administration (based at Washburn University in Topeka); director of university police at Pittsburg State University (Kansas); acting director of public safety, University of Nevada, Reno; and assistant professor of criminal justice at Wichita State University. He has authored or coauthored 28 textbooks (relating to general policing, community policing, criminal justice administration, police supervision and management, and women in law enforcement), two historical books (on Kansas temperance and bootlegging), and more than 60 journal articles and invited book chapters. He recently served as general editor for SAGE's *Encyclopedia of Community Policing and Problem Solving*, and also is past chairman of the Police Section of the Academy of Criminal Justice Sciences and president of the Western and Pacific Association of Criminal Justice Educators. He received two gubernatorial appointments to statewide criminal justice committees while residing in Kansas and holds a doctorate from the University of Kansas.

PART I

CRIMINAL JUSTICE AS A SYSTEM: THE BASICS

This part consists of four chapters. Briefly, **Chapter 1** examines why it is important to study criminal justice, the foundations and politics of criminal justice, an overview of the criminal justice process and the offender's flow through the system, and how discretion and ethics apply to the field.

Chapter 2 considers the sources and nature of law (including substantive and procedural, and criminal and civil), the elements of criminal acts, felonies and misdemeanors, offense definitions and categories, and legal constructs and defenses that are allowed under the law.

Chapter 3 examines some of the attempts to explain why people commit crimes (including the classical, positivist, biological, psychological, and socio-cultural theories) as well as prevailing methods in use for trying to measure how many crimes are committed.

Chapter 4 looks at definitions and types of ethics in general, and then examines ethical dilemmas that confront the police, the courtroom work group, and corrections staff. Included are legislative enactments and judicial decisions involving ethics at the federal, state, and local levels.

 Author Introduction to the Course

FUNDAMENTALS OF CRIMINAL JUSTICE:
Essential Themes and Practices

LEARNING OBJECTIVES

As a result of reading this chapter, the student will be able to:

1 Explain the importance of studying and understanding our criminal justice system

2 Describe the foundations of our criminal justice system, including its legal and historical bases

3 Define the crime control and due process models of criminal justice

4 Review the influence of politics on our criminal justice system, as well as what can constitute "good politics" and "bad politics"

5 Relate the importance of citizen responses to crime and willingness to become involved in the criminal justice process

6 Describe the fundamentals of the criminal justice process—the offender's flow through the police, courts, and corrections components, and the functions of each component

7 Explain the "wedding cake" model of criminal justice

8 Describe the importance of discretion and ethics throughout the justice system

CHAPTER

01

The true administration of justice is the firmest pillar of good government.

—Inscription on the New York State
Supreme Court, Foley Square, Manhattan, New York

When we pull back the layers of government services, the most fundamental and indispensable virtues are public safety and social order.

—Hon. David A. Hardy, Washoe
County District Court, Reno, Nevada

INTRODUCTION

Author Introduction:
Chapter 1

The criminal justice system as we know it has existed for more than a century and a half. However, since their childhood, most Americans have witnessed countless fictional "cops-and-robbers" programs in film media, and yet they are unable to read or watch actual crime news stories and comprehend what is taking place. Our justice system remains a mystery to many of us, as do the reasons people commit crimes, what is being done about homeland security, the purposes of punishment, our protections under the Bill of Rights, and so on. Therefore, for purely cognitive reasons, this system needs to be studied and understood.

Another reason for understanding the criminal justice system is the precarious situation in which Americans find themselves in the aftermath of September 11, 2001; since that fateful day, we can no longer take domestic well-being for granted. Americans also learned on 9/11 that crime is an international problem. Crime now easily transcends national borders, and the manner in which our federal, state, and local criminal justice agencies must organize and plan in order to deal with crime has also changed in many ways, as later chapters will show.

ASSESS YOUR AWARENESS:

Test your knowledge of criminal justice fundamentals by first reading and responding to the following seven true-false items; check your answers after reading this chapter's materials.

1. Under the U.S. system of justice, people basically join together, form governments (thus surrendering their rights of self-protection), and receive governmental protection in return.

2. Very little if any political or discretionary behavior or authority exists in the field of criminal justice; its fixed laws and procedures prevent such influences.

3. "Three-strikes laws" basically refer to state statutes sentencing offenders with three qualifying felonies to a minimum of 25 years in prison.

4. All prosecutions for crimes begin with a grand jury indictment.

5. Police make the final decisions concerning the actual crimes with which a suspect will be charged.

6. *Parolee* is the term used to describe one who has served time in prison.

7. The U.S. system of criminal justice is intended to function, and indeed does function in all respects, like a "well-oiled machine."

Answers can be found on page 401.

In addition, odds are that you and most Americans will be affected by crime during your lifetime. There are about 10.2 million Part I crimes (defined in Chapter 2) reported to the Federal Bureau of Investigation each year in the United States,[1] and millions more that are less serious in nature, as well as millions that go unreported. Americans thus also need to understand the flow of the offender through the police, judicial, and corrections processes, as well as their legal rights in a democracy.

Finally, your tax dollars will support criminal justice in federal, state, and local governments (which now spend about $228 billion annually and employ approximately 2.5 million persons).[2] The resources required to support our criminal justice system are staggering. But as the French novelist Alain-René Lesage stated several centuries ago, "Justice is such a fine thing that we cannot pay too dearly for it."[3]

This chapter looks at the underpinnings of our criminal justice system—the "big picture"—including the foundations of criminal justice (legal and historical bases), two models of crime, the politics of criminal justice, citizens' responsibility for addressing crime, an overview of one's flow through the criminal justice process, and how discretion and ethics permeate the system. The chapter contains "Focus On" and "You Be the Judge" features to engage the reader, and concludes with a summary, key terms and concepts, review questions, and several scenarios and activities that provide opportunities for you to "learn by doing."

FOUNDATIONS OF CRIMINAL JUSTICE: LEGAL AND HISTORICAL BASES

In July 1993, Richard Allen Davis was paroled halfway into his 16-year sentence for kidnapping—his latest in a long line of violent felonies he had committed over four decades. Several months later, Davis kidnapped, sexually assaulted, and murdered 12-year-old Polly Klaas in Petaluma, California. After his capture, many Americans began asking how someone like him, with such a long and horrific criminal record, could have been paroled. California lawmakers responded by proposing the first of the nation's **three-strikes laws**, which California voters overwhelmingly approved. Within two years, more than 20 states and the federal government had done the same.[4]

The law's original premise was simple: A violent offender who was convicted of a qualifying felony and had two prior qualifying felony convictions had to serve a minimum of 25 years.[5] Proponents of the law predicted it would curb crime and protect society by incapacitating the worst offenders for a long period of time, while opponents argued that three-strikes defendants would demand trials (rather than plea bargain) and explode prison populations.[6]

 Criminal Law

The law that was finally enacted in California was vastly different from what was originally intended—and with many negative and unanticipated repercussions.[7] According to the *New York Times*, the law was unfairly punitive and

created a cruel, Kafkaesque criminal justice system that lost all sense of proportion, doling out life sentences disproportionately to black defendants. Under the statute, the third offense that could result in a life sentence could be any number of low-level felony convictions, like stealing a jack from the back of a tow truck, shoplifting a pair of work gloves from a department store, pilfering small change from a parked car or passing a bad check.[8]

Three-strikes law: a crime control strategy whereby an offender who commits three or more violent offenses will be sentenced to a lengthy term in prison, usually 25 years to life.

We've Lost Our Dad Because of a Petty Theft 25 to life

Three strikes laws, while differing in content somewhat from state to state, all have a simple premise: making violent offenders with three qualifying convictions serve lengthy prison sentences.

Other studies of the California law found that prisoners added to the prison system in one decade's time would cost taxpayers an additional $8.1 billion in prison and jail expenditures.[9] Furthermore, three-strikes inmates sentenced for nonviolent offenses would serve 143,439 more years behind bars than if they had been convicted prior to the law's passage.[10]

In November 2012, Californians voted to soften the sentencing law, to impose a life sentence only when the third felony offense is serious or violent, as defined in state law. The law also authorizes the courts to resentence thousands of people who were sent away for low-level third offenses and who present no danger to the public,[11] and provides redress to mentally ill inmates—who were estimated to compose up to 40 percent of those inmates with life sentences under the three-strikes rule.[12]

The Polly Klaas murder, as cruel and senseless as it was, and the events in its aftermath nevertheless serve to provide an excellent illustration of the U.S. criminal element, the legislative process, and the democratic system of criminal justice that exists to deal with offenders. California's experience with "three strikes" also allows us an opportunity to consider, given that our system of justice is founded on a large, powerful system of government, the following questions: From whence are such legislative and law enforcement powers derived? How can governments presume to maintain a system of laws that effectively governs its people and, moreover, a legal system that exists to punish persons who willfully violate those laws? On what basis can states legally construct prisons to restrain anyone—and especially the high numbers of individuals who will no doubt be incarcerated as a result of tough new laws? We now consider those questions.

The Consensus-Versus-Conflict Debate

Our society contains innumerable lawbreakers—many of whom are more violent than Richard Davis. Most of them are dealt with by the police in a cooperative manner, without challenging the legitimacy of the law if arrested and incarcerated. Nor do they challenge the system of government that enacts the laws or the justice agencies that carry them out. The stability of our government for more than 200 years is a testimony to the existence of a fair degree of consensus as to its legitimacy.[13] Thomas Jefferson's statements in the Declaration of Independence are as true today as the day when he wrote them and are accepted as common sense:

> We hold these truths to be self-evident, that all men are created equal, that they are endowed by their Creator with certain inalienable Rights, that among these are Life, Liberty and the pursuit of Happiness—That to secure these rights, Governments are instituted among Men, deriving their just powers from the consent of

the governed. That whenever any Form of Government becomes destructive of these ends, it is the Right of the People to alter or abolish it.

The principles of the Declaration are almost a paraphrase of John Locke's Second Treatise on Civil Government, which justifies the acts of government on the basis of Locke's social contract theory. In the state of nature, people, according to Locke, were created by God to be free, equal, and independent, and to have inherent inalienable rights to life, liberty, and property. Each person had the right of self-protection against those who would infringe on these liberties. In Locke's view, although most people were good, some would be likely to prey on their fellows, who in turn would constantly have to be on guard against such evildoers. To avoid this brutish existence, people joined together, forming governments to which they surrendered their rights of self-protection. In return, they received governmental protection of their lives, property, and liberty. As with any contract, each side has benefits and considerations; people give up their rights to protect themselves and receive protection in return. Governments give protection and receive loyalty and obedience in return.[14]

Castle Doctrine

Locke believed that the chief purpose of government was the protection of property. Properties would be joined together to form a commonwealth. Once the people unite into a commonwealth, they cannot withdraw from it, nor can their lands be removed from it. Property holders become members of that commonwealth only with their express consent to submit to its government. This is Locke's famous theory of tacit consent: "Every Man . . . doth hereby give his tacit consent, and is as far forth obliged to Obedience to the Laws of the Government."[15] Locke's theory essentially describes an association of landowners.[16]

Author Video: The Sovereign Citizen Movement

Another theorist connected with the social contract theory is Thomas Hobbes, who argued that all people were essentially irrational and selfish.

John Locke, an English philosopher and physician and one of the most influential thinkers of his day, developed two influential theories concerning government and natural law: social contract and tacit consent. Another English philosopher and social contract theorist, Thomas Hobbes, believed in individual rights and representative government.

you be the... JUDGE

THE SOVEREIGN CITIZEN MOVEMENT

Shawn Rice, a 50-year-old Arizona man who rejects government authority as a member of the "sovereign citizen movement," was sentenced to 98 months in a federal prison and ordered to forfeit more than $1.29 million in assets. Rice was convicted on 1 count of conspiracy to commit money laundering, 13 counts of money laundering, and 4 counts of failure to appear, and ordered to pay $98,782 in restitution once he leaves prison.[17]

Rice and other members of this movement believe that the U.S. government is illegitimate and that they should not have to pay taxes or be subject to federal laws. Most of them have their own constitution, bill of rights, and government officials.

Members of the group often commit financial fraud crimes, or "paper terrorism." However, they are extremely dangerous and violent, and have been tied to a number of shootouts with, and killings of, police officers.[18]

It is estimated that "hundreds of thousands" of sovereign citizens currently live throughout the United States.[19] They are such a threat that the FBI maintains a website on these citizens.[20]

1. Looking only at their beliefs and not the violent acts that are committed by some members of the sovereign citizen movement, are such people truly U.S. "citizens"?

2. Do their beliefs have any redeemable merit?

3. What types and amounts of punishment, if any, do you believe are justified for sovereign citizens?

Jean-Jacques Rousseau, a Genevan conflict theorist, argued that while the co-existence of human beings in equality and freedom is possible, it is unlikely that humanity can escape alienation, oppression, and lack of freedom: "Everywhere he is in chains."

He maintained that people had just enough rationality to recognize their situation and to come together to form governments for self-protection, agreeing "amongst themselves to submit to some Man, or Assembly of men, voluntarily, on confidence to be protected by him against all others."[21] Therefore, they existed in a state of consensus with their governments.

Jean-Jacques Rousseau, a conflict theorist, differed substantively from both Hobbes and Locke, arguing that "man is born free, but everywhere he is in chains."[22] Like Plato, Rousseau associated the loss of freedom and the creation of conflict in modern societies with the development of private property and the unequal distribution of resources. Rousseau described conflict between the ruling group and the other groups in society, whereas Locke described consensus within the ruling group and the need to use force and other means to ensure the compliance of the other groups.[23]

Thus, the primary difference between the consensus and conflict theorists with respect to their view of government vis-à-vis the governed concerns their evaluation of the legitimacy of the actions of ruling groups in contemporary societies. This debate is important because it plays out the competing views of humankind toward its ruling group; it also has relevance with respect to the kind of justice system (or process) we have. As mentioned earlier, goals are not shared by the system's three components, and the system may move in different directions. Therefore, the systems approach is part of **consensus theory**, which assumes that all parts of the system work toward a common goal.[24] **Conflict theory**, holding that agency interests tend to make actors within the system self-serving, provides the other approach. This view notes the pressures for success, promotion, and general accountability, which together result in fragmented efforts of the system as a whole, leading to a criminal justice nonsystem.[25]

CRIME CONTROL AND DUE PROCESS: DO ENDS JUSTIFY MEANS?

In 1968, Herbert Packer described two now-classic models of the criminal justice process in terms of two competing value systems: crime control and due process (see Figure 1.1).[26] The **due process model**—likened to an "obstacle course" by some authors—essentially holds that criminal defendants should be presumed innocent, that the courts' first priority is protecting the constitutional rights of the accused, and that granting too much freedom to law enforcement officials will result in the loss of freedom and civil liberties for all Americans. Therefore, each court case must involve formal fact-finding to uncover mistakes by the police and prosecutors. This view also stresses that crime is not a result of individual moral failure, but is the result of social influences (such as unemployment, racial discrimination, and other factors that disadvantage the poor); thus, courts that do not follow this philosophy are fundamentally unfair to these defendants. Furthermore, rehabilitation will prevent further crime.

In contrast is the **crime control model**, which is a much more traditional philosophy and which Packer likened to an "assembly line." This model views crime as a breakdown of individual responsibility. It places the highest importance on repressing criminal conduct and thus protecting society. Persons who are charged are presumed guilty, and the courts should not hinder effective enforcement of the laws; rather, legal loopholes should be eliminated and offenders swiftly punished. Under this philosophy, the police and prosecutors should have a high degree of discretion. Punishment will deter crime, so there must be speed and finality in the courts to ensure crime suppression.

Although Packer indicated that neither of these models would be found to completely dominate a particular community or control U.S. crime policy,[27] even to say that one of these models is superior to the other requires an individual to make a value judgment. How much leeway should be given to the police? Should they be allowed to "bend" the laws just a little bit in order to get criminals off the streets? Does the end justify the means? These are important questions; note that these questions will be revisited in discussions of ethics in Chapter 4 and police discretion in Chapter 6.

Consensus theory: said to exist where a society functions as a result of a group's common interests and values, which have been developed largely because the people have experienced similar socialization.

Conflict theory: said to exist in societies where the worker class is exploited by the ruling class, which owns and controls the means of production and thus maintains the constant state of conflict between the two classes.

Crime control model: a model by Packer that emphasizes law and order and argues that every effort must be made to suppress crime, and to try, convict, and incarcerate offenders.

Due process model: Packer's view that criminal defendants should be presumed innocent, courts must protect suspects' rights, and there must be some limits placed on police powers.

 FIGURE 1.1

Packer's Crime Control and Due Process Models

	CRIME CONTROL MODEL	DUE PROCESS MODEL
Views criminal justice system as an:	Assembly line	Obstacle course
Goal of criminal justice system	Controlling crime	Protecting rights of defendants
Values emphasized	Efficiency, speed, finality	Reliability
Process of adjudication	Informal screening by police and prosecutor	Formal, adversarial procedures
Focus on	Factual guilt	Legal guilt

POLITICS AND CRIMINAL JUSTICE

As the above discussion of California's three-strikes law demonstrates, and as with society in general, politics permeates the field of criminal justice. Governing boards and politicians appropriate laws and budgets to cover policy making; the construction of new police stations, courthouses, jails, and prisons; and other operations of police, courts, and corrections organizations at the national, state, and local levels of government. Certainly politics and policy making are intrinsic to our form of government and affect every aspect of our lives.

Permeating the Field

Data-Mining Programs

No doubt many politicians want to do what is right and proper for society as well as the justice system; however, it is also true that many times, their coming out forcefully against crime may be prompted more out of a desire to merely grandstand for votes or a "knee-jerk" response to a high-profile criminal event; politicians may react out of anger or political expediency, or with limited information about a problem (see the three-strikes law, discussed above).

With regard to the police, where chiefs of police serve at the pleasure of their city councils and sheriffs must run for election, the potential for political patronage and influence is obvious. Indeed, as will be seen in Chapter 5, the history of policing is so replete with politics that it even experienced a formal political "era." Perhaps because society perceives the police as a very powerful entity, this is an aspect of policing that is often overlooked.

Our courts are certainly bound closely to the laws and budgets that politicians put in force. And while it is generally believed that the federal courts (where judges receive life appointments) are, or at least can be, removed from local political influence, state and local judges (like police chiefs and sheriffs) are often appointed by city councils or elected. The latter issue—judges having to run for election and thus be compelled to accept campaign contributions and run under a political party label—has led many states to opt for a merit selection plan for judges, which is discussed in Chapter 10. Certainly the same can be said for directors of state correctional systems and their prison wardens, both of which may be appointed by, and serve at the pleasure of, their governors.

Mid-Chapter Quiz: Fundamentals of Criminal Justice

Good Politics, Bad Politics

There can be "good" politics as well as "bad" politics. **Political influence** can range from major beneficial policy, personnel, and budgetary decisions to the overzealous city manager or city council member who wants to micromanage the police department and even appears unexpectedly at night at a crime scene (overheard on his or her police scanner) to "help" the officers. Norm Stamper, former chief of police in Seattle, Washington, provided a succinct yet excellent example of how politics can be good or bad; although he speaks in the context of policing, his comments are certainly applicable in other criminal justice systems—and in society-at-large:

Dragnet Era

> *Everything* about policing is ultimately political. Who gets which office: political. Which services are cut when there's a budget freeze: political. Who gets hired, fired, promoted: political, political, political. I hire my brother-in-law's cousin, a certifiable doofus, because he's got a bass boat I wouldn't mind borrowing—bad politics. I promote a drinking buddy—bad politics. I pick an individual because he or she will add value to the organization and will serve the community honorably—good politics.[28]

Political influence: matters taken into account for developing public policies, allocating funds and other resources, and choosing among preferred alternatives.

CITIZENS' RESPONSES TO CRIME

In order to function properly, the law and the criminal justice system need citizens to be willing to "get involved." These two aspects of an ordered society would be largely ineffectual if citizens were unwilling to report crimes that come to their attention; to serve as witnesses, complainants, and jurors; and to come to the aid of their neighbors. A large proportion of criminal justice responses to crimes are initiated by the police, but certainly many responses to crime are initiated by the private sector—as individuals or families, neighborhood associations, businesses, industries, agriculture, educational institutions, the news media, and so on.

The "Focus On" box describes a sad as well as poor example of citizen responses to crime; the Kitty Genovese story has become a classic example in this regard, and her story demonstrates the very worst that can happen when people are not willing to come forward either to assist one of their fellow humans or to aid the law in the identification and apprehension of an offender. Today the Kitty Genovese case still begs the question: "If we need help, will those around us stand around and let us be destroyed, or will they come to our aid?"

THE CRIMINAL JUSTICE PROCESS: AN OVERVIEW OF FLOW AND FUNCTIONS

As a voter and taxpayer, you also participate in criminal justice through the policy-making process that affects how the criminal justice process operates, the resources available to it, and its goals and objectives.

Neighborhood Watch, a crime prevention program launched in the U.S. in 1972, involves citizens working with law enforcement to be vigilant for criminal activities in their communities.

FOCUS ON   KITTY GENOVESE

The victim, a bar manager, was returning home from her work at 3 a.m. on March 14, 1964, in Queens, New York, when suddenly a man overtook and stabbed her. She screamed, "Oh, my God, he stabbed me! Please help me!" Her pleas for help were heard by several neighbors, but on a cold night with the windows closed, only a few of them recognized the sound as a cry for help. When one of the neighbors shouted at the attacker, he ran away, and she slowly made her way toward her own apartment around the end of the building. She was seriously injured and now out of view of those few who may have had reason to believe she was in need of help.

The attacker returned about 10 minutes later, systematically searched the area, followed her trail of blood, and ultimately found her lying barely conscious in a hallway at the back of the building. He then proceeded to attack her again, stabbing her several more times. And there, while the defenseless victim lay semiconscious, incoherent from pain and loss of blood, he cut off her bra and underwear and sexually assaulted her. He stole about $49 from her and left her dying in the hallway. The attacks spanned approximately half an hour. Later investigative accounts revealed that none of the neighbors who

had witnessed her killer's attacks had come to her aid or called the police. The police commander of Queens detectives said that nothing in his 25 years of police work had shocked him so much as the apathy encountered on the Genovese murder during the 35-minute ordeal.

The victim was Catherine "Kitty" Genovese, age 28; her name would become symbolic in the public mind, standing for the proposition that, on occasion, Americans are too indifferent, frightened, alienated, or self-absorbed to "get involved" in helping a fellow human being in dire trouble. Genovese's attacker, Winston Moseley, 29, was a business-machine operator who lived with his wife and two children and had no criminal record. He was convicted and sentenced to life imprisonment. Over the years, there have been various scholarly studies of the case, including conferences on "Bad Samaritanism."

Source: Adapted from Michael Dorman, "The Killing of Kitty Genovese," *Newsday.com,* May 9, 2006, http://www.envisionacademy.org/blogs/english/kitty.pdf (accessed March 4, 2013); also see Michael Gansberg, "Thirty-Eight Who Saw Murder Didn't Call the Police," *New York Times,* March 27, 1964, http://www2.selu.edu/Academics/Faculty/scraig/gansberg.html (accessed February 15, 2013).

Police Academy

At every stage of the process from the original formulation of objectives to the decision about where to locate jails and prisons to the reintegration of inmates into society, the private sector has a role to play.

The Offender's Pathway Through the Process

What follows is a brief description of the **criminal justice flow and process** in the United States. Figure 1.2 shows a flowchart of that system and summarizes the major events, including entry into the criminal justice system, prosecution and pretrial services, adjudication, sentencing and sanctions, and corrections. Note that *all* of the discussions in the following chapters of this book are based on the *people* and *processes* that are included in this concise sequence of events.

As we follow the path of the offender through the process, note, however, that Figure 1.2 also depicts vertical pathways out of the criminal justice system. That is because many crimes fall out of the system for one of a variety of reasons: The crime is not discovered or reported to the police (the so-called shadow of crime); no perpetrator is identified or apprehended; or, in some instances, a suspect is arrested, but later the police determine that no crime was committed, and he or she is released from custody.

Law Enforcement: Entry Into the System

The flowchart in Figure 1.2 begins with "reported and observed crime." Law enforcement agencies learn about crime from the reports of victims or other citizens, from discovery by a police officer in the field, from informants, or from investigative and intelligence work. Once a law enforcement agency has established that a crime has been committed, the perpetrator must be identified and apprehended in order for the case to proceed through the system. Sometimes, the offender is apprehended at the scene; at other times, however, identification of the offender requires an extensive investigation.

Court-Appointed Attorneys

Prosecution and Pretrial Activities

Next we enter the **prosecution** and pretrial services phase of the process—and the realm of the powerful who "control the floodgates" of the judicial process. After an arrest, law enforcement agencies present information concerning the case and the accused (typically in the form of an official offense/arrest report) to the prosecutor, who will decide if formal charges will be filed with the court. If no charges are filed, the accused must be released. The prosecutor can also elect, after initially filing charges, to drop charges (*nolle prosequi*) if he or she determines that the probable cause and/or evidence in the matter is weak. (**Probable cause**, discussed more fully in Chapter 8, is a legal term that basically refers to information that would lead a reasonable person to believe that a person has committed, is committing, or is about to commit a crime.)

Persons charged with a crime must be taken before a judge or magistrate without unnecessary delay (the amount of time will normally be specified in the state's statutes or municipal ordinances) to an initial appearance, where the judge will inform them of the charges and decide whether there is probable cause to detain them. If the offense is not very serious, the determination of guilt and assessment of a penalty may also occur at this stage.

Often, the defense counsel is also assigned at the initial appearance. All defendants who are prosecuted for serious crimes have a right to be represented by an attorney. If the court determines the defendant is indigent and cannot afford such representation, the court will assign counsel at the public's expense. A pretrial-release decision may also be made at this initial appearance, but may occur at other hearings as well; the court often bases its decision of whether to release the defendant on such factors as drug use, residence,

Criminal justice flow and process: the horizontal movement of defendants and cases through the criminal justice process, beginning with the commission of a crime, investigation, arrest, initial appearance, arraignment, trial, verdict, sentencing, and appeal (to include vertical movement, as when a case is dropped or for some other reason one leaves the system)

Prosecution: the bringing of charges against an individual, based on probable cause, so as to cause the matter to go to court.

Prosecuting attorney: a federal, state, or local prosecutor who represents the people, particularly victims.

The Sequence of Events in the Criminal Justice System

What is the sequence of events in the criminal justice system?

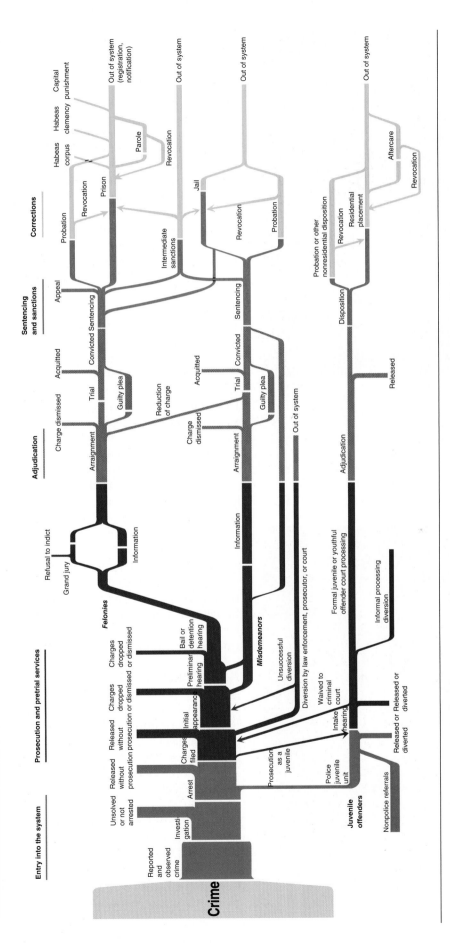

Source: Adapted from *The challenge of crime in a free society.* President's Commission on Law Enforcement and Administration of Justice, 1967. This revision, a result of the Symposium on the 30th Anniversary of the President's Commission, was prepared by the Bureau of Justice Statistics in 1997.

Note: This chart gives a simplified view of caseflow through the criminal justice system. Procedures vary among jurisdictions. The weights of lines are not intended to show actual size of caseloads.

Under the United States' system of justice, all criminal defendants who are prosecuted for serious crimes have the right to be represented by an attorney.

James Holmes, accused in the July 2012 shootings that killed 12 people and injured 70 in an Aurora, Colorado, movie theater, changed his plea to not guilty by reason of insanity.

employment status, and family ties. If he or she appears to be a good risk for appearing at trial and not fleeing the area, the court may decide that the accused should be released on recognizance (often termed "ROR," meaning that the defendant is released without having to provide bail, upon promising to appear and answer the criminal charge) or into the custody of a third party after the posting of a financial bond.

The next step is to determine whether there is probable cause to believe the accused committed the crime and whether he or she should be tried. Depending on the jurisdiction and the case, this determination is made in one of two ways. First, in many jurisdictions, the initial appearance may be followed by a preliminary hearing, where a judge determines if there is probable cause to believe that the accused committed the crime and, if so, moves the case forward to trial, also known as "binding the defendant over" for trial. If the judge does not find probable cause, the case is dismissed.

Second, in other jurisdictions/cases, a grand jury hears evidence against the accused presented by the prosecutor and decides if there is sufficient evidence to bring the accused to trial. If the grand jury finds sufficient evidence, it submits to the court an "indictment," a written statement of the essential facts of the offense charged against the accused. Misdemeanor cases and some felony cases proceed by the issuance of an information, which is a formal, written accusation submitted to the court by a prosecutor (rather than an indictment from the grand jury). In some jurisdictions, indictments may be required in felony cases. Grand juries are discussed more in Chapter 9.

Furthermore, in some jurisdictions, defendants, often those without a prior criminal record, may be eligible for diversion from prosecution subject to the completion of specific conditions such as drug treatment. Successful completion of the conditions may result in charges being dropped or the record of the crime being expunged (meaning to legally strike or erase).

Adjudication

Next, in the middle of the flowchart shown in Figure 1.2, is the **adjudication** process. Once an indictment or information has been filed with the trial court, the accused is scheduled for arraignment. At the arraignment, the accused is informed of the charges, advised of the rights of criminal defendants, and asked to enter a plea to the charges.

If the accused pleads guilty or *nolo contendere* (accepts penalty without admitting guilt), the judge may accept or reject the plea. If the plea is accepted, no trial is held, and the offender is sentenced at this proceeding or at a later date. Note it is a commonly accepted fact that approximately 90 percent of criminal defendants plead guilty as a result of plea bargaining between the prosecutor and the defendant; therefore, contrary to popular media depictions, trials are very rare.

However, if the accused pleads not guilty or not guilty by reason of insanity, a date is set for the trial. A person accused of a serious crime is guaranteed a trial by jury. However, the accused may instead request a bench trial, where the judge alone, rather than a jury, will hear both sides of the case. In both instances the prosecution and defense present evidence by questioning witnesses, while the judge decides on issues of law. The trial results in an acquittal (not guilty) or a conviction (guilty) on the original charges or on lesser included offenses.

Sentencing and Sanctions, Generally

After a conviction, a sentence is imposed. With the exception of capital cases where the death penalty is being sought and the jury decides the punishment, the judge determines the sentence.

In arriving at an appropriate sentence, a sentencing hearing may be held at which time evidence of **aggravating** or **mitigating circumstances** is considered (aggravators are elements that tend to increase the offender's blame, such as use of torture; mitigators tend to reduce blame, such as youthfulness and lack of prior criminal record; these are discussed more in Chapter 11). Here the court may rely on presentence investigations by probation agencies, and consider victim impact statements (a written or oral statement by the victim concerning the pain, anguish, and financial devastation the crime has caused).

The sentencing choices that may be available to judges and juries include one or more of the following:

The United States Supreme Court has held that trial juries may hear and consider victim impact statements (concerning such factors as the pain, anguish, and suffering the defendant's crime has caused) when making sentencing decisions.

- The death penalty

- Incarceration in a prison, a jail, or another confinement facility

- Probation—allowing the convicted person to remain at liberty but subject to certain conditions and restrictions such as drug testing or drug treatment

- Fines—primarily applied as penalties in minor offenses

- Restitution—requiring the offender to pay compensation to the victim

- "Intermediate sanctions" (used in some jurisdictions)—alternatives to incarceration that are considered more severe than straight probation but less severe than a prison term (for example, boot camps, intense supervision often with drug treatment and testing, house arrest and electronic monitoring, and community service)

Sentences and punishment are discussed in Chapter 11, while intermediate **sanctions**, probation, and parole are examined in Chapter 14.

Appellate Review

Following trial and sentencing, a defendant may request appellate review (requesting that a higher court look at the arrest, trial, and so forth) of the conviction or sentence. The appellate process provides checks on the

Mitigating circumstances: circumstances that would tend to lessen the severity of the sentence, such as one's youthfulness, mental instability, not having a prior criminal record, and so on.

Aggravating circumstances: elements of a crime that enhance its seriousness, such as the infliction of torture, killing of a police or corrections officer, and so on.

Adjudication: the legal resolution of a dispute—for example, when one is declared guilty, or a juvenile is declared to be dependent and neglected—by a judge or jury.

Sanction: a penalty or punishment.

Convicted offenders who are to be incarcerated will either serve time in a local jail (typically for misdemeanants serving less than one year) or a federal or state prison (for felons, and usually for more than one year).

Recidivism

Indeterminate sentencing: a scheme whereby one is sentenced for a flexible time period (e.g., 5–10 years) so as to be released when rehabilitated or the opportunity for rehabilitation is presented.

Parole: early release from prison, with conditions attached and under supervision of a parole agency.

criminal justice system by ensuring that errors at trial (except for those considered to be "harmless") did not adversely affect the fairness of trial processes and the defendant's constitutional rights. In some cases, appeals of convictions are automatic; *all* states with the death penalty provide for automatic appeal of cases involving a death sentence. In other cases, whether or not the appeal will be taken up for consideration is subject to the discretion of the appellate court.

Corrections

The next phase into which the offender enters is corrections, as shown in Figure 1.2. Offenders sentenced to incarceration usually serve time in a local jail or a state prison. Offenders sentenced to less than one year generally go to jail; those sentenced to more than one year go to prison.

A prisoner may become eligible for parole after serving a portion of his or her **indeterminate sentence** (a range, such as 5–10 years). **Parole** is the conditional release of a prisoner before the prisoner's full sentence has been served. The decision to grant parole is made by an authority such as a parole board, which has power to grant or revoke parole (i.e., return the parolee to prison) or to discharge a parolee altogether. In some jurisdictions, offenders serving what is termed a **determinate sentence**—a fixed number of years in prison—will not come before a paroling authority, because each offender is required to serve out his or her full sentence prior to release, less any "good time credits" (a reduction in the actual time served in jail or prison due to good behavior, participation in programs, and so on) received.

If released by a parole board or by mandatory release, the parolee will be under the supervision of a parole officer in the community for the balance of his or her unexpired sentence. This supervision is governed by specific conditions of release, and the parolee may be returned to prison ("parole revocation") for violations of such conditions.

Once a person who is suspected of committing a crime is released from the jurisdiction of a criminal justice agency, he or she may commit a new crime (recidivate) and thus need to be processed again through the criminal justice system. Studies show that individuals with prior criminal histories are more likely to be rearrested.

The Juvenile Justice System

Juvenile courts usually have jurisdiction over matters concerning children, including delinquency, neglect, and adoption. They also handle "status offenses" such as truancy and running away, which are not applicable to adults. State statutes define which persons are under the original jurisdiction of the juvenile court. The upper age of original juvenile court jurisdiction in delinquency matters is 17 in most states.[29] Chapter 15 is devoted to an examination of the juvenile justice system.

THE WEDDING CAKE MODEL OF CRIMINAL JUSTICE

The criminal justice system flowchart shown in Figure 1.2 makes it easy to see the steps through which the offender moves through the process horizontally. It is also helpful to see how the system treats cases differently by viewing it vertically, as shown in the "wedding cake" in Figure 1.3, which was developed by Samuel Walker.[30]

This approach begins with the premise that not all criminal cases are viewed or handled in the same manner—by either the police or the judiciary. The type of treatment given to a particular case, including its outcome, may well be determined in large measure by such factors as the seriousness of the charge, the current policy implications, and the defendant's celebrity and resources. In other words, some cases are run-of-the-mill, and will be treated as such, as opposed to more high-profile crimes and/or criminals, commanding much more attention.

As shown in Figure 1.3, this model divides the proceedings in the criminal justice system into four different categories: celebrated cases, serious felonies, lesser felonies, and misdemeanors. This partitioning of cases allows for a closer analysis of the manner in which they are dealt with by the criminal justice system.

FIGURE 1.3

The Wedding Cake Model of Crime

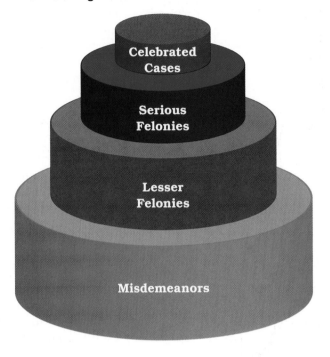

Layer 1: Celebrated Cases

The top layer of the **wedding cake model** includes the "celebrated cases." These cases command a great deal of media attention because the crimes are unusual (such as Andrea Yates, the Texas woman who drowned her five children) or because the defendants are celebrities or high-ranking officials (consider Michael Jackson; O. J. Simpson, the celebrated athlete and actor whose "trial of the century" is discussed in Chapter 2; and Bernie Madoff, the operator of a Ponzi scheme who bilked investors out of billions of dollars). The manner in which the criminal justice system deals with these types of cases is not different from that of the "usual" case, and because of their complexity or high-profile nature, many more resources will be devoted in the form of forensic tests, use of expert witnesses, jury sequestering (seclusion), cameras in the courtroom, and crowd control. At the same time, there will be extra care to ensure that the defendant's rights are protected—and, hopefully, because these cases are so public in nature and used as examples of U.S. justice in action, that the accused is not being given preferential treatment.

Layer 2: Serious Felonies

The second layer of the wedding cake includes serious felonies, which are violent crimes committed by people with lengthy criminal records and who often prey on people they do not know. These are viewed by the police and prosecutors as the cases that are most deserving of "heavy" treatment and punishment, and there is not as great a chance that the defendant will be allowed to enter into a plea agreement before trial.

Layer 3: Lesser Felonies

On the third layer of the wedding cake are the lesser felonies, which tend to be nonviolent and typically viewed as less important than the felonies in Layer 2. Here, the offender may have no criminal record, may have had a prior relationship with the victim, and may be charged with drug-related, financial, or other such crimes. A good portion of these cases will be filtered out of the system prior to trial, and end in plea agreements.

Determinate sentence: a specific, fixed-period sentence ordered by a court.

"Wedding cake" model of criminal justice: a model of the criminal justice process whereby a four-tiered hierarchy exists, with a few celebrated cases at the top, and lower tiers increasing in size as the severity of cases become less (serious felonies, felonies, and misdemeanors).

Layer 4: Misdemeanors

Layer 4 consists of misdemeanor cases, which make up about 90 percent of all criminal matters. They include the so-called "junk" crimes: public drunkenness, minor theft, disturbing the peace, and so on. Police may deal with them informally, and where arrests are made, they will be handled by the lower courts—where speed is of the essence and thus trials are rare. Many misdemeanor cases are resolved with plea agreements and penalties that involve fines, probation, or short-term jail sentences.[31]

DISCRETION AND ETHICS THROUGHOUT THE CRIMINAL JUSTICE SYSTEM

Crime Commission

Discretion is exercised throughout the criminal justice system, and the limits of discretion vary from jurisdiction to jurisdiction. Legislative bodies understand that they cannot anticipate the range of circumstances surrounding each crime, anticipate local attitudes and priorities concerning crime control, and enact laws that clearly encompass all conduct that is criminal and all that is not. Nor does any jurisdiction have all the human and financial resources it needs to respond equally to all forms of crime. Therefore, persons charged with the day-to-day response to crime are expected to exercise their own judgment within limits set by law. Basically, they must decide whether to take action, which official response is appropriate, the community's attitude toward specific types of criminal acts, and so forth.

The President's Commission on Law Enforcement and Administration of Justice (published in 1967 and commonly known as the *Crime Commission*) made a very pertinent comment in this regard:

> Crime does not look the same on the street as it does in a legislative chamber. How much noise or profanity makes conduct "disorderly" within the meaning of the law? When must a quarrel be treated as a criminal assault: at the first threat, or at the first shove, or at the first blow, or after blood is drawn, or when a serious injury is inflicted? How suspicious must conduct be before there is "probable cause," the constitutional basis for an arrest? Every [officer], however sketchy or incomplete his education, is an interpreter of the law.[32]

Applying the Law on the Streets

Certainly the police have tremendous amounts of discretionary authority on their beats, largely unsupervised, in dealing with people in the community—to stop or not stop, to search or not search, and to arrest or not arrest; for these reasons, police discretion can be a source of controversy. In the prosecutor's office, assistant district attorneys have considerable discretion in determining which cases to prosecute fully. Judges have broad discretion in the exercise of their functions, including sentencing (even with sentencing guidelines, discussed in Chapter 11).

Ethics and Character: Constant Dilemmas

Robert F. Kennedy, in his 1960 book, *The Enemy Within: The McClellan Committee's Crusade Against Jimmy Hoffa and Corrupt Labor Unions*, stated that

> in the fall of 1959 I spoke at one of the country's most respected law schools. The professor in charge of teaching ethics told me the big question up for discussion among his students was whether, as a lawyer, you could lie to a judge. I told the professor . . . that I thought we had all been taught the answer to that question when we were six years old.[33]

Discretion: authority to make decisions in enforcing the law based on one's observations and judgment ("spirit of the law") rather than the letter of the law.

As Kennedy, the late U.S. Attorney General and U.S. Senator, implied, by the time they reach the point of being college or university students, hopefully everyone—and those who are studying the field of criminal justice in particular—will have had deeply ingrained in them the need to practice exemplary and ethical behavior. Ethical behavior is often emphasized in postsecondary education in the form of instructors explaining the need for academic honesty. Later, at some point in your life, it will likely be emphasized in terms of how you are to conduct yourself in terms of dealing with others as well as perhaps with the property and responsibility that has been entrusted to you.

Character in the criminal justice arena is of foremost importance, for, without it, nothing else matters. "Character," it might be said, "is who we are when no one is watching." So having character means that people would never betray their fellow human beings, or violate their oath of office or public trust. Unfortunately, character of mind and actions cannot be implanted in someone in a college or university classroom, nor can it be inoculated in a doctor's office or be administered intravenously or with a pill.

Prior to commencing your journey into the field of criminal justice (and, later, reading Chapter 4, concerning ethics), you might do well to first ask yourself these questions: Should police officers receive free coffee from restaurants and quick-stop establishments? Free or half-priced meals? What about judges? Prison wardens? If we do not "reward" judges, wardens, school-teachers, plumbers, pizza delivery persons, or others with "freebies," then should establishments compensate police officers in such a manner? On what grounds do many police officers expect such favored treatment? And can this lead to ethical problems with respect to their work?

At its root, the field of criminal justice is about people and their activities; and in the end, the primary responsibilities of people engaged in this field is to ensure that they be of the highest ethical character and treat everyone with dignity and respect. Therefore, as indicated above, this textbook, unlike most or all others of its kind, devotes an entire chapter to the subject of **ethics**—or what essentially constitutes "correct" behavior in criminal justice.

Police Ethics

Chapter Quiz: Fundamentals of Criminal Justice

Ethics: a set of rules or values that spell out appropriate human conduct.

you be the... JUDGE

IS OUR JUSTICE SYSTEM ALWAYS "JUST"?

Nancy Black, a California marine biologist, also captains a whale watching ship. She was with some watchers in 2005 when a member of her crew whistled at a nearby humpback whale, hoping the whale would linger. Meanwhile, on land, one of Black's employees contacted a national oceanographic organization to see if the whistling was in fact harassment of a marine mammal—an environmental crime. Black provided a videotape of the incident, slightly edited to show the whistling; for the editing, she was charged with a felony under the 1863 False Claims Act. She was also charged with a federal crime involving the feeding of killer whales (orcas)—having rigged an apparatus that would stabilize a slab of blubber to better photograph the orca while feeding on a dead gray whale. Since the charges were filed, Black has spent more than $100,000 in legal fees and could be sentenced to 20 years in prison.

1. Does this case represent the conflict or consensus model of justice?

2. Assume Black were to be convicted: Would the end justify the means? Conversely, would the means justify the end result (i.e., having such federal laws, compelling such exorbitant legal fees)?

3. Do you believe politics played a part in this case?

4. Where would this type of case fit on the "wedding cake" model of criminal justice?

5. Should the prosecutor have the discretion to drop all charges in this case?

Source: For more information, see "Nancy Black, Indicted Marine Biologist, Denies Feeding Orcas," *Huffington Post*, February 1, 2012, http://www.huffingtonpost.com/2012/02/01/indicted-marine-biologist-nancy-black_n_1247284.html (accessed March 4, 2013).

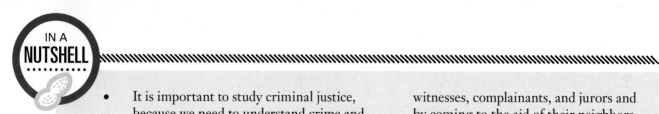

- It is important to study criminal justice, because we need to understand crime and criminal justice generally, and given that all of us are potential victims, witnesses, and taxpaying supporters of our justice system; particularly since 9/11, we have also learned that we are no longer safe within our borders. Furthermore, we need to be able to understand the processing of criminals and the rights we enjoy under law in a democracy.

- The consensus-versus-conflict debate concerns challenges to the legitimacy of the law, the system of government that enacts the laws, and the justice agencies that carry them out. The stability of our government for more than 200 years is a testimony to the existence of consensus as to its legitimacy, although some theorists described long ago the conflicts between the ruling group and the other groups in society, and the need to use force and other means to ensure the compliance of the other groups.

- The due process model of criminal justice basically holds that criminal defendants should be presumed innocent, and constitutional rights of the accused should be upheld. Conversely, the crime control model, likened to an "assembly line," emphasizes repressing criminal conduct and protecting society; legal loopholes should be eliminated and offenders swiftly punished, and the police and prosecutors should be given a high degree of discretion. Neither of these models, however, completely dominates a particular community or U.S. crime policy.

- Politics permeates the field of criminal justice, from governing boards and politicians to enacting laws and budgets; everything—who is hired and elected as officeholders; the construction of new police stations, courthouses, jails, and prisons; and other operations at the national, state, and local levels of government—is driven by politics.

- In order to function properly, the law and the criminal justice system need citizens to be willing to "get involved" by their willingness to report crimes and serve as witnesses, complainants, and jurors and by coming to the aid of their neighbors. Furthermore, most crimes are reported to the police by citizens. The Kitty Genovese case stands as an example of what can happen when people are unwilling to become engaged in the crime control effort.

- Although the path of the offender through the criminal justice process may be viewed as horizontal in nature, there are many points throughout where he or she takes a vertical pathway out of the system, and for a variety of reasons: Much of our crime is not discovered or reported to the police (the so-called shadow of crime); in some cases no perpetrator is identified or apprehended; and, in other instances, a suspect is arrested, but later the police determine that no crime was committed, and he or she is released from custody.

- The wedding cake model of criminal justice argues that not all criminal cases are viewed or handled in the same manner by either the police or the judiciary. The type of treatment given to a particular case is determined by such factors as the seriousness of the charge, the current policy implications, and the defendant's celebrity and resources. The processing of cases by the criminal justice system is divided into four categories: celebrated cases, serious felonies, lesser felonies, and misdemeanors.

- Discretion is exercised throughout the criminal justice system, because violations of laws vary in their seriousness, and there are not enough human and financial resources to enforce all laws equally. Therefore, persons charged with enforcing laws, adjudicating cases, and punishing offenders exercise considerable judgment in terms of deciding whether to take action, which official response is appropriate, the community's attitude toward specific types of criminal acts, and so forth.

- Ethical considerations are also at the root of criminal justice; the people engaged in this field must be of the highest ethical character and treat everyone with dignity and respect.

Adjudication	Discretion	Prosecution
Aggravating circumstances	District attorney	Recognizance
Appeal	Due process model	Sanctions
Conflict theory	Ethics	Sentence
Consensus theory	Indeterminate sentencing	Three-strikes laws
Corrections	Mitigating circumstances	"Wedding cake" model of
Crime control model	*Nolo contendere*	criminal justice
Criminal justice flow and	Parole	
process	Political influence	
Determinate sentences	Probable cause	

STUDY SITE

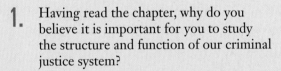

Sharpen your skills with **SAGE edge** at **edge.sagepub.com/peak**. **SAGE edge for students** provides a personalized approach to help you accomplish your coursework goals in an easy-to-use learning environment. Access the videos, audio clips, quizzes, cases and SAGE journal and reference articles that are noted in this chapter.

REVIEW QUESTIONS?

1. Having read the chapter, why do you believe it is important for you to study the structure and function of our criminal justice system?

2. How would you describe the crime control and due process models of criminal justice? What indicators might be present in your local community for determining which particular model is apparently dominant?

3. How would you characterize the influence of politics on our criminal justice system? What might be an example of "good politics" and "bad politics"?

4. Why is it important for citizens to be willing to "get involved" with crime and the criminal justice process? In what ways can you become so involved?

5. What are the major points where the offender is dealt with in the criminal justice process, as he or she moves through the police, courts, and corrections components?

6. Do you believe there exists a true criminal justice "system"? Explain your answer.

7. How would you characterize the importance of discretion and ethics throughout the justice system?

As indicated in this textbook's Preface, this "Learn by Doing'" section, as well as those at the ends of all other chapters of this book, is an outgrowth of teachings by famed educator John Dewey, who advocated the "learning by doing" or problem-based approach to education. It also follows the popular learning method espoused by Benjamin Bloom in 1956, known as "Bloom's Taxonomy," in which he called for "higher-order thinking skills"—critical and creative thinking that involves analysis, synthesis, and evaluation.[34]

The following scenarios and activities will shift your attention from textbook-centered instruction and move the emphasis to student-centered projects. By being placed in these hypothetical situations, you can thus learn—and apply—some of the concepts covered in this chapter, develop skills in communication and self-management, at times become a problem solver, and learn about/address current community issues.

1. Assume that you are an officer in your campus criminal justice honor society and are invited to speak at the society's monthly meeting concerning your view of how crime is perceived and dealt with in your community. You opt to approach the question from Packer's crime control/due process perspectives. Given what you know about crime and criminal justice in your community, what will you say in your presentation?

2. As a member of your campus criminal justice honor society, you are asked to speak at a meeting of your local police department's Citizens' Police Academy, focusing on the general need for citizens to "become involved" in addressing crime. What will you say (include the Kitty Genovese case in your presentation)?

3. Your criminal justice professor asks you to prepare your own succinct diagram of the criminal justice process, including brief descriptions of each of the major stages (arrest, initial appearance, and so on) as a case flows through the process; what will your final product look like?

4. As part of a class group project concerning the nature of crime and punishment, you are asked by your fellow group members to develop a 10-minute presentation on the "wedding cake" model of crime. How will you describe it?

FOUNDATIONS OF LAW AND CRIME:
Nature, Elements, and Defenses

LEARNING OBJECTIVES

As a result of reading this chapter, the student will be able to:

1 Briefly explain how modern-day law evolved from English common law, and the differences between criminal and civil law

2 Explain the difference between substantive and procedural law

3 Provide examples of how outdated, unenforced laws are not always repealed from the statutes and ordinances

4 Review two critical elements of the criminal law—criminal intent (*mens rea*) and the physical commission of the criminal act (*actus reus*)

5 Delineate the definitions of, and distinctions between, felonies and misdemeanors, and Part I and Part II crimes

6 Discuss the various defenses that citizens may offer to reduce or eliminate their criminal liability

CHAPTER

02

The Constitution of the United States was made not merely for the generation that then existed, but for posterity-unlimited, undefined, endless, perpetual posterity.

—Henry Clay

INTRODUCTION

Author Introduction:
Chapter 2

John Adams famously said we have a "government of laws and not of men," meaning that our democracy is not ruled on the whim of kings or rulers or demagogues. As explained in Chapter 1, Americans willfully give up some of their rights to their elected governments to create laws and to receive protection for their persons and property. It thus becomes important that Americans possess at least a fundamental knowledge of the rule of law; however, most of us probably fall quite short of having such knowledge.

As examples, we often hear someone screaming "I've been robbed!" on television or in the movies after returning home and discovering it has been entered and ransacked (he or she was not robbed). Or, someone discovers a dead body and states "He's been murdered!" (a person may have indeed been killed, but many killings are not criminal in nature; only a judge or jury can decide). Another common error is when a news reporter states that "John Jones, a convicted murderer, was sentenced to jail today" (Jones will actually serve his sentence in a prison, not a jail). As French philosopher Voltaire wrote, "If you wish to converse with me, define your terms." That statement represents the major purpose of this chapter.

The reader should bear in mind, however, that several important components of the rule of law will not be discussed here, either because they go beyond the reach of an introductory textbook or given space limitations. Persons wishing to inquire more deeply into the law—for example, in such areas as conspiracies, attempted crimes, omissions, and causation—would be wise to enroll in criminal law and procedure courses.

ASSESS YOUR AWARENESS:

Test your knowledge of the nature of law and crime by first reading and responding to the following seven true-false items; check your answers after reading this chapter's materials.

1. The U.S. legal system is based on English common law.

2. A person returning home, discovering her premises has been illegally entered and valuables removed, will correctly tell police "I've been robbed."

3. Under current U.S. laws, one can only be charged with criminal acts he or she actually performs, and not for failure to act or perform in some manner.

4. Today, as opposed to English common law, one may use force, even deadly force, if he or she reasonably believes that an attack against him or her is imminent.

5. Intoxication will generally always be a successful defense and excuse one from guilt.

6. There is no particular amount of time necessary for one to legally premeditate a murder.

7. Basically there are only two defenses one can use against being charged with a crime: "I didn't know it was a crime," and/or "I was too intoxicated to know what I was doing."

Answers can be found on page 401.

In addition to a number of examples, several criminal cases are intermingled to challenge the reader's knowledge of chapter materials. A summary, key terms and concepts, review questions, and "Learn by Doing" exercises conclude the chapter.

COMMON LAW AND ITS PROGENY

Hammurabi

Rules were laid out in ancient societies. As examples, the law can be traced back to the reign of Hammurabi (1792–1750 B.C.E.), the sixth king of the ancient empire of Babylon (which set out crimes and punishments based on *lex talionis*—"an eye for an eye, a tooth for a tooth"), and a more recent source of law found in the Mosaic Code of the Israelites (1200 B.C.E.) (in which, according to tradition, Moses—acting as an intermediary for God—passed on the law to the tribes of Israel).

Common Law

But the system of law as we know it today (except for Louisiana's, which is based on the French civil code) is based on the common law: collections of rules, customs, and traditions of medieval England, created during the reign of Henry II (1154–1189 C.E.), who began the process of unifying the law. Henry established a permanent body of professional judges who traveled a "circuit" and sat as tribunals in shires throughout the Crown's realm; these judges eventually gave the Crown jurisdiction over all major crimes, and sowed the seeds of the trial by jury and the doctrine of *stare decisis*.[1]

The latter doctrine, **stare decisis** (Latin for "to stand by things settled"), is perhaps the most distinctive aspect of Anglo-American common law. According to the simple definition in *Black's Law Dictionary*, *stare decisis* is the doctrine stating that, when a court has once laid down a principle of law as applicable to a certain state of facts, it will adhere to that principle—and apply it in the same manner to all future cases where facts are substantially the same.[2] This doctrine binds courts of equal or lower status or levels in its jurisdiction to the principles established by the higher appellate courts within the same jurisdiction.

For example, a federal district court in Maryland is required to follow the decisions of the Fourth Circuit Court of Appeals, of which it is a part, as well as those of the U.S. Supreme Court, but it is not bound by the decisions of other district courts or by the Maryland state courts.[3] Note, however, that our system of law still must remain flexible and capable of change, and thus courts can also revisit earlier decisions and set a new precedent.

The Code of Hammurabi, written in about 1780 B.C.E., set out crimes and punishments based on *lex talionis*—"an eye for an eye, a tooth" – is the earliest-known example of a ruler setting forth a body of laws arranged in orderly groupings.

CRIMINAL AND CIVIL LAW

Another important distinction is between criminal and civil law. Simply put, **criminal law** applies to criminal matters, when someone breaks a criminal law against committing robbery, for example. **Civil law** applies to civil matters,

Criminal law: the body of law that defines criminal offenses and prescribes punishments for their infractions.

when two parties have a property dispute or want to get divorced. These two distinct types of law differ in several critical ways.

First, each type involves different parties. When someone commits a crime, the state or government—through the prosecutor or district attorney—prosecutes the person on behalf of the people (because the criminal law represents what we as a people have decided is criminal behavior and crimes are considered harmful to all of us, as a society). A typical criminal case name is something like *U.S. v. Jones* or *State of Nevada v. Smith*. In a civil matter, two individuals (or business entities like a corporation) are on either side. In a property dispute, such as when A erects a fence five feet along the property line of B, one neighbor brings a lawsuit against the other so the court can referee their dispute. Or if a person is injured using a product like a blow dryer, that person can bring a civil case against the manufacturer, probably a corporation. A typical civil law case name is something like *Jones v. Smith* or *Jones v. ABC Corporation*. In the former example, Jones is the party bringing the suit—the **plaintiff**—and Smith is the party defending against the suit—the **defendant**.

Not surprisingly, these two types of cases are heard in different courts, and most courthouses have separate criminal and civil "divisions," where judges are more experienced in either of these particular type of cases.

Another important difference involves how these cases are decided. In a criminal case, the prosecutor or the state has the burden of proving—the **burden of proof**—the defendant's guilt "beyond a reasonable doubt." This sometimes heavy burden is designed to force the government—the prosecutor—to prove its case because, again, underlying our rule of law in the United States is the all-important concept that one is innocent until proven guilty (technically, one is innocent until the prosecution proves him or her guilty). Sometimes the burden shifts to the defense to prove something, as with self-defense claims, discussed below. In a civil case, the burden on the party seeking damages or a remedy is less than in a criminal matter—those representing this party must prove their case by a "preponderance of the evidence." These two terms can be hard to distinguish, even for experienced lawyers.

Reasonable doubt can be difficult to explain; in fact, several courts prefer to not attempt to give the jury any explanation at all. However, in most cases reasonable doubt means that, after hearing all of the evidence, jurors do not possess an abiding conviction—to a moral certainty—that the charges brought against the defendant are true. This does not necessarily mean absolute certainty—there can still be some doubt, but only to the extent that it would *not* affect a "reasonable person's" belief that the defendant is guilty. On the other hand, if such doubt *does* affect a "reasonable person's" belief that the defendant is guilty, then the prosecution has not met its burden of proof, and the judge or jury must acquit—find the defendant not guilty.

The civil standard of "preponderance of the evidence" is a much less difficult burden to meet and is often referred to as the "50 percent plus a feather" test. It asks jurors to decide which way the evidence causes the scales of justice to tip, toward guilt or innocence, and to decide the case on that basis.

But the major difference between civil and criminal matters is the penalty. In a criminal case, the state or prosecutor seeks to punish a defendant with prison or jail time, a monetary fine, or both (or perhaps a community-based punishment such as probation, discussed in Chapter 14). In a civil matter, one party is seeking "damages" (money or some legal remedy) from the other party rather than trying to send him or her to jail or prison. In the property dispute example, A would be required to tear down or move the fence and perhaps pay for the legal fees incurred in bringing the suit. And in the hair dryer example, the corporation could be ordered to pay the consumer's medical expenses and legal fees.

Some conduct can give rise to both a criminal and a civil matter as the cases of O. J. Simpson and others illustrate.

Civil law: a generic term for all noncriminal law, usually relating to settling disputes between private citizens.

Plaintiff: the party who is bringing a lawsuit or initiating a legal action against someone else.

Defendant: a person against whom a criminal charge is pending; one charged with a crime.

Burden of proof: the requirement that the state must meet to introduce evidence or establish facts.

Reasonable doubt: the standard used by jurors to arrive at a verdict—whether or not the government (prosecutor) has established guilt beyond a reasonable doubt.

FOCUS ON   REASONABLE DOUBT

In 2008 R&B star R. Kelly was put on trial for 14 charges of child pornography with a 13-year-old girl. The prosecution showed a 27-minute videotape of someone they said was Kelly having sex with the girl, arguing that a mole of the back of the person on the tape was similar to one on his back. The defense, meanwhile, argued that the mole on the tape was actually not a mole at all, but instead was a shadow created by the light of the camera. Although several family members identified the girl as being the female in the tape, not all relatives identified her as such. The girl refused to cooperate with the prosecution and did not testify. After several split votes, the jury unanimously found Kelly not guilty because they had reasonable doubt concerning whether the mole was indeed Kelly's. This example demonstrates that, although someone may have committed a crime (the videotape seemed to show Kelly engaged in the criminal conduct), he or she may not be convicted if the prosecution does not establish guilt beyond a reasonable doubt.

Source: Adapted from Steven Gray, "The Acquittal of R. Kelly," *Time,* June 13, 2008, http://www.time.com/time/nation/article/0,8599,1814568,00.html (accessed February 21, 2013).

A few examples might serve to explain the difference—and how the two can cause problems for the police and misunderstanding by the public. Assume that Jane calls the police to her home and tells the officer that she and her husband, Bill, recently separated and he recently went to their home and removed some furniture and other goods that she does not believe he should have taken. The officer must inform Jane that there is nothing he can do—at this point, this is a *civil*, not a criminal, matter. Jane may be upset with the officer, but legally the police have no jurisdiction in such disputes. Assume, however, that Bill goes to the home and makes serious threats of injury toward Jane, and she then goes to court and obtains a temporary protection order (TPO) commanding Bill to avoid any form of contact with her; Bill disregards the TPO and stalks Jane at her place of employment. Because he violated the court's order, this has now become a *criminal* matter, and the police may arrest Bill.

Or, look again at the example of someone erecting a fence that cuts across his neighbor's property by 5 feet. The neighbor refuses to move or tear down the fence, so the matter is taken to court. This is a civil cause of action. Both sides have a dispute that the courts will resolve if they cannot reach an agreement. Assume further that the neighbors cannot resolve the fence matter, and one day while one of them is working in his yard the other attacks him with a club. Now the situation has become *criminal* in nature.

Table 2.1 shows the primary differences between civil and criminal law.

TABLE 2.1

Differences Between Civil and Criminal Law

	CIVIL	CRIMINAL
Burden of proof	"Preponderance of evidence"	"Beyond a reasonable doubt"
Nature of crime	A private wrong	A public wrong
Parties	Case is filed by an individual party	Some level of government files charges against the individual
Punishment	Usually in the form of monetary compensation for damages caused; no incarceration	Jail, fine, prison, probation, possibly death
Examples	Landlord/tenant dispute, divorce proceeding, child custody proceeding, property dispute, auto accident	Person accused of committing some crime (or, perhaps, neglecting a duty to act)

FOCUS ON   CRIMINAL AND CIVIL TRIALS—THE SIMPSON CASE

O. J. Simpson, once a wealthy college and professional football player and actor, was acquitted at his criminal trial for stabbing to death his estranged wife and her friend, but was later found responsible for their deaths in the ensuing civil trial.

O. J. Simpson was once a wealthy and admired college and professional football player as well as a movie and television personality. But in 1994 he was charged with stabbing to death his estranged wife, Nicole, and her friend, Ron Goldman. The media covered the trial live as California prosecutors put on evidence of Simpson's history of domestic abuse and damning DNA evidence from the crime scene, while Simpson's "Dream Team" of high-caliber defense attorneys cross-examined the state's witnesses and dissected their evidence in hopes of creating

reasonable doubt about Simpson's guilt. After the nearly yearlong trial, the jury deliberated only four hours before returning not-guilty verdicts on all charges. One year later, the victims' parents filed a civil suit against Simpson, alleging that he caused the victims' wrongful deaths and seeking millions of dollars in damages for those deaths. Many people wondered how the families could hope to win when Simpson had been found not guilty in the criminal trial. The answer lies in the differences between the criminal and civil cases. In the civil case, the burden of proof on the families was less than the burden on the prosecutors in the criminal case. The families needed to show only by a "preponderance of the evidence"—rather than beyond a reasonable doubt—that Simpson killed the victims. The civil jurors needed to decide only which way the scales of justice tipped, toward guilt or innocence, not whether the state had proven Simpson's guilt beyond a reasonable doubt. Indeed, the civil jury found Simpson responsible for the deaths and awarded the families $33.5 million in damages. So while Simpson was acquitted in the criminal trial and did not serve any prison time, he was adjudged responsible in the civil trial and ordered to pay money damages for his conduct.

Source: For a complete analysis of the Simpson case, see, for example, Jeffrey Toobin, *The Run of His Life: The People v. O. J. Simpson* (New York: Random House, 1998); Lawrence Schiller and James Willwerth, *American Tragedy: The Uncensored Story of the O. J. Simpson Defense* (New York: Random House, 1996); Joseph Bosco, *A Problem of Evidence: How the Prosecution Freed O. J. Simpson* (New York: William Morrow, 1996); CNN.com, *O. J. Simpson Main Page,* http://www.cnn.com/US/OJ/ (accessed March 26, 2013).

SUBSTANTIVE AND PROCEDURAL LAW

Substantive law: the body of law that spells out the elements of criminal acts.

Procedural law: rules that set forth how substantive laws are to be enforced, such as those covering arrest, search, and seizure.

Substantive law is the written law that defines criminal acts—the very "substance" of the criminal law. Examples are laws that define and prohibit murder and robbery. **Procedural law** (discussed in detail in Chapter 8) sets forth the procedures and mechanisms for processing criminal cases. The Fourth Amendment (requiring police officers to obtain search and arrest warrants, except in certain situations) is procedural law, as is the requirement that officers give the *Miranda* warning before a suspect is interrogated while in custody (Fifth and Sixth Amendments) and the right to an attorney at key junctures during processing through the criminal justice system. (Note that these requirements are not criminal laws in the way the law prohibits robbery or murder, but rather these laws govern how police officers, lawyers, judges, corrections officers, and a host of others do their work in the justice system.) Procedural law also prescribes rules concerning jurisdiction, jury selection, appeal, evidence presented to a jury, order of conducting a trial, representation of counsel, and so on.

MODERN-DAY SOURCES AND HIERARCHY OF LAW

In addition to the two primary types of law—criminal and civil—the U.S. legal system features different sources of law and jurisdictions where those laws are enforced and administered. As you would expect to find in our federal system of government, we have federal and state laws with corresponding federal and state courts to preside over such cases. Within those two legal arenas, laws—criminal and civil—are organized hierarchically, with different priorities and legal effects depending on their source and application.

Again, terminology is critical to understanding law. Generally speaking, a *statute* is a law enacted by Congress (a federal law) or by a state legislature (a state law). Statutes are also known as *statutory law*. A *code* or *ordinance* typically refers to a law enacted by a local lawmaking body—a county board or a city council, for example (municipal laws). These and other types of laws are prioritized as follows:

Federal Law

1. The U.S. Constitution—"the supreme law of the land," which takes precedence over state constitutions and law even if they conflict

2. Federal statutes—civil and criminal laws enacted by Congress

3. Administrative laws—orders, directives, and regulations for federal agencies, such as workplace laws promulgated by the Occupational Safety and Health Administration (OSHA)

4. Federal common law—published decisions from the U.S. Supreme Court and the U.S. Circuit Courts of Appeal, which, like the common law from England (discussed above), establish legal "precedence" and must be followed by lower courts in the federal and state systems (Chapter 9 describes how the Supreme Court decides to hear cases and render its decisions.)

Procedural law sets forth the mechanisms for processing criminal cases, such as the requirement that officers give the Miranda warning before a suspect is interrogated.

Sources of federal law include the U.S. Constitution, the U.S. Supreme Court, and those enacted by Congress.

State Law

Precedence

1. State constitutional law—state constitutional rulings (from a state's highest court) that may give greater protection or rights than the federal constitution but may not give less, and that contain protections similar to the U.S. Constitution—civil rights and liberties, separation of powers, and checks and balances[4]

2. State statutes—laws enacted by state legislatures, including criminal laws like a statute prohibiting murder or robbery

3. State common law—precedent established in published opinions by state appellate judges when deciding civil or criminal cases

City/County Law

Municipal ordinances or codes govern many aspects of our daily lives, including all of the following:

- Building and construction standards

- Rent control

- Noise and nuisance regulations

- Public health and safety

- Business licenses

- Civil rights and antidiscrimination

ESSENTIAL ELEMENTS: *MENS REA* AND *ACTUS REUS*

Intent, specific: a purposeful act or state of mind to commit a crime.

Motive: the reason for committing a crime.

The Latin term for criminal intent is *mens rea*, or "guilty mind," and its importance cannot be overstated. Our entire legal system and criminal laws are designed to punish only those actors who intend to commit their acts, and as will be seen below in the law of homicide, clearly intentional, premeditated acts (murder in the first degree) are punished most severely, while those acts that are less intentional and/or accidental are punished less harshly. For example, assume Bill, while hunting deer, shoots another hunter while out in the woods; if the prosecutor believes the shooting was purely accidental in nature, Bill will not be charged with unlawful killing.

Mens Rea: Intent Versus Motive to Commit Crime

An important distinction to be made concerns the difference between *intent* and *motive*. One's specific **intent** concerns what he is seeking to do and is connected to a purpose or goal; **motive** refers to one's reason for doing something. For example, when a poverty-stricken woman steals milk for her child, her intention is to steal, but

One's criminal intent is a major consideration in our legal system; for example, one who intentionally kills someone during a robbery may well be charged with premeditated murder, while a hunter who accidentally (without intent) shoots and kills another normally would not.

her motive is to provide for her child. Therefore, motive (the "why" someone is stirred to perform an action) is primarily grounded in psychology; intent, conversely, is the result of one's motive, is grounded in law, and carries a higher degree of blameworthiness because a harmful act was committed. Anyone who watches crime movies can attest that much ado is often made of one's possible motive for committing a particular crime. However, as one law professor put it, "As any first year law student will tell you, motive is irrelevant in determining criminal liability. Unlike in the television show . . . in the perceived real world of criminal liability, motive is just a bit player, appearing only in limited circumstances, usually as a consideration in certain defenses. Ordinarily, the only real questions at trial are (1) did the defendant commit the illegal act and (2) did she have the necessary mental state (*mens rea*)?[5]

One's intent while committing a crime is not always easy to prove. As will be seen below with the crime of homicide, when A shoots B, there are a variety of possible outcomes, and the prosecutor will "look behind the act" to determine what was going on in the mind of the killer, and whether to reduce what appears to be a charge of murder in the first degree (an intentional killing) down to manslaughter (an accidental killing).

Actus Reus: The Act

Another critical feature of the U.S. criminal justice system is that we do not punish people for merely thinking about committing criminal acts; rather, the law generally requires a voluntary, overt act or an intentional *failure* to act where there is a legal duty to do so (known as an "omission," such as a parent failing to feed a child or give him or her medical attention).

you be the... JUDGE

MENS REA AND *ACTUS REUS*

The Nebraska Revised Statutes set forth the following statutory provisions. Read them carefully and then respond to the questions posed.

28-306. Motor vehicle homicide; penalty.

(1) A person who causes the death of another unintentionally while engaged in the operation of a motor vehicle in violation of the law of the State of Nebraska or in violation of any city or village ordinance commits motor vehicle homicide.

60-6,213. Reckless driving, defined.

Any person who drives any motor vehicle in such a manner as to indicate an indifferent or wanton disregard for the safety of persons or property shall be guilty of reckless driving.

60-6,214. Willful reckless driving, defined.

Any person who drives any motor vehicle in such a manner as to indicate a willful disregard for the safety of persons or property shall be guilty of willful reckless driving.

1. What is the *mens rea* element under Section 1 of the motor vehicle homicide statute (and what word[s] defines the *mens rea* element)?

2. Provide an example of what would qualify as motor vehicle homicide under Section 1.

3. A woman who is texting while driving strikes and kills a pedestrian who is crossing the street. The woman was not speeding. Can she be charged for a violation of Section 1? Why or why not?

4. Which word(s) supplies the *mens rea* element under Section 60-6,213 (reckless driving)? Define and provide examples of the word(s).

5. Do the same as above (Item 4) for Section 60-6,214.

Source: Pamela M. Everett, personal communication, March 25, 2013.

The rule for establishing criminal liability is to prove that the defendant committed the *actus reus* element (the criminal act) with the *mens rea* ("guilty mind") set forth in the particular criminal law. The prosecutor must prove both elements beyond a reasonable doubt—a question of fact for the jury to decide.

Mid-Chapter Quiz: Foundations of Law and Crime

FELONIES AND MISDEMEANORS

Crimes are also classified into two broad categories based on the severity of the criminal act and the corresponding punishment. **Felonies** are offenses punishable by death or that have a possible sentence of more than one year of incarceration in prison. Many states further divide their felonies into different classes; for example, under Arizona's laws, first-degree murder is a Class 1 felony and is punishable by death or life imprisonment; forcible rape is a Class 2 felony (the number of years for which one may be sentenced to prison for this and other offenses will differ, depending on an offender's prior record); aggravated robbery (the offender has an accomplice) is a Class 3 felony; forgery is a Class 4 felony; and so forth.[6]

A **misdemeanor** is a less serious offense and is typically punishable by incarceration for less than one year in a local jail. Like felonies, misdemeanors are often classified under state laws. In Arizona, shoplifting is a Class 1 misdemeanor (if the value of items taken is less than $250); reckless driving is a Class 2 misdemeanor; a vehicle driver who leaves the scene of an accident is guilty of a Class 3 misdemeanor; and so on.[7]

OFFENSE DEFINITIONS AND CATEGORIES

The Federal Bureau of Investigation (FBI) maintains a Uniform Crime Reporting (UCR) program (discussed more in Chapter 3) dividing offenses into two groups, Part I and Part II crimes. Each month, contributing agencies voluntarily submit information to the FBI concerning the number of Part I offenses reported to them, as well as those offenses that were cleared by arrest, and the age, sex, and race of persons arrested for each of the offenses.

Next is further discussion of Part I and II offenses.

Part I Offenses

Part I or "index" crimes are composed of eight serious felonies—murder, forcible rape, robbery, aggravated assault, burglary, larceny-theft, motor vehicle theft, and arson. About 10.2 million such crimes are reported each year (about 1.2 million being violent and 9 million, property).[8] The first four of these eight offenses—the **crimes against persons**—and their approximate annual rates are discussed briefly below to illustrate how crimes are defined and how the elements of *mens rea* and *actus reus* operate.

Crimes Against Persons

Crimes Against Persons

Violent crime is composed of four offenses: murder and non-negligent manslaughter, forcible rape, robbery, and aggravated assault. Violent crimes are defined in the UCR as those offenses that involve force or threat of force.

Murder and Homicide: The taking of a human life—homicide—is obviously the most serious act that one can perpetrate against another person. But not every killing is criminal in nature as the following demonstrate:

- Justifiable homicide—acts of war, self-defense, legal state or federal executions, and where a police officer uses lawful lethal force
- Excusable homicide—killings that are accidental, such as a person who runs over an unseen toddler in the driveway behind his car

Felony: a serious offense with a possible sentence of more than a year in prison.

Misdemeanor: a lesser offense, normally punishable by a fine or up to one year in a local jail.

Crime against persons: a violent crime, to include murder, rape, robbery, and assault.

The term *murder*, however, includes only intentional killings, which are categorized by degrees.

As mentioned earlier, under our system of justice, the premise underlying homicide is that "when A shoots B, there are a variety of possible outcomes." The prosecutor must attempt to determine the shooter's intent, which can result in criminal charges ranging from murder in the first degree to involuntary manslaughter.

- *Murder in the first degree* (sometimes termed "murder one") is the unlawful, intentional killing of a human being with *premeditation/deliberation* (often termed "P&D") and *malice aforethought* (note that federal and state statutes define murder and its elements differently, but generally they all require the elements of intent, P&D, and malice aforethought). P&D means the defendant thought about committing the act before doing so. Courts generally look at the following factors to determine P&D: evidence of planning, the manner of killing, and the prior relationship between the defendant and the victim.[9] Courts also look at the *time* a defendant may have contemplated or planned to determine whether premeditation existed, but courts differ on this issue. The federal courts have held that *no* minimum time period is necessary, and a jury can determine from the facts whether or not a defendant premeditated murder.[10]

Excusable killings include those that are accidental in nature, such as when a driver strikes and kills a toddler who darts out into the street; in such cases the driver will not be deemed culpable (blameworthy).

Malice aforethought is often said to be shown where someone acts with "a depraved heart," evidenced by one's shooting a gun, stabbing with a knife, and so on. Malice is discussed more below, under second-degree murder.

Dangerous conduct can also be prosecuted as first-degree murder under the **felony-murder rule**, which provides that if a death occurs during the commission of a felony, the defendant will be charged with murder in the first degree, regardless of his or her intent (a crime that does not require a *mens rea* element is known as a "strict liability" crime—see also the discussion of statutory rape below). The classic example is where multiple defendants rob a bank and during the robbery the bank security guard dies from a heart attack. In that case, all the defendants may be charged with first-degree murder under the felony-murder rule. Likewise, if one of the bank robbers panics and shoots a security guard, all of the defendants will be charged with first-degree murder even though the robbers intended only to rob, not to kill anyone.

Murder

- *Murder in the second degree* ("murder two") is distinguished from first-degree murder in that it is also intentional—with malice—yet *impulsive*, without P&D. An example would be where two men get into an argument at a bar, and one pulls a knife and stabs the other to death. He intended to stab the other man, but the killing did not involve premeditation. Furthermore, while the intent to kill is an essential element of both first- and second-degree murder, a defendant can also be found guilty of second-degree murder if his actions show gross recklessness, a disregard for human life is high, and there is extreme risk of death. Although it will depend on the jury's views, such acts as allowing a dangerous pit bull dog to run at large (which then bites and kills a child), intentionally shooting a gun into a crowd of people, throwing a heavy object off of a roof onto a crowded street below, and playing Russian roulette (loading a gun and intentionally firing it at another person) have been found to lead to conviction for second-degree murder.[11]

Felony-murder rule: the legal doctrine that says if a death occurs during the commission of a felony, the perpetrator of the crime may be charged with murder in the first degree.

FOCUS ON   THE "NIGHT STALKER," SERIAL KILLER, DIES IN PRISON

Some people are thought to be purely evil, such as Richard Ramirez, whose murderous crime spree in the mid-1980s included 13 murders — many of which were particularly heinous and included reports of satanic symbols at bloody crime scenes.

Richard Ramirez, the serial killer known as the "Night Stalker" and the subject of books and movies, and who went on a one-year murderous crime spree in southern California in the mid-1980s, died in June 2013 of natural causes (age 53) while awaiting execution.

Ramirez had been on San Quentin's death row since 1989 after being convicted for committing 13 murders, 5 attempted murders, 11 sexual assaults, and 14 burglaries. Many of his crimes were particularly heinous, and there were reports of satanic symbols at bloody crime scenes. According to a prison spokesperson, since 1978, when California reinstated capital punishment, 13 condemned inmates have been put to death, 59 have died from natural causes, 22 have committed suicide, and 6 have died from other causes.

Source: Patrick Garrity, "'Night Stalker,' Serial Killer in 1980s, Dies in Prison," NBCNews. com, June 7, 2013, http://usnews.nbcnews.com/_news/2013/06/07/18829118-night-stalker-serial-killer-in-1980s-dies-in-prison?lite (accessed June 7, 2013).

Second-degree murder involves an intentional yet spontaneous, impulsive killing, without premeditation but with malice—such as when two individuals are arguing and one stabs the other to death.

- *Voluntary manslaughter* is an intentional killing but involves (at least in the eyes of the law) no malice; instead, there is "heat of passion" to a degree that a "reasonable person" might have been provoked into killing someone. The best example is where one comes home early in the day and finds his or her significant other in the arms of another person, becomes enraged, grabs a gun, and kills one or both of them. The killer acted in the heat of passion rather than intentionally. A killing can be downgraded to voluntary manslaughter only if the actor was adequately provoked (generally, words alone—as in an argument—are not enough to provoke, but seeing something like a cheating spouse is), and the actor must not have had time to "cool off." The person discovering his cheating spouse cannot leave, go to a bar and drink a few beers, and then return to the scene and kill the offending couple (this would be first-degree murder, as explained above). The "passion" that aroused the person to kill must have arisen immediately in time and continued until the time of the criminal act.

- *Involuntary manslaughter* is typically established in two ways: (1) acts of negligence, such as when one is driving too fast on a slick road and kills a pedestrian, and (2) the misdemeanor-manslaughter rule—similar to the felony-murder rule, but the crime involved is a misdemeanor. A man enters a convenience store and shoplifts a six-pack of beer; the clerk chases him out the door but slips and falls, striking his head on the sidewalk and dying from the force of the impact. The shoplifter may be charged with involuntary manslaughter, as his actions caused the clerk's death.

Each year there are about 14,000 homicides reported to the police in the United States.[12] As seen in Table 2.2, however, crimes of murder have been declining since 2008.

TABLE 2.2

Declining Rates of Murders Committed in the United States

YEAR	POPULATION	MURDER AND NON-NEGLIGENT MANSLAUGHTER	MURDER AND NON-NEGLIGENT MANSLAUGHTER RATE
2007	301,621,157	17,128	5.7
2008	304,059,724	16,465	5.4
2009	307,006,550	15,399	5.0
2010	309,330,219	14,722	4.8
2011	311,591,917	14,612	4.7

Source: Adapted from Federal Bureau of Investigation, "Table 1. Volume and Rate per 100,000 Inhabitants, 1992–2011," *Crime in the United States—2011* (Washington, D.C.: Uniform Crime Reporting Program), http://www.fbi.gov/about-us/cjis/ucr/crime-in-the-u.s/2011/crime-in-the-u.s.-2011/tables/table-1 (accessed February 15, 2013).

Consider the facts in "A Tale of Two Shootings," the following "You Be the Prosecutor" case (based on an actual incident in a western state). Then determine the likely homicide charges that will be filed.

Forcible Rape (or "Sexual Assault" under Most State Laws Today): Forcible rape is defined as the carnal knowledge of a female forcibly and against her will (the UCR does not list rapes against men, nor does it list same-sex rape, but

Rape

you be the... PROSECUTOR

A TALE OF TWO SHOOTINGS

One Sunday summer afternoon, Charles, leaving a swap meet and very intoxicated, is driving his van and decides to park and "sleep it off" in a parking lot of a mechanic's garage. The two brothers who own the garage show up and become upset that the van is parked there, and begin to shake the van in an attempt to awaken the man inside and force him to leave. As the brothers shake the van violently, Charles awakens and becomes very frightened, not comprehending what is occurring. He grabs his pistol, exits the van, and immediately shoots and kills one brother who is standing beside the van. Seeing this, the second brother runs away and manages to enter the garage (with Charles still in pursuit) and attempts to reach a desk telephone; Charles continues chasing this brother inside the garage, and then shoots and kills him as well.

1. What charges will likely be filed against Charles by the prosecutor for the shooting of the *first* brother? Brother 2?

you be the...
PROSECUTOR

THE ELEMENTS OF RAPE

Three men are spending an evening drinking in bars. In one bar, one of them begins dancing with a young woman who is intoxicated and soon collapses in his arms on the dance floor. The men offer to drive the woman to her home, and place her in the back seat of their car. Once in the car, they each sexually assault the woman while she is still unconscious in the back seat. Some time later, when the woman fails to regain consciousness, the men become concerned about her well-being and drive her to a nearby service station, where medical personnel are contacted. Eventually, it is determined that the woman is dead—and was most likely deceased at the point of her collapse on the dance floor due to a serious congenital heart condition.

1. What is the *primary* legal issue in this case? Also consider the essential elements that must be proven to establish the crime of rape (discussed above).

2. On what grounds could the prosecutor justify the decision to charge the men with conspiracy to commit rape? What would be the *defense* arguments in their behalf?

3. If the three men were to be found *not* to have committed an actual rape (i.e., the required elements of the crime were not met), is there another crime(s) for which they might be charged and convicted?

most modern state statutes include both of these acts as crimes). Assaults and attempts to commit rape by force or threat of force are also included; however, statutory rape (a "strict liability" crime with no mens rea element, requiring only a "victim" of a certain age, typically between 12 and 16, and a "perpetrator" who is older, typically 19 and above) and other sex offenses are excluded. Approximately 80,000 forcible rapes are annually reported to police.[13]

Note the above definition of rape and then consider "The Elements of Rape" in the "You Be the Prosecutor" case study above, again based on an actual event.

Robbery involves the taking, or attempting to take, anything of value from another person by force or threat of force or violence, where the victim is in fear of injury or death.

Robbery: Robbery is the taking of or attempt to take anything of value from the care, custody, or control of a person or persons by force or threat of force or violence and/or by putting the victim in fear. About 350,000 robberies are reported to the police annually in the United States.[14] As stated in the opening chapter section, many times people who come home to find their houses have been broken into claim they have been "robbed" when they obviously have not (they have been burglarized), given that robbery requires a face-to-face taking—a combination of theft and assault.

Aggravated Assault: Aggravated assault is an unlawful attack upon another for the purpose of inflicting severe or aggravated bodily injury. This offense is usually accompanied by the use of a weapon or by other means likely to produce death or great bodily harm. When aggravated assault (or even regular assault, as long as there is a threat) and larceny-theft occur together, the offense falls under the category of robbery. Each year about 750,000 aggravated assaults are reported in the United States.[15]

As discussed above with homicide crimes, criminal justice students often have difficulty understanding the "ladder" of assault crimes. A few examples will help to clarify the differences.

First, the mere placing of someone in fear for their safety is an assault; if Joe yells at Jack threateningly, "I'm going to beat your brains out," this is an assault. An *assault*, then, occurs when one person makes threatening gestures that alarm someone and makes him feel under attack; actual physical contact is not necessary; threatening gestures that alarm someone can constitute an assault.

But if Joe intentionally strikes Jack on his cheek, the intentional physical contact intended to harm raises this conduct to the crime of *assault and battery*.

Finally, if Joe gets a lug wrench out of his car and strikes Jack with it several times, inflicting severe injury, Joe has now committed an *aggravated assault*.

Crimes Against Property

Crimes against property that are included in the FBI's *Uniform Crime Reports* are burglary, larceny-theft, motor vehicle theft, and arson. Next is a brief definition of each.

Crimes Against Property

Burglary: Burglary is the unlawful entry of a structure to commit a felony or theft. To classify an offense as a burglary, the use of force to gain entry need not have occurred, nor does anything of value have to have been stolen. The UCR definition of "structure" includes an apartment, a barn, a house trailer or houseboat when used as a permanent dwelling, an office, a railroad car (but not an automobile), a stable, and a vessel (i.e., ship). Annually, about 2.2 million burglaries are reported in the United States.[16]

Larceny-Theft: Larceny-theft is the unlawful taking, carrying, leading, or riding away of property from the possession of another; it includes attempted thefts as well as thefts of bicycles, motor vehicle parts and accessories, shoplifting, pocket-picking, or the stealing of any property or article that is not taken by force and violence or by fraud. The value of the item stolen is significant, and in all states the monetary worth will determine whether or not the larceny-theft is a felony or misdemeanor; each state's statutes will set forth its limits. Using Nevada statutes as examples, if the item is worth more than $250, it is a felony; Iowa, however, has several classifications: It is a "serious misdemeanor" if the item stolen is valued between $200 and $500, an "aggravated misdemeanor" if worth between $500 and $1,000, and a felony if worth more than $1,000.[17] Each year there are about 6.26 million larceny-thefts reported to the police in the United States.[18]

Motor Vehicle Theft: Motor vehicle theft is the theft or attempted theft of a motor vehicle. The UCR defines a motor vehicle as a self-propelled vehicle that runs on land surfaces and not on rails. Examples of motor vehicles include sport utility vehicles, automobiles, trucks, buses, motorcycles, motor scooters, all-terrain vehicles, and snowmobiles (but not farm equipment, bulldozers, airplanes, construction equipment, or watercraft such as motorboats, sailboats, houseboats, or Jet Skis). There are about 715,000 motor vehicle thefts reported each year to police in the United States.[19]

Arson: Arson is any willful or malicious burning or attempting to burn, with or without intent to defraud, a dwelling house, a public building, a motor vehicle or aircraft, personal property of another, and so forth. There are different

Crime against property: a crime where no violence is perpetrated, such as burglary, theft, auto theft, and arson.

types of arsonists, with very different motives for setting fires. Each year about 43,500 arsons are reported to police, with an average dollar loss per event of about $13,000. About half (45.9 percent) of all arsons involve structures (residential, storage, public, and so on).[20]

TABLE 2.3

Definitions of the FBI's UCR Part I (Index) Crimes

Murder

Murder in the First Degree

A killing with premeditation and deliberation ("P&D")—planned, with malice aforethought (intent to do serious bodily harm, an "evil heart") (felony-murder rule may also be applicable)

Murder in the Second Degree

An impulsive and spontaneous yet intentional killing, with malice aforethought

Voluntary Manslaughter

An intentional killing, under "heat of passion" and with provocation; no "cooling-off" period

Involuntary Manslaughter

An unintended killing involving negligence (the misdemeanor-manslaughter rule may also be applied)

Forcible Rape

Carnal knowledge of a female forcibly and against her will

Robbery

The taking of or attempt to take anything of value from the care, custody, or control of a person or persons by force or threat of force or violence and/or by putting the victim in fear

Aggravated Assault

An unlawful attack by one person upon another for the purpose of inflicting severe or aggravated bodily injury; usually accompanied by the use of a weapon or by other means likely to produce death or great bodily harm

Burglary

The unlawful entry of a structure to commit a felony or theft

Larceny-Theft

The unlawful taking, carrying, leading, or riding away of property from the possession or constructive possession of another

Auto Theft

The theft or attempted theft of a motor vehicle

Arson

Any willful or malicious burning or attempting to burn, with or without intent to defraud, a dwelling house, a public building, a motor vehicle or aircraft, personal property of another, and so forth

The FBI's annual *Uniform Crime Reports* contain a "Crime Clock" that depicts the average time intervals between Part I crimes; a sample Crime Clock is shown in Figure 2.1.

Part II Offenses

In addition to information concerning the aforementioned eight Part I offenses, the FBI provides arrest-only data for about 20 Part II offenses—simple assaults, forgery, embezzlement, prostitution, vandalism, drug violations, and so forth (for more information, see http://www.fbi.gov/about-us/cjis/ucr/crime-in-the.u.s/2011/crime-in-the.u.s.-2011/offense-definitions).

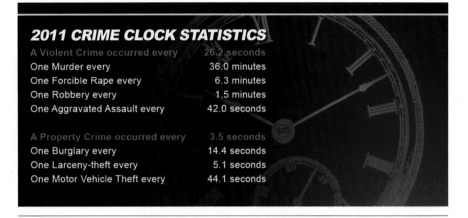

FIGURE 2.1

FBI's UCR "Crime Clock"

2011 CRIME CLOCK STATISTICS

A Violent Crime occurred every	26.2 seconds
One Murder every	36.0 minutes
One Forcible Rape every	6.3 minutes
One Robbery every	1.5 minutes
One Aggravated Assault every	42.0 seconds
A Property Crime occurred every	3.5 seconds
One Burglary every	14.4 seconds
One Larceny-theft every	5.1 seconds
One Motor Vehicle Theft every	44.1 seconds

DEFENSES

In the U.S. system of justice, criminal defendants have the opportunity to defend their actions by asserting **affirmative defenses**, in which the defendant admits to the criminal conduct but offers his or her reasons for acting. Because the defendant asserts such defenses, he or she typically has the burden to prove them. These **defenses** fall under two categories, excuses and justifications. In the former, defendants admit to the criminal act but claim they are not legally responsible—they are excused—because they are too young or insane, for example. In the latter, defendants argue they were justified in acting because, for example, they were defending themselves or others, or they were a police officer who had to injure a fleeing felon.

Affirmative defense: the defendant admits he or she committed the act charged, but for some mitigating reason (self-defense, mental illness, duress, mistake, intoxication) should be treated more lightly (or excused) under the law.

Defense: the response by a defendant to a criminal charge, to include denial of the criminal allegations in an attempt to negate or overcome the charges.

you be the... PROSECUTOR

HOMICIDE

Using Table 2.2 and the preceding discussions, for each of the following questions apply your knowledge of the elements of murder and determine whether the facts primarily indicate murder in the first degree, murder in the second degree, or manslaughter (voluntary or involuntary).

I. Jill, returning home early one afternoon, finds her husband Jack on the sofa, embracing the next-door neighbor, Sue. In a blind rage, Jill takes a knife from the kitchen and stabs them both to death. As discussed in this chapter, she will most likely be convicted of which form of murder?

II. Assume instead that, upon witnessing the lovers in each other's arms, Jill departs from the home and drives around in her car for an hour brooding about her husband's infidelity. She then returns to the home, finds a shotgun in the garage, and shoots and kills Jack and Sue. What is the offense for which she will now most likely be convicted?

FOCUS ON   "STAND YOUR GROUND" LAWS

The fatal shooting of Trayvon Martin by George Zimmerman in Sanford, Florida, generated tremendous controversy because of its racial overtones and the state's "stand your ground" law; Zimmerman was acquitted in July 2013 for the shooting.

The killing in Florida of Trayvon Martin by George Zimmerman in February 2012 caused a major controversy that, by its nature, implicates the entire criminal justice system and binds the police and prosecutors under a controversial statute known as the "stand your ground" law, which essentially expands the common law "castle doctrine" that allows a homeowner to use deadly force against an intruder. "Stand your ground" became law in Florida in 2005; at least 25 states have since enacted some version, extending the common law to the outside of one's home and to any other place where he or she has a right to be. Under the law, when killers state they acted in self-defense, they cannot be convicted of homicide unless it can be proven *beyond a reasonable doubt* (the highest legal standard) that the victim did not attack the killer. The laws were originally intended to give citizens a presumption of innocence when defending themselves, while also generally banning police from detaining someone if they have evidence that the shooter was attacked "in a place he had a right to be." Prosecutors largely despise the law because of the aforementioned burden of proof, while defense attorneys have found it to be a means of defending people who claim they had a right to meet force with force.

Source: John Arnold, "The Law Heard Round the World," *Time*, April 9, 2012, http://www.time.com/time/magazine/article/0,9171,2110471,00.html (accessed March 9, 2013); also see "Trayvon Martin Case (George Zimmerman)," *New York Times*, July 19, 2012, http://topics.nytimes.com/top/reference/timestopics/people/m/trayvon_martin/index.html (accessed March 9, 2013).

Self-Defense

Author Video: Stand Your Ground Law

Self-defense is a necessity defense, where the defendant argues that he or she had to commit the act because it was necessary to avoid some greater harm. Under early common law of England, people had a "duty to retreat," also known as "retreat to the wall," prior to using force to defend themselves. In effect, a person could not respond to an attacker until he or she was "cornered" and had no other retreat option available. Today, most state laws do not impose a duty to retreat and, in fact, provide in many situations that people may "stand their ground" (see discussion in the "Focus On" box, above).

Further, under modern laws, one may use force, even deadly force, without first "retreating to the wall" against another person if he or she reasonably believes that an attack against him or her is imminent, but defensive actions must be proportionate to the threatened harm and not unreasonable for the circumstances. One cannot respond to an attack with a tree branch by using a shotgun.

Age

Juveniles

The infancy defense excuses the acts of children age 7 and under because they are too young to be criminally responsible for their actions—they are too young to form the requisite *mens rea*. Minors between ages 7 and 14 are presumed incapable of committing a crime, but prosecutors may challenge that assumption in certain cases. Minors over age 14 have no infancy defense, but those under 16 at the time of the crime are typically tried in juvenile court. But under some state statutes, serious felony cases are automatically transferred to adult court, or the prosecutor has the option to seek such a transfer if the juvenile is not a suitable candidate for the more lenient and protective philosophy and law of the juvenile court.

Entrapment

If the police induced a person to commit a crime that he or she would otherwise not have attempted, the defendant can claim the defense of **entrapment**.[21] But it is not always clear what constitutes entrapment. A state supreme court deemed that police officers posing as homeless persons with cash sticking out of their pockets was entrapment because it could tempt even honest persons who were not otherwise predisposed to committing theft. But the U.S. Supreme Court did not find entrapment where undercover drug agents provided an essential chemical to defendants who were already planning to manufacture illegal drugs.[22] Nor is it entrapment when a drug agent sells drugs to a suspect, who then sells it to government agents. The defense of entrapment will fail where the government has merely set the scene for people to commit a crime they are predisposed to commit anyway.

Intoxication

The intoxication defense is rooted in the concept of *mens rea*, and defendants must show that they were operating under such "diminished capacity" that they could not know what they were doing and cannot be held responsible. The defense is not available in cases of voluntary intoxication (except in some cases of severe alcoholism where *mens rea* is permanently impaired) and is only successful—albeit rarely—in cases of involuntary intoxication (the spiked drink or slipped drug), where the intoxicant was ingested without awareness of its intoxicating nature or where the consumption was coerced. The burden on the defendant is high in these cases, and defense attorneys generally have a difficult time convincing juries that defendants should be excused (although diminished capacity can be useful for defense attorneys to seek reduced charges or punishment).

Duress

The duress defense is an excuse with defendants claiming that they committed the act only because they were not acting of their own free will. The wife of a bank president calls her husband and informs him that someone has broken into their home and put a gun to her head, and if he does not bring money home immediately, she will be killed. The husband then removes the money from his bank in order to supply the ransom. The husband could claim that he acted under duress, only to save his wife. Other actual cases include a person who was forced by gangsters to commit certain criminal acts or be killed, a drug smuggler who argued that his family would have been killed if he did not do what he was told,[23] and a Texas prison inmate whose three cellmates planned an escape and threatened to slit his throat if he did not accompany them.[24] Again, the burden will be on the accused to convince the jury they committed the act under duress.

Double Jeopardy

The Fifth Amendment to the U.S. Constitution states that no person shall be "subject for the same offense to be twice put in jeopardy of life or limb," prohibiting the government from prosecuting someone for the same offense more than once (**double jeopardy**). Other than some specific exceptions (a mistrial, a reversal on appeal, or a situation in which the crime violates laws of separate jurisdictions such as civilian/military or federal/state), the government has only one attempt to obtain a conviction; if a defendant is acquitted, the prosecution may not appeal that conviction or retry the defendant.

Entrapment: police tactics that overly encourage or entice individuals to commit crimes they normally would not commit.

Double jeopardy: subjecting an accused person to be tried twice for the same offense; prohibited by the Fifth Amendment.

John Hinckley Jr. attempted to assassinate President Ronald Reagan in 1981, but was later found not guilty by reason of insanity; he claimed he had done so in an effort to impress actress Jodie Foster.

Mental Illness/Insanity

Several notorious criminal trials over the past few decades have put the mental illness/insanity defense under the microscope. First, in 1981, John Hinckley Jr. attempted to assassinate President Ronald Reagan but was found not guilty by reason of insanity after he claimed he had done so in an effort to impress actress Jodie Foster and after psychiatrists testified at length about his childhood.[25]

Then, in 1986, Steve Roth hired two men who slashed model Marla Hanson's face with razors after Hanson rejected Roth's sexual advances. Her injuries required more than 100 stitches. Roth's insanity defense—based on the psychiatric effects of his short stature—failed, and all three men were convicted.[26]

More recently, the 2008 movie *Milk* recalled the so-called Twinkie defense from the trial of Dan White, who in 1978 murdered Harvey Milk, a San Francisco gay rights activist and politician. Although the defense never even mentioned Twinkies during White's trial, the media coined the term following psychiatric testimony that White had been depressed and consuming junk food and sugar-laden soft drinks—allegedly "blasting sugar through his arteries and driving him into a murderous frenzy."[27]

Despite these high-profile cases, the insanity defense is raised in less than 1 percent of felony cases and is successful in only a fraction of those.[28] State laws set forth the applicable test for legal insanity; for example, the M'Naghten Rule, in effect in the majority of the states, requires in part that "to establish a defense on the ground of insanity, it must be clearly proven that, at the time of the committing of the act, the party accused was laboring under such a defect of reason, from disease of mind, as not to know the nature and quality of the act he was doing; or if he did know it, that he did not know he was doing what was wrong."[29] This is often termed the **right-wrong test**.

Another test that has been used in some states is the "irresistible impulse test," requiring a showing that the defendant could not control his impulses or volition.

After John Hinckley's trial, many states shifted the burden of proving insanity to the defense, requiring them to show either clear and convincing evidence or a preponderance of the evidence that the defendant was legally insane at the time of the crime. Consider the following notorious cases in which the insanity defense failed:

- Jeffrey L. Dahmer, the serial killer who claimed that necrophilia drove him to murder and dismember/cannibalize 15 men and boys, was convicted in 1992.[30]

- David Berkowitz, known as the "Son of Sam" killer (receiving messages from the devil through a neighbor's dog, Sam) who murdered six people in New York in the mid-1970s, was deemed fit by the trial court to stand trial (despite a psychiatric report that found him paranoid and delusional).[31]

- John Wayne Gacy, the Chicago-area so-called Killer Clown who murdered more than 30 youths, pleaded not guilty by reason of insanity but was convicted and executed in 1994.[32]

Insanity Defense Reform Act

Ashe v. Swenson

Chapter Quiz: Foundations of Law and Crime

Right-wrong test: the test of legal insanity, asking whether the defendant understood the nature and quality of his or her act and, if so, if he or she understood it was wrong.

The Hinckley verdict also generated the creation of "guilty but mentally ill" verdicts in some states, allowing mentally ill defendants to be found guilty but to receive psychiatric treatment while incarcerated or, alternatively, to be placed in a mental hospital until they are well enough to be moved to a prison to serve their sentences.[33]

IN A NUTSHELL

- Substantive law is the written law that defines or regulates our rights and duties. Procedural law sets forth the procedures and mechanisms for processing criminal cases.

- Our legal system is based on the English common law: collections of rules, customs, and traditions; at its core is the doctrine of *stare decisis*, meaning that when a court has decided a case based on a set of facts, it will adhere to that principle, and other courts will apply that decision in the same manner to all future cases where facts are substantially the same.

- There are both civil and criminal laws at the federal, state, and local levels. Many more laws are enacted each year by the U.S. Congress, state legislatures, and city councils.

- Many of our laws are outdated and no longer applicable to modern society; although our legislative bodies enact countless new laws, they are not always responsible in repealing those that have clearly outlived their applicability.

- Two essential elements that underlie our system of law are *mens rea* (criminal intent) and *actus reus* (a criminal act or a failure to act where there is a legal duty).

- Each year the FBI reports on eight Part I ("Index") crimes in its Uniform Crime Reporting (UCR) program, published in *Crime in the United States* (the elements for each of those eight offenses are provided in the chapter); the FBI also reports arrest data for Part II offenses.

- Our system of justice allows for persons charged with crimes to offer defenses for their behavior; one can argue that his or her acts were justified (such as when a police officer injures a suspect during a lawful arrest); or the accused can admit wrongdoing but argue that he or she is not deserving of blame due to circumstances surrounding the offense (self-defense, entrapment, mental illness, and so forth).

KEY TERMS & CONCEPTS

Actus reus	Defense	Motive
Affirmative defense	Double jeopardy	Plaintiff
Burden of proof	Entrapment	Procedural law
Civil law	Felony	Reasonable doubt
Crimes against persons	Felony-murder rule	Right-wrong test
Crimes against property	Intent, specific	*Stare decisis*
Criminal law	*Lex talionis*	Substantive law
Defendant	Misdemeanor	

REVIEW QUESTIONS

1. What are the differences between criminal law and civil law?

2. How would you define and explain the importance and contributions of *mens rea* and *actus rea* as they operate in our legal system?

3. What is the difference between one's motive and one's intent to commit a crime, and which is the most important in our legal system?

4. A Nebraska law states the following: Any person who knowingly or intentionally causes or permits a child or vulnerable adult to ingest methamphetamine, a chemical substance used in manufacturing methamphetamine, or paraphernalia is guilty of a Class I misdemeanor. The *mens rea* for this crime is _____; the *actus reus* element of this crime is _____.

5. What is double jeopardy, why does this area of law exist, and what are some examples of exceptions to this area of law?

6. How can age, entrapment, intoxication, and duress each be used as a criminal defense?

LEARN BY DOING

Below are several additional case studies, all of which are grounded in actual case facts and chapter materials (concerning double jeopardy, self-defense, and causation, respectively). While studying each scenario, first assume that you are the *prosecuting* attorney and decide which charge(s), if any, should be brought against the accused on the basis of the facts. Next, assume the role of the *defense* attorney and explain, given the facts, what defenses should legitimately be made against the crime(s) charged. Remember that the Sixth Amendment entitles every defendant to the "guiding hand" of effective counsel, whose job it is to ensure that all legal protections are afforded. Answers and/or outcomes for each case are provided in the Notes section. For purposes of discussion, however, approach all of them as if there are no absolute, totally correct answers.

Six men are playing poker one night when four masked men enter their home and rob each of them of their money, watches, and other items of value. The robbers are later caught and charged with six separate robberies—one for each of the six poker players. One of the robbers, Everett, is charged and tried for robbing *one* of the poker players, and he is acquitted. Next, the prosecutor files new charges against Everett, this time for robbing *another* poker player. This time a different jury finds him guilty.

1. What is the *primary* legal issue in this case?

2. After Everett was acquitted for the first robbery, was it legally proper for the prosecutor to then file new charges for robbing a second poker player?

3. How many actual robberies have been committed here?

4. How many individual *acts* (or "counts" to be charged) of robbery are there in this case (taken from *Ashe v. Swenson*, 1970)?[34]

―――――――――――――

Peterson is relaxing at home when he hears noises in the alley behind his house; he looks in that direction and sees three men who are removing parts from his parked vehicle. Peterson approaches the men and tells them to stop what they are doing; he then runs inside his home, obtains a pistol, and returns to the alley. By now the three men are back in their vehicle and preparing to drive away. Peterson approaches them and tells them not to move, or he will shoot. The driver exits the car and, with a wrench in his hand, begins advancing toward Peterson; Peterson then warns the driver not to come any closer. Still carrying the wrench, the man continues to move toward Peterson, who then shoots and kills him (see *U.S. v. Peterson*, 1973).[35]

1. What is the *primary* legal issue here?

2. Also consider:
   o What charge should the prosecutor bring against Peterson: Murder in the first degree? Second degree? Manslaughter?
   o Did Peterson act in self-defense?
   o What other options might have been

available to Peterson, aside from obtaining a gun and returning to the alley? Besides shooting the driver?

―――――――――――――

A young man knocks on the door of a young woman's home and asks her to go out with him. She refuses, and he then stabs her four times with a knife and runs away. The victim collapses at a neighbor's home and is taken to a hospital, where she is informed that she must have a blood transfusion in order to survive the attack. She refuses to accept blood, on the ground that that would be contrary to her religious beliefs. She is then told by the doctor that if she does not accept blood, she will likely die; again she refuses it, and also acknowledges her refusal in writing. The woman then perishes (see *Regina v. Blaue*, 1975).[36]

1. What is the *primary* legal issue in this case?

2. What, if any, form of murder might the man be charged with under the law (if need be, reflect again on the elements of murder discussed in this chapter)?

3. Look at this series of events as links in a chain—the act, her refusal to accept blood, and her ensuing death. Did the girl's refusal to accept a blood transfusion *break* the chain of causation between the stabbing and her death, and therefore eliminate the man's contribution to her death? Or, alternatively, did her refusal *not* break the chain of causation, leaving him criminally responsible for her death?

4. Should the victim's religious beliefs be given any weight in this case? If so, how much?

5. What would be the defense arguments on the man's behalf?

6. If he were to not be charged with some type of murder, is there another crime(s) for which he might be charged?

THEORIES OF CRIME AND MEASURING VICTIMIZATION

LEARNING OBJECTIVES

As a result of reading this chapter, the student will be able to:

1 Explain early beliefs concerning the causes of crime prior to the mid-1700s

2 Describe how Beccaria and the classical school formed the foundation for our explaining crime in more rational terms

3 Delineate how the positivist school of criminology attempted to explain criminality

4 Delineate the various biological theories of crime, to include Lombroso's "born criminal," the "criminal" chromosome, and studies of body type, twins, and adopted children

5 Review the psychological influences of crime that have been put forth

6 Discuss the several social and cultural explanations of crime—generally how people's living in social groups might shape their behavior

7 Review the fundamental aspects of feminist theory—explanation for women becoming much more engaged in criminal activities since the 1970s

8 Describe the nature and types of white-collar crime

9 Explain the three primary methods for measuring crime and advantages/disadvantages of each

CHAPTER

03

Children will watch anything, and when a broadcaster uses crime and violence and other shoddy devices to monopolize a child's attention, it's worse than taking candy from a baby.

—Newton N. Minow, Chairman,
Federal Communications Commission

Crimes are not to be measured by the issue of events, but by the bad intentions of men.

—Marcus Tullius Cicero

INTRODUCTION

Author Introduction:
Chapter 3

What causes some people to devote much or most of their lives to preying on and harming others? Is it their "nature" or how they were "nurtured"? How could someone enter an elementary school and kill 26 children and teachers? Or shoot up a movie theater, leaving 12 dead and 57 wounded?[1] Are such people just base and cruel? Is crime a product of poverty and need? Congenital defects? Greed? Vengeance?

We humans have always sought to better understand the world around us, and so we seek answers to such questions—the "Rosetta Stone" (the Nile River Delta stone found in 1799 that furnished Egyptologists with the key to deciphering hieroglyphics) of crime. As with the stone, we have long sought to unravel the mysteries of human behavior and nature,[2] and many books have been written that attempt to explain these mysteries. This chapter will briefly address some of those questions. Included is a discussion of the three means we have of measuring how many crimes are committed by this criminal element.

First is a look at the two major, original schools of criminological thought: classical and positivist. Next is an overview of the biological, psychological, and sociocultural theories that have been put forth to explain criminal behavior,

ASSESS YOUR AWARENESS:

Test your knowledge of crime theories and measurement by first reading and responding to the following eight true-false items; check your answers after reading this chapter's materials.

1. Studies show that the "root" of all crime lies in one's biological makeup.

2. Research shows that nearly all male offenders carry an extra Y chromosome—the "criminal" chromosome.

3. Scholarly studies have revealed that identical twins have a greater preponderance to having criminal records.

4. "White-collar crime" was first introduced in 1939 when a criminologist discovered many crimes were committed by persons of respectability and high social status.

5. The best, most widely used, and most accurate reporting of crimes in the United States is that which is published by the FBI, in the *Uniform Crime Reports*.

6. Increases in labor force participation of women are related to their significantly higher crime rates.

7. If a burglar enters a premises and also commits an aggravated assault and a murder while inside, per reporting rules the police will only report the crime of murder to the FBI.

8. Carjacking is now one of the FBI's eight "Part I" crimes on which it thoroughly reports annually.

Answers can be found on page 401.

followed by a consideration of the unique role played by women in criminality. Then, having looked at these explanations put forth by learned theorists over the past two and a half centuries to explain crime, a brief review is afforded of the motivations for selected crimes—forcible rape, armed robbery, burglary, and carjacking—in the words of offenders. Following that is a discussion of a companion concept: how crimes are measured; included are three primary approaches to measuring crime, and the advantages and shortcomings of each. The chapter concludes with a summary, key terms and concepts, review questions, and several scenarios and activities that provide opportunities for you to "learn by doing."

Punishment

Jeremy Bentham

CLASSICAL AND POSITIVIST THEORIES

Until the 18th century, criminal behavior was explained by most Europeans in supernatural terms. In other words, people who committed criminal acts were "possessed" by the devil. Coupled with that was the fact that defendants had few rights. Persons accused of crimes typically were not allowed to put forth a defense, confessions could be obtained through the use of torture, and the penalty for most offenses of that time was some form of physical punishment or death.

The Classical School

In 1764 the first attempt was put forth to explain crime in more rational terms. Cesare Beccaria published his classic *Essays on Crime and Punishments*, in which he bemoaned that potential criminals had no way of anticipating the whimsical nature of the criminal law; attempted to expose the injustices in, and arbitrariness of, the administration of law and punishment; and encouraged reform in the way law was enforced so as to be more consistent and rational. Classical criminology (the **classical school**) evolved from this movement, the main principles of which were as follows:

1. Criminal behavior is rational, and most people have the potential to engage in such behavior.

2. People may choose to commit a crime after weighing the costs and benefits of their actions.

3. Fear of punishment is what keeps most people law-abiding; therefore, the severity, certainty, and speed of punishment affect the crime rate.

4. The punishment should fit the crime rather than fit the offender.

5. The criminal justice system must be predictable, with laws and punishments known to the public.

Beccaria's contemporary, Jeremy Bentham, argued that the laws should provide "the greatest good for the greatest number," saw the purpose of punishment to be deterrence rather than vengeance, and emphasized the certainty of punishment over its severity.[3]

Although classical criminology laid the cornerstone of modern western criminal law as it was formulated from 1770 to 1812,[4] its ideas began to decline in the 19th century, largely because of the rise of science and in part because its principles did not take into account differences among individuals or the manner in which crimes were committed.[5]

Classical school (of criminology): a perspective indicating that people have free will to choose between criminal and lawful behavior, and that crime can be controlled by sanctions and should be proportionate to the offense.

Cesare Beccaria, an Italian jurist, philosopher, and politician who is best known for his essays on crime and punishment, believed that punishment should be proportional to the crime, that it is better to prevent crimes than to punish them, and that crimes are more effactually prevented by the *certainty* than the *severity* of punishment.

Neoclassical Criminology

Classical ideas began to take on new life in the 1980s, when scholars again began arguing that crimes may result from the rational choice of people who have weighed the benefits to be gained from the crime against the costs of being caught and punished (**neoclassical criminology**). They also argued that the criminal law must take into account the differences among individuals. To a large extent, sentencing reform, criticisms of rehabilitation, and greater use of incarceration sprung from this renewed interest in classical ideas. However, the positivist school of thought, discussed next, is what has dominated U.S. criminology since the beginning of the 20th century.

Positivist Criminology

Prison Therapy

By the middle of the 19th century, the classical school seemed to be old-fashioned in large part because of the expansion of science; instead, positivist criminology—a philosophical approach proposed by French sociologist Auguste Comte—emphasized the criminal actor rather than the criminal act,[6] and also used science to study the body, mind, and environment of the offender. Positivists seek to uncover the basic cause of crime, have strong faith in scientific experts, and believe in rehabilitating "sick" offenders rather than punishing them.[7] They also believe that science can explain why offenders commit crimes and how they can be rehabilitated. Following are some of the tenets of this viewpoint:

1. Human behavior is controlled by physical, mental, and social factors, not by free will.

2. Criminals are different from non-criminals.

3. Science can be used to discover the true causes of crime and to treat offenders.[8]

What also became evident was that possessing an understanding of the causes of crime is important, because that will affect how laws are enforced, how one's guilt is determined, and how punishment is meted out.

The major types of positivism—biological and psychological—are discussed next. As both theories are described, consider their potential to affect public policy making with respect to crime.

Positivists seek to find the basic cause of one's crimes and believe in rehabilitating offenders rather than punishing them. Prison therapy groups focus on rehabilitation.

BIOLOGICAL DETERMINISM

Neoclassical criminology: the accused is viewed as exempted from conviction if circumstances prevented the exercise of free will.

Biological theories of crime have persisted over time. These theories have their foundation in the belief that the causes of crime are found in the biological determinants—or "original nature"—of the offender and are the result of some biological element or defect, and that criminals are *born* and not *made* by their home or social environment.

A Throwback?

In the 19th century, Italian criminologist Cesare Lombroso gave life to the anthropological study of crime and criminals, believing that offenders were a product of their physical stigmata—or "atavism," a throwback to some earlier stage in the evolution of humans or to an apelike ancestor, and the "born criminal." Having been influenced by the evolutionary doctrines of Charles Darwin, Lombroso saw in criminals some of the same characteristics that were found in "savages" or "prehuman people": a slanting forehead, abnormal teeth, excessively long arms and dimensions of the jaw and cheekbones, ears of unusual size, a sparse beard, a twisted nose, woolly hair, recessed eyes (and pronounced supraorbital ridges, or bony structures surrounding the eye sockets), fleshy and swollen lips, excessive vanity, or the presence of tattoos.[9]

Lombroso's theories, however, failed to explain crime fully—obviously, many offenders did not possess any, much less all, of these "born criminal" characteristics—so over time these "revelations" fell out of favor. Nonetheless, for his groundbreaking work that forced people to consider the makeup of the criminal in addition to his or her offense, Lombroso is today known as "the father of criminology."[10]

Related to Lombroso's views are those of Charles Goring and Henry Goddard, both of whom began publishing their theories in the early 1900s. Goring compared "criminals" and "noncriminals" and determined that criminals were, in general, shorter, they weighed less, and, more importantly, they were "mentally defective" or "feebleminded." Goddard compared offspring of a Revolutionary War militiaman who had fathered children with two wives, one a "barwench" and the other a "respectable" woman. He found the children of the former to be feebleminded and deviant, while children of the latter were moral and relatively intelligent. He thus deemed that crime was caused by feeblemindedness, and was the first to coin the term *moron*.[11]

Italian criminologist Cesare Lombroso saw in criminals a pattern of physical characteristics that were found in "savages" or "prehuman people."

Aberrant or "Criminal" Chromosomes

During the second half of the 20th century, advances in the field of molecular biology led to the belief that a link might exist between chromosomal abnormality and criminal behavior. Most females have two X chromosomes, and the majority of males have an XY set. Much speculation and research has been done with respect to males carrying an extra Y chromosome (**XYY chromosome**), or the "criminal" chromosome. Some scientists have hypothesized that the extra male chromosome produces tall men, generally with below-average intelligence, who behave aggressively or antisocially.

However, a number of studies—including an international review of relevant research by R. G. Fox—failed to be conclusive regarding differences between XYY and XY males.[12] Fox stated that "the information gleaned from research so far provides . . . a flimsy suggestion that an XYY constitution produces a disposition toward deviant behavior." Fox called for "some form of longitudinal study of XYY persons" that, "with the aid of computers, could ascertain and record the chromosome structure of all new-born infants in a large hospital over a period of time and subsequently check police records to determine the significance of any criminal patterns that may develop in the population."[13]

 Somatotypes

XYY chromosome: the so-called criminal chromosome, where criminal behavior is felt to be caused in some offenders who possess an extra Y chromosome—believed to cause agitation, aggression, and greater criminal tendencies—as opposed to the "passive" X chromosome.

Other Biological Studies

Other theories and studies grounded in what might be termed biocriminology have been offered over time and bear mention as well; next we touch on some that have been more enduring: studies involving body type, heredity, twins, and adoptions.

Body Type and Heredity Studies

What might also be termed anthropological criminology or constitutionalism theories, **body type studies** are essentially a continuation of Lombroso's work, described above and continued by William Sheldon. Sheldon, who focused his studies primarily on juvenile delinquents, believed that human beings can be separated into three distinct body types, or somatotypes (with varying degrees for each)[14]:

1. Endomorphic persons have a wide waist and a large bone structure (and are usually referred to as fat).

2. Mesomorphic persons have medium bones, a solid torso, low fat levels, and wide shoulders with a narrow waist; they are athletic and commonly viewed as muscular.

3. Ectomorphic persons have long, thin muscles and limbs, with low fat storage; they are commonly referred to as slim.

Sheldon believed that every individual has elements of all three body types, but that one type usually predominates. He also determined, in examining 200 Boston delinquents, that the more serious offenders tended to be athletically built, or mesomorphic. Later studies of Sheldon's work confirmed the relationship between mesomorphy and delinquency.

However, Sheldon's body type or constitutionalist theories in criminology have largely been discredited because they have little value in predicting criminal behavior; if indeed there is a relationship between body type and crime, it is more likely a result of social factors that are involved—for example, more muscular (mesomorphic) individuals might well be recruited into gangs. Another problem concerns this theory's policy implication: Imagine applying the concept of eugenics, whereby reproduction of the criminally prone and unfit is to be prevented; here, the only way that mesomorphy could be dealt with would be either to isolate these individuals from society through imprisonment, or to execute them—not viable choices for policy makers.

William H. Sheldon believed that human beings can be separated into three distinct body types, and that more serious offenders tended to be athletically built, or mesomorphic.

Body type studies: 19th- and 20th-century theorists argued that body types led to patterns of criminal behavior; currently outmoded.

Twin studies: criminological research that uses identical twins to look for possible genetic transmission of criminal traits or tendencie

Twin Studies

Such books as *Evil Twins: Chilling True Stories of Twins, Killing and Insanity*[15] would have us believe that crime is hereditary; the proof lies in the fact that twins—identical twins in particular, which are the product of a single egg—engage in criminal acts to a greater degree than do fraternal twins (the product of two eggs fertilized by two sperm) or regular siblings. The logic is that if there is greater similarity in criminal records among identical twins than between fraternal twins, then the behavior must be due to heredity, since their environments were much the same. As it turns out, scholarly studies have revealed that identical twins have a greater preponderance to having criminal records. However, a problem with these **twin studies** is with their environmental influences: Identical twins tend to spend more time together, be treated more alike by their families and friends, and share more of a common identity than do fraternal twins.

Adoption Studies

The most recent and sophisticated studies in the crime-as-heredity realm concern **adoption studies**. These studies, as the name suggests, examine people who have been adopted from their natural parents and raised by a different set of parents. The thesis is that, if there is a strong genetic influence over criminal behavior, children who are adopted will share more of those characteristics with their natural parents than with their adoptive parents; conversely, if people are inclined to criminal acts more as a result of their environment, then they would share the characteristics of their adoptive parents.[16]

Findings of these studies typically indicate that the percentage of adoptees who are criminal is greater when the biological father has a criminal record than when the adoptive father has one. However, as with twin studies, there are certain limitations with adoption studies that must be accounted for. First, children who are adopted may be placed in environments that are similar to those from which they were adopted; second, many children are adopted many months or years after their birth, which raises the possibility that their early life experiences may have contributed to their criminality.

Policy implications here are similar to those that flow from the twin studies and other studies showing that criminals are biologically inferior: selective incapacitation—either imprisoning or executing people who have been adopted and whose natural fathers had a criminal record, which is of course repugnant to our sense of justice and values unless one has in fact committed a heinous crime. Some may argue instead that neurological defects may be identified through CAT scan, and that medications can suppress violent tendencies. There may be help in the future in this regard, however, as scientists come closer to being able to identify and remove or alter defective genes through genetic engineering; furthermore, one could argue that persons with learning disabilities may be helped by receiving special education and counseling.

Researchers who argue that crime is hereditary have attempted to show that identical twins engage in criminal acts to a greater degree than do fraternal twins or regular siblings.

PSYCHOLOGICAL RATIONALES

Mental conditions have also been thought to be the reason (**psychological rationale**) for criminal behavior, by either a personality disorder or limited intellect. Sigmund Freud (1856–1939), who is credited with the development of psychoanalytic theory, argued that all humans have natural drives and urges repressed in the unconscious, and have criminal tendencies. Using case studies, Freudians document examples of the Oedipus complex, the death wish, the inferiority complex, birth trauma, castration fears, and penis envy, and believe that crime represents a substitute response to goals that are blocked or repressed during childhood as well as hostility to male

Adoption studies: criminological research that looks at whether adopted children share criminal tendencies with their natural or adoptive parents.

Psychological rationales for crime: explanations of crime that link it to mental states or antisocial personality.

Sigmund Freud argued that all humans have natural drives and urges repressed in the unconscious, and have criminal tendencies.

authority symbols.[17] Through the process of socialization, however, these tendencies are curbed by the development of inner controls that are learned through childhood experience. Freud hypothesized that the most common element that contributed to criminal behavior was faulty identification by a child with her or his parents. The improperly socialized child may develop a personality disturbance that causes her or him to direct antisocial impulses inward or outward. The child who directs them outward becomes a criminal, and the child that directs them inward becomes a neurotic.[18]

In 1931, Edwin Sutherland examined approximately 350 studies of the relationship between intelligence and delinquency and criminality. He concluded from this review that although intelligence may play a role in individual cases, the distribution of the intelligence scores of criminals was roughly the same as the distribution of such scores for the general population. In other words, intelligence was not a predictor of crime.[19]

The 1970s saw a resurgence of interest in the debate, however, and several studies reported that there was such a relationship—that IQ was as important a predictor of juvenile delinquency as race or social class. The studies found an 8-point difference in IQ levels between delinquent and nondelinquent youths[20]; of note—and what these studies failed to point out—however, is the fact that both IQs with the 8-point difference were within the normal range.

Certainly the policy implications for the psychological theories—if indeed found to be solid predictors of criminality—would include treatment for those persons found to have mental disorders, to include psychotherapy and counseling, as well as individual and group therapy.

SOCIOCULTURAL EXPLANATIONS

While the psychological approaches to studying crime as laid out by Freud focus on one's mental condition, the sociocultural explanations look at how people's living in social groups might shape their behavior. Sociologists argue that criminality is not innate in one's biological makeup, but instead is caused by external social factors. They believe that one's contact with the world—and such related factors as poverty, age, race, gender, family, problems faced by immigrants, and so on—will foster crime; in sum, criminals are made, not born.

Next we discuss three of the many theories that stress the influence of social factors on crime: social structure theory, social process theory, and critical theory.

Social Structure Theory

Social structure theory: generally attempts to explain criminality as a result of the creation of a lower-class culture based on poverty and deprivations, and the subsequent response of the poor to the situation

Robert Merton is perhaps the primary proponent of **social structure theories**, which maintain that criminal behavior is related to culture and social class—and provides, he wrote, a "basis for determining the nonbiological conditions which induce deviations from prescribed patterns of conduct."[21] Merton built on the concept of anomie—a state of normlessness, in which the existing rules and values of society have little impact—which was first introduced by the famed French sociologist Émile Durkheim in the late 19th century. Merton argued that social change often leads to anomie, when rules are unclear or they cannot achieve their goals. Criminologists who have incorporated the concept of anomie into theories of criminal behavior are known as "strain theorists," who believe that crime is caused by the strain (frustration, hopelessness, anger, and so on) that comes from living in disadvantaged, dysfunctional, and generally normless families and/or communities where legitimate opportunities for success and prosperity are nearly if not altogether out of reach. Therefore, Merton argued, in order to relieve this strain, the individual in such an environment will turn to crime as a means of alleviating this strain and to reach his or her goals.[22] Furthermore, the anger that is caused by strain—as well as the child abuse, unemployment, victimization, and family problems—can lead to crime and delinquency. Merton believed that

> the extreme emphasis upon the accumulation of wealth as a symbol of success in our own society militates against the completely effective control of institutionally regulated modes of acquiring a fortune. Fraud, corruption, vice, crime, in short, the entire catalogue of proscribed behavior, becomes increasingly common.[23]

Social structure theory certainly has strong policy implications if decision makers believe it is a solid explanation of criminality. If crime is indeed grounded in a number of social conditions that serve to breed crime (e.g., poverty, unemployment, and discrimination), then those conditions might well be addressed by educational (including vocational) programs and governmental programs that will enhance the living conditions in terms of housing, health care, employment opportunities, and so forth.

Strain theorists argue that crime is caused by frustration, hopelessness, and anger resulting from living in disadvantaged and dysfunctional families and/or communities, where opportunities for success and prosperity are largely nonexistent.

Social Process Theories

Many criminologists believe that the aforementioned social structure theory places too much responsibility for crime on the shoulders of the poor, and too much emphasis on the offender's being in a state of poverty. Subsequently, they do not believe that social structure theory adequately explains crime that is committed by more affluent, middle- or upper-class people. Therefore, **social process theories** argue that any person, regardless of social class, education, or nature of the family, neighborhood, or community, can learn to become a criminal.

There are three primary social process theories: learning theory, control theory, and labeling theory.

Learning Theories

In 1934, Edwin Sutherland first put forth in his book, *Criminology*, his theory of differential association. When Sutherland died in 1950, Donald Cressey continued to popularize the theory. The existence of white-collar crime and professional theft led them to believe that there were social learning processes that could turn anyone into a criminal, anytime or anywhere. Following are some of the major points of **learning theory**:

- Criminal behavior is learned, in interaction with others, in a process of communication.

- Learning criminal behavior occurs within primary groups (family, friends, peers, one's most intimate, personal companions) and involves learning their techniques, motives, drives, rationalizations, and attitudes.

Learning Theory

Social process theory: argues that criminality is a normal behavior and that everyone has the potential to commit crime, depending on the influences that compel them toward or away from crime and in view of how they are viewed by others.

Learning theory (of crime): any school of thought that suggests criminal behaviors are learned from associating with others and from social interactions and social experiences.

- A person becomes a criminal when there is an excess of definitions favorable to violation of law over definitions unfavorable to violation of law (this is the principle of differential association).

- Differential associations vary in frequency, duration, priority, and intensity (frequent contacts, long contacts, age at first contact, important or prestigious contacts).[24]

Sutherland's theory was tested mainly on juveniles because delinquency is largely a group crime. One of the problems with such research is in determining which comes first, the delinquency or delinquent friends. It may be that "birds of a feather flock together" and delinquency "causes" delinquent friends, but delinquent friends do not cause delinquency. Another problem is that the theory does not explain, nor does it even attempt to explain, the point at which, or cause for which, the initial inclination to commit a crime occurred.

Control Theories

Walter Reckless and Travis Hirschi began proposing a new theory of criminality in the 1960s known as **social control theory**—also known as containment theory—in which it is argued that people are essentially rational beings but that they also are motivated by a desire to maximize pleasure and minimize pain. Therefore, external pressures (poor living conditions or economy, lack of legitimate opportunities), sensitivity to the opinions of others, and belief in the values expressed by friends and relatives will influence one to either obey or disobey the law. Lawbreaking occurs due to the weakness, breakdown, or absence of these social bonds or socialization processes that are presumed to encourage law-abiding conduct.[25]

Labeling Theory

Howard Becker observed that society creates deviance, and thus criminality, "by making the rules whose infraction constitutes deviance and by applying those rules to particular people and labeling them outsiders."[26] In simpler terms, **labeling theory** means in the extreme that no act that we deem to be criminal in and of itself is deviant; rather, it is deviant—and labeled as a crime—only because some group has determined that the behavior is different and should be criminalized.

Why is the possession of cocaine labeled a criminal act, while possession and even home manufacturing of alcohol is not? Why is a corporate executive who commits a white-collar crime less likely to receive a prison term than one who is caught in the act of committing a burglary? Why is it that one who shoots a bald eagle is guilty of committing a felony federal offense (with maximum penalties of up to $100,000 and/or one year in federal prison)[27] while the same man who, the day before, killed a large elk might well be labeled a skilled "sportsman" and praised for his marksmanship? Such questions underscore the labeling theory and compel us to consider how different acts may be labeled as criminal, be applied to individuals, and result in their losing their freedom.

A companion issue that arises in labeling theory is the notion that being labeled as a criminal *promotes* individuals' identification with their stigmatized status. When they have been labeled, they begin to believe the label is true, and then they may adopt a deviant identity and begin acting in deviant ways—a self-fulfilling prophecy of sorts.

Social process theory is obviously broad in its reach and includes a number of possible explanations for crime. Policy implications need to focus on the various means by which crime is learned, and address the aforementioned problems of control, association, and labeling by striving to provide programs that have positive role models and will reinforce the proper value system and norms.

Labeling

Social control theory: a theory arguing that deviant behavior results when social controls are weakened or break down, so that people are not motivated to conform to them.

Labeling theory (of crime): a theory holding that persons acquire labels or defined characteristics that are deviant or criminal; thus, perceiving themselves as criminals, they follow through and commit crimes.

Critical Theory

In the mid-1960s, the biological, psychological, and sociological theories described above were challenged by scholars whose theories became known as critical criminology. These theorists argued that crime is defined in terms of the concept of oppression.

Critical theorists maintain, perhaps first and foremost, that the criminal justice system acts in the interests of the dominant groups and classes of a society, and that the police can do nothing more than act repressively against potential and real challenges to the established order.[28] Conversely, the working class—women (particularly those who are single heads of household and are socially isolated) and ethnic minorities (those from non-English-speaking backgrounds and refugees, in particular)—are the most likely to suffer oppressive treatment based upon class division, sexism, and racism. In other words, the criminal laws are designed by those who are in power, and the laws are intended to oppress those who are not in power. These theorists argue that people of means commit as many crimes as do the oppressed, but the latter groups are more likely to be apprehended and punished.

A theory that can be said to be within the critical criminology arena is the social conflict theory, which maintains that crime is the result of conflict between competing interest groups: rich against poor, management against labor, whites against minorities, men against women, adults against children, and so on. In many of these conflicts, the competing interest groups are not equal in power and resources, so one group will be dominant, the other subordinate. One of the earliest conflict theorists was George B. Vold, who believed that many behaviors are defined as crimes because it is in the best interest of the dominant groups to do so.[29]

To them, in order to understand crime, one must view it as a product of group struggle. Humans are by nature social beings, forming groups out of shared interests and needs. The criminal law serves the goals of the dominant group—which is successful in achieving control of the legislative process—and contains the "crime norms," inappropriate behavior and its punishment. At the same time, the "conduct norms" of the subordinate groups often come into conflict with the crime norms; this in turn leads to the production of deviant or criminal definitions surrounding the everyday behavior of the individual members of these less powerful groups.[30]

Policy implications for the **critical theory** of crime—where the system itself foments crime—are certainly challenging. Decision makers must attempt to provide minorities with programs that will lessen or alleviate the injustices of the criminal justice system that might be found at the hands of the police, courts, or corrections system—while also making the system more equitable by meting out punishment more equally among upper-class as well as lower-class offenders.

Table 3.1 provides a synopsis of the theorists and theories discussed above.

In closing this chapter section on classical crime theories, it should be mentioned that there are many more theories that attempt to explain criminality than are discussed here; furthermore, the number and thrust of such theories continue to expand and broaden. It is probably beneficial that such is the case, for no one theory has as yet been found that can explain all forms of criminal behavior. Some criminologists still believe that there are aspects of the biological theories that have merit, while others may argue that there are elements of the psychological or sociocultural theories that have some basis in fact. In truth, each of these theories may explain in part why someone commits a criminal act.

Critical theory: a school of thought in criminology arguing that crime is largely a product of capitalism, that laws are created to separate haves and have-nots and are wielded by those in power.

TABLE 3.1

A Synopsis of Crime Theories

THEORY TYPE	THEORY SUMMARY	MAJOR THEORISTS
Classical	Criminals are rational and responsible for their crimes (free will).	Cesare Beccaria and Jeremy Bentham
Positivist: Biological	One can genetically inherit a trait or propensity toward crime.	
Physical stigmata, atavism		Cesare Lombroso
Mental deficiency		Charles Goring
Feeble-mindedness		Henry H. Goddard
Somatotypes (endomorphs)		William Sheldon
XYY chromosomes, brain disorders, etc.		
Positivist: Psychological	Crime is a result of mental problems, psychological determinism, or criminal personality.	
Unconscious repression of sexual instincts; crime as a result of blocked goals		Sigmund Freud
Postivist: Sociological	Groups and social interactions explain human misconduct.	
Anomie: normlessness lessens social control		Emile Durkeheim
Gap between goals and means creates deviance		Robert Merton
Social control (containment): crime is learned through interaction with intimates		Edwin Sutherland
Social pressures pull an individual either toward or away from crim		Walter Reckless and Travis Hirschi
Labeling: societal reaction to crime, not intrinsic behavior, causes crime		Howard Becker
Critical theory: society, composted of competeing interest groups, uses the law to serve the needs of the more powerful groups		

WOMEN AND CRIME

Mid-Chapter Quiz: Theories of Crime and Measuring Victimization

Although it has often been said that "crime is a young man's game,"[31] and women commit far fewer crimes (especially violent crimes) than their male counterparts, women are not to be overlooked in our consideration of theories of crime. This area of criminality, sometimes termed **feminist theory**, is felt to be a part of the broader area of the aforementioned critical theory. Freda Adler, criminologist and author of *Sisters in Crime*,[32] wrote the following in 1975:

> Women are no longer indentured to the kitchens, baby carriages, or bedrooms of America. There will be no turning back to the days when women found it necessary to justify their existence by producing babies or cleaning houses. Women have chosen to desert those kitchens and plunge exuberantly into the formerly all-male quarters of the working world.

Feminist theory: a theory that emphasizes gender involvement in crime.

At about the time Adler wrote those words, women were indeed beginning to "desert those kitchens" and enter the labor force in large numbers. With passage of the Equal Employment Opportunity Act in 1972,[33] women were given the right to compete with men for jobs and promotions, and to receive the same compensation upon being hired. Later, the Pregnancy Discrimination Act of 1978,[34] which required employers to treat pregnancy, childbirth, and related medical conditions in the same manner as any other temporary disability, and the Family and Medical Leave Act of 1993,[35] allowing employees to take 12 weeks of unpaid leave for the birth or adoption of a child, helped women to enter the labor force. And, by extension, these increases in labor force participation of women would become related to their significantly higher crime rates.[36]

Female Inmates

Adler also believed that the arrival of a wave of feminism during the 1970s consequently coincided with a "dramatic" upsurge in women's criminal activity. She claimed that while

> women have demanded equal opportunity in the fields of legitimate endeavors, a similar number of determined women have forced their way into the world of major crime such as white collar crime, murder and robbery.[37]

That women criminals today represent a "new breed" can be demonstrated, according to Adler, by evidence of the changing nature of female involvement in a wide variety of crimes. This "new female criminal" engaged in predatory crimes of violence and corporate fraud has broken into a man's world.[38] For example, female white-collar crime increased following the "liberation" of women. Adler also suggested that as women were "climbing up the corporate business ladder," they were making use of their "vocational liberation" to pursue careers in white-collar crime (discussed below).[39] Adler's theory has invited much criticism from other feminist writers, who argue instead that feminism has made female crime more visible through increased reporting, policing, and sentencing of female offenders.[40]

Girls' Sentencing

Irrespective of how women became engaged in crime, as a result of these and many studies of women and their criminality, feminist theory is among the newest in criminology. With gender as its central focus, it recognizes that the study of crime has historically focused on male offenders; as a result, criminal behavior by women and young girls tended to be ignored. Adler's work as well as Rita Simon's *Women and Crime*[41] proposed that the emancipation of women and increased economic opportunities for women allowed women to be as crime-prone as men. Again, there is disagreement on the emancipation or liberation thesis, and some scholars argue that there is absolutely no empirical evidence that exists for it.[42]

Two important questions have yet to be answered, however; first, do the traditionally male-centered theories of crime that apply to men apply to women as well? And second, what explains the long-standing fact that women commit far fewer crimes than men? And, it might be argued, if women were socialized in the same manner as men, then one would also expect their rates of criminal offending to be about the same. Another criticism of feminist criminology is that it fails to take into account the experiences between white women and women of color. A number of scholars are now attempting to address these questions and omissions.[43]

The study of crime has historically focused on male offenders, but the recent extent and nature of female criminality — more predatory and violent — has brought them more attention by criminologists as well.

Table 3.2 shows a five-year arrest trend for women for selected crimes; it is seen that, as with the nation at large, arrests of women have declined overall—with the exception of property crimes, which increased 14 percent overall (largely as a result of increased arrests for larceny-theft).

TABLE 3.2

Five-Year Arrest Trend for Women

OFFENSE CHARGED	TOTAL		
	2007	2011	PERCENT CHANGE
TOTAL	2,338,839	2,203,165	-5.8
Murder and non-negligent manslaughter	854	850	-0.5
Forcible rape	158	152	-3.8
Robbery	9,695	8,817	-9.1
Aggravated assault	62,504	59,227	-5.2
Burglary	31,231	32,296	+3.4
Larceny-theft	329,777	388,209	+17.7
Motor vehicle theft	13,761	8,126	-40.9
Arson	1,630	1,443	-11.5
Violent crime	73,211	69,046	-5.7
Property crime[1]	376,399	430,074	+14.3
Other assaults	230,849	239,369	+3.7
Forgery and counterfeiting	27,531	18,173	-34.0
Fraud	81,600	48,202	-40.9
Embezzlement	8,316	5,510	-33.7
Stolen property; buying, receiving, possessing	17,320	13,035	-24.7
Vandalism	35,368	32,361	-8.5
Weapons; carrying, possessing, etc.	9,986	8,572	-14.2
Prostitution and commercialized vice	34,377	23,567	-31.4
Sex offenses (except forcible rape and prostitution)	4,302	3,552	-17.4

[1]Property crimes include burglary, larceny-theft, motor vehicle theft, and arson.

Source: Adapted from Federal Bureau of Investigation, "Table 35. Five-Year Arrest Trends by Sex, 2007–2011," Crime in the United States—2011 (Washington, D.C.: Uniform Crime Reporting Program), http://www.fbi.gov/about-us/cjis/ucr/crime-in-the-u.s/2011/crime-in-the-u.s.-2011/tables/table-35 (accessed July 28, 2013).

WHITE-COLLAR CRIME

Today it seems inconceivable that anyone would attempt to rob a bank or burglarize a home—possibly to be met with a fortified premises that includes guard dogs, security patrols, and/or video cameras—when he or she could engage in any of several dozen if not hundreds of less hazardous forms of illegal activity. These approaches—under the broad umbrella of property crimes—are termed white-collar or **corporate crimes**, which can and do make some people financially comfortable if not wildly rich for their efforts.

Theoretical Foundation

Certainly the social control theory discussed earlier—in which it is argued that people are essentially rational beings but motivated by a desire to maximize pleasure and minimize pain—would appear to explain this type of unlawful behavior. White-collar crime also challenges many of the traditional assumptions concerning criminality—that is, that it occurs in the streets and is mostly committed by criminals who are lower class and uneducated. White-collar crime is also the largest and most costly type of crime in the United States; as criminologist Frank Hagan put it, "All the other forms of criminal behavior together do not equal the costs of occupational and organizational (corporate) crime."[44]

White-Collar Crime

Perhaps John D. Rockefeller, the famed industrialist, explained the nature of the white-collar criminal well in a lecture he reportedly gave often to his Sunday school classes:

> The growth of a large business is merely the survival of the fittest. The American Beauty rose can be produced in the splendor and fragrance which bring cheer to its beholder only by sacrificing the early buds which grow up around it.[45]

But Rockefeller could not have envisioned how that would have led to the many forms of criminality that occur today in the "suites" of the corporate world. Table 3.3 provides an often-cited typology of such crimes, as developed by Herbert Edelhertz in 1970.

Origin and Measurement Problems

The concept of white-collar crime was first introduced in 1939 in an address to the American Sociological Association by Edwin Sutherland, who defined it as "a crime committed by a person of respectability and high social status in the course of his occupation."[46] Sutherland, after examining 40 years of records held by regulatory agencies, courts, and commissions, reported that of the 70 largest industrial and mercantile corporations, all of them violated at least one law and had an adverse decision lodged against it for false advertising, patent abuse, wartime trade violations, price fixing, fraud, or intended manufacturing and sale of faulty goods. Many of them were recidivists, and those that were recidivists averaged eight such violations apiece.[47]

Author Video: White-Collar Criminality

While today we recognize and frequently hear of white-collar criminals, for several reasons the actual extent of white-collar crime remains shrouded in darkness. First, collecting accurate data is difficult, and official statistics of the *Uniform Crime Reports* (discussed below) and victim surveys generally do not include much information concerning this type of crime. And, for obvious reasons, corporations zealously guard their public image and thus prefer to regulate themselves and maintain a code of silence. In addition, the police, social scientists, and members of the media are often inexperienced in the ways of corporate crime, which itself is made even more complicated by the very web of complex corporations that exist. Furthermore, while the Sherman Antitrust Act (1890) and hundreds of laws and regulatory agencies exist to police corporations—and can use recalls, warnings, consent agreements, injunctions, fines, and criminal proceedings—and to keep white-collar crime in check, guilty companies often maintain legions of attorneys and accountants who possess considerable expertise in seeing their bosses are seldom if ever punished.[48]

Corporate crime: crimes committed by wealthy or powerful individuals in the course of their professions or occupations; includes price-fixing, insider trading, and other "white-collar" crimes.

TABLE 3.3

Edelhertz's (1970) Typology of White-Collar Crime

Edelhertz's typology of white-collar crime details a variety of offenses

Crimes committed in the course of their occupations by those operating inside business, government, or other establishments in violation of their duty of loyalty and fidelity to employer or client

1. Commercial bribery and kickbacks (i.e., by and to buyers, insurance adjusters, contracting officers, quality inspectors, government inspectors, and auditors)
2. Bank violations by bank officers, employees, and directors
3. Embezzlement or self-dealing by business or union officers and employees
4. Securities fraud by insiders trading to their advantage by the use of special knowledge
5. Employee petty larceny and expense account fraud
6. Frauds by computer, causing unauthorized payments
7. "Sweetheart contracts" entered into by union officers
8. Embezzlement or self-dealing by attorneys, trustees, and fiduciaries
9. Fraud against the government:
   a. Padding of payrolls
   b. Conflict of interest
   c. False travel, expense, or per diem claims

Crimes incidental to and in furtherance of business operations, but not the central purpose of the business

1. Tax violations
2. Antitrust violations
3. Commercial bribery of another's employee, officer, or fiduciary (including union officers)
4. Food and drug violations
5. False weights and measures by retailers
6. Violations of Truth in Lending Act by misrepresentation of credit terms and prices
7. Submission or publication of false financial statements to obtain credit
8. Use of fictitious or overvalued collateral
9. Check kiting to obtain operating capital on short-term financing
10. Securities Act violations (i.e., sale of nonregistered securities to obtain operating capital, false proxy statements, manipulation of market to support corporate credit or access to capital markets)
11. Collusion between physicians and pharmacists to cause the writing of unnecessary prescriptions
12. Dispensing by pharmacists in violation of law, excluding narcotics trafficking
13. Immigration fraud in support of employment agency operations to provide domestics
14. Housing code violations by landlords
15. Deceptive advertising
16. Fraud against the government:
    a. False claims
    b. False statements
       (1) Statements made to induce contracts
       (2) Aiding fraud
       (3) Housing fraud
       (4) Small Business Administration fraud, such as bootstrapping, self-dealing, and cross-dealing, or obtaining direct loans by use of false financial statements
    c. Moving contracts in urban renewal
17. Labor violations (Davis-Bacon Act)
18. Commercial espionage

Types

Certainly such celebrated cases as the $50 billion fraudulent Ponzi scheme (where one basically uses new investors' funds to pay early investors, rather than using profits earned by the individual or organization running the operation) perpetrated by Bernie Madoff (who was sentenced to 150 years in prison)[49] and the conviction of businesswoman/author/ television personality Martha Stewart (for committing/ lying about insider trading in which she sold stock that plunged in price soon after her trade)[50] are permanently seared in the annals of white-collar crime. But white-collar crime can take many more forms, such as the following:

- A Swiss pharmaceutical company pleaded guilty and paid a record $500 million in fines for price fixing on vitamins.

- Medical quackery and unnecessary surgical procedures victimize more than 2 million Americans, cost $4 billion, and result in 12,000 deaths per year. Fee splitting and "ping-ponging" (doctors referring patients to other doctors in the same office) also occur.

- A major auto manufacturing company, aware that a defect (which would cost $11 to repair) in one of its vehicles could result in a fiery explosion during a rear-end collision (even at low speeds), decided it would be cheaper to not recall the vehicles and make repairs, but instead to pay drivers' injury and death claims.[51]

- Lawyers engage in "ambulance-chasing," file unnecessary lawsuits, and falsify evidence.

- Corporations dump or release toxic chemicals and hazardous materials into the environment to cut costs and avoid regulatory laws.

- Companies steal secrets and patents from one another and thus commit corporate espionage.

Bernie Madoff, a former stockbroker and financial advisor, was convicted of operating a Ponzi scheme that is considered to be the largest of its kind in U.S. history.

Related Fraudulent Acts

The aforementioned social control theorists, Walter and Travis Hirschi, and others in that camp would nod their heads knowingly when told of other such schemes people have concocted over time, motivated by a desire to maximize pleasure and minimize pain and committing what might be said are "cousins" of white-collar crimes.

First is the broad category of identity theft, wherein the offender assumes someone else's identity, uses the other person's stolen credit cards, steals his or her login credentials, and performs countless other such ruses. These cost some 40.5 million Americans about $1.5 billion per year in losses.[52]

Other fraudulent acts, all of which would fit within Edelhertz's typology, can involve businesses while some are run at home, and include the following:

- Postal schemes: Very widespread, they involve everything from leaving town with payments for orders, to offering to arrange a "guaranteed" business loan or employment for an "advance fee," to chain letters, to work-at-home schemes, to fraudulent sales of property.

FOCUS ON   THE GREAT SAVINGS AND LOAN SCANDAL

The biggest, most costly white-collar crime in U.S. history, costing an estimated $500 billion, was the scandal involving the savings and loan industry during the 1980s. To simplify the matter in very basic terms, the scandal had its genesis in the 1930s when the federal government, seeking to protect banking and savings and loan (S&L) customers, began guaranteeing their deposits (eventually up to $100,000). At the same time, the government strictly limited S&Ls to financing home mortgages and smaller loans. By the 1970s, double-digit inflation wreaked havoc on the S&L industry, which was strapped with 6 percent, 30-year mortgages when inflation was 14 to 16 percent; so in 1982 the government decided to deregulate them, allow them to charge more competitive interest rates, and invest

in other commercial and banking enterprises. Still, more than 300 federally insured S&Ls collapsed from 1980 to 1986, leaving the government holding the bag. Meanwhile, Congress and Washington were distracted by a presidential election, so the deregulation of S&Ls created a climate of criminal opportunity—a "junk bond" (high-risk) speculative environment with federal depositors' insurance money. Criminals such as Charles Keating and Michael Milken robbed the S&Ls and were aided by some of the best and brightest financial and legal talent in the United States (80 law firms represented Keating), which were described as a "financial mafia of swindlers, mobsters, greedy SL executives and con men [who] capitalized on regulatory weaknesses and thoroughly fleeced the thrift industry."[53]

- Religious cons: Here, religious cults, televangelists, or organizers skim money from the church.
- Phony accident claims: In this one of many forms of insurance fraud, people fake accidents or forge accident claims.
- Nigerian letter scams: Often e-mailed, these are pleas to help transfer money from Nigeria or some other part of the world, for which the recipients will be handsomely rewarded (after providing their banking information); see http://www.fbi.gov/scams-safety/fraud.
- Paper hanging: This includes passing bad checks, forgery, and other such fraudulent acts.
- Phony fund-raising: Offenders may target victims of natural disasters or other types of victims.
- Cons: These are offenses involving nonexistent home electrical or plumbing repairs, fortune tellers who persuade people to bury their money in a cemetery so as to lift its "curse," and so on.
- Hundreds of other assorted swindles: Consider schemes, frauds, deceptions, stings, rip-offs, hoaxes, and rackets.

IN THEIR OWN WORDS: OFFENDERS SPEAK

Having looked at some of the major criminological theories posited over time as to why men and women commit crimes, this is a good opportunity to consider the motives and methods offered from offenders themselves for their criminal behavior. Using a variety of field-research methods (including interviews with active offenders, incarcerated individuals, and probationers and parolees), researchers have allowed us to learn from actual criminals—armed robbers, burglars, and carjackers—and thus narrow the "distance" between students and their criminal subjects. Certainly the motive underlying the crime of armed robbery is clear: Financial gain (and another long-standing dynamic—temptation) is discussed in Chapter 4 and should not

FOCUS ON   APPLICATION OF CRIME THEORIES

For each of the following scenarios, determine which of the theories described in this chapter might be applied in order to understand the person's motivation for engaging in criminal behavior:

• An employee in a county treasurer's office has developed a means of "juggling the books" and circumventing expenditure controls in such a way as to embezzle county funds. She examines the risks of doing so (i.e., engaging in unethical behavior, getting arrested) against the benefits that would be derived from committing the crimes. Also considered are the benefits: converting to her possession perhaps hundreds of thousands of dollars in a very short period of time. She has also determined that punishment for such crimes is not "swift and certain" because her methods would be difficult to detect (and, to her knowledge, embezzlers receive relatively light punishments). She also perceives that she lives in a society that values people who are financially successful, and that the legal means for attaining such success are otherwise unavailable to her. She thus embezzles the funds.

• A young girl attending college desires to complete her education and enter into a successful career. With financial obstacles in the way, she weighs the benefits and drawbacks of employment with a local "dating service," which she has learned is actually a cover for girls to engage in acts of prostitution. One deterrent, however, is that if arrested, she would be deemed a less-than-acceptable member of society; however, she also perceives that degrees of punishment in such cases are normally light. On the other hand, she is aware that society reveres those who become educated, obtain a good position, and live comfortably. To do so, however, she must somehow find the means of affording her tuition and living expenses. In the end, she opts to take the position with the "dating service," thus risking being arrested and labeled as an outcast, in order to achieve her goals.

• A 16-year-old boy is contemplating whether or not to drop out of school and join a local gang. He knows that to do so he will have to suffer painful initiation rites, and that the lifestyle poses considerable dangers. Conversely, he is also aware that his city's policing of gangs is relatively lax, punishment is not certain, and financial rewards are promising. He is also aware that his legal options for obtaining lucrative employment and financial comfort are limited if not altogether blocked, given his likewise limited (i.e., below-average) education and training. After considering his options and looking at both the benefits and potential disadvantages, he decides the benefits outweigh the deterrents, and he joins the gang.

be overlooked. Unlike most forms of street crime, armed robbers are never secret or ambiguous. And, like the crime of carjacking, discussed below, the crime of robbery bridges property and violent crimes.[54] The armed robber must also create the illusion of impending death in the mind of the victim.

By announcing their intentions to rob, armed robbers believe they are committing themselves irrevocably to the offense; that is the "make or break" moment, and they must establish dominance over the victims and convince them they are not in a position to resist, and displaying a weapon usually precludes the need to do much talking.[55]

The most difficult aspect of armed robberies, according to those who commit them, is the transfer of goods. Here, the robber must keep the victim under strict control while attempting to make sure he has obtained everything of value; it must be done quickly, lest the police or a passerby discover the act.[56] Finally, the robber must make his escape—another difficult stage of the robbery. Armed robbers must maintain their control over their victims while increasing their distance from them. A robber can either flee—possibly bringing attention to himself or allowing the victim to raise an alarm—or force the victim to flee. The latter allows the offender to leave the scene in a leisurely manner.[57]

Burglars, like armed robbers, are primarily motivated by money in order to maintain their "high-living" lifestyle; however, they may also be motivated by noneconomic reasons, including the "thrill" of the act, as well as by revenge.[58] Burglars, then, while usually being prompted by a perceived need for cash, may also derive psychic rewards as a secondary benefit, finding the crime to be exciting. Some also commit residential burglaries in order to get even with someone for a real or imagined wrong—an attack on one's status, identity, or self-esteem. For example, a burglar can have an argument over a traffic or parking matter, and then follow the victim home; later, after learning the victim's routine, he may burglarize the person's home to settle the "grudge"— possibly even destroying more goods than he removes.[59]

According to one study,[60] with the exception of homicide, "probably no offense is more symbolic of contemporary urban violence than carjacking." Indeed, following the 1992 murder of a woman when two men commandeered her car in Washington, D.C., carjacking was made a federal crime punishable by up to 25 years in prison.[61] Unlike most robberies, carjacking is directed at an object rather than a person; still, weapons are used in two-thirds to three-fourths of carjackings.[62]

Carjackers are motivated by two primary objectives: opportunity (i.e., weighing potential risks and rewards) and situational inducements (peer pressure, need for cash or drugs, or revenge). They normally have a precarious day-to-day existence, exacerbated by "boom or bust" cycles, and are always under some degree of financial pressure. The sale of stolen vehicles and parts can be very lucrative, with carjackers either selling the car parts or delivering the car to a "chop shop," where it will be stripped; items of value include tire rims, hubcaps, and stereos—for which the average carjacker will be paid about $1,750 per car.[63]

HOW MUCH CRIME IN THE UNITED STATES? DEPENDS ON WHOM YOU ASK

Mark Twain once said, rather famously, that there are "lies, damn lies, and statistics."[64] Unfortunately, that assessment of statistics is somewhat (if not significantly) accurate with respect to U.S. reported crime figures. One example that will make the point is two different data sets reporting hate crimes. Specifically, in a recent year the Federal Bureau of Investigation's (FBI's) *Uniform Crime Reports* (discussed below) reported a total of 6,222 hate crimes (with 7,713 victims).[65] However, the National Crime Victimization Survey (NCVS, also discussed below) reported an annual average of *169,000* violent hate crime victimizations. This large discrepancy is largely due to the fact that about 54 percent of victims in the NCVS did not report their crimes to the police. Furthermore, in the NCVS, hate-related victimizations are based on victims' suspicion of the offenders' motivation, rather than the suspicion of the police.[66] Thus it is emphasized that crime figures must be viewed with more than a hint of suspicion.

Errors and variations notwithstanding, in order to comprehend the impact of crime on our society, criminologists, victimologists, sociologists, psychologists, and members of other related disciplines have need of such information for their research and for making recommendations concerning planning and policy making. Knowing the nature and extent of crime also assists toward an understanding of the social forces that are driving those offenses and aggregated trends. Furthermore, measuring crime is one of the best ways of attempting to determine the policies and effectiveness of our agencies of criminal justice. We can better examine the structure and functions of the police (by looking at reported crimes and the proportion of crimes that are solved by arrest or other means), the courts (to determine the types of punishment and treatment that offenders are receiving), and corrections organizations (to

Hate Crimes

ascertain, among other things, whether or not our offenders are being returned to prisons and jails)

Having crime data also allows for calculations of a national *crime rate* (discussed below), which in turn provides us with a "victim risk rate" of sorts—the odds that we (or relatives and friends) will become a victim of a serious crime.

Discussed first is the FBI's **Uniform Crime Reports**, and following is a review of a more in-depth method of capturing and analyzing reported crimes: the National Incident-Based Reporting System; finally, the National Crime Victimization Survey is examined. Unfortunately, as shown above, these three sources of crime information are very different in their approaches and findings.

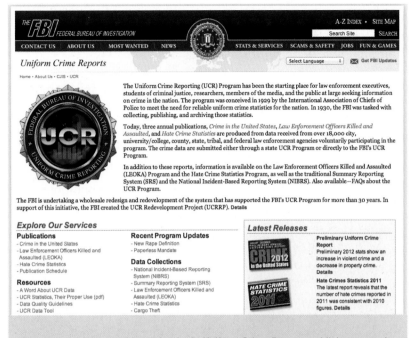

The Federal Bureau of Investigation's *Uniform Crime Reports* publishes annual crime data for selected crimes as reported to the police in the United States.

The FBI's *Uniform Crime Reports*

The Uniform Crime Reporting (UCR) Program was conceived in 1929 by the International Association of Chiefs of Police to meet a need for reliable, uniform crime statistics for the nation. In 1930, the FBI was tasked with collecting, publishing, and archiving those statistics. Today, several annual statistical publications, such as the comprehensive *Crime in the United States*, are produced from data provided by nearly 17,000 law enforcement agencies across the United States.

Other annual publications, such as *Hate Crime Statistics* and *Law Enforcement Officers Killed and Assaulted*, address specialized facets of crime such as hate crime or the murder and assault, respectively, of law enforcement officers.[67] Special studies, reports, and monographs prepared using data mined from the UCR's large database are published each year as well. In addition to these reports, information about the *National Incident-Based Reporting System (NIBRS)*, answers to general UCR questions, and answers to specific UCR questions are available on this site.

Cautions and Criticisms of UCR Data

Each year when the FBI's *Crime in the United States* is published, many people and groups with an interest in crime rush to use the crime figures in attempts to rank and compare crimes in cities and counties. The FBI is quick to point out each year in its UCR that making such comparisons is very ill advised, due to the variety of characteristics of different states, counties, and communities.

Many variables can contribute to the amount of crime occurring in a specific jurisdiction. First, it is important to understand a jurisdiction's industrial/economic base, its dependence on neighboring jurisdictions, its transportation system, its reliance on tourism and conventions, its proximity to military installations and correctional facilities, and so forth. Indeed, the strength and aggressiveness of the local police are also key factors in understanding the nature and extent of crime occurring in an area.

In addition to the crime theories discussed above, other factors known to affect the volume and type of crime are largely outside the control of the criminal justice system:

- Population density and degree of urbanization

- Variations in composition of the population, particularly youth concentration

- Stability of the population with respect to residents' mobility, commuting patterns, and transient factors

- Modes of transportation and highway system

- Economic conditions, including median income, poverty level, and job availability

- Cultural factors and educational, recreational, and religious characteristics[68]

Critics of UCR data—who include any person engaged in serious research into crime, criminology, victimology, and so on—commonly note its shortcomings, as noted in Figure 3.1.[69]

FIGURE 3.1

Limitations of the *Uniform Crime Reports*

Although the FBI's *Uniform Crime Reports* include several unique publications such as special reports providing statistics on hate crimes and law enforcement officers killed and assaulted,

- offense data are available only for a small number (8) of all crimes committed in the United States;

- the UCR data only list crimes reported to law enforcement agencies (not all crimes that occur are known to the police);

- reporting of citizens' reports of crime by the police is voluntary, and therefore police may choose to not report or might report inaccurately (thus UCR data may be affected by the reporting practices of local law enforcement);

- the hierarchy rule (discussed below) is employed, meaning that where a number of crimes are committed as part of a single criminal act, only the most serious offense of all of them is reported to the UCR;

- attempted crimes are combined with completed crimes;

- when computing crime rates, the UCR counts incidents involving all kinds of targets (for example, crimes of burglary are against businesses and residents, not against "populations"); and

- UCR includes very little information concerning crime victims.

Source: A complete UCR handbook may be viewed at http://www.fbi.gov/about-us/cjis/ucr/additional-ucr-publications/ucr_handbook.pdf/view.

The Hierarchy Rule: Definition and Application

In tabulating how many crimes occur each year, law enforcement agencies are instructed by the FBI to use what is known as the **hierarchy rule**, which basically says that when more than one Part I offense is committed during a criminal event, the law enforcement agency must identify and report only the offense that is highest on the hierarchy list.[70]

Put another way, the hierarchy rule requires counting only the most serious offense and ignoring all others. Note, however, that this rule applies only to the crime reporting process; it does *not* affect the number of charges for which the defendant may be prosecuted in the courts.

The next "Focus On" box contains several exercises that will test your knowledge of the hierarchy rule; prior to addressing them, however, it might be beneficial for you to first review the definitions of the eight Part I offenses, discussed in Chapter 2.

Hierarchy rule: in the FBI *Uniform Crime Reports* reporting scheme, the practice whereby only the most serious offense of several that are committed during a criminal act is reported by the police.

FOCUS ON   THE HIERARCHY RULE

To better understand the hierarchy rule in these exercises, you may wish to first revisit the definitions of the eight Part I offenses in Chapter 2, which are commonly listed in terms of their severity. Now consider the following example:

1. Assume that Doe, during the daytime hours, enters Smith's home through an unlocked back door and removes furniture that is valued at about $10,000. If Doe is apprehended, under the hierarchy rule the *only* crime that the police will report to the FBI is

   a. burglary;   c. robbery; or

   b. theft, as it occurred in the daytime;   d. felony theft.

2. Further assume that Smith returns home and finds Doe inside; after briefly scuffling, Doe strikes Smith sharply with a candlestick holder, rendering Smith unconscious and near death. Then Doe, fearing he will be caught and returned to prison if Smith testifies against him, picks up a nearby vase and strikes enough blows to end Smith's life.

What crime(s) has Doe committed? Under the UCR's hierarchy rule, which crime(s) will be reported by the police to the FBI?

Crime Rate

A fundamental aspect of the calculating and understanding of crime concerns how the FBI calculates the **crime rate**.

The formula used is not complicated in nature; it is as follows: number of crimes reported, divided by the population of the jurisdiction in question, then multiplied by 100,000; this renders the number of crimes reported for each 100,000 population. It is depicted thusly:

$$\frac{\text{Number of offenses}}{\text{Population of the jurisdiction}} \times 100{,}000 = \frac{\text{Number of offenses per}}{100{,}000 \text{ population}}$$

As an example, assume, as in a recent year, that there were about 1,203,000 violent crimes reported to the police in the United States; also for that year the nation's reported population was 311,600,000; using the above formula, the resulting crime rate for that year was 386 violent crimes per 100,000 population.[71]

The crime rate formula can also be considered a "victim risk rate," or the chances of one becoming a victim; therefore, the chances of one's being a victim of a violent Part I offense for that recent year were about 386 in 100,000.

The National Incident-Based Reporting System

Being aware of the criticisms that have been leveled over time against the UCR, described above, in 1988 the U.S. Department of Justice launched the **National Incident-Based Reporting System (NIBRS)** (see Table 3.4). Although the UCR collects and analyzes data for eight Part I offenses, the NIBRS furnishes crime data provided by nearly 6,500 participating federal, state, and local law enforcement agencies for 46 specific crimes (called Group A offenses) in the following major crime categories: terrorism, white-collar crime, weapons offenses, missing children where criminality is involved, drug/narcotics offenses, drug involvement in all offenses, hate crimes, spousal abuse, abuse of the elderly, child abuse, domestic violence, juvenile crime/gangs, parental abduction, organized crime, pornography/child pornography, driving under the influence, and alcohol-related offenses.[72]

Crime rate: the number of reported crimes divided by the population of the jurisdiction, and multiplied by 100,000 persons; developed and used by the FBI *Uniform Crime Reports.*

National Incident-Based Reporting System: a crime reporting system in which police describe each offense in a crime as well as describing the offender.

Furthermore, with the NIBRS, legislators, municipal planners/administrators, academicians, sociologists, and the public will have access to more comprehensive, detailed, accurate, and meaningful crime information than the traditional UCR system can provide. Furthermore, with such information, law enforcement can better make a case to acquire the resources needed to fight crime. The NIBRS also enables agencies to locate similarities in crime-fighting problems so that agencies can work together to develop solutions or discover strategies for addressing the issues. Several NIBRS manuals, studies, and papers are available on the UCR Program's website at www.fbi.gov/ucr/ucr.htm.

Another change is that the "hierarchy rule" (discussed above) does not apply in the NIBRS; if more than one crime was committed by the same person or group of persons and the time and space intervals were insignificant, all of the crimes would be reported as offenses within the same incident.

In addition to having the UCR's two crime categories—crimes against persons (e.g., murder, rape, and aggravated assault) and crimes against property (e.g., robbery, burglary, and larceny-theft), the NIBRS includes a third crime category, crimes against society, to represent society's prohibitions against certain types of activities (e.g., drug or narcotic offenses). As shown in Table 3.4, the NIBRS also collects more comprehensive data about drug offenses than the summary reporting system.

The National Crime Victimization Survey

NCVS

The **National Crime Victimization Survey (NCVS)**, created to address some of the shortcomings with the UCR as delineated above, has been collecting data on personal and household victimization since 1973. The NCVS claims on its website to be "the nation's primary source of information on criminal victimization." Each year, data are obtained from a nationally representative sample of about 40,000 households comprising nearly 75,000 persons on the frequency, characteristics, and consequences of criminal victimization in the United States. Each household is interviewed twice during the year. The survey enables the Bureau of Justice Statistics to estimate the likelihood of victimization by rape, sexual assault, robbery, assault, theft, household burglary, and motor vehicle theft for the population as a whole as well as for segments of the population such as women, the elderly, members of various racial groups, city dwellers, or other groups. The NCVS provides the largest national forum for victims to describe the impact of crime and characteristics of violent offenders.[73]

The survey—which asks respondents to report crime experiences occurring in the past six months—is administered by the U.S. Census Bureau (under the U.S. Department of Commerce) on behalf of the Bureau of Justice Statistics (under the U.S. Department of Justice).

The four primary objectives of the NCVS are to

1. develop detailed information about the victims and consequences of crime,

2. estimate the number and types of crimes not reported to the police,

3. provide uniform measures of selected types of crimes, and

4. permit comparisons over time and types of areas.[74]

The NCVS categorizes crimes as "personal" or "property." Personal crimes cover rape and sexual attack, robbery, aggravated and simple assault, and purse-snatching/pocket-picking, while property crimes cover burglary, theft, motor vehicle theft, and vandalism.

National Crime Victimization Survey: a random survey of households that measures crimes committed against victims; includes crimes not reported to police.

TABLE 3.4

Crime data collected by NIBRS

NIBRS offenses

Group A Offenses

The following offense categories, known as Group A offenses, are those for which extensive crime data are collected in the National Incident-Based Reporting System.

- Arson
- Assault Offenses—Aggravated Assault, Simple Assault, Intimidation
- Bribery
- Burglary/Breaking and Entering
- Counterfeiting/Forgery
- Destruction/Damage/Vandalism of Property
- Drug/Narcotic Offenses—Drug/Narcotic Violations, Drug Equipment Violations
- Embezzlement
- Extortion/Blackmail
- Fraud Offenses—False Pretenses/Swindle/Confidence Game, Credit Card/Automatic Teller Machine Fraud, Impersonation, Welfare Fraud, Wire Fraud
- Gambling Offenses—Betting/Wagering, Operating/Promoting/Assisting Gambling, Gambling Equipment Violations, Sports Tampering
- Homicide Offenses—Murder and Non-negligent Manslaughter, Negligent Manslaughter, Justifiable Homicide
- Kidnapping/Abduction
- Larceny/Theft Offenses—Pocket-Picking, Purse-Snatching, Shoplifting, Theft from Building, Theft from Coin-Operated Machine or Device, Theft from Motor Vehicle, Theft of Motor Vehicle Parts or Accessories, All Other Larceny
- Motor Vehicle Theft
- Pornography/Obscene Material
- Prostitution Offenses—Prostitution, Assisting or Promoting Prostitution
- Robbery
- Sex Offenses, Forcible—Forcible Rape, Forcible Sodomy, Sexual Assault with an Object, Forcible Fondling
- Sex Offenses, Nonforcible—Incest, Statutory Rape
- Stolen Property Offenses (Receiving, etc.)
- Weapon Law Violations

Group B Offenses

There are 11 additional offenses, known as Group B offenses, for which only arrest data are reported.

- Bad Checks
- Curfew/Loitering/Vagrancy Violations
- Disorderly Conduct
- Driving Under the Influence
- Drunkenness
- Family Offenses, Nonviolent
- Liquor Law Violations
- Peeping Tom
- Runaway
- Trespass of Real Property
- All Other Offenses

Source: Federal Bureau of Investigation, "NIBRS General Frequently Asked Questions," *Uniform Crime Reports* (Washington, D.C.: U.S. Department of Justice), http://www.fbi.gov/ucr/nibrs_general.html (accessed February 17, 2013).

Chapter Quiz: Theories of Crime and Measuring Victimization

A potential problem with the NCVS is that it makes estimates of crime based on a representative sample; therefore, it is subject to sampling error. There is also the possibility of nonsampling error, such as with respondents' inability to recall in detail the crimes that occurred during the six months prior to the interview, when the crimes occurred, and other details of the crimes.[75]

IN A NUTSHELL

- The classical and neoclassical schools of criminology were the first attempt to explain crime in rational terms. They postulated that criminal behavior is rational, and most people have the potential to engage in such behavior; punishment should fit the crime rather than fit the offender, and justice must be predictable. To a large extent, sentencing reform, criticisms of rehabilitation, and greater use of incarceration sprung from these classical ideas.

- Later, the positivist school of thought, which has dominated U.S. criminology since the beginning of the 20th century, used science to study the body, mind, and environment of offenders and how they could be rehabilitated. Human behavior is controlled by physical, mental, and social factors, not by free will.

- Biological theories of crime offer that the causes of crime are found in the biological determinants—or "original nature"—of the offender and are the result of some biological element or defect; criminals are *born* and not *made* by their home or social environment. Included here are studies of the influence of chromosomes, body types, twins, and adopted children.

- Psychological rationales for crime argue that mental conditions are the reason for criminal behavior, either by a personality disorder or limited intellect. The improperly socialized child may develop a personality disturbance that causes her or him to have antisocial and criminal impulses.

- Social and cultural explanations for crime argue that living in social groups might shape criminal behavior; criminality is not innate in one's biological makeup, but instead is caused by external social factors through one's contact with the world. Factors such as poverty, age, race, gender, family, problems faced by immigrants, and so on will foster crime. Theories that stress the influence of social factors on crime are social structure theory, social process theory, and critical theory.

- The wave of feminism during the 1970s consequently gave women equal opportunity and brought female involvement in a wide variety of crimes—sometimes termed *feminist theory*—as well as new studies and questions of that involvement: Do the traditionally male-centered theories of crime apply to women as well? And what explains the long-standing fact that women commit far fewer crimes than men?

- In their own words, criminals explain and rationalize their acts in a variety of ways, including financial gain, the need to maintain street status and a partying lifestyle, revenge, and "thrill seeking."

- Crimes in the United States are measured and reported in three primary ways: the FBI's *Uniform Crime Reports*, the National Incident-Based Reporting System, and the National Crime Victimization Survey. Each has its unique approaches as well as advantages and disadvantages.

Adoption studies
Biological determinism
Body type studies
Classical school
Control theories
Corporate crime
Crime rate
Critical theory
Feminist theory

Hierarchy rule
Labeling theory
Learning theory
National Crime
  Victimization Survey
National Incident-Based
  Reporting System
Neoclassical
  criminology

Positivist school
Psychological
  rationales for crime
Social process theory
Social structure theory
Twin studies
Uniform Crime Reports
XYY chromosome

STUDY
SITE

$SAGE edge™

Sharpen your skills with **SAGE edge** at edge.sagepub.com/peak. **SAGE edge for students** provides a personalized approach to help you accomplish your coursework goals in an easy-to-use learning environment. Access the videos, audio clips, quizzes, cases and SAGE journal and reference articles that are noted in this chapter.

REVIEW
QUESTIONS
?

1. What were the prevailing beliefs concerning the causes of crime prior to the mid-1700s?

2. How did Cesare Beccaria and the classical school form the foundation for explaining crime in more rational terms?

3. What were the major contributions of the positivist school of criminology in attempting to explain criminality?

4. How would you describe the tenets of the biological theories of crime, including the "born criminal," the "criminal" chromosome, and studies of body type, twins, and adopted children?

5. What were the central psychological explanations of crime as explained by personality disorder and limited intellect?

6. What, in your opinion, are the most compelling of the several social and cultural explanations of crime?

7. What explanations have been offered for women becoming much more engaged in criminal activities since the 1970s?

8. What is white-collar crime, and how/why does it function and persist?

9. What are the three primary methods of measuring the extent of crime, and what have been offered as disadvantages for some of them?

1. Assume that our legal system is neoclassical: People make a rational choice to commit crimes after weighing the benefits to be gained against the costs of being caught and punished, but the criminal law must take into account the differences among individuals. You are engaged in a class debate concerning the following resolution: "Our legal system has struck an excellent balance between its holding people responsible for their crimes and allowing them to be excused for their crimes." Choose a side, and stake out your argument.

2. Your criminal justice professor hands out the following scenario: John, a youth of 14, is on an errand for his parents (who are lower in socioeconomic class) when he decides to stop at a crafts shop and look at model cars and airplanes—a hobby he greatly enjoys. While in the store, he puts two small bottles of model paint in his pockets and leaves, but he is quickly stopped by a clerk as he attempts his escape. Explain the possible reasons for John's actions in view of the biological, psychological, and sociocultural theories of crime as discussed in this chapter.

3. As part of a criminal justice honor society paper to be presented at a local

conference, you are asked to use the Internet and determine how many crimes were reported for your city, your county, your state, and the United States during the past calendar year. How will you proceed?

4. Ellen believes Sally prevented her from receiving a Best Citizen Award and is extremely upset. Ellen confronts Sally on the street and verbally threatens to "beat her within an inch of her life," and then hits her with her purse, causing a bloody nose. Ellen then grabs a sharp nail file in the bottom of her purse, and after briefly contemplating whether or not to stab Sally with it, decides not to do so and then runs away. Sally goes to the district attorney's office to file charges. As the prosecutor, what crime(s) do you believe Ellen has actually committed?

5. Your criminal justice professor is working on a journal article concerning the dangers of police work, and she a sks you to obtain some information on police deaths and assaults. Using the FBI's UCR website and its supplemental report, *Law Enforcement Officers Killed and Assaulted* (at http://www.fbi.gov/ ucr/ucr.htm#leoka), what would you report?

ETHICAL ESSENTIALS:
"Doing Right When No
One Is Watching"

LEARNING OBJECTIVES

As a result of reading this chapter, the student will be able to:

1 Articulate legitimate ethical dilemmas that arise with police, courts, and corrections practitioners

2 Describe the codes and canons of ethics that exist in police, courts, and corrections

3 Explain the philosophical foundations that underlie and mold modern ethical behavior

4 Explain why the "ends justify means" type of thinking poses problems for criminal justice and society

5 Discuss and provide examples of absolute and relative ethics

6 Define noble cause corruption

7 Review the utilitarian approach to ethics

8 Clarify the controversy surrounding the acceptance of gratuities, as well as a proposed model for determining whether or not such acceptance is corrupt in nature

9 Delineate the unique kinds of ethical considerations and obligations that exist with federal employees

10 Discuss the need for, and application of, ethical standards as they concern police, courts, and corrections practitioners

CHAPTER

04

Watch your thoughts, for they become words.
Watch your words, for they become actions.
Watch your actions, for they become habits.
Watch your habits, for they become character.
Watch your character, for it becomes your destiny.

—Unknown

INTRODUCTION

Author Introduction:
Chapter 4

As regular practice is essential to being a renowned musician, and a perfect cake is to a beautiful wedding, so too is ethics essential to being a criminal justice practitioner. A Latin term that might be used to describe this relationship is *sine qua non*—"without which, nothing." Given that, a fundamental knowledge of ethics, as well as some guideposts concerning what constitutes unethical behavior, is an important topic in today's society and for all criminal justice students—not only to guide their own behavior but also in light of the fact that unethical behavior at times appears to permeate the spheres of contemporary U.S. politics/government, business, and sports.

What specific behaviors are clearly unethical for criminal justice employees? What kinds of criteria should guide these employees in their work? To what extent, if any, should the public allow criminal justice employees to violate citizens' rights in order to maintain public order?

This chapter attempts to address these questions and examine many types of ethical problems that can and do arise in police departments, courts, and corrections agencies. The focus will necessarily be on the police, who will find themselves in many more situations where corruption and brutality can occur than will the judges and corrections personnel.

This is not a black-and-white area of study; in fact, it will be seen that there is definitely a "shade of gray" for many people where ethics is called into question. Also problematical is that some people who are hired into criminal

ASSESS YOUR AWARENESS:

Test your knowledge of ethics by first reading and responding to the following seven true-false items; check your answers after reading this chapter's materials.

1. The term *ethics* is rooted in the ancient Greek idea of *character*.

2. The "ends justify the means" philosophy is normally a good, safe philosophy for the police and judges to follow.

3. At times, communities seemingly tolerate questionable police behavior, if there is a greater public good (such as dealing with violent gang members).

4. During an oral interview, applicants for policing jobs should *never* state that they would be willing to "snitch out" another officer whom they observe doing something wrong.

5. The receipt of gratuities by criminal justice personnel is a universally accepted practice.

6. Whistleblowers exposing improper acts of their coworkers now enjoy no legal protection.

7. Because of their constitutional obligations, prosecutors and defense attorneys are not bound to ethical standards as are other criminal justice employees.

Answers can be found on page 401.

justice positions simply are not of good character. Furthermore, as stated in Chapter 1, we cannot *train* people to have high ethical standards; nor can we infuse ethics intravenously. In sum, character and ethics are largely something that someone either has or does not have.

Included are several scenarios and activities, providing you with opportunities to put the chapter's materials into practice; among them are several "learn by doing" exercises. Note, too, that police brutality, judicial misconduct, and related problems in corrections will be discussed in Chapters 6, 10, and 13, respectively.

GOOD EXAMPLES OF BAD EXAMPLES

To frame the concept of ethics and demonstrate how one's value system can easily be challenged in criminal justice work, consider the following scenarios, all of which are true, and what might be an appropriate punishment (if any) for each (outcomes for each are provided in the notes at chapter's end):

Unique Ethical Considerations

- *Police*: Upon seeing a vehicle weaving across the center line of the highway, Officer A stops the car, approaches the driver's door, and immediately detects a strong odor of alcohol. The motorist is removed from the car and joins Officer A and a backup, Officer B, on the roadside. Officer A decides to use a portable breath test device to confirm his suspicions of driving under the influence, or DUI, and he gives a sterile plastic mouthpiece to the driver to blow into. The driver attempts to thwart the test by appearing (but failing) to blow into the mouthpiece. Irritated by this attempt, Officer A yanks the mouthpiece away, throws it on the ground, and arrests the driver for DUI. At trial, the driver claims the mouthpiece was flawed (blocked) so he was unable to blow through it; Officer A testifies under oath that it was not blocked, and as "evidence," he takes a mouthpiece out of his pocket, stating it is the mouthpiece he used for the test that night. Officer B, sitting in the room, hears this testimony and knows differently, having seen Officer A impatiently throw the mouthpiece on the ground and leave it at the scene.[1]

- *Courts*: For several weeks, a wealthy divorcée receives menacing telephone calls that demand dates and sexual favors. The caller's voice is electronically disguised. The suspect also begins stalking the woman. After working some clues and tailing a suspect, a federal agent finally makes contact with a suspect, determining that he is the chief judge of the state's supreme court. Upon confronting him, the agent is told by the judge to "forget about it, or you'll be checking passports in a remote embassy."[2]

- *Corrections*: A corrections officer in a minimum-security facility for young offenders is working the night shift when a youth is admitted. The youth is frightened because this is his first time in custody, and the officer places him in isolation because the youth told the staff he is feeling suicidal. Over the next several days, the officer develops a friendship with the youth. Looking through the youth's file, the officer learns that the boy does not wish to remain male; rather, he wants to become a female. One day while doing a routine cell search, the officer observes the youth stuffing women's panties into his pillowcase. With a terrified and pleading look, the youth explains he prefers them to boxer shorts and begs the officer not to mention this incident to other staff or youths in the facility. The officer ponders what to do; surely the boy would be seriously ridiculed if others knew of the panties, and it does not seem to be a "big deal."

On the other hand, if the officer does not report the event and the boy's choice of underwear is revealed later, the officer knows he will be accused of being lax and not watching over the youths as he should have, and at the very least lose credibility with other staff and the administration.[3]

PHILOSOPHICAL FOUNDATIONS

Ethical Theories

The term **ethics** is rooted in the ancient Greek idea of *character*. Ethics involves doing what is right or correct and is generally used to refer to how people should behave in a professional capacity. Many people would argue, however, that no difference should exist between one's professional and personal behavior. Ethical rules of conduct should apply to everything a person does.

A central problem with understanding ethics concerns the questions of "whose ethics" and "which right." This becomes evident when one examines controversial issues such as the death penalty, abortion, use of deadly force, and gun control. How individuals view a particular controversy largely depends on their values, character, or ethics. Both sides of controversies such as these believe they are morally right. These issues demonstrate that to understand behavior, the most basic values must be examined and understood.

Deadly Force
Controversy

Another area for examination is **deontological ethics,** which does not consider consequences but instead examines one's duty to act. The word *deontology* comes from two Greek roots, *deos*, meaning "duty," and *logos*, meaning "study." Thus, deontology means the study of duty. When police officers observe a violation of law, they have a duty to act. Officers frequently use this as an excuse when they issue traffic citations that appear to have little utility and do not produce any great benefit for the rest of society. For example, when an officer writes a traffic citation for a prohibited left turn made at two o'clock in the morning when no traffic is around, the officer is fulfilling a departmental duty to enforce the law. From a utilitarian standpoint (where we judge an action by its consequences), however, little if any good was served. Here, duty and not good consequences was the primary motivator.

Immanuel Kant, an 18th-century philosopher, expanded the ethics of duty by including the idea of "good will."[4] People's actions must be guided by good intent. In the previous example, the officer who wrote the traffic citation for an improper left turn would be acting unethically if the ticket was a response to a quota or some irrelevant motive. On the other hand, if the citation was issued because the officer truly believed that it would result in some good outcome, it would have been an ethical action.

Some people have expanded this argument even further. Richard Kania[5] argued that police officers should be allowed to freely accept **gratuities** because such actions would constitute the building blocks of positive social relationships between the police and the public. In this case, duty is used to justify what under normal circumstances would be considered unethical. Conversely, if officers take gratuities for self-gratification rather than to form positive community relationships, then the action would be considered unethical by many.

Types of Ethics

Ethics usually involves standards of fair and honest conduct; what we call conscience, the ability to recognize right from wrong; and actions that are good and proper. There are absolute ethics and relative ethics. **Absolute ethics** has only two sides—something is either good or bad, black or white. Some examples in police ethics would be unethical behaviors such as bribery, extortion, excessive force, and perjury, which nearly everyone would agree are unacceptable behaviors by the police.

Ethics: a set of rules or values that spell out appropriate human conduct.

Deontological ethics: one's duty to act.

Gratuities: the receipt of some benefit (a meal, gift, or some other favor) either for free or for a reduced price.

Absolute ethics: the type of ethics where there are only two sides—good or bad, black or white; some examples would be unethical behaviors such as bribery, extortion, excessive force, and perjury, which nearly everyone would agree are unacceptable for criminal justice personnel.

Relative ethics is more complicated and can have a multitude of sides with varying shades of gray. What is considered ethical behavior by one person may be deemed highly unethical by someone else. Not all ethical issues are clear-cut, however, and communities *do* seem willing at times to tolerate extralegal behavior if there is a greater public good, especially in dealing with problems such as gangs and the homeless. This willingness on the part of the community can be conveyed to the police. Ethical relativism can be said to form an essential part of the community policing movement, discussed more fully later.

A community's acceptance of relative ethics as part of criminal justice may send the wrong message: that there are few boundaries placed on justice system employee behaviors and that, at times, "anything goes" in their fight against crime. As John Kleinig[6] pointed out, giving false testimony to ensure that a public menace is "put away" or illegally wiretapping an organized crime figure's telephone might sometimes be viewed as "necessary" and "justified," though illegal; this is the essence of the crime control model of criminal justice (discussed in Chapter 1). Another example is that many police believe they are compelled to skirt along the edges of the law—or even violate it—in order to arrest drug traffickers. The ethical problem here is that even if the action could be justified as morally proper, it remains illegal. For many persons, however, the protection of society overrides other concerns.

This viewpoint—the "principle of double effect"—holds that when one commits an act to achieve a good end and an inevitable but intended effect is negative, then the act might be justified. A long-standing debate has occurred about balancing the rights of individuals against the community's interest in calm and order.

These special areas of ethics can become problematic and controversial when police officers use deadly force or lie and deceive others in their work. Police could justify a whole range of activities that others may deem unethical simply because the consequences resulted in the greatest good for the greatest number—the *utilitarian* approach (or **utilitarianism**). If the ends justified the means, perjury would be ethical when committed to prevent a serial killer from being set free to prey on society. In our democratic society, however, the means are just as important as, if not more important than, the desired end.

The community—and criminal justice administrators—cannot tolerate completely unethical behavior but may seemingly tolerate extralegal behavior if there is a greater public good, especially with regard to violent gang members. As examples, citizens in some jurisdictions may not object to the police "hassling" suspected gang members—pulling them over in their cars, say, and doing a field interview—or telling homeless people who are loitering in front of a heavy tourism area or public park to "move along."

It is no less important today than in the past for criminal justice employees to appreciate and come to grips with ethical essentials. Indeed, ethical issues in policing have been affected by three critical factors[7]: (1) the growing level of temptation stemming from the illicit drug trade; (2) the potentially compromising nature of the organizational culture—a culture that can

One of the ethical responsibilities of police officers is to testify truthfully in court concerning what they saw, heard, and did during the performance of their duties.

Relative ethics: the "gray" area of ethics that is not so clear-cut, such as releasing a serious offender in order to use him later as an informant.

Utilitarianism: in ethics, as articulated by John Stuart Mill, a belief that the proper course of action is that which maximizes utility—usually defined as that which maximizes happiness and minimizes suffering

exalt **loyalty** over integrity, with a "code of silence" that protects unethical employees; and (3) the challenges posed by decentralization (flattening the organization and pushing officers' decision making downward) through the advent of community-oriented policing and problem solving (the community era of policing will be discussed in Chapter 5).

Noble Cause Corruption

When relative ethics and the "principle of double effect," described above, are practiced by the police, it is known as **noble cause corruption**—what Thomas Martinelli,[8] perhaps gratuitously, defined as "corruption committed in the name of good ends, corruption that happens when police officers care too much about their work." This viewpoint has been termed the "principle of double effect." It basically holds that when an act is committed to achieve a good end (such as an illegal search) but its outcome is negative (the person who is searched eventually goes to prison), the act might still be justified.

Although noble cause corruption can occur anywhere in the criminal justice system, we might look at the police for examples. Officers might "bend the rules," such as not reading a drunk person his rights or performing a field sobriety test; planting evidence; issuing "sewer" tickets—writing a person a ticket but not giving it to him, resulting in a warrant issued for failure to appear in court; "testilying"; or "using the magic pencil," where police officers write up an incident in a way that criminalizes a suspect; this is a powerful tool for punishment. Noble cause corruption carries with it a different way of thinking about the police relationship with the law; here, officers operate on a standard that places personal morality above the law, become legislators *of* the law, and act as if they *are* the law.[9] Such activities can be rationalized by some officers, however; as a Philadelphia police officer put it, "When you're shoveling society's garbage, you gotta be indulged a little bit."[10] Nonetheless, when officers participate in such activities and believe the ends justify the means, they corrupt their own system.

Obviously the kinds of "ends justify means," noble cause behaviors mentioned above often involve arrogance on the part of the police and ignore the basic constitutional guidelines their occupation demands. Administrators and middle managers must be careful to take a hard-line view that their subordinates always tell the truth and follow the law. A supervisory philosophy of discipline based on due process, fairness, and equity, combined with intelligent, informed, and comprehensive decision making, is best for the department, its employees, and the community.[11]

Police and the Truth

ETHICS IN POLICING

Having defined the types of ethics and some dilemmas, next we discuss in greater detail some of the ethical issues faced by police leaders and their subordinates.

Oral Interview

A Primer: The Oral Interview

During oral interviews for a position in policing, applicants are often placed in a hypothetical situation that tests their ethical beliefs and character. For example, they are asked to assume the role of a police officer who is checking on foot an office supplies retail store that was found to have an unlocked door during early morning hours. On leaving the building, the officer observes another officer, Smith, removing a $100 writing pen from a display case and placing it in his uniform pocket. What should the officer do?

This kind of question commonly befuddles the applicant: "Should I rat on my fellow officer? Overlook the matter? Merely tell Smith never to do that again?" Unfortunately, applicants may do a lot of "how am I *supposed* to

Noble cause corruption: a situation where one commits an unethical act but for the greater good; for example, a police officer violates the Constitution in order to capture a serious offender.

respond" soul searching and second-guessing with these kinds of questions.

Bear in mind that criminal justice agencies do not wish to hire someone who possesses ethical shortcomings; it is simply too potentially dangerous and expensive, from both legal and moral standpoints, to take the chance of bringing into an agency someone who is corrupt. That is the reason for such questioning and a thorough background investigation of applicants.

Before responding to a scenario like the one concerning Officer Smith, the applicant should consider the following issues: Is this likely to be the first time that Smith has stolen something? Don't the police arrest and jail people for this same kind of behavior?

In short, police administrators should *never* want an applicant to respond that it is acceptable for an officer to steal. Furthermore, it would be incorrect for an applicant to believe that police do not want an officer to "rat out" another officer. Applicants should never acknowledge that stealing or other such activities are to be overlooked.

New York City police officer Frank Serpico testified before the Knapp Commission in 1971 concerning the extent of corruption within the NYPD.

Police Corruption

"For as long as there have been police, there has been police corruption."[12] Thus observed Lawrence Sherman about one of the oldest problems in U.S. policing. Indeed, the Knapp Commission investigated police corruption there in the early 1970s, finding that there are two primary types of corrupt police officers: the "meat-eaters" and the "grass-eaters." Meat-eaters spend a good deal of their working hours aggressively seeking out situations that they can exploit for financial gain, including gambling, narcotics, and other lucrative enterprises.

Grass-eaters, the commission noted, constitute the overwhelming majority of those officers who accept payoffs; they are not aggressive but will accept gratuities from contractors, tow-truck operators, gamblers, and the like. Although such officers probably constitute a small percentage of the field, any such activity is to be identified and dealt with sternly.

Police corruption can be defined broadly, from major forms of police wrongdoing to the pettiest forms of improper behavior. Another definition is "the misuse of authority by a police officer in a manner designed to produce personal gain for the officer or for others."[13] Police corruption is not limited to monetary gain, however. Gains may be made through the acceptance of services received, status, influence, prestige, or future support for the officer or someone else.[14]

Law Enforcement and Corruption

Code of Silence

To Inform or Not to Inform: The Code of Silence

To continue with the above scenario, Officer Brown witnesses another officer putting an expensive ink pen in his pocket after they found an unlocked office supplies retail business on the graveyard shift. If reported, the misconduct will ruin the officer, but if not reported, the behavior could eventually cause enormous harm. To outsiders, this is not a moral dilemma for Brown at all; the only proper path is for him to report the misconduct. However, arguments exist both for and against Officer Brown's informing on his partner. Reasons for informing include the fact that the harm caused by a scandal would be outweighed by the public knowing that the police department is free of corruption; also, individual

Police corruption: misconduct by police officers that can involve but is not limited to illegal activities for economic gain, gratuities, favors, and so on.

you be the... OFFICER

DILEMMAS OF GIFTS AND GRATUITIES

Although their receipt is prohibited by policy in many if not most police agencies, it is not uncommon for retail businesses, especially restaurants and convenience stores, to offer police officers free or reduced prices for meals and drinks. Proponents argue that it compensates officers for their hard work—a "fringe benefit" of the job. Opponents argue that even the smallest gratuities can lead to greater corruption (the "slippery slope" argument) and create an expectation of some patronage or favor in return. Former New York Police Commissioner Patrick V. Murphy was one of those who "drew the short line," telling his officers that "except for your pay check, there is no such thing as a clean buck."[15] Furthermore, gratuities are not received by other persons in professional positions (e.g., doctors, lawyers, educators) for performing their duties, and thus policing cannot be considered a true profession as long as police accept gratuities.

Assume the county sheriff's department has the following policy concerning the solicitation and acceptance of gifts: "No personnel shall accept any gift, gratuity, loan, fee, or thing of value which might tend to improperly influence their actions in any matter of police business, or which might tend to cast an adverse reflection on the department."

A deputy sheriff has been using a variety of problem-solving approaches to address problems at a shopping mall where juveniles have been loitering, engaging in acts of vandalism, dumping trash, and generally causing traffic problems after hours in the parking lot. Now the mall manager, Mr. Chang, feels morally obligated to express his appreciation to the deputy. Mr. Chang has made arrangements for the deputy and family to receive a 15 percent discount while shopping at any store in the mall. Also, as part owner of a children's toy store in the mall, Mr. Chang offers the deputy a bicycle for his young daughter. Knowing that the agency policy requires that such offers be declined, the deputy is also aware that Mr. Chang will be very hurt or upset if the proffered gifts are refused.

1. Are Mr. Chang's motives honorable?

2. Should the deputy accept the offered discount? The bicycle?

3. Do you believe the department's policy should be modified to accommodate such situations?

Author Video:
Ethical Dilemmas

Mid-Chapter Quiz:
Ethical Essentials

episodes of corruption would be brought to a halt. The officer, moreover, has a sworn duty to uphold the law. Reasons against Officer Brown's informing include the fact that, at least in Brown's mind, the other officer is a member of the "family," as well as that a skilled police officer is a valuable asset whose social value far outweighs the damage done by moderate corruption.[16]

A person who is in charge of investigating police corruption would no doubt take a punitive view, because police are not supposed to steal, and they arrest people for the same kinds of acts every day. Still, the issue—and a common question during oral boards when citizens are being tested for police positions—is whether or not Brown would come forth and inform on his fellow officer.

It is necessary to train police recruits on the need for a corruption-free department. The creation and maintenance of an internal affairs unit and the vigorous prosecution of lawbreaking police officers are also critical to maintaining the integrity of officers.

The Law Enforcement Code of Ethics and Oath of Honor

The Law Enforcement Code of Ethics (LECE) was first adopted by the International Association of Chiefs of Police (IACP) in 1957, and it has been revised several times since then. It is a powerful proclamation, and tens of thousands of police officers across the nation have sworn to uphold this code upon graduating from their academies. Unfortunately, however, the LECE is also quite lengthy, covering rather broadly the following topics as they relate to police officers: primary responsibilities, performance of one's duties, discretion, use of force, confidentiality, integrity, cooperation with other officers and agencies, personal/professional capabilities, and private life.

Recently the IACP adopted a separate, shorter code that would be mutually supportive of the LECE but also easier for officers to remember and call to mind when they come face-to-face with an ethical dilemma. It is the Law Enforcement Oath of Honor, and the IACP is hoping the oath will be implemented in all police agencies and by all individual officers. It may be used at swearing-in ceremonies, graduation ceremonies, promotion ceremonies, beginnings of training sessions, police meetings and conferences, and so forth. It is presented in Figure 4.1.[17]

Accepted and Deviant Lying

In many cases, no clear line separates acceptable from unacceptable behavior in policing. The two are separated by an expansive "gray" area that comes under relative ethics. Some observers have referred to such illegal behavior as a **"slippery slope"**: People tread on solid or legal ground but at some point slip beyond the acceptable into illegal or unacceptable behavior.

Criminal justice employees lie or deceive for different purposes and under varying circumstances. In some cases, their misrepresentations are accepted as an essential part of a criminal investigation, whereas in other cases they are viewed as violations of law. David Carter[18] examined police lying and perjury and found a distinction between accepted lying and deviant lying. **Accepted lying** includes police activities intended to apprehend or entrap suspects. This type of lying is generally considered to be trickery. **Deviant lying**, on the other hand, refers to occasions when officers commit perjury to convict suspects or

"Slippery slope": the idea that a small first step can lead to more serious behaviors, such as the receipt of minor gratuities by police officers believed to eventually cause them to desire or demand receipt of items of greater value.

Accepted lying: police activities intended to apprehend or entrap suspects. This type of lying is generally considered to be trickery.

Deviant lying: occasions when officers commit perjury to convict suspects or are deceptive about some activity that is illegal or unacceptable to the department or public in general.

● ● ● **FIGURE 4.1**

Law Enforcement Code of Ethics and Law Enforcement Oath of Honor

The Law Enforcement Code of Ethics (LECE) was first adopted by the International Association of Chiefs of Police in 1957 and has been revised several times since then. It is a powerful proclamation, and tens of thousands of police officers across the United States have sworn to uphold this code upon graduating their academies.

Because the original version is quite lengthy, the IACP recently adopted a separate, shorter code that would be mutually supportive of the LECE—but also easier for officers to remember and call to mind when they come face-to-face with an ethical dilemma. It is the Law Enforcement Oath of Honor, and the IACP is hoping this oath will be implemented in all police agencies and by all individual officers. It may be used at swearing-in ceremonies, graduation ceremonies, promotion ceremonies, beginnings of training sessions, police meetings and conferences, and so forth.

The Law Enforcement Oath of Honor is as follows:

On my honor,

I will never betray my badge,

my integrity, my character,

or the public trust.

I will always have

the courage to hold myself

and others accountable for our actions.

I will always uphold the constitution,

my community and the agency I serve.

Source: Based on International Association of Chiefs of Police, "What Is the Law Enforcement Oath of Honor," www.theiacp.org/PoliceServices/ExecutiveServices/ProfessionalAssistance/Ethics/WhatistheLawEnforcement OathofHonor/tabid/150/Default.aspx (accessed March 7, 2013).

MEXICO: WHERE POLICE "ETHICS" MATTERS LITTLE

Mexico has long been involved in fighting an epidemic of corruption as drug cartels bribe poorly paid police officers and state officials.

Massive firings of police for corruption is not uncommon: In mid-2010 more than 3,200 Mexican federal police were fired for failing to do their work or being linked to corruption; of those, 465 were charged with crimes, and more than 1,000 officers faced disciplinary proceedings for failing confidence exams.[19] Another 500 officers were dismissed in late 2012 after failing tests specifically targeted at weeding out corrupt officials.[20]

The problem is real and goes beyond involvement in drug crime: Municipal officers have killed their own mayors, state jailers have assisted inmates who escape, federal agents are forced to rise up against corrupt commanders, and officers themselves have been murdered because they work for gangster rivals.[21]

Nor have substantial amounts of U.S. aid and training under the Mérida Initiative (a cooperative agreement between the governments of the United States and Mexico to combat drug trafficking,

Mexican police have long been known to engage in graft and corruption, as drug cartels have bribed and exploited many of the poorly paid officers.

organized crime, and money laundering) worked; Mexico's 32,000 federal police remain understaffed and replete with graft.

Lying and deception have long been used by the police to identify and arrest criminals; this undercover DEA agent is posing as a student as part of a drug investigation.

are deceptive about some activity that is illegal or unacceptable to the department or public in general.

Deception has long been practiced by the police to ensnare violators and suspects. For many years, it was the principal method used by detectives and police officers to secure confessions and convictions. *Accepted lying* is allowed by law, and to a great extent, it is expected by the public. Gary Marx[22] identified three methods police use to trick a suspect: (1) performing the illegal action as part of a larger, socially acceptable, and legal goal; (2) disguising the illegal action so that the suspect does not know it is illegal; and (3) morally weakening the suspect so that the suspect voluntarily becomes involved. The courts have long accepted deception as an investigative tool. For example, in *Illinois v. Perkins*,[23] the U.S. Supreme Court ruled that police undercover agents are not required to administer the *Miranda* warning to incarcerated inmates when investigating crimes. Lying, although acceptable by the courts and the public in certain circumstances, does result in an ethical dilemma. It is a dirty means to accomplish a good end—the police using untruths to gain the truth relative to some event.

In their examination of lying, Thomas Barker and David Carter[24] identified two types of *deviant lying*: lying that serves legitimate purposes and lying that conceals or promotes crimes or illegitimate ends. Lying that serves legitimate goals occurs when officers lie to secure a conviction, obtain a search warrant, or conceal omissions during an investigation. Barker[25] found that police officers believe that almost one fourth of their agency would commit perjury to secure a conviction or to obtain a search warrant. Lying becomes an effective, routine way to sidestep legal impediments. When left unchecked by supervisors, managers, and administrators, lying can become organizationally accepted as an effective means to nullify legal entanglements and remove obstacles that stand in the way of convictions. Examples include using the services of nonexistent confidential informants to secure search warrants, concealing that an interrogator went too far, coercing a confession, or perjuring oneself to gain a conviction.

Mexican Law
Enforcement

Illinois v. Perkins

Lying to conceal or promote criminality is the most distressing form of deception. Examples range from when the police lie to conceal their use of excessive force when arresting a suspect to obscuring the commission of a criminal act.

Accepting Gratuities

Gratuities are commonly accepted by many police officers as a part of their job. Restaurants frequently give officers free or half-price meals and drinks, and other businesses routinely give officers discounts for services or merchandise. While some officers and their departments accept the receipt of such gratuities as a legitimate part of their job, other agencies prohibit such gifts and discounts but seldom attempt to enforce any relevant policy or regulation. Finally, some departments attempt to ensure that officers do not accept free or discounted services or merchandise and routinely enforce policies or regulations against such behavior.[26]

There are two basic arguments *against* police acceptance of gratuities. First is the slippery slope argument, discussed earlier, which proposes that gratuities are the first step in police corruption. This argument holds that once gratuities are received, police officers' ethics are subverted and they are open to additional breaches of their integrity. In addition, officers who accept minor gifts or gratuities are then obligated to provide the donors with some special service or accommodation. Furthermore, some propose that receiving a gratuity is wrong because officers are receiving rewards for services that, as a result of their employment, they are obligated to provide. That is, officers have no legitimate right to accept compensation in the form of a gratuity. If the police ever hope to be accepted as members of a full-fledged profession, then they must address whether the acceptance of gratuities is professional behavior.

Figure 4.2 is an example of a policy developed by a sheriff's office concerning gratuities.

Greed and Temptation

Edward Tully[27] underscored the vast amount of temptation that confronts today's police officers and what police leaders must do toward combating it:

> Socrates, Mother Teresa, or other revered individuals in our society never had to face the constant stream of ethical problems of a busy cop on the beat. One of the roles of [police leaders] is to create an environment that will help the officer resist the temptations that may lead to misconduct, corruption, or abuse of power. The executive cannot construct a work environment that will completely insulate the officers from the forces which lead to misconduct. The ultimate responsibility for an officer's ethical and moral welfare rests squarely with the officer.

FIGURE 4.2

Example of a Sheriff's Office Policy Concerning Gratuities

1. Without the express permission of the Sheriff, members shall not solicit or accept any gift, gratuity, loan, present, or fee where there is any direct or indirect connection between this solicitation or acceptance of such gift and their employment by this office.

2. Members shall not accept, either directly or indirectly, any gift, gratuity, loan, fee, or thing of value, the acceptance of which might tend to improperly influence their actions, or that of any other member, in any matter of police business, or which might tend to cast an adverse reflection on the Sheriff's Office.

3. Any unauthorized gift, gratuity, loan, fee, reward, or other thing falling into any of these categories coming into the possession of any member shall be forwarded to the member's commander, together with a written report explaining the circumstances connected therewith. The commander will decide the disposition of the gift.

Most citizens have no way of comprehending the amount of temptation that confronts today's police officers. They frequently find themselves alone inside retail businesses after normal business hours, clearing the building after finding an open door or window. A swing or graveyard shift officer could easily obtain considerable plunder during these occasions, acquiring everything from clothing to tires for his personal vehicle. At the other end of the spectrum is the potential for huge payoffs from drug traffickers or other big-money offenders who will gladly pay the officer to look away from their crimes. Some officers, like the general public, find this temptation impossible to overcome (see Figure 4.3).

The organization's culture is also important in this regard. The police culture often exalts loyalty over integrity. Given the stress usually generated more from within the organization than from outside and the nature of

FIGURE 4.3

Yielding to Lying and Temptation: Engrained?

Certainly a related aspect of crime that should not be overlooked in discussions of greed, opportunity for crime, and so on, concerns two other long-standing traits of humans: lying and succumbing to temptation. First, regarding lying, experts note that we humans begin lying at around age 4 or 5, when we gain an awareness of the use and power of language. This early lying is not malicious, but rather to find out, or test, what can be manipulated in the child's environment. As this lying continues, rightly or wrongly, it leads to cynicism in the criminal justice system.[1] As an example, as noted police researchers Carl Klockars and Stephen Mastrofski observed, although traffic violators frequently offer what they feel are very good reasons for the officer to overlook their offense, "every police officer knows that, if doing so will allow them to escape punishment, most people are prepared to lie through their teeth."[2] Regarding temptation, researchers have long known that the best way to establish a causal relationship is through setting up an experiment; however, it would be unethical to create new opportunities for burglary or robbery, then sit back to see what happens. But some researchers have undertaken such experiments using more minor transgressions. For example, in the 1920s, researchers gave schoolchildren the opportunity to cheat on tests, to lie about cheating, and to steal coins from puzzles that were used. What they discovered was that only a few children resisted all these temptations. In fact, most behaved dishonestly some of the time, supporting the idea that opportunities cause crime. In another experiment, researchers disseminated stamped and addressed letters in the streets to see whether people would pick them up and mail them. It was found that people were less likely to mail the letters they found that contained money, again showing their response to opportunity. Furthermore, people were more likely to place in the mail letters that were addressed to males rather than females, indicating that a person gives some thought and makes a conscious decision whether to respond to temptation.[3]

Sources: 1. Gail Saltz, "Why people lie—and How To Tell If They Are," *Today Health*, January 31, 2004, http://www.today.com/id/4072816/ns/today-today_health/t/why-people-lie-how-tell-if-they-are/#.Ua-ko-Dn_cs (accessed June 4, 2013); 2. Carl B. Klockars and Stephen D. Mastrofski, "Police Discretion: The Case of Selective Enforcement," in *Thinking about Police: Contemporary Readings*, 2nd ed., ed. Carl B. Klockars and Stephen D. Mastrofski (Boston: McGraw-Hill, 1991), p. 331; 3. Hugh Hartshorne and Mark A. May, *Studies in Deceit* (New York: Macmillan, 1928); David P. Farrington and Barry J. Knight, "Stealing from a 'lost' Letter," *Criminal Justice and Behavior* 7 (1980), pp. 423–436.

life-and-death decisions they must make daily, even the best officers who simply want to catch criminals may become frustrated and vulnerable to bending the rules for what they view as the greater good of society.

ETHICS IN THE COURTS

Although the public tends to think of criminal justice ethics primarily in terms of the police, certainly other such criminal justice professionals—including the court work group—have expectations in this regard as well. The ethical standards and expectations—and some examples of failings—of those individuals are discussed next.

The Evolution of Standards of Conduct

The first call during the 20th century for formalized standards of conduct in the legal profession came in 1906, with Roscoe Pound's speech "The Causes of Popular Dissatisfaction with the Administration of Justice."[28] However, the first canons of judicial ethics probably grew out of a professional baseball scandal in 1919, in which the World Series was "thrown" to the Chicago White Sox by the Cincinnati Reds. Baseball officials turned to the judiciary for leadership and hired U.S. District Court Judge Kenesaw Mountain Landis as baseball commissioner—a position for which Landis was paid $42,500, compared to his $7,500 earnings per year as a judge. This affair prompted the 1921 American Bar Association (ABA) convention to pass a resolution of censure against the judge and appoint a committee to propose standards of judicial ethics.[29]

In 1924, the ABA approved the Canons of Judicial Ethics under the leadership of Chief Justice William Howard Taft, and in 1972, the ABA approved a new **Model Code of Judicial Conduct**; in 1990, the same body adopted a revised model code. Nearly all states and the District of Columbia have promulgated standards based on the code. In 1974, the United States Judicial Conference adopted a Code of Conduct for United States Judges, and Congress over the years enacted legislation regulating judicial conduct, including the Ethics Reform Act of 1989.

The Judge

Judges will be discussed generally in Chapter 10; however, here the focus is on their ethical responsibilities. Ideally, our judges are flawless, not allowing emotion or personal biases to creep into their work, treating all cases and individual litigants with an even hand, and employing "justice tempered with mercy." The perfect judge has been described as follows:

> The good judge takes equal pains with every case no matter how humble; he knows that important cases and unimportant cases do not exist, for injustice is not one of those poisons which . . . when taken in small doses may produce a salutary effect. Injustice is a dangerous poison even in doses of homeopathic proportions.[30]

Not all judges, of course, can attain this lofty status. Judges can become embroiled in improper conduct or overstep their bounds in many ways: abuse of judicial power (against attorneys or litigants); inappropriate sanctions and dispositions (including showing favoritism or bias); not meeting the standards of impartiality and competence (discourteous behavior, gender bias and harassment, incompetence); conflict of interest (bias; conflicting financial interests or business, social, or family relationships); and personal conduct (criminal or sexual misconduct, prejudice, statements of opinion).[31]

Model Code of Judicial Conduct: adopted by the House of Delegates of the American Bar Association in 1990, it provides a set of ethical principles and guidelines for judges.

Following are examples of some true-to-life ethical dilemmas involving the courts[32]:

1. A judge convinces jailers to release his son on a nonbondable offense.

2. A judge is indicted on charges that he used his office for a racketeering enterprise.

3. Two judges attend the governor's $500-per-person inaugural ball.

4. A judge is accused of acting with bias in giving a convicted murderer a less severe sentence because the victims were homosexual.

5. A judge whose car bears the bumper sticker "I am a pro-life Democrat" acquits six pro-life demonstrators of trespassing at an abortion clinic on the grounds of necessity to protect human life.

Such incidents certainly do little to bolster public confidence in the justice system. People expect more from judges, who are "the most highly visible symbol of justice."[33]

Unfortunately, codes of ethical conduct have not served to eradicate these problems or allay concerns about judges' behavior. Indeed, one judge who teaches judicial ethics at the National Judicial College in Reno stated that most judges attending the college admit never having read the Model Code of Judicial Conduct before seeking judicial office.[34] According to the American Judicature Society, during one year 25 judges were suspended from office, and more than 80 judges resigned or retired either before or after formal

FOCUS ON   JUDGES' ETHICAL MISCONDUCT

A former county juvenile court judge in Pennsylvania was sentenced to prison for 28 years after being convicted on federal racketeering charges—specifically, sentencing juveniles to a detention facility for minor crimes while accepting more than $1 million in kickbacks from the private company that built and maintained the facility.[35]

One fourth of this judge's juvenile defendants were sentenced to detention centers, as he routinely ignored requests for leniency made by prosecutors and probation officers. Some of the nearly 5,000 sentenced juveniles were as young as 10. One girl, who described the experience as a "surreal nightmare," was sentenced to three months of "hard time" for posting spoofs about an assistant school principal on the Internet. Some juveniles even committed suicide following their commitment.[36] The judge was said to have maintained a culture of intimidation in which no one was willing to speak up about the sentences he was handing down. Although he pleaded guilty to the charges, he denied sentencing juveniles who did not deserve it or receiving remuneration from the detention centers.[37]

The matter also raised concerns about whether juveniles should be required to have counsel

Former Pennsylvania Judge Mark Ciavarella, Jr., convicted of racketeering, was sentenced to a federal prison for 28 years.

either before or during their appearances in court: It was revealed that more than 500 juveniles had appeared before the judge without representation. Although juveniles have long had a right to counsel,[38] Pennsylvania, like at least 20 other states, allows children to waive counsel, and about half of these Pennsylvania youths had chosen to do so.[39]

charges were filed against them; 120 judges also received private censure, admonition, or reprimand.[40]

The key to judicial ethics is to identify the troublesome issues and to create an "ethical alarm system" that responds.[41] Perhaps the most important tenet in the code and the one that is most difficult to apply is that judges should avoid the *appearance* of impropriety—in other words, it is not enough that judges *do* what is just; they must also avoid conduct that would create in the public's mind a perception that their ability to carry out responsibilities with integrity, impartiality, and competence is impaired.

By adhering to ethical principles, judges can maintain their independence and follow the ancient charge Moses gave to his judges:

> Hear the causes between your brethren, and judge righteously. Ye shall not respect persons in judgment; but ye shall hear the small as well as the great; ye shall not be afraid of the face of man; for the judgment is God's; and for the cause that is too hard for you, bring it unto me, and I will hear it.[42]

Ethical requirements for the federal judiciary and other federal employees are discussed below.

Prosecutors

Given their power and authority to decide which cases are to be prosecuted, prosecuting attorneys must closely guard their ethical behavior. It was decided over 75 years ago (in *Berger v. United States*, 1935) that the primary duty of a prosecutor is "not that he shall win a case, but that justice shall be done."[43]

Miller v. Pate

Instances of prosecutorial misconduct were reported as early as 1897[44] and are still reported today. One of the leading examples of unethical conduct by a prosecutor is *Miller v. Pate*,[45] in which the prosecutor concealed from the jury in a murder trial the fact that a pair of undershorts with red stains contained not blood but red paint.

According to Elliot Cohen,[46] misconduct works: Oral advocacy is important in the courtroom and can have a powerful effect. Another significant reason for such conduct is the harmless error doctrine, in which an appellate court can affirm a conviction despite the presence of serious misconduct during the trial. Only when appellate courts take a stricter, more consistent approach to this problem will it end.[47]

Defense Attorneys

Defense attorneys, too, must be legally and morally bound to ethical principles as agents of the courts. Cohen[48] suggested the following moral principles for defense attorneys:

1. Treat others as ends in themselves and not as mere means to winning cases.

2. Treat clients and other professional relations in a similar fashion.

3. Do not deliberately engage in behavior apt to deceive the court as to truth.

4. Be willing, if necessary, to make reasonable personal sacrifices of time, money, and popularity for what you believe to be a morally good cause.

5. Do not give money to, or accept money from, clients for wrongful purposes or in wrongful amounts.

6. Avoid harming others in the course of representing your client.

7. Be loyal to your client and do not betray his or her confidence.

Other Court Employees

Other court employees have ethical responsibilities as well. For example, an appellate court judge's secretary is asked by a good friend who is a lawyer whether the judge will be writing the opinion in a certain case. The lawyer may be wishing to attempt to influence the judge through his secretary, renegotiate with an opposing party, or engage in some other improper activity designed to alter the case outcome.[49] Bailiffs, court administrators, court reporters, courtroom clerks, and law clerks all fit into this category. It would be improper, say, for a bailiff who is accompanying jurors back from a break in a criminal trial to mention that the judge "sure seems annoyed at the defense attorney" or for a law clerk to tell an attorney friend that the judge she works for prefers reading short bench memos.[50]

ETHICAL CONDUCT OF FEDERAL EMPLOYEES

Whistleblowing

The laws governing the ethical conduct of federal employees are contained in a variety of statutes, the two major sources of which are Title 18 of the United States Code and the Ethics in Government Act of 1978 (enacted following the Watergate scandals of the early 1970s to promote public confidence in government). The latter act has been amended a number of times, with its most significant revision occurring in the Ethics Reform Act of 1989 (Public Law 101-194). A brief general description of that law, as well as expectations of the federal judiciary, is provided next.

The Ethics Reform Act

The Ethics Reform Act addresses a number of areas of ethical concern, including the receipt of gifts, financial conflicts involving employees' position, personal conflicts that may affect their impartiality, misuse of position (for private gain), and outside activities or employment that conflicts with their federal duties (such as an expert witness, payment for speaking, writing, and teaching).

In 1989 the **Whistleblower Protection Act**, known as the WPA (Public Law 101-12), strengthened the protections provided in the Ethics Reform Act. These whistleblower protection laws prohibit reprisal against federal employees who reasonably believe that their disclosures show "a violation of law, rule, or regulation, gross mismanagement, a gross waste of funds, an abuse of authority, or a specific and substantial danger to public health and safety."

Whistleblower Protection Act: a federal law prohibiting reprisal against employees who reveal information concerning a violation of law, rule or regulation, gross mismanagement or waste of funds, an abuse of authority, and so on.

FOCUS ON   PROTECTING WHISTLEBLOWERS

An example of protecting whistleblowers under federal law is the case of John Kopchinski, in what would become the largest health fraud settlement in U.S. history. Kopchinski, a sales representative for pharmaceutical giant Pfizer, Inc., discovered widespread deceptive advertising in connection with Bextra, an anti-inflammatory painkiller; he was fired by the company in 2003 (by then he was already talking with lawyers about evidence he had accumulated).

Pfizer eventually pleaded guilty to numerous criminal and civil charges and paid the U.S. government a total of $2.3 billion. Kopchinski and five other relators split another $102 billion in civil penalties.

Source: Scott Hensley, "Pfizer Whistleblower Tells His Bextra Story," *Shots: Health News from NPR,* September 3, 2009, http://www.npr.org/blogs/health/2009/09/pfizer_whistleblower_tells_his.html (accessed March 26, 2013); also see Whistleblower Info, "What Is a Federal Whistleblower?" http://www.whistleblowingprotection.org/?q=node/40 (accessed March 26, 2013).

The Federal Judiciary

Federal judges have the authority to resolve significant public and private disputes. Occasionally, however, a matter assigned to them may involve them or their families personally, or affect individuals or organizations with which they have associations outside of their official duties. In these situations, if their impartiality might be compromised, they must disqualify (or recuse) themselves from the proceeding.

Disqualification is required under Canon 3C(1) of the Code of Conduct for United States Judges of the ABA if the judge

- has personal knowledge of disputed facts;

- was employed in a law firm that handled the same matter while he or she was there;

- has a close relative who is a party or attorney;

- personally owns, or has an immediate family member who owns, a financial interest in a party; or

- as a government official, served as a counsel in the case.

The next "Focus On" box shows the canons of ethical conduct for federal judges as set forth by the Administrative Office of the United States Courts.

ETHICS IN CORRECTIONS

Corrections personnel confront many of the same ethical dilemmas as police personnel. Thus, prison and jail administrators, like their counterparts in the police realm, would do well to understand their occupational subculture and its effect on ethical decision making.

 Officer Deviance

The strength of the corrections subculture correlates with the security level of a correctional facility and is strongest in maximum-security institutions. Powerful forces within the correctional system have a stronger influence over the behavior of correctional officers than the administrators of the institution, legislative decrees, or agency policies.[51] Indeed, it has been known

FOCUS ON   CANONS OF ETHICS FOR THE FEDERAL JUDICIARY

Following are the canons of the Code of Conduct for United States Judges:

CANON 1: A judge should uphold the integrity and independence of the judiciary.

CANON 2: A judge should avoid impropriety and the appearance of impropriety in all activities.

CANON 3: A judge should perform the duties of the office impartially and diligently.

CANON 4: A judge may engage in extrajudicial activities that are consistent with the obligations of judicial office.

CANON 5: A judge should refrain from political activity.

Implicit in these canons are restrictions on judges' soliciting or accepting gifts, outside employment, and payment for appearances, speeches, or written articles.

Source: Administrative Office of the United States Courts, *Code of Conduct for United States Judges*, http://www.uscourts.gov/RulesAndPolicies/CodesOfConduct/CodeConductUnitedStatesJudges.aspx (accessed March 8, 2013); further guidance appears in Federal Judicial Center, *Guide to Judiciary Policies and Procedures: Volume 2. Maintaining the Public Trust: Ethics for Federal Judicial Law Clerks* (Washington, D.C.: Author, 2002).

for several decades that the exposure to external danger in the workplace creates a remarkable increase in group solidarity.[52]

Some of the job-related stressors for corrections officers are similar to those the police face: the ever-present potential for physical danger, hostility directed at officers by inmates and even by the public, unreasonable role demands, a tedious and unrewarding work environment, and dependence on one another to effectively and safely work in their environment.[53] For these reasons, several norms of corrections work have been identified: always go to the aid of an officer in distress; do not "rat"; never make another officer look bad in front of inmates; always support an officer in a dispute with an inmate; always support officer sanctions against inmates; and do not wear a "white hat" (participate in behavior that suggests sympathy or identification with inmates).[54]

Officer Code

Security issues and the way in which individual correctional officers have to rely on each other for their safety make loyalty to one another a key norm. The proscription against ratting out a colleague is strong. In one documented instance, two officers in the Corcoran, California, state prison blew the whistle on what they considered to be unethical conduct by their colleagues: Officers were alleged to have staged a gladiator-style fight among inmates from different groups in a small exercise yard. The two officers claimed that their colleagues would even place bets on the outcome of the fights, and when the fights got out of hand, the officers would fire shots at the inmates. Since the institution had opened in 1988, eight inmates had been shot dead by officers, and numerous others had been wounded. The two officers who reported these activities were labeled by colleagues as "rats" and "no-goods" and had their lives threatened; even though they were transferred to other institutions, the labels traveled with them. Four correctional officers were indicted for their alleged involvement in these activities, but all were acquitted in a state prosecution in 2001.[55]

In another case, a female corrections officer at a medium-security institution reported some of her colleagues for sleeping on the night shift. She had first approached them and expressed concern for her safety when they were asleep and told them that if they did not refrain from sleeping, she would have to report them to the superintendent. They continued sleeping, and she reported them. The consequences were severe: Graffiti was written about her on the walls, she received harassing phone calls and letters, her car was vandalized, and some bricks were thrown through the windows of her home.[56] Obviously, she deserved better, both in terms of protection during these acts, and with the investigation and prosecution of the parties involved.

It would be unfair to suggest that the kind of behavior depicted here reflects the behavior of corrections officers in all places and at all times. The case studies do demonstrate, however, the power and loyalty of the group, and correctional administrators must be cognizant of that power. It is also noteworthy that the corrections subculture, like its police counterpart, provides several positive qualities, particularly in crisis situations, including mutual support and protection, which is essential to the emotional and psychological health of officers involved; there is always the "family" to support you.

Like police officers, correctional officers in jails and prisons at times must exercise force—which raises ethical considerations and concerns for them as well.

you be the... OFFICER

ETHICAL DILEMMA IN CORRECTIONS

Correctional Officer Ben Jones has worked for one year in a medium-security housing unit in a state prison and has gotten on friendly terms with an inmate, Stevens. Known to have been violent, manipulative, and associating with a similarly rough crowd while on the outside, now Stevens appears to be a model inmate; in fact, Officer Jones relies heavily on Stevens to keep him informed of the goings-on in the unit as well as to maintain its overall cleanliness and general appearance. Over time, the two address each other on a first-name basis and increasingly discuss personal matters; Jones occasionally allows Stevens to get by with minor infractions of prison rules (e.g., being in an unauthorized area or entering another inmate's cell). Today Stevens mentions that he is having problems with his fiancé—specifically, that he has received a "Dear John" letter from her, stating that she is dating other men and is "moving on." Upon arriving home from work that evening, Jones finds a case of wine on his porch. There is no card left on the case of wine, but at work the next morning Stevens winks at Jones and asks if he "ventured into the vineyard last night."

1. Should Officer Jones report the incident?

2. Has Jones's behavior thus far violated any standards of ethics for correctional officers? If so, what form of punishment (if any) would be appropriate?

3. What should be the relationship between Jones and Stevens in the future?

4. What could Jones have done differently, if anything?

ETHICS TESTS FOR THE CRIMINAL JUSTICE STUDENT

Following are some tests to help guide you, the criminal justice student, to decide what is and is not ethical behavior[57]:

- *Test of common sense.* Does the act make sense, or would someone look askance at it?

- *Test of publicity.* Would you be willing to see what you did highlighted on the front page of the local newspaper?

- *Test of one's best self.* Will the act fit the concept of oneself at one's best?

- *Test of one's most admired personality.* What would one's parents or minister do in this situation?

- *Test of hurting someone else.* Will it cause pain for someone?

- *Test of foresight.* What is the long-term likely result?

Other questions that the officer might ask are "Is it worth my job and career?" and "Is my decision legal?"

Another tool is that of "the bell, the book, and the candle": Do bells or warning buzzers go off as I consider my choice of actions? Does it violate any laws or codes in the statute or ordinance books? Will my decision withstand the light of day or spotlight of publicity (the candle)?[58]

In sum, all we can do is seek to make the best decisions we can and be a good person and a good justice system employee, one who is consistent and fair. We need to apply the law, the policy, the guidelines, or whatever it is we dispense in our occupation without bias or fear and to the best of our ability, being mindful along the way that others around us may have lost

"The bell, the book, and the candle" test can be used as a guide against making unethical decisions.

Chapter Quiz: Ethical Essentials

their moral compass and attempt to drag us down with them. To paraphrase Franklin Delano Roosevelt, "Be the best you can, wherever you are, with what you have."

In closing, it might be good to mention that ethics is important to all criminal justice students and practitioners, not only because of the moral/ethical issues and dilemmas they confront each day, but also because they have a lot of discretion with the people with whom they are involved—such as the discretion to arrest or not arrest, to charge or not charge, to punish or not punish, and even to shoot or not shoot.

IN A NUTSHELL

- The term *ethics* is rooted in the ancient Greek idea of *character* and involves doing what is right or correct in a professional capacity. Deontological ethics examines one's duty to act. Immanuel Kant expanded the ethics of duty by including the idea of "good will." People's actions must be guided by good intent.

- There are absolute ethics and relative ethics. Absolute ethics has only two sides—something is either good or bad, black or white. Relative ethics is more complicated and can have a multitude of sides with varying shades of gray. What is considered ethical behavior by one person may be deemed highly unethical by someone else.

- The "principle of double effect"—also known as noble cause—holds that when one commits an act to achieve a good end

and an inevitable but intended effect is negative, then the act might be justified. The community cannot tolerate completely unethical behavior but may seemingly tolerate extralegal behavior if there is a greater public good, such as with gang members.

- The Knapp Commission identified two primary types of corrupt police officers: the "meat-eaters" and the "grass-eaters." The branch of the department and the type of assignment affect opportunities for corruption. Stoddard, who coined the term *blue-coat crime*, described eight different forms of deviant practices among police. Officers' code of silence can exacerbate the efforts of police leadership to uncover police corruption.

- The Law Enforcement Code of Ethics (LECE) was first adopted in 1957; recently a separate, shorter code was adopted, easier for officers to remember when they come face-to-face with an ethical dilemma; it is the Law Enforcement Oath of Honor.

- *Accepted lying* includes police activities intended to apprehend or entrap suspects. This type of lying is generally considered to be trickery. *Deviant lying* refers to occasions when officers commit perjury to convict suspects or are deceptive about some activity that is illegal or unacceptable to the department or public in general.

- There are two basic arguments *against* police acceptance of gratuities. First is the slippery slope argument, which proposes that gratuities are the first step in police corruption. In addition, officers who accept minor gifts or gratuities are then obligated to provide the donors with some special service or accommodation.

- The first call for formalized standards of conduct in the legal profession came in 1906, with Roscoe Pound's speech "The Causes of Popular Dissatisfaction with the Administration of Justice." In 1924, the ABA approved the Canons of Judicial Ethics, and in 1972 the ABA approved a new Model Code of Judicial Conduct; in 1990, the same body adopted a revised model code. Nearly all states and the District of Columbia have promulgated standards based on the code.

- In 1974, the United States Judicial Conference adopted a Code of Conduct for United States Judges, and Congress over the years has enacted legislation regulating judicial conduct, including the Ethics Reform Act of 1989.

- Judges can engage in abuse of judicial power (against attorneys or litigants); present inappropriate sanctions and dispositions (including showing favoritism or bias); not meet the standards of impartiality and competence; engage in conflict of interest (bias; conflicting financial interests or business, social, or family relationships); and be unethical in their personal conduct (criminal or sexual misconduct, prejudice).

- Prosecutors and defense attorneys, too, must be legally and morally bound to ethical principles as agents of the courts.

- Federal employees are governed by the Ethics Reform Act of 1989 (Public Law 101-194). The Ethics Reform Act addresses a number of areas of ethical concern, including the receipt of gifts, financial conflicts involving an employee's position, personal conflicts that may affect employees' impartiality, misuse of position (for private gain), and outside activities or employment that conflicts with their federal duties (such as an expert witness, payment for speaking, writing, and teaching).

- Corrections personnel confront many of the same ethical dilemmas as police personnel.

- The strength of the corrections subculture correlates with the security level of a correctional facility and is strongest in maximum-security institutions.

KEY
TERMS
···· & ····
CONCEPTS

$SAGE edge™

REVIEW QUESTIONS

1. How would you define *ethics*?

2. What are examples of relative and absolute ethics?

3. What specific examples of legitimate ethical dilemmas arise with police, courts, and corrections practitioners in the course of their work?

4. How would you describe the codes and canons of ethics that exist in police departments, courts, and corrections? What elements do they have in common?

5. How does the principle of double effect—"ends justify means" type of thinking—pose problems for criminal justice and society?

6. Why was the Law Enforcement Oath of Honor developed recently, and how does it differ from the Code of Ethics?

7. What constitutes police corruption? What are its types, and what are the most difficult ethical dilemmas presented in the case studies? Consider the issues presented in each.

8. Do you believe criminal justice employees should be allowed to accept minor gratuities? Explain your reasoning.

9. In what ways can judges, defense attorneys, and prosecutors engage in unethical behaviors?

10. What forms of behavior by corrections officers in prisons or jails may be unethical?

11. What are some components of the ethics "test" for criminal justice students?

LEARN BY DOING

Following are several brief, real-life case studies involving criminal justice employees. Having read this chapter's materials, determine for each the ethical dilemmas involved, and explain what you believe is the appropriate outcome.

1. You are sitting next to a police officer in a restaurant. Upon the officer's attempt to pay for the meal, the waiter says, "Your money is no good here. An officer just visited my son's school and made quite an impression. Plus, I feel safer having cops around." Again the officer offers to pay, but the waiter refuses to accept payment. The police department has a policy prohibiting the acceptance of free meals or gifts.

2. A municipal court judge borrows money from court employees, publicly endorses and campaigns for a candidate for judicial office, conducts personal business from chambers (displaying and selling antiques), directs other court employees to perform personal errands for him during court hours, suggests that persons appearing before him contribute to certain charities in lieu of paying fines, and uses court

employees to perform translating services at his mother's nursery business.

3. A judge often makes inappropriate sidebar comments and uses sexist remarks or jokes in court. For example, a woman was assaulted by her husband who beat her with a telephone; from the bench the judge said, "What's wrong with that? You've got to keep her in line once in a while." He begins to address female lawyers in a demeaning manner, using such terms as *sweetie*, *little lady lawyer*, and *pretty eyes*.[59]

4. (a) An associate warden and "rising star" in the local prison system has just been stopped and arrested for driving while intoxicated in his personal vehicle and while off-duty. There are no damages or injuries involved, he is very remorseful, and he has just been released from jail. His wife calls you, the warden, pleading for you to allow him to keep his job. (b) One week later, this same associate warden stops at a local convenience store after work; as he leaves the store, a clerk stops him and summons the police—the individual has just been caught shoplifting a package of cigarettes. You have just been informed of this latest arrest.

PART II

THE POLICE

This part consists of four chapters. **Chapter 5** discusses the organization and operation of law enforcement agencies at the local, state, and federal levels; included are discussions of their English and colonial roots, the three eras of policing in the United States, and local (municipal police and sheriff's offices), state, and selected federal law enforcement agencies. Also included are brief considerations of Interpol and functions of the private police.

Chapter 6 focuses on the kinds of work that police do; after looking at their recruitment and training, considered next are the patrol and investigative functions, to include the dangers of the job, the traffic function, and the use of police discretion, as well as the work of criminal investigators.

Chapter 7 broadly examines several policing issues that exist today: use of force, corruption, civil liability, stress, some police technologies, and women and minorities in the field.

Chapter 8 examines the constitutional rights of the accused as well as limitations placed on the police under the Fourth, Fifth, and Sixth Amendments; the focus is on arrest, search and seizure, the right to remain silent, and the right to counsel.

POLICE ORGANIZATION:
Structure and Functions

LEARNING OBJECTIVES

As a result of reading this chapter, the student will be able to:

1 Describe the four major police-related offices and their functions that came to America from early England

2 Discuss the three eras of policing

3 Review events and problems that led to the current community era

4 Diagram and explain the elements of the basic organizational structure of a local police agency

5 Distinguish between structure and functions of municipal police departments and county sheriff's offices

6 Explain the primary duties and titles of state-level law enforcement organizations

7 Describe the functions of the major federal law enforcement organizations that compose the Department of Homeland Security, the Department of Justice, and other selected federal agencies

8 Relate the purposes, functions, and contributions of Interpol

9 Explain how and why private policing was developed, and the contemporary purposes and issues of the private police

CHAPTER

05

We are born in organizations, educated by organizations, and most of us spend much of our lives working for organizations. We spend much of our leisure time paying, playing, and praying in organizations. Most of us will die in an organization, and when the time comes for burial, the largest organization of all—the state—must grant official permission.

—Amitai Etzioni

INTRODUCTION

Author Introduction:
Chapter 5

How did the police come into being? How are they "designed" to do their job? These are legitimate questions.

The primary intention of this chapter is to accomplish two aims—looking at the early development of policing, while also informing the reader about the role and functions of contemporary federal, state, and local agencies, as well as the private police.

The chapter begins with a brief history of the evolution of four primary criminal justice officers—sheriff, constable, coroner, and justice of the peace—from their roots in early England to their coming to America. Following is an overview of the three eras of policing in the United States, and the events and shortcomings that were a part of the first two eras, thus leading to today's *community* era. Discussed next are the structures and functions of the major **organizations** that compose the Department of Homeland Security, and then discussions are held of the major agencies within the Department of Justice. Then the primary duties of state-level law enforcement organizations are covered. Following is a review of local law enforcement—municipal police and county sheriff's agencies.

Finally, a brief examination is included of private policing, including how and why it was developed and some of its contemporary purposes and issues.

Organization: an entity of two or more people who cooperate to achieve an objective(s).

ASSESS YOUR AWARENESS:

Test your knowledge of police organization and functions by first reading and responding to the following seven true-false items; check your answers after reading this chapter's materials.

1. The four primary criminal justice officials of early England—the sheriff, constable, coroner, and justice of the peace—remain in existence today.

2. The creation of the Department of Homeland Security in 2002 (and the integration of federal departments and agencies in 2003) was the most significant transformation of the U.S. government in over a half-century.

3. Full-time professional policing, as it is generally known today, began in the late 1800s in New York City.

4. The patrol function may be said to represent the backbone of policing.

5. State law enforcement agencies typically perform one function: patrolling state highways.

6. Interpol is the oldest, best known, and probably only truly international crime-fighting organization.

7. The U.S. Coast Guard and Transportation Security Administration do not possess law enforcement authority.

Answers can be found on page 401.

The chapter concludes with a summary, key terms and concepts, review questions, and several scenarios and activities that provide opportunities for you to "learn by doing."

ENGLISH AND COLONIAL ROOTS: AN OVERVIEW

All four of the primary criminal justice officials of early England—the sheriff, constable, coroner, and justice of the peace—either still exist or existed until recently in the United States. Accordingly, it is important to grasp a basic understanding of these offices, including their early functions in England and, later, in America. Following is a brief discussion of each.

Policing History

Sheriff

The word **sheriff** is derived from *shire-reeve—shire* meaning "county" and *reeve* meaning "agent of the king." The shire-reeve appeared in England before the Norman Conquest of 1066. His job was to maintain law and order in the tithings (groupings of ten households). At the present time in England, a sheriff's only duties are to act as officer of the court, summon juries, and enforce civil judgments.[1]

The first sheriffs in America appeared in the early colonial period. Today, the American sheriff remains the basic source of rural crime control.

Constable

Like the sheriff, the **constable** can be traced back to Anglo-Saxon times. The office began during the reign of Edward I, when every parish or township had a constable. As the county militia turned more and more to matters of defense, only the constable pursued felons. Hence the ancient custom of citizens raising a loud "hue and cry" and joining in pursuit of criminals lapsed into disuse. The constable had a variety of duties, including collecting taxes, supervising highways, and serving as magistrate. The office soon became subject to election and was conferred upon local men of prominence. However, the creation of the office of justice of the peace around 1200 quickly changed this trend forever; soon the constable was limited to making arrests only with warrants issued by a justice of the peace. As a result, the office, deprived of social and civic prestige, was no longer attractive. It carried no salary, and the duties were often dangerous.[2] In the American colonies, the position fell into disfavor largely because most constables were untrained and believed to be wholly inadequate as officials of the law.[3]

Coroner

The office of **coroner** has been used to fulfill many different roles throughout its history and has steadily changed over the centuries since it began functioning by the end of the 12th century. From the beginning, the coroner was elected; his duties included oversight of the interests of the Crown, including criminal matters. In felony cases, the coroner could conduct a preliminary hearing, and the sheriff often came to the coroner's court to preside over the coroner's jury. This "coroner's inquest" determined the cause of death and the party responsible for it. Initially, coroners were given no compensation, yet they were elected for life. Soon, however, they were given the right to charge fees for their work.[4] The office was slow in gaining recognition in America, as many of the coroners' duties were already being performed by the sheriffs and justices of the peace. By 1933, the coroner was recognized as a separate office in two-thirds of the states. By then, however, the office had been stripped of many of its original functions. Today, in many states, the

Sheriff: the chief law enforcement officer of a county, normally elected and frequently operating the jail as well as law enforcement functions.

Constable: in England, favored noblemen who were forerunners of modern-day U.S. criminal justice functionaries; largely disappearing in the United States by the 1970s.

Coroner: an early English court officer; today one (usually a physician) in the United States whose duty it is to determine cause of death.

Changes in Law Enforcement

coroner legally serves as sheriff when the elected sheriff is disabled or disqualified. However, since the early part of this century, the coroner has basically performed a single function: determining the causes of all deaths by violence or under suspicious circumstances.[5]

Justice of the Peace

The **justice of the peace (JP)** can be traced back as far as 1195 in England. Early JPs were wealthy landholders. The duties of JPs eventually included the granting of bail to felons, which led to corruption and criticism as the justices bailed out people who clearly should not have been released into the community. By the 16th century, the office came under criticism again because of the caliber of the people holding it (wealthy landowners who bought their way into office).[6] By the early 20th century, England had abolished the property-holding requirement, and many of the medieval functions of the JP's office were removed. Thereafter, the office possessed strictly extensive criminal jurisdiction but no civil jurisdiction whatsoever. This contrasts with the American system, which gives JPs limited jurisdiction in both criminal and civil cases. By 1930, the office had constitutional status in all of the states. JPs have long been allowed to collect fees for their services. As in England, it is typically not necessary to hold a law degree or to have pursued legal studies in order to be a JP in the United States.[7]

Police Reform in England and the United States, 1829–1860

In England, after the end of the Napoleonic Wars in 1815, workers protested against new machines, food riots, and an ongoing increase in crime. The British army, traditionally used to disperse rioters, was becoming less effective as people began resisting its commands. In 1822, England's ruling party, the Tories, moved to consider new alternatives. The prime minister appointed Sir Robert Peel to establish a police force to combat the problems. Peel, a wealthy member of Parliament,[8] finally succeeded in 1829 when Parliament passed the Metropolitan Police Act. The London police are nicknamed "bobbies" after Sir Robert Peel.[9] Peel's remark that "the police are the public, and the public are the police" emphasized his belief that the police are first and foremost members of the larger society.[10]

Sir Robert Peel's "bobbies" were established in London in 1829.

POLICING COMES TO THE UNITED STATES

The following section provides an overview of the three eras of U.S. policing—political, reform, and community—that were shaped and defined by the varying goals and philosophies of each over time.

The Political Era, 1840s–1930s

In 1844, the New York State legislature passed a law establishing a full-time preventive police force for New York City. However, this new body came into being in a very different form than in Europe. The American version, as begun in New York City, was deliberately placed under the control of the city government and city politicians. The American plan required that each ward in the

Justice of the peace (JP): a minor justice official who oversees lesser criminal trials; one of the early English judicial functionaries.

city be a separate patrol district, unlike the European model, which divided the districts along the lines of criminal activity. The process for selecting officers was also different. The mayor chose the recruits from a list of names submitted by the aldermen and tax assessors of each ward; the mayor then submitted his choices to the city council for approval. This system resulted in most of the power over the police going to the ward aldermen, who were seldom concerned about selecting the best people for the job. Instead, the system allowed and even encouraged political patronage and rewards for friends.[11]

This was the **political era** of policing, from the 1840s to the 1930s. Politics were played to such an extent that even nonranking patrol officers used political backers to obtain promotions, desired assignments, and transfers.

Police corruption also surfaced at this time. Corrupt officers wanted beats close to the gamblers, saloonkeepers, madams, and pimps—people who could not operate if the officers were "untouchable" or "100 percent coppers."[12] Political pull for corrupt officers could work for or against them; the officer who incurred the wrath of his superiors could be transferred to the outposts, where he would have no chance for financial advancement.

Still, it did not take long for other cities to adopt the general model of the New York City police force. New Orleans and Cincinnati adopted plans for a new police force in 1852, Boston and Philadelphia followed in 1854, Chicago in 1855, and Baltimore and Newark in 1857.[13] By 1880, virtually every major American city had a police force based on Peel's model.

The Reform Era, 1930s–1980s

During the early 20th century, reformers sought to reject political involvement by the police, and civil service systems were created to eliminate patronage and ward influences in hiring and firing police officers. In some cities, officers were not permitted to live in the same beat they patrolled in order to isolate them as completely as possible from political influences.[14] However, policing also became a matter viewed as best left to the discretion of police executives. Any noncrime activities police were required to do were considered "social work." The **reform era** (also termed the professional era) of policing would soon be in full bloom.

The crime-fighter image gained popularity under the reform model of policing, when officers were to remain in their "rolling fortresses," going from one call to the next with all due haste. Much of police work was driven by *numbers*—numbers of arrests, calls for service, response time to calls for service, number of tickets written and miles driven by a patrol officer during a duty shift, and so on. For many people, like Los Angeles Chief of Police William Parker, the police were the "thin blue line," protecting society from barbarism. He viewed urban society as a jungle, needing the restraining hand of the police; the police had to enforce the law without fear or favor. Parker opposed any restrictions on police methods. The law, he believed, should give the police wide latitude to use wiretaps and to conduct search and seizure.[15]

Political era (of policing): from the 1840s to the 1930s, the period of time when police were tied closely to politics and politicians, dependent on them for being hired, promoted, and assignments—all of which raised the potential for corruption.

Reform era (police): also the professional era, from the 1930s to 1980s, when police sought to extricate themselves from the shackles of politicians, and leading to the crime-fighter era—with greater emphases being placed on *numbers* of arrests, citations, response times, and so on.

Community era: beginning in about 1980, a time when the police retrained to work with the community to solve problems by looking at their underlying causes and developing tailored responses to them.

Los Angeles Chief of Police William Parker believed the police were the "thin blue line," protecting society from barbarism.

Community Policing

Community Policing

The Community Era, 1980s–Present

Today policing is in the **community era**, practicing community policing and problem solving. This strategy was born because of the problems that overwhelmed the reform era, which actually began occurring in the 1960s. During the reform era, officers had little long-term effect in dealing with crime and disorder; they were neither trained nor encouraged to consider the underlying causes of problems on their beats.[16]

In addition, several studies struck at the very heart of traditional police methods. For example, it was learned that response time had very little to do with whether or not an arrest was made at the scene; detectives were greatly overrated in their ability to solve crimes[17]; less than 50 percent of an officer's time was committed to calls for service (CFS); and of those calls handled, over 80 percent were noncriminal incidents.[18] As a result, a new "common wisdom" of policing came into being. The police were trained to work with the community to solve problems by looking at their underlying causes and developing tailored responses to them. Community policing and problem solving are discussed more thoroughly in Chapter 6.

SELECTED FEDERAL AGENCIES

This section describes the major law enforcement arms of the federal government, most of which are found within Department of Homeland Security and the Department of Justice. Table 5.1 shows the federal agencies that employ full-time officers with authority to carry firearms and make arrests.

Department of Homeland Security

Homeland Security

Within one month of the attack on U.S. soil on September 11, 2001, President George W. Bush issued a proposal to create a new **Department of Homeland Security (DHS)**—which was established in November 2002 and became the most significant transformation of the U.S. government in over a half-century. All or part of 22 different federal departments and agencies were combined, beginning in January 2003, and 80,000 new federal employees were immediately put to work.[19] Congress committed $32 billion toward safeguarding the nation, developing vaccines to protect against biological or chemical threats, training and equipping first responders (local police, firefighters, and medical personnel), and funding science and technology projects to counter the use of biological weapons and assess vulnerabilities. Since 2003, more than $635 billion has been appropriated by the federal government to support homeland security.[20]

Figure 5.1 shows the current organizational structure of DHS.

Following are brief descriptions of the major law enforcement agencies that are organizationally located within the DHS; all of them have full law enforcement authority:

Border Patrol

- *Customs and Border Protection (CBP)* is one of the largest federal law enforcement agencies, with more than 60,000 agents. CBP is responsible for preventing terrorists and terrorist weapons from entering the United States while facilitating the flow of legitimate trade and travel. The CBP protects nearly 7,000 miles of border with Canada and Mexico and 95,000 miles of shoreline.[21]

- *Immigration and Customs Enforcement (ICE)* is the largest investigative arm of DHS with about 12,500 sworn employees in more than 40 offices worldwide. ICE is responsible for identifying and shutting down vulnerabilities both in the nation's borders and in economic, transportation, and infrastructure security.[22]

TABLE 5.1

Federal Law Enforcement Agencies With Arrest and Firearm Authority

AGENCY	NUMBER OF OFFICERS
Federal Bureau of Prisons	16,835
Federal Bureau of Investigation	12,760
U.S. Immigration and Customs Enforcement	12,446
U.S. Secret Service	5,213
Administrative Office of the U.S. Courts*	4,696
Drug Enforcement Administration	4,308
U.S. Marshals Service	3,313
Veterans Health Administration	3,128
Internal Revenue Service, Criminal Investigation	2,636
Bureau of Alcohol, Tobacco, Firearms and Explosives	2,541
U.S. Postal Inspection Service	2,288
U.S. Capitol Police	1,637
National Park Service—Rangers	1,404
Bureau of Diplomatic Security	1,049
Pentagon Force Protection Agency	725
U.S. Forest Service	644
U.S. Fish and Wildlife Service	598
National Park Service—U.S. Park Police	547
National Nuclear Security Administration	363
U.S. Mint Police	316
Amtrak Police	305
Bureau of Indian Affairs	277
Bureau of Land Management	255
TOTAL	36,863

*Limited to federal probation officers employed in federal judicial districts that allow officers to carry firearms.

Source: Brian Reaves, *Federal Law Enforcement Officers, 2008* (Washington, D.C.: U.S. Department of Justice, Bureau of Justice Statistics, June 2012), p. 2, http://bjs.ojp.usdoj.gov/content/pub/pdf/fleo08.pdf (accessed January 2, 2013).

Homeland Security is in actuality composed of multiple law enforcement agencies, including officers performing both customs and border protection duties.

●● FIGURE 5.1

Department of Homeland Security Organizational Structure

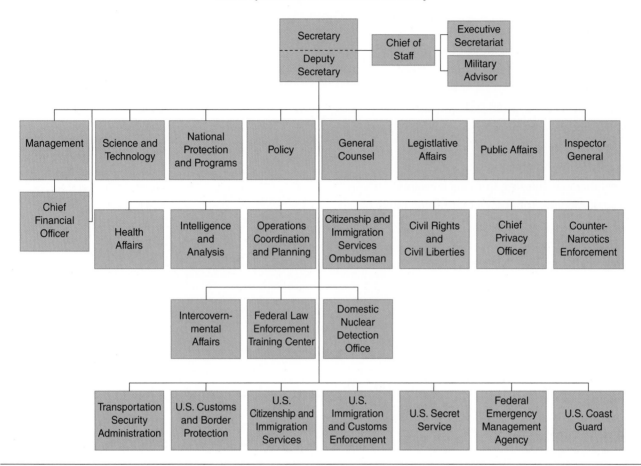

U.S. Department of Homeland Security

- The *Transportation Security Administration (TSA)* protects the nation's transportation systems. TSA employs 48,000 personnel at 457 airports who screen approximately 2 million people per day to ensure travel safety. Agents also inspect air carrier operations to the United States, assess security of airports overseas, fly air marshal missions, and train overseas security personnel.[23]

- The *Coast Guard* is the nation's leading maritime law enforcement agency; it protects the public, the environment, and U.S. economic interests in the nation's ports, on its waterways, along the coast, on international waters, or in any maritime region as required to support national security.[24]

- The *Secret Service* protects the president and other high-level officials and investigates counterfeiting and other financial crimes, including financial institution fraud, identity theft, computer fraud, and computer-based attacks on our nation's financial, banking, and telecommunications infrastructure. The Secret Service's Uniformed Division protects the White House complex and the vice president's residence as well as foreign e mbassies and missions in the Washington, D.C., area. The Secret Service has agents assigned to approximately 125 offices located in cities throughout the United States and in select foreign cities.[25]

Because its roles and purpose are closely related to the protection of the United States against terrorism and other crimes, a discussion of **Interpol** is provided in the next "Focus On" box.

International Policing

FOCUS ON   INTERPOL

Interpol is the oldest, the best known, and probably the only truly international crime-fighting organization for crimes committed on an international scale, such as drug trafficking, bank fraud, money laundering, and counterfeiting. Interpol agents do not patrol the globe, nor do they make arrests or engage in shootouts. They are basically intelligence gatherers who have helped many nations work together in attacking international crime since 1923.

Lyon, France, serves as the headquarters for Interpol's crime-fighting tasks and its 190 member countries. Today Interpol has six priority crime areas: corruption, drugs and organized crime, financial and high-tech crime, fugitives, public safety and terrorism, and trafficking in human beings. It also manages a range of databases with information on names and photographs of known criminals, wanted persons, fingerprints, DNA profiles, stolen or lost travel documents, stolen motor vehicles, child sex abuse images, and stolen works of art. Interpol also disseminates critical crime-related data through its system of international notices. There are seven kinds of notices, of which the most well known

is the Red Notice, an international request for an individual's arrest.

Interpol has one cardinal rule: It deals only with common criminals; it does not become involved with political, racial, or religious matters. It has a basic three-step formula for offenses that all nations must follow for success: pass laws specifying the offense is a crime, prosecute offenders and cooperate in other countries' prosecutions, and furnish Interpol with and exchange information about crime and its perpetrators. This formula could reverse the trend that is forecast for the world at present: an increasing capability by criminals for violence and destruction. The following crimes, because they are recognized as crimes by other countries, are covered by almost all U.S. treaties of extradition: murder, rape, bigamy, arson, robbery, burglary, forgery, counterfeiting, embezzlement, larceny, fraud, perjury, and kidnapping.[26]

Source: "Interpol: Global Crackdown on Illicit Online Pharmacies," October 4, 2012, http://www.interpol.int/News-and-media/News-media-releases/2012/PR077 (accessed October 7, 2012); also see Interpol, "Overview," http://www.interpol.int/About-INTERPOL/Overview (accessed January 15, 2013).

Department of Justice

The **Department of Justice** is headed by the attorney general, who is appointed by the U.S. president and approved by the Senate. The president also appoints the attorney general's assistants and the U.S. attorneys for each of the judicial districts. The U.S. attorneys in each judicial district control and supervise all federal criminal prosecutions and represent the government in legal suits in which it is a party. These attorneys may appoint committees to investigate other governmental agencies or offices when questions of wrongdoing are raised or when possible violations of federal law are suspected or detected.

The Department of Justice is the official legal arm of the government of the United States. Within the Justice Department are several law enforcement organizations that investigate violations of federal laws; we will discuss the Federal Bureau of Investigation; Bureau of Alcohol, Tobacco, Firearms and Explosives; Drug Enforcement Administration; and U.S. Marshals Service.

Figure 5.2 shows the organizational chart for the Department of Justice.

Mid-Chapter Quiz: Police Organization

Federal Bureau of Investigation

The Federal Bureau of Investigation (FBI) was created and funded through the Department of Justice Appropriation Act of 1908. A new era was begun for the FBI in 1924 with the appointment of J. Edgar Hoover, who was determined to professionalize the organization, as director. Special agents were college graduates, preferably with degrees in law or accounting. During his tenure in office many notorious criminals, such as Bonnie Parker, Clyde

Interpol: the only international crime-fighting organization, it collects intelligence information, issues alerts, and assists in capturing world criminals; it has nearly 200 member countries.

FIGURE 5.2

Department of Justice Organizational Chart

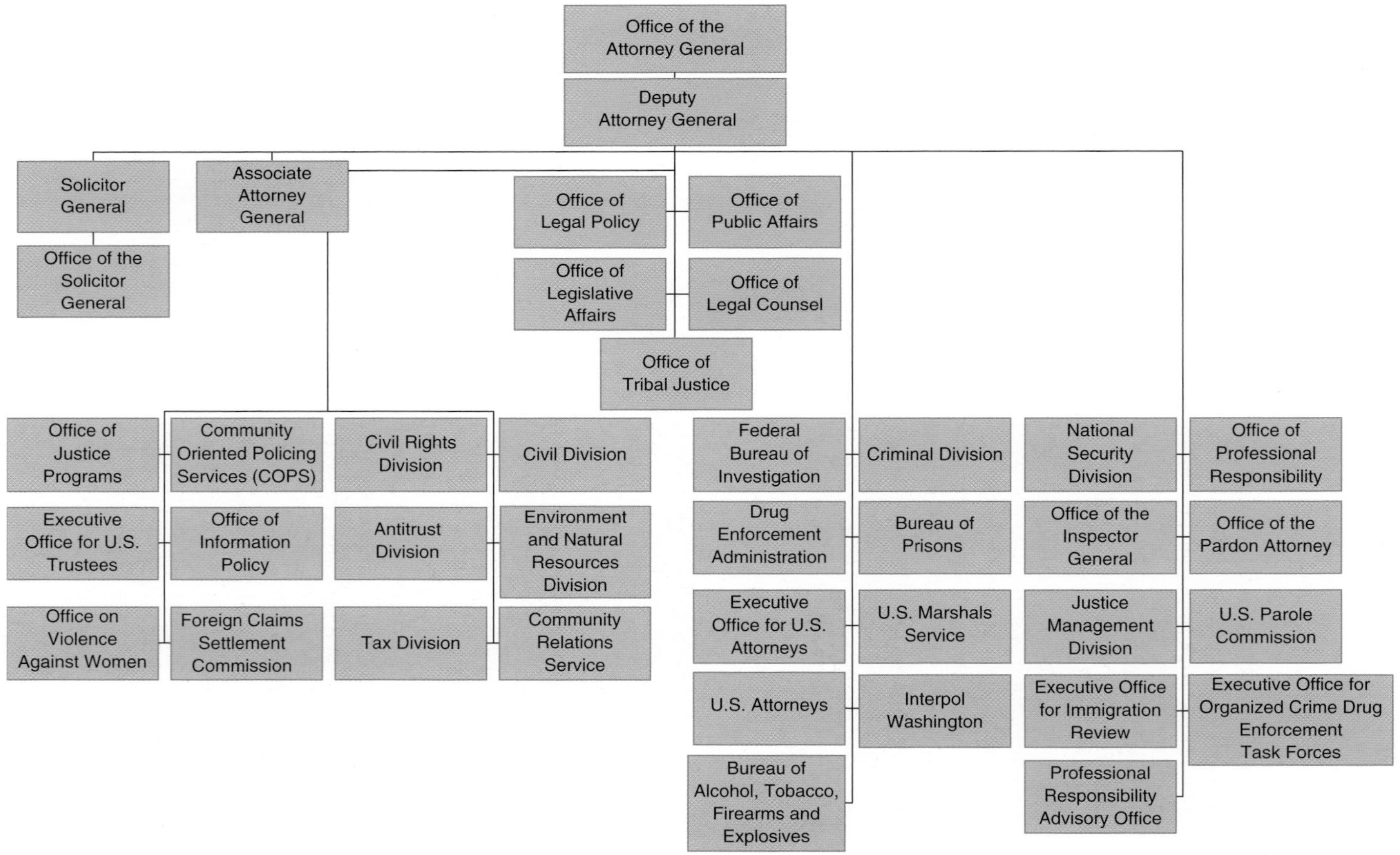

Barrow, and John Dillinger, were tracked and captured or killed.[27] The bureau's top three priority areas are as follows[28]:

1. Protect the United States from terrorist attack

2. Protect the United States against foreign intelligence operations and espionage

3. Protect the United States against cyber-based attacks and high-technology crimes

Figure 5.3 shows an organizational chart for the FBI.

To combat terrorism, the bureau can now monitor Internet sites, libraries, churches, and political organizations. In addition, under revamped guidelines, agents can attend public meetings for the purpose of preventing terrorism.[29] The FBI's laboratory examines blood, hair, firearms, paint, handwriting, typewriters, and other types of evidence—at no charge to state police and local police agencies. The FBI also operates the National Crime Information Center (NCIC), through which millions of records—including wanted persons as well as stolen vehicles and all kinds of property items or about anything with an identifying number—are entered.

A synopsis of the hiring process of the FBI is shown in Table 5.2 although simplistic in its appearance, each phase involves a number of individual activities by applicants and FBI personnel.

J. Edgar Hoover was the first Director of the Federal Bureau of Investigation and served in that capacity from 1924 until his death in 1972, at age 77.

Bureau of Alcohol, Tobacco, Firearms and Explosives

The Bureau of Alcohol, Tobacco, Firearms and Explosives (ATF) originated as a unit within the Internal Revenue Service in 1862, when certain alcohol and tobacco tax statutes were created. Like the FBI and several other federal agencies, the ATF has a rich and colorful history, much of which has involved capturing bootleggers and disposing of illegal whiskey stills during Prohibition. The ATF administers the U.S. criminal code provisions concerning alcohol and tobacco smuggling and diversion. ATF also maintains a U.S. Bomb Data Center (to collect information on arson- and explosives-related incidents) and a Bomb and Arson Tracking System, which allows local, state, and other federal agencies to share information about bomb and arson cases.[30]

Drug Enforcement Administration

Today's Drug Enforcement Administration (DEA) had its origin with the passage of the Harrison Narcotics Tax Act, signed into law on December 17, 1914, by President Woodrow Wilson.[31] It was created as the DEA by President Richard Nixon in July 1973 in order to create a single federal agency to coordinate and enforce the federal drug laws. In 1982 the organization was given primary responsibility for drug and narcotics enforcement, sharing this jurisdiction with the FBI.

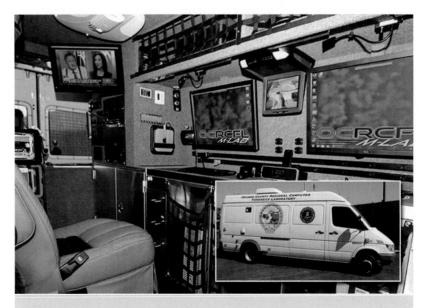

Some agencies operate mobile forensic crime laboratories in addition to those that are fixed.

FIGURE 5.3

FBI Organizational Chart

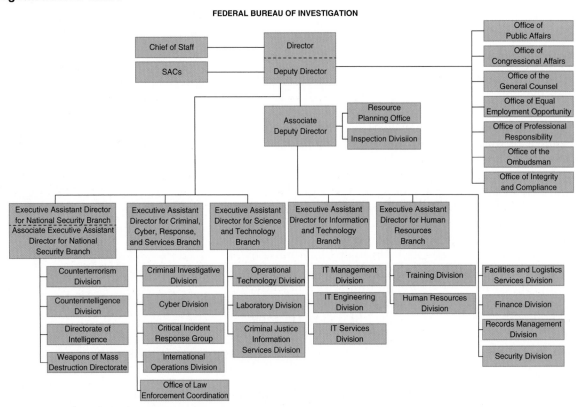

FEDERAL BUREAU OF INVESTIGATION

U.S. Marshals Service

The U.S. Marshals Service (USMS) is one of the oldest federal law enforcement agencies, established under the Judiciary Act of 1789. Today the USMS has 94 U.S. marshals, one for each federal court district. Deputy U.S. Marshals transport federal prisoners and track fugitives, while also protecting federal judges, prosecutors, and witnesses; they also conduct courthouse threat analyses and investigations, and perform security, rescue, and recovery activities for natural disasters and civil disturbances. Each district headquarters office is managed by a politically appointed U.S. marshal and a chief deputy U.S. marshal, who direct a staff of supervisors, investigators, deputy marshals, and administrative personnel. The USMS also operates the Witness Security Program. Federal witnesses are sometimes threatened by defendants or their associates; if certain criteria are met, the USMS will provide a complete change of identity for witnesses and their families, including new Social Security numbers, residences, and employment.[32]

Deputy U.S. Marshals perform many duties, including transporting federal prisoners, tracking fugitives, and protecting federal judges, prosecutors, and witnesses.

TABLE 5.2

The FBI Special Agent Selection System (SASS)

STAGE	DESCRIPTION	TIME FRAME
Phase I Test	Consists of three (3) sections—**Biodata Inventory**, **Logical Reasoning**, and **Situational Judgment**—that are designed to assess the competencies that successful Special Agents possess. Invited candidates complete the computerized test in a proctored environment. Candidates who pass Phase I are required to submit a PFT self-evaluation within 30 days of passing the test.	Candidates receive pass/fail notification within one hour of completing the test.
Meet and Greet	The Applicant Coordinator or other HR staff in your processing field office reviews online applications and evaluates applicant qualifications in person. Those deemed **most competitive** will be selec ted for Phase II testing.	Approximately 4-6 weeks after passing Phase I.
Phase II Test	Phase II consists of a structured interview conducted by a panel of three (3) Special Agents. Phase II also consists of a written exercise.	Approximately 4-6 weeks after passing Phase I. (Note: Phase II testing occurs on an as-needed basis.)
Conditional Appointment Offer (CAO)	Candidates who pass Phase II will receive a Conditional Appointment Offer (CAO). Actual hiring is contingent on the successful completion of the remaining SASS components (medical, background investigation, polygraph etc.).	Approximately two weeks after passing Phase II.
Physical Fitness Test (PFT)	The PFT assesses a candidate's physical fitness level relative to the essential tasks performed by FBI Special Agents. An official PFT will be conducted at your local Field Office by trained FBI personnel.	Within approximately two weeks of issuance of a CAO.
Background Investigation (BI)	The BI consists of a Personnel Security Interview, polygraph examination, and medical examination, followed by a thorough background investigation.	The BI process generally takes four months to complete.
New Agent Training (NAT)	Candidates who successfully complete the entire SASS, as described above, are eligible to be scheduled for New Agents Training at the FBI Academy in Quantico, VA. Assignment to NAT is based on the needs of the bureau.	NAT training is twenty weeks in duration.

Source: Federal Bureau of Investigation, *Candidate Information* Packet (revised 8/2011), p. 7; available at https://www.fbijobs.gov/1121 .asp.

Other Federal Agencies

Two other significant federal agencies outside of the Department of Justice with unique missions and contributions to the enforcement of the United States Code are the Central Intelligence Agency and Internal Revenue Service; they are discussed next.

Office of Law Enforcement Coordination

Central Intelligence Agency

Although not a law enforcement agency, the Central Intelligence Agency (CIA) is of significance at the federal level to the nation's security and warrants a brief discussion. The National Security Act of 1947 established the National Security Council, which in 1949 created a subordinate organization, the CIA. Considered the most clandestine government service, the CIA participates in undercover and covert operations around the world for the purposes of managing crises and providing intelligence during the conduct of war.[33]

DEA

you be the... JUDGE

ONE NATIONAL POLICE ORGANIZATION?

Most European and many Asian countries have police organizations that are centralized into one national police force. On a smaller scale, centralizing or combining some police functions is not new in the United States: since the 1960s, many police and sheriff's departments located in the same county have consolidated their units into one, thus avoiding the duplication of several expensive functions (e.g., records, communications, and jail).

The idea of a national police force is attractive to some Americans who believe that the nation is already drifting in that direction given the creation of the Department of Homeland Security and local police devoting more and more energy to protecting the nation's borders, scanning the Internet for cybercrimes, engaging in searches and seizures at seaports, and enforcing immigration laws. They argue that the current decentralization of law enforcement into federal, state, municipal, county, and even private police (or security) entities is inefficient and fragmented, and that a single, national police force would be better able to train their personnel, have fewer laws to uphold, be more accountable, and realize considerable cost savings if eliminating the current duplication of effort.

In the other camp are those who see such centralization as a huge danger to democracy as well as personal freedom. They believe a national force would be more disengaged from the community, involve a loss of local control and oversight over the police, and be vulnerable to abuse by the central government.

1. What do you think? Would implementing a single, national police force such as that found in many other countries work in the United States? Why or why not?

Author Video:
National Police Force

Internal Revenue Service

The Internal Revenue Service (IRS) has as its main function the monitoring and collection of federal income taxes from American individuals and businesses. Since 1919, the IRS has had a Criminal Investigation (CI) division employing "accountants with a badge." While other federal agencies also have investigative jurisdiction for money laundering and some bank secrecy act violations, the IRS is the only federal agency that can investigate potential criminal violations of the Internal Revenue Code.[34]

STATE AGENCIES

As with federal law enforcement organizations, a variety of organizations, duties, and specialization can be found in the 50 states—although, generally, state troopers and highway patrol officers actually perform a lot of the same functions as their county and municipal counterparts: enforcing state statutes, investigating criminal and traffic offenses (and, by virtue of those roles, knowing and applying laws of arrest, search, and seizure), making arrests, testifying in court, communicating effectively in both oral and written contexts, using firearms and self-defense tactics proficiently, and effectively performing pursuit driving, self-defense, and lifesaving techniques until a patient can be transported to a hospital. Such agencies also maintain a wide array of special functions, including special weapons and tactics (SWAT) teams, drug units and task forces, marine and horse patrol, and so on.[35]

Tactics Teams

Patrol, Police, and Investigative Organizations

State police organizations are typically tasked, under state statute, to perform more general law enforcement functions than are highway patrol troopers, to include criminal investigations as well as highway patrol, traffic control, crash investigations, and related functions. The latter, public safety organizations, are often more complex and may encompass several agencies or divisions. For example, the Hawaii Department of Public Safety, by statute, includes a Law Enforcement Division (with general arrest duties, narcotics division, sheriff division,

State police: a state agency responsible for highway patrol and other duties as delineated in the state's statutes; some states require their police to investigate crimes against persons and property.

and executive protection unit), a Corrections Division (inmate intake, incarceration, paroling authority, and industries), and a victim compensation commission.[36]

State bureaus of investigation (SBIs), as their name implies, are investigative in nature and might be considered a state's equivalent to the FBI; they investigate all manner of cases assigned to them by their state's laws and usually report to the state's attorney general. SBI investigators are plainclothes agents who usually investigate both criminal and civil cases involving the state and/or multiple jurisdictions. They also provide technical support to local agencies in the form of laboratory or record services and may be asked by the city and county agencies to assist in investigating more serious crimes (e.g., homicide).

Some state troopers primarily patrol their state's highways, while others are authorized by state statute to perform more general law enforcement functions, to include criminal investigations.

Other Special-Purpose State Agencies

In addition to the traffic, investigative, and other units mentioned above, several other special-purpose state agencies, including police and other law enforcement organizations, have developed over time to meet particular needs. For example, many state attorney general's offices have units and investigators that investigate white-collar crimes; fraud against or by consumers, Medicare providers, and food stamp recipients; and crimes against children and seniors.[37]

As shown in Table 5.3, states may also have limited-purpose units devoted to enforcing the following:

- Alcoholic beverage laws (regarding the distribution and sale of such beverages, monitoring bars and liquor stores, and so on)

- Fish and game laws (relating to hunting and fishing, to ensure that persons who engage in these activities have proper licenses and do not poach, hunt, or fish out of season, exceed their limit, and so on)

- State statutes and local ordinances on college and university campuses

- Agricultural laws, to include cattle brand inspection and enforcement

- Commercial vehicle laws, such as those federal and state laws pertaining to weights and permits of interstate carriers (i.e., tractor-trailer rigs) and ordinances applying to taxicabs

Most of these organizations have their own training academies, but some—campus police officers and fish and game agents, for example—may attend the regular police academies that train county deputies and local police officers.

LOCAL AGENCIES: MUNICIPAL POLICE AND SHERIFF'S DEPARTMENTS

Today Sir Robert Peel (discussed earlier in this chapter) would be amazed because there are about 17,000 general-purpose municipal police departments and county sheriff's departments in the United States.[38] The municipal agencies are composed of about 463,000 sworn full-time police officers,[39] and sheriff's offices employ about 183,000 sworn full-time deputies.[40] Next we focus on the organization and functions of these local agencies.

State bureau of investigation: a state agency that is responsible for enforcing state highway laws and investigating crimes involving state statutes; they may also be called in to assist police agencies in serious criminal matters, and often publish state crime reports.

TABLE 5.3

Special Jurisdiction Law Enforcement Agencies and Full-Time Sworn Personnel, by Type of Jurisdiction, 2008

TYPE OF SPECIAL JURISDICTION	AGENCIES	FULL-TIME SWORN PERSONNEL
Total	1,733	56,968
Public buildings/facilities	**1,126**	**21,418**
4-year university/college	508	10,916
Public school district	250	4,764
2-year college	253	2,648
State government buildings	29	1,138
Medical school/campus	18	747
Public hospital/health facility	48	715
Public housing	13	250
Other state-owned facilities	7	240
Natural resources	**246**	**14,571**
Fish and wildlife conservation laws	56	5,515
Parks and recreational areas	124	4,989
Multi-function natural resources	16	2,926
Boating laws	10	461
Environmental laws	7	368
Water resources	18	185
Forest resources	9	65
Levee district	6	62
Transportation systems/facilities	**167**	**11,508**
Airports	103	3,555
Mass transit system/railroad	18	3,214
Transportation–multiple types	5	2,000
Commercial vehicles	12	1,320
Harbor/port facilities	25	876
Bridges/tunnels	4	543
Criminal investigations	**140**	**7,310**
State bureau of investigation	22	3,527
County/city investigations	66	2,006
Fraud investigations	13	636
Fire marshal/arson investigations	21	478
Tax/revenue enforcement	6	177
Other/multiple types	12	486
Special enforcement	**54**	**2,161**
Alcohol/tobacco laws	22	1,280
Agricultural laws	12	387
Narcotics laws	5	233
Gaming laws	10	231
Racing laws	5	30

Note: Excludes agencies employing less than one full-time officer or the equivalent in part-time officers.

What Local Agencies Do: Basic Operations

Municipal police departments employ an average of 2.3 officers per 1,000 population; about 1 in 8 of these sworn employees is a woman, and 1 in 4 is a member of a racial or ethnic minority. For recruiting qualified personnel, 86 percent of these agencies use physical agility tests, 82 percent use written aptitude tests, and two-thirds employ personality inventories. On average, these officers receive 760 hours of recruit training in their academy. Significantly, about half of local police agencies employ fewer than 10 sworn personnel. Two-thirds of these agencies require their officers to wear protective body armor at all times while on duty; 61 percent use video cameras in patrol cars, three-fourths authorize the use of electronic control devices (such as a Taser), and more than 90 percent of agencies serving 25,000 or more residents use in-car computers. More information concerning municipal police agencies may be obtained from the Bureau of Justice Statistics.[41]

In county sheriff's departments, about 1 in 8 sworn employees is a woman, and 19 percent are members of a racial or ethnic minority. For recruiting qualified personnel, 74 percent of these agencies use physical agility tests, 68 percent use written aptitude tests, and 52 percent employ personality inventories. On average, new deputy recruits receive about 580 hours of academy training. About three-fifths of sheriff's departments employ fewer than 25 sworn personnel. Fifty-seven percent of these agencies require their officers to wear protective body armor at all times while on duty; two-thirds use video cameras in patrol cars, 79 percent authorize the use of electronic control devices (such as a Taser), and about 80 percent of agencies use in-car computers. More information concerning county sheriff's departments may be obtained from the Bureau of Justice Statistics.[42]

For those persons interested in a police career, Figure 6.1 and Table 6.1, in Chapter 6, describe the kinds of screening methods that tend to be used in hiring new officers, as well as typical topics covered in basic recruit academies.

Organization of Local Agencies

Every police agency, no matter what its size, has an **organizational structure**, which is often prominently displayed for all to see in the agency's facility—or perhaps not even written down at all. Even a community with only a town marshal has an organizational structure, although the structure will be very horizontal, with the marshal performing all of the functions displayed in Figure 5.4, the basic organizational chart for a small agency.

Municipal police department: a police force that enforces laws and maintains peace within a specified city or municipality.

Organizational structure or chart: a diagram of the vertical and horizontal parts of an organization, showing its chain of command, lines of communication, division of labor, and so on.

FIGURE 5.4

A Basic Police Organizational Structure

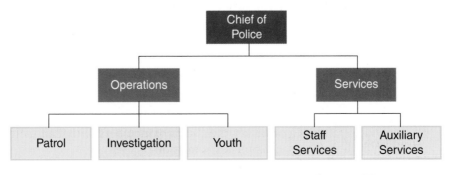

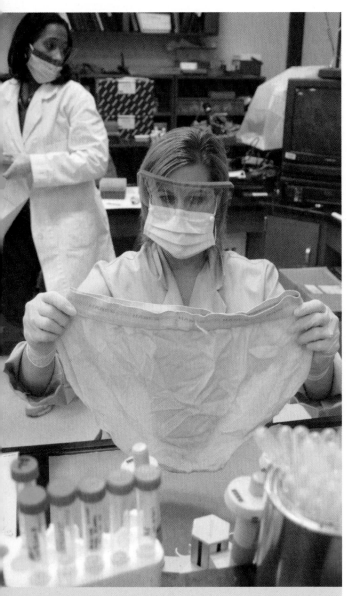

An example of a police organization's auxiliary services is the work done by crime laboratory services.

Operations, or the line-element, personnel are engaged in active police functions in the field. They may be subdivided into primary and secondary operations elements. The patrol function—often called the backbone of policing—is the primary operational element because of its major responsibility for policing. (The patrol function is examined in Chapter 6.) In most small police agencies, patrol forces are responsible for all operational activities: providing routine patrols, conducting traffic and criminal investigations, making arrests, and functioning as generalists. The investigative and youth functions are the secondary operations elements. (The investigative function is discussed in Chapter 6 and juvenile rights in Chapter 15). The support (or nonline) functions and activities can become quite numerous, especially in a large agency. These functions fall within two broad categories: staff (or administrative) services and auxiliary (or technical) services. The staff services usually involve personnel and include such matters as recruitment, training, promotion, planning and research, community relations, and public information services. Auxiliary services are the kinds of functions that civilians rarely see. They include jail management, property and evidence, crime laboratory services, communications, and records and identification. Many career opportunities exist for those who are interested in police-related work but who cannot or do not want to be a field officer.

Obviously, the larger the agency, the greater the need for specialization and the more vertical the organizational chart will become. With greater specialization comes the need and opportunity for officers to be assigned to different tasks, often rotating from one assignment to another after a fixed interval. For example, in a medium-sized department serving a community of 100,000 or more, it would be possible for a police officer with 10 years of police experience to have been a dog handler, a motorcycle officer, a detective, and a traffic officer while simultaneously holding a slot on the special-weapons or hostage-negotiation team.

Consider the organizational structure for a larger police organization, such as the Portland, Oregon, Police Bureau (PPB) (see Figure 5.5). This structure not only shows the various components of the organization, but also does the following:

- Apportions the workload among members and units according to a logical plan

- Ensures that lines of authority and responsibility are as definite and direct as possible

- Places responsibility and authority and, if responsibility is delegated, holds the delegator responsible

- Coordinates the efforts of members so that all will work harmoniously to accomplish the mission

Chain of command: vertical and horizontal power relations within an organization, showing how one position relates to others.

In sum, this structure establishes the **chain of command** and determines lines of communication and responsibility.

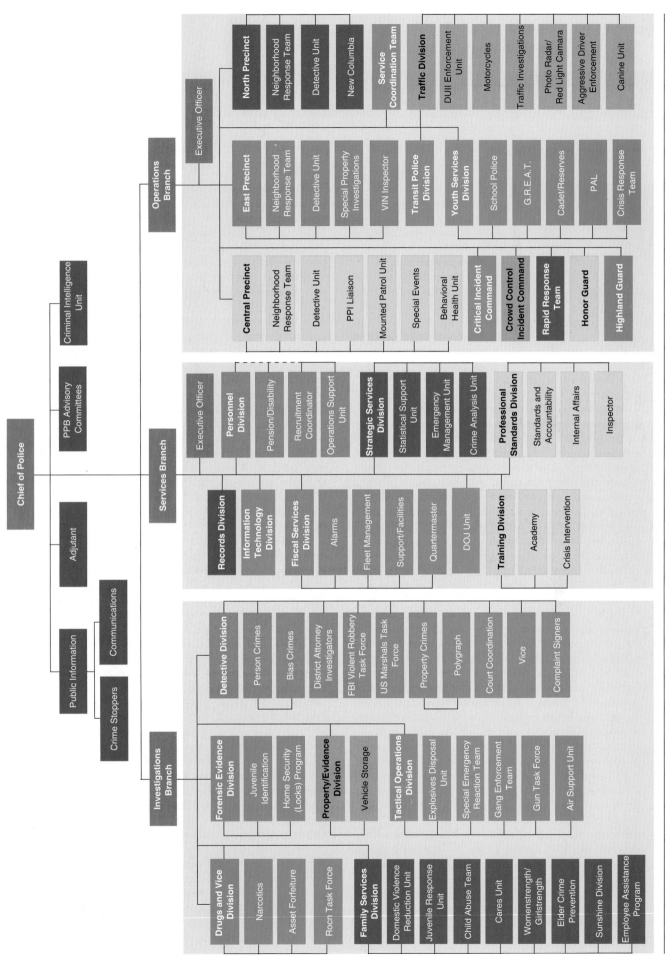

FIGURE 5.5

Portland Police Bureau Organizational Chart

Source: Printed with the permission of Chief Michael Reese, The City of Portland, Oregon, Police Bureau.

PRACTITIONER'S PERSPECTIVE

POLICE CHIEF

Name: Michael A. Davis
Current position: Chief of Police
City, state: Brooklyn Park, Minnesota
College attended/ academic major: Concordia University/MA, organizational management; BA, criminal justice
How long have you been a practitioner in this criminal justice position?

Five years as a police chief, 21 years in law enforcement

My primary duties and responsibilities as a practitioner in this position are:

To create and then lead the police department toward a cogent vision of outcomes in the community related to public safety and service. As a police chief, I also have a vital role in the community as a leader, facilitator, and expert on issues related to community livability, social fabric, and crime control. With a community of just under 80,000 residents I also work quite closely with other department heads to ensure that the whole organization is moving in lockstep in service to our community members.

The qualities/characteristics that are most helpful for one in this career are:

Based on what my earlier career as a major in the U.S. Army taught me, the most important trait of an effective leader is vision. At that time, I didn't perceive "vision" as being all that important because as a supervisor my job (so I thought) was to execute my duties in accordance with the paradigm set by others of much higher rank. As police chief, however, vision has everything to do with my success. In this context, vision is the ability not only to project measurable outcomes for an organization but also to have the knowledge and intuition to lead people toward that vision. As a police chief, I also must possess the ability to distill problems down to their root cause and coalesce the talents of those around me to come up with the best possible solution. My success depends on me effectively leveraging the strengths, capacities, passions, and skills of all stakeholders to achieve the vision. Finally, a person in my position must have an unwavering moral compass both personally and professionally along with an intense passion for bettering the community he or she serves.

In general, a *typical day* for a practitioner in this career would include:

First, being far from an 8-hour day or a set schedule, spending considerable time engaged in personal development activities. These activities include reading, research, and communicating with my professional network of fellow chiefs, scholars, and experts in various fields related to community building. A typical day for me consists of first reviewing all the significant activity from the night before. This task is typically done from home early in the morning. Here I'm looking for not only what events occurred but more importantly how we as an organization responded to those events. My expectation is that we consistently demonstrate not only competence and compassion in our work but also the ability to challenge those conditions that led to the event in the first place. I encourage each member of our department to take ownership of not just his or her tasks but the outcomes that we are collectively seeking in the community. Upon my arrival at work I spend much of my time in communication with police staff, community members, and other stakeholders. While there are a number of formal meetings on my calendar, perhaps my most productive time is spent in the hallways, doorways, and common spaces talking to people. Much of my work is the confluence of effective task management and relationship building. Both are critical to my success as a police chief.

My advice to someone either wishing to study, or now studying, criminal justice to become a practitioner in this career field would be:

Anyone seeking a career in criminal justice must first have an understanding of what his or her "telos" (or purpose/goal) is for seeking a career of this type. The question one should ask is "How do my passions, capacities, and strengths fit into the work I seek to do?" Often times a person's perception of the work he or she seeks and the real outcomes of that work are incongruous. People often forget that the criminal justice system is just that—a "system" designed to produce the exact results that it produces. My satisfaction is derived from the way in which I do my work within the construct of the criminal justice system. It is the autonomy that I exercise in how my work is done that creates a sense of purpose for me. I understand that my work is slow and incremental and often stalled with unexpected challenges, but it is the process of creating a future both for the department and for the community distinct from the past that drives me in this work. If people are not driven for outcomes they control within the criminal justice system, then I suggest they find other work, as there are some practitioners in the field who have not found their "telos" and thus satisfaction in their careers. The work of the criminal justice system is to protect our democracy and requires that all who work within it to have an intense passion for this work.

On Guard: The Private Police

Much has certainly changed in society and the private security industry since 1851, when Allan Pinkerton initiated the Pinkerton National Detective Agency, specializing in railroad security. Pinkerton established the first private security contract operation in the United States. His motto was "We Never Sleep," and his logo, an open eye, was probably the genesis of the term private eye.

Private Police

Today, according to the late loss-prevention expert Saul Astor, "We are a nation of thieves"[43]—and, it might be added, a nation that needs to be protected against would-be terrorists, rapists, robbers, and other dangerous people. According to the National Crime Victimization Survey, there are about 5.8 million violent-crime victimizations and 17.1 million property crime victimizations each year in this nation.[44] As a result, and especially since 9/11, this nation has become highly security minded concerning its computers, lotteries, celebrities, college campuses, casinos, nuclear plants, airports, shopping centers, mass transit systems, hospitals, and railroads. Such businesses, industries, and institutions have recognized the need to conscientiously protect their assets against threats of crime and other disasters—as well as the limited capabilities of the nation's full-time sworn officers and agents to protect them—and have increasingly turned to the "other police"—those of the private sector—for protection.

In-house security services, directly hired and controlled by the company or organization, are called proprietary services; contract services are those outside firms or individuals hired by the individual or company to provide security services for a fee. The most common security services provided include contract guards, alarm services, private investigators, locksmith services, armored-car services, and security consultants.

Chapter Quiz: Police Organization

Although some of the duties of the security officer are similar to those of the public police officer, their overall powers are entirely different. First, because security officers are not police officers, court decisions have stated that the security officer is not bound by the *Miranda* decision concerning suspects' rights. Furthermore, security officers generally possess only the same authority to effect an arrest as does the common citizen (the exact extent of citizen's arrest power varies, however, depending on the type of crime, the jurisdiction, and the status of the citizen). In most states, warrantless arrests by private citizens are allowed when a felony has been committed and reasonable grounds exist for believing that the person arrested committed it. Most states also allow citizen's arrests for misdemeanors committed in the arrester's presence.

The tasks of the **private police** are very similar to those of their public counterparts: protecting executives and employees, tracking and forecasting security threats, monitoring alarms, preventing and detecting fraud, conducting investigations, providing crisis management and prevention, and responding to substance abuse.[45]

Still, there are concerns about the field: As one author noted, "Of those individuals involved in private security, some are uniformed, some are not; some carry guns, some are unarmed; some guard nuclear

Our society has increasingly turned to the "other police"—those of the private sector—for protection.

energy installations, some guard golf courses; some are trained, some are not; some have college degrees, some are virtually uneducated."[46] Studies have shown that security officer recruits often have minimal education and training; because the pay is usually quite low, the jobs often attract only those people who cannot find other jobs or seek temporary work. Thus much of the work is done by the young and the retired, and the recruitment and training of lower-level private security personnel can present a real concern.[47] Clearly, today's security officer needs to be highly trained and competent.

Another long-standing issue that concerns private police is whether or not they should be armed. In the past, much has been made about security officers who have received little or no prior training or have undergone no checks on their criminal history records but are carrying a weapon. Twenty-three hours of firearms instruction is recommended for all security personnel, as well as another twenty-four hours on general matters and proper legal training.[48]

Private police/security: all nonpublic officers, including guards, watchmen, private detectives, and investigators; they have limited powers and only the same arrest powers as regular citizens.

IN A NUTSHELL

- All four of the primary criminal justice officials of early England—the sheriff, constable, coroner, and justice of the peace—either still exist or existed until recently in the United States.

- In 1829, Sir Robert Peel established professional policing as it is known today, under the Metropolitan Police Act of 1829. Later, in 1844, the New York State legislature passed a law establishing a full-time preventive police force for New York City. However, this new body took a very different form than in Europe. The U.S. version was placed under the control of the city government and city politicians, thus launching the first era of policing, the political era, from the 1840s to the 1930s.

- The reform (also known as the professional) era of policing, from the 1930s to the 1980s, sought to remove police from political control. Civil service systems were created, and soon the crime-fighter image was projected; much of police work was driven by *numbers*—arrests, calls for service, response time to calls for service, number of tickets written, and so on. The police were the "thin blue line," but crimes continue to increase, and the police were becoming increasingly removed from their communities.

- The community era of policing, 1980s to present, was born because of the problems that overwhelmed the reform era. The police were trained to work with the community to solve problems by looking at their underlying causes and developing tailored responses to them.

- Today there are approximately 17,000 police agencies, each with an organizational structure, divided into a number of operations and support functions.

- State law enforcement agencies are of two primary types: general law enforcement agencies engaged in patrol and related functions, and state bureaus of investigation.

- At the federal level, agencies of the Department of Homeland Security were formed in 2003 to combat terrorism; agencies of the Department of Justice and other federal agencies support that and other efforts as well.

- Interpol is the oldest, the best known, and probably the only truly international crime-fighting organization for crimes committed on an international scale; its agents do not patrol the globe, nor do they make arrests or engage in shootouts. They are basically intelligence gatherers who have helped many nations work together in attacking international crime since 1923.

- The field of private policing or security is much larger than public policing, and is divided into in-house security services, called *proprietary* services, and *contract* services, where outside firms or individuals are hired by the individual or company to provide security services for a fee. Private security officers are not bound by court decisions that govern the public police, but security officers generally possess the same authority to make an arrest as a private citizen. Issues with this industry involve training, the carrying of weapons, and criminal background checks of personnel.

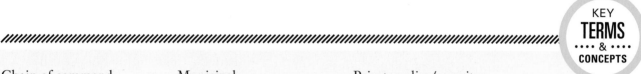

KEY TERMS & CONCEPTS

Chain of command
Community era
Constable
Coroner
Interpol
Justice of the peace (JP)

Municipal
  police department
Organization
Organizational structure or
  chart
Political era (of policing)

Private police/security
Reform era (police)
Sheriff
State bureau of investigation
State police

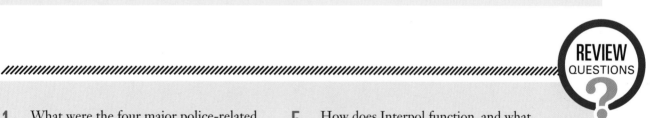

REVIEW QUESTIONS

1. What were the four major police-related offices and their functions during the early English and colonial periods?

2. What are the three eras of local policing, and what primary problems of the first two eras led to the development of the current community era?

3. What are the major agencies within the Department of Homeland Security and the Department of Justice, and what are their primary functions?

4. What functions do the Central Intelligence Agency and the Internal Revenue Service perform?

5. How does Interpol function, and what are its primary contributions to crime-fighting?

6. Why were the private police organizations developed, and what are their contemporary purposes and issues?

7. Using a simple organizational structure that you have drawn, how would you describe the major functions of a local (i.e., municipal or county) police agency?

8. How would you describe the primary differences between federal and state law enforcement agencies?

1. Assume that you are part of a group that is studying the creation of a national police force in the United States, such as those found in many countries around the world. All state, county, and municipal police organizations would be abolished in favor of having only this single national agency, with one governing board, one set of laws to enforce and agency policies to uphold, and standardized training and pay/benefits. Develop an argument both pro and con for this proposal, perhaps including the history of policing, all possible positive and negative consequences that might occur from this single entity, its political pitfalls and favor with the general public, and whether or not you would support this proposal.

2. Describe (if they exist in your area) the duties of the four early English policing offices: sheriff, constable, justice of the peace, and coroner.

3. You have been assigned to describe federal and state law enforcement agencies for a class presentation. Prepare a lecture outline covering the major agencies—including their functions—that compose both the Department of Justice and the Department of Homeland Security; include the complementary roles of Interpol.

POLICE AT WORK:
Patrolling and Investigating

LEARNING OBJECTIVES

As a result of reading this chapter, the student will be able to:

1 Describe the ideal traits typically sought among people who are hired into policing

2 Explain the kinds of topics that are taught in the recruit academy and overall methods for preparing recruits for a career in policing

3 Delineate the methods and purposes of the FTO concept

4 Describe the several basic *tasks* and distinctive *styles* of policing

5 Explain what is meant by a police working personality, including how it is developed and operates

6 Clarify how the work of policing can be perilous in nature

7 Discuss the nature of the police traffic function

8 Define police discretion, how and why it is allowed to function, and some of its advantages and disadvantages

9 Explain the current era of policing, the community era, and the prevailing philosophy and strategies of community policing and problem solving

10 Review the qualities, myths, and methods that involve investigative personnel

CHAPTER
06

You gain strength, courage, and confidence by every experience in which you really stop to look fear in the face. You are able to say to yourself, "I lived through this horror. I can take the next thing that comes along." . . . You must do the thing you think you cannot do.

—Eleanor Roosevelt

Murder, though it have no tongue, will speak.

—Shakespeare, *Hamlet*, Act II, Scene 2

INTRODUCTION

Author Introduction:
Chapter 6

How do I become a police officer? A detective? A criminal profiler? How do I qualify to work in forensics? Do police have to arrest everyone they see breaking the law?

These are all legitimate, oft-heard questions as posed by university students. Unfortunately, owing in large measure to Hollywood's portrayals of police work and investigations, there are many misperceptions about the field. First, the odds of one becoming a criminal profiler are virtually nil—as are the odds of some federal agent academy trainee being brought out to help investigate a serial killer case (as was the plot in a major movie starring Jodie Foster). Second, one who wishes to work in a forensics lab must have a background in chemistry, biology, or a related natural science field (e.g., biochemistry or microbiology). Finally, in order to become a detective, one must normally begin as a regular officer; then, with years of training, experience, and often testing or at least an oral examination, one might be deemed worthy of being an investigator. This chapter hopes to remedy those misperceptions at least in part by looking at some of the primary roles and functions of the individuals who work in police organizations; included are

ASSESS YOUR AWARENESS:

Test your current knowledge of police patrol and investigations by first reading and responding to the following seven true-false items; check your answers after reading this chapter's materials.

1. Of several high-risk occupations—including commercial fishing, logging, and piloting airplanes—policing ranks highest in terms of danger.

2. The terms *forensic science* and *criminalistics* are often used interchangeably, but they have quite different meanings.

3. As typically shown in movie and television portrayals, detective work is primarily action-packed and involves a successful search for offenders.

4. The four basic tasks of policing as involves the public include patrolling, tracking, arresting, and appearing in court.

5. What is termed the "CSI effect" has actually helped jurors to become more knowledgeable and thus widely improved the quality of justice in the United States.

6. DNA is the most sophisticated and reliable type of physical evidence.

7. Police officers, being governed by laws and procedure manuals, actually have very little discretion.

Answers can be found on page 401.

the point of their being recruited and trained, and eventually going to work either as officers on patrol or as criminal investigators.

First is a review of the types of persons who are sought for and hired into policing, as well as their initial training at the academy; included is a consideration of how one's occupational personality is formed—the subculture of the "cop's world." The roles and tasks of the police are discussed, as is their discretionary use of authority in enforcing the law. Finally, those who investigate crimes, the detectives, are examined; included is a review of the nature of their work, some myths and attributes, and how advances in DNA have assisted in achieving their goals. A summary, key terms and concepts, review questions, and several scenarios and activities that provide opportunities for you to "learn by doing" will conclude the chapter.

FROM CITIZEN TO PATROL OFFICER

The Hiring Process

The idea of a police subculture was first proposed by William Westley in his 1950 study of the Gary, Indiana, Police Department, where he found, among many other things, a high degree of secrecy and violence.[1] The police develop traditions, skills, and attitudes that are unique to their occupation because of their duties and responsibilities. Next we consider how citizens are brought into, and socialized within, the police world.

Recruiting the Best

Recruiting an adequate pool of applicants is an extremely important facet of the police hiring process. August Vollmer, the renowned Berkeley, California, police innovator and administrator, said that law enforcement candidates should

> have the wisdom of Solomon, the courage of David, the patience of Job and leadership of Moses, the kindness of the Good Samaritan, the diplomacy of Lincoln, the tolerance of the Carpenter of Nazareth, and, finally, an intimate knowledge of every branch of the natural, biological and social sciences.[2]

Police officers are solitary workers, spending most of their time on the job unsupervised. At all times they must be able to make sound decisions and adjust quickly to changing situations during periods that are unpredictable and unstable, chaotic, or high-stress—all the while acting ethically and in keeping with the U.S. Constitution, their state statutes, and their agency's policy and procedures manual. For these reasons, police agencies must attempt to attract the best individuals possible.

Figure 6.1 shows the general kinds of screening and testing methods that are used with new recruits in the United States. Obviously the goal is to bring the most qualified and capable people into the field (as well as more women and minorities, generally, discussed in Chapter 7). Then an example of an agency's hiring process is provided in the accompanying "Focus On" case study, setting forth the components of the hiring process as used by the Kansas City, Missouri, Police Department.

Recruit Training

Police recruits are taught a wide variety of subjects in **academy training** (see Table 6.1). They are taught to nurture a **"sixth sense"**: suspicion. A suspicious nature is as important to the street officer as a fine touch is to

Academy training: police and corrections personnel are trained in the basic functions, laws, and skills required for their positions

"Sixth sense": in policing, the notion that an officer can "sense" or feel when something is not right, as in the way a person acts, talks, and so on.

FIGURE 6.1

Local Police Officers Employed by a Department Using Selected Screening Methods in the Hiring Process, 2003 and 2007

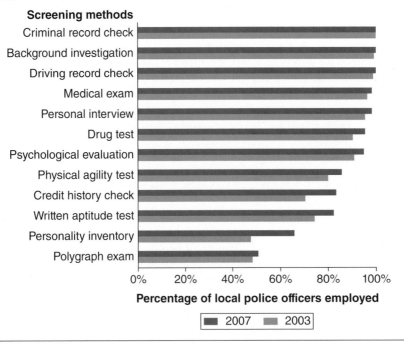

Source: Brian A. Reaves, *Local Police Departments, 2007* (Washington, D.C.: U.S. Department of Justice, Bureau of Justice Statistics, December 2010), p. 11, http://bjs.ojp.usdoj.gov/content/pub/pdf/lpd07.pdf (accessed August 4, 2013).

FOCUS ON THE POLICE HIRING PROCESS IN KANSAS CITY, MISSOURI

Following are the types of examinations and activities involved in the hiring process for the Kansas City, Missouri, Police Department (KCPD) (as well as many other police agencies). The entire process, which includes a substance abuse questionnaire (not shown), may require several months to complete.

- *Written Examination:* All applicants begin with and must take the Police Officer Selection Test (POST). A review for this exam is generally given within one month prior to the written examination, and a sample test is available upon request.

- *Physical Abilities Test:* This is an obstacle course designed to simulate challenges that could be encountered during an officer's tour of duty. Applicants must demonstrate their ability to maneuver through the course with minimal errors.

- *Preemployment Polygraph Examination:* The polygraph examination is administered by a qualified polygraph examiner and covers criminal activity, drug usage, integrity, truthfulness, and employment history.

- *Background Investigation:* The background investigation will cover pertinent facts regarding the applicant's character, his or her work history, and any criminal or traffic records.

- *Ride-Along:* To expose applicants to the actual duties performed by KCPD officers, during the background investigation, the applicant will be required to ride with an officer on a weekend for a full tour of duty during the evening or night shift.

- *Oral Board:* This interview consists of questions designed to allow the KCPD to assess an applicant's overall abilities as they relate to the field of law enforcement.

- *Psychological Examination:* This interview is conducted by a certified psychologist, after a job offer has been made.

- *Physical Examination:* Applicants undergo a complete medical and eye examination performed by a licensed physician, after a job offer has been made.

Source: Kansas City, Missouri, Police Department, "Hiring Process," http://www.kcmo.org/police/AboutUs/Departments/Administration/HumanResources/EmploymentSection/HiringProcess/index.htm (accessed May 30, 2013).

a surgeon. The officer should be able to visually recognize when something is wrong or out of the ordinary. As a Chicago Police Department bulletin stated,

> Actions, dress, or location of a person often classify him as suspicious in the mind of a police officer. Men loitering near schools, public toilets, playgrounds and swimming pools may be sex perverts. Men loitering near . . . any business at closing time may be robbery suspects. Men or youths walking along looking into cars may be car thieves or looking for something to steal.[3]

Table 6.1 displays the predominant topics included in training new officers and the median length of training for each. A considerably high percentage of police agencies use physical agility tests, perform psychological evaluations, and provide educational incentive pay to officers, and municipal police officers receive about 55 additional hours of initial (i.e., academy and field) training.

Police recruits undergo training in a wide variety of subjects during their many weeks in the academy.

Field Training Officer

Once the recruits leave the academy, they are not merely thrown to the streets to fend for themselves in terms of upholding the law and maintaining order. Another very important part of this acquisition process is being assigned to a veteran officer for initial field instruction and observation. This veteran is sometimes called a **field training officer (FTO)**.[4] This training program provides recruits with an opportunity to make the transition from the academy to the streets under the protective arm of a veteran officer. Recruits are on probationary status, normally ranging from six months to one year; they may be immediately terminated if their overall performance is unsatisfactory during that period.

Most FTO programs consist of three identifiable phases:

1. An introductory phase (the recruit learns agency policies and local laws)

2. Training and evaluation phases (the recruit is introduced to more complicated tasks that patrol officers confront)

3. A final phase (the FTO acts strictly as an observer and evaluator while the recruit performs all the functions of a patrol officer)[5]

The length of time rookies are assigned to FTOs will vary. A formal FTO program might require close supervision for a range of 1–12 weeks.

Most police officers also receive in-service training throughout their careers, because their states require a minimum number of hours of such training. News items, court decisions, and other relevant information can also be covered at roll call before the beginning of each shift. Short courses ranging from a few hours to several weeks are available for in-service officers through several such means as videos and nationally televised training programs.

To assist in their transition from the training academy to the street, new officers are typically assigned to work with a veteran field training officer for a period of time before being released to act on their own.

TABLE 6.1

Topics Included in Basic Training of State and Local Law Enforcement Training Academies

TOPICS	PERCENTAGE OF ACADEMIES WITH TRAINING	MEDIAN NUMBER OF HOURS OF INSTRUCTION
Operations		
Report writing	100	20
Patrol	99	40
Investigations	99	40
Basic first aid/CPR	99	24
Emergency vehicle operations	97	40
Computers/information systems	58	8
Weapons/self-defense		
Self-defense	99	51
Firearms skills	98	60
Nonlethal weapons	98	12
Legal		
Criminal law	100	36
Constitutional law	98	12
History of law enforcement	84	4
Self-improvement		
Ethics and integrity	100	8
Health and fitness	96	46
Stress prevention/management	87	5
Basic foreign language	36	16
Community policing		
Cultural diversity/human relations	98	11
Basic strategies	92	8
Mediation/conflict management	88	8
Special topics		
Domestic violence	99	14
Juveniles	99	8
Domestic preparedness	88	8
Hate crimes/bias crimes	87	4

Source: Brian A. Reaves, *State and Local Law Enforcement Training Academies, 2006* (Washington, D.C.: U.S. Department of Justice, Bureau of Justice Statistics, February 2009), p. 6, http://bjs.ojp.usdoj.gov/content/pub/pdf/slleta06.pdf (accessed August 4, 2013).

Field training officer (FTO): one who is to oversee and evaluate the new police officer's performance as he or she transitions from the training academy to patrolling the streets.

HAVING THE "RIGHT STUFF": A WORKING PERSONALITY

Since the publication of Westley's aforementioned examination of police subculture in 1950, the notion of a police personality has become a popular area of study. In 1966, Jerome Skolnick[6] described what he termed the working personality of the police. He determined that the police role contained two important variables: danger and authority. Danger is a constant feature of police work. Police officers, constantly facing potential violence, are warned at the academy to be cautious. They are told many war stories of officers shot and killed at domestic disturbances or traffic stops. Consequently, they develop "perceptual shorthand," Skolnick said, that they use to identify certain kinds of people as "symbolic assailants"—individuals whom the officer has come to recognize as potentially violent based on their gestures, language, and attire.

Policing Routines

John Broderick[7] presented another view of the working personality of the police. He believed that there are actually four types of police personalities: enforcers, idealists, realists, and optimists.

- *Enforcers* are officers who believe that the job of the police consists primarily of keeping their beats clean, making good arrests, and sometimes helping people. These officers have sympathy for the homeless, the elderly, the working poor, and others whom they see as basically good people.

- *Idealists* are officers who put high value on individual rights and due process. They also believe that it is their duty to keep the peace, protect citizens from criminals, and generally preserve the social order. As a group with a high percentage of college graduates, their commitment to the job is the lowest of the four groups, and they are less likely to recommend the job to a son or daughter.

- *Realists* place relatively little emphasis on either social order or individual rights. They seem less frustrated, having found a way to come to terms with a difficult job. For them, the reality of the job consists of manila envelopes and properly completed forms. Realists see many problems in policing, such as special privileges given to politicians. They work well in the ordered, predictable environment of a police records room.

- *Optimists* also place a relatively high value on individual rights. Like idealists, they see their job as people oriented instead of crime oriented, providing opportunities to help people; they find it rewarding to spend the majority of their time in service activities. Optimists are committed to the job and would choose policing as a career all over again. They enjoy the mental challenge of problem solving.

Traits That Make a "Good" Officer

It is not too difficult to identify bad police officers through their unethical or criminal behavior. But what are the traits of good officers?

Dennis Nowicki[8] acknowledged that while certain characteristics form the foundation of a police officer—honesty, ethics, and moral character—no scientific formula can be used to create a highly effective officer. However, he compiled 12 qualities that he believes are imperative for entry-level police officers:

- Enthusiasm: Believing in what one is doing and going about even routine duties with a certain vigor that is almost contagious

- Good communication skills: Having highly developed speaking and listening skills and the ability to interact equally well with a wealthy person or someone lower on the socioeconomic ladder

A sense of humor, the ability to communicate, and job enthusiasm even for routine duties are some of the crucial traits required for police officers to be successful.

- Good judgment: Having wisdom and the ability to make good analytic decisions based on an understanding of the problem

- Sense of humor: Being able to laugh and smile, to help oneself cope with regular exposure to human pain and suffering

- Creativity: Using creative techniques to place oneself in the mind of the criminal and accomplish legal arrests

- Self-motivation: Making things happen, proactively solving difficult cases, and creating one's own luck

- Knowing the job and the system: Understanding the role of a police officer, the intricacies of the justice system, and what the administration requires; using both formal and informal channels to be effective

- Ego: Believing one is a good officer; having self-confidence that enables one to solve difficult crimes

- Courage: Being able to meet physical and psychological challenges; thinking clearly during times of high stress; admitting when one is wrong; standing up for what is right

- Understanding discretion: Enforcing the spirit of the law, not the letter of the law; not being hard-nosed, hardheaded, or hard-hearted; giving people a break; showing empathy

- Tenacity: Staying focused; seeing challenges, not obstacles; viewing failure not as a setback but as an experience

- A thirst for knowledge: Being aware of new laws and court decisions; always learning (from the classroom but also through informal discussions with other officers)

DEFINING THE ROLE

Crime and Media

What are the police supposed to do? Often this question is given such oversimplified answers as "They enforce the law" or "They 'serve and protect.'"[9] But policing is much more complex, and most Americans probably do not have an accurate idea of what the police really do. In reality, the police are called on to perform an almost countless number of tasks.

One of the greatest obstacles to understanding the American police is the crime-fighter image. Because of film and media portrayals, many people believe that the role of the police is confined to the apprehension of criminals.[10] However, only about 20 percent of the police officer's typical day is devoted to fighting crime per se.[11] And, as Jerome Skolnick and David Bayley point out, the crimes that terrify Americans the most—robbery, rape, burglary, and homicide—are rarely encountered by police on patrol. In their words:

> Only "Dirty Harry" has his lunch disturbed by a bank robbery in progress. Patrol officers individually make few important arrests. The "good collar" is a rare event. Cops spend most of their time passively patrolling and providing emergency services.[12]

Also, many individuals enter police work expecting it to be exciting and rewarding, as depicted on television and in the movies. Later they discover that much of their time is spent with boring, mundane, and trivial tasks—and that paperwork is seldom stimulating.

Four Basic Tasks

Patrol officers may be said to perform four basic **tasks of policing**:

1. *Enforce the laws*—although this is a primary function of the police, as we saw above, they actually devote a very small portion of their time to "chasing bad guys."

Police Functions
and Duties

2. *Perform welfare tasks*—throughout history, the police have probably done much more of this type of work than the public (or the police themselves) realize; following are some of them:

   • "Check the welfare of" kinds of calls, where someone has not been seen or heard from for some time and may be either deceased, ill, missing, or in distress

   • "Be on the lookout" (BOLO) calls, where someone has wandered away from a nursing or an assisted living home, is a juvenile runaway, and so forth

   • Delivering death messages

   • Delivering blood to hospitals (particularly in more rural areas where blood banks are not available)

   • Assisting firefighters and animal control units

   • Reporting burned-out street lights or damaged traffic signs

   • Performing all manner of errands simply because they are available—locking and unlocking municipal parking lots, collecting receipts from municipal entities such as golf courses, delivering agendas to city/county commissioners, and so forth

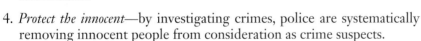

As opposed to Hollywood's portrayals, very little police work is action-packed; these officers are, by their mere presence, preventing crime and assisting with crowd control at a street fair.

3. *Prevent crime*—this function of police involves engaging in random patrol and providing the public with crime prevention information.

4. *Protect the innocent*—by investigating crimes, police are systematically removing innocent people from consideration as crime suspects.

Three Distinctive Styles

James Q. Wilson also attempted to clarify what it is that the police are supposed to do; Wilson maintained that there are three distinctive **policing styles**[13]:

1. The *watchman* style involves the officer as a "neighbor." Here, officers act as if order maintenance (rather than law enforcement) is their primary function. The emphasis is on using the law as a means of maintaining order rather than regulating conduct through arrests. Police ignore many common minor violations, such as traffic and juvenile offenses. These violations and so-called victimless crimes, such as gambling and prostitution, are tolerated; they will often be handled informally. Thus the individual officer has wide latitude concerning whether to enforce the letter or the spirit of the law; the emphasis is on using the law to give people what they "deserve."

Tasks of policing (four basic): enforce the law, prevent crime, protect the innocent, and perform welfare tasks.

Policing styles: James Q. Wilson argued that there are three styles of policing: watchman, legalistic, and service.

2. The *legalistic* style casts the officer as a "soldier." This style takes a much harsher view of law violations. Police officers issue large numbers of traffic citations, detain a high volume of juvenile offenders, and act vigorously against illicit activities. Large numbers of other kinds of arrests occur as well. Chief administrators want high arrest and ticketing rates not only because violators should be punished but also because it reduces the opportunity for their officers to engage in corrupt behavior. This style of policing assumes that the purpose of the law is to punish.

3. The *service* style views the officer as a "teacher." This style falls in between the watchman and legalistic styles. The police take seriously all requests for either law enforcement or order maintenance (unlike in the watchman-style department) but are less likely to respond by making an arrest or otherwise imposing formal sanctions. Police officers see their primary responsibility as protecting public order against the minor and occasional threats posed by unruly teenagers and "outsiders" (tramps, derelicts, out-of-town visitors). The citizenry expects its service-style officers to display the same qualities as its department store salespeople: They should be courteous, neat, and deferential. The police will frequently use informal sanctions instead of making arrests.

Mid-Chapter Quiz:
Police at Work

Perils of Patrol

Although several occupations—commercial fishing, logging, piloting airplanes, farming, and ranching in particular—have workers dying at much higher rates than policing,[14] police officers' lives are still rife with

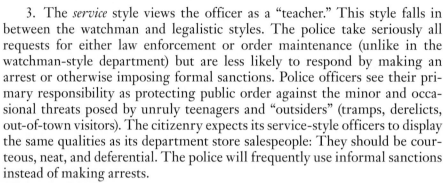

SAUDI ARABIA: LITTLE TO DO ON PATROL

The police in Saudi Arabia assist with enforcing the very cruel (by Western standards) Islamic law, which is governed by the Koran and can include amputations of limbs, which are conducted in many cities and with some frequency on the Justice Square in Riyadh. Believing that public beheadings and amputations deter other prospective offenders, people in the vicinity of the square are encouraged by the police to witness these events. When a thief's right hand is cut off in public, a string is tied to the middle finger and the hand is hung from a hook high on a streetlight pole on Justice Square for all to see. Because there is a near total absence on Saudi Arabian streets of gangs, drive-by shootings, purse snatchings, and contraband, the police patrol the streets in Chevrolets, BMWs, and Volvos, looking for minor infractions of the law.[15]

Owing to the aforementioned harsh criminal code, there is little for the Saudi police to do in

terms of crime prevention or investigation. The religious police—the *Mutawin*—patrol and stroll in their white cotton robes and sandals and look, as one writer observed, like "desert nomads who have stumbled unexpectedly into the 20th century." They look for people who are improperly dressed or women who have a loose strand of hair falling across their face or who need to adjust their *tarhas* (head coverings). Around-the-clock patrols ensure that shops are closed in time for daily prayers and that only married couples are sitting in family sections of restaurants. The patrols often follow persons suspected of being involved in what is deemed immoral behavior, such as drug use, homosexuality, gambling, and begging. Teams of religious police will also destroy home satellite dishes, which bring uncensored Western television broadcasts into Saudi homes.[16]

occupational hazards. Each year, about 70 police officers die through felonious means; the average age of the slain officers is about 38 years, they had worked in law enforcement for about 12 years, and about two-thirds were assigned to patrol duties. Another 50 or so officers die through accidental means.[17] Officers seldom know for certain whether a citizen whom they are about to confront is armed, high on drugs or alcohol, or perhaps even planning to die at the hands of the police using a technique known as "suicide by cop." This danger is heightened during the graveyard (night) shift, when patrol officers encounter burglars looking to invade homes and businesses, people who are intoxicated from a night of partying, and so on, all under cover of darkness.

By its nature, policing carries a high potential for danger; this funeral procession escorts an officer who was killed during routine traffic stop.

A STUDY OF PATROL EFFECTIVENESS

The best known study of patrol efficiency, the Kansas City Preventive Patrol Experiment, was conducted in Kansas City, Missouri, in 1973. Researchers—wanting to know if random patrol had any significant effect on crime, police response rates to crime, or citizen fear of crime—divided the city into 15 beats, which were then categorized into 5 groups of 3 matched beats each. Each group consisted of neighborhoods that were similar in terms of population, crime characteristics, and calls for police services. In one beat area, there was no preventive patrol (police only responded to calls for service); another beat area had increased patrol activity (2 or 3 times the usual amount of patrolling); in the third beat there was the usual level of patrol service. Citizens were interviewed and crime rates were measured during the year the experiment was conducted.

The study found that the deterrent effect of policing was not reduced by the elimination of routine patrolling; nor were citizens' fear of crime, their attitudes toward the police, or the ability of the police to respond to calls reduced. The Kansas City Preventive Patrol Experiment (depicted in Figure 6.2) indicated that the traditional assumption of "Give me more cars and more money, and we'll get there faster and fight crime" was probably not a very viable argument.[18]

THE TRAFFIC FUNCTION

No one enjoys being on the receiving end of a traffic citation, but traffic hazards (especially drunk or texting drivers) pose a major problem, and thus traffic control is part of the police role. Indeed, traffic stops account for about half (52 percent) of the contact Americans have with the police.[19] Citizens are often unhappy about having to pay a traffic fine or possibly go to court, and may verbally

FIGURE 6.2

Schematic Representation of the Kansas City Preventive Patrol Experiment

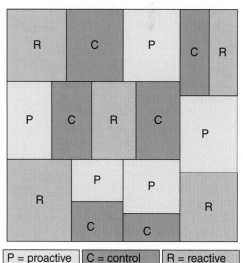

| P = proactive | C = control | R = reactive |

Source: George L. Kelling, Tony Pate, Duane Dieckman, and Charles E. Brown, The Kansas City Preventative Patrol Experiment: A Summary Report. Washington, DC: Police Foundation, 1974. Reprinted with permission of the Police Foundation.

PRACTITIONER'S PERSPECTIVE

PATROL OFFICER

Name: Tony Moore
Current position: Drug Interdiction Task Force Detective
City, state: Reno, Nevada
College attended/ academic major: University of Nevada, Reno/BA, criminal justice
Most significant career achievement: Selected by peers for the distinguished rank of Master Police Officer.

How long have you been a practitioner in the criminal justice system?

17 years (6 years as patrol officer, 10 years as gang officer and detective, 1 year as drug interdiction detective)

My primary duties and responsibilities as a patrol officer include:

Generally, providing safety for the public. As a citizen, I expect the same from my police. Also, the patrol officer is the first responder to every emergency, ranging from something very minor (such as a stalled vehicle) to rescuing children and adults from violent attacks, in-progress felonies, or burning buildings and vehicles.

With every response or arrest comes responsibility for making the right decisions. The patrol officer must know applicable laws and procedures so the correct actions are taken and decisions made. Bad decisions or inappropriate actions can lead to civil liability, departmental discipline, or the officer or another person being injured or killed.

Proactive policing is another aspect of the patrol officer's role. The officer must address problems and crime trends in his or her area, including traffic enforcement, drug activity, warrant arrests, gang activity, or investigations that extend beyond merely taking a crime report.

In addition, problem solving is the patrol officer's responsibility. Arrests are not the only solutions to neighborhood problems, so officers must understand crime theories and study crime trends, environmental factors leading to crime, and so on—while also using community resources such as residents, businesses, schools, hospitals, the news media, and treatment programs.

Although about one-third of my career has been as a patrol officer, that was my most influential assignment. The patrol function is where officers learn a style of policing; accumulate the basic skills to be a safe, productive, and effective officer; and develop the skills for accomplishing the above tasks as well as for more specialized assignments. Even interviewing skills are learned while working the street.

The qualities/characteristics that are most helpful for a patrol officer include:

Integrity, good decision making skills, the desire to work, and the physical ability to perform. Integrity is absolutely essential, as it guides the officer to make good decisions, especially under difficult circumstances.

Good decision-making skills are necessary for making dozens or hundreds of critical decisions daily. These decisions affect people, and involve criminal procedures and laws, safety concerns, civil liability, and departmental guidelines. Not every situation and decision the patrol officer is faced with is covered by clearly defined standards or laws, so the ability to effectively use discretion is an essential element of good decision making.

Anyone can learn a skill or information, but the desire and drive to work is far more valuable. A very knowledgeable officer who chooses not to fully apply his or her skills is far less effective and productive and useful than a less skilled officer who works hard.

Remaining physically fit will also prepare one for a long career in law enforcement. This is essential because, inevitably, the officer will be involved in fights with suspects, foot pursuits, climbing over fences, lifting arrestees, and performing searches.

In general, a typical day for a patrol officer would include:

A shift briefing at the outset, where the previous day's or shift's significant events are discussed, and might include short training segments, discussions of crime trends and persons of interest, and departmental business. Once the patrol officer is in service, he or she will first respond to any high-priority calls for service (e.g., a traffic accident with injuries, an escalating domestic disturbance, a burglary in progress, a bank robbery, a fight, a shooting, a missing child, or a suicidal subject), and then may assist the officers still on calls from the previous shift. Then the officer will respond to lower-priority calls, such as "cold" burglary or larceny reports, traffic problems, graffiti reports, tenant/landlord civil disputes, or shoplifting cases. From there, a wide variety of occurrences is possible (i.e., there is no "typical" day): The day may begin in a calm and structured manner, and then become very chaotic. For example, while completing a crime report, the officer might be sent across town to assist other officers in a fight, then immediately go to another area for a violent domestic dispute, and then go assist the fire department—all in the span of an hour or so.

As indicated above, the patrol officer must also designate time for proactive policing and problem solving. Patrol officers are also expected to be extremely familiar with their assigned areas and the people within them.

Developing communication skills is also important, as most reported crimes or significant actions taken by the patrol officer will be documented through official reporting. Paperwork is often a very unpopular, time-consuming task, and reports are plentiful, but they are important, are expected to be accurate and detailed, and must typically be completed before the end of the shift.

My advice to someone either wishing to study, or now studying, criminal justice to become a practitioner in this career field would be:

To be certain that you want to be a police officer and are willing to begin working in patrol. While very rewarding, the patrol officer's role is inherently dangerous, is at times quite stressful and difficult, and involves great successes and terrible tragedies. If you cannot function in this environment, then you may want to consider a different career.

Also, you should become familiar with every aspect of policing and patrol assignments. My education was instrumental in preparing me for employment with my department. In addition to providing me with an overall education and view into the criminal justice system, I took opportunities for internships at different agencies that afforded firsthand experience, and also helped me to identify the department that was most desirable to me. This is a good means of preparing for patrol work and policing prior to entering the academy. The educational resources, literature, and training opportunities that you can use prior to being hired are endless.

Finally, identify those patrol officers and law enforcement practitioners who are successful, and apply the traits and skills that make them successful. Surround yourself with others like you who want to have a successful career. Be a positive example for your peers, and know that your actions and attitudes are contagious. And never compromise your integrity.

express their displeasure: "You should be out catching bank robbers," "I'm a taxpayer, and I pay your salary," or "I know the police chief!" Because this traffic encounter may be the citizen's one and only contact with a police officer, the officer's display of a professional and courteous demeanor may well have long-term significance for community policing, and strict traffic enforcement policies can also negatively impact police-community relations.[20]

By trying to enforce traffic laws and investigating traffic collisions, the police endeavor to reduce traffic deaths and injuries and generally make vehicular travel safer; on its face, this is a noble undertaking. In this era of accountability and litigation—and the vast amounts of damage done to people and property each year as a result of traffic accidents—it is essential that officers competently investigate traffic collisions and cite the guilty party, not only from a law enforcement standpoint but also in the event that the matter is taken to civil court.

One of the **traffic functions** for which the police receive public support is in their efforts to identify, apprehend, and convict the hit-and-run (or "phantom") driver. No one thinks highly of these offenders—who are often intoxicated—who collide with another innocent party's vehicle or strike a pedestrian and then leave the scene. In fact, this matter quickly becomes more of a criminal investigation than a mere collision investigation for the police. In most states, the killing of a human being by someone driving under the influence (DUI) is a felony. Physical evidence and witness statements must be collected in the same fashion as in a conventional criminal investigation; paint samples and automobile parts left at the scene are sent to crime laboratories for examination. The problem for the police is that unless the driver of the vehicle is identified—by physical evidence, an eyewitness, or a confession—the case can be lost.

As will be seen in Chapter 7, the police traffic function also carries tremendous potential for liability, particularly in the area of high-speed pursuits; examples are provided in that chapter.

POLICE DISCRETION

The power to use **discretion** in performing one's role is at the very core of policing. However, as will be seen below, this power can be controversial—and used for both good and bad.

The Myth of Full Enforcement

The municipal police chief or county sheriff is asked during a civic club luncheon speech which laws are and are not enforced by his or her agency. The official response will inevitably be that *all* of the laws are enforced equally, all of the time. Yet the chief and sheriff know that full enforcement of the laws is a myth—that there are neither the resources nor the desire to enforce them all, nor are all laws enforced impartially. There are legal concerns as well. For example, releasing some offenders (to get information about other crimes, because of a good excuse, etc.) cannot be the official policy of the agency (and letting an offender go is a form of discretion as well); however, the chief or sheriff cannot broadcast that fact to the public. Indeed, it has been stated that "the single most astonishing fact of police behavior is the extent to which police do *not* enforce the law when they have every legal right to do so."[21]

Attempts to Define Discretion

The way police make arrest decisions is largely unknown (see possible determining factors, below). What *is* known, however, is that when police observe something of a suspicious or an illegal nature, two important decisions must be made: (1) whether to intervene in the situation and (2) how to intervene. The kinds, number, and possible combinations of interventions are virtually limitless. What kinds of decisions are available for an officer who makes a routine traffic stop? David Bayley and Egon Bittner observed long ago that officers have as many as 10 actions to select from at the initial stop (for example, order the driver out of the car), 7 strategies appropriate during the stop (such as a roadside sobriety test), and 11 exit strategies (for instance, releasing the driver with a warning), representing a total of 770 different combinations of actions that might be taken![22]

Criminal law has two sides—the formality and the reality. The formality is found in the statute books and opinions of appellate courts. The reality is found in the practices of enforcement officers. In some circumstances, the choice of action to be taken is relatively easy, such as arresting a bank robbery suspect. In other situations, such as quelling a dispute between neighbors or determining how much party noise is too much, the choice is more difficult.[23]

Our system tends to treat people as individuals. One person who commits a robbery is not the same as another person who commits a robbery. Our system also

Author Video: Discretion

Traffic function: the aggregate of motor vehicles, pedestrians, streets, and highways, for which police must investigate and apply laws to provide safe travels for citizens in their jurisdiction.

Discretion: authority to make decisions in enforcing the law based on one's observations and judgment ("spirit of the law") rather than the letter of the law.

Although at times very unpopular with the public, the police function includes enforcing traffic laws and investigating traffic collisions, to reduce traffic deaths and injuries and to make streets and highways safer.

takes into account why and how a person committed a crime (his or her intent, or *mens rea*, discussed in Chapter 2). The most important decisions take place on the streets, day or night, generally without the opportunity for the officer to consult with others or to carefully consider all the facts.

Determinants of Discretionary Actions

The power of discretionary policing can be awe-inspiring. Kenneth Culp Davis, an authority on police discretion, writes, "The police are among the most important policy makers of our entire society. And they make far more discretionary determinations in individual cases than does any other class of administrators; I know of no close second."[24]

Street-Level
Police Discretion

What determines whether the officer will take a stern approach (enforcing the letter of the law with an arrest) or will be lenient (issuing a verbal warning or some other outcome short of arrest)? Several variables enter into the officer's decision:

1. The *law* is indeed a factor. For example, many state statutes and local ordinances now mandate that the police arrest for certain suspected offenses, such as driving under the influence or domestic violence.

2. The *officer's attitude* can also be a factor. First, some officers are more willing to empathize with offenders who feel they deserve a break than others. Also, as Carl Klockars and Stephen Mastrofski observed, although violators frequently offer what they feel are very good reasons for the officer to overlook their offense, "every police officer knows that, if doing so will allow them to escape punishment, most people are prepared to lie through their teeth."[25] Furthermore, police, being human, can bring to work either a happy or an unhappy disposition. Personal viewpoints can also play a role; for example, perhaps the officer is fed up with juvenile crimes that have been occurring of late and thus will not give any leniency to youths he or she confronts who are involved in even minor crimes.

Discretion

3. Another major consideration in the officer's choice among options is the *citizen's* attitude. If the offender is rude and condescending, denies having done anything wrong, or uses some of the standard clichés that are almost guaranteed to rankle the officer—such as "You don't know who I am" (someone who is obviously very important in the community), "I'll have your job," "I know the chief of police," or "I'm a taxpayer, and I pay your salary"—the probable outcome is obvious. On the other hand, the person who is honest with the officer, avoids attempts at intimidation and sarcasm, and does not try to "beat the rap" may fare better.

Pros and Cons of Discretion

Having discretionary authority carries several advantages for the police officer: First, because the law cannot (and should not) cover every sort of situation the officer encounters, discretion allows the officer to have the flexibility to treat different situations in accordance with humanitarian and practical goals. For example, assume an officer pulls over a speeding motorist, only to learn that the car is en route to the hospital with a woman who is about to deliver a baby. While the agitated driver is endangering everyone in the vehicle as well as other motorists on the roadway, discretion allows the officer to be compassionate and empathetic, giving the car a safe escort to the hospital rather than issuing a citation for speeding. In short, discretionary use of authority allows the police to employ a philosophy of "justice tempered with mercy."

Lawful Policing

One disadvantage of discretionary authority is that those officers who are the least trained and experienced have the greatest amount of discretion to exercise. In other words, as the rank of the officer *increases*, the amount of discretion that he or she can employ normally *decreases*. The patrol officer or deputy, being loosely supervised on the streets, makes many discretionary decisions about whether or not to arrest, search, frisk, and so forth. Conversely, the chief of police or sheriff will be highly constrained by department policies and procedures, union agreements, affirmative-action laws, and/or governing board guidelines and policies. Another disadvantage is that allowing police to exercise such discretion belies their need to appear impartial—treating people differently for committing essentially the same offense. Critics of discretion also argue that such wide latitude in decision making may serve as a breeding ground for police corruption; for example, an officer may be offered a bribe to overlook an offense.

See the two case studies in the accompanying "You Be the Officer" box and respond to the questions posed for each of them.

COMMUNITY POLICING AND PROBLEM SOLVING

Community
Policing

Chapter 5 discussed the three eras of policing, which led to today's "community era." Following is a brief description of policing in terms of how it moved from the political and reform eras—both of which experienced problems in terms of recognizing and working with the community. The seeds of community policing and problem solving were sown in London in 1829, when the architect of London's police force, Sir Robert Peel, offered that "the police are the public and . . . the public are the police," and that by establishing patrol beats, officers could get to know their citizens and thus be better able to gather information about neighborhood crime and disorder. As was seen in Chapter 5, however, in the United States that close police-public association over time

you be the... OFFICER

POLICE DISCRETION

A. Assume a police officer pulls over a vehicle for swerving across the center line. The driver is a 17-year-old college student who is an elementary education major who admits she's been drinking at a party. The breathalyzer test reveals a .07 blood alcohol concentration. In this state, .07 can result in a charge of either "driving after having consumed alcohol" or a more serious "driving while ability is impaired." There are two other girls in the car: One has a badly swollen jaw after having fallen at the party; the driver is attempting to get her to the Urgent Care facility. Another girl, the older sister of the driver, is visibly pregnant.

1. What discretionary issues are presented? What discretionary options are presented? In the final analysis, how do you believe the officer should deal with the driver?

B. A flashpoint for many citizens is racial profiling— also known as biased policing—in which police appear to be pulling over drivers simply on the basis of their race. (Racial profiling began to loom as a major issue in policing in the early 2000s,

driving a deep wedge between the police and minorities, many of whom claimed to be victims of this practice. Indeed, a New Jersey state police executive was fired for statements that were perceived as racially insensitive concerning racial profiling.) Assume there have been a number of complaints against police for racial profiling in your city, and a number of minority groups are very vocal about wanting the situation stopped. At the same time, there has also been a serious problem of violent crimes being committed in shopping malls against jewelry salespeople delivering gems. Based on descriptions provided by victims and informant information, it appears the robbers are Colombians—not Latinos, African Americans, or other immigrants—and it seems a group of about a dozen Colombians is committing these crimes. Assume two police officers see four men who fit this physical description sitting in a car in front of a jewelry boutique and who appear to be closely watching people with briefcases.

2. How should the officers address this situation?[26]

often led to powerful political influences and corruption (in terms of who was hired, who was promoted, and who could bring elected officials the most votes), which in turn led to the onset of the reform era in the 1930s (which attempted the removal of police from the community and political influence, the creation of civil service systems, and so forth). The community era of policing recognized that the public has a vested interest in addressing—as well as vital information concerning—neighborhood crime and disorder, and thus a return to Peel's principles were needed and the two entities should work hand in glove to resolve problems.

Problem-oriented policing, which began to develop in the mid-1980s, was grounded in principles different from, but complementary to, those of community-oriented policing. Problem-oriented policing is a strategy that puts the community policing philosophy into practice. It advocates that police examine the underlying causes of recurring incidents of crime and disorder. The problem-solving process helps officers to identify problems, analyze them completely, develop response strategies, and assess the results. Police must be equipped to define more clearly and to understand more fully the problems they are expected to handle. They must recognize the relationships between and among incidents—for example, incidents involving the same behavior, the same address, or the same people. The police must therefore develop a commitment to analyzing problems—gathering information from police files, the minds of experienced officers, other agencies of government, and private sources as well. It can also require conducting house-to-house surveys and talking with victims, complainants, and offenders. It includes an uninhibited search for the most effective response to each problem, looking beyond just the criminal justice system to a wide range of alternatives; in sum, police must try to design a customized response that holds the greatest potential for dealing effectively with a specific problem in a specific place under specific conditions.

Community Policing

Thousands of police agencies have thus broken away from their reactive, incident-driven methods that characterized the reform era—where police would race from call to call, take an offense report, and leave the scene without seeking any resolution to problems or achieving any long-term benefits. This change in philosophy and strategies goes far beyond merely creating a "crime prevention specialist" position, a "community relations unit," a foot or bicycle patrol, or a neighborhood mini-station. Today, community-oriented policing and problem solving involves radical changes in police organizational culture and structures, management styles, and external relationships. It requires a cultural transformation within the entire police agency, involving changes in recruiting, training, awards systems, evaluation, and promotions. New technologies have also been designed to help effect this transition, while personnel training, evaluation, and reward systems have been altered to fit this philosophy. At its core, this approach fosters more long-term, thoughtful crime control and prevention strategies.

Finally, what every criminal justice employee knows is that there are three

As part of their community policing and problem solving efforts, many agencies use bicycle patrols to focus on crime prevention and greater interaction with the community.

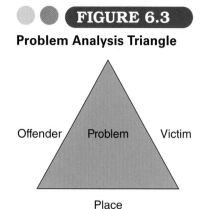

FIGURE 6.3

Problem Analysis Triangle

Offender   Problem   Victim

Place

elements that must exist in order for a crime to occur: an offender, a victim, and a location, as shown in Figure 6.3, the problem analysis triangle. The triangle helps officers visualize the problem and understand the relationship between these three elements. Additionally, it helps officers to analyze problems, it suggests where more information is needed, and it assists with crime control and prevention. Simply put, if there is a victim and he or she is in a place where crimes occur but there is no offender, no crime occurs. If there is an offender and he or she is in a place where crimes occur but there is nothing or no one to be victimized, then no crime will occur. If an offender and a victim are not in the same place, there will be no crime. Part of the analysis phase involves finding out as much as possible about the victims, offenders, and locations where problems exist in order to understand what is prompting the problem and what can be done about it.

FOCUS ON   COMMUNITY POLICING AND PROBLEM SOLVING

In the following scenario, compare how the police would have handled the problem using traditional methods versus the contemporary community-oriented policing and problem-solving approach. In the latter, the police use what is termed the SARA problem-solving process (see Figure 6.4), which is composed of the following four steps: scanning (officers first identify a problem and look for a pattern or persistent repeat incidents), analysis (here, officers thoroughly examine the nature and causes of the problem in order to identify possible responses), response (the officer develops creative solutions that will address the problem), and assessment (later, officers look at the problem and neighborhood to see if their responses were effective, examining such indicators as numbers of reported crimes, calls for service to the area, and citizen fear of crime).

In a relatively quiet neighborhood, police have recently had to respond to a series of disturbances. All of the disturbances—loud music, fighting, screeching tires, people displaying lewd behavior on and near the premises—appear to be related to a recently opened live-music dance club. In a month's time, police officers have been sent to the club to restore order on more than 50 occasions. Under the traditional policing model, typically the swing (evening) shift officers would respond to the club and restore order for a short period of time; later, graveyard (night) shift officers often would have to return to the club to again restore calm. Usually when officers arrive, however, the offenders are already gone, so a report is taken, and the officer leaves. This problem—with police basically showing up, taking a disturbance or noise complaint report, and leaving—persists for months on end.

Under the community policing and problem-solving approach, however, following are examples of activities that might occur toward getting the problem resolved. First, information is gathered concerning possible zoning and health department violations. Officers arrange a meeting with the club manager/operator and representatives from the city's business licensing division, during which the consequences for continued problems are explained. This also results in the manager's removal of an unsavory employee and his "following" of drug users and other undesirable characters at the club. The hours of the club's live music are limited, and the manager and employees are trained in relevant sections of the municipal code covering disturbing the peace, minors in liquor establishments, trespassing laws, disorderly behaviors, and so on. The officers also arrange a meeting with the club's landlord, who agrees to install more lights in the parking lots and a "sound wall" around the business to buffer the area residents. A later assessment reveals that a reduction in call for service in the area was realized, and area residents, although not entirely happy with the continuing existence of the business, acknowledged satisfaction from their complaints; no further newspaper stories appeared regarding the noise and disorder in the neighborhood.

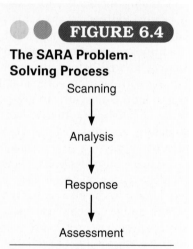

FIGURE 6.4

The SARA Problem-Solving Process

Scanning

↓

Analysis

↓

Response

↓

Assessment

Source: John E. Eck and William Spelman, Problem-Solving: *Problem-Oriented Policing in Newport News* (Washington, D.C.: U.S. Department of Justice, National Institute of Justice, 1987), p. 43.

THE WORK OF FORENSICS AND DETECTIVES

The challenges involved with investigating crimes may well be characterized by a quote from Ludwig Wittgenstein: "How hard I find it to see what is right in front of my eyes!"[27] Certainly the art of sleuthing has long fascinated the American public; furthermore, the expanding uses of DNA in the news and such television series as *CSI: Crime Scene Investigation* have done much to capture the public's fascination with criminal investigation and forensic science in the 21st century. This interest in "sleuthing" is not a recent phenomenon, however; for decades, Americans have feasted on the exploits of dozens of fictional masterminds, like Sherlock Holmes, Agatha Christie's Hercule Poirot and Miss Marple, Clint Eastwood's portrayal of Detective "Dirty Harry" Callahan, and Peter Falk's Columbo, to name a few.

In reality, investigative work is largely misunderstood, often boring, and generally overrated; it results in arrests only a fraction of the time; and it relies strongly on the assistance of witnesses and even some luck.

Forensic Technology

Evidence

Forensic Science and Criminalistics: Defining the Terms

The terms *forensic science* and *criminalistics* are often used interchangeably. **Forensic science** is the broader term; it is that part of science used to answer legal questions. It is the examination, evaluation, and explanation of physical evidence in law. Forensic science encompasses pathology, toxicology, physical anthropology, odontology (development of dental structure and dental diseases), psychiatry, questioned documents, ballistics, tool work comparison, and serology (the reactions and properties of serums), among other fields.[28]

Criminalistics is one branch of forensic science; it deals with the study of physical evidence related to crime. From such a study, a crime may be reconstructed. Criminalistics is interdisciplinary, drawing on mathematics, physics, chemistry, biology, anthropology, and many other scientific fields.[29]

Basically, the analysis of physical evidence is concerned with identifying traces of evidence, reconstructing criminal acts, and establishing a common origin of samples of evidence. The types of information that physical evidence can provide are as follows[30]:

- Information on the *corpus delicti* (or "body of the crime") is physical evidence showing that a crime was committed, such as tool marks, a broken door or window, a ransacked home, and missing valuables in a burglary or a victim's blood, a weapon, and torn clothing in an assault.

- Information on the *modus operandi* (or method of operation) is physical evidence showing means used by the criminal to gain entry, tools that were used, types of items taken, and other signs—items left at the scene, an accelerant used at an arson scene, the way crimes are committed, and so forth.

- *Linking a suspect with a victim* is one of the most important linkages, particularly with violent crimes. It includes hair,

Forensic science: the study of causes of crimes, deaths, and crime scenes.

Criminalist: a police crime scene analyst or laboratory examiner skilled in criminalistics or forensics aspects of investigation.

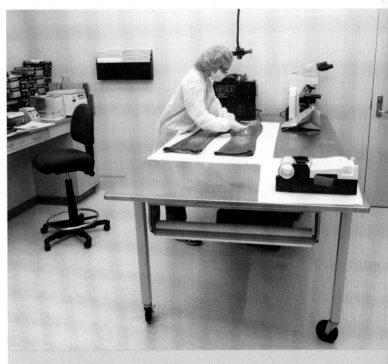

Forensic scientists examine of all kinds of articles and substances in their search for physical evidence that will link persons to their crimes.

blood, clothing fibers, and cosmetics that may be transferred from victim to perpetrator. Items found in a suspect's possession, such as bullets or a bloody knife, can also be linked to a victim.

- *Linking a person to a crime scene* is also a common and significant linkage. It includes fingerprints, glove prints, blood, semen, hairs, fibers, soil, bullets, cartridge cases, tool marks, footprints or shoeprints, tire tracks, and objects that belonged to the criminal. Stolen property is the most obvious example.

- In terms of *disproving or supporting a witness's testimony*, evidence can indicate whether or not a person's version of events is true. An example is a driver whose car matches the description of a hit-and-run vehicle. If blood is found on the underside of the car and the driver claims that he hit a dog, tests on the blood can determine whether the blood is from an animal or from a human.

- One of the best forms of evidence for *identification of a suspect* is DNA evidence, which proves "individualization." Without a doubt, that person was at the crime scene.

Investigative Stages and Activities

The police, more specifically investigators and criminalists, operate on the age-old theory that there is no such thing as a perfect crime; criminals either leave a bit of themselves or take something away from the crime scene. This is termed **Locard's exchange principle**, which asserts that when any person comes into contact with an object or another person, a cross-transfer of evidence—in the form of fingerprints, hairs, fibers, and all manner of residue or other materials—will occur.[31] An example is when a victim is strangled to death (by an assailant who is not wearing gloves), the suspect may well have the victim's skin cells under his nails, the victim's hair on his clothing, and other such residual material on his person. In the apprehension process, when a crime is reported or discovered, police officers respond, conduct a search for the offender, and check out suspects. If the search is successful, evidence for charging the suspect is assembled, and the suspect is apprehended.[32] Cases not solved in the initial phase of the apprehension process are assigned either to an investigative specialist or, in smaller police agencies, to an experienced uniformed officer who functions as a part-time investigator. Following are the basic investigative stages[33]:

- *The preliminary investigation:* Duties include establishing whether a crime has been committed; securing from any witnesses a description of the perpetrator and his or her vehicle; locating and interviewing the victim and all witnesses; protecting the crime scene (and searching for and collecting all items of possible physical evidence); determining how the crime

Investigative Interviewing

Locard's exchange principle: the notion that offenders both leave something at the crime scene and take something from it; the crime scene analyst or investigator's job is to locate that evidence and use it in the investigation.

Fingerprint identification has been used since the late 19th century to identify both crime suspects and victims.

was committed and what the resulting injuries were, as well as the nature of property taken; recording in field notes and sketches all data about the crime; and arranging for photographs of the crime scene.

- *The continuing investigation:* This stage includes follow-up interviews; developing a theory of the crime; analyzing the significance of information and evidence; continuing the search for witnesses; beginning to contact crime lab technicians and assessing their analyses of the evidence; conducting surveillances, interrogations, and polygraph tests, as appropriate; and preparing the case for the prosecutor.

- *Reconstructing the crime:* The investigator seeks a rational theory of the crime. Most often, inductive reasoning is used: The collected information and evidence are carefully analyzed to develop a theory. One of the major traits of criminals is vanity; their belief in their own cleverness, not chance, is the key factor in their leaving a vital clue. Investigators look for mistakes.

- *Focusing the investigation:* When this stage is reached, all investigative efforts are directed toward proving that one suspect (perhaps with accomplices) is guilty of the crime. This decision is based on the investigator's analysis of the relationship between the crime, the investigation, and the habits and attitudes of the suspect.

 CSI Effect

 Forensic Science

Myths and Attributes of Detectives

Detectives/investigators are members of police agencies who investigate crimes by obtaining evidence and information relating to illegal activities; furthermore, by extension—and what is often overlooked in their role—they ultimately present in court the findings of their investigation. To be effective, detectives must be trained in such general areas as the laws of arrest, search, and seizure; investigative principles and practices; judicial proceedings; and oral and written communications. More specialized training will often be required if individuals are specializing in such areas as sex crimes, family crimes, homicide investigation, and gang and drug enforcement.

Several myths surround police detectives, who are often portrayed in movies as rugged, confident (sometimes overbearing), independent, streetwise individualists who bask in glory, are rewarded with big arrests, and are adorned by beautiful women. In reality, detective work

Detective/investigator: a police officer who is assigned to investigate reported crimes, to include gathering evidence, completing case reports, testifying in court, and so on.

you be the... DETECTIVE

SUICIDE OR MURDER?

As the coach opened the door to the locker room, the only light that shone was from the players' large shower area. Upon flipping the light switch, he saw the body of his once "ace" pitcher, Hines, lying on the floor in the shower. In his pale left hand he held a gun. There was a bullet wound in his left temple. Under his tanned right hand was a note saying "My pitching days are gone, my debts and humiliation more than I can bear. Sorry." His nearby locker contained a half-empty bottle of beer, his uniform, an uneaten stadium hot dog, a picture of his two children, and his Acme-brand ball glove with "RH" stamped in the webbing. Wet footprints were observed walking in and out of the shower. Upon surveying the scene, the responding detective said "I do not believe this was a suicide."

1. What fact(s) led to this conclusion?

Police detectives must be skilled interviewers; this detective is interviewing college students after a gunman opened fire at a college in California.

is seldom glamorous or exciting. Investigators, like their bureaucratic cousins, often wade in paperwork and spend many hours on the telephone. Furthermore, studies have not been kind to detectives, showing that their vaunted productivity is overrated. Not all cases have a good or even a 50-50 chance of being cleared by an arrest. Indeed, in a study of over 150 large police departments, a RAND research team learned that only about 20 percent of their crimes could have been solved by detective work.[34] Another study, involving the Kansas City Police Department, found that fewer than 50 percent of all reported crimes received more than a minimal half-hour's investigation by detectives. In many of these cases, detectives merely reported the facts discovered by the patrol officers during the preliminary investigations.[35]

Yet the importance and role of detectives should not be understated. Detectives know that a criminal is more than a criminal. As Paul Weston and Kenneth Wells said,

John, Jane and Richard are not just burglar, prostitute and killer. John is a hostile burglar and is willing to enter a premises that might be occupied. Jane is a prostitute who wants a little more than pay for services rendered and is suspected of working with a robbery gang and enticing her customers to secluded areas. Richard is an accidental, a person who, in a fit of rage, killed the girl who rejected him.[36]

FOCUS ON   THE "CSI EFFECT"

Television programs focusing on criminal investigations and forensic techniques may be creating unrealistic courtroom expectations among jurors that cannot be achieved in real life. This phenomenon has been labeled the "CSI effect." Some court officers believe this "effect" is truly present: Prosecutors indicate that jurors want to see all evidence subjected to substantial forensic examination, whether warranted in a specific case or not, while some defense attorneys believe that jurors deem all scientific evidence to be flawless and thus establish guilt. The *voir dire* jury selection process may also be altered to ensure that those jurors who are unduly influenced by shows like *CSI* are screened from jury service. Such modifications to the usual process could result in longer trials and increased use of expert witnesses to aid the jury in understanding the presence or absence of physical evidence.[37]

A survey of Kentucky circuit court judges found that the impact has been strong—but not in areas

where one might expect. First, three-fourths of the judges indicated that jurors have come to expect more forensic evidence; furthermore, 82 percent of the judges believed that "shows like *CSI* have distorted the public's perception of time needed to obtain forensic results." In that same connection, a slight majority (53.4 percent) believed that the popularity of shows like *CSI* has made it harder to convict defendants. The responding judges also perceived that these television programs create unrealistic representations concerning the state of the forensic art in their jurisdiction, as well as the speed of forensic testing.[38]

In one Illinois case, jurors acquitted the defendant of a rape charge—even when presented with DNA evidence and strong testimony from the victim and an emergency room nurse—because no test was performed to see if "debris" found in the victim matched soil from the park where the crime occurred.[39]

To be successful, the investigator must possess four personal attributes to enhance the detection of crime: an unusual capability for observation and recall; extensive knowledge of the law, rules of evidence, scientific aids, and laboratory services; power of imagination; and a working knowledge of social psychology.[40] Successful detectives (and even patrol officers) also appear to empathize with the suspect; if a detective can appear to understand why a criminal did what he did, a rapport is often established that results in the suspect's telling the officer his or her life history—including how and why he or she committed the crime in question. Perhaps first and foremost, however, detectives need logical skills, the ability to exercise deductive reasoning, to assist in their investigative work.

Using DNA Analysis

Today **DNA** is the most sophisticated and reliable type of physical evidence (see Figure 6.5); police are now able to submit to laboratories work that until recently was not even possible to examine: "touch" evidence, utilizing DNA analysis to see whether a defendant even touched a

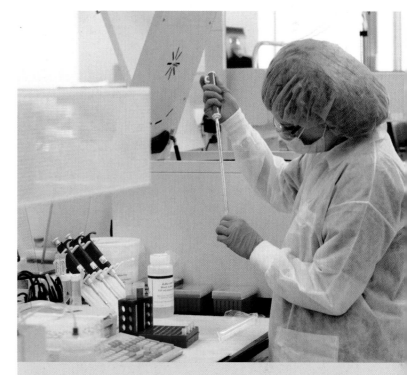

Today the power of what can be done with DNA, as well its variety of uses, is incredible.

FIGURE 6.5

"What Is DNA?"

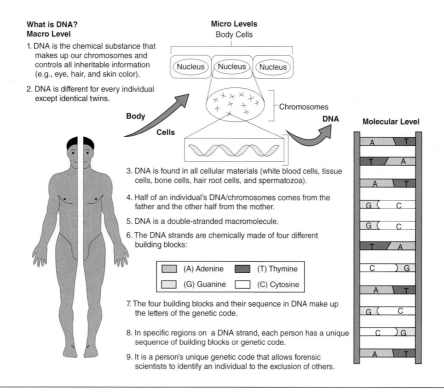

What is DNA?
Macro Level

1. DNA is the chemical substance that makes up our chromosomes and controls all inheritable information (e.g., eye, hair, and skin color).

2. DNA is different for every individual except identical twins.

Micro Levels
Body Cells

Nucleus   Nucleus   Nucleus

Chromosomes

Body
Cells

DNA

Molecular Level

3. DNA is found in all cellular materials (white blood cells, tissue cells, bone cells, hair root cells, and spermatozoa).

4. Half of an individual's DNA/chromosomes comes from the father and the other half from the mother.

5. DNA is a double-stranded macromolecule.

6. The DNA strands are chemically made of four different building blocks:

| (A) Adenine | (T) Thymine |
| (G) Guanine | (C) Cytosine |

7. The four building blocks and their sequence in DNA make up the letters of the genetic code.

8. In specific regions on a DNA strand, each person has a unique sequence of building blocks or genetic code.

9. It is a person's unique genetic code that allows forensic scientists to identify an individual to the exclusion of others.

Chapter Quiz:
Police at Work

weapon; DNA evidence from steering wheels; finding drugs on the floor of a room and analyzing them to determine which hand threw them down on the floor.[41]

A testimonial of DNA's promise in investigations is offered by a former supervising criminalist of the Los Angeles County Sheriff's Department:

> The power of what we can look for and analyze now is incredible. It's like magic. Every day we discover evidence where we never thought it would be. You almost can't do anything without leaving some DNA around. DNA takes longer than fingerprints to analyze, but you get a really big bang for your buck.[42]

DNA: deoxyribonucleic acid, or the acids found in all cells; used in forensics to match evidence (hair, semen) left at a crime scene with a particular perpetrator.

Furthermore, DNA has allowed investigative personnel to exonerate people who were convicted in the past for crimes they did not commit. Indeed, in April 2007 it was reported that the 200th person—a former Army cook who spent nearly 25 years in prison for a rape he did not commit—was exonerated by DNA evidence (the 100th exoneration since January 2002).[43]

PRACTITIONER'S PERSPECTIVE

FORENSIC SCIENTIST (CRIMINALIST)

Name: Renee Romero
Current position: Director, Forensic Science Division, Washoe County Sheriff's Office
City, state: Reno, Nevada
College attended/ academic major: Michigan State University/BA, chemistry, forensic science; University of Nevada, Reno/ MS, cell and molecular biology

How long have you been a practitioner in this criminal justice position? Since 1989—24 years

My primary duties and responsibilities as a practitioner in this position are:

Being responsible for the management of the Forensic Science Division at the Sheriff's Office. This entails managing budgets, planning for future forensic technology changes, and ensuring we are meeting our accreditation standards. Prior to becoming the director in 2008, I was a practicing forensic scientist (criminalist). While I have limited controlled substances experience, the majority of my experience is in the DNA field. The primary duty of a forensic scientist is to examine evidence from criminal cases. This evidence can range from drugs, firearms, toxicology, and DNA to shoe prints, tire tracks impressions, and latent fingerprints. A forensic scientist usually specializes in one specific discipline. After examining the evidence the forensic scientist must issue the findings to the investigating agency and then work with the district attorney's office to prepare for expert testimony when the cases go to trial.

The qualities/characteristics that are most helpful for one in this career are: Attention to detail, organization, and excellent communication skills.

In general, a *typical day* for a practitioner in this career would include:

Spending time in the laboratory examining evidence, reviewing findings, and writing reports. The day may be interrupted with changing priorities based on the investigative needs of new cases as they arise.

My advice to someone either wishing to study, or now studying, criminal justice to become a practitioner in this career field would be:

To obtain a scientific degree. If you believe you are interested in toxicology or controlled substances, then work toward a chemistry degree. If you think you are interested in the DNA field, then work toward a molecular biology degree—and you must also earn college credits in genetics, molecular biology, and biochemistry. The field of forensic science is getting more competitive, so obtaining a master's degree would be beneficial as well.

- The idea of a police subculture was first proposed in 1950 by William Westley, who found a high degree of secrecy and violence.

- Recruit academy training covers a wide variety of subjects; neophyte officers learn how to use a variety of lethal and less lethal weapons, and how to deal with criminal suspects, offenders, victims, and witnesses; hands-on training and simulated situations are also employed.

- After leaving the academy, new officers are assigned to a veteran officer—a "field training officer"—for initial field instruction and observation; this phase of training helps recruits to make the transition from the academy to the streets under the protective arm of a veteran officer, while on probationary status.

- Jerome Skolnick said officers develop a working personality, and that the police role contains two important variables: danger and authority. Consequently, they develop a "perceptual shorthand" to identify certain kinds of people as "symbolic assailants"—those who pose a physical threat to them.

- John Broderick presented another view of the working personality of the police, believing that there are actually four types of police personalities: enforcers, idealists, realists, and optimists. Dennis Nowicki stated that honesty, ethics, and moral character make a highly effective officer, and offered 12 additional qualities for entry-level police officers.

- Police have four basic tasks: enforcing the laws, performing welfare tasks, preventing crimes, and protecting the innocent.

- James Q. Wilson maintained that there are three distinctive policing styles: the *watchman* style, the *legalistic* style, and the *service* style.

- Although several occupations have workers die at much higher rates than policing, this occupation still has many occupational hazards.

- The traffic function is an important part of policing; as officers enforce traffic laws and investigate traffic collisions, they attempt to reduce traffic deaths and injuries.

- Full enforcement of the laws by police is a myth; they typically have considerable discretion in whether or not to arrest someone. Determining factors include the law (e.g., some ordinances mandate arrest for certain offenses, such as domestic violence), the officer's attitude (concerning the law that is violated, as well as toward the offender), and the citizen's attitude toward the officer.

- Today, under the community policing philosophy, officers are trained to examine the underlying causes of problems in the neighborhoods on their beats and to involve citizens in the long-term resolution of neighborhood problems.

- The fields of forensic science and criminalistics are the most rapidly developing areas in policing—and probably in all of criminal justice.

- Several myths surround police detectives, who often perform mundane duties and are often unsuccessful in their search for the offender.

- DNA is the most sophisticated and reliable type of physical evidence and has resulted in hundreds of arrestees being exonerated.

Academy training
Criminalistics
Detective/investigator
Discretion
DNA
Field training officer (FTO)

Forensic science
Kansas City Preventive
  Patrol Experiment
Locard's exchange principle
Policing styles
"Sixth sense"

Tasks of policing (four basic)
Traffic function
Welfare tasks
Working personality

REVIEW QUESTIONS

1. What ideal traits are sought among those persons wishing to enter policing?

2. How are police recruits socialized into the police subculture while in academy training, and what are some topics that are studied by trainees while attending the academy?

3. What are the methods and purposes of the FTO concept?

4. What is meant by the working personality, how was the concept developed, and how does it function?

5. What traits or qualities are said to make a "good" officer?

6. What are the primary tasks and styles of policing?

7. How would you describe the activities that are involved in the police traffic function?

8. What examples can you provide of police use of discretion? What are some pros and cons of police use of discretionary authority?

9. What are the qualities, myths, and methods that tend to revolve around investigative personnel?

LEARN BY DOING

1. You are a patrol sergeant lecturing to your agency's Citizens' Police Academy about the patrol function. Someone asks: "Sergeant, your officers obviously can't enforce all of the laws all of the time. Which laws are always enforced, and which ones are not?" How do you respond to her (without saying something absurd like "We enforce all of the laws, all of the time," which of course would be untrue)? How would you fully explain police discretion to the group?

2. The "Crime & Investigation Network," based in the United Kingdom, advertises on its website that it "investigates the darker corners of human life" and "offers viewers stories of real life crime" that "open the door to real crime labs, police archives and courtrooms, allowing viewers to join detectives as they examine

evidence and piece together clues." You can access and participate in solving a number of different crimes at http://www.crimeandinvestigation.co.uk/games/solve-the-murder.html.

3. For a practical view of traffic problems and solutions, go to http://www.popcenter.org/problems/street_racing/ and/or go to http://www.popcenter.org/problems/drunk_driving/. These are guides published by the federal Center for Problem-Oriented Policing. Read and describe the kinds of problems that are caused by illegal street racing and/or drunk driving. As importantly, consider what efforts are described in the guides that police are using to successfully address these problems.

POLICING METHODS AND CHALLENGES

LEARNING OBJECTIVES

As a result of reading this chapter, the student will be able to:

1 Describe what constitutes the inappropriate use of force by the police, as well as the use of force continuum that helps to determine the amount of force that is justified

2 Explain the law concerning police high-speed vehicle pursuits

3 Review the types of acts that constitute police brutality

4 Explain the meaning and applications of U.S. Code Title 42, Section 1983, and the types of police actions that are vulnerable to Section 1983 lawsuits

5 Discuss how police officers—and their supervisors—might be held criminally liable for their misconduct

6 Explain the law as well as areas of police liability concerning police high-speed pursuits

7 Explain the status and advantages of women and minorities in policing

8 Delineate several types of technologies that are assisting police in large measure toward investigating crimes and identifying their perpetrators

CHAPTER

07

INTRODUCTION

Author Introduction:
Chapter 7

How much force can the police use in performing their duties? What constitutes police liability? How have technologies affected policing? This chapter addresses such questions as well as others that often arise today.

The topics covered in this chapter strike at the very heart of policing today. They concern police behaviors that can greatly affect all Americans. Following a discussion of police use of force, next are discussions of police civil liability, the challenges of bringing more women and minorities to the field, and selected technologies (including police use of social networking sites). (Note: A major related issue, police corruption, was discussed in Chapter 4.) Concluding the chapter are a summary, key terms and concepts, review questions, and several scenarios and activities that provide opportunities for you to "learn by doing."

USE OF FORCE: A SACRED TRUST

Use of Force

Throughout our history, police agencies have faced allegations of brutality and corruption. In the late 19th century, New York police sergeant Alexander "Clubber" Williams epitomized police brutality; he spoke openly of using his nightstick to knock a man unconscious, batter him to pieces, or even kill him. Williams supposedly coined the term *tenderloin* when he commented, "I've had nothing but chuck steaks for a long time, and now I'm going to have me a little tenderloin."[1] Williams was referring to opportunities for graft in an area in downtown New York that was the heart of vice and nightlife, often termed Satan's Circus. This was Williams's beat, where his reputation for using force and brutality became legendary.[2] Next we look at its permissible use, restrictions, and types.

Use of force continuum: a guide for deciding which level of force is appropriate for a police officer to deploy based on the actions of the suspect.

The Force Prerogative

Our society recognizes three legitimate and responsive forms of force on the **use of force continuum**: the right of self-defense (including the use of lethal force in order to protect oneself from harm), the power to control those for whom one is responsible (such as a prisoner or a patient in a mental hospital), and the relatively unrestricted authority of police to use force as required. Police work is dangerous; a routine arrest may result in a violent confrontation, sometimes triggered by drugs, alcohol, or mental illness. To confront those situations, police officers are given the unique right to use force, even deadly force, against others. There are, of course, limitations on when an officer may exercise deadly and nondeadly force; they are discussed later in this chapter.

The exercise of force by police can take several forms, ranging from a simple verbal command to the use of lethal force. Next is discussed a means for determining which type of force to apply, and under what circumstances.

Preventing
Abuse of Authority

What Type of Force to Use? A Model

A new approach to determining proper use of force has recently been developed by two special agents of the Federal Bureau of Investigation and attempts to help officers to have clear and consistent guidelines in the use of force. This approach is known as the dynamic resistance response model (DRRM), where *dynamic* indicates that the model is fluid, and *resistance* demonstrates that the suspect controls the interaction. In this view, the suspect's level of resistance determines the officer's response.[3] The model also delineates suspects into one of four categories (see Figure 7.1).

As shown in Figure 7.1, if a passively resistant suspect fails to follow commands and perhaps attempts to move away from the officer or escape, appropriate responses include using a firm grip, control holds, and pressure points to gain compliance. However, an aggressively resistant suspect—one who is taking offensive action by attempting to push, throw, strike, tackle, or physically harm the officer—would call for such responses as the use of personal weapons (hands, fists, feet), batons, pepper spray, and a stun gun. Finally, because a deadly resistant suspect can seriously injure or kill the officer or another person, the officer is justified in using force, including deadly force, as is *objectively reasonable* to overcome the offender.

In the DRRM, a suspect's lack of resistance (compliance) is in the center of the triangle, which is emphasized as the goal of every encounter. If a suspect's resistance level places him or her on one of the three corners of the triangle, the officer's response is intended to move the suspect's behavior to the center of the triangle and compliance. The sole purpose of the application of force is to gain compliance.

The U.S. Supreme Court has also addressed police use of force, particularly that which is lethal in nature. In *Tennessee v. Garner*[4] (1985), the court held that a police officer, when pursuing a fleeing suspect, may use deadly force only to prevent escape if the officer has probable cause to believe that the suspect poses a significant threat of death or serious physical injury to the officer or others.

FIGURE 7.1

Dynamic Resistance Response Model

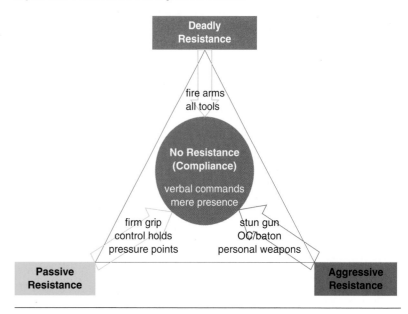

Typical configuration of the dynamic resistance response model with traditional use-of-force options

Persons who aggressively resist arrest can require that police response with weaponless defense tactics (hands, fists, feet), batons, chemical sprays, and/ or an electronic control device.

Police Brutality

Many people contend that there are actually three means by which the police can be "brutal." There is the literal sense of the term, which involves the physical abuse of others. There is the verbal abuse of citizens, exemplified by slurs or epithets. Finally, for many who feel downtrodden, the police symbolize brutality because the officers represent the majority group's law, which serves to keep the minority groups in their place. It is perhaps the latter form of **police brutality** that is of the greatest concern for anyone who is interested in improving community relations; because it is a philosophy or frame of mind, it is probably the most difficult to overcome.

Citizen use of the term *police brutality* encompasses a wide range of practices, from the use of profane and abusive language to the actual use of physical force or violence.[5] While no one can deny that some police officers use brutal practices, it is impossible to know with any degree of accuracy how often and to what extent these incidents occur. They are low-visibility acts, and many victims decline to report them. It is doubtful that police brutality will ever disappear forever. There are always going to be, in the words of A. C. Germann, Frank Day, and Robert Gallati,[6] "Neanderthals" who enjoy their absolute control over others and become tyrannical in their arbitrary application of power.

Police Brutality

WHEN FAILING THE PUBLIC TRUST: CIVIL LIABILITY

The specter of **civil liability** looms large every workday for people who are engaged in police work. With the possible exception of professionals working in the medical field, no group of workers is more susceptible to litigation and liability than police (and prison) employees. Frequently cast into confrontational situations, and given the complex nature of their work and its requisite training needs, they will from time to time act in a manner that evokes public scrutiny, complaints, and financial remuneration to persons who have suffered as a result (see Figure 7.2). As we will see, the price of failure among public servants can be quite high, in both human and financial terms.

Torts and Negligence

A **tort** is the infliction of some injury on one person by another. Three categories of torts generally cover most of the lawsuits filed against criminal justice practitioners: negligence, intentional torts, and constitutional torts.

Negligence can arise when a criminal justice employee's conduct creates a danger to others. In other words, the employee did not conduct his or her affairs in a manner so as to avoid subjecting others to a risk of harm and may be held liable for the injuries caused to others.[7]

Police brutality: unnecessary use of force by police against citizens, resulting in injury.

Civil liability: in tort law, the basis for which a cause of action (e.g., fine) is made to recover damages; in criminal justice, where a police or corrections officer, for example, violates someone's civil rights.

Tort: a civil wrong or infraction; the remedy will be damages awarded in civil trial.

Negligence: failure to perform a duty owed.

PRACTITIONER'S PERSPECTIVE

POLICE INTERNAL AFFAIRS INVESTIGATOR

Name: David Schofield, Police Officer/Detective
Current position: Investigator, Professional Standards Section
City, state: Cincinnati, Ohio
College attended/academic major: University of Cincinnati/BA, economics; MS, criminal justice

How long have you been a practitioner in this criminal justice position?

Since May 2006

My primary duties and responsibilities as a practitioner in this position are:

I investigate allegations of criminal conduct, sexual misconduct, serious misconduct, excessive use of force, unnecessary pointing of firearms, improper searches and seizures, and discrimination by sworn and nonsworn department members of the Cincinnati Police Department.

The qualities/characteristics that are most helpful for one in this career are:

- Honesty/integrity
- High moral values
- Confidence
- Professionalism
- Accountability
- Strong work ethic
- Ability to perform well during dangerous situations
- High level of physical fitness
- Ability to read and write well
- Ability to speak well in front of others
- Ability to be readily available for various shifts
- Ability to work long, often stressful hours

In general, a *typical day* for a practitioner in this career would include:

Interviewing citizens and police officers regarding allegations of officer misconduct. Decisions must be made on which investigative leads ought to be given priority and how best to pursue those leads.

Investigators are given considerable freedom to pursue their investigation how they deem necessary. This requires self-motivation to stay on task and complete the assignment properly. Investigators also must find and develop witnesses for further investigation, while some investigative techniques require covert operations investigating fellow police officers. Other investigative techniques may involve hours of mundane fact-finding. Honesty and integrity are crucial to conduct fair investigations and gain the trust of the public.

Investigators must be able to put the mission of the police department first—even when it involves sustaining serious allegations of misconduct by fellow officers. Investigators must also be able to present their findings in court, disciplinary hearings, the media, and other venues using verbal and written communication. Oftentimes, long hours are spent documenting the findings of an investigation. Information gathered must be documented fairly and concisely. Considerable time is also spent investigating erroneous complaints; however, investigations can be as important as legitimate complaints when the integrity of a police employee is called into question.

My advice to someone either wishing to study, or now studying, criminal justice to become a practitioner in this career field would be:

To research what type of employment you desire. Once that is determined, candidates ought to determine what actual practitioners did in order to get there.

Uniform patrol is the backbone of policing. Most local sworn law enforcement positions require candidates to perform exceptionally well as patrol officers prior to attaining other duties such as investigations, canine, or special operations. If a candidate must be a patrol officer for several years before attaining the position of an investigator, the candidate must be willing to fulfill that requirement.

Prior to gaining employment with a police agency, candidates must protect their reputation and abstain from questionable behavior. Many dreams are lost due to a bad, single decision.

Candidates must also do well in high school and college, as one's academic standing is a strong reflection of his or her work ethic. The lack of a quality education and strong academic background can prevent candidates from achieving their goals.

FIGURE 7.2

When Police Fail the Public Trust

Following are recent examples, as reported by ABC News, of the kinds of police actions that lead to liability; none of these cases were tried by a jury, being settled out of court instead:

- Two women mistakenly shot by Los Angeles police during a manhunt in early 2013 reached a $4.2 million settlement. A woman and her daughter were delivering newspapers when police officers fired about 100 bullets at their pickup truck—which did not match the suspect's vehicle. The city attorney opined that the settlement allowed the city to get out "pretty cheaply all things considered."

- A dancer on a boat chartered for a gay pride party in San Diego jumped into the San Diego Bay and was shot and killed by Harbor Police during an altercation as they tried to get him out of the water. Police said the man fought with an officer and tried to grab his gun, but the man's parents argued he was unarmed and shot in the back; they settled the case for $2.5 million.

- In 2011, a 37-year-old homeless man with schizophrenia was stopped by two Fullerton, California, officers for allegedly trying to break into cars at a bus depot. Officers beat the man and used a Taser several times; he died five days later. The city awarded $1 million to the victim's mother.

- Heavily armed police entered a home in Connecticut with guns drawn and flash grenades exploding, and then shot and killed a man who was watching television at the time. The raid reportedly occurred because police were under pressure to "do something" about the man, who entertained exotic dancers in his home and was considered a blot on the neighborhood. His family settled their lawsuit for $3.5 million in early 2013.

Source: Adapted from Albert Sabaté, "6 Police Misconduct Settlements Worth Millions," *ABC News*, May 1, 2013, http://abcnews.go.com/ABC_Univision/News/police-misconduct-settlements-worth-millions/story?id=19077115# (accessed June 6, 2013).

Public Trust

Intentional torts occur when an employee engages in a voluntary act that has a substantial likelihood of resulting in injury to another; examples are assault and battery, false arrest and imprisonment, malicious prosecution, and abuse of process. *Constitutional torts* involve employees' duty to recognize and uphold the constitutional rights, privileges, and immunities of others; violations of these guarantees may subject the employee to a civil suit, most frequently brought in federal court under 42 U.S. Code Section 1983, discussed below.[8]

Assault, battery, false imprisonment, false arrest, invasion of privacy, negligence, defamation, and malicious prosecution are examples of torts that are commonly brought against police officers. **False arrest** is the arrest of a person without probable cause. False imprisonment is the intentional illegal detention of a person, not only in jail, but any confinement to a specified area. For example, the police may fail to release an arrested person after a proper bail or bond has been posted, they can delay the arraignment of an arrested person unreasonably, or authorities can fail to release a prisoner after they no longer have authority to hold him or her.

Respondeat Superior

A single act may also be a crime as well as a tort. If Officer Smith, in an unprovoked attack, injures Jones, the state will attempt to punish Smith in a criminal action by sending him to jail or prison, fining him, or both. The state would have the burden of proof at criminal trial, having to prove Smith guilty "beyond a reasonable doubt." Furthermore, Jones may sue Smith for money damages in a civil action for the personal injury he suffered. In this civil suit, Jones would have the burden of proving Smith's acts were tortious by a "preponderance of the evidence"—a lower standard than that in a criminal court and thus easier to satisfy.

Section 1983 Legislation

The primary civil instrument that can be used against the police is **Section 1983**. Following the Civil War and in reaction to the activities of the Ku Klux Klan, Congress enacted the Ku Klux Klan Act of 1871, later codified as Title 42, U.S. Code, Section 1983. It states that:

False arrest: unlawful physical restraint by a police officer, for no valid reason.

Section 1983: a portion of the U.S. Code that allows a legal action to be brought against a police officer or other person in position of authority who, it is believed, used his position ("acted under color of law") to violate one's civil rights.

Every person who, under color of any statute, ordinance, regulation, custom, or usage of any State or Territory, subjects, or causes to be subjected, any citizen of the United States or any other person within the jurisdiction thereof to the deprivation of any rights, privileges, or immunities secured by the Constitution and laws, shall be liable to the party injured in an action at law, suit in equity, or other proper proceeding for redress. A trend is for such litigants to cast a wide net in their lawsuits, suing not only the principal actors in the incident, but agency administrators and supervisors as well; this breadth of suing represents the notion of **"vicarious liability"** or the doctrine of *respondeat superior*, an old legal maxim meaning, "let the master answer." In sum, an employer can be found liable in certain instances for wrongful acts of the employee.

An example is the 1991 case of Rodney King, who, following a vehicle pursuit, was kicked, stomped, and beaten with batons (totaling 56 blows, all of which was caught on an 81-second videotape) by three Los Angeles police officers.[9] King sued the officers and the city under Section 1983, and was awarded $3.8 million for his injuries.[10]

Police *supervisors* have also been found liable for injuries arising out of an official policy or custom of their department. Injuries resulting from a chief's verbal or written support of heavy-handed behavior resulting in the use of excessive force by officers have resulted in such liability.[11]

The 1991 beating of Rodney King by Los Angeles police officers resulted in King's being awarded $3.8 million for his injuries.

Vicarious liability: a legal doctrine whereby responsibility rests upon one person for the actions of another and is to exercise reasonable and prudent care in supervising that person.

FOCUS ON   U.S. CODE TITLE 42, SECTION 1983

The University of California at Davis agreed to pay about $1 million to settle a lawsuit filed by students who were pepper-sprayed by campus police during an nonviolent protest on campus in November 2011.

The University of California at Davis agreed in September 2012 to pay about $1 million to settle a lawsuit filed by students who were pepper-sprayed by campus police during an Occupy-style protest on campus in November 2011. The university agreed to pay $30,000 to each of the 21 current and former students who were sprayed or arrested, $250,000 for attorneys' fees, and a set-aside fund of $100,000 for other persons who could prove they were either arrested or pepper-sprayed during the incident. An investigation blamed the incident on poor communication and planning throughout the campus chain of command. Although the officers who engaged in spraying the protesters did not face criminal charges, several involved officers were terminated or resigned their positions under fire.

Source: Adapted from NBCNews.com, "University of California to Pay Nearly $1 Million in Deal with 21 Pepper-Sprayed UC-Davis Occupy Protesters," http://usnews.nbcnews.com/_news/2012/09/26/14112860-university-of-california-to-pay-nearly-1-million-in-deal-with-21-pepper-sprayed-uc-davis-occupy-protesters?lite (accessed February 16, 2013).

General Areas of Liability

To help to conceptualize what is meant by police civil liability, following are some general areas in which police liability may be found.

Proximate Cause

Proximate cause is basically something that causes an event, particularly an injury due to negligence or an intentional wrongful act. In other words, the injury caused would not have occurred but for the cause. As an example, it is established by asking "but for the officer's conduct, would someone have been injured or killed?" If the answer to this question is no, then proximate cause is established, and the officer can be held liable for the damage or injury. An example is where an officer is inappropriately and negligently involved in a high-speed chase and the fleeing driver strikes an innocent third party.[12] Proximate cause also may be found in such cases as an officer leaving the scene of an accident aware of dangerous conditions (e.g., spilled oil, smoke, vehicle debris, stray animals) without proper warning to motorists.[13]

Persons in Custody and Safe Facilities

Courts generally rule that police officers have a **duty of care** to persons in their custody, including a legal responsibility to take reasonable precautions to keep detainees free from harm, render medical assistance when necessary, and treat detainees humanely.[14] This duty, however, normally does not include self-inflicted injury or suicide, because these acts are normally considered to result from the detainee's own intentional conduct.[15] However, if a prisoner's suicide is "reasonably foreseeable" from his actions or statements, then the jailer has a duty of care to help prevent that suicide.

Police also need to provide safe facilities. For example, the construction of a Detroit jail's holding cell did not allow officers to observe detainees' movements; there were no electronic monitoring devices for observing detainees, and there was an absence of detoxification cells required under state department of corrections rules. Therefore, following a suicide in this facility, the court held that these building defects in effect contributed to the detainee's death.[16]

Failure to Protect

This form of negligence may occur if a police officer fails to protect a person from a known and foreseeable danger. Claims of **failure to protect** most often involve battered women. However, police informants, witnesses, and other people dependent on the police can be a source of police liability if an officer fails to take reasonable action to prevent them from being victimized.

Vehicle Pursuits

Vehicle pursuits are of great concern because they involve tremendous potential for injury, property damage, and liability. As one police manual describes it, "The decision by a police officer to pursue a citizen in a motor vehicle is among the most critical that can be made,"[17] putting innocent third parties—other drivers and bystanders—at risk. Police policy and procedure manuals are very thorough where pursuits are concerned, and typically order the supervisor to shut down the pursuit unless there is probable cause to believe the suspect presents a clear and immediate threat to the safety of others, or has committed or is attempting to commit a violent felony.

Two cases explain the law of high-speed pursuits. The first involves two Sacramento County, California, deputies who pursued a motorcyclist for a traffic violation at speeds greater than 100 miles per hour, with the motorcycle crashing; the deputies' vehicle could not stop in time, striking and killing the bike's passenger. The passenger's family claimed in a civil suit that the

Vehicle Persuits

County of Sacramento
v. Lewis

Proximate cause: a factor that contributed heavily to an event, such as an auto crash or death.

Duty of care: a legal obligation imposed on someone; in the case of the police, they have a legal responsibility to see that persons in their custody are free from harm, given necessary medical assistance when necessary, and treated humanely.

Failure to protect: a situation where police place someone in jeopardy, such as giving out the location of a battered spouse or names of victims or witnesses.

you be the... OFFICER

LIABILITY FOR FAILURE TO PROTECT?

What, if any, legal obligation is held by the police to protect someone from his or her estranged spouse who has been served with a legal restraining order? That question was at the crux of a lawsuit from Castle Rock, Colorado, which was ultimately heard by the U.S. Supreme Court. Jessica Gonzales's restraining order required her husband to remain at least 100 yards from her and their three daughters except during specified visitation times. One evening the husband took possession of the three children in violation of the order; Mrs. Gonzales repeatedly urged the police to search for and arrest her husband, but they took no immediate action (due to Jessica's allowing her husband to take the children at various hours). At approximately 3:20 a.m., the husband appeared at the city police station and instigated a shoot-out with the police (he died). A search of his vehicle revealed the corpses of the three daughters,

whom the husband had killed prior to his arrival. U.S. cities are generally immune from lawsuits, so in this case the Supreme Court was asked to decide whether Jessica Gonzales could sue the city because of inaction by its police officers.

1. Were the police *morally* responsible for the deaths of the three girls?

2. Were the police *legally* responsible for their deaths?

3. If you believe Jessica should be allowed to sue the city, and the police were liable, how much financial compensation should Jessica receive?

See the Notes section at the end of the book for the outcome and whether or not the city was deemed as liable for its police department's actions.[18]

pursuit violated the crash victim's due process rights under the Fourteenth Amendment. The U.S. Supreme Court, in *County of Sacramento v. Lewis* (1998),[19] held that the proper standard in such cases is whether the officer's conduct "shocks the conscience"—was the conduct offensive to a reasonable person's sense of moral goodness? The Court felt that in this case, deputies had

Mid-Chapter Quiz: Police Methods and Challenges

no intent to harm the suspects and thus their behavior did not "shock the conscience." Then, in 2007 the Supreme Court heard another case involving the level of force used by police in such pursuits. A deputy's pursuit of a 19-year-old Georgia youth, driving at speeds up to 90 miles per hour for 9 miles, ended in a violent crash that left the youth a quadriplegic. His lawyers argued that the Fourth Amendment protects against the use of excessive force—and that when high-speed drivers have their cars stopped in pursuits, a "seizure" occurs for Fourth Amendment purposes. The Supreme Court held that an officer's attempt to terminate a dangerous high-speed car chase that threatens the lives of innocent bystanders "does not violate the Fourth Amendment, even when it places the fleeing motorist at risk of serious injury or death" (*Scott v. Harris*, 2007).[20]

High-speed police pursuits carry a number of potential dangers and cause for police liability, so they must be closely supervised and governed by written policies and procedures.

Scott v. Harris

Still, it is important to remember that a police pursuit is justified only when the necessity of apprehension outweighs the degree of danger created by the pursuit.

NEEDED: MORE WOMEN AND MINORITIES

Although this chapter section could have been included in the discussion of recruitment in Chapter 6, certainly a *challenge* for today's police in our increasingly diverse society is for the police to be represented by women and minorities. But practically since its beginning, as reflected by the numbers, policing has been a predominantly male- and non–minority-dominated occupation. Next we briefly examine the status of women and minorities in the field.

Author Video: Women and
Minorities in Policing

Gains and Obstacles for Women

Over the last 30 years, the proportion of women police officers has grown steadily. During the 1970s, some formal barriers to hiring women were eliminated, such as height requirements; in addition, subjective physical agility tests and oral interviews were modified. Some job discrimination suits further expanded women's opportunities. Women now represent about 12 percent of the sworn personnel in local (municipal and county) police agencies.[21] State agencies as a whole have a much lower percentage of female officers than either local or federal law enforcement agencies, 6.5 percent.[22] Women account for about 15 percent of all federal sworn officers, which is a bit higher than local agencies.[23]

Female Officers

In addition to helping to diversify the police labor force, there are certainly practical advantages to having women in uniform (see Figure 7.3); according to a report by the National Center for Women and Policing:

1. *Female officers are proven to be as competent as their male counterparts.* The center notes that several evaluations of the effectiveness of female officers in a number of work-related areas in several large cities (e.g., Washington, D.C., St. Louis, New York City, Denver, Philadelphia) concluded that men and women were equally capable of successful performance as patrol officers.

2. *Female officers are less likely to use excessive force.* As with their competency, research both in the United States and in international venues demonstrates that female officers utilize a less authoritarian style of policing that relies less than men's style on physical force—and their communication skills allow them to defuse situations.

3. *Female officers implement "community-oriented policing."* Community policing and problem solving emphasizes communication and cooperation with citizens as well as informal problem solving. The center believes that, in addition to their communication skills, women officers demonstrate empathy toward others and interacting in a way that is not designed to "prove" something.

4. *More female officers will improve law enforcement's response to violence against women.* It is critical that the police properly respond to problems

Certainly one of the challenges facing police agencies today is greater representation by female and minority police officers.

of sexual and physical assaults against women; the price of failure is high, not only in terms of crimes against the victims, but also in terms of the risk of litigation (particularly in domestic violence). The center cites studies indicating that female officers have long been viewed as more effective in responding to crimes against women than their male counterparts.

5. *Increasing the presence of female officers reduces problems of sex discrimination and harassment within a law enforcement agency.*

FIGURE 7.3

Women in Policing: Dawn of a New Era?

Peter Horne, a noted author in the field of women in policing, maintains that women have gone well beyond making contributions in community policing and proving to be as effective as men; now they are changing attitudes about their working in the field. Specifically:

- Beginning with *Cagney & Lacey* in the mid-1980s and later in *Hill Street Blues, NYPD Blue, Third Watch,* and *Law & Order: SVU,* as well as the various CSI shows, female detectives and uniformed officers are portrayed as competent, valuable members of the police force, and other characters treat their presence as unexceptional. This has occurred in movies as well.

- Attitudes are changing. The mass media has put a positive spin on the portrayal of policewomen in the last 15 years or so, and the print media do not run sensational front-page stories about the first policewoman hired or promoted. Articles about women in policing are more matter-of-fact or routine.

- There is a growing acceptance by the public for females in the law enforcement role. Especially noteworthy is that most people are no longer skeptical of women's ability to handle violent situations.

- More than two-thirds of male criminal justice students are supportive of female officers overall; a good number of these students will be going on to careers in policing where they may well be working with female colleagues.

- It is not uncommon for male police officers to acknowledge that women make good cops. A number of larger and midsize police agencies are actively recruiting, employing, and promoting more women.

- A number of state, regional, national, and international associations have emerged to give support to female officers and give them an organized voice: The International Association of Women Police (IAWP) has approximately 3,000 members; the National Association of Women Law Enforcement Executives has some 400 voting members at the rank of lieutenant or higher; the National Center for Women and Policing has several hundred members and produces and disseminates research on issues relevant to women in law enforcement; and Women in Federal Law Enforcement (WIFLE) also has several hundred members.

Source: Adapted from Peter Horne, "Policewomen: Their First Century and the New Era," *The Police Chief* (May 2013), http://www.policechief magazine.org/magazine/index.cfm?fuseaction=display&article_id=1000 (accessed June 6, 2013).

A primary challenge to seeing more women in policing begins with the fact that most women never consider such a career to begin with, perhaps owing to their misunderstanding of the nature of the job and the macho image portrayed in the media. Then, if hired, women may face discrimination, sexual harassment, or even peer intimidation, and possibly enter an agency where there might be few women role models or mentors to help them adjust and to move up the ranks.[24] Certainly these are issues that must be addressed before women are fully represented and provide the aforementioned benefits to the field.

Women and Minorities in Policing

Overcoming the History of Police-Minority Relations

As with women, it is increasingly important and advantageous to have minorities serving communities in police uniforms. However, to understand some of the challenges involved with recruiting minorities—African Americans in particular—it is necessary to possess at least a basic knowledge of the history of police-minority relations in the United States.

Racial Profiling

Race riots during the 1960s, such as the one in Watts, California, often pitted police against protesting members of the community.

Because of widespread discrimination and disparate treatment, during the 1960s major race riots occurred in Harlem, New York; Watts, California; Newark, New Jersey; and Detroit (often fomented by such violent militant groups as the Black Panthers). There were 75 civil disorders involving African Americans and the police in 1967 alone, with at least 83 people killed. A number of presidential commissions were created to study riots, campus disorder, and minority relations in general. One such commission, the National Advisory Commission on Civil Disorders (also known as the Kerner Commission) stated in 1968 that "our nation is moving toward two societies, one black, one white—separate and unequal."[25] Then, in the late 1980s and early 1990s, police-community relations appeared to worsen again, with major riots, looting, and burning in Miami, Florida; Los Angeles; Atlanta; Las Vegas; Washington, D.C.; and St. Petersburg, Florida, as well as in other cities.

The police were involved in all of these incidents, at times using force against protesting minority groups,[26] and often being viewed in many communities as an "occupying force"; for example, prominent sociologist James Baldwin wrote that the very presence of the police in Harlem "is an insult, and it would be, even if they spent their entire day feeding gumdrops to children."[27]

Then the new millennium arrived, and bias-based policing—also known as racial profiling or "driving while black or brown" (DWBB)—became a hot-button issue. A 2007 study released by the Bureau of Justice Statistics (BJS) found that while black, Hispanic, and white drivers were equally likely to be pulled over by the police, black and Hispanic drivers were much more likely to be searched and arrested, and police were much more likely to threaten or use force against black and Hispanic drivers than against white drivers in any encounter. Even though some police executives lost their jobs because of their officers' racial profiling, the BJS report warned that the findings do not prove that police treat people differently along racial lines and that the differences could be explained by driver conduct or other circumstances.[28]

Thus, members of both groups have had a tenuous and at times violent and deadly coexistence. The term *police-community relations*, as police expert Samuel Walker wrote, is really a euphemism for *police-race relations*.[29]

Given this historical backdrop, minority citizens naturally pose a challenge in terms of recruitment into policing, but will also feel more secure in their communities when they see and know police officers of their own race. At present, however, only about 12 percent of all local police officers are African American, and 10 percent are Hispanic/Latino.[30] Probably the most difficult barrier has to do with the image that police officers have in the minority communities.

Recruiting minority police officers not only diversifies the agency but also provides a positive impact on community relations.

POLICE TECHNOLOGIES

Technologies historically have had a tremendous impact on policing, greatly expanding and changing the work of patrol officers, criminal investigators, forensics, and other specialized assignments (e.g., bomb disposal). This chapter section provides a sampling of such technologies for addressing old crime and security problems.

Wireless Technology

Many U.S. police departments, including small agencies, are using laptop computers with wireless connections to access crime and motor vehicle databases. These systems are believed to pay for themselves in increased fines and officer safety. Officers can access court documents, in-house police department records, and a system of computer-aided dispatching (CAD) and can enter license numbers into their computers. Through a national network of motor vehicle and criminal history databases, they can locate drivers with outstanding warrants, expired or suspended licenses, and so on. Furthermore, rather than using open radio communications, police officers use their computers to communicate with one another via e-mail.[31]

Crime Mapping

Computerized crime mapping combines geographic information from global positioning satellites with crime statistics gathered by a department's CAD system and demographic data provided by private companies or the U.S. Census Bureau. The result is a picture that combines disparate sets of data for a whole new perspective on crime. For example, maps of crimes can be overlaid with maps or layers of causative data: unemployment rates in the areas of high crime, locations of abandoned houses, population density, reports of drug activity, or geographic features (such as alleys, canals, or open fields) that might be contributing factors.[32] Furthermore, the hardware and software are now available to nearly all police agencies for a few thousand dollars. In 1997 the national Crime Mapping Research Conference was established to promote research, evaluation, development, and dissemination of geographic information systems technology for criminal justice research and practice.[33]

Locating Serial Offenders

Most offenders operate close to home and tend to operate in target-rich environments to "hunt"

Police agencies are equipped with many forms of high-technology. This officer's police car uses a computer to scan license plate numbers and locate stolen vehicles or persons who have outstanding arrest warrants.

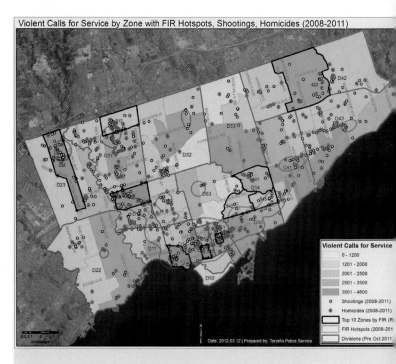

Using computerized crime mapping, police can obtain a wide perspective on crime. (FIR stands for field information reports.)

Police Technology

Police Technology

Technology
and Policing

Tasers

for their prey. Geographic profiling analyzes the geography of such locations and the sites of the victim encounters, the attacks, the murders, and the body dumps, and maps the most probable location of the suspect's home.[34] Washington State uses a homicide investigation and tracking system (HITS) that links crime-related databases to vice and gang files, sex offender registries, corrections and parole records, and department of motor vehicle databases. Then, when an agency has a major crime occur, a central system scans every database to compare eyewitness descriptions of a suspect and vehicle, and then builds a data set containing profiles of the offender, the victims, and the incidents. The data set then goes into a geographic information system (GIS), where the program selects and maps the names and addresses of those suspects whose method of operation fits the crimes being investigated.[35]

Smartphones

Unquestionably, social media are changing the way police operate as well (see Figure 7.4). One smartphone app now allows officers responding to calls for service to determine instantly if previously reported incidents and convicted criminals are associated with a particular address. Officers can point their phone at a particular location and, using the phone's global positioning system (GPS), check the arrest history or officer safety hazard information of the address in question. When looking for a missing child, an icon appears if any sex offenders are living nearby. The app can also track the location of police units, allowing the officer to determine distances of backup units.[36]

Electronic Control Devices

A federal survey found that about 60 percent of local police departments, employing 75 percent of all officers, and 30 percent of sheriffs' offices authorized their officers to use handheld electronic control devices (ECDs, also known as conducted energy devices, or CEDs), such as a Taser or stun gun.[37] These ECDs have become smaller and easier for police to carry, and more effective to use (including a range of up to 35 feet). A new Taser Cam has been introduced, which allows the Taser ECD's deployment to be recorded with full audio and video, even in zero light conditions. Also new is the Taser X3, a multishot ECD that can engage multiple targets and display warning arcs while loaded.

●● FIGURE 7.4

Social Media and Crime Fighting

Minutes after a shooting near the Oakland Airport (which killed seven people), the gunman was on the loose. A police sergeant quickly fired off a flurry of text alerts to thousands of nearby residents through a social media tool for law enforcement agencies, warning them to stay out of the area and, eventually, informing them the danger had passed and the shooter was in custody.

Across the country, police agencies are using social media as crime-fighting tools, providing residents with real-time alerts on crimes in progress, traffic messes, and missing children. And it works: Police in Amarillo, Texas, captured a fugitive wanted for aggravated robbery, and a robbery suspect in Fayetteville, North Carolina, was caught after an alert was sent out.

A survey found that about 9 of 10 agencies use some form of social media; some, like Nixle, have security features that make them less susceptible to hacking than some social media. This tool allows police to send out alerts and advisories to its subscribers either citywide or just to a specific neighborhood within a quarter-mile radius. Subscriptions typically spike when populaces suffer crises such as tornadoes, wildfires, and major violent crimes.

Source: Adapted from Terry Collins, "Police Embrace Emerging Social Media Tool," *Associated Press*, August 11, 2012, http://news.yahoo.com/police-embrace-emerging-social-media-tool-150141734.html.

you be the... JUDGE

YOUR CELL PHONE AND THE STORED COMMUNICATIONS ACT

In February 2001 a businessman was gunned down in Fort Lauderdale, Florida; four years later the prosecutor charged three men with the murder. The three suspects awaited trial for over five years, and the evidence to be used turned on the admissibility of two of the suspects' cell phone records—specifically, an analysis of the location data contained in them (which placed two of the men within 500 feet of the murder as it occurred). The defense argued that the use of such evidence violated the defendants' constitutional rights, but the judge refused to suppress the cell phone records on grounds that cell phone users have no reasonable expectation of privacy in location information gathered by the police.[38]

One survey found that there are now about 1.3 million such requests for cell phone tracking data each year. The potential for tracking data to assist police investigations is undeniable. However, the issue is whether or not law enforcement agencies, phone manufacturers, cell carriers, and software makers should be exploiting users' personal privacy data without their knowledge.[39]

The **Stored Communications Act**,[40] enacted in 1986, speaks to these issues. Essentially, while the Fourth Amendment to the U.S. Constitution protects people's right to be secure against unreasonable searches and seizures in their houses, papers, and effects, the amendment's protections do not apply to electronically stored information in part because Americans do not have a "reasonable expectation of privacy" in an online context. Furthermore, users of such devices generally entrust the security of online information to a third party, an Internet service provider (ISP), and in doing so, many courts have held that users relinquish any expectation of privacy.

At present, the Stored Communications Act allows law enforcement access to electronic messages greater than 180 days old without a warrant (or, with a court order or subpoena, such access may be obtained for messages less than 180 days old). The government does not need to establish probable cause, but must only offer facts showing that the information sought is material to an ongoing criminal investigation.[41]

1. Which side do you believe can make the most compelling argument: one's right to privacy, or the need for law enforcement agencies to use such technologies to identify and arrest offenders?

Robotics

Recent advances in robotics ("bots" in tech-speak) have allowed policing (and soldiering) to become safer. Robots are now fitted with odor sensors; video capability, including night vision; a camera (also useful for photographing crime scenes); a Taser ECD; and even the ability to engage in two-way communications.[42] Robots with 7-foot arms (that scan the inside and undercarriage of vehicles for bombs), lights, video cameras (that zoom and swivel), obstacle-hurling flippers, and jointed arms (that have hand-like grippers to disable or destroy bombs) are even relatively commonplace. A recent application of such a robot for policing is discussed in the next "Focus On" exhibit.

Traffic Functions

A multicar traffic collision (also termed a traffic crash) can turn a street or highway into a parking lot for many hours, sometimes even days. The police must collect evidence relating to the collision including measurements and sketches of the scene, vehicle and body positions, skid marks, street or highway elevations, intersections, and curves. Some police agencies have begun using

Electronic control devices, such as the Taser, are expanding in usage among and capabilities for the police.

FOCUS ON   USING ROBOTS FOR A MASS SHOOTER

James Eagan Holmes stands accused of one of the worst mass shootings in American history: killing 12 people and wounding 58 at an Aurora, Colorado, movie theater on July 20, 2012, during a late-night screening of a Batman movie. After being arrested, Holmes informed police that his apartment was booby-trapped, so local, state, and federal police officers, firefighters, and bomb-squad experts converged on Holmes's apartment to evacuate neighbors and search for additional evidence.

The officers' first action was to send in a bomb-removal robot to disarm a tripwire guarding the apartment's front door. The robot then neutralized potential explosive devices, incendiary devices, and fuel found near the door. Next, the robot's camera—which revealed numerous containers with accelerants and trigger mechanisms—searched for computers or any other evidence to be removed

before attempting to disarm additional explosives. Eventually, 30 aerial shells filled with gunpowder, two containers filled with liquid accelerants, and numerous bullets left to explode in the resulting fire were found in the apartment. Evidence was collected and sent to the FBI laboratory's Terrorist Explosive Device Analytical Center in Quantico, Virginia. Later, another bomb-disposal robot was sent to a potentially related threat on the University of Colorado at Denver's medical campus in Aurora, where Holmes could have shipped some of the items used in the attack.

Source: John Ingold, "James Holmes Faces 142 Counts, Including 24 of First-Degree Murder," *The Denver Post*, July 30, 2012, http://www.denverpost.com/breakingnews/ci_21191265/hearing-underway-man-suspected-killing-12-aurora-theater; also see Larry Greenmeier, "Bomb-Disarming Robot Was First to Enter Alleged Aurora Shooter's Apartment, " *Scientific American,* July 25, 2012, http://blogs.scientificamerican.com/observations/2012/07/25/bomb-disarming-robot-was-first-to-enter-alleged-aurora-shooters-apartment/ (accessed December 4, 2012).

Tennesee v. Garner

Chapter Quiz: Police Methods and Challenges

GPS to determine such details as vehicle location and damage, elevation, grade, radii of curves, and critical speed. A transmitter takes a series of "shots" to find the exact locations and measurements of collision details like skid marks, area of impact, and debris. That information is then downloaded into the system, and the coordinates are plotted on an aerial shot of the intersection or roadway. Using computer technology, the details are then superimposed on the aerial shot, thus re-creating the collision scene to scale. Digital photos of the collision are incorporated into the final product, resulting in a highly accurate depiction of the collision.[43]

Computer technologies now assist police in investigating traffic crashes; this officer is using collision reconstruction software.

Databases for Fingerprints and Mug Shots

Though perhaps not as exotic as DNA identification, fingerprints are still a reliable means of positively identifying someone, and advances continue to be made in the field. Throughout the country, filing cabinets are filled with ink-smeared cards that hold the keys to countless unsolved crimes if only the data could be located. An automated fingerprint identification system (AFIS) allows this legacy of data to be rapidly shared. One such system is the Western Identification Network (www.winid.org), established by nine states as a way to share their 17 million fingerprint records. These states were later joined by local agencies and the Federal Bureau of Investigation, the Internal Revenue Service, the Secret Service, and the Drug Enforcement Administration. The system can generally provide a match within a few hours and has helped solve more than 5,000 crimes. A digital photo exchange facility known as WinPho is now being added to supplement fingerprint data.[44]

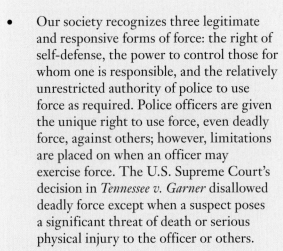

- Our society recognizes three legitimate and responsive forms of force: the right of self-defense, the power to control those for whom one is responsible, and the relatively unrestricted authority of police to use force as required. Police officers are given the unique right to use force, even deadly force, against others; however, limitations are placed on when an officer may exercise force. The U.S. Supreme Court's decision in *Tennessee v. Garner* disallowed deadly force except when a suspect poses a significant threat of death or serious physical injury to the officer or others.

- Use of force continuums guide officers in deciding which level of force is appropriate for the situation; having evolved for more than three decades, they are depicted from the very simple to the more elaborate forms. Clearly, nothing can inflame a community and raise tensions like police shootings.

- Historically, three forms of police brutality have been recognized: the physical abuse of others, the verbal abuse of citizens, and officers representing the majority group's law.

- The specter of civil liability looms large over police work. Often being in confrontational situations, police officers may from time to time act in a manner that evokes public scrutiny and complaints. They and their superiors may be sued for a variety of reasons if a citizen believes his or her rights were violated; the primary civil instrument that can be used against the police is Section 1983.

- High-speed vehicle pursuits by police are legally permissible, but are to be used only when certain conditions are met.

- Although women and minority representation in policing has grown over the past decades, these groups are still underrepresented overall; greater numbers of both women and minorities are needed—as is greater accommodation—if the police are to become diversified like the rest of society.

- Technology has improved the capabilities of nearly every aspect of police patrol and investigations—bringing with it some concerns with citizens' right to privacy.

Civil liability
Duty of care
Failure to protect
False arrest
Negligence

Police brutality
Proximate cause
Respondeat superior
Section 1983
Stored Communications Act

Tort
Use of force continuum
Vicarious liability

Sharpen your skills with **SAGE edge** at **edge.sagepub.com/peak. SAGE edge for students** provides a personalized approach to help you accomplish your coursework goals in an easy-to-use learning environment. Access the videos, audio clips, quizzes, cases and SAGE journal and reference articles that are noted in this chapter.

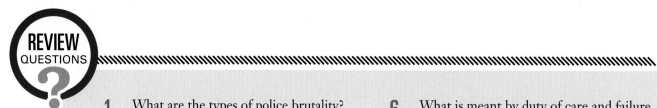

1. What are the types of police brutality? Which one is most problematic for the police?

2. What do you believe constitutes inappropriate use of force by the police?

3. How would you describe the DRRM and its uses and benefits?

4. What kinds of police behaviors are deemed to be corrupt in nature?

5. How would you define U.S. Code Title 42, Section 1983?

6. What is meant by duty of care and failure to protect, and what are some examples as they apply to police supervisors and officers?

7. How might the police be deemed liable if they are involved in vehicle pursuits?

8. What challenges exist with bringing more women and minorities into the field?

9. How have technologies assisted police investigative functions? Patrol operations?

1. In the past six months there has been a spike in the number of complaints from citizens in your community concerning inappropriate use of force by police. As your police department's community liaison, you are asked to describe how newly adopted DRRM policy to the city commission might help. How will you describe the model?

2. Your criminal justice professor assigns your class a group project wherein you are to argue which technologies provide the greatest usefulness in crime fighting. How will you respond, and why?

3. Your police chief assigns you the task of developing a new method for recruiting both women and minority police officers. Money is no object, because the mayor has made agency diversity a top priority for the coming year; what will you recommend be done in terms of reaching these individuals in markets that are not normally recruited?

EXPOUNDING THE CONSTITUTION:
Laws of Arrest, Search, and Seizure

LEARNING OBJECTIVES

As a result of reading this chapter, the student will be able to:

1 Outline the general protections enjoyed by citizens under the Fourth, Fifth, and Sixth Amendments

2 Define and provide examples of probable cause

3 Explain the rationale for, ramifications of, and exceptions to the exclusionary rule

4 Distinguish between arrests and searches and seizures with and without a warrant

5 Explain the rights of—and limitations on—the police with regard to searching a person's home, immediate area, body, and vehicle

6 Discuss some significant ways in which the *Miranda* decision has been eroded

7 Review what is meant by "stop and frisk"

8 Explain generally to what extent the police may use electronic devices in order to obtain information from members of the public

9 Describe what rights are held by criminal defendants regarding the right to counsel, for both felony and misdemeanor arrests

CHAPTER

08

We must never forget that it is a constitution we are expounding.
—John Marshall, *McCulloch v. Maryland* (1819)[1]

Author Introduction:
Chapter 8

McCulloch v. Maryland

Fourth Amendment: in the Constitution, it contains the protection against unreasonable searches and seizures and protects people's homes, property, and effects.

Fifth Amendment: in the Constitution, among other protections, it guards against self-incrimination and double jeopardy.

Sixth Amendment: in the Bill of Rights, it guarantees the right to a speedy and public trial by an impartial jury, the right to effective counsel at trial, and other protections.

INTRODUCTION

What constitutional rights do Americans possess regarding arrest, search, and seizure? At the same time, how are the police constrained by those rights? If the police have a search warrant for a friend you are accompanying, can they search you as well? If the police knock on your apartment door, must you allow them to enter if you do not see a search warrant in their possession? These are certainly challenging questions if someone is not familiar with the Bill of Rights; after reading this chapter, however, the answers should be clear.

Most college and university students probably have few opportunities to witness police actions that concern the U.S. Constitution. Although they may become directly and innocently involved with arrest, search, and seizure by being present at parties, in friends' vehicles, or at their place of employment, most Americans' knowledge of the Bill of Rights probably comes from movies and television crime shows—which are questionable at best in terms of how they portray police conduct. This chapter will serve to clarify any such confusion.

The foci of this chapter will be three of the ten amendments that constitute the Bill of Rights: the **Fourth Amendment** (probable cause, the exclusionary rule, arrest, search and seizure, electronic surveillance, and lineups), the **Fifth Amendment** (confessions and interrogations), and the **Sixth Amendment** (right to counsel and interrogation). (Note: The Eighth Amendment, prohibiting cruel and unusual punishment, applies to jails and prisons; furthermore, the Fourteenth Amendment states that we are entitled to due process, as spelled out in the criminal justice system flow in Chapter 1. These two amendments are not examined in detail in this chapter, however.) Several challenging boxed exhibits are located throughout the chapter. The chapter concludes with a summary, key terms

ASSESS YOUR AWARENESS:

Test your knowledge of your constitutional rights regarding arrest, search, and seizure by first reading and responding to the following seven true-false items; check your answers after reading this chapter's materials.

1. The standard for a legal arrest, search, and seizure is probable cause.

2. The exclusionary rule requires that evidence obtained by police in violation of the Fourth Amendment may *not* be used against the defendant in a criminal trial.

3. There are essentially two ways for the police to make an arrest: with a warrant and without a warrant.

4. The courts grant police greater latitude in searching automobiles, which can be used to help make a getaway and to hide evidence.

5. The *Miranda* warning remains intact from its original version; no deviations in its explanation or practice by police are permitted.

6. Generally, police do not have to "search" for things they see in plain view.

7. Nowhere is the law harsher than in the Middle East, particularly in Saudi Arabia.

Answers can be found on page 401.

and concepts, review questions, and several scenarios and activities that provide opportunities for you to "learn by doing." Also note that the law as it pertains to juvenile offenders is quite different from that for adults; juvenile law is covered in Chapter 15.

SOME CAVEATS

Students of criminal justice might do well to remember the classical words of John Adams, who stated in 1774 that a republic is "a government of laws, and not of men."[2] The Bill of Rights was enacted largely to protect all citizens from excessive governmental power.

As was seen in previous chapters of this book, criminal justice practitioners have far-reaching powers. Furthermore, agencies of criminal justice have the added benefit of using expert witnesses, forensic crime laboratories, undercover agents, informants, and so forth. Therefore, the Bill of Rights serves as an important means of "balancing the scales"— controlling the police and others so that they conduct themselves in a manner as is suited to a democratic society. Criminal justice professionals must conform their behavior to the rule of law as set forth not only in the U.S. Constitution but also in the state constitutions, statutes enacted by state legislatures, municipal ordinances, and the precedent of prior interpretations by the courts.

It would also be good to remember that the law is *dynamic*—that is, constantly changing—by virtue of acts by federal and state courts as well as their legislative bodies. Therefore, it is imperative that criminal justice practitioners keep abreast of such changes and have formal mechanisms for imparting these legal changes to their employees. In the best case, agencies will have either an in-house assistant district attorney—or, at the least, one who is on call—to render advice concerning legal matters.

A final note: Anyone who believes our legal system to be unduly harsh and restrictive might wish to read the brief discussion of Islamic law, below. Remember that governments—through their criminal justice systems (and, too often, their military forces)—may employ many methods to maintain order and attempt to maintain "justice." In China or Saudi Arabia, however, the methods used would be far different from those in the United States. But would "justice" really result? And would many Americans want to *live* in one of those venues? As noted above, see the boxed "Going Global" exhibit near the chapter's end for a foretaste of how "justice" appears in venues that follow Islam's law of sharia.

 4th Amendment

 Probable Cause

 Exclusionary Rule

THE FOURTH AMENDMENT

The right of the people to be secure in their persons, papers, and effects, against unreasonable **searches and seizures**, shall not be violated, and no Warrants shall issue, but upon probable cause, supported by Oath or affirmation, and particularly describing the place to be searched, and the persons or things to be seized.

The Fourth Amendment is intended to limit overzealous behavior by the police. Its primary protection is the requirement that a neutral, detached magistrate, rather than a police officer, issue **warrants for arrest** and search; the legal right to search is best decided by a neutral judicial officer, not by an agent of the police.[3]

Search and seizure: in the Fourth Amendment, the term refers to an officer's searching for and taking away evidence of a crime.

Warrant, arrest: a document issued by a judge directing police to immediately arrest a person accused of a crime.

Probable Cause

The standard for a legal arrest, as well as for **search and seizure**, is **probable cause**. This important concept is elusive at best; it is often quite difficult for professors to explain and even more difficult for students to understand. One way to define probable cause is to say that for an officer to make an arrest or conduct a search of someone's person or effects, he or she must have a **reasonable suspicion** that a crime has been or is about to be committed by that individual (which, in the case of a search, can include his or her merely possessing some form of illegal contraband).

That definition still may not help much to understand this concept. However, if you read carefully the example provided in the next "Focus On" box (which is an actual case), you should have a better understanding of this concept—and how it is applied in the field.

Of course, the facts of each case and the probable cause indicators present are different; the court will examine the type and amount of probable cause that the officer had at the time of the arrest. It is important to note that a police officer cannot add to the probable cause used to make the arrest after making the arrest; the judge will then determine whether or not sufficient probable cause existed to arrest the individual based on the officer's knowledge of the facts at the time of the arrest.

The Supreme Court has upheld convictions when probable cause was provided by a reliable informant,[4] when it came in an anonymous letter,[5] and when a suspect fit a Drug Enforcement Administration profile of a drug courier.[6]

The Exclusionary Rule

As observed in Chapter 7, the Fourth Amendment protects people's right to be secure against unreasonable searches and seizures in their houses, papers, and

Weeks v. United States

Mapp v. Ohio

Probable cause: reasonable suspicion or belief that a crime has been, or is about to be, committed by a particular person.

Reasonable suspicion: suspicion that is less than probable cause but more than a mere hunch that a person may be involved in criminal activity.

FOCUS ON   PROBABLE CAUSE

At midnight, a 55-year-old woman, having spent several hours at a city bar, wished to leave the bar and go to a nightclub in a rural part of the county. A man offered her a ride, but rather than driving directly to the nightclub, he drove to a remote place and parked the car. There he raped the woman and forced her to sodomize him. She fought him and later told the police she thought she had broken the temples (side pieces) of his black glasses. After the act, he drove her back to town; when she got out of the car, she saw the license plate number and thought that the hood of the car was colored red. Her account of the crime and her physical description of the rapist led the officers to have a suspect in mind, so they immediately conducted a photograph lineup with the victim; a known rape/sodomy suspect's picture was shown to her (along with those of several other men who were of similar physical description). She tentatively identified the suspect in the mug shot, but she was not absolutely certain (the suspect's mug shot had been taken several years earlier).

With this information and without an arrest or search warrant, two police officers hurried to the suspect's home to question him. Upon entering the suspect's driveway, the officers observed a beige car—but it had a red hood; next the officers noted that the vehicle's license number matched the one given by the victim; finally, as the suspect came out of the home, the officers observed that the front of his eyeglasses frame was black plastic, but the side pieces were gold aluminum.

Queries:

1. Upon entering the suspect's driveway, what observations did the officers make that might lead "a reasonable person" to believe that the suspect had committed the offenses?

2. Do the officers have enough probable cause to make a warrantless arrest of the individual?

3. Is there anything else they could legally do to further establish the suspect's guilt?

effects. However, simple as that may sound, the manner in which the amendment is applied on the street is more complicated. First of all, not *all* searches are prohibited—only those that are unreasonable. Another issue has to do with how to handle evidence that is illegally obtained. Should murderers be released, Justice Benjamin Cardozo asked, simply because "the constable blundered"?[7] The Fourth Amendment says nothing about how it is to be enforced; this is a problem that has stirred a good amount of debate for a number of years. Most of this debate has focused on the constitutional necessity for the so-called **exclusionary rule**, which basically requires that all evidence obtained in violation of the Fourth Amendment must be excluded from government use in a criminal trial.

The exclusionary rule first appeared in the federal criminal justice system when the Supreme Court ruled in *Weeks v. United States* (1914) that all illegally obtained evidence was barred from use in federal prosecutions.[8] Then, in *Mapp v. Ohio* (1961),[9] the Court applied the doctrine to the states' courts (see the next "Focus On" box).

The exclusionary rule requires that evidence obtained improperly by the police may not be used in a criminal trial, These two officers wait outside a jewelry store for a search warrant to be signed by a judge so they may then search the property for stolen goods.

Exclusionary rule: the rule (see *Mapp v. Ohio*, 1961) providing that evidence obtained improperly cannot be used against the accused at trial.

FOCUS ON   THE EXCLUSIONARY RULE

In May 1957, three Cleveland police officers went to the home of Dollree Mapp to follow up on an informant's tip that a suspect in a recent bombing was hiding there. They also had information that a large amount of materials for operating a numbers game would be found. Upon arrival at the house, officers knocked on the door and demanded entrance, but Mapp, after telephoning her lawyer, refused them entry without a search warrant.

Three hours later, the officers again attempted to enter Mapp's home, and again she refused them entry. They then forcibly entered the home. Mapp confronted the officers, demanding to see a search warrant; an officer waved a piece of paper at her, which she grabbed and placed in her bosom. The officers struggled with Mapp to retrieve the piece of paper, at which time Mapp's attorney arrived at the scene. The attorney was not allowed to enter the house or to see his client. Mapp was forcibly taken upstairs to her bedroom, where her belongings were

searched. One officer found a brown paper bag containing books that he deemed to be obscene.

Mapp was charged with possession of obscene, lewd, or lascivious materials. At the trial, the prosecution attempted to prove that the materials belonged to Mapp; the defense contended that the books were the property of a former boarder who had left his belongings behind. The jury convicted Mapp, and she was sentenced to an indefinite term in prison.

In June 1961, the U.S. Supreme Court overturned the conviction, holding that the Fourth Amendment's prohibition against unreasonable search and seizure had been violated and that as

the right to be secure against rude invasions of privacy by state officers is . . . constitutional in origin, we can no longer permit that right to remain an empty promise. We can no longer permit it to be revocable at the whim of any police officer who, in the name of law enforcement itself, chooses to suspend its enjoyment.

Police officers may perform warrantless arrests and searches under certain circumstances if they have probable cause to do so.

Miranda Rights

Affidavit: any written document in which the signer swears under oath that the statements in the document are true.

Exigent circumstance: an instance where quick, emergency action is required, such as searching for drugs before they are removed or destroyed.

Arrests With and Without a Warrant

It is always best for a police officer to arrest someone with a warrant, because that means a neutral magistrate—rather than a police officer—has examined the facts and determined that the individual should be arrested in order to make an accounting of the charge(s). To obtain an arrest warrant, the officer or a citizen swears in an **affidavit** (as an "affiant") that he or she possesses certain knowledge that a particular person has committed an offense. This person might be, as an example, a private citizen who informs police or the district attorney that he or she attended a party at a residence where drugs or stolen articles were present. Or, as is often the case, a detective gathers physical evidence or interviews witnesses or victims and determines that probable cause exists to believe that a particular person committed a specific crime. In either case, a neutral magistrate, if believing that probable cause exists, will issue the arrest warrant. Officers will execute the warrant, taking the suspect into custody to answer the charges.

Furthermore, the Supreme Court has required police officers to obtain a warrant when making a felony arrest, unless exigent circumstances are present.[10] **Exigent circumstances** means that immediate action is required—to prevent danger to life or serious damage to property, the escape of a suspect, or the destruction of evidence—and that the officer possesses probable cause. Patrol officers, unlike detectives, rarely have the time or opportunity to perform an arrest with a warrant in hand because the suspect is generally trying to escape, dispose of evidence, and so on. Although the actual situation described in the "You Be the Officer" box involves consent to search, it will serve as a good example.

Police may not randomly stop a single vehicle to check the driver's license and registration; there must be probable cause for stopping drivers.[11] However, in 1990, the Supreme Court ruled that the stopping of all vehicles passing through sobriety checkpoints—a form of seizure—did not violate the Constitution, although singling out individual vehicles for random stops without probable cause is not authorized.[12] Several days later, it ruled that police were not required to give drunk-driving suspects a *Miranda* warning and could videotape their responses.[13]

The Supreme Court held also that police may arrest *everyone* in a vehicle in which drugs are found,[14] and that police may set up roadblocks to collect information from motorists about crime. Short stops, "a very few minutes at most," are not too intrusive considering the value in crime solving, the Court noted.[15]

Search and Seizure in General

An old saying holds that "a person's home is his castle," and the police are held to a high Fourth Amendment standard when wanting to enter and search someone's domicile. Regarding what have become known as "knock and announce" cases, the Supreme Court has determined that the Fourth Amendment does require the police to first knock and announce their presence before entering a person's home for the purpose of executing a warrant; the Court allows exceptions, however, if knocking and announcing would be likely to endanger the officers or lead to the destruction of evidence. In mid-2011 the U.S. Supreme Court expanded the ability of police

you be the... OFFICER

SEARCHES BASED ON PROBABLE CAUSE

One spring afternoon a police officer was dispatched to the residence of several university students, who were hosting a keg party for about 20 guests. They reported that three unknown men (two white, one African American) entered the home, had a few beers, and quickly left. Soon thereafter, a party guest also left, and discovered that the stereo had been taken from his car, parked in the back yard. A description of the men and their vehicle was given to the officer, who soon (within 20 minutes and a mile from the crime scene) observed a vehicle and three men, all of whom matched the description that was given. The officer stopped the vehicle, informed the dispatcher of the stop and location, and approached the vehicle.

1. Are exigent circumstances and probable cause sufficient for the officer to search the vehicle without a warrant or the men's consent? If you believe not, how do you propose the three men be handled while a warrant is being sought from a judge?

2. Assume the officer asks the vehicle's driver for permission to search the vehicle, and consent is given; what is the officer's next move? Instead, assume the driver of the vehicle refuses to give the officer permission to search the vehicle; what action(s) do you believe the officer can then legally take?

3. Assume the officer, with or without a warrant, locates the stolen stereo equipment inside the vehicle under the driver's seat; can the officer then arrest only the vehicle's driver, or should all other occupants be arrested as well?

4. Following the arrest of one or more of the occupants, can they then be searched (if necessary, see the section below, "Searches Incidental to Lawful Arrest")?

5. What other issues (e.g., his or her safety) arise for the officer once an arrest is made of one or more of the occupants?

to enter a home without a warrant—but under exigent circumstances. In *Kentucky v. King*,[16] police in Lexington were pursuing a drug suspect and banged on the door of an apartment where they thought they smelled marijuana. After identifying themselves, the officers heard movement inside the apartment and, suspecting that evidence was being destroyed, kicked in the door and found King smoking marijuana. King, convicted of multiple drug crimes, appealed, and Kentucky's highest court ruled there were no "emergency circumstances" present and thus the drugs were inadmissible as police should have sought a search warrant. The U.S. Supreme Court disagreed, saying that the police acted reasonably: When police knock on a door and there is no response, and then hear movement inside that suggests evidence is being destroyed, they are justified in breaking in.

Kentucky v. King

In other Fourth Amendment cases, the Court has upheld a warrantless search and seizure of garbage in bags outside the defendant's home,[17] as well as approaching seated bus passengers and asking permission to search their luggage for drugs (because, they reasoned, such persons should feel free to refuse the officer's request).[18] The Court also decided that no "seizure" occurs (and therefore the Fourth

The U.S. Supreme Court has ruled that the stopping of all vehicles passing through sobriety checkpoints—a form of seizure—does not violate the Constitution.

Amendment does not apply) when a police officer is in a foot pursuit (here, a juvenile being chased by an officer threw down an object, later determined to be crack cocaine).[19]

Searches and Seizures With and Without a Warrant

Search Warrants

As with arrests, the best means by which the police can search a person or premises is with a search warrant that has been issued by a neutral magistrate; after hearing evidence from an affiant, the determination has been made that probable cause exists to believe the named person possesses the fruits or instrumentalities of a crime, or that the fruits are present at a particular location. Again, as with an arrest with a warrant, typically it is the detectives who have the "luxury" of searching and seizing with a warrant after interviewing victims and witnesses, perhaps obtaining analyses at a forensics laboratory, and so on, and gathering enough available evidence to request a search warrant. Patrol officers rarely have the opportunity to perform such a search, as the flow of events normally requires quick action to prevent escape and to prevent the evidence from being destroyed or hidden.

Mid-Chapter Quiz: Expounding the Constitution

Figure 8.1 shows the pertinent parts of a search and seizure warrant form for persons or property that is used by the U.S. District Courts, for execution by agents of the federal government.

Five types of searches may be conducted without a warrant: (1) searches incidental to lawful arrest, (2) searches during field interrogation (stop-and-frisk searches), (3) searches of automobiles under special conditions, (4) seizures of evidence that is in "plain view," and (5) searches when consent is given.

Searches Incidental to Lawful Arrest

Chimel v. California

In *Chimel v. California* (1969), officers arrested Chimel without a warrant in one room of his house and then searched his entire three-bedroom house, including the garage, attic, and workshop. The Supreme Court said that searches incidental to a lawful arrest are limited to the area within the arrestee's immediate control or that area from which he or she might obtain

Florida v. Harris

---

you be the... JUDGE

DO DRUG-SNIFFING DOGS VIOLATE THE FOURTH AMENDMENT?

In early 2013 the Supreme Court considered two Florida cases that involved the constitutionality of police using trained drug-sniffing dogs. *Florida v. Jardines*[20] involved the use of a dog outside of a home to determine the presence of drugs within. After receiving a tip that marijuana was being grown in a house, officers from the Miami-Dade Police Department approached the premises with a drug dog. The Labrador retriever alerted officers to the presence of marijuana in the house; subsequently officers obtained a search warrant and discovered the plants inside.

The second such case heard by the Court, *Florida v. Harris,*[21] concerned a traffic stop during which

a trained police dog alerted, which gave officers probable cause to further search the occupant's vehicle; the search uncovered methamphetamine ingredients inside.

1. Does the use of a drug-sniffing dog near one's home violate the Fourth Amendment (and thus require a search warrant before doing so)?

2. Can a drug-sniffing dog be used in traffic stops without a warrant?

The Supreme Court's decisions for both cases are provided in the Notes section at the end of the book.

FIGURE 8.1

Federal Court Search and Seizure Warrant Form, U.S. District Courts

AO 93 (Rev. 12/09) Search and Seizure Warrant

UNITED STATES DISTRICT COURT

for the

In the Matter of the Search of *(Briefly describe the property to be searched or identify the person by name and address)*	))) Case No.)))

SEARCH AND SEIZURE WARRANT

To: Any authorized law enforcement officer

An application by a federal law enforcement officer or an attorney for the government requests the search of the following person or property located in the _____ District of _____
(identify the person or describe the property to be searched and give its location):

The person or property to be searched, described above, is believed to conceal *(identify the person or describe the property to be seized)*:

I find that the affidavit(s), or any recorded testimony, establish probable cause to search and seize the person or property.

YOU ARE COMMANDED to execute this warrant on or before _____
                                                                                                  (not to exceed 14 days)

❏ in the daytime 6:00 a.m. to 10 p.m.   ❏ at any time in the day or night as I find reasonable cause has been established.

Unless delayed notice is authorized below, you must give a copy of the warrant and a receipt for the property taken to the person from whom, or from whose premises, the property was taken, or leave the copy and receipt at the place where the property was taken.

The officer executing this warrant, or an officer present during the execution of the warrant, must prepare an inventory as required by law and promptly return this warrant and inventory to United States Magistrate Judge

_____ .
                    (name)

❏ I find that immediate notification may have an adverse result listed in 18 U.S.C. § 2705 (except for delay of trial), and authorize the officer executing this warrant to delay notice to the person who, or whose property, will be searched or seized *(check the appropriate box)* ❏ for _____ days *(not to exceed 30).*

                              ❏ until, the facts justifying, the later specific date of _____ .

Date and time issued: _____   _____
                                                                                            Judge's signature

City and state: _____   _____
                                                                              Printed name and title

(Continued)

FIGURE 8.1

(Continued)

AO 93 (Rev. 12/09) Search and Seizure Warrant (Page 2)

	Return	
Case No.:	*Date and time warrant executed:*	*Copy of warrant and inventory left with:*
Inventory made in the presence of :		
Inventory of the property taken and name of any person(s) seized:		

Certification
I declare under penalty of perjury that this inventory is correct and was returned along with the original warrant to the designated judge.

Date: _____

_____
Executing officer's signature

_____
Printed name and title

a weapon. Therefore, if the police are holding a person in one room of the house, they cannot search and seize property in another part of the house, away from the arrestee's immediate physical presence.[22]

Another advantage given the police was the Court's allowing a warrantless, in-home "protective sweep" of the area in which a suspect is arrested to reveal the presence of anyone else who might pose a danger. Such a search, if justified by the circumstances, is not a full search of the premises and may only include a cursory inspection of those spaces where a person could be hiding.[23]

In April 2009, the Supreme Court held that, where an individual has been arrested and is in police custody away from his vehicle, unable to access his vehicle, officers may not then search the vehicle without a warrant. Here, the officers did so, and discovered a handgun and a plastic bag of cocaine; the Court overturned nearly three decades of such a police practice, saying it is a violation of the Fourth Amendment's protection against unreasonable searches and seizures.[24] In essence, the Court is saying that police may search the passenger compartment of a vehicle incident to a recent occupant's arrest only if it is reasonable to believe that the arrestee might access the vehicle at the time of the search or that the vehicle contains evidence of the offense of arrest.

Finally, in mid-2013, in a decision that Justice Samuel Alito described as "the most important criminal procedure case this court has heard in decades," the Supreme Court held that police can collect DNA from people arrested but not yet convicted. The majority compared taking a DNA swab to fingerprinting, viewing it as a reasonable search that can be considered a routine part of a booking procedure.[25]

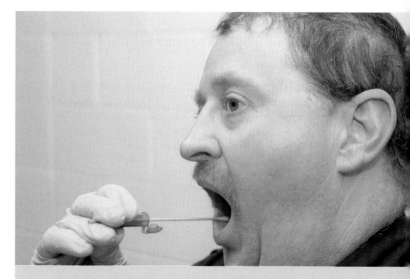

In mid-2013 the U.S. Supreme Court held that police can collect DNA from people arrested but not yet convicted.

Terry v. Ohio

Stop and Frisk

Minnesota v. Dickerson

Racial Profiling

Maryland v. Wilson

Stop and Frisk

In 1968 the U.S. Supreme Court heard *Terry v. Ohio*, which involved on-the-spot police searches and questioning of a suspect who was apparently "casing" a store for robbery (see the next "Focus On" box for more on "stop and frisk").

An important extension of the *Terry* doctrine was handed down in 1993 in *Minnesota v. Dickerson*,[26] in which a police officer observed a man leave a notorious crack house and then try to evade the officer. The man was eventually stopped and patted down, or frisked, during which time the officer felt a small lump in the man's front pocket that was suspected to be drugs. The officer removed the object—crack cocaine wrapped in a cellophane container—from the man's pocket. Although the arrest and conviction were later thrown out as not being allowed under *Terry*, the Court also allowed such seizures in the *future* when officers' probable cause is established by the sense of touch.

Another important Supreme Court decision in February 1997 took officer safety into account. In *Maryland v. Wilson*,[27] the Court held that police may order passengers out of vehicles they stop, regardless of any suspicion of wrongdoing or threat to the officer's safety. Citing statistics showing officer assaults and murders during traffic stops, the Court noted that the "weighty interest" in officer safety is present whether a vehicle occupant is a driver or a passenger.

FOCUS ON   STOP AND FRISK, PER *TERRY V. OHIO*

Cleveland Detective McFadden, a veteran of 19 years of police service, first noticed Terry and another man who appeared to be "casing" a retail store. McFadden observed the suspects making several trips down the street, stopping at a store window, walking about a half-block, turning around and walking back again, pausing to look inside the same store window. At one point they were joined by a third party, who spoke with them and then moved on. McFadden claimed that he followed them because he believed it was his duty as a police officer to investigate the matter further.

Soon the two rejoined the third man; at that point McFadden decided the situation demanded direct action. The officer approached the subjects and identified himself, then requested that the men identify themselves as well. When Terry said something inaudible, McFadden "spun him around so that they were facing the other two, with Terry between McFadden and the others, and patted down the outside of his clothing." In a breast pocket of Terry's overcoat, the officer felt a pistol. McFadden found another pistol on one of the other men. The two men were arrested and ultimately convicted for concealing deadly weapons. Terry appealed on the grounds that the search was illegal and that the evidence should have been suppressed at trial.

The U.S. Supreme Court disagreed with Terry, holding that the police have the authority to detain a person briefly for questioning even without probable cause if they believe that the person has committed a crime or is about to commit a crime. Such detention does not constitute an arrest, and a person may be frisked for a weapon if an officer reasonably suspects the person is carrying a weapon and fears for his or her life.

See *Terry v. Ohio,* 319 U.S. 1 (1968).

Searches of Automobiles

Author Video: Stop and Frisk

The third general circumstance allowing a warrantless search is when an officer has probable cause to believe that an automobile contains criminal evidence. The Supreme Court gives the police greater latitude in searching automobiles, because a vehicle can be used to effect a getaway and to hide evidence. In *Carroll v. United States* (1925), officers searched the vehicle of a known bootlegger without a warrant but with probable cause, finding 68 bottles of illegal booze. On appeal, the Court ruled that the seizure was justified. *Carroll* established two rules, however: First, to invoke the *Carroll* doctrine, the police must have enough probable cause that if there had been enough time, a search warrant would have been issued; second, urgent circumstances must exist that require immediate action.[28]

The Court also allows the police the right to enter an impounded vehicle following a lawful arrest in order to inventory its contents (*Harris v. United States*, 1968),[29] and has stated that a person's general consent to a search of the interior of an automobile also justifies a search of any closed container found inside the car that might reasonably hold the object of the search.[30] And, when an officer has probable cause to search a vehicle, the officer may search objects belonging to a passenger in the vehicle, provided the item the officer is looking for could reasonably be in the passenger's belongings[31] (such as finding drugs in a passenger's purse). Finally, motorists have no expectation of privacy during a traffic stop if contraband is hidden in a vehicle and detected by a drug-sniffing dog.[32]

The courts have held that motorists have no expectation of privacy during a traffic stop if contraband hidden in a vehicle is detected by a drug-sniffing dog.

MEASURING THE RULE OF LAW AROUND THE WORLD

The rule of law consists of a framework of rules and rights that provide for a fair society in which no one person or government is above the law, fundamental rights are protected, and justice is accessible to all.[33]

The World Justice Project (WJP), based in Washington, D.C., works to advance and enhance the rule of law worldwide, develop programs at the community level, and increase public awareness about the concept. One of its primary contributions is to score countries' practice of rule of law on the following eight factors: (1) limited government powers (e.g., government powers are limited by the legislature and judiciary; government officials are punished for corruption); (2) absence of corruption (e.g., government officials do not use office for public or private gain); (3) order and security (e.g., crime is effectively controlled); (4) fundamental rights (e.g., equal treatment, due process of law, freedom of belief and religion); (5) open government (e.g., laws are publicized and stable); (6) regulatory enforcement (e.g., regulations are enforced without influence); (7) civil justice (e.g., affordable, free of corruption and influence); and (8) criminal justice (investigation, adjudication are effective; impartial, free of corruption, due process). Then each is scored (using an independent assessment conducted by the European Commission Joint Research Centre) on each of the factors and subfactors of the index.

The WJP Rule of Law Index® is a quantitative assessment tool offering a detailed and comprehensive picture of the extent to which countries adhere to the rule of law in practice. Viewers can click on any of the 97 countries shown on the map to see the rule of law score.

More information is available at http://worldjusticeproject.org/rule-law-index-map.

Source: World Justice Project, *Rule of Law Index Map,* http://world justiceproject.org/rule-law-index-map (accessed August 9, 2013).

In 2012 the U.S. Supreme Court ruled[34] that police violated the Constitution when they attached a global positioning system (GPS) device to a suspect's vehicle without a search warrant. Police had followed a drug trafficking suspect for a month and eventually found nearly 100 kilograms of cocaine and $1 million in cash when raiding the suspect's home in Maryland. Justice Antonin Scalia noted that the Fourth Amendment's protection of "persons, houses, papers, and effects, against unreasonable searches and seizures" extends to automobiles as well, and that even a small trespass, if committed in "an attempt to find something or to obtain information," constitutes a "search" under the Fourth Amendment. This decision is anticipated to primarily affect major narcotics investigations.

Carroll v. United States

Harris v. United States

Plain-View and Open-Field Searches

Essentially, police do not have to search for items that are seen in plain view. If police are lawfully on the premises and the plain-view discovery is inadvertent, then they may seize the contraband. For example, if an officer has been admitted into a home with an arrest or search warrant and sees drugs and paraphernalia on a living-room table, he or she may arrest the occupants on drug charges as well as the earlier ones. Or, if an officer during a traffic stop observes drugs in the backseat of the car, he may arrest for that as well. Furthermore, fences and the posting of "No Trespassing" signs afford no expectation of privacy and do not prevent officers from viewing open fields without a search warrant.[35] Nor are police prevented from making a naked-eye aerial observation of a suspect's backyard or other curtilage (the grounds around a house or building).[36] Finally, where an officer found a gun under

Consent Searches

a car seat while looking for the vehicle identification number, the Court upheld the search and the resulting arrest as being a plain-view discovery.[37]

Consent to Search

Another permissible warrantless search involves situations where citizens consent to a search of their persons or effects—provided that the defendant's consent is given voluntarily (see the next "Focus On" box). However, police cannot deceive people into believing they have a search warrant when they in fact do not.[38] Nor can a hotel clerk give a valid consent to a warrantless search of the room of one of the occupants; hotel guests have a reasonable expectation of privacy, and that right cannot be waived by hotel management.[39]

What if one occupant of a home consents to a search while the other occupant refuses? In a recent case, a wife gave police permission to search for her husband's drugs, but the husband refused to give such permission; the officers went ahead and searched and found cocaine. The Supreme Court reversed his conviction, saying the Constitution does not ignore the privacy rights of an individual who is present and asserting his rights.[40] However, an occupant may still give police permission to search when the other resident is absent or does not protest.

Electronic Surveillance

Katz v. United States (1967) held that any form of electronic surveillance, including wiretapping, is a search and violates a reasonable expectation of privacy.[41] The case involved a public telephone booth, deemed by the Court to be a constitutionally protected area where the user has a reasonable expectation of privacy. This decision expressed the view that the Constitution protects people, not places. Thus the Court has required that warrants for electronic surveillance be based on probable cause, describe the conversations that are to be overheard, be for a limited period of time, name subjects to be overheard, and be terminated when the desired information is obtained.[42] However, the Court has also held that electronic eavesdropping (that is, an informant wearing a "bug," or hidden microphone) does not violate the Fourth Amendment.[43]

Looking at the plain-view doctrine, assume police officers are lawfully inside a home to execute an arrest warrant on a suspected bank robber. If, by chance, they happen to observe this illegal marijuana operation, the officers could then also arrest the occupant on drug charges.

Surveillance

FOCUS ON   CONSENT SEARCHES

Following are two examples of police performing warrantless searches with **informed consent**:

- A 25-year-old Wisconsin woman was stopped by police for driving while her license was suspended. Police then asked if they could search her vehicle, to which she replied, "Yeah, sure." Police then found illegal prescription drugs, a small bag of cocaine, marijuana, and drug paraphernalia. She allegedly told police that the cocaine and marijuana belonged to a friend and the prescription drugs were her father's.[44]

- State troopers in Nevada stopped two men in a California pickup for speeding and not staying in its lane on an interstate; a trooper became suspicious of the driver, and asked his permission to search the vehicle. Both verbal and written permission were granted. The search turned up 1.1 pounds of cocaine, worth $50,000. The two were booked for suspicion of trafficking a controlled substance, possession of a controlled substance for sale, possession of drug paraphernalia, and transporting drugs across a state line.[45]

you be the... JUDGE

CONSTITUTIONALITY OF BLOOD TESTS

In January 2013 the U.S. Supreme Court heard arguments in a landmark Fourth Amendment case involving nearly 50 years of uncertainty over whether or not police securing blood tests (for people who might be driving under the influence) without a suspect's consent is constitutional. Because of the frequency of drunk-driving stops, this decision is felt to have far-reaching effects.

The case involves Tyler McNeely, of Cape Girardeau, Missouri, who was pulled over for speeding. McNeely refused an on-scene breath test, so the trooper took him to a hospital, where McNeely again refused a test. The trooper told the lab technician to take a blood sample anyway, without a warrant. McNeely's blood-alcohol level was almost double the legal limit. Complicating the case is the fact that, earlier in 2010, the Missouri legislature changed the state's "implied consent" law to say that when people drive on Missouri's roads, they automatically consent to take a sobriety test.

1. What do you believe will/should be the outcome in this case?

Source: Adapted from M. Alex Johnson, "Supreme Court to Decide Whether Police Can Take Your Blood Without Your Permission," *U.S. News,* January 8, 2013, http://usnews.nbcnews.com/_news/2013/01/08/16416051-supreme-court-to-decide-whether-police-can-take-your-blood-without-your-permission?lite (accessed February 21, 2013).

THE FIFTH AMENDMENT

No person shall be held to answer for a capital, or otherwise infamous crime, unless on a presentment or indictment of a Grand Jury, except in cases arising in the land or naval forces, or in the Militia, when in actual service in time of war or public danger; nor shall any person be subject for the same offense to be twice put in jeopardy of life or limb; nor shall be compelled in any criminal case to be a witness against himself, nor be deprived of life, liberty, or property, without due process of law; nor shall private property be taken for public use, without just compensation.

Interrogation: police questioning of a suspect about a particular crime(s); the suspect may have an attorney present if he or she desires (see *Escobedo v. Illinois,* 1964).

Application

Today, the Fifth Amendment applies not only to criminal defendants but also to any witness in a civil or criminal case and anyone testifying before an administrative body, a grand jury, or a congressional committee. However, the privilege does not extend to blood samples, handwriting exemplars, and other such items not considered as testimony.[46]

The right against self-incrimination is one of the most significant provisions in the Bill of Rights. Basically it states that no criminal defendant shall be compelled to take the witness stand and/or give evidence against himself or herself. See the next "Focus On" box.

Once a suspect has been placed under arrest, the *Miranda* warning must be given before **interrogation** for any offense, be it a felony or a misdemeanor. An exception is the brief, routine traffic stop; however, a custodial interrogation of

The Fifth Amendment does not apply to criminal defendants' handwriting exemplars, blood samples, and other such items not considered to be testimony.

FOCUS ON   THE *MIRANDA* WARNING

While walking to a Phoenix, Arizona, bus stop on the night of March 2, 1963, 18-year-old Barbara Ann Johnson was accosted by a man who shoved her into his car, tied her hands and ankles, and drove her to the edge of the city, where he raped her. He then drove Johnson to a street near her home, letting her out of the car and asking that she pray for him. The Phoenix police subsequently picked up Ernesto Miranda for investigation of Johnson's rape and included him in a lineup at the police station. Miranda was identified by several women; one identified him as the man who had robbed her at knifepoint a few months earlier, and Johnson thought he was the rapist.

Miranda was a 23-year-old eighth-grade dropout with a police record dating back to age 14, and he had also served time in prison for driving a stolen car across a state line. During questioning, the police told Miranda that he had been identified by the women; Miranda then made a statement in writing that described the rape incident. He also noted that he was making the confession voluntarily and with full knowledge of his legal rights. He was soon charged with rape, kidnapping, and robbery.

At trial, officers admitted that during the interrogation the defendant was not informed of his right to have counsel present and that no counsel was present. Nonetheless, Miranda's confession was admitted into evidence. He was convicted and sentenced to serve 20 to 30 years for kidnapping and rape.

On appeal, the U.S. Supreme Court overturned Miranda's conviction, stating that

the current practice of incommunicado interrogation is at odds with one of our Nation's most cherished principles—that the individual may not be compelled to incriminate himself. Unless adequate protective devices are employed to dispel the compulsion inherent in custodial surroundings, no statement obtained from the defendant can truly be the product of free choice.

See *Miranda v. Arizona*, 384 U.S. 436 (1966).

Miranda v. Arizona

a DUI (driving under the influence) suspect requires the *Miranda* warning.[47] Moreover, after an accused has invoked the right to counsel, the police may not interrogate the same suspect about a different crime.[48] Once a "Mirandized" suspect invokes his or her right to silence, interrogation must cease. The police may not readminister *Miranda* and interrogate the suspect later unless the suspect's attorney is present. If, however, the suspect initiates further conversation, any confession he or she provides is admissible.[49]

Decisions Eroding *Miranda*

It has been held that a second interrogation session held after the suspect had initially refused to make a statement did not violate *Miranda*.[50] The Court also decided that when a suspect waived his or her *Miranda* rights, believing the interrogation would focus on minor crimes, but the police shifted their questioning to a more serious crime, the confession was valid; there was no police deception or misrepresentation.[51] And when a suspect invoked his or her right to assistance of counsel and refused to make written statements, then voluntarily gave oral statements to police, the statements were admissible.[52] Finally, a suspect need not be given the *Miranda* warning in the exact form as it was outlined in *Miranda v. Arizona*. In one case, the waiver form said the suspect would have an attorney

Once a suspect has been arrested, the *Miranda* warning must be given before interrogation for any offense.

appointed "if and when you go to court." The Court held that as long as the warnings on the form reasonably convey the suspect's rights, they need not be given verbatim.[53]

Bill of Rights

Lineups and Other Pretrial Identification Procedures

A police **lineup** or other face-to-face confrontation after the accused has been arrested is considered a critical stage of criminal proceedings; therefore, the accused has a right to have an attorney present. If counsel is not present, the evidence obtained is inadmissible.[54] However, the suspect is not entitled to the presence and advice of a lawyer before being formally charged.[55]

Identification Procedure

Lineups that are so suggestive as to make the result inevitable violate the suspect's right to due process (for example, the suspect being much taller than the others in the lineup, or being the only person wearing a leather jacket similar to that worn by the robber).[56] In sum, lineups must be fair to suspects; a fair lineup guarantees no bias against the suspect.

THE SIXTH AMENDMENT

In all criminal prosecutions the accused shall enjoy the right to a speedy and public trial, by an impartial jury of the State and district wherein the crime shall have been committed, which district shall have been previously ascertained by law, and to be informed of the nature and cause of the accusation; to be confronted with the witnesses against him; to have compulsory process for obtaining witnesses in his favor, and to have the assistance of counsel for his defense.

Lineup: a procedure in which police ask suspects to submit to a viewing by witnesses to determine the guilty party, based on personal and physical characteristics; information obtained may be used later in court.

going GLOBAL

THE MIDDLE EAST: THE LAW OF SHARIA

Nowhere in the Middle East is the law harsher than in Saudi Arabia. To describe Saudi law is to speak of the country's religion, culture, and customs, all of which are bound closely together. Islam means complete submission to the will of God, and to provide a well-ordered society. Alcohol is forbidden in Saudi Arabia, and possessing of even small amounts of hashish or marijuana can carry a punishment of two years' imprisonment or deportation.

The law of Islam (the Sharia) is the fundamental code in Saudi Arabia. For the crime of theft, even for the first offense, the penalty may be amputation of the left hand at the wrist. The penalty for slander is flogging, usually with 80 lashes, and the same penalty may be applied for consuming alcohol. The penalty for adultery is flogging 100 times. A woman who engages in adultery is liable to flogging or burial to the waist in a pit; stoning may follow. Highway robbery is punishable by execution or crucifixion, the amputation of opposite hands and feet, or exile from the land. Transgression will be confronted by the Saudi armed forces until the foes of the imam are defeated, and apostasy carries the death penalty. Public executions are commonplace in Saudi Arabia. Hundreds of worshippers, including children and women, often gather to observe these and other punishments. The crowd usually applauds after the execution, and some bystanders spit on the blood of the dead persons and curse them.

Source: See Saudi Arabian International Schools, "An Introduction to the Kingdom of Saudi Arabia" (Debbie Cross, personal correspondence, October 19, 1985), p. 17; Adel Mohammed el Fikey, "Crimes and Penalties in Islamic Criminal Legislation," *CJ International* 2 (July–August 1986), p. 13.

Many people believe our greatest protection is the right to have the "guiding hand" of legal counsel, not only when facing felony charges but also in certain cases involving misdemeanor charges.

Right to Counsel

Many people believe that the **Sixth Amendment** right of the accused to have the assistance of counsel before and during trial is the greatest right we enjoy in a democracy.

Over seventy years ago, in *Powell v. Alabama* (1932), it was established that in a capital case, when the accused is poor and illiterate, he or she enjoys the right to assistance of counsel for his or her defense and due process.[57] In *Gideon v. Wainwright* (1963), the Supreme Court mandated that all indigent people charged with felonies in state courts be provided counsel.[58] *Gideon* applied only to felony defendants, however; but in 1973, *Argersinger v. Hamlin* extended the right to counsel to indigent people charged with *misdemeanor* crimes if they face the possibility of incarceration (however short the incarceration may be).[59]

Another landmark decision concerning the right to counsel is *Escobedo v. Illinois* (1964).[60] Danny Escobedo's brother-in-law was fatally shot in 1960; Escobedo was arrested and questioned at police headquarters; his request to confer with his lawyer was denied, even after the lawyer arrived and asked to see his client. The questioning of Escobedo lasted several hours, during which time he was handcuffed and forced to remain standing. Eventually, he admitted being an accomplice to murder. At no point was Escobedo advised of his rights to remain silent or to confer with his attorney. Escobedo's conviction was ultimately reversed by the Supreme Court, based on a violation of his right to counsel. However, the real thrust of the decision was his Fifth Amendment right not to incriminate himself and to be informed of his rights; when a defendant is scared, flustered, ignorant, alone, and bewildered, he or she is often unable to effectively make use of protections granted under the Fifth Amendment without the advice of an attorney. Note that *Miranda*, decided two years later, simply established the guidelines for the police to inform suspects of all of these rights.

The Sixth Amendment's provision for a speedy and public trial is discussed in Chapter 9.

Gideon v. Wainwright

Escobedo v. Illinois

Chapter Quiz: Expounding the Constitution

IN A NUTSHELL

- The Fourth Amendment protects the right of the people to be secure in their persons, papers, and effects, against unreasonable searches and seizures, and no search or arrest warrants shall be issued without probable cause, describing the place to be searched, and disclosing the persons or things to be seized.

- The standard for a legal arrest, search, and seizure is **probable cause,** meaning that for an officer to make an arrest or conduct a search of someone's person or effects, he or she must have a reasonable suspicion that a crime has been or is about to be committed by that individual (which, in the case of a search, can include his or her merely possessing some form of illegal contraband).

- The exclusionary rule requires that all evidence obtained in violation of the

Fourth Amendment may not be used against the defendant in a criminal trial.

- There are two ways for the police to make an arrest: with a warrant, and without a warrant. It is always best for a police officer to arrest someone with a warrant, because a neutral magistrate has examined the facts and determined that the individual should be arrested in order to make an accounting of the charge(s).

- Police officers must obtain a warrant when making a felony arrest, unless exigent circumstances are present (immediate action being required) and the officer possesses probable cause to make the arrest.

- As with arrests, the best means by which the police can *search* a person or premises is with a search warrant issued by a neutral magistrate; the process for obtaining a search warrant is the same as for an arrest warrant, and a determination is made, after hearing evidence from an affiant, whether probable cause exists to believe a person possesses the fruits or instrumentalities of a crime.

- The police may detain a person briefly for questioning even without probable cause if they believe that the person has committed a crime or is about to commit a crime, and the person may be frisked for a weapon if an officer reasonably suspects the person is carrying a weapon and fears for his or her life. An extension of that rule involves

the "plain feel" doctrine, where police, having reasonable cause to believe a person possesses drugs and feels what resembles such an object on his or her person, may remove the object and make an arrest.

- The police have greater latitude in searching automobiles, because they can be used to effect a getaway and to hide evidence.

- The police may search incidental to lawful arrest, and do not have to search for items that are seen in plain view where citizens gives police consent to search their persons or effects.

- Police may use drug-sniffing dogs at traffic stops but not near homes without a warrant; they may also collect DNA swabs from arrestees as part of a routine booking procedure.

- The right against self-incrimination, under the Fifth Amendment, states that no criminal defendant shall be compelled to take the witness stand and give evidence against himself or herself. Once a suspect is arrested, the *Miranda* warning must be given before interrogation for any offense, be it a felony or a misdemeanor, takes place.

- The Sixth Amendment guarantees the accused the right to have the assistance of counsel during custodial interrogation and during trial.

KEY TERMS & CONCEPTS

REVIEW QUESTIONS

1. What protections are afforded citizens by the Fourth, Fifth, and Sixth Amendments?

2. What is an example of probable cause?

3. What, from both the police and community perspectives, are the ramifications of having and not having the exclusionary rule?

4. How would you distinguish between arrests and searches and seizures with and without a warrant? Which method for arresting or searching is always best?

5. In what significant ways has the *Miranda* decision been eroded, and what is its long-term outlook, given the shifting composition of judges on the Supreme Court?

6. What limitations are placed on the police in their ability to use high-tech electronic equipment in order to listen in on conversations? Search for drugs?

7. What are two major court decisions concerning right to counsel, and how do they apply in everyday life?

LEARN BY DOING

1. Your criminal justice professor has assigned a class project wherein class members are to determine which amendment to the Bill of Rights—the Fourth, Fifth, or Sixth—contains the most important rights that are protected by citizens under a democracy. You are to analyze the three and present your findings as to which one is the most important.

2. As part of a criminal justice honor society exercise, you are debating which period of legal history was the most important: the so-called due process revolution of the Warren Court (when the Supreme Court granted many additional rights to the accused through *Gideon, Miranda,* *Escobedo,* and so forth), or the more conservative era that followed under the Rehnquist Court (during which time many Warren Court decisions were eroded, and more rights were given to the police). Choose a side, and defend your opinion.

3. From the time of his confirmation in 1969, Chief Justice Warren Burger viewed the exclusionary rule as an unnecessary and unreasonable intrusion on law enforcement. Assume that as part of a group project, you are to prepare a pro-con paper that examines why there should and should not be an exclusionary rule as a part of our system of justice. What will be your arguments, pro and con??

PART III

THE COURTS

This part consists of three chapters. **Chapter 9** examines court organization and functions at the federal, state, and trial court levels; included are discussions of pretrial preparations, the actual trial process, and the jury system.

Chapter 10 looks at the courtroom work group: the judges, prosecutors, and defense attorneys.

Chapter 11 discusses sentencing, punishment, and appeals. Included are the types and purposes of punishment, types of sentences convicted persons may receive, federal sentencing guidelines, victim impact statements, capital punishment, and some court technologies.

COURT ORGANIZATION:
Structure, Functions, and the Trial Process

LEARNING OBJECTIVES

As a result of reading this chapter, the student will be able to:

1 Define what is meant by the terms *decor* and *decorum*, as they relate to the courts

2 Explain the methods and purposes of the adversarial system

3 Describe the influence of courts on policy making

4 Explain the kinds of jurisdiction that courts possess

5 Describe trial courts of general and limited jurisdictions

6 Relate the activities that occur during the pretrial process as attorneys prepare for trial

7 Explain the gravity of a defendant's right to a speedy trial—and what can happen when this right is denied

8 Distinguish advantages and disadvantages of plea negotiation

9 Review why our jury system exists, and how a jury is formed

10 Delineate the entire trial process, from opening statements through conviction and appeal

11 Describe the organization and operation of our dual—federal and state—court system

12 Review the nature of international law and the International Court of Justice

13 Delineate the role and some of the traditions of the U.S. Supreme Court

CHAPTER

09

The place of justice is a hallowed place.

—Francis Bacon

Courts are at the center of life's important moments.
—Howard Conyers, former Washoe County,
Nevada, District Court Administrator

INTRODUCTION

Author Introduction:
Chapter 9

Courts have existed in some form for thousands of years. The court system has survived the dark eras of the Inquisition and the Star Chamber (which, in England during the 1500s and 1600s, without a jury or public view, enforced unpopular political policies and meted out severe punishment, including whipping, branding, and mutilation). The U.S. court system developed rapidly after the American Revolution and led to the establishment of law and justice on the western frontier.

To set the tone and underscore how important and revered the U.S. court system is, first are considerations of courtroom decor and decorum, the adversarial system the courts employ, and how the courts influence our lives as policy-making bodies. Then the focus shifts to the several levels of courts found in the United States. First are the trial courts; included here are the several processes that occur *pre*trial, including booking, initial appearance, bail, preliminary hearing, formal charging, and arraignment. The influence of plea negotiation, the jury system, and discovery is included, as is a review of the entire **trial process**, from opening statements by the prosecution and defense attorneys through conviction, sentencing, and appeal. Next, the organization, jurisdiction, and functions of the dual court system—including both state and federal courts—is examined; the discussion of the state court system centers on both the courts of last resort and appeals courts, while the foci of the **federal court system** is on the supreme, appeals, and district courts; included is a brief overview of international law and the International

Trial process: all of the steps in the adjudicatory process, from indictment or charge to conviction or acquittal.

Federal court system: the four-tiered federal system that includes supreme courts, circuit courts of appeal, district courts, and magistrate courts.

ASSESS YOUR AWARENESS:

Test your knowledge of court structure and functions as well as the trial process and jury system by first reading and responding to the following seven true-false items; check your answers after reading this chapter's materials.

1. America's court system relies on the adversarial system, which includes, among other things, the cross-examination of witnesses.

2. America's court system consists of a national system of federal courts as well as 50 state court systems plus the District of Columbia and territories.

3. Federal judges are nominated by the president and confirmed by the Senate, and have a lifetime appointment.

4. All courts generally have unlimited jurisdiction, to hear civil/criminal trials as well as appeals.

5. The Sixth Amendment gives the accused the right to a trial by an impartial jury of peers—meaning 12 people who are "similar in nearly all regards" to the defendant.

6. The International Court of Justice is under the United Nations and applies international law to settle legal disputes.

7. A convicted person may quickly and easily—and at any time—leave the state court appellate system and appeal in a federal court.

Answers can be found on page 401.

Court of Law. Your attention is drawn to the case of Barry Kibbe, presented near the chapter's end; this case provides a rare look at the entire criminal trial and appeals process, all the way to the U.S. Supreme Court.

The chapter concludes with a chapter summary, key terms and concepts, review questions, and several scenarios and activities that provide opportunities for you to "learn by doing."

COLONIAL COURTS: AN OVERVIEW

Our nation's colonial courts began modestly. Thomas Olive, deputy governor of West Jersey in 1684, described the prevailing court system when he wrote that he was "in the habit of dispensing justice sitting in his meadow."[1] As the population of the colonies grew, however, formal courts of law appeared in Virginia, Massachusetts, Maryland, Rhode Island, and Connecticut, among other venues. The colonies drew on the example set by the English Parliament in that the colonial legislatures became the highest courts.[2]

Beneath the legislatures were the superior courts, which heard both civil and criminal cases. Over time, some colonies established trial courts headed by a chief justice and several associate justices. Appeals from the trial courts were heard by the governor and his council in what were often called "courts of appeals."[3]

Courts established at the county level played a key role in both the government and the social life of the colonies. In addition to having jurisdiction in both civil and criminal cases, county courts fulfilled many administrative duties, including setting and collecting taxes, supervising the building of roads, and licensing taverns.

Eventually, however, the founders of the new republic had profound concerns about the distribution of power between courts and legislatures, and between the states and the federal government. Coming from the experience of living under English rule, they feared the tyranny that could flow from the concentration of governmental power. On the other hand, they were also living with the problems associated with a weak centralized government. This conflict prompted the delegates to the Constitutional Convention of 1787 to create a federal judiciary that was separate from the legislative branch of government. As a result, today we have the **dual court system**—one implemented by the state courts (inherited directly from the Crown of England) and the other created by Congress and entrusted to the federal courts.[4]

Both state and federal courts composing this dual court system are discussed below.

Independent Judiciary

INSIDE THE COURTS: DECOR, DECORUM, ADVERSARIES

It is important to first understand the status and role of the courts in the U.S. criminal justice system. Discussed next are the general "hallowed" nature of our courts and how their physical appearance and required demeanor of court participants are essential for conveying that nature, as well as the role of the courts in achieving justice and policy making in our society.

Hallowed Places
Practically everything one sees and hears in an American courtroom is intended to convey the sense that the courtroom is a hallowed place in our society. Alexis de Tocqueville, in his famous study of the United States more than a

Dual court system: a term basically meaning there are both state and federal court systems.

century and a half ago, observed the extent to which our legal system permeates our lives:

> Scarcely any political question arises in the United States that is not resolved, sooner or later, into a judicial question. Hence all parties are obliged to borrow, in their daily controversies, the ideas, and even the language, peculiar to judicial proceedings. [T]he spirit of the law, which is produced in the schools and courts of justice, gradually penetrates beyond their walls into the bosom of society, where it descends to the lowest classes, so that at last the whole people contract the habits and the tastes of the judicial magistrate.[5]

The physical trappings and demeanor—the **decor**—one finds in the courts convey this sense of importance. On their first visit, citizens often are struck by the court's high ceilings, ornate marble walls, and comparatively expensive furnishings.

A formalized level of **decorum** is accorded this institution. All people must rise when the judge enters the courtroom; permission must be granted before a person can approach the elevated bench; and a general air of deference is granted the judge. A vitriolic utterance that could lawfully be directed to the president of the United States could, if directed to a judge, result in the utterer's being jailed for contempt of court.

The design of the courtroom, although generally dignified in nature, also provides a safe, functional space that is conducive to efficient and effective court proceedings. The formal arrangement of the participants and furnishings reflects society's view of the appropriate relationships between the defendant and judicial authority. The courtroom must accommodate judges, court reporters, clerks, bailiffs, witnesses, plaintiffs, defendants, attorneys, juries, and spectators, as well as police officers, social workers, probation officers, *guardians ad litem*, interpreters, and the press. Space must also be allotted for evidence, exhibits, recording equipment, and computers. Judges and court staff now may require high-technology audiovisual equipment and computer terminals to access automated information systems.

Decor, court: The physical aspects of courtroom facilities, which are to convey an image of dignity and solemnity in a facility is which justice is rendered.

Decorum: the manner in which one must conduct his or her behavior in a courtroom—for example, obtaining permission to speak to the judge or to approach the bench.

Justice in the Eye of the Beholder

Whether or not justice is done in the courtrooms depends on the interests or viewpoints of the affected or interested parties. A victim may not agree with a jury's verdict; a "winner" in a civil case may not believe that he or she received an adequate sum of money for the suffering or damages involved. Thus, because "justice" is not always agreed on, the courts must *appear* to do justice. The court's responsibility is to provide a fair hearing, with all rights accorded to the parties that are embodied in the due process clause and the other amendments, and thus result in a just outcome.[6] Several citizens' groups interested in reforming the system have engaged in court-watching efforts; such groups include Mothers Against Drunk Driving and the League of Women Voters.

The physical trappings and demeanor—the decor and decorum—of America's courts are intended to convey their sense of great importance and lofty status in our society.

Seeking Truth in an Adversarial Arena

Ralph Waldo Emerson stated that "every violation of truth . . . is a stab at the health of human society.[7] Certainly, most people would agree that the traditional, primary purpose of our courts is to provide a forum for seeking and—through the **adversarial system**—obtaining the truth. Indeed, the U.S. Supreme Court declared in 1966 in *Tehan v. United States ex rel. Shott*[8] that "the basic purpose of a trial is the determination of truth."

Our American court system relies on the adversarial system, which uses several means to get at the truth. First, evidence is tested under this approach through cross-examination of witnesses. Second, power is lodged with several different people; each courtroom actor is granted limited powers to counteract those of the others. If, for example, the judge is biased or unfair, the jury can disregard the judge and reach a fair verdict. If the judge believes the jury has acted improperly, he or she can set aside the jury's verdict and order a new trial. Furthermore, both the prosecuting and defense attorneys have certain rights and authority under each state's constitution. This series of checks and balances is aimed at curbing misuse of the criminal courts.

The American court system relies on the adversarial system of justice in attempting to discern the truth; this includes the questioning (examination) and cross-examination of witnesses.

The Influence of Courts in Policy Making

Determining what the law says and providing a public forum involve the courts in policy making. **Policy making** can be defined as choosing among alternative choices of action. The policy decisions of the courts affect virtually all of us in our daily living. In recent decades, the courts have been asked to deal with issues that previously were within the purview of the legislative and executive branches. Because many of the Constitution's limitations on government are couched in vague language, the judicial branch must eventually deal with potentially volatile social issues, such as those involving prisons, abortion, and schools.[9]

U.S. Supreme Court decisions have also dramatically changed race relations, resulted in the overhaul of juvenile courts, increased the rights of the accused, prohibited prayer and segregation in public schools, legalized abortion, and allowed for destruction of the U.S. flag. State and federal courts have together overturned minimum residency requirements for welfare recipients, equalized school expenditures, and prevented road and highway construction from damaging the environment. They have eliminated the requirement of a high school diploma for a firefighter's job and ordered increased property taxes to desegregate public schools. The only governmental area that has not witnessed judicial policy making since the Civil War is foreign affairs. Cases in which courts make policy determinations usually involve government, the Fourteenth Amendment, and the need for equity—the remedy most often used against governmental violations of law. Recent policy-making decisions by the judicial branch have been based not on the Constitution, but rather on federal statutes concerning the rights of the disadvantaged and consumers and the environment.[10]

Adversarial system: a legal system wherein there is a contest between two opposing sides, with a judge (and possibly jury) sitting as an impartial arbiter, seeking truth.

Policy making: the act of creating laws or setting standards to govern the activities of government; the Supreme Court, for example, has engaged in policy making in several areas, such as affirmative action, voting, freedom of communication and expression, and so on.

Court Justices

Perhaps nowhere have the nation's courts had more of an impact than in the prisons—from which about 52,000 prisoner petitions are filed each year in the U.S. District Courts (approximately 80 percent of them filed by state prisoners—and the bulk of those are fairly split between inmates' perceived civil rights violations and habeas petitions).[11] Among these accomplishments of judicial intervention have been extending recognized constitutional rights of free speech, religion, and due process to prisoners; abolishing the South's plantation model of prisons; accelerating the professionalization of U.S. correctional managers; encouraging a new generation of correctional administrators more amenable to reform; reinforcing the adoption of national standards for prisons; and promoting increased accountability and efficiency of prisons. The only failure of judicial intervention has been its inability to prevent the explosion in prison populations and costs.[12]

It may appear that the courts are overbroad in their review of issues. However, it should be remembered that judges "cannot impose their views . . . until someone brings a case to court, often as a last resort after complaints to unresponsive legislators and executives."[13] Plaintiffs must be truly aggrieved or have *standing*. The independence of the judicial branch, particularly at the federal court level, at which judges enjoy lifetime appointments, allows the courts to champion the causes of the underclasses: those with fewer financial resources or votes (by virtue of, say, being a minority group) or without a positive public profile.[14] It is also important to note that the judiciary is also the "least dangerous branch," having no enforcement powers. Moreover, the decisions of the courts can be overturned by legislative action. Thus, the judicial branch depends on a perception of legitimacy surrounding its decisions.[15]

WHERE THE VAST MAJORITY OF CASES BEGIN: TRIAL COURTS

The courts at the lower end of the judicial hierarchy—those that handle traffic and all manner of criminal and civil cases—actually perform the bulk of the work in adjudicating cases in the United States. These courts are described next.

General Jurisdiction: The Major Trial Courts

Trial courts of general jurisdiction are usually referred to as the major trial courts. There are an estimated 2,000 major trial courts in the 50 states and the District of Columbia, staffed by more than 11,000 judges. The term *general jurisdiction* means that these courts have the legal authority to decide all matters not specifically delegated to lower courts; this division of **jurisdiction** is specified in law. The most common names for these courts are district, circuit, and superior.[16]

Each court has its own support staff consisting of a clerk of court, a sheriff, and others. In most states the trial courts of general jurisdiction are also grouped into judicial districts or circuits. In rural areas these districts or circuits encompass several adjoining counties, and the judges are true generalists who hear a wide variety of cases and literally ride the circuit; conversely, larger counties have only one circuit or district for the area, and the judges are often specialists assigned to hear only certain types of cases.[17]

The great majority of the nation's judicial business occurs at the state, not the federal, level. State courts decide primarily street crimes. The more serious criminal violations are heard in the trial courts of general jurisdiction.

Jurisdiction, court: the power of a court to hear a particular type of case; also, the territory where a court may conduct its work—city, county, state, or federal.

State courts must also process a rising volume of drug-related offenses. Over the last 15 years, criminal cases filed in general jurisdiction courts have increased by 25 percent; most criminal cases do not go to trial, and thus the dominant issue in the trial courts of general jurisdiction is not guilt or innocence, but what penalty to apply to the guilty.[18]

Figure 9.1 shows an organizational structure for a county district court serving a population of 300,000. Note the variety of functions and programs that exist in addition to the basic court role of hearing trials and rendering dispositions.

It should also be noted that within the trial courts, a number of specialty courts or problem-solving courts, such as drug, family, mental health, and domestic violence courts, have become more common; in fact, today there are drug courts in 49 states.[19]

Limited Jurisdiction: Lower Courts

At the lowest level of state courts are trial courts of limited jurisdiction, also known as inferior courts or lower courts. There are more than 13,500 trial courts of limited jurisdiction in the United States, staffed by about 18,000 judicial officers. The lower courts constitute 85 percent of all judicial bodies in the United States.[20]

FOCUS ON COURTHOUSE VIOLENCE

Today's courts are no longer the criminal justice system's safest sanctuaries. Due to recent budget cuts, court security officers and metal detectors are being taken out of service, and some judges have even begun keeping handguns under their bench for protection—as one judge in Birmingham, Alabama, put it, to avoid becoming "a sitting duck."[21] Consider the following acts committed in what were once our nation's "hallowed halls":

- A gunman apparently on a suicide mission opens fire in a federal courthouse in Las Vegas, killing a security officer and wounding a deputy U.S. marshal.[22]

- A sniper shoots a family court judge who had presided over his divorce proceedings in Reno, Nevada, as the judge is standing at a window in his chambers.[23]

- A prisoner steals a deputy's gun and fatally shoots a judge, his court reporter, and a deputy sheriff in Atlanta.[24]

- A federal district court judge finds her husband and mother shot dead in the basement of her Chicago home, less than a year after a white supremacist was convicted of trying to have her murdered for holding him in contempt of court.[25]

These are but a few of many such incidents of **courthouse violence** that occur across the nation. Reality television programs are full of scenarios that show people attacking victims, witnesses, judges, and attorneys. It appears people are not deterred by metal-detection screening devices or security officers: A study by the Los Angeles County Superior Court found that during a recent year, officers at security screening stations detected and confiscated more than 50,000 knives, 21,000 razors, 8,200 handcuffs, and 114 stun guns from its 48 court facilities.[26]

Some individuals have no intention of engaging in violence but, either during or at the conclusion of the court proceeding, become incensed and act out in the courtroom or public corridors. Other individuals expressly intend to launch a deliberate attack on certain individuals or the judiciary itself.[27] Still others send judges inappropriate communications containing threatening activity, and state and local government buildings have been bombed as well.[28]

The problem with enhancing courthouse security is its cost. Today the cost to replace a judge's window with bullet-resistant glass would be over $1,500 for the window frame and $120 per square foot for the glass. Another problem is that such glass can weigh up to 224 pounds a square foot, and not all buildings can support such weight.[29]

Several U.S. senators introduced legislation, the Court Security Improvement Act of 2006, that would have provided funds for both federal and state court security measures, but the bill was not passed before the Congress adjourned.[30]

FIGURE 9.1

Organizational Structure for a District Court Serving a Population of 300,000

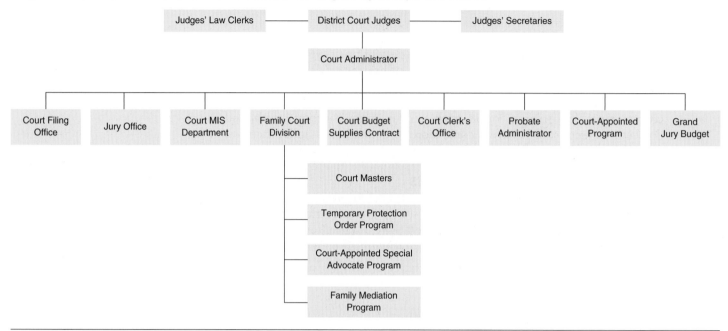

Note: (MIS = Management Information Systems)

Variously called district, justice, justice of the peace, city, magistrate, or municipal courts, the lower courts decide a restricted range of cases. These courts are created and maintained by city or county governments and therefore are not part of the state judiciary. The caseload of the lower courts is staggering—more than 61 million a year, an overwhelming number of which are traffic cases (more than 41 million in any given year).[31]

The workload of the lower courts can be divided into felony criminal cases, nonfelony criminal cases, and civil cases. In the felony arena, lower court jurisdiction typically includes the preliminary stages of felony cases. Therefore, after an arrest, a judge in a trial court of limited jurisdiction will hold the initial appearance, appoint counsel for indigents, and conduct the preliminary hearing. Later, the case will be transferred to a trial court of general jurisdiction (discussed above) for trial (or plea) and sentencing.[32]

Table 9.1 shows the caseload trends for both limited and jurisdiction criminal trial courts in the United States. As with crime in general, it is seen that the caseloads are declining in the trial courts.

MAKING PREPARATIONS: PRETRIAL PROCESSES

Pretrial Process

In Chapter 1 we briefly discussed the sequence of major events that compose the U.S. criminal justice system, from the point of entry of the offender into the system and through the related police, courts, and corrections components. In this chapter section we will focus on the trial process, including the events that occur prior to the actual trial itself. (Also note that we will discuss judges as well as the roles and strategies of prosecution and defense attorneys in Chapter 9.)

TABLE 9.1

State Court Criminal Caseloads, 2001–2010

	TOTAL INCOMING CRIMINAL CASELOADS REPORTED BY STATE COURTS, ALL STATES, 2001-2010									
	2001	**2002**	**2003**	**2004**	**2005**	**2006**	**2007**	**2008**	**2009**	**2010**
General Jurisdiction*	5,809,621	5,966,919	6,203,554	6,468,820	6,601,232	6,548,996	6,686,364	6,557,361	6,240,335	6,294,665
Limited Jurisdiction*	13,124,710	13,626,024	14,235,685	13,966,177	14,042,962	14,834,781	14,513,603	14,474,297	14,240,290	14,143,184
Total Incoming	18,934,331	19,592,943	20,439,239	20,434,997	20,644,194	21,383,777	21,199,967	21,031,658	20,480,625	20,437,849
Criminal Cases per 100,000 Population										
Total	6,556	6,723	6,954	6,889	6,897	7,076	6,950	6,832	6,596	6,528

*Courts of general jurisdiction go by many names—superior court, circuit court, district court, court of chancery, court of common pleas, and more; they are the highest trial court in the state for the matters they hear. Felony criminal cases are heard in these courts. Courts of limited jurisdiction (which also go by many names) typically have jurisdiction over misdemeanors and ordinance violations. Juvenile and domestic relations cases are heard in both general and limited jurisdiction courts depending on the state.

Source: R. LaFountain, R. Schauffler, S. Strickland & K. Holt. *Examining the Work of State Courts: An Analysis of 2010 State Court Caseloads* (National Center for State Courts 2012).

Booking, Bail, Initial Appearance, Preliminary Hearing

As stated in Chapter 1, the criminal justice process is engaged when one is arrested. Following that, the accused will then proceed through the following steps:

• **Booking**: Basically a clerical function, booking usually involves taking the suspect to a police station or sheriff's office, where he may be fingerprinted, photographed, questioned, read his rights, and possibly be given a bail amount that must be paid in order to gain release until the next stage in the process. Meanwhile, the prosecutor will be sent a copy of the offense report written by the police, and will be considering whether or not enough probable cause (discussed in Chapter 8) exists to believe the suspect committed the offense.

• **Initial appearance**: Within a reasonable time after arrest, the suspect is taken before a judge where he will be asked to enter a plea, given formal notice of the charge(s) against him, advised of his rights, and (if the judge allows) permitted to post bail. If, at this stage, the judge does not believe enough evidence has been provided to establish probable cause, the case will be dismissed.

More on pleas: Regarding defendants' pleas, they may be "not guilty," "guilty," or "no contest" (also known as *nolo contendere*). A "not guilty" plea means the defendant claims innocence for all charges made in the arrest. This plea still permits the defendant to be charged and tried; however, in criminal cases it has a similar effect as a guilty verdict, with one exception: The *nolo* plea cannot be used against him later in a civil case (because he has not admitted guilt). The court must always approve a plea of *nolo contendere.*

Booking: basically a clerical procedure for when an arrestee is taken to jail and a record is made of his or her name, address, charge(s), arresting officers, time and place of arrest, and so on.

Initial appearance: a formal proceeding during which the accused is read his or her rights, informed of the charges, and given the amount of bail required to secure pretrial release.

Bail Bond

- **Bail**: Bail is simply release pending trial, and it is guaranteed by the Constitution's Eighth Amendment except for in cases of "capital crimes," and it must not be "excessive." Certainly the defendant hopes to be released, to avoid jail, help prepare his defense, maintain ties with his family and job, and so forth. The judge must balance this right against all of the following:

✓ The risk of flight

✓ The presumption of innocence

✓ The safety of the community

The amount of a bail bond is determined by a judge, and a bail hearing will occur within the first few days (usually 48 hours) following an arrest. The courts have a bail bond schedule that sets forth the typical bail bond amounts for certain crimes. There are several ways to make bail, all of which are to ensure that the accused will later appear in court (if so, the court will refund the bail bond; if not, the court will keep the bail bond money and issue a warrant for the defendant's arrest). The defendant may make bail using any of the following:

1. Cash.

2. A secured bail bond. Here, a secured ("property") bail bond requires that the defendant use some form of security, such as the title to property equal in worth to the amount of the bail bond.

3. An unsecured (surety) bail bond, which does not require that money up front; a defendant (or perhaps a relative) signs a bond stating his or her promise to appear before the court, and, if failing to do so, promising to later pay the court an agreed-upon bail bond amount.

4. Signature or own recognizance (OR), which, like an unsecured bond, also does not require that collateral be posted or promised.

Jury

A bail bond company may also bail out the defendant, typically for 10 percent of the total amount of the bail bond as a service fee, for the risk taken to post the bail bond money.

- **Preliminary hearing**: This hearing (which the defendant may choose to waive in some jurisdictions) allows a magistrate to decide whether or not probable cause is sufficient against the person charged to proceed to trial. Before a judge only (no jury is present) the prosecutor will offer enough pertinent physical evidence and testimony to try to get the accused "bound over" for trial; the defendant may offer evidence on his own behalf. If finding enough probable cause, the judge will order the accused to appear at trial, and next the prosecutor will bring formal charges. The accused can benefit greatly at the preliminary hearing, hearing the state's case against him; because of this, some states allow the prosecutor to present the case before a sitting—and secretive—grand jury, discussed below.

Bail: surety (e.g., cash or paper bond) provided by a defendant to guarantee his or her return to court to answer to criminal charges.

Preliminary hearing: a stage in the criminal process conducted by a magistrate to determine whether a person charged with a crime should be held for trial based on probable cause; does not determine guilt or innocence.

Charging by Prosecutor or Grand Jury

By this point, the prosecutor will be preparing a formal document setting forth the charge against the defendant; this document is known as an information.

About half of all states use a **grand jury** to bring formal charges, rather than the prosecutor's doing so unilaterally.[33] He or she presents evidence to the grand jury, which also looks for probable cause to charge the defendant with a crime (the functions of the grand jury are described in the next "Focus On" box). If finding sufficient probable cause to charge the accused, an "indictment" is rendered—a formal charge—and trial will ensue.

Table 9.2 shows the use and powers of grand juries in state criminal courts.

Grand jury: a body that hears evidence and determines probable cause regarding crimes and can return formal charges against suspects; use, size, and functions vary among the states.

TABLE 9.2

State Grand Juries Used

STATE	GRAND JURY SIZE	NUMBER TO INDICT	QUORUM SIZE	INDICTMENT REQUIRED
Alabama	18	12	13	Yes
Alaska	12–18	Majority	12	Yes
Arizona	12–16	9	9	No
Arkansas	16	12	12	No
California	23/19/11	14/12/8	14/12/8	No
Colorado	23/12	12/9	12/9	No
Connecticut	1–3	Grand jury does not have authority to indict	1–3	No
Delaware	15/10	9/7	9/7	Yes
District of Columbia	16–23	12	16	Yes
Florida	15–21	12	12	Yes
Georgia	16–23	12	16	Yes
Guam	23	3/4 of the jury	16	Yes
Hawai'i	16	3/4 of the jury	8	No
Idaho	16	12	12	No
Illinois	16	9	12	No
Indiana	6	5	5	No
Iowa	7	5	5	No
Kansas	15	12	12	No
Kentucky	12	9	9	Yes
Louisiana	12	9	9	No
Maine	13-23	12	13	Yes
Maryland	23	12	12	No
Massachusetts	23	12	12	No
Michigan	13-17	9	13	Yes
Minnesota	16-23	12	16	Yes
Mississippi	15-20	12	15	Yes
Missouri	12	9	12	No
Nebraska	16	12	12	No
Nevada	17	12	12	No
New Hampshire	13-23	12	13	Yes
New Jersey	23	12	12	Yes

(Continued)

TABLE 9.2

(Continued)

STATE	GRAND JURY SIZE	NUMBER TO INDICT	QUORUM SIZE	INDICTMENT REQUIRED
New Mexico	12 - 16	8	12	No
New York	16-23	12	16	No
North Carolina	12 - 18	12	12	Yes
North Dakota	8-11	6	8	Yes
Northern Mariana Islands	1	0	1	No
Ohio	15	12	9	Yes
Oklahoma	12	9	12	No
Oregon	7	5	5	Yes
Pennsylvania	30-38	Grand jury does not have authority to indict	15	No
Puerto Rico	0		0	No
Rhode Island	13-23	13	13	No
South Carolina	18	12	12	Yes
South Dakota	6-10	6	6	Yes
Tennessee	13	12	12	Yes
Texas	12	9	9	Yes
Utah	9-15	3/4 of the jury	9	No
Vermont	0	0	0	No
Virginia	5-7	4	5	Yes
Washington	12	3/4 of the jury	12	No
West Virginia	16	12	15	Yes
Wisconsin	17	12	14	No
Wyoming	12	9	9	Yes

Source: Adapted from U.S. Department of Justice, Bureau of Justice Statistics, *State Court Organization 2004 (2006), pp. 215-216,.* at: http://bjs.gov/content/pub/pdf/sco04.pdf

Arraignment: a criminal court proceeding where a formally charged defendant is informed of the charges and asked to enter a formal plea of guilty or not guilty.

Plea negotiation (or bargaining): a preconviction process between the prosecutor and the accused in which a plea of guilty is given by the defendant, with certain specified considerations in return—having several charges or counts tossed out, a plea by the prosecutor to the court for leniency or shorter sentence, and so on.

Arraignment

After being formally charged, the accused will again be advised of his or her rights, and is given one more opportunity prior to trial to enter a plea. If the plea at this **arraignment** is "not guilty," a trial must occur (unless plea bargaining takes place, discussed below).

Plea Negotiation

When defendants enter a "guilty" or "no contest" plea, they often do so through a **plea negotiation**, or bargain. In fact, the great majority of criminal convictions—up to 90 percent—are obtained without any courtroom fact-finding, because a plea is struck beforehand. In essence, in exchange for the defendants' plea of guilty, the government is willing to give the defendant certain concessions.

There are several forms of plea bargaining. The accused can engage in *charge bargaining* (offering to plead guilty to a lesser offense than the one charged, thus hoping for a lighter sentence), *count bargaining* (pleading guilty to, say, three of the charged counts and having the remaining

FOCUS ON   GRAND JURY POWERS

The primary function of the modern grand jury is to review the evidence presented by the prosecutor and determine whether there is probable cause to return an indictment.

The Fifth Amendment to the U.S. Constitution requires that a grand jury indictment be brought to commence all federal criminal charges, so in virtually every federal jurisdiction, there is at least one grand jury sitting every day. Federal grand juries have extraordinary investigative power, which is the source of much of the criticism against grand juries: that they simply act as a rubber stamp for the prosecutor. And, unlike potential jurors in regular trials, grand jurors are not screened for biases or other improper factors.

For federal cases involving complex and long-term investigations (such as those involving organized crime, drug conspiracies, or political corruption), "long-term" grand juries will be impaneled. In most jurisdictions, grand jurors are drawn from the same pool of potential jurors as are any other jury panels, and in the same manner.

The Federal Rules of Criminal Procedure provide that the prosecutor, grand jurors, and the grand jury stenographer are prohibited from disclosing what happened before the grand jury, unless ordered to do so in a judicial proceeding. Secrecy prevents

the escape of people whose indictment may be contemplated, ensures that the grand jury can deliberate without outside pressure, prevents witness tampering prior to trial, and encourages people with information about a crime to speak freely.

A prosecutor can obtain a subpoena to compel anyone to testify before a grand jury, without showing probable cause and, in most jurisdictions, without even showing that the person subpoenaed is likely to have relevant information.

In the federal system, a witness cannot have his or her lawyer present in the grand jury room, although witnesses may interrupt their testimony and leave the grand jury room to consult with their lawyer. A few states do allow a lawyer to accompany the witness. A witness who refuses to appear before the grand jury risks being held in contempt of the court.

If the grand jury refuses to return an indictment, the prosecutor can try again; double jeopardy does not apply to the grand jury. No judge is present in the grand jury room when testimony is being taken.

All states have some form of grand jury, but only about half the states now use grand juries routinely for bringing criminal charges.

Source: Adapted from the American Bar Association, "Frequently Asked Questions About the Grand Jury System," http://www.abanow.org/2010/03/faqs-about-the-grand-jury-system/ (accessed February 19, 2013).

six counts thrown out), or negotiating how they will serve their sentence (e.g., two five-year terms to be served concurrently, as opposed to consecutively).

As the defendant benefits from plea bargaining, so does the government. The prosecutor "wins" a conviction while reducing the time, money, and uncertainty involved in taking the case to trial; it also helps to avoid a crowded court docket, eases the burden on witnesses and prospective jurors, and can reduce the overcrowding of jails. Certainly there are many reasons why a high percentage of cases are bargained out of the system, and one can only imagine the havoc that would be caused in the court system if nine of ten cases that are plea bargained had to be tried. However, by signing off the deal and pleading guilty, the defendant waives a number of constitutional protections (see some of them enumerated in the next "Focus On" box). But consider the realities of a typical barroom killing. There might be evidence of premeditation and malice that is sufficient enough to justify a jury verdict of murder in the first degree. Or, the defendant's long-time status as an alcoholic might convince the jury that he was unable to form the necessary intent to be heavily punished. Perhaps the defendant may indicate that he acted in "heat of passion," pointing to a verdict of manslaughter, or even that he acted in self-defense. When such cases are given to the jury to decide, a variety of possible outcomes is possible. Therefore, the reality is that plea negotiations allow the prosecutor

In 2009 Chris Brown, recording artist, dancer, and actor, used a plea negotiation to avoid jail time for the felony assault that he committed against his one-time girlfriend, recording artist Rihanna.

and defense to arrive at some middle ground of what experience has shown to be "justice," without the defense running the risk of heavy punishment for the defendant, and the government not having to devote many days in trial—with the risk of the defendant being acquitted.[34]

Jury Trials

Most civilizations—even the most primitive in nature—have used some means to get at the truth: to tell right from wrong, guilt from innocence, and so forth. In Burma, each suspected party to a crime had to light a candle, and the person whose candle burned the longest was not punished.[36] In Borneo, suspects poured lime juice on a shellfish; whoever's shellfish squirmed first was the guilty party.[37] The "trial by ordeal" method was also used around the world, with people's guilt or innocence determined by subjecting them to a painful task (often using fire and water); the idea was that God would intercede and help the innocent by performing a miracle on their behalf.[38]

FOCUS ON   PLEA BARGAINING

Some authors believe plea bargaining reduces the courthouse to something akin to a Turkish bazaar, where people barter over the price of copper jugs. They see it as justice on the cheap. Others believe that plea bargaining works to make the job of the judge, the prosecutor, and the defense attorney much easier, while sparing the criminal justice system the expense and time to conduct many more trials.

No matter where one stands on the issue, however, it is ironic that both police and civil libertarians oppose plea bargaining, but for different reasons. Police and others in the crime control camp view plea bargaining as undesirable because defendants can avoid conviction and responsibility for crimes they actually committed when allowed to plead guilty to (and be sentenced for) lesser and/ or fewer charges; police, in the crime control camp, would prefer to see the defendant convicted for the crime actually committed.

Civil libertarians and other supporters of the due process model also oppose plea bargaining, but for different reasons: When agreeing to negotiate a plea, the accused forfeits a long list of legal protections afforded under the Bill of Rights: the presumption of innocence; the government's burden of proof (beyond a reasonable doubt); and the rights to face one's accuser, testify, and present witnesses in one's defense, have an attorney and a trial by jury (except for lesser offenses), appeal if convicted, and so on. Another concern is that an innocent defendant might be forced to enter a plea of guilty.

1. In your opinion, does plea bargaining sacrifice too many of the defendant's rights?

2. Or, does justice suffer by giving too many benefits to guilty persons?[35]

The U.S. Constitution ensures that our method is more civilized, however; its Sixth Amendment provides for the defendant to have a trial by an impartial jury of his or her peers. It is felt by many people that the jury is the most sacred aspect of our criminal justice system, because it is where common citizens sit as a forum to determine the truth and assess the punishment to be meted out. Not all criminal defendants are guaranteed a right to trial by jury (i.e., if charged with a *lesser misdemeanor*—one that has a penalty of less than six months in jail); furthermore, the defendant may waive the right to jury trial and be tried by a judge alone (known as a *bench trial*). There are advantages and disadvantages to each, and a wise defendant will want to discuss them with an attorney.

Criminal trials in the United States often involve a jury of one's peers to hear the evidence; then, if rendering a conviction, the same jury may be used to determine the proper form and extent of punishment.

The method of selection of 12 citizen *peers* to hear the evidence is important. First, in most states a questionnaire is mailed to people (whose names were obtained from voter, taxpayer, driver, or other lists), to determine who is qualified to serve or not; certain exemptions are given. Those who are qualified to serve are then sent a *summons* to compose a jury pool; from this pool a smaller number of prospective jurors is selected, usually about 20, for *voir dire*. This group (or *panel*) will then appear in court to be questioned further concerning their suitability to serve—that is, whether they can be fair and impartial, decide the case based upon the evidence presented, and so on. With the judge overseeing the selection process, both the prosecution and defense can challenge and have removed an unlimited number of jurors *for cause*, meaning for some reason one is prejudiced against their side. Finally, both the prosecution and defense also receive a limited (usually set by statute) number of *peremptory challenges*, which allow them to remove jurors without any reason or explanation.

Generally, 12 jurors and 2 alternates are selected for a criminal trial, but that number is not required by the Constitution. In *Williams v. Florida*,[39] the U.S. Supreme Court said that the decision to fix the size of a jury at 12 "appears to have been a historical accident" and that a 6-member jury satisfied the constitutional requirement. Nor is a unanimous verdict by the jury required by either the U.S. Constitution or the U.S. Supreme Court, so in some states a majority of "votes" from the jurors will support a verdict.[40]

Figure 9.2 shows several aspects of jury service and trials in the United States as reported by the Center for Jury Studies: the estimated number of jury trials, the percentage of actual trials by case type, and the estimated number of adults involved in jury service each year.

Pretrial Motions

Prior to the trial, either the defendant or the prosecutor may file **pretrial motions/processes** with the court in order to be better positioned for trial. Possible defense motions include to suppress evidence (e.g., the defense believes that a police search, physical evidence or a confession, and so on was

Mid-Chapter Quiz: Court Organization

Williams v. Florida

Pretrial motions/processes: any number of motions filed by prosecutors and defense attorneys prior to trial, to include quashing of evidence, change of venue, discovery, to challenge a search or seizure, to raise doubts about expert witnesses, to exclude a defendant's confession, and so on.

FOCUS ON   JURY DUTY AND EXCUSED ABSENCES

There seems to be no end to the lengths some potential jurors will go to avoid jury duty.

A Bronx, New York, woman informed the court that she could not serve on a murder case because she had been a murder victim herself. Other proffered excuses include these:

"I have too much to do."

"I have a lunch date with my buddies each month—I can't miss that."

"I'm sick of this BLEEP! I'll serve, but I'm going to find everyone guilty!"

Then there was a woman who said she couldn't possibly serve on a jury and leave her dogs home alone.[41]

Such excuses can severely test the courts' patience, possibly result in prosecution, and earn an angry rebuke from the judge: When a Cape Cod man claimed he was homophobic, racist, and a habitual liar to avoid jury duty, the judge referred the case to prosecutors for possible charges. "In 32 years of service in courtrooms, as a prosecutor, as a defense attorney and now as a judge, I have quite frankly never confronted such a brazen situation of an individual attempting to avoid juror service," stated Superior Court Judge Gary Nickerson.[42]

FIGURE 9.2

Jury Trials and Service in U.S.

Estimated Number of Jury Trials in All U.S. State Courts

Estimated number of jury trials* 148,558

Trial rate per 100k population 59

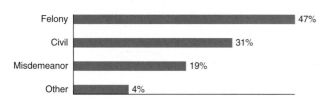

Percentage of trials by case type

Felony — 47%
Civil — 31%
Misdemeanor — 19%
Other — 4%

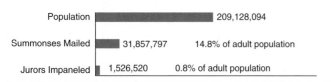

Estimated number of adults involved in jury selection annuallay

Population — 209,128,094
Summonses Mailed — 31,857,797   14.8% of adult population
Jurors Impaneled — 1,526,520   0.8% of adult population

*This estimate was extrapolated using survey results for 1,546 counties representing 70% of the U.S. population.

Source: Reprinted with permission from The National Center for State Courts, Center for Jury Studies.

obtained illegally), to reduce bail (if the accused is still in jail awaiting trial), discovery (discussed below), change of venue (to move the trial to another city, if a highly publicized or emotional crime is charged), and continuances.

Discovery

No member of the court work group—including judges, prosecutors, and defense attorneys—likes major surprises or "bombshell" evidence coming to light in the courtroom. **Discovery** is simply the exchange of information between prosecution and defense, in order to promote a fair adversarial contest between the two sides and help the truth come to light. Essentially, each side is entitled to learn the strengths and weaknesses of the other, as well as what evidence and theories will be relied on.

Discovery has become quite controversial in recent years, with prosecutors often being accused of withholding evidence that should have been provided to the defense. This has even gotten to the point that many jurisdictions have individuals—normally attorneys, skilled in the laws of evidence—serving as "discovery masters" to ensure fair exchange of information by both sides. Generally, the prosecution has a higher burden of providing "exculpatory" evidence (that which tends to support the defendant's innocence) (see *Brady v. Maryland*, 1963).[43] However, because the Supreme Court has only required exculpatory evidence be disclosed, this has become a confusing area of law and formal/informal policy—with some states adopting conservative, others liberal, and still others "middle ground" rules of discovery[44]—so that the question of what is to be exchanged is not at all clear-cut.

Diversion Programs

In some jurisdictions, prior to trial, some defendants—typically young offenders who have no significant or particularly violent criminal records—may be allowed to enter a diversion program such as a drug court, mental health court, or military veterans court; such courts are now beginning to appear across the country. Normally, if the individual successfully completes the conditions of a program, such as remaining "clean," obtaining counseling, or attending specified classes, either no charges will be filed, or any charges filed will be dismissed. However, a defendant who violates the terms of the program will likely have charges reinstated and be taken to trial.

THE TRIAL PROCESS

After all pretrial processes have been addressed, the next challenge lies with getting the case into the courtroom in a timely manner and then seeing that certain rules and defendants' rights are followed. These aspects of the trial process are discussed next.

Jelani Gaynor addresses the jury during final arguments in Teen Court in Greenville, North Carolina. First-time offenders may use this specialized diversion program, which allows defendants ages 11 through 15 to appear before a jury of their peers to avoid a formal hearing in juvenile court.

Right to a Speedy Trial: "Justice Delayed . . ."

Swift justice is a term that is fairly well emblazoned in our collective psyche—and has been the title for a number of books, movies, and even some television series. Doing justice in a timely manner is felt to be essential for sending a meaningful message to the offender, to likewise convey a message of deterrence to the general public, maintain public confidence in the judicial process, and generally help the criminal justice system better do its job.

Similarly, the adage that "justice delayed is justice denied" says much about the long-standing goal of processing court cases with due deliberate speed. Charles Dickens condemned the practice of slow litigation in 19th-century England.[45] Dickens was considerably harsh toward England's Chancery Courts in his novel *Bleak House*,[46] and Shakespeare mentioned "the law's delay" in *Hamlet*.[47] Most importantly, even our Founding Fathers saw fit to hasten the movement of criminal matters into the courtroom: The Sixth Amendment to the Constitution states in part, "In all criminal prosecutions, the accused shall enjoy the right to a speedy and public trial." As a result, the consequences of **delay** to society are potentially severe: The U.S. Supreme Court has ruled that if the defendant's right to a speedy trial has been violated, then the indictment must be dismissed and/or the conviction overturned.[48]

Certainly there will be some criminal defendants who want their trial dates continued as long as possible—in order for the community emotion surrounding the crime to subside, the memories of its victims and witnesses to fade, and so on. Others, however—particularly those who cannot post bail and are awaiting trial in a jail, and/or have jobs and family to return to—want their "day in court" to arrive as soon as possible.

Brady v. Maryland

Trial Process

Discovery: a procedure wherein both the prosecution and the defense exchange and share information as to witnesses to be used, results of tests, recorded statements by defendants, psychiatric reports, and so on, so that there are no major surprises at trial; known as "Brady material," based on *Brady v. Maryland* (1963

Delay (trial): an attempt (usually by defense counsel) to have a criminal trial continued until a later date.

FOCUS ON AN INSIDER'S VIEW OF A LOWER COURT

On his website, the Honorable Kevin Higgins, a lower court judge in Nevada, provided compelling realism and insight—as well as a bit of humor—in describing the workings and proper decorum of people and lawyers who are about to litigate cases in his courtroom:

We tend to be the fast-food operators of the court system—high volumes of traffic for short visits with a base of loyal repeat customers. Don't plan on having a private conversation with your client or a witness amidst the throngs of other people trying to do the same thing. Prepared attorneys can be in and out in short order. Meeting your client for the first time after calling out his name in the lobby can take longer.

Patience is a virtue and communication with the bailiffs and court staff will keep everyone happy. We coordinate the court's calendar, your calendar, and opposing counsel's calendar with the availability of the witnesses.

Here are a few other "do's" and "don'ts" for successfully navigating this Court:

- Everyone goes through the metal detector. Having to go back to your car to stow your Leatherman, linoleum cutting knife, stun gun, giant padlock or sword-cane (all items caught by security) can be annoying.

- I once ruled against a very sweet elderly lady who reminded me of my own grandmother. She simply didn't have a case and I thought I had ruled fairly and gently. As she slowly walked by the front of the bench on the way out of the courtroom, she looked up and said, "Aw, go ---- yourself," and walked out the door. My mouth was hanging open; I just didn't know what to do. I'm fairly sure that this is the first and last time someone will get away with this, so even if the judge rules against you, smile on the way out. You can mutter to yourself all you want on the way back to the office rather than the holding cell in the back of the courthouse.

- I once watched a gentleman in the back row feed his parrot peanuts while it was sitting on his shoulder. I assumed I had a parrot case in the pile somewhere, but after the last case was called, the parrot left without testifying. I asked the security officer why he let the man with the parrot come into court. I was told that the man had been there to watch a friend's case and that his sick parrot needed to be fed every 15 minutes. While admiring the logic of his decision, I have advised our new court security officers that unless an animal is actually a service animal, various beasts, fish, and fowl are not allowed in simply to watch court.

- Expect the unexpected. Recent interesting events include a live pipe bomb being left at the front door by a concerned citizen; a gentleman dancing on top of his motor home in the parking lot while his laundry hung from the trees and his morning coffee perked on the propane stove he had set up in the next space; and the occasional ammonia discharges into the holding cell by one of the neighboring businesses.

1. Are you surprised by Judge Higgins's comments concerning the manner in which some people conduct themselves in a court of law?

Source: Adapted from Hon. Kevin Higgins, "An Insider's View of Justice Court," *Nevada Lawyer* 16, no. 8 (August 2008), p. 21. Reprinted with permission.

Speedy Trial Act of 1974: later amended, it originally was enacted to ensure compliance with the Sixth Amendment's provision for a speedy trial by requiring that a federal case be brought to trial no more than 100 days following the arrest.

But what does "speedy trial" mean in practice, and how does an appellate court know if the right has been denied? Those questions have been addressed at the *federal* level, with Congress enacting the **Speedy Trial Act of 1974**.[49] This act mandates a 30-day limit from the point of arrest to indictment and 70 days from indictment to trial. Thus, federal prosecutors have a total of 100 days from the time of arrest until trial.

However, there is very little in the way of fixed, enforced time limits at the *state* level, and the Supreme Court has refused to give the concept of a "speedy trial" any precise time frame.[50] Also, where they exist, most state laws fail to provide the courts with adequate and effective enforcement mechanisms; furthermore, if a prosecutor has clearly taken excessively long to bring a case to trial, existing time limits may be waived due to the court's own congested dockets. As a result, there are no "teeth" in state statutes concerning the time limits, so state-level speedy trial laws are often not followed in practice.

The concern, then, is with *unnecessary* delay. Where a court must determine whether or not the defendant's right to a speedy trial was violated, the Supreme Court in *Barker v. Wingo*[51] established the following test:

1. *Length of delay*: A delay of a year or more from the date of arrest or indictment, whichever occurs first, was termed "presumptively prejudicial"; however, as noted above, the Supreme Court has never explicitly ruled that any absolute time limit applies.

2. *Reason for the delay*: The prosecution may not excessively delay the trial for its own advantage; however, a trial may be delayed for good reason, such as to secure the presence of a key witness.

3. *Time and manner in which the defendant has asserted his right*: If a defendant agrees to the delay when it works to his own benefit, he cannot later claim that he has been unduly delayed.

4. *Degree of prejudice to the defendant which the delay has caused.*[52]

Author Video: Right to a Speedy Trial

Barker v. Wingo

Trial Protocols

After the judge has given the jury its preliminary instructions—emphasizing the defendant is presumed innocent until proven guilty—and other pretrial issues have been settled, typically the pattern of the trial process is as follows:

1. *Opening statements*: The prosecutor goes first, as he or she has the burden of proof (and must prove every element of the crimes charged—beyond a reasonable doubt), followed by the defense (although in many jurisdictions the defense can opt to defer making its opening statements until later, when it presents its main case, or waive it altogether). The purpose of this step is to succinctly outline the facts they will try to prove during the trial—and it is *not* a time to argue with the other side.

2. *Prosecution's case*: The prosecution will present its side of the case, presenting and questioning its witnesses and admitting relevant evidence. The defense may cross-examine these prosecution witnesses. A "redirect" allows the prosecution to reexamine its witnesses. Once the prosecution has finished presenting its evidence, it will rest its case.

3. *Motion to dismiss*: As a formality, at this point during a criminal trial the defense will often make a motion to dismiss all charges. This request is generally denied by the judge, opening the way for the defense case.

4. *Defense's case*: Next, the defense presents its main case through direct examination of their chosen witnesses. The prosecution is then given an opportunity to cross-examine the defense witnesses, and, during redirect, the defense may reexamine its witnesses. The defendant cannot be compelled to testify against himself, but he has the right to testify in his own defense if he chooses to do so. The defense then rests.

5. *Prosecution rebuttal*: The prosecution may offer evidence to refute the arguments made by the defense.

6. *Closing arguments*: This is a time for both sides to arrange the evidence so it is not so confusing, so the jury can weigh and understand it. The order of closing arguments varies by jurisdiction. In some jurisdictions, the state always argues first; in others it is the defense.[53] The prosecution will offer reasons why the evidence points to the defendant's guilt, and the defense will explain why the defendant should be acquitted. This is *not* the time for the prosecutor to offer personal opinion, make inflammatory or discriminatory remarks, or comment on the defendant's failure to testify; any of these forms of misconduct may result in a reversal of a conviction, and retrial.

7. *Jury instructions*: The judge's instructions to the jury are very important and, if improper, may later be grounds for a reversal and new trial.

Closing arguments are used by both prosecutors and defense attorneys attempt to arrange the evidence and make it more understandable for the jurors.

A head juror—sometimes termed its "foreperson," "foreman" or "presiding juror"—may be selected by the judge or by vote of the jurors, pose questions to the judge on behalf of the jury, and sometimes read the jury's verdict at the end of the trial.

The judge will explain the law that is applicable to that particular criminal case and the possible verdicts, and will typically include general comments concerning the presumption of the defendant's innocence, that guilt be proved beyond a reasonable doubt, that the jury may not draw inferences from the fact that the defendant did not testify in his own behalf, and so on.

8. *Jury deliberations and verdict*: The jury will deliberate for as long as it takes to reach a verdict. In most states, unanimous agreement must be met for a verdict to be reached (however, as noted above, a unanimous verdict is not required by the Constitution). Once the jury has determined its verdict, either guilty or not guilty for each crime in question, it will be read to the court. Then, either side, or the judge, may "poll the jury," asking all jurors individually if the verdict as read is theirs; if not unanimous, the jury may be returned to its room to deliberate again, or be discharged. If the jury acquits the defendant, the case is usually over (the prosecutor not being able to appeal an acquittal). The jury may, instead, convict the defendant of some charges while acquitting of others.

9. *Posttrial motions*: If the jury delivers a guilty verdict, the defense will usually ask the judge to override the jury's decision and acquit the defendant or grant him a new trial. This motion is almost always denied.

  a. *Sentencing*: If the defendant was convicted of the crime(s), sentencing will be determined by the judge immediately after the verdict is read or at a later court date. In arriving at a sentence, the judge will likely take into account the severity and nature of the crimes; also, to assist in arriving at a proper sentence the judge may order a presentence investigation (PSI) by probation or court services personnel, to look at the history of the person convicted, any extenuating circumstances, a review of his or her criminal record, and a review of the specific facts of the crime. The person or agency doing the PSI makes a recommendation to the court about the type and severity of the sentence. The judge may, however, be limited by federal and state sentencing guidelines (discussed in Chapter 1); some crimes carry a mandatory minimum sentencing requirement, while other sentences may be largely based on the discretion of the judge.

  b. *Punishments*: After a conviction, and upon receiving the PSI or using sentencing guidelines, the judge may opt for one of the following punishments:

- Incarceration
- Probation
- Fines
- Restitution
- Community service

10. Appeal: After conviction, the defendant may challenge the outcome. Potential grounds for appeal in a criminal case include legal error (e.g., improperly admitted evidence, improper jury instructions), juror misconduct, ineffective counsel, or lack of sufficient evidence to support a guilty verdict. If this error affected the outcome of the case, the appeal will stand, and a retrial will be ordered (or the prosecutor may choose to drop charges); if the error would not have affected the outcome, then the errors are considered harmless.[54] Note also that, for the *first* appeal, the U.S. Supreme Court has said that if the person convicted is indigent, then free, appointed counsel must be provided.[55] However, the Court later ruled that, if losing the initial appeal, he or she is *not* entitled to free appointed counsel for any subsequent appeals.[56]

STATE COURTS

Courts of last resort are usually referred to as the state supreme court. The specific names differ from state to state, however, as do the number of judges (from a low of 5 to as many as 9). Unlike the intermediate appellate courts (discussed below), these courts do not use panels in making decisions; rather, the entire court sits to decide each case. All state supreme courts have a limited amount of original jurisdiction in dealing with such matters as disciplining lawyers and judges.[57]

State Supreme Court

In those 11 states not having **intermediate courts of appeals**, the state supreme court has no power to choose which cases will be placed on its docket. However, the ability of most state supreme courts to choose which cases to hear makes them important policy-making bodies. Whereas intermediate appellate courts review thousands of cases each year, looking for errors, state supreme courts handle a hundred or so cases that present the most challenging legal issues arising in that state.

Nowhere is the policy-making role of state supreme courts more apparent than in deciding death penalty cases—which, in most states, are automatically appealed to the state's highest court, thus bypassing the intermediate courts of appeal. The state supreme courts are also the ultimate review board for matters involving interpretation of state law.[58]

Like their federal counterparts, state courts have experienced a significant growth in appellate cases that threatens to overwhelm the state supreme court; therefore, to alleviate the caseload burden on courts of last resort, state officials in 39 states have responded by creating intermediate courts of appeals, or ICAs (the only states not having an ICA are sparsely populated with low volumes of appeals). There are about 1,000 such judges in the nation today. The ICAs must hear all properly filed appeals.[59]

The structure of the ICA varies; in most states these bodies hear both civil and criminal appeals; and like their federal counterparts, these courts typically use rotating three-judge panels. Also like the federal appellate courts, the state ICAs' workload is demanding as well: According to the National Center for State Courts, state ICAs report that about 273,000 are cases filed annually.[60] ICAs engage primarily in error corrections; they review trials to make sure that the law was followed; the overall standard is one of fairness.

Court of last resort: the last court that may hear a case at the state or federal level.

Intermediate courts of appeal: a level of courts in state courts that stand between trial courts and courts of last resort; they typically have appellate jurisdiction only.

The ICAs represent the final stage of the process for most litigants; very few cases make it to the appellate court in the first place, and of those cases, only a small proportion will be heard by the state's court of last resort.[61]

Table 9.3 shows the trend of caseloads for all states in both their courts of last resort and their courts of appeals—all of which will be seen to be declining as of 2006.

TABLE 9.3

Caseloads of State Courts of Last Resort and Appellate Courts, 2001–2010

TOTAL INCOMING CASES IN STATE APPELLATE COURTS									
2001	2002	2003	2004	2005	2006	2007	2008	2009	2010

	2001	2002	2003	2004	2005	2006	2007	2008	2009	2010
Total Incoming	277,894	278,006	281,363	280,221	282,298	283,443	282,728	280,535	273,061	272,975

TOTAL INCOMING CASES IN STATE APPELLATE COURTS, BY COURT TYPE, 2001–2010									
2001	2002	2003	2004	2005	2006	2007	2008	2009	2010

	2001	2002	2003	2004	2005	2006	2007	2008	2009	2010
Court of Last Resort*	88,845	90,849	91,641	89,914	88,964	91,735	89,495	87,231	82,125	81,439
Intermediate Appellate Courts	189,049	187,157	189,722	190,307	193,334	191,708	193,233	193,304	190,936	191,536

*The court of last resort in a state can go by many names—superior court, supreme court of appeals, appeals court—but whatever its name, it is the highest trial court in the state for the matters they hear.

Source: National Center for State Courts, Court Statistics Project, Examining the Work of State Courts: An Analysis of 2010 State Court Caseloads, September 2012.

THE FEDERAL COURTS

Henderson v. Kibbe

Habeas Corpus

In order to better understand the court system of the United States, it is first important to know that this country has both a national system of federal courts (to include the District of Columbia and U.S. territories) and 50 state courts systems. Although often sharing similar names, they operate under different constitutions and laws. This dual court system of the United States is discussed next.

A Dual Court System

The next "You Be the Judge" box contains an excellent *procedural* case that uniquely demonstrates the entire appellate process through the dual state and federal court systems, going through the state courts and all the way to the U.S. Supreme Court. Read the case and respond to the queries posed at its conclusion (answers are provided in the Source note). This case could have fit in Chapter 2 as well, under the law of **causation**, but it is included here to showcase how our appellate system operates as well as some important legal concepts.

Next the federal court system and the general structure and functions of the state courts are briefly described.

U.S. Supreme Court

The **Supreme Court of the United States,** as the highest court in the nation, has ultimate jurisdiction over all federal courts as well as over state

Causation: a link between one's act and the injurious act or crime, such as one tossing a match in a forest and igniting a deadly fire.

U.S. Supreme Court: the court of last resort in the United States, also the highest appellate court; it consists of nine justices who are appointed for life.

you be the... JUDGE

THE APPEALS PROCESS OF BARRY KIBBE

On a very cold night in Rochester, New York, Barry Kibbe and a friend met Stafford at a bar. Stafford had been drinking so heavily that the bartender refused to serve him more alcohol, so Kibbe offered to take him barhopping elsewhere. They visited other bars, and at about 9:30 p.m., Kibbe and his friend drove to a remote point on a highway and demanded Stafford's money; they also forced Stafford to lower his trousers and remove his boots to show he had no money hidden. Stafford was then abandoned on the highway, in the cold. A half-hour later, a man driving his truck down the highway saw Stafford standing in the highway, waving his arms for him to stop; seeing him too late, the driver struck and killed Stafford.

State Court Actions: Kibbe was arrested and convicted, in *State v. Kibbe*, of robbery and murder in the second degree. At trial, the judge did *not* instruct the jury on the subject of causation (e.g., that the government had to prove Kibbe had actually caused Stafford's death). On appeal to New York's appeals court, in *Kibbe v. Henderson*, Kibbe argued that the judge *should* have given the jury such an instruction to consider, but the appellate court affirmed his conviction. Then, on appeal to New York's supreme court, the conviction was also affirmed; both courts found that there was sufficient evidence of causation.

Federal Court Actions: Having *exhausted all possible state* remedies, Kibbe then sought redress in the federal court, filing a *writ of habeas* corpus with the U.S. District Court having jurisdiction and arguing that the trial judge had violated his due process rights by not giving the jury instruction; the district court denied the *habeas* petition, saying that no constitutional question had been raised.

Next, Kibbe appealed to the Second U.S. Circuit Court of Appeals, making the same argument. This court, however, *reversed* his conviction, saying that Kibbe *had been* deprived of due process because of the trial judge's failure to instruct the jury on causation. Next, the *government* appealed, this time to the U.S. Supreme Court; in *Henderson v. Kibbe*, the Supreme Court, issuing a *writ of certiorari* (defined below) to the lower court, decided to hear the case.

1. How do you believe the U.S. Supreme Court should rule—for or against Kibbe? Why?

2. Who was Henderson (Kibbe's adversary) in this case?

3. What is meant by "exhausting all possible state remedies"?

4. What is meant by *habeas corpus?*

Again, answers to these questions are provided in the Source note below.

Source: The U.S. Supreme Court reversed the decision of the lower court (i.e., Circuit Court), saying the lack of an instruction on causation by itself in this case was not a violation of due process rights. The Court also said, notably, that "a person who is aware of, and consciously disregards a risk, must foresee the ultimate harm involved." See *Kibbe v. Henderson*, 534 F.2d 493 (1976). Kibbe's adversary (the appellee) in this case, Henderson, was the superintendent at Auburn Correctional Facility in New York. *Habeas corpus* (sometimes termed "the great writ") is a Latin term for "you have the body"; it is the inmate's means of asking a court to grant a hearing to determine whether or not he or she is being held illegally. The term *exhausting all possible state remedies* is a legal doctrine meaning that the *state's* appeals courts are to be given the opportunity to correct any defects that occurred at trial before a party may pursue a case in federal court. This is basically the rule of comity, or courtesy—the federal courts to defer to state courts to correct any defects prior to those claims being raised in a federal court.

courts in cases involving issues of federal law; it is the final interpreter of federal constitutional law. The court, as will be seen below, is also richly steeped in tradition. Also briefly discussed are its jurisdiction, practices, workload, and administration.

Judges and Advocacy

The Supreme Court, formed in 1790, and other federal courts have their basis in Article III, Section 1, of the Constitution, which provides that "the judicial Power of the United States, shall be vested in one supreme Court, and in such inferior Courts as the Congress may from time to time ordain and establish."[62] The Supreme Court is composed of nine justices: one chief justice and eight associate justices. As with other federal judges appointed under Article III, they are nominated to their post by the president and confirmed by the Senate, and serve for life.[63] Each new term of the Supreme Court begins, by statute, on the first Monday in October.

Court Justices

The United States Supreme Court, in Washington, D.C., is where the court's nine justices meet, deliberate, and render the law of the land.

Defense attorney Johnnie Cochran is shown with gloves on during O. J. Simpson's criminal trial: "If it doesn't fit, you must acquit." For many people this trial stands as the primary example of how trials can become a media "circus" and why cameras should not be allowed in the courtroom

Not just any lawyer may advocate a cause before the high court; all who wish to do so must first secure admission to the Supreme Court bar. Applicants must submit an application form that requires applicants to have been admitted to practice in the highest court of their state for a period of at least three years (during which time they must not have been the subject of any adverse disciplinary action), and must appear to the Court to be of good moral and professional character. Applicants must also swear or affirm to act "uprightly and according to law, and . . . support the Constitution of the United States."[64]

Inside the Court: Traditions and Practices

The Court building, constructed in 1935 and most impressive in its design, has emblazoned over its main entrance the words "Equal Justice Under Law." Many thousands of visitors to the U.S. Supreme Court have been struck by the sight and the might of the building and its jurists. Justice Robert Jackson once described the Court's uniqueness, saying, "We are not final because we are infallible, but we are infallible because we are final."[65]

In many respects the Court is the same institution that first met in 1790. Since at least 1800, it has been traditional for justices to wear black robes while in session. White quills are placed on counsel tables each day that the Court sits, as was done at the earliest sessions of the Court. The "conference handshake" has been a tradition since the late 19th century. When the justices assemble to go on the bench each day and at the beginning of the private conferences at which they discuss decisions, each justice shakes hands with each of the other eight—a reminder that differences of opinion on the Court did not preclude overall harmony of purpose. When the Court is in session, the following seating arrangement exists for each justice: The chief justice always sits in the middle, with four associate justices on each side. The justice who is senior in terms of service sits on the chief's immediate right as the justice face out; the justice who is second in seniority occupies the position on the chief's left; thereafter, the justices are seated alternately right and left according to time served. The junior justice is always on the chief's extreme left.[66]

Conferences and Workload

The Supreme Court does not meet continuously in formal sessions during its nine-month term. Instead, the Court divides its time into four separate but related activities. First, some amount of time is allocated to reading through

you be the... JUDGE

SHOULD CAMERAS BE BANNED FROM CRIMINAL TRIALS?

Although the topic is not played out much in the public eye, there has been a long-standing debate concerning whether or not cameras should be allowed in courtrooms. Those in favor of cameras argue that they provide greater transparency; that people have a right to see what is happening in court—especially given that their tax dollars help to pay for courtrooms and trials; and that cameras will assist the media in reporting cases to the public.

Conversely, many people complain that cameras can and do cause a distraction and could even be dangerous: An angry public might wish to exact vigilante justice against one who is convicted if his face has been in the news. No doubt the same could happen to victims, witnesses, and jurors—and therefore a public safety crisis could arise in that fewer people would wish to serve in any of those three capacities in the future. They also argue that televising courtroom proceedings transforms them into a form of public entertainment for the public, which is not what our system of jurisprudence should be about.[67]

Certainly there is historical support for those who are opposed to the idea. The widely televised trial of O. J. Simpson beginning in late 1994 (termed "the trial of the century") clearly caused rethinking about whether cameras should be allowed in courtrooms. Perceptions that Simpson's lawyers (commonly termed the "Dream Team") played to the cameras apparently had an impact in several

highly publicized cases that followed: By the late 1990s, however, despite the Simpson trial backlash, opposition cooled; a study found that four of every five television requests were approved by judges in California.[68]

Supporters of the concept, conversely, maintain that televising trials has an educational value, providing the public with a firsthand view of how court proceedings operate. Indeed, studies have found that viewers of a television trial of moderate interest became more knowledgeable about the judicial process.

The Supreme Court has unanimously held that electronic media and still-photographic coverage of public judicial proceedings does not violate a defendant's right to a fair trial; states are therefore free to set their own guidelines. Only 2 states prohibit all forms of electronic coverage of criminal trial proceedings, whereas 35 states allow electronic coverage of criminal trials.[69] The remaining states are as yet undecided on the issue. The lingering question is whether cameras are an asset or a liability in the courtroom. To answer, one must determine whether their value as a tool of education and publicity overcomes the potential liabilities.[70]

1. Should those who favor the use of cameras in courtrooms prevail? Those who are against the practice? Explain.

---

the thousands of petitions for review of cases that come annually to the Court—usually during the summer and when the Court is not sitting to hear cases. Second, the Court allocates blocks of time for oral arguments—the live discussion in which lawyers for both sides present their clients' positions to the justices. During the weeks of oral arguments the Court sets aside its third allotment of time, for private discussions of how each justice will vote on the cases they have just heard. Time is also allowed for the justices to discuss which additional cases to hear. These private discussions are usually held on Wednesday afternoons and Fridays during the weeks of oral arguments. The justices set aside a fourth block of time to work on writing their opinions.[71]

The Court has complete discretion to control the nature and number of the cases it reviews by means of the *writ* (order) *of certiorari*—an order from a higher court directing a lower court to send the record of a case for review. The Court considers requests for *writs of certiorari* according to the *rule of four;* if four justices decide to "grant cert," the Court will agree to hear the case. Several criteria are used to decide if a case requires action: First, does the case concern an issue of constitutional or legal importance? Does it fall within the Court's jurisdiction (the Court can only hear cases that are mandated by Congress or the Constitution)? Does the party bringing a case have **standing**—a strong vested interest in the issues raised in the case and in its outcome?[72]

Standing: a legal doctrine requiring that one must not be a party to a lawsuit unless he has a personal stake in its outcome.

The Court hears only a tiny fraction of the thousands of petitions that come before it. When it declines to hear a case, the decision of the lower court stands as the final word on the case. The Court's caseload has been steadily increasing; today the Court has about 10,000 cases on the docket per term, and formal written opinions are delivered in 80 to 90 cases.[73]

Administration

The chief justice orders the business of the Supreme Court (a description of the chief justice's role is provided in Chapter 10) and administers the oath of office to the president and vice president upon their inauguration. According to Article 1, Section 3, of the Constitution of the United States, the chief justice is also empowered to preside over the Senate in the event that it sits as a court to try an impeachment of the president.

The clerk of the Court serves as the Supreme Court's chief administrative officer, supervising a staff of 30 under the guidance of the chief justice. The marshal of the Court supervises all building operations. The reporter of decisions oversees the printing and publication of the Court's decisions. Other key personnel are the librarian and the public information officer. In addition, each justice is entitled to hire four law clerks, almost always recent top graduates of law schools, many of whom have served clerkships in a lower court the previous year.[74]

U.S. Courts of Appeals

Circuit Court

The **federal courts of appeals** (or circuit courts) hear appeals from the district courts within their respective federal judicial circuit, and are considered to be very powerful and influential in their own right, second only to the Supreme Court of the United States. Those courts are discussed next.

Judges and Jurisdiction

U.S. Attorneys

The courts of appeals are the intermediate appeals for the **federal court system**. Eleven of the circuits are identified by number, and another is called the D.C. Circuit (see Figure 9.3). A court of appeals hears appeals from the district courts located within its circuit, as well as appeals from decisions of federal administrative agencies.

The courts of appeals are staffed by 179 judges nominated by the president and confirmed by the Senate. As with the U.S. district courts, discussed below, the number of judges in each circuit varies, from 6 in the First Circuit to 28 in the Ninth, depending on the volume and complexity of the caseload. Each circuit has a chief judge (chosen by seniority) who has supervisory responsibilities. Several staff positions aid the judges in conducting the work of the courts of appeals. A circuit executive assists the chief judge in administering the circuit. The clerk's office maintains the records. Each judge is also allowed to hire three law clerks. In deciding cases, the courts of appeals may use rotating three-judge panels. Or, by majority vote, all the judges in the circuit may sit together to decide a case or reconsider a panel's decision. Such "en banc" hearings are rare, however.[75]

U.S. District Courts

The U.S. **district courts,** like their counterparts in the state court system, may be fairly described as the "workhorses" of the federal judiciary, because nearly all civil or criminal cases heard in the federal courts are initiated at the district court level.

Federal court system: the four-tiered federal system that includes supreme courts, circuit courts of appeal, district courts, and magistrate courts.

District courts: trial courts at the county, state, or federal levels with general and original jurisdiction.

FIGURE 9.3

Geographic Boundaries of U.S. Courts of Appeals and District Courts

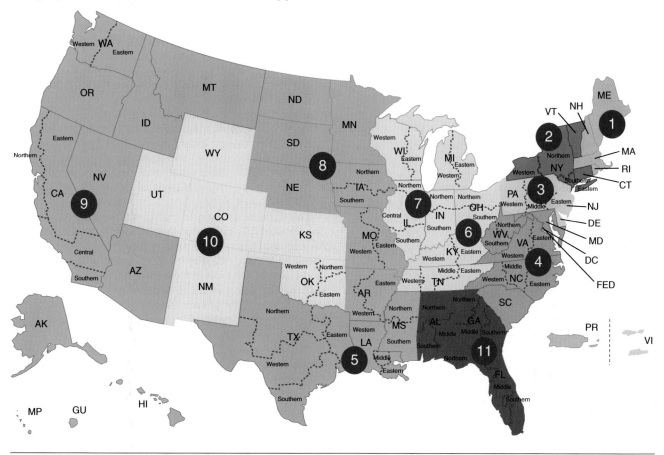

Judges and Jurisdiction

The locations of the U.S. district courts may also be seen in Figure 9.3 (sometimes designated by region—"northern" or "eastern," for example). Congress created 94 U.S. district courts, 89 of which are located within the 50 states. There is at least one district court in each state (some states have more, such as California, New York, and Texas, all of which have four). Congress has created 678 district court judgeships for the 94 districts. As with the other federal court judges discussed previously, the president nominates district judges, who must then be confirmed by the Senate; they then serve for life unless removed for cause. In the federal system, the U.S. district courts are the federal trial courts of original jurisdiction for all major violations of federal criminal law (some 500 full-time magistrate judges hear minor violations).[76]

District court judges are assisted by an elaborate supporting cast of clerks, secretaries, law clerks, court reporters, probations officers, pretrial services officers, and U.S. marshals. The larger districts also have a public defender. Another important actor at the district court level is the U.S. attorney; there is one U.S. attorney in each district. The work of district judges is significantly assisted by 352 bankruptcy judges, who are appointed for 14-year terms by the court of appeals in which the district is located.

Much of the caseload of these courts concerns prisoner petitions, which were discussed earlier.

Chapter Quiz:
Court Organization

FOCUS ON   INTERNATIONAL LAW AND THE INTERNATIONAL COURT OF JUSTICE

International law has no defined area or governing body, but the United Nations is recognized as an influential international organization, with the **International Court of Justice** (ICJ) as its judicial counterpart. International law includes a number of laws, rules, and customs governing the legal interactions between different nations, their governments, businesses, and organizations. Therefore, without a single governing entity, examining matters under international law is largely voluntary, and the power of enforcement only exists when the parties involved consent to abide by an agreement.[77]

International law may be divided into *public* law and *private* law. The former covers the rules, laws, and customs that govern and monitor the conduct and dealings between nations and/or their citizens. Conversely, private international law concerns disputes between private citizens of different nations. International law also includes both common law (case law) and civil law (statutes created by governing bodies), with their jurisdiction including substantive law, procedure, and remedies. The UN deals largely with public international law. Private international law is concerned with disputes between private citizens of different nations.[78]

The ICJ is the principal judicial entity of the UN and was established in June 1945. The ICJ's home is in The Hague (Netherlands). The Court's role, following international law, is to settle legal disputes submitted to it by its member nations and to render advisory opinions on legal questions referred to it by authorized UN members and agencies. The Court is composed of 15 judges who serve nine-year terms and are elected by the UN General Assembly and the Security Council.[79]

The ICJ acts as a world court, and recently about one-third of its cases have involved disputes between African countries. Since its inception, it has rendered about 90 judgments, dealing with such matters as land frontiers and maritime boundaries, territorial sovereignty, the nonuse of force, noninterference in the internal affairs of countries, diplomatic relations, rites of passage, nationality, hostage-taking, the right of asylum, and economic matters. There is no enforcement system for these ICJ decisions; however, a matter could be referred to the UN Security Council, where it would be vulnerable to the veto system of the five permanent members.[80]

IN A NUTSHELL

- As the population of the colonies grew, formal courts of law appeared based on the English system; however, fearing tyranny from this concentration of governmental power, a federal judiciary was created that was separate from the legislative branch of government; we now have the dual court system—one implemented by the state courts, the other created by Congress and entrusted to the federal courts.

- Practically everything one sees and hears in a U.S. courtroom is intended to convey the sense that the courtroom is a hallowed place in our society, including the physical trappings (decor) and people's demeanor (decorum).

- The courts must *appear* to do justice—and provide rights that are embodied in the due process clause. Our court system relies on the adversarial system, using several means to get at the truth: Evidence is tested through cross-examination of witnesses, and power is lodged with several different people. This series of checks and balances is aimed at curbing misuse of the criminal courts.

- Federal judges are nominated by the president and confirmed by the Senate, and serve for life. The Supreme Court has complete discretion to control the nature and number of the cases it reviews, and it hears only a tiny fraction of the thousands of petitions that come before it. The chief justice orders the business of the Supreme Court.

- There are 11 circuit courts of appeals plus the D.C. Circuit; they hear appeals from the federal district courts located within their circuit, as well as appeals from decisions of federal administrative agencies.

- There are 94 U.S. district courts, which are trial courts of original jurisdiction for all major violations of federal criminal law.

- Each state has a court of last resort, all but 11 states have an appellate court, and there are trial courts of general jurisdiction that decide all matters not specifically delegated to lower courts.

- Lower state trial courts have limited jurisdiction, but after an arrest, the judges conduct the initial appearance, appoint counsel for indigents, and conduct the preliminary hearing.

- The criminal justice process is engaged when one is arrested. Following that, the accused will then proceed through a series of steps; at some point, the prosecutor will prepare an information setting forth the charge against the defendant; some jurisdictions use a grand jury to bring formal charges, rather than the prosecutor doing so unilaterally.

- The Sixth Amendment gives defendants a trial by an impartial jury of his or her peers. The jury system is felt by many to be the most sacred aspect of our criminal justice system, because it is where common citizens sit as a forum to determine the truth and assess the punishment to be meted out.

- Discovery is the pretrial exchange of information between prosecution and defense, in order to promote a fair adversarial contest between the two sides and help the truth come to light.

- The Sixth Amendment guarantees the accused the right to a speedy and public trial. Although there are fixed, enforced time limits at the federal level, the Supreme Court has never defined a "speedy trial" with precise time frames at the state level; rather, courts must determine whether or not the defendant's right to a speedy trial was violated using a test.

- The policy decisions of the courts affect virtually all of us in our daily living. Perhaps nowhere have the nation's courts had more of an impact than in the prisons.

KEY TERMS & CONCEPTS

Adversarial system
Arraignment
Bail
Booking
Causation
Circuit courts
Courthouse violence
Court of last resort
Decor, court
Decorum
Delay (trial)
Discovery

District courts
Diversion programs
Dual court system
Federal
  court system
Grand jury
Initial appearance
Intermediate
  courts of appeal
International
  Court of Justice
Jurisdiction, court

Plea negotiation (or
  bargaining)
Policy making
Preliminary hearing
Pretrial motions/
  processes
Speedy
  Trial Act of 1974
Standing
State court system
Trial process
U.S. Supreme Court

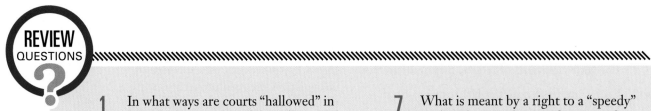
REVIEW QUESTIONS

1. In what ways are courts "hallowed" in our society in terms of their decor and decorum?

2. How is the adversarial system of justice related to the truth-seeking function of the courts?

3. How do the courts influence public policy making?

4. What are the structure and function of the trial courts of general and limited jurisdiction?

5. What are the types of, and reasons for, courts having a specific type(s) of jurisdiction?

6. What are some of the pretrial activities that occur?

7. What is meant by a right to a "speedy" trial? What are the ramifications of a defendant's being denied this right?

8. Why does our jury system exist, and how is a jury formed?

9. What are the major points of the trial process, from opening statements through appeal?

10. What are the roles of the state court systems?

11. What are some of the traditions of the U.S. Supreme Court, and what functions do they provide?

12. How would you describe what is meant by international law, as well as the functions of the International Court of Justice?

LEARN BY DOING

1. Your local League of Women Voters is establishing a new study group to better understand the court system as it relates to political affairs. You are asked to explain the dual (federal and state) court system. You opt to use *Kibbe v. Henderson* (discussed above) as a good—and rare—example of a convicted offender's flow through both systems. Prepare your presentation.

2. You have been invited to appear at a luncheon meeting of a local group of court watchers. Someone poses the following question to you: Why are such U.S. Supreme Court traditions as black robes, white quill pens, the "conference handshake," and even a fixed seating arrangement for each justice necessary? How would you reply?

3. Your criminal justice professor has assigned the class to debate the pros and cons of plea negotiation. What do you believe will be the prominent arguments presented by each side?

THE BENCH AND THE BAR:
Those Who Judge,
Prosecute, and Defend

LEARNING OBJECTIVES

As a result of reading this chapter, the student will be able to:

1 Explain the five methods of judicial selection, and why the subject of judicial selection has come under scrutiny

2 Describe why courtroom civility is important, as well as the meaning of "good judging"

3 Review the problems encountered by judges, particularly those who are new to the role

4 Relate the major duties of prosecutors and defense attorneys (to include their roles in plea negotiation)

CHAPTER

10

our things belong to a Judge:
To hear courteously,
To answer wisely,
To consider soberly, and
To decide impartially.

—Socrates

Fiat justitia ruat coelum [Let justice be done, though heaven should fall].

—Emperor Ferdinand I, 1563

INTRODUCTION

Author Introduction:
Chapter 10

Having looked at the general nature of courts and judges in the previous chapter, this chapter expands that discussion, focusing more on judges and other key personnel who are involved in the courts and their operation.

It is a part of our human nature that we hate losing. Therefore, even though in theory attorneys in a criminal courtroom are engaged in a truth-seeking process, make no mistake: They are *competing* from beginning to end—trying to convince the judge to include or exclude evidence or witnesses, to persuade the judge or jury of the guilt or innocence of the defendant, to sway the judge or jury that the convicted person should or should not be severely punished, and so on. This adversarial legal process is what drives our criminal justice system. Indeed, renowned defense attorney Percy Foreman is said to have remarked, "The best defense in a murder case is that the deceased should have been killed."[1] In a murder case where a woman was charged with shooting her husband, Foreman so slandered the victim that "the jury was ready to dig up the deceased and shoot him all over again."[2]

ASSESS YOUR AWARENESS:

Test your knowledge of the duties of judges, prosecutors, and defense attorneys by first reading and responding to the following seven true-false items; check your answers after reading this chapter's materials.

1. Studies indicate that there really is no difference in terms of how judges are selected, so in all states they are simply elected.

2. In recent years, people involved with courtroom matters have become much less friendly and well-behaved.

3. The prosecutor may be fairly said to be the single most powerful person in the American criminal justice system.

4. A prosecutor's primary duty is not to convict, but to see that justice is done.

5. One's transition from public or private attorney to the role of judge can involve a number of psychological problems and issues.

6. Because courts have existed for centuries, their administration is the most easily understood and accomplished area of criminal justice administration.

7. To allow more time for trials, no judges typically have to administer or preside over their courts' budget, and so on; instead, they hire nonjudicial personnel to do so.

Answers can be found on page 401.

As will be seen in this chapter, the challenges (and criticisms) facing today's judges are several. They must successfully serve many masters and occupy many roles; as one person noted:

> The "grand tradition" judge, the aloof brooding charismatic figure in the Old Testament tradition, is hardly a real figure. The reality is the working judge who must be politician, administrator, bureaucrat, and lawyer in order to cope with a crushing calendar of cases.[3]

The chapter opens by considering the means by which judges ascend to the bench. This once simple task has come under intense scrutiny—particularly the partisan election of judges, for which they must often solicit campaign contributions. Then we discuss the benefits and problems that occur when one becomes a judge, as well as the kinds of personal and professional problems one often faces when assuming the role; following that is the need for courtroom civility, and then we look at judicial misconduct.

The roles and strategies of two other very important court figures—prosecutors and defense attorneys—are reviewed next. The chapter concludes with a chapter summary, key terms and concepts, review questions, and several scenarios and activities that provide opportunities for you to "learn by doing."

THOSE WHO WOULD BE JUDGE: SELECTION METHODS AND ISSUES

The manner in which state and local court judges assume the bench matters—and it differs widely from state to state. The method used to select judges is important for at least four reasons: The type of judicial selection system affects judges' experience level; it determines the ability of qualified, but less politically connected, individuals to serve; it affects the gender and racial diversity of the judiciary; and it affects the public's perception of judicial impartiality and independence.[4] Across the United States at least five methods of **judicial selection** are used, but it is important to note that no two states use exactly the same selection method. In many states, more than one method of selection is used—for judges at different levels of the court system and even among judges serving at the same level. And when the same method is used, there are still variations in how the process works in practice.

Methods of Selection in State Courts

As noted in Chapter 9, all federal judges are nominated by the president and confirmed by the Senate, then serve for life (unless they resign or are impeached). When a vacancy (due to death, retirement, or resignation of a judge)[5] occurs at the state level, however, candidates are as likely to face an election as part of their selection process as not. This becomes particularly important given that 97 percent of the cases heard in the United States are handled by state judges. Furthermore, every year, millions of Americans find themselves in state courts, whether called for jury service, to address a minor traffic offense, as a crime victim, or in a small claims case.[6]

Next is a discussion of these five methods of selection,[7] which are also depicted in Figure 10.1.

1. Commission-based appointment (also known as **merit selection** or the **Missouri Plan**): Judicial applicants are evaluated by a nominating commission, which then sends the names of the best qualified

Merit selection: a means of selecting judges whereby names of interested candidates are considered by a committee and recommendations are then made to the governor, who then makes the appointment; known also as the Missouri Plan.

FIGURE 10.1

Initial Selection of State Judges (Trial Courts of General Jurisdiction)

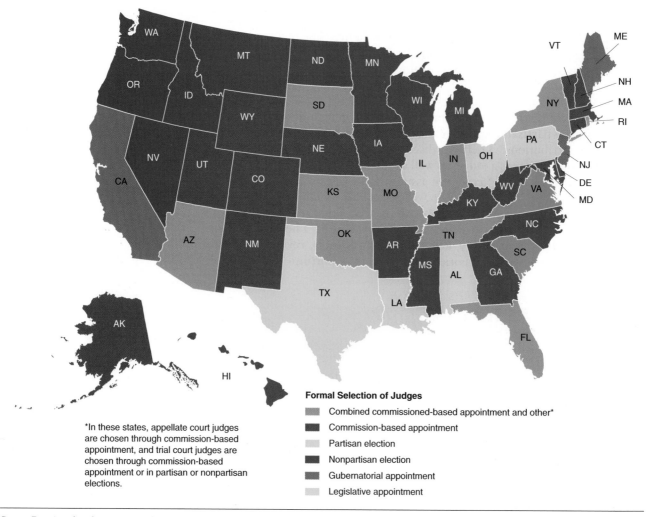

Formal Selection of Judges
- Combined commissioned-based appointment and other*
- Commission-based appointment
- Partisan election
- Nonpartisan election
- Gubernatorial appointment
- Legislative appointment

*In these states, appellate court judges are chosen through commission-based appointment, and trial court judges are chosen through commission-based appointment or in partisan or nonpartisan elections.

Source: Reprinted with permission from Institute for the Advancement of the American Legal System and American Judicature Society.

candidates to the governor, who appoints one of those nominees. In most commission-based appointment systems, judges run unopposed in periodic retention elections, where voters are asked whether the judge should remain on the bench.

2. Partisan election: In a partisan election multiple candidates may seek the same judicial position. Voters cast ballots for judicial candidates as they do for other public officials, and candidates run with the official endorsement of a political party. The candidate's party affiliation is listed on the ballot.

3. Nonpartisan election: In a nonpartisan election a judicial candidate's party affiliation, if any, is not designated on the ballot.

4. Gubernatorial appointment: A judge is appointed by the governor (without a judicial nominating commission). The appointment may require confirmation by the legislature or an executive council.

5. Legislative appointment/election: This is the process by which judges are nominated and appointed or elected by legislative vote only.

State Judges

Debating Judges and Politics

"They're awful. I hate them." Thus spoke former U.S. Supreme Court Justice Sandra Day O'Connor in May 2009 at an American Bar Association summit concerning her views of judicial elections.[8] O'Connor added that the public is growing increasingly skeptical of elected judges in particular, with surveys showing that more than 70 percent of the public are considerably more distrustful of their judges than they have been in the past. At risk, O'Connor said, is the perception by the public that judges are "just politicians in robes."[9] O'Connor also said in November 2007 that "if I could wave a magic wand, I would wave it to secure some kind of merit selection of judges across the country."[10]

Our courts make decisions every day that affect nearly every aspect of our lives. Therefore, to a large extent, the quality of justice Americans receive depends on the quality of the judges who dispense it. Next we turn our attention to the increasingly controversial issue of politics and money in the selection and election of our state and local judges.

The debate over how America chooses its judges has escalated in the 21st century. Consider this: In March 2009 the U.S. Supreme Court heard oral arguments concerning a newly elected West Virginia Supreme Court of Appeals justice, Brent Benjamin, who voted on a mining company dispute; the mining company contributed $3 million in an election campaign to help Benjamin get elected. Instead of removing himself from the vote (known in the courts as *recusal*), Benjamin instead possibly cast the deciding vote in the 3-2 case—in favor of the mining company. There is no law in West Virginia saying a judge can't hear a case involving someone who financed his or her campaign. During oral arguments in the case, former Justice David Souter said, "The system . . . is not working well."[11]

Chief Justice John Roberts, of the Supreme Court of the United States.

FOCUS ON DUTIES OF THE CHIEF JUSTICE OF THE UNITED STATES

The **chief justice** of the United States has 53 duties enumerated in the U.S. Code, the Constitution, and other sources. Following is a listing of a small number of those duties:

- Approve appointments and salaries of some court employees
- Direct the publication of Supreme Court opinions
- Approve rules for the Supreme Court library
- Select company to handle the printing and binding of court opinions
- Send appeals back to lower courts, if justices cannot agree on them
- Approve appointments of employees to care for the Supreme Court building and grounds as well as regulations for their protection
- Call and preside over an annual meeting of the Judicial Conference of the United States

and report to Congress the conference's recommendations for legislation (the Judicial Conference is composed of 27 federal judges who represent all the levels and regions of the federal judiciary; the conference meets twice a year to discuss common problems and needed policies and to recommend to Congress measures for improving the operation of the federal courts)

- Report to Congress on changes in the Federal Rules of Criminal Procedure
- Report to the president if certain judges have become unable to discharge their duties
- Designate a member of the Smithsonian Institution

Source: The Supreme Court Historical Society, "How the Court Works: The Chief Justice's Role," http://www.supremecourthistory.org/how-the-court-works/how-the-court-work/the-chief-justices-role/ (accessed February 22, 2013).

Judicial
Elections

Several states are now evaluating their judicial selection systems with a view to altering their current processes. And, perhaps by taking up the West Virginia case, the Supreme Court may well be putting a spotlight on this issue—one that has already been settled in about two dozen states by eliminating political fund-raising by their judicial candidates through the use of various "merit selection" systems.[12]

"Investing" in Judges?

Certainly adding fuel to the controversy over judicial selection is the amount of money now being spent to fund judges' elections, which has skyrocketed in state supreme courts since 1990, rising from $6.2 million then to $43.2 million in 2008. Furthermore, a recent survey found that 44 percent of these contributions came from business groups, and 21 percent came from lawyers.[13] Special interest groups have ramped up their efforts to influence the composition of state courts, making contributions to candidates, funding television ads, and pressuring candidates to speak publicly about their political views.

JURISTS' BENEFITS, TRAINING, AND CHALLENGES

Recommendations
for Court

Judges enjoy several distinct benefits of office, including life terms for federal positions and in some states. Ascending to the bench can be the capstone of a successful legal career for a lawyer, even though a judge's salary can be less than that of a lawyer in private practice. Judges certainly warrant a high degree of respect and prestige as well; from arrest to final disposition, the accused face judges at every juncture involving important decisions about their future: bail, pretrial motions, evidence presentation, trial, punishment.

Although it would seem that judges are the primary decision makers in the courts, such is not always the case. Judges often accept recommendations from others who are more familiar with the case—for example, bail recommendations from prosecutors, **plea negotiations** struck by prosecuting and defense counsels, and sentence recommendations from the probation officer.

FOCUS ON THE NATIONAL JUDICIAL COLLEGE

At the National Judicial College (NJC) in Reno, Nevada, the underlying message rings loud: Wearing a black robe alone does not a judge make. At the judicial college, the goal is not only to coach lawyers on how to be judges, but to teach veteran judges how to be better arbiters of justice. For many lawyers, the move to the other side of the bench is an awesome transition. "Judges aren't born judges," said former U.S. Supreme Court Justice Sandra Day O'Connor. She recalled her anxieties the first time she assumed the bench: "It was frightening, really. There was so much to think about and to learn." Justice Anthony M. Kennedy, who is on the judicial college's faculty, states that

judicial independence cannot exist unless you have skilled, dedicated, and principled judges. This leads to so many different areas—judicial demeanor, how to control a courtroom, basic rules of civility, how to control attorneys. These

are difficult skills for judges to learn. They're not something judges innately have. Judges have to acquire these skills.

The NJC offers about 65 on-site and online courses each year, ranging from a few days' duration to several weeks. Regular curriculum includes courses on courtroom technology; dealing with jurors; courtroom disruptions; domestic violence; managing complex cases; death penalty issues; traffic cases; ethics; mediation; family law; forensic, medical, and scientific evidence; and opinion writing. Certificates as well as extension, administrative law, courts and media, international, and other types of specialized programs are also offered.

Source: The National Judicial College, "Course Planner," http://www.judges.org/planner.html (accessed February 24, 2013); information also taken from Sandra Chereb, "Judges Must Train to Take the Bench," *Reno Gazette-Journal,* May 28, 1996, pp. 1B, 5B. Used with permission.

These kinds of input are frequently accepted by judges in the kind of informal courtroom network that exists. Although judges run the court, if they deviate from the consensus of the courtroom work group, they may be sanctioned: Attorneys can make court dockets go awry by requesting continuances or by not having witnesses appear on time.

Newly elected judges are not simply "thrown to the wolves" and expected to immediately begin to conduct trials, listen to arguments, understand rules of evidence, render verdicts and sentences, and possibly write opinions, without the benefit of training or education. Many states mandate judicial education at the beginning or even prior to their assuming the role, as well as mandatory in-service or continuing education thereafter (see Table 10.1).

Judicial
Challenges

Other challenges can await a new jurist-elect or appointee. Judges who are new to the bench commonly face three general problems:

1. *Mastering the breadth of law they must know and apply.* New judges would be wise, at least early in their career, to depend on other court staff, lawyers who appear before them, and experienced judges for invaluable information on procedural and substantive aspects of the law and local court procedures. Through informal discussions and formal meetings, judges learn how to deal with common problems. Judicial training schools and seminars have also been developed to ease the transition into the judiciary.

2. *Administering the court and the docket while supervising court staff.* One of the most frustrating aspects of being a presiding judge is the heavy caseload and corresponding administrative problems. Instead of having time to reflect on challenging legal questions or to consider the proper sentence for a convicted felon, trial judges must move cases. They can seldom act like a judge in the "grand tradition."[14] Judges are required to be competent administrators, a fact of judicial life that comes as a surprise to many new judges. One survey of 30 federal judges found that three-fourths had major administrative difficulties on first assuming the bench, while half complained of heavy caseloads. One judge maintained that it takes about 4 years to "get a full feel of a docket."[15]

3. *Coping with the psychological discomfort that accompanies the new position.* Most trial judges experience psychological discomfort on assuming the bench. Three-fourths of new federal judges acknowledged having psychological problems in at least one of five areas: maintaining a judicial bearing both on and off the bench, the loneliness of the judicial office, sentencing criminals, forgetting the adversary role, and local pressure. One judge remembers his first day in court: "I'll never forget going into my courtroom for the first time with the robes and all, and the crier tells everyone to rise. You sit down and realize that it's all different, that everyone is looking at you and you're supposed to do something."[16] Like police officers and probation and parole workers, judges complain that they "can't go to the places you used to. You always have to be careful about what you talk about. When you go to a party, you have to be careful not to drink too much so you won't make a fool of yourself."[17] And the position can be a lonely one:

> After you become a . . . judge some people tend to avoid you. For instance, you lose all your lawyer friends and generally have to begin to make new friends. I guess the lawyers are afraid that they will someday have a case before you and it would be awkward for them if they were on too close terms with you.[18]

Judges frequently describe sentencing criminals as the most difficult aspect of their job: "This is the hardest part of being a judge. You see so many pathetic people and you're never sure of what is a right or a fair sentence."[19]

TABLE 10.1

Provisions for Mandatory Judicial Education

| | APPELLATE COURT JUDGES | | | | | |
| | INITIAL/PRE-BENCH EDUCATION | | | CONTINUING EDUCATION | | |
	REQUIRED	MANDATED HOURS	SOURCES OF FUNDING	REQUIRED	MANDATED HOURS	SOURCES OF FUNDING
Alabama		None	~		None	~
Alaska		None	S	■	None	S
Arizona	■	~	~	■	16	S/T
Arkansas		None	S	■	12	S
California	■	None	S		None	S
Colorado		60	~	■	15	S
Connecticut		None	~		None	~
Delaware		None	~	■	23	S
District of Columbia		None	~		None	~
Florida	■	40	F	■	10	F
Georgia		None	~	■	12	S
Hawaii		None	~	■	32	S
Idaho		None	~	■	None	S
Illinois		None	~		None	~
Indiana		None	S	■	36	S/T
Iowa		None	~	■	15	S
Kansas		None	S	■	12	S
Kentucky		None	~	■	25	S
Louisiana		None	~	■	12.5	T
Maine		None	~		12	~
Maryland	■	None	S	■	28	S
Massachusetts		None	S		None	S
Michigan		6.5	S	~	None	S
Minnesota		None	S	■	15	S
Mississippi	■	None	S/F	■	12	S/F
Missouri		None	S		15	S

APPELLATE COURT JUDGES					
	INITIAL/PRE-BENCH EDUCATION			COUNTINUING EDUCATION	
	REQUIRED	MANDATED HOURS	SOURCES OF FUNDING	REQUIRED	MANDATED HOURS	SOURCES OF FUNDING
Montana		None	~	■	15	S
Nebraska		None	S		20(every 2 yrs)	S
Nevada		16	F/S	■	12	F/S
New Hampshire		None	~	■	12	S
New Jersey		None	~	■	15	S
New Mexico		None	~	■	15	S/F/T
New York		None	~	■	12	S
North Carolina		None	~	■	15	S
North Dakota		None	~	■	15	S
Ohio		None	S	■	20	S/L/T
Oklahoma		None	~		12	S
Oregon		None	~	■	45	T
Pennsylvania		None	~		None	~
Puerto Rico	■	None	S	■	None	S
Rhode Island	■	None	S	■	10	S
South Carolina	■	6	S	■	15	S/T
South Dakota		None	~	■	None	S
Tennessee		None	S	■	15	S
Texas	■	30	S	■	16	S/L
Utah		None	~	■	30	S
Vermont	■	50	S	■	64	S
Virginia		None	~	■	12	S
Washington		None	S	■	15	S
West Virginia		None	~	■	15	S
Wisconsin		None	~	■	30	S
Wyoming		None	~	■	15	S

Note: Details on the types of requirements and how they are fulfilled vary greatly from state to state. The above is a summary of general education provisions.

Legend: ~ = Not applicable; N/S = None stated; S = State; L = Local; F = Fees; T = Tuition; ■ = Yes

JUDGES AND COURTROOM CIVILITY

Mid-Chapter Quiz:
The Bench and the Bar

Decision Making

What traits make for "good judging"? Obviously, judges should treat each case and all parties before them in court with absolute impartiality and dignity while providing leadership as the steward of their organization in all of the court management areas described in the following section. In addition to those official duties, however, other issues and suggestions have been put forth.

"Good Judging"

For example, a retired jurist with 20 years on the Wisconsin Supreme Court stated that the following qualities define the art and craft of judging:

- Judges are keenly aware that they occupy a special place in a democratic society. They exercise their power in the most undemocratic of institutions with great restraint.

- They are aware of the necessity for intellectual humility—an awareness that what we think we know might well be incorrect.

- They do not allow the law to become their entire life; they get out of the courtroom, mingle with the public, and remain knowledgeable of current events.[20]

Other writers believe that judges should remember that the robe does not confer omniscience or omnipotence; as one trial attorney put it, "Your name is now 'Your Honor,' but you are still the same person you used to be, warts and all."[21] As if it weren't difficult enough to strive for and maintain humility, civility, and balance in their personal lives, judges must also enforce courtroom civility. Many persons have observed that we are becoming an increasingly uncivil society; the courts are certainly not immune to acts involving misconduct (see the discussion of courthouse violence in Chapter 9).

Personal character attacks by lawyers, directed at judges, attorneys, interested parties, clerks, jurors, and witnesses, both inside and outside the courtroom, in criminal and civil actions have increased at an alarming rate in the last 15 years.[22] For example, an attorney stated that opposing and other attorneys were "a bunch of starving slobs," "incompetents," and "stooges."[23] Such behavior clearly does not enhance the dignity or appearance of justice and propriety that is so important to the courts' public image and function. The **Model Code of Judicial Conduct** addresses these kinds of behaviors; Canon 3B(4) requires judges to be "patient, dignified, and courteous to litigants, jurors, witnesses, lawyers, and others with whom the judge deals in an official capacity," and requires judges to demand "similar conduct of lawyers, and of staff, court officials, and others subject to the judge's direction and control."[24]

At a minimum, judges need to attempt to prevent such behavior, and discipline offenders when it occurs. Some means judges have at their disposal to control errant counsel includes attorney disqualifications, new trials, and reporting of attorneys to disciplinary boards.[25]

Model Code of Judicial Conduct: adopted by the House of Delegates of the American Bar Association in 1990, it provides a set of ethical principles and guidelines for judges.

The Model Code of Judicial Conduct requires judges to be "patient, dignified, and courteous" to all persons engaged in court business.

PRACTITIONER'S PERSPECTIVE

JUDGE, LIMITED-JURISDICTION COURT

Name: Diana L. Sullivan
Current position: Justice of the Peace, Las Vegas Justice Court
City, state: Las Vegas, Nevada
College attended/ academic major: University of Nevada, Reno/BA, criminal justice; University of San Diego School of Law/Juris Doctorate

How long have you been a practitioner in this career? Four years

The primary duties and responsibilities of a limited-jurisdiction court judge are:

For misdemeanor cases, making the ultimate determination of guilt or innocence. For an offender who is found guilty of a misdemeanor, the magistrate also determines the punishment within the range allowed by law. Justice Court justices also oversee preliminary proceedings in felony cases.

In most sentences, I include jail time that is suspended while the offender satisfies his other sentencing requirements. Once the offender satisfies his other sentencing requirements and stays out of trouble, the suspended jail sentence is vacated and the case is closed. If, on the other hand, the offender fails to successfully complete the other sentencing requirements or fails to stay out of trouble, the offender's suspended jail sentence is imposed. In felony cases, a retributive-based sentence by a district court or jury is often appropriate and warranted. My philosophy in sentencing misdemeanor offenders, however, is not one of retribution but one aimed at deterrence and rehabilitation. I am mindful of the harsh reality that even a short jail sentence of 30 days can drastically affect an offender's life circumstances, such as his employment, residence, or visitation rights of children. Hence, based upon the offender's charge, criminal history, family dynamics, employment status, and remorse (if any), my goal is to sentence the offender to just enough punishment to hopefully prevent future criminal activity. My sentences often include requirements alternative to—and hopefully in lieu of—any jail time, such as monetary fines, community service, counseling programs, and informal probation orders.

Our pretrial detention decisions are some of our most important roles in the entire criminal process. Decisions on an accused's custody status or bail setting while he awaits trial on serious charges are difficult because the magistrate must consider and weigh various factors in determining whether to release an accused person pending trial. Factors to be considered in making pretrial custody determinations include the accused's length of residence in the community; his employment status and criminal history; the serious nature of the charged offense; the likelihood of conviction and range of punishment if convicted; the likelihood of reoffending while awaiting trial; and the risk that the accused will fail to appear for future court appearances. These decisions must be made promptly after arrest and with very limited and sometimes unsupported information, always keeping in mind the constitutional presumption of innocence. Even though these initial custody decisions are made quickly, an accused's custody status can be revisited at any stage of the criminal case.

The qualities/characteristics that are most helpful for one in a career as a judge in this court are:

The study and practice of criminal justice—which is, simply put, fascinating. Each and every day something occurs that makes today different from yesterday.

In general, a typical day for a judge in a limited-jurisdiction court would include:

Handling my caseload, which, at any given time, surpasses 8,000 nontraffic criminal cases. Thus, it is typical for me to have anywhere from 50 to 80 cases on my court docket each morning. I handle the majority of these tasks quickly and summarily, such as initial arraignments and postsentencing compliance hearings. Other types of daily hearings, such as misdemeanor trials and felony preliminary evidentiary hearings, can take several hours.

When not handling my court docket, other daily tasks include reviewing probable cause reports for recent and future arrests, and researching and ruling on motions filed by parties. I also handle administrative duties, such as overseeing certain personnel and serving on committees for the improvement of local court rules and procedural processes. Lastly, as a public official I volunteer my time to the community, focusing on our local youth. I mentor at-risk high school students, participate in career fairs, and judge high school mock trial competitions.

My advice to someone either wishing to study, or now studying, criminal justice to become a practitioner in this career field would be:

To have at least a minimal understanding of psychology, sociology, cultural differences, and generational indigence. Anyone who wants to litigate either criminal or civil cases should also acquire training in public speaking, debate, and eventually trial advocacy.

Problems With Judicial Misconduct

What types of **judicial misconduct** must the judiciary confront? Sometimes medications may affect a judge's cognitive process or emotional temperament, causing him or her to treat parties, witnesses, jurors, lawyers, and staff poorly. Some stay on the bench too long; such judges will ideally have colleagues who can approach them, suggest retirement, and explain why this would be to their benefit. And sometimes, according to one author, judicial arrogance (sometimes termed "black robe disease" or "robe-itis") is the primary problem. This is seen when judges "do not know when to close their mouths, do not treat people with dignity and compassion, do not arrive on time, or do not issue timely decisions."[26]

Some bar associations or judicial circuits perform an anonymous survey of a sample of local attorneys who have recently argued a case before a particular judge and then share the results with the judge. Sometimes these surveys are popularity contests, but a pattern of negative responses can have a sobering effect on the judge and encourage him or her to correct bad habits. Many judges will be reluctant to acknowledge they have such problems as those described above. In such cases, the chief judge may have to scold or correct a subordinate judge. Although difficult, it may be imperative to do so in trying to maintain good relations with bar associations, individual lawyers, and the public. A single judge's blunders and behaviors can affect the reputation of the entire judiciary as well as the workloads of the other judges in his or her judicial district. Chief judges must therefore step forward to address such problems formally or informally.[27]

Judicial
Misconduct

Author Video: Bias

THE ATTORNEYS

Next we look at the roles and strategies of attorneys who serve on both sides of the aisle in court—as prosecutors and defense attorneys.

"Gatekeeper" of the Justice System: Prosecutor

The prosecutor may be fairly said to be the single most powerful person in the American criminal justice system—and to have tremendous discretion

Judicial misconduct:
inappropriate behavior by a judge.

---

you be the... JUDGE

THE *APPEARANCE* OF JUSTICE

In early 2013 a South Hackensack, New Jersey, municipal court judge held a unique part-time job—as a stand-up comedian on a major network's hidden-camera program. But the judge was told his part-time job—which is his primary source of income—conflicts with his judicial work and violates rules the state's judges are to follow. He pleaded his case to the state's supreme court.

One of the issues raised was whether or not the average person understands the difference between a character and an actor—as with movie actors, whether or not someone is seen as expressing his or her true self or following a fictional script. A deputy attorney general argued that the judge's comedy program—which includes portraying racist and homophobic characters—may not know the judge is

acting; in addition, the judge could meet defendants who are familiar with his comic routine and might not believe he's a serious judge. The state also argued that municipal court judges are the face of the judiciary for most citizens, and it is vital that such judges maintain the confidence of the public and the impartiality, dignity, and integrity of the court.

1. What do you think? It is often said that judges and courts must at all times "*appear* to do justice." Should the judge be able to "moonlight" as a comedian on his own time?

2. Or, alternatively, do you agree with the state's arguments—that judges are never truly "off duty," and are thus obligated to avoid such activities?

in what he or she does. As described by the Southern Poverty Law Center, "Prosecutorial discretion is a necessary and important part of our system of justice—it allocates sparse prosecutorial resources, provides the basis for plea-bargaining and allows for leniency and mercy in a criminal justice system that is frequently harsh and impersonal. They literally have unchecked power to decide who will stand trial for crimes."[28]

Prosecutorial Discretion

Prosecutors represent the people, the victims in particular, and investigate crimes—often out in the field, having been called to the scene of a particularly heinous crime by the police. Still, it is important to remember that the primary role of the **prosecuting attorney**, as set forth by the U.S. Supreme Court (and as noted in Chapter 4), is "not that he shall win a case, but that justice shall be done."[29]

Once a preliminary investigation has been completed by the police, the prosecutor evaluates the offense report and other documents to determine whether there is sufficient evidence to bring charges (and also have the ability to scold officers who have not done their work properly—perhaps failing to have the requisite probable cause prior to making a search or an arrest—and quashing the arrest report). They have contact with the person suspected of the crime, the victim and witnesses, and the police. For them, the overarching question is "Can I prove that a defendant committed a particular criminal act beyond a reasonable doubt?" If so, the prosecutor's office files charges and handles the case through pretrial negotiations (if any) and ultimately takes the case to trial.

Other determining factors concerning how to handle a case are

- the type of crime charged (personal or property crime);
- the prior criminal record of the person accused;
- the number of counts in the complaint (the more counts there are, the stiffer the sentence sought);
- whether there are aggravating or mitigating circumstances in the case; and
- the victim's attitude—what he or she wants done with the case (this is particularly important in crimes of violence).

Prosecuting attorney: one who brings prosecutions, representing the people of the jurisdiction.

Good prosecutors will also try to establish a good rapport with the victim prior to trial, to personalize the justice system. If possible, take the victim to the court and show him or her the courtroom and witness stand, where the offender will be seated, and so on.

"Guiding Hand of Counsel": Defense Attorney

In many foreign countries, one who finds himself mired in some stage of a legal proceeding might also find himself standing alone in the courtroom, overwhelmed by fear and his mind befuddled with the activities swirling around him. Not so under our democratic system, where the fundamental principles of liberty and justice require that all Americans, even the poorest among us, will be given the "guiding hand of counsel" at all critical stages of a criminal proceeding. Next we discuss that cherished right.

Prosecutors at trial must thoroughly question witnesses – not, the Supreme Court has said, to win a case, but to "see that justice shall be done."

PRACTITIONER'S PERSPECTIVE

PROSECUTING ATTORNEY

Name: Katherine Elizabeth Pridemore
Current position: Assistant Prosecuting Attorney/Division Chief, Juvenile Division, Hamilton County
City, state: Cincinnati, Ohio
College attended/ academic major: University of Cincinnati/BA, political science/prelaw

How long have you been a practitioner in this criminal justice position?

Since March 2001; from 1998 to 2001, Assistant Attorney General for the State of Ohio in the Non-Capital Crimes/Habeas Corpus/1983 Actions Section

My primary duties and responsibilities as a practitioner in this position are:

First, as felony prosecutor, I prosecute high-level felonies including homicides, sexual assaults, child endangerings, shootings and other felonious assaults, and media cases; also, as Felony Assistant Supervisor, I teach assistant prosecutors the fundamentals of felony prosecutions, trial work, the art of plea bargaining, and how to interview victims/ witnesses/police officers and effectively prosecute and resolve felony cases. I also cover the offices of other assistant prosecutors when they are out of the office in all of the above, plus going to trial on any and all felonies (drug trafficking, drug possession, burglaries, robberies, domestic violence, gun charges, etc.).

The qualities/characteristics that are most helpful for one in this career are:

In no particular order, to possess the following abilities: (1) to communicate in a meaningful manner with "all walks of life" kinds of people—victims, witnesses, officers, business owners, the homeless, lower economics, higher economics, and different ethnicities, races, genders, and sexual orientations;

(2) to analyze a felony case and determine the best resolution for the case; (3) to keep work life and personal life separate (because felony work can be extremely difficult and frustrating, and you don't want to take that home with you), and thus maintain a good balance between work and home; (4) to think on your feet, and use reason and common sense; (5) to use good interpersonal skills when dealing with the public, the judges, the defense bar, and the court staff; and (4) to remain ethical and professional at all points in time!

In general, a *typical day* for a practitioner in this career would include:

(1) Going to court and addressing a docket that consists of a variety of cases that include different charges, settings, and actions, such as sentencings, jury trials, bench trials, plea or trial settings, initial case settings, and reports; (2) interacting with the public, the court staff, the judges, the defense bar, and possibly the media; (3) possibly going to trial—if no trial, then office tasks include returning phone calls from witnesses, victims, defense attorneys, and officers; (4) responding to e-mail from the same groups, and doing paperwork (including requests for additional evidence, follow-ups on investigations, discovery, issuing subpoenas); (5) devoting time to trial preparation for upcoming trials; and (6) meeting with witnesses for upcoming trials.

My advice to someone either wishing to study, or now studying, criminal justice to become a practitioner in this career field would be:

To be prepared to take a vow of poverty! Honestly, though, be prepared for the fact that employment in the public sector yields very little money unless you are an elected public official. Sometimes the work can be very hard on your home life, especially if you really care about the cases and are gearing up for, or are in, trial. Be prepared to experience much of the public (at least in urban settings) resenting you, distrusting you, ignoring subpoenas, and being hostile toward you—and that the prosecution of criminal defendants rarely, if ever, results in anyone thanking you.

Duties and Strategies

As noted in Chapter 8, many people believe that the Sixth Amendment's provision for effective counsel is the most important right we enjoy in a democracy. The law is complicated, and by requiring the state to prove its case and helping defendants understand their options in the criminal justice system, **defense attorneys** can help ensure that the state does not commit innocent people to jail or prison. Furthermore, defendants have the right to counsel during all "critical stages" of the proceedings—those in which rights could be lost—which include interrogation, jury selection, arraignment, trial, sentencing, and first appeal of conviction (but not the initial appearance, where the judge simply informs the defendant of his or her charges and rights), as well as pretrial testing of fingerprints, blood samples, clothing, hair, and so on (*Maine v. Moulton*, 1985).[30]

What does "ineffective counsel" mean in practice? Basically it means the attorney was deficient in his or her performance, and in being so, the resulting prejudice to the defendant was so serious as to bring the outcome of the proceeding into question.[31] Examples would include one's failures to investigate an alibi defense, investigate prosecution witnesses, obtain experts to challenge the prosecution's physical evidence, or even attend or stay awake for hearings.[32] The burden of proving ineffective counsel is high, and is on the defendant to show that "a reasonable probability" exists that, but for counsel's unprofessional errors, the result of the proceeding would have been different (see *Strickland v. Washington*, 1984).[33] But it is possible to do so: In one Texas case, a defense attorney claimed he did not believe he needed to go into "sleazy bars to look for witnesses"; the appeals court basically informed him that that's precisely what he would do, if doing so was required to locate witnesses for the defendant, persons to confirm the defendant's alibi, and so on.[34]

When one is charged with a crime, a defense lawyer, either hired or court-appointed, should

- explain the offense the accused is charged with, including the possible punishments and probation options;

- advise the accused of his or her rights, ensure those rights are upheld, and inform the accused of what to expect during the different stages of the criminal process;

- investigate the facts of the case;

- explain what is likely to happen if the case goes to trial;

- if beneficial for the accused, attempt to negotiate a plea bargain with the prosecutor (bear in mind that more than 90 percent of criminal convictions come from negotiated pleas of guilty, which must be approved by the judge; therefore, less than 10 percent of criminal cases go to trial)[35]—this can involve arranging for reduced charges, a shorter sentence, serving sentences for different crimes consecutively instead of concurrently, probation and/or a disposition that avoids certain imprisonment, and/or other consideration, in exchange for entering a plea of guilty; and

- cross-examine government witnesses, object to improper questions and evidence, and present applicable legal defenses if the case goes to trial.[36]

Defense Attorney

Defense attorney: one whose responsibility is to see that the rights of the accused are upheld prior to, during, and after trial; the Sixth Amendment provides for "effective" counsel, among other constitutionally enumerated rights that defense attorneys must see are upheld.

Defense attorneys must cross-examine the government's witnesses. This witness is being questioned at trial concerning recording artist Michael Jackson's death.

Other defense strategies might include

- trying to make the victim appear to be the aggressor, or someone who "deserved what he got" (the general rule is that the defense attorney wants to try to overlook the victim's story, while the victim wishes to punish the defendant, and will also try to engender sympathy; particularly if the victim appears to have precipitated or participated in the crime, the defense will attack his or her faults at trial (within legal bounds);

- coming up with ways to compensate the victim (will he or she accept restitution, or be satisfied if the defendant will attend counseling?); and

- to keep getting continuances (key witnesses move away, emotions and local publicity surrounding the crime will diminish, and so forth).

Indigent Services

In *Griffin v. Illinois* (1956),[37] the U.S. Supreme Court observed that "there can be no equal justice where the kind of trial a man gets depends on the amount of money he has." There are basically three systems for providing legal representation to indigent persons in criminal prosecutions: the public defender system, the assigned counsel system, and the contract system.[38]

Public defenders, like prosecutors, are paid government employees—most commonly found in larger jurisdictions—whose sole function is to represent indigent defendants. Public defenders perform many of the duties of prosecutors, described above. They provide representation to people, who not only are indigent but also may be illiterate, uneducated, and uncooperative, while managing a large caseload. Public defenders might also represent juveniles charged with acts of delinquency (offenses that would be a felony if committed by an adult) as well as children in child abuse and neglect cases.

The assigned counsel system uses private attorneys appointed on an as-needed basis by the court. A primary problem with assigned counsel is that the attorney may have little or no experience handling the criminal matter at hand; indeed, it may have been long ago that the assigned counsel studied such subjects as criminal law, criminal procedure, rules of evidence, and so on, and such attorneys may have limited knowledge about their state's criminal statutes.

The contract system is one whereby an attorney, a law firm, or a nonprofit organization contracts for a certain dollar amount—often after engaging in competitive bidding—with a unit of government to represent its indigent defendants. Advantages of this system can include reduced and predictable costs, streamlining of the counsel appointment process, and greater expertise of the attorneys. Potential disadvantages are related to the above: Obtaining legal counsel from the "lowest bidder" may result in inadequate

Public Private Attorney

Public defender: an attorney whose full-time job is to represent indigent defendants.

Legal aid attorneys provide free legal advice for defendants. This Legal Aid attorney meets with her client before an arraignment in Brooklyn's Criminal Court.

PRACTITIONER'S PERSPECTIVE

CRIMINAL DEFENSE ATTORNEY

Name: Michelle E. Beck

Current position: Criminal Defense Attorney

City, state: Houston, Texas

College attended/academic major: Rice University/BA, political science; Thurgood Marshall School of Law, Texas Southern University, Juris Doctorate

How long have you been a practitioner in this criminal justice position? 10 years as an assistant district attorney in Harris County, Texas; 8 years as a criminal defense attorney

My primary duties and responsibilities as a practitioner in this position are: To represent clients charged with felony and misdemeanor criminal offenses; to appear in court to advocate on behalf of the defendant in court with the judge, prosecutor, and jury; and to explain to my client the procedures of the criminal justice system and his constitutional rights.

The qualities/characteristics that are most helpful for one in this career are:

A desire to advocate on behalf of another; written and verbal communication skills; a passion for justice; empathy for those being accused of very serious offenses—which could possibly lead to loss of freedom; patience; ability to think quickly; tenacity; and knowledge of criminal law and procedure.

In general, a *typical day* for a practitioner in this career would include:

Making court appearances for several clients in felony and misdemeanor courts where I review the contents of the state's file to see what evidence the state has to attempt to prove my client's guilt; communicate plea bargain offers between client and the prosecutor; file necessary motions with the court; interview witnesses, along with the investigator, relevant to the offense; research case law and relevant topics pertinent to the alleged offense; examine physical evidence collected in the case; visit those clients who are incarcerated in jail; and prepare for trial if that becomes necessary.

If in trial, duties include representing the client in court/jury trial, cross-examining the state's witnesses and questioning defense witnesses if necessary; ensuring that the state meets its burden of proving my client guilty beyond a reasonable doubt; and objecting to violations of the rules of evidence and procedure by the court and the prosecutors during such proceedings.

My advice to someone either wishing to study, or now studying, criminal justice to become a practitioner in this career field would be:

To have a complete knowledge of criminal law and the code of criminal procedure; attend law school and pass the state bar exam; observe other defense attorneys in court, especially during trials; develop a passion and empathy for the accused and their right to have a fair trial and effective legal representation, no matter how heinous the alleged offense; shore up on oratory, communication, and people skills; and expose yourself to other socioeconomic and cultural experiences and perspectives (so that you can relate to potential witnesses and experiences that you may otherwise not be familiar with).

or ineffective legal services—which may, of course, implicate the Sixth Amendment right to effective counsel and be the basis for appealing a conviction.

As with many things in life, it is said that with regard to legal representation, "You get what you pay for." Obviously, people with financial means to do so will normally "go to the marketplace" and hire the best-trained legal counsel they can afford to represent them for their particular criminal matter. Conversely, at the opposite end of this continuum is the *pro se* defendant who chooses instead to represent himself. In such cases there is an old adage: "He who represents himself at trial has a fool for a client."

 Self-Representation

 Chapter Quiz: The Bench and the Bar

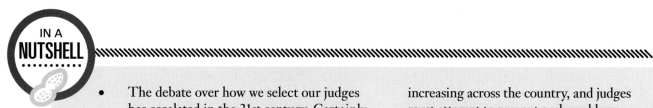

IN A NUTSHELL

- The debate over how we select our judges has escalated in the 21st century. Certainly adding fuel to the controversy over judicial selection is the amount of money now being spent by judges to fund their elections; across the nation, states use five basic methods of judicial selection; one of the more popular methods is the merit plan (or "Missouri Plan").

- Judges enjoy several distinct benefits of office, including life terms for federal positions and a high degree of respect and prestige. But problems can await new judges as well: mastering the breadth of law they must know and apply; administering the court and the docket; supervising court staff; and coping with the psychological discomfort and loneliness that accompanies the new position. Courtroom violence is also increasing across the country, and judges must attempt to prevent such problems.

- The prosecutor is probably the most powerful person in our criminal justice system, controlling the floodgates in determining whether or not to file charges (and these attorneys also have the ability to scold officers who fail to do their work properly). The prosecutor also interacts with the person suspected of the crime, the victim, and witnesses.

- Defense attorneys require the state to prove its case, help defendants understand their options in the criminal justice system, and attempt to ensure that the entire slate of rights owed to the defendant is upheld. As with prosecutors, defense attorneys have a number of strategies at their disposal.

KEY TERMS & CONCEPTS

Chief justice
Defense attorney
Judicial misconduct
Judicial selection (methods of)

Merit selection
Model Code of Judicial Conduct
Plea negotiation (or bargaining)

Prosecuting attorney
Public defender

STUDY SITE

$SAGE edge™

Sharpen your skills with **SAGE edge** at **edge.sagepub.com/peak**. **SAGE edge for students** provides a personalized approach to help you accomplish your coursework goals in an easy-to-use learning environment. Access the videos, audio clips, quizzes, cases and SAGE journal and reference articles that are noted in this chapter.

1. What are the five methods by which judges are selected?

2. Why is the partisan election method of selecting judges currently under severe criticism?

3. What are the key points of the merit selection plan for selecting judges?

4. What is meant by "good judging," and why is courtroom civility so important?

5. How might judges receive training for their roles?

1. Your local League of Women Voters is establishing a new study group to better understand the "merit selection," or so-called Missouri Plan for selecting judges, so as to be better informed when the matter comes up for a referendum. You are asked to explain this system of selecting judges, including its pros and cons when compared with, say, judges running for election on a partisan ticket. Develop your presentation.

2. Some foreign countries do not subscribe to the adversarial process as part of their court system, believing that it is too combative, slow, and cumbersome, and can lead to a "win at all cost" mentality among the lawyers. Rather, they use a nonadversarial or inquisitorial system, where the court or a part of the court is actively involved in determining the facts of the case (as opposed to the court being primarily an impartial referee in the adversarial system). Your instructor asks you to participate in a pro-con group project concerning the adversarial process. Choose a side and make your defense.

3. You have been requested by your criminal justice department chairperson to participate in the annual "Career Day" program that the faculty conducts; the focus is on different careers in law enforcement, courts, and corrections. Because the faculty members know you recently completed an internship with your local prosecutor's office, they ask you to make a presentation on the functions and challenges that exist for a prosecutor. Develop and organize into a 20-minute speech what you will say in your comprehensive presentation.

COURT METHODS AND CHALLENGES:
Sentencing and Punishment

LEARNING OBJECTIVES

As a result of reading this chapter, the student will be able to:

1 Delineate the four purposes of punishment

2 Explain the factors that influence the type of punishment that a convicted person will receive

3 Describe the historical development of, and different philosophies regarding, crime and punishment from the colonial era to today, and how different types of prisons were built accordingly

4 Review the forms of punishment that are used around the world, and a sense of whether or not the punishment that is used is always suited to the offense committed

5 Describe the differences between, and purposes of, both determinate and indeterminate sentences

6 Review the federal sentencing guidelines

7 Explain the law and purposes surrounding the use of victim impact statements

8 Describe the fundamental arguments for and against capital punishment, including key Supreme Court decisions concerning its existence and application, methods of execution, and DNA exonerations from death sentences

9 Describe aggravating and mitigating circumstances as they apply to sentencing decisions

10 Explain the right to appeals by those who are convicted

11 Review how technologies are making the courts more efficient

CHAPTER

11

If you are going to punish a man retributively, you must injure him. If you are going to reform him, you must improve him. And men are not improved by injuries.

—George Bernard Shaw[1]

INTRODUCTION

Author Introduction:
Chapter 11

For what reasons and purposes are people punished? Do punishments always fit the crimes committed? Does capital punishment work? Certainly punishing those who violate the right to life, liberty, and property of their fellow human beings is one of the primary functions of the American criminal justice system. However, there are many questions concerning the "how" and "how much" to be addressed. As the above quote by G. B. Shaw might indicate, an enigma for our time is what might best be done with people who must be punished for their transgressions. As will be seen in this chapter, sentencing and punishment are complicated issues, with both having financial and societal factors that must be included in these discussions.

Also consider that, while violent crimes are declining at the outset of the new millennium, people are increasingly being victimized by intelligent white-collar criminals, identity thieves, and cybercriminals. How should our society deal with these new types of offenders? Into this complicated mix might also be added the adage that "it is better to let a hundred guilty people go free than to convict one innocent person." Finally, the federal and state sentencing guidelines discussed in this chapter indicate how much concern and effort have recently gone into sentencing and punishment.

As shown in the above chapter outline, this chapter approaches sentencing and punishment from several perspectives, including their purposes, types, and methods, as well as the recent influence of DNA. Included are several scenarios and activities that provide opportunities for you to "learn by doing."

PURPOSES OF PUNISHMENT

The need to punish some of our fellow citizens has existed since the beginning of time—at least since biblical times, and likely much earlier. It would seem

ASSESS YOUR AWARENESS:

Test your knowledge of criminal sentencing and punishment by first reading and responding to the following seven true-false items; check your answers after reading this chapter's materials.

1. Historically, people have been punished for one purpose only: retribution.

2. A small number of offenders commit a disproportionately large number of offenses.

3. Today American society adheres to the "rehabilitation model," which states that criminals have been failed by society and emphasizes offender treatment.

4. Offenders' sentences can be served in determinate/indeterminate and concurrent/consecutive configurations.

5. Prosecutors and defense attorneys can influence judges' sentencing decisions.

6. Victims' families are not allowed to present impact statements in court at the time of sentencing.

7. Federal sentencing guidelines are to be merely advisory and not mandatory.

Answers can be found on page 401.

there have always been attempts—by a variety of methods and for a variety of reasons—to convince people that they should change their behavior and either obey the customs and laws of their society or suffer the consequences. Very often those attempts at changing behaviors meant that—by one means or another, such as imprisonment, banishment, or death—offenders would be removed from society in such a way that they were no longer in a position to do further harm to their fellow citizens. Next we discuss the four goals of punishment—some or all of which are hoped to be achieved by all societies, even the most primitive. Furthermore, we will see that throughout history, crimes and criminals have been viewed and punished differently, depending on several factors (some of those factors that determine punishment today are included in the discussions of the "wedding cake" and crime control/due process models of crime, in Chapter 1).

Four Goals

Following are the historical reasons and goals for **punishment** of our fellow citizens—what is hoped will be achieved (note that all of these goals and justifications may also be achieved by methods employed in *community-based corrections*, discussed in Chapter 14):

1. Retribution: **Retribution** has its roots in Old Testament law where, in Exodus 21:24, the "eye for eye, tooth for tooth, hand for hand, foot for foot" quote appears for the first time—labeled *lex talionis*, the law of equitable retribution. Death penalty supporters also quote this often as justification for their position. However, neither the "eye for eye" quote nor the verse itself is a complete sentence, nor do they mention the death penalty. However, the "eye for eye" quote for many people dictates that offenders should be punished in an equal manner reflecting their crime: It is instinctive for people to want to get even when wronged by another, and it is deeply engrained within ourselves and our society that punishment should be meted out when someone offends the law.

2. Deterrence: A second traditional purpose of criminal punishment is **deterrence**, which probably makes more sense than retribution in terms of betterment of society because it is not grounded on our primal human emotions and instincts. In essence, because people will typically avoid unpleasant things, they are much less likely to commit a crime if they know that punishment will occur if they get caught. Deterrence therefore has two components: general and specific. By seeing others being punished for their crimes, there is a general deterrent effect because the general public can also see what will befall them should they engage in similar behavior. Specific deterrence, conversely, involves using punishment against specific offenders for their criminal acts in order to discourage them from committing such acts again in the future.

3. Incapacitation: **Incapacitation**, by its very meaning, is beneficial in that it prevents

Punishment (and its purposes): penalties imposed for committing criminal acts, to accomplish deterrence, retribution, incapacitation, and/or rehabilitation.

Retribution: a goal of punishmentt that states the offender ought to be made to experience revenge for his actions.

Deterrence, general/specific: actions that are designed to prevent crimes from occurring

Incapacitation: rendering someone as unable to act or move about, either through incarceration or by court order.

Placing people in stocks was used internationally and during medieval, Renaissance, and colonial American times as a form of physical punishment as well as for public humiliation.

criminals from victimizing others by virtue of their being placed in a situation where they cannot physically commit crimes. The best examples, of course, are imprisonment in jails and prisons as well as execution. Bear in mind, however, that one can still commit crimes while in a state of incarceration. Using that analogy, the methods of community corrections—probation and parole and other alternatives to incarceration—are forms of incapacitation, which also aims to protect the innocent from committing new crimes.

4. Rehabilitation: Almost since its beginning, the modern criminal justice system has had as a primary goal—indeed a responsibility—to change criminals so that they become law-abiding; in other words, to *rehabilitate* them. In fact, for most of the 20th century, **rehabilitation** was the system's primary goal in terms of how it was to function and be organized. However, during the last half-century, that ideology has been modified to the point that it is hardly recognizable.[2] The reasons for this ideological change are several, and include changing governmental priorities, other concerns of the public (as revealed in national polls), and institutional and political resistance to change.[3] Furthermore, politicians can point to the "nothing works" idea put forth by Robert Martinson, who studied prison programs (discussed in Chapter 12). Still, a wide array of correctional programs (i.e., vocational, educational, counseling) continues to be offered in prisons and jails, and with marked success. One cost-benefit analysis of 14 correctional treatment programs found that in all but one of the programs, program benefits outweighed program costs. Such programs can be crucial for assisting offenders to reenter society and not recidivate (commit more crimes).[4]

Sentencing and punishment must accomplish one or more of these goals if the public is to be supportive of them. If increases in prison and jail sentences do not provide effective means of preventing crime, then a more cost-effective strategy must be found that will target the offenders most likely to commit serious crimes at high rates. As a federal report noted:

> It is frequently observed that a small number of offenders commit a disproportionately large number of offenses. If prison resources can be effectively targeted to high-rated offenders, it should be possible to achieve . . . levels of crime control. The key to such a policy rests on an ability to identify high-rate offenders . . . and at relatively early stages in their careers.[5]

Factors Influencing Punishment

As noted above, sentencing and punishment involve issues concerning their financial and societal benefit. For example, on average it costs about $31,000 per year to house an inmate in prison.[6] For that amount of money, society expects to be able to accomplish one or more of the four functions described. Regarding the cost-benefit effect of prisons, some researchers argue that prisons should be used to greater advantage, believing it is at least twice as costly to let a prisoner be loose in society than it is to lock him up. For example, comparing the cost of incarceration with the human and financial toll of crime, prison expert John DiIulio Jr. believes that prisons are a "real bargain."[7]

In addition to victims making their wishes known early on to the prosecution concerning punishment, as well as victim impact statements and aggravating/mitigating circumstances involved in a crime (both of which are discussed below), there are other factors that influence sentencing and punishment. First, the U.S. Constitution speaks briefly but forcefully regarding the use of punishment. The Eighth Amendment provides that incarceration will not involve "cruel and unusual punishment," and that fines will not be

Influencing Punishment

Rehabilitation: attempts to reform an offender through vocational and educational programming, counseling, and so forth, so he is not a recidivist and does not return to crime/prison.

excessive. Furthermore, the Thirteenth Amendment states that U.S. citizens have a right against involuntary servitude.

Prosecutors can influence the sentencing decision by agreeing to engage in plea negotiation in terms of the number of charges filed, to limit the maximum penalty the judge may impose, by explaining to the sentencing judge that the offender was particularly cruel in his crime or, alternatively, was very cooperative with the police and/or remorseful for the crime; in many states, prosecutors can also make a specific sentencing recommendation to the court that has been agreed upon with the defense.

Defense attorneys probably carry less influence over sentencing decisions than prosecutors. Nonetheless, they can seek to obtain the lightest sentence possible, including probation or other alternatives to sentencing, as well as emphasize prior to sentencing such things as the defendant's minor involvement in the crime, the victim's participation, and so on.

Certainly the seriousness of the offense is the most important factor in determining the sentencing one receives for his or her offense; a violent crime against a person certainly warrants a more harsh penalty than an offense against one's property, and certainly the judge, jury, prosecutor, and defense attorney must take into account the suffering of the victim when carrying out their roles in arriving at a proper punishment.

Next in importance to the seriousness of the offense, where sentencing is concerned, is the defendant's prior criminal record. Certainly the existence of a lengthy criminal record—particularly a record of violence, or even habitual crimes against property, such as home invasion—can weigh heavily in terms of sentencing and punishment. [Many states have habitual offender laws (see the next "You Be the Judge" box), which are related to and often viewed the same as three-strikes laws (discussed in Chapter 1), which vary widely from state to state but typically apply only to felonies and require third-time felons to serve a mandatory 25 years to life. Furthermore, many police departments have repeat offender units dedicated solely to surveilling known offenders.]

you be the... JUDGE

HABITUAL OFFENDERS

A habitual offender is essentially one who has been convicted of a crime several times (either a misdemeanor or a felony, and normally at least twice). Habitual offender laws normally impose additional punishments on such offenders. Such laws can even address traffic violations. For example, a first-time driving under the influence (DUI) offense is usually a misdemeanor that results in a fine and jail time of less than one year. However, upon being arrested for a second or third DUI, the offender may be charged with a felony (depending on state law). Being classified as a habitual offender can thus result in higher criminal fines, longer jail or prison sentences, and loss of various rights and privileges (e.g., the right to own a firearm or to possess a driver's license).

An example is a Florida law stating that "if you receive three (3) or more convictions of serious offenses on separate occasions you will be deemed a habitual offender. Examples of serious traffic offense include voluntary manslaughter while driving, involuntary manslaughter while driving, [and] felony while driving. Other serious traffic offenses include not stopping at an accident with a personal injury or death, or driving with a suspended or revoked license. Three convictions of these offenses and you will be considered a habitual traffic offender."

1. Do you agree with the spirit and intent of such laws?

2. Are such laws too harsh or too lenient?

Source: See LegalMatch, "What Is a Habitual Offender," http://www .legalmatch.com/law-library/article/what-is-a-habitual-offender.html (accessed March 25, 2013); also see Florida Drivers Association, "How to Get a Hardship License for Habitual Offenders," http://www.123driving.com/ habitual-offender.shtml (accessed March 25, 2013).

Plantation
Prisons

Models, Methods, and Reforms

Philosophies of crime and punishment have changed significantly since the late 1700s, when American society was relatively sparsely populated and predominantly rural. However, with the Industrial Revolution came a new concept of criminal punishment embracing various correctional methods, including the following[8]:

1. The colonial model (1600s–1790s): During the colonial period most Americans lived under laws that were transferred from England; Puritans rigorously punished violations of religious laws, and banishment from the community, fines, death, and other punishments were the norm; use of the death penalty was common.

What is often termed the "first American penitentiary," if not the first in the world, was established in Philadelphia, in 1790: the Walnut Street Jail.

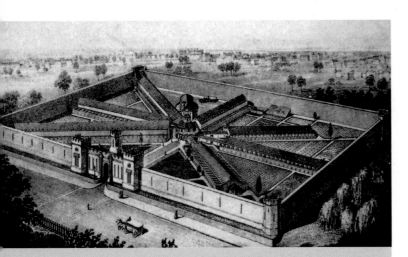

Built in 1829, Eastern State Penitentiary, a huge fortress near Philadelphia, emphasized complete solitary confinement.

2. The penitentiary model (1790s–1860s): With the Industrial Revolution—and increasing populations—came a new concept of criminal punishment. Criminal offenders were to be isolated from the bad influences of society and from one another so that, while engaged in productive labor, they might reflect on their past misdeeds, and be "penitent" or remorseful for their crimes. As a result, what has been termed "the first American penitentiary, if not the first one in the world," was established in Philadelphia, in 1790, in the Walnut Street Jail. This penitentiary introduced the institutional pattern of outside cells with a central corridor and the use of solitary confinement as the central method of reforming inmates to "the good life." Inmates were also segregated according to "age, sex, and the type of the offenses charged against them."[9] Auburn Prison, built in New York in 1821, reflected this shift, emphasizing individual cell-block architecture to create an environment to rehabilitate and reform, separate criminals from all contact with corruption, and teach them moral habits, by means of severe discipline. Inmates worked as contract convict labor 10 hours per day, 6 days per week. The Auburn model influenced the emergence of reform schools and workhouses in the 1820s. Then, Eastern State Penitentiary, a huge fortress with thick walls near Philadelphia, was built in 1829, emphasizing complete solitary confinement rather than Auburn's contract labor. New inmates wore hoods when marched to their cells to avoid seeing other prisoners. Regimentation included use of the lockstep and marching in close order single file shuffling with head turned right, practices that continued into the 1930s. No visitors or mail or newspapers were allowed. The design of this prison became the most influential in U.S. history

3. The reformatory model (1870s–1890s): By the middle of the 1800s, reformers became disillusioned with the results of the penitentiary

movement, and soon a new generation of reform came to the fore, motivated by humanitarian concerns. This new approach to penology emphasized inmate change and indeterminate sentences. Fixed sentences, lockstep (marching everywhere in single file), silence, and isolation were seen as destructive to inmate initiative. This wave of prison reform began with the founding of today's American Correctional Association in 1879 and the building of Elmira Reformatory in 1876. At Elmira, Zebulon Brockway began classification and segregation of prisoners, as well as providing vocational training, and rewards for good behavior—including early release for good behavior and parole. This—Brockway's "New Penology"—included the creation of specialized institutions to care for the young, female, and mentally impaired. Also created at this time was the juvenile court system, in Chicago in 1899, that gave wide discretionary powers to judges, and Indiana's Female Prison and Reformatory Institution for Girls and Women in Indianapolis in 1874. Inmates began producing license plates, constructing public highways, and working at prison farms and factories that produced food and items for internal consumption. In 1927 the first federal prison for women opened in Alderson, West Virginia, a minimum-security campus-like prison with residential cottages. Elsewhere, the camps that housed inmates working on roads became models for minimum-security prisons that emerged in the 1930s. Then, with Congress recognizing the need to build federal penitentiaries, the Three Prisons Act of 1891 authorized the first federal penitentiaries. The old army prison at Fort Leavenworth, Kansas, became the first United States penitentiary in 1895; the second opened in 1902 at Atlanta, Georgia, and the third was located at the old territorial prison on McNeil Island in Puget Sound, Washington.

Penitentiary Model

4. The progressive model (1890s–1930s): The first two decades of the 20th century saw the Progressives coming from upper-status backgrounds, being benevolent and philanthropic, and wanting to understand and cure crime—first by improving social conditions that appeared to breed crime, and second by treating criminals so that they would lead crime-free lives. Treatment would be focused on the individual and his or her specific problem. Probation was launched as an alternative to incarceration, allowing offenders to be treated in the community under supervision, and indeterminate sentences came into being.

5. The medical model (1930s–1960s): This model generally included the idea that criminals are mentally ill, and the emphasis of corrections shifted to treatment; criminals were seen as persons whose social, psychological, or biological deficiencies had caused them to engage in illegal activity and who should be treated; rehabilitation took on national legitimacy and became the primary purpose of incarceration. The Federal Bureau of Prisons (discussed in Chapter 12) was established in 1930 to oversee the 11 federal prisons then in existence. In 1933 Alcatraz was acquired from the U.S. Army for a federal prison. The gangster era was in full swing, and national Prohibition wrought violent crime waves, and Alcatraz was the ideal solution—serving the dual purpose of holding public enemies and being a visible icon to warn this new brand of criminal; under Warden James A. Johnston, Alcatraz's rules of conduct were among the most rigid in the correctional system, and harsh punishments were delivered to inmates who defied prison regulations. Then, more in keeping with the medical model was the appointment of James V. Bennett as director of the Federal Bureau of Prisons in 1937; in 1941 he built the Federal Correctional Institution at Seagoville, Texas, a prison without walls, that became widespread in the 1960s. Different treatment programs were offered to prisoners, and the Federal Prison Industries program began in 1934, allowing inmates to be furloughed out of prison for work and other purposes.

6. The community model (1960s–1970s): Following the inmate riot and hostage taking at New York State's Attica Correctional Facility in 1971, prisons were seen as artificial institutions that interfered with the offender's ability to develop a crime-free lifestyle. Community reintegration was the dominant idea until the 1970s, when it gave way to a new punitive stance in criminal justice.

7. The crime control model (1970s–2000s): The pendulum swung again, with the public during the late 1900s—and still today—being concerned about rapidly rising crime rates and studies of inmate treatment programs challenging their success and worth. Critics attacked the indeterminate sentence and parole, calling for longer sentences for career criminals and violent offenders. Legislators, judges, and officials responded with determinate sentencing laws, "three-strikes laws," mandatory sentencing laws (e.g., doubling one's sentence for a crime committed with a weapons), and so forth. (Regarding the accompanying changes in prisons, in 1961 Texas prison system director George Beto, in opposition to the medical model, began emphasizing strict discipline; in 1972, David Ruiz sued the Texas prison system, claiming that the system constituted "cruel and unusual punishment" prohibited by the Eighth Amendment to the U.S. Constitution; his class action suit was settled in 1980, the longest-running prisoners' lawsuit in U.S. history.)

In 1941 James V. Bennett, director of the Federal Bureau of Prisons oversaw construction of the Federal Correctional Institution at Seagoville, Texas, a prison without walls.

Making Punishment Fit the Crime

Crime Control Model

We might consider punishment from this perspective: A recent report by Amnesty International discusses capital punishment around the world, including beheadings in Saudi Arabia; hangings in Japan, Iraq, Singapore, and Sudan; firing squads in Afghanistan, Belarus, and Vietnam; stonings in Iran; and "the only country in the Americas that regularly executes: the United States." Amnesty reports that in the 58 countries retaining the death penalty around the world, at least 18,750 people are now under sentence of death, and at least 680 people were executed worldwide in 2011, excluding China (which does not release its figures).[10]

Although the death penalty is administered to about 50 people each year in the United States (and that number has been declining since 2000),[11] certainly "justice" and acts deserving of punishment in those foreign nations—where people are executed, for example, for their political thoughts, apostasy (improper religious beliefs), and "highway robbery," or flogged 80 times for possessing alcohol, or, as in Singapore, flogged with a rattan cane for vandalism[12]—mean something altogether different from the way in which they are perceived in the United States; and while the crime rates in those venues are likely to be relatively low, the question to be asked is this: Given a choice, would you opt to *live* in any of those countries?

Looking at the use of incarceration in the United States, it is suggested in a later chapter, Chapter 12, that for many people, being sentenced to prison is a "step up," partly because there they receive "three hots and a cot" without having to support a family, and might even be surrounded by their family members, "homies," and gang-banger friends. If that sad commentary on American life is true, then one is left to wonder how our society can allow that to happen—or, perhaps, why we devote the time, effort, and money—$53.5 billion annually for state corrections expenditures prisons alone[13]—to basically "warehouse" 1.3 million people.[14]

Some might say we should abandon the warehousing approach and make every effort to try to identify those individuals for whom the prison experience can be beneficial; then, while they are a "captive audience" in prison, make all manner of rehabilitative educational/vocational programming available to them. Or, alternatively, some might argue that those inmates for whom prison is a "step up" should be put to work at hard labor, in order to make prison life less attractive and thus stop repeat offending. But which way should the pendulum swing?

The next "You Be the Judge" box poses some thought-provoking questions regarding punishment options. As you read them, consider the four functions of punishment that are discussed above, as well as your own philosophy concerning punishment.

TYPES OF SENTENCES TO BE SERVED

How offenders serve their sentences—in a determinate or indeterminate, as well as a concurrent or consecutive, fashion—is a crucial distinction, particularly in terms of how long an offender must remain in prison and where parole is concerned. Next we distinguish between these types.

Determinate and Indeterminate Sentences

First, *determinate* **sentencing** is either legislatively determined or judicially determined. In states using a determinate sentencing structure, convicted offenders are sentenced for a fixed term, such as 10 years; therefore, there is

Determinate sentence: a specific, fixed-period sentence ordered by a court.

---

you be the... JUDGE

IS PUNISHMENT APPROPRIATE?

Given that many people have philosophical and practical disagreements with the four stated purposes of punishment, above, consider the following questions and determine where you stand on these "issues."

- Do you support corporal punishment—the deliberate infliction of pain against someone through spanking? Would you alter your opinion if you knew that corporal punishment is legal in schools in 22 states? Does the end justify the means?

- Would your opinion be changed if you were told that the U.S. Supreme Court refused to hear a case arguing that beating students is constitutionally impermissible? Does it change your thinking to know that the student in the above case was an 18-year-old adult?

- Does punishment generally fail to stop, and even increase, the problem behavior?

- Does punishment typically arouse strong emotional responses, including anxiety, apprehension, and guilt?

- Does punishment teach people to have and use internal controls at all times, or only when other people are present?

- Does the infliction of pain arouse aggression toward the source of the pain?

- Can punishment be effective when it is used sporadically, or must it be regularly practiced?

- Can punishment ever become abuse?

Source: Adapted from "The School Law Blog," *Education Week,* http://blogs .edweek.org/edweek/school_law/2008/06/the_supreme_court_and_corporal .html (accessed February 19, 2013).

Inmates often appear before their parole board to express remorse for their crimes, to explain how they have progressed while in prison, and to offer reasons why they should be released and placed on parole.

no opportunity for a paroling authority to make adjustments in time served when making release decisions; offenders are released at the expiration of their term, minus any good time credits. Under a legislatively determined structure, the legislature fixes by law the penalty for specific offenses or offense categories. In a judicially determined system, the judge has broad discretion to choose a sanction, but once imposed, it is not subject to change.

Conversely, in an **indeterminate sentencing** format, the convicted individual will be sentenced for a set range of time, such as 5–10 years, so that his or her conduct inside the prison system, amenability to rehabilitative efforts (e.g., educational and vocational programs, counseling), apparent remorsefulness, and so forth can be taken into account in terms of deciding a release date. The legislature sets a broad range of time, expressed as minimum and maximum sentences, for a particular offense or category of offenses, and the responsibility for determining the actual term of incarceration is divided between the judge and the parole board. The judge's sentence is also made in terms of a minimum and maximum term.

The authority of a parole board to grant discretionary release to a prisoner before the expiration date of the maximum term varies from state to state. The parole board determines the actual release date, typically using a formula for determining earliest parole eligibility, which may occur after a percentage of the minimum, after a percentage of the maximum, or after the entire minimum has been served, depending on the state.[15]

Those persons supporting the rehabilitative ideal for offenders will obviously be more in favor of indeterminate sentencing, which allows room for the length of sentence to fit the offender's positive responses to treatment and programs.[16]

Consecutive and Concurrent Sentences

Assume that a man is convicted for committing three separate offenses as part of a night's crime spree: He unlawfully entered a couple's home (burglary), stole several valuable items (a felony theft), and violently assaulted the husband in making his escape. Depending on the sentencing court's decision, the offender will then serve his three sentences for those crimes either concurrently or consecutively:

- A *concurrent* sentence means he will serve all three sentences together, in a sort of "stacked" manner, or all at once.

- If he serves the three sentences in a *consecutive* manner, each sentence will be served separately—in other words, when he finishes serving the sentence for the first crime, he immediately begins serving the sentence for the second crime, and so on.

FEDERAL SENTENCING GUIDELINES

The growing complexity and importance of the **sentencing guidelines** now found in criminal justice pose a bit of a dilemma for this introductory course textbook: On the one hand, they are too complicated to discuss

Intermediate Sentencing

Mid-Chapter Quiz: Crime Control Model

Indeterminate sentencing: a scheme whereby one is sentenced for a flexible time period (e.g., 5–10 years) so as to be released when rehabilitated or the opportunity for rehabilitation is presented.

Sentencing guidelines: an instrument developed by the federal government that uses a grid system to chart the seriousness of offense, criminal history, and so forth and thus allow the court to arrive at a more consistent sentence for everyone.

comprehensively or in great detail; on the other hand, they are far too important to ignore. Therefore, this chapter section will strive to achieve an appropriate balance by looking at the guidelines in summary form; some hands-on exercises are also provided.

Background: Legislation and Court Decisions

In the mid- to late 1970s and early 1980s, many people were becoming discontented with the above discussed indeterminate sentencing process; they witnessed inmates often being released after serving only a fraction of their sentences (some jurisdictions even allowing 30 days of "good time" reduction of a sentence for each 30 days served). That, coupled with renewed concern about the rising crime rate throughout the nation, resulted in wide experimentation with sentencing systems by many states and the creation of sentencing guidelines at the federal level. So, after more than a decade of research and debate, Congress decided that (1) the sentencing discretion given federal trial judges needed to be structured; (2) the administration of punishment needed to be more certain; and (3) specific offenders (e.g., white-collar and violent, repeat offenders) needed to be targeted for more serious penalties.[17] As a result, Congress abolished indeterminate sentencing at the federal level and created a determinate sentencing structure through the federal sentencing guidelines. The Sentencing Reform Act[18] was enacted to ensure that similarly situated defendants were sentenced in a more uniform fashion rather than depending on the judge to which they happened to be assigned,[19] and reformed the federal sentencing system by

Sentencing Guidelines

1. dropping rehabilitation as one of the goals of punishment;

2. creating the U.S. Sentencing Commission and charging it with establishing sentencing guidelines;

3. making all federal sentences determinate; and

4. authorizing appellate review of sentences.[20]

A long line of legal challenges ensued involving these sentencing guidelines. The first such challenge came from the state of Washington, where the petitioner had pled guilty to kidnapping. Under Washington's law, the maximum penalty for that offense is 10 years. A separate range-of-sentence provision limited the maximum allowable sentence to 53 months, but it authorized an upward departure for "exceptional" judge-determined factors. The trial judge increased the sentence to 90 months because the crime was committed with deliberate cruelty. Because the facts supporting the enhanced penalty were neither admitted by the petitioner nor found by a jury, the Supreme Court held that the sentence violated the Sixth Amendment right to trial by jury.[21] This decision, however, only applied to Washington.

Then, six months later, the Supreme Court decided *United States v. Booker*,[22] this time addressing sentencing guidelines nationally. The defendant, Booker, was found guilty by a jury of possessing at least 50 grams of crack cocaine (he actually had 92.5 grams). Under those facts, the guidelines required a possible 210- to 262-month sentence. Although the jury never heard any such evidence, the judge, finding by a preponderance of the evidence that Booker possessed the much larger amount of cocaine, rendered a sentence that was almost 10 years longer than what the guidelines prescribed. By a 5 to 4 vote, the U.S. Supreme Court found that the U.S. sentencing guidelines violated the Sixth Amendment by allowing judicial, rather than

Victim Impact Statements

//

Victim impact statements: information provided prior to sentencing by the victims of a crime (or, in cases of murder, the surviving family members) about the impact the crime had on their lives; allowed by the U.S. Supreme Court.

A homicide victim's brother is overcome with emotion while making his victim impact statement to the court.

jury, fact-finding to form the basis for the sentencing; in other words, letting in these judge-made facts is unconstitutional. The guidelines also allowed judges to make such determinations with a lesser standard of proof than the jury's "beyond a reasonable doubt" and to rely on hearsay evidence that would not be admissible at trial.[23]

The Court did not discard the guidelines entirely. The guidelines, the Court said, are to be merely advisory and not mandatory. Thus, the guidelines are a resource a judge can look at, but may choose to ignore. Although courts still must "consider" the guidelines, they need not follow them. In addition, sentences for federal crimes will become subject to appellate review for "unreasonableness," allowing appeals courts to clamp down on particular sentences that seem far too harsh.

Finally, in late 2007 the U.S. Supreme Court went further and explained what it meant in 2005 by "advisory" and "reasonableness," deciding two cases that together restored federal judges to their traditional central role in criminal sentencing. The Court found that district court judges do not have to justify their deviations from the federal sentencing guidelines, and have broad discretion to disagree with the guidelines and to impose what they believe are reasonable sentences—even if the guidelines call for different sentences. Both cases—*Gall v. United States*[24] and *Kimbrough v. United States*[25]—were decided by the same 7-2 margin and chided federal appeals courts for failing to give district judges sufficient leeway.

State-Level Sentencing Guidelines

Several states have enacted sentencing guidelines. As an example, Table 11.1 shows the sentencing grid used by the State of Washington, which has developed a very sophisticated and objective sentencing tool called *The Adult Sentencing Guidelines Manual*.[26] This manual provides comprehensive information on adult felony sentencing as set forth under state law, identifying the seriousness level of the offense and "scoring" the offender's criminal history. The seriousness of crimes ranges from Level I (which includes such offenses as simple theft, malicious mischief, attempting to elude a pursuing police vehicle, and possessing stolen property) to Level XVI (aggravated murder, which includes a first degree murder with one or more of a number of aggravating circumstances).

VICTIM IMPACT STATEMENTS

Victim impact statements are written or oral information provided in court—most commonly at sentencing—and at offenders' parole hearings concerning the impact of the crime on the victim and the victim's family. These statements generally inform the court of the financial, emotional, psychological, and/or physical impact on their lives that was caused by the crime, and provide a means for the court to refocus its attention on the human cost of the crime, as well as for the victim to participate in the criminal justice process. The right to make an impact statement is generally available not only to the victim, but also to homicide survivors, the parent or guardian of a minor victim, and a person representing an incompetent or incapacitated victim.

TABLE 11.1

State of Washington Sentencing Grid

Seriousness Level	OFFENDER SCORE 0	1	2	3	4	5	6	7	8	9+
LEVEL XVI	LIFE SENTENCE WITHOUT PAROLE/DEATH PENALTY									
LEVEL XV	180-240	187.5-249.75	195.75-260.25	203.25-270.75	210.75-280.5	218.25-291	234-312	253.5-337.5	277.5-369.75	308.25-411
LEVEL XIV	92.25-165	100.5-175.5	108-183	115.5-190.5	123.75-198.75	131.25-206.25	146.25-221.25	162-237	192.75-267.75	223.5-297.75
LEVEL XIII	92.25-123	100.5-133.5	108-144	115.5-153.75	123.75-164.25	131.25-174.75	146.25-195	162-216	192.75-256.5	223.5-297.75
LEVEL XII	69.75-92.25	76.5-102	83.25-110.25	90-120	96.75-128.25	103.5-138	121.5-162	133.5-177	156.75-207.75	180-238.5
LEVEL XI	58.5-76.5	64.5-85.5	71.25-93.75	76.5-102	83.25-110.25	90-118.5	109.5-145.5	119.25-158.25	138.75-183.75	157.5-210
LEVEL X	38.25-51	42.75-56.25	46.5-61.5	50.25-66.75	54-72	57.75-76.5	73.5-97.5	81-108	96.75-128.25	111.75-148.5
LEVEL IX	23.25-30.75	27-36	30.75-40.5	34.5-45.75	38.25-51	42.75-56.25	57.75-76.5	65.25-87	81-108	96.75-128.25
LEVEL VIII	15.75-20.25	19.5-25.5	23.25-30.75	27-36	30.75-40.5	34.5-45.75	50.25-66.75	57.75-76.5	65.25-87	81-108
LEVEL VII	11.25-15	15.75-20.25	19.5-25.5	23.25-30.75	27-36	30.75-40.5	42.75-56.25	50.25-66.75	57.75-76.5	65.25-87
LEVEL VI	9-10.5	11.25-15	15.75-20.25	19.5-25.5	23.25-30.75	27-36	34.5-45.75	42.75-56.25	50.25-66.75	57.75-76.5
LEVEL V	4.5-9	9-10.5	9.75-12.75	11.25-15	16.5-21.75	24.75-32.25	30.75-40.5	38.25-51	46.5-61.5	54-72
LEVEL IV	2.25-6.75	4.5-9	9-10.5	9.75-12.75	11.25-15	16.5-21.75	24.75-32.25	32.25-42.75	39.75-52.5	47.25-63
LEVEL III	0.75-2.25	2.25-6	3-9	6.75-9	9-12	12.75-16.5	16.5-21.75	24.75-32.25	32.25-42.75	38.25-51
LEVEL II	0-67.5 days	1.5-4.5	2.25-6.75	3-9	9-10.5	10.5-13.5	12.75-16.5	16.5-21.75	24.75-32.25	32.25-42.75
LEVEL I	0-45 days	0-67.5 days	1.5-3.75	1.5-4.5	2.25-6	3-9	9-10.5	10.5-13.5	12.75-16.5	16.5-21.75

Source: Reprinted with permission, copyright © 2012 State of Washington/John C. Steiger, PhD.

A recent survey by the National Center for Victims of Crime found that 80 percent of all victims rated their ability to make a victim impact statement at sentencing and at parole hearings as "very important."[27]

Victim impact statements were upheld in 1991 by the U.S. Supreme Court, in *Payne v. Tennessee*.[28] Payne was convicted of two counts of murder for stabbing to death a mother and her 2-year-old daughter and also wounding her 3-year-old son. During the sentencing hearing, the boy's grandmother described how the killings affected the surviving grandson. On appeal, the Supreme Court held 7-2 that the victim has a right to be heard, and quoted from a 1934 opinion by Justice Benjamin Cardozo: "Justice, though due to the accused, is due to the accuser also."[29] See the next "Focus On" box for more discussion and an example of such a statement.

Payne v. Tennessee

FOCUS ON   VICTIM IMPACT STATEMENTS

Following is an example of a victim impact statement as prepared by Ken and Sue Antrobus following the shooting death of their daughter Vanessa Quinn (the person named in the statement, Hunter, was the person who sold the gun to the person who then went on a shooting spree in a mall).

How has this affected my family? [T]o be honest I don't know yet, I can only tell you how it has affected us to this point in time. My Mom gave up her fight for life, 6 weeks after Vanessa was taken from us, and my youngest daughter Susanna had a miscarriage the same night my Mom passed away. My husband and I cry every day, we struggle to get through each and every day, you wake up with it, you carry it through your day and it goes to bed with you every night. If you're old enough at 18 to give your life up for this country, you're old enough to know what you're doing when you sell an illegal weapon to a minor. I am asking and pleading with this court to give Mr. Hunter the maximum sentence to send a message to the people of this country and people like Mr. Hunter, that if you chose to engage in illegal weapons to minors you will be held responsible for your actions. It cost us 7,000 dollars to lay our daughter Vanessa to rest. . . . I think I deserve to give an impact statement, since Vanessa is not here to speak for herself, I don't think 10 minutes is asking for much considering what we've lost for a life time. . . .

1. Should victim impact statements be allowed in court? Why or why not?

Source: *In re Antrobus,* 519 F.3d 1123 (10th Cir. 2008); also see *Salt Lake City News,* "Victim Status Rejected in Trolley Gun Case," http://www.deseretnews.com/article/695241253/Victim-status-rejected-in-Trolley-gun-case.html?pg=all (accessed March 25, 2013).

CAPITAL PUNISHMENT

Author Video: Victim Impact Statements

Because of its finality, debate concerning the death penalty has always been emotionally charged. Certainly there are strong arguments put forth by those who favor and are opposed to **capital punishment**.

Arguments For and Against

As will be seen in the discussion below, for a politician or political entity to try to fashion a state or national policy on the death penalty that would definitively—and once and for all—appeal to most Americans would be nearly impossible. The U.S. Supreme Court has halted death sentences and then approved them, and several states have done likewise (largely due to the fact that many convicted murderers on death row have been found to be innocent); some studies indicate that the death penalty works to prevent crimes of murder, and other studies show the opposite; and Americans themselves seem fickle in their views of whether or not killers should be put to death.

Figure 11.1 shows the percentage of Americans who favor and are opposed to the death penalty, per Gallup Inc. It is seen that the percentages of people in favor of the death penalty rose steadily for the most part from about 1967 to 1995; from that point, however, there has been an overall decline in such support, reducing from about 80 percent to about 65 percent. Meanwhile, the percentage of people saying they are in opposition to the death penalty has remained fairly stable since 1937, ranging from 31 percent to 38 percent (with a spike in 1967 to 42 percent).

Death Penalty

Arguments in Favor

People who support the death penalty often believe that it deters other people from committing murder, while others base their stand on theological grounds—the commandment "Thou shalt not kill." Others favor capital punishment because of the retribution it provides to family members and friends of the victim; "getting even" is a proper punishment in the eyes of

Capital punishment: a sentence of death, or carrying out same via execution of the offender.

FIGURE 11.1

Percentage of Americans Favoring and Opposing the Death Penalty

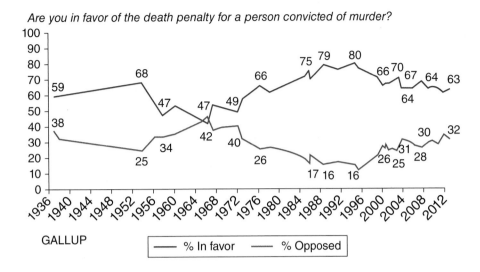

Are you in favor of the death penalty for a person convicted of murder?

GALLUP   —— % In favor   —— % Opposed

many people, rather than some "rehabilitative" ideal. It is society's nod to *lex talionis*—"eye for eye": "If you kill one of us, we will kill you." One thing the death penalty most certainly accomplishes, however, is the prevention of future murders. As James Q. Wilson noted, "Whatever else may be said about the death penalty, it is certain that it incapacitates."[30]

Does the existence of a death penalty deter individuals from committing murder? That is an important question, and one that is at the tip of the spear in this debate. The answer, unfortunately, is elusive, and it largely depends on which set of studies one looks at and gives credence to. Beginning in 2003, a number of studies were published that reportedly demonstrated the death penalty saves lives by acting as a deterrent to murder. One study that garnered a large amount of attention was conducted by H. Naci Mocan and R. Kaj Gittings[31], who analyzed 6,143 death sentences imposed in the United States between 1977 and 1997. Their results indicated that each execution resulted in five fewer murders, and each commutation of a death sentence to a long or life prison term resulted in five additional homicides. Further, each additional removal from death row when one's sentence is vacated resulted in one additional homicide.

Another 2003 study by professors at Emory University, using a panel data set of over 3,000 counties from 1977 to 1996, found that each execution results in 18 fewer murders, and that the implementation of state moratoria is associated with the increased incidence of murders.[32] Then, two studies by a Federal Communications Commission economist also supported the deterrent effect of capital punishment, finding that each additional execution, on average, results in 14 fewer murders,[33] and that executions conducted by electrocution are the most effective at providing deterrence.[34] However, as will be seen below, the findings of these studies were challenged by other criminologists.

Death Penalty

Arguments in Opposition

Arguments against the death penalty include that it does not have any deterrent value, that it is discriminatory against minorities, that retribution is unfitting for a civilized society, and that it can (and does) claim the lives of innocent people.

As indicated above, at least two criminologists have found serious flaws in the Mocan-Gittings study, which found that each execution resulted in five fewer murders. Richard Berk, using Mocan and Gittings's original data set, removed the Texas data and ran the model exactly as the original authors did for the other 49 states, and found that the deterrent effect disappeared.[35]

A second reexamination of the Mocan-Gittings study was conducted by Jeffrey Fagan, who, by modifying their measure of deterrence, also found that all the deterrent effects disappeared. Rather than prove that Mocan and Gittings erred in their assumptions, Fagan showed that small changes in their assumptions could produce wild fluctuations in their deterrence estimates.[36] Regarding the contention that the death penalty is discriminatory, many people would agree with a finding by the U.S. General Accounting Office that there is "a pattern of evidence indicating racial disparities in the charging, sentencing, and imposition of the death penalty."[37] Amnesty International argues, furthermore, that "from initial charging decisions to plea bargaining to jury sentencing, African-Americans are treated more harshly when they are defendants, and their lives are accorded less value when they are victims. All-white or virtually all-white juries are still commonplace in many localities."[38] Following are other findings regarding the death penalty discrimination thesis:

• A report sponsored by the American Bar Association concluded that one-third of African American death row inmates in Philadelphia would have received sentences of life imprisonment if they had not been African American.

• A study of death sentences in Connecticut conducted by Yale University School of Law revealed that African American defendants receive the death penalty at three times the rate of white defendants in cases where the victims are white. In addition, killers of white victims are treated more severely than people who kill minorities, when it comes to deciding what charges to bring.

Furman v. Georgia

A study released by the University of Maryland concluded that race and geography are major factors in death penalty decisions. Specifically, prosecutors are more likely to seek a death sentence when the race of the victim is white and are less likely to seek a death sentence when the victim is African American.[39]

Finally, of course, is the argument that innocent people can be—and have been—executed for crimes they never committed, which is discussed below.

Key Supreme Court Decisions

In *Furman v. Georgia* (1972), by vote of 5 to 4, the U.S. Supreme Court, for the first time, struck down the death penalty under the cruel and unusual punishment clause of the Eighth Amendment. The decision involved not only Furman, convicted for murder, but also two other men (in Georgia and Texas), convicted for rape; juries at the trials of all three men had imposed the death penalty without any specific guides or limits on their discretion. The justices

Many people oppose capital punishment and express their disapproval by protesting against it – especially when someone is about to be executed.

for the majority found this lack of guidelines or limits on jury discretion to be unconstitutional, as it resulted in a random pattern among those receiving the death penalty; one justice also felt that death was disproportionately applied to the poor and socially disadvantaged, and felt those groups were denied equal protection under the law.[40]

Four years after *Furman*, the Supreme Court rendered another major death penalty decision. A Georgia jury had found Troy Gregg guilty of armed robbery and murder and sentenced him to death. Gregg challenged his death sentence, claiming that it was, *per se*, a "cruel and unusual" punishment that violated the Eighth and Fourteenth Amendments. In a 7-2 decision, the Court held that a punishment of death did not violate the Constitution. Where a defendant has been convicted of deliberately killing another person, the careful and judicious use of the death penalty may be appropriate if carefully employed. The Court noted that Georgia's death penalty statute required a bifurcated proceeding (where the trial and sentencing are conducted separately), as well as specific jury findings as to the severity of the crime and the nature of the defendant and a comparison of aggravating and mitigating circumstances.[41]

Roper v. Simmons

Witherspoon v. Illinois

Another significant decision was rendered by the Supreme Court in 2005, in *Roper v. Simmons*, holding that the Eighth and Fourteenth Amendments forbid the execution of offenders who were under the age of 18 when their crimes were committed.[42] In addition, the Supreme Court has held that

- the Eighth Amendment prohibits the *execution of insane people*[43];

- the death penalty cannot be applied to *adults who rape children* (and, more broadly, that a state cannot impose the death penalty for a crime that did not result in the death of the victim, except for crimes committed against the state—i.e., espionage, treason)[44];

- in order to show their *legal counsel* was ineffective, defendants in capital cases must prove that the attorney's performance was less than reasonable (e.g., counsel did not present mitigating circumstances), and that there is a reasonable likelihood that this substandard performance changed the outcome of the trial[45]; and

- people who are opposed to the death penalty cannot be automatically excluded from serving on juries in capital cases; however, people whose opposition is so strong as to "prevent or substantially impair the performance of their duties" (*Witherspoon v. Illinois*, 1968) may be removed from the jury pool during *voir dire* (preliminary examination).[46]

Methods of Execution

Earlier we discussed the major forms of execution that were used throughout history. Here we discuss the methods of execution that are in use today in the United States. Those methods of execution are shown in Table 11.2. Lethal injection is authorized in a majority of the states, 36, followed by electrocution, in 9 states; gas is authorized in 3, hanging in 3, and firing squad in 2. The table also shows that 16 states authorize two methods of execution.

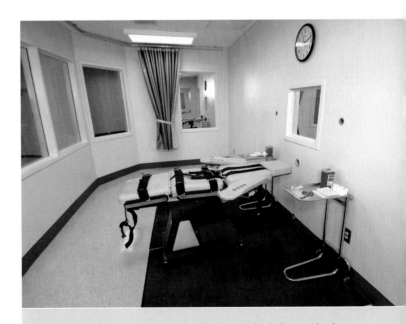
Lethal injection is the most commonly used method of execution in the United States. Shown here is the lethal execution chamber at San Quentin prison in California.

TABLE 11.2

Method of Execution, by State, 2010

JURISDICTION	LETHAL INJECTION	ELECTROCUTION	LETHAL GAS	HANGING	FIRING SQUAD
Total	36	9	3	3	2
Alabama	X	X			
Arizona[a]	X		X		
Arkansas[b]	X	X			
California	X				
Colorado	X				
Connecticut	X				
Delaware[c]	X			X	
Florida	X	X			
Georgia	X				
Idaho	X				
Illinois[d]	X	X			
Indiana	X				
Kansas	X				
Kentucky[e]	X	X			
Louisiana	X				
Maryland	X				
Mississippi	X				
Missouri	X		X		
Montana	X				
Nebraska	X				
Nevada	X				
New Hampshire[f]	X			X	
New York	X				
North Carolina	X				
Ohio	X				
Oklahoma[g]	X	X			X
Oregon	X				
Pennsylvania	X				
South Carolina	X	X			
South Dakota	X				
Tennessee[h]	X	X			
Texas	X				
Utah[i]	X				X
Virginia	X	X			
Washington	X			X	
Wyoming	X		X		

Source: BJS, National Prisoner Statistics Program.

Note: The method of execution of federal prisoners is lethal injection, pursuant to 28 CFR, Part 26. For offenses prosecuted under the Violent Crime Control and Law Enforcement Act of 1994, the execution method is that of the state in which the conviction took place (18 U.S.C. 3596).

[a]Authorizes lethal injection for persons sentenced after November 15, 1992; inmates sentenced before that date may select lethal injection or gas.

[b]Authorizes lethal injection for those whose offense occurred on or after July 4, 1983; inmates whose offense occurred before that date may select lethal injection or electrocution.

[c]Authorizes hanging if lethal injection is held to be unconstitutional by a court of competent jurisdiction.

[d]Authorizes electrocution only if lethal injection is held illegal or unconstitutional.

[e]Authorizes lethal injection for persons sentenced on or after March 31, 1998; inmates sentenced before that date may select lethal injection or electrocution.

[f]Authorizes hanging only if lethal injection cannot be given.

[g]Authorizes electrocution if lethal injection is held to be unconstitutional, and firing squad if both lethal injection and electrocution are held to be unconstitutional.

[h]Authorizes lethal injection for those whose capital offense occurred after December 31, 1998; inmates whose offense occurred before that date may select electrocution by written waiver.

[i]Authorizes firing squad if lethal injection is held unconstitutional. Inmates who selected execution by firing squad prior to May 3, 2004, may still be entitled to execution by that method.

Although death by lethal injection has widely been thought to be much more humane than other methods, several challenges to this method of execution have been raised in the Supreme Court in recent years. Such challenges typically claim that the drugs used in the executions cause extreme and unnecessary pain, while masking the pain being experienced by the inmate, and thus violate the Eighth Amendment's ban on cruel and unusual punishment. Most recently, in *Baze v. Rees*,[47] the U.S. Supreme Court held that the three-drug "cocktail" used by 35 states and the federal government did not violate the Eighth Amendment; Chief Justice John G. Roberts observed that a method of execution would only violate the constitution if it was "deliberately designed to inflict pain." Two years earlier, Clarence Hill, an inmate on Florida's death row, challenged the use of lethal injection *per se* as causing unnecessary pain contrary to contemporary standards of decency; however, by a vote of 5-4, the U.S. Supreme Court denied a stay of execution (Justice Antonin Scalia noting that "lethal injection is much less painful than hanging"), and Hill was executed in September 2006.[48]

Methods of Execution

DNA Exonerations—and Moratoria

Being convicted of a crime is no guarantee that one is guilty as charged; indeed, according to the Death Penalty Information Center, since 1973, 142 persons on death row in the United States have been exonerated; furthermore, according to the Innocence Project, **DNA** led to 18 of those death row **exonerations**.[49] Furthermore, looking at all crimes for which people were convicted and imprisoned (not just capital offenses), according to the Innocence Project, there have been 249 postconviction DNA exonerations in the United States.[50] What the above shows is that humans certainly are not infallible.

Exonerations

These exonerations of convicted murderers did not go unnoticed. Indeed, from 2000 to 2008, Illinois, Nebraska, Indiana, New Jersey, and Maryland placed moratoria on capital punishment while reviews of the process were being conducted; Indiana and Maryland also declared moratoria until studies could be completed.[51] Furthermore, during that time the U.S. Supreme Court held that the execution of mentally retarded persons (generally defined as having an IQ less than 70) is cruel and unusual punishment,[52] and that the finding of an aggravating factor justifying a death sentence must be made by a jury, not merely by the sentencing judge.[53]

DNA: deoxyribonucleic acid, or the acids found in all cells; used in forensics to match evidence (hair, semen) left at a crime scene with a particular perpetrator.

Exoneration: to absolve someone of criminal blame, or find someone not guilty.

FOCUS ON DNA EXONERATIONS

In November 1994 the naked body of Nina Glover was discovered in a dumpster on Chicago's South Side. Glover, a drug abuser and prostitute, had been brutally raped and murdered; an autopsy concluded she had been killed by strangulation. Four months later, 18-year-old Jerry Fincher walked into a police station; volunteered that he had participated in the abduction, rape, and murder of Glover; and implicated Michael Saunders, 15, and three other minors.

Saunders and the others were arrested, with each eventually confessing to luring Glover to a basement, taking turns vaginally raping her, beating her over the head with a shovel, strangling her, and dumping her body in a dumpster. No physical evidence connected any of the teenagers to the crime. However, pretrial DNA testing was performed and excluded all of the charged teenagers as the source of the semen.

Nevertheless, in May 1998, Saunders and three of the youths were tried (charges against Fincher were dropped due to coerced evidence against him being suppressed), with the only significant evidence being their own confession. All three defendants were convicted; Saunders was sentenced to 40 years.

In December 2010, Saunders successfully filed a motion for a more advanced form of DNA testing to be performed than was done pretrial, and in May 2011 the Illinois State Police reported a match with another person in the state DNA database—a deceased man, who was one of the first people that police interviewed about Glover's murder. On November 16, 2011, based on the DNA evidence, a judge vacated the convictions of Saunders (who had served 14 years in prison) and the three others.

Source: Adapted from The Innocence Project, "Know the Cases," http://www .innocenceproject.org/Content/Michael_Saunders.php (accessed March 25, 2013).

DNA analysis has been used to exonerate more than 100 persons in prison. After serving more than 25 years in prison for a rape conviction, Larry Fuller leaves a Dallas courthouse after DNA evidence exonerated him. At left is Innocence Project lawyer Vanessa Potkin; at right is Innocence Project director Barry Scheck.

AGGRAVATING AND MITIGATING CIRCUMSTANCES

In passing sentence, judges (and, in death penalty cases, the jury) will look at factors other than the crime itself. They consider the manner in which the crime was committed, in order to determine whether or not they should increase or decrease the severity of the punishment.

In other words, the judge or jury might "look behind" the crime to see if, for example, the victim was tortured prior to being killed or, on the other hand, the defendant played a minor role in the offense.

These are termed aggravating and mitigating circumstances or factors. Examples of each, as commonly exist in the states, are shown in the next "Focus On" box.

Under the Supreme Court's decision in *Gregg v. Georgia*, discussed above, the judge will also instruct the jury members that they may not impose the death penalty unless they first determine the existence of one or more statutory aggravating circumstances beyond a reasonable doubt, as well as determine that the aggravating circumstances outweigh the mitigating circumstances beyond a reasonable doubt.

FOCUS ON   AGGRAVATING AND MITIGATING CIRCUMSTANCES

Following are examples of the kinds of aggravating and mitigating circumstances that are found in state statutes (note that not all factors shown exist in all states; nor is the list exhaustive):

Aggravating Circumstances

- The murder was committed by a person with a weapon, knowingly creating a great risk of death to more than one person.
- The murder was committed while the person was committing, or attempting to commit, specified felonies.
- The murder was committed to avoid or prevent a lawful arrest or to escape from custody.
- The murder was committed for hire.
- The murder victim was a peace officer or firefighter who was engaged in the performance of his official duty ("peace officer" also includes corrections officers).

- The murder was committed by a person while in prison.[54]

Mitigating Circumstances

- The defendant has no significant history of prior criminal activity.
- The murder was committed while the defendant was under the influence of extreme mental or emotional disturbance.
- The victim was a participant in the defendant's criminal conduct or consented to the act.
- The defendant was an accomplice in a murder committed by another person, and his participation in the murder was relatively minor.
- The defendant acted under duress or under the domination of another person.
- The defendant was a youth at the time of the crime.[55]

CRIMINAL APPEALS

In an appeal, one who has been convicted for a crime attempts to show that the trial court made a legal error that affected the decision in the case, or that he had ineffective counsel or some other violation of due process; he now asks a higher (appellate) court to review the transcript of the case for such errors—and possibly have the conviction overturned or be granted a retrial. In addition, the defendant may contest the trial court's sentencing decision without actually challenging the underlying conviction. Then, if the appellate court grants the appeal, it may reverse the lower court's decision in whole or in part. However, if the appellate court denies the appeal, the lower court's decision stands.[56]

Gregg v. Georgia

Article I, Section 9, of the Constitution speaks only briefly and indirectly to criminal appeals, saying that the privilege of the writ of *habeas corpus* (discussed in Chapter 9 in the case of *Kibbe v. Henderson*) shall not be suspended, "unless when in Cases of Rebellion or Invasion the public Safety may require it." This writ, often referred to as "the great writ," is Latin for "you have the body," and is the inmate's means of asking a court to grant a hearing to determine whether or not the inmate is being held illegally.

Convicted persons who are indigent (poor) are entitled to free legal counsel for their initial appeal,[57] and a free copy of their trial transcript.[58] (However, the Supreme Court has held that prison inmates are not entitled to free legal counsel for subsequent "discretionary" appeals.[59]) Furthermore, as will be noted in Chapter 12, prison inmates also have a right to access to law libraries, and many law schools have defender clinics in which law students represent state and federal prisoners in appellate and postconviction litigation in state and federal courts. This is in addition to prison "writ-writers"—inmates who over time develop considerable expertise in constitutional law and means of filing writs and petitions.

Inmates are not only able to challenge their criminal conviction on a variety of grounds (the evidence that was introduced against them; the police arrest, search, and seizure of their person and property; the judge's instructions to the jury; and so on), but after being incarcerated they may attempt to obtain what are called postconviction remedies—making what are termed "collateral attacks." These lawsuits are civil in nature (unlike the original appeal of their conviction) and challenge, for example, the conditions of their confinement; they often list the prison warden as the appellee, and can involve the inmate's filing a *writ of habeas corpus*, typically in a federal court having jurisdiction over his or her place of incarceration.

TECHNOLOGIES IN THE COURTS

As with the police, the courts are unveiling new technologies that will hopefully provide more efficient and effective operations. Below some of those technologies are described.

Achieving Paper on Demand

A major goal for all courts in the United States is to go "paper on demand" (POD)—denoting an environment in which the routine use of paper no longer exists in general; rather, paper may be used for court business only rarely, and as a last resort. The ultimate goal is that there are no more lost files, all receipts are issued electronically, all police citations are issued electronically, all filing formats and forms are standardized, all judges use POD, and there are no more folders in the courtroom.

Toward that end, electronic case filing has been possible for many years and allows courts to realize dramatic increases in efficiency and reductions in related costs—in clerical staff alone. Electronic filing also enables some court services—such as the payment of fines and fees, collection of fines and penalties, providing case information and documents to the public, and jury management—to be centralized or regionalized for improved efficiency and service. In addition, an electronic case file enables a court to better distribute its workload across the system.

Emerging Technologies

Following are two other areas in which court technologies are emerging or have already been put in place:

Chapter Quiz:
Court Organization

Digital Recording. Significant savings can be realized by replacing court stenographers with digital audio- or video-recording equipment. Many states have used digital recording extensively, and some states have used digital recording exclusively for many years without experiencing significant issues.

Conducting Hearings via Videoconferencing. Videoconferencing has rapidly improved in both cost and quality over the last few years. Prices for basic capabilities have been reduced considerably, while the quality of the networks has steadily improved.

FOCUS ON HIGH-TECH COURTROOM CAPABILITIES

The National Judicial College in Reno, Nevada, has a state-of-the-art model courtroom—including a digital audio-video system, an evidence presentation system, and a convenient cable management system—that serves as a blueprint for other courtrooms. The 2,700-square-foot courtroom has a false floor allowing for a computer lab and hidden wires within. The audio-video system enables web conferencing and records everything going on in the courtroom; the system includes five voice-activated cameras and a tape backup system, which eliminates the need for a court reporter. Evidence can be digitally displayed to jurors so that the evidence can be viewed more closely without having to be passed around.

As a safety feature, the judge's bench is fully armored; it not only deflects bullets, but it *catches* them, protecting everyone against bullet ricochets. Teleconferencing ability saves the attorneys and the court money; if a trial is not in session and the judge is deciding motions, attorneys can be in court without physically driving there.

Source: Adapted from Heather Singer, "Court Technology Partners," *Case in Point,* Winter/Spring 2005. Reprinted with permission from The National Judicial College. Copyright protected. www.judges.org.

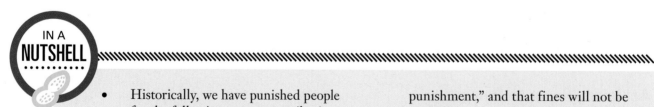

IN A NUTSHELL

- Historically, we have punished people for the following reasons: retribution, deterrence, incapacitation, and rehabilitation. The U.S. Constitution speaks only briefly but forcefully regarding the use of punishment. The Eighth Amendment provides that incarceration will not involve "cruel and unusual punishment," and that fines will not be excessive.

- Prosecutors can influence the sentencing decision by agreeing to engage in plea negotiation concerning the number of charges filed, to limit the maximum penalty the judge may impose, explaining that the accused was very cooperative with the police and/or remorseful for the crime, and so on. Defense attorneys can seek to obtain the lightest possible sentence, or other alternatives to sentencing, as well as emphasize such things as the defendant's minor involvement in the crime.

- The seriousness of the offense is the most important factor in determining the sentencing one receives for his or her offense, followed by the defendant's prior criminal record.

- Philosophies of crime and punishment have changed significantly since the late 1700s; today people are calling for longer sentences for career criminals and violent offenders. Legislators, judges, and officials have responded with determinate sentencing laws, "three-strikes laws," mandatory sentencing laws (e.g., doubling one's sentence for a crime committed with a weapon), and so forth.

- Under *determinate* sentencing, convicted offenders are sentenced for a fixed term, such as 10 years; therefore, there is no opportunity for a paroling authority to make adjustments in time served; conversely, in an *indeterminate* sentencing format, the convicted individual will be sentenced for a set range of time, such as 5–10 years, allowing for the length of sentence to be adjusted to fit the offender's positive responses to treatment and programs.

- Becoming discontented with the sentencing process and the rising crime rate throughout the nation, Congress abolished indeterminate sentencing at the federal level and created a determinate sentencing structure through the federal Sentencing Reform Act; the U.S. Supreme Court found that the guidelines violated the constitution by allowing judicial, rather than jury, fact-finding to form the basis for the sentencing. The Court did not discard the guidelines entirely, however; the guidelines, the Court said, are to be merely advisory and not mandatory. Thus, the guidelines are a resource a judge can look at, but may choose to ignore.

- Victim impact statements are written or oral information provided in court—most commonly at sentencing—and at offenders' parole hearings concerning the impact of the crime on the victim and the victim's family. These statements generally inform the court of the financial, emotional, psychological, and/or physical impact on their lives that was caused by the crime.

- Supporters of the death penalty often believe that it deters other people from committing murder, while others base their stand on theological grounds—"Thou shalt not kill." Others favor capital punishment because of the retribution it provides to family members and friends of the victim— "getting even," and *lex talionis*. Arguments against the death penalty include that it does not have any deterrent value, that it is discriminatory against minorities, that retribution is unfitting for a civilized society, and that it can (and does) claim the lives of innocent people. There is some, but not unanimous, research in support of the deterrence argument.

- In 1972, the U.S. Supreme Court struck down all death penalty laws as being cruel and unusual punishment, due to the manner in which the sanction was being administered. The Court later approved the death sentence in concept. Today lethal injection is the method of execution authorized in a majority of the states.

- Since 1973 there have been 142 persons exonerated on death row in the United States; furthermore, according to the Innocence Project, DNA led to 18 of those death row exonerations. Such exonerations resulted in several states placing a moratorium on their executions until capital punishment studies could be completed.

- Early in American history, sentenced prisoners had little opportunity to appeal their convictions due to the costs for attorneys, trial transcripts, filing fees, and so forth. That situation changed during the 1960s, with the U.S. Supreme Court deciding that indigent persons should not be prevented from an appellate review of their conviction. Therefore, convicted, indigent persons are now entitled to free legal counsel for their initial appeal as well as a free copy of their trial transcript. However, the Court later held that prison inmates are not entitled to free legal counsel for subsequent "discretionary" appeals.

- The courts are well on their way to becoming reliant on technologies to make their work more efficient—eventually becoming primarily electronic if not totally paperless in the future.

REVIEW QUESTIONS

1. How would you describe the four purposes of punishment? Which one of them do you believe works the best? Which purpose or function is now predominant in our society?

2. What are the factors that influence the degree—and harshness—of the punishment that a convicted person will receive?

3. How would you delineate the different philosophies regarding crime and punishment that evolved from the colonial era to today? How did prison construction change in accordance with those changes in punishment models?

4. What forms of punishment used around the world would you point to that are clearly excessive in terms of the offenses committed? Explain your answer.

5. What are the differences between, and purposes of, both determinate and indeterminate sentences? Which is likely used when the crime control model or due process model is more predominant in a community?

6. How would you explain the rationale for, and operation of, the federal sentencing guidelines?

7. What is the interesting legal history of victim impact statements? How do such statements work, and for what purpose?

8. What are the fundamental arguments for and against capital punishment? What did the Supreme Court say about capital punishment in *Furman* and *Gregg*?

9. What are the prevailing methods of execution in use today?

10. What changes have been brought by DNA with regard to the death penalty?

11. What are examples of both aggravating and mitigating circumstances, and how do they apply to sentencing decisions? To the death penalty?

12. What rights are possessed by a convicted person regarding access to legal counsel, trial transcripts, and law libraries?

13. How are technologies advancing court operations?

LEARN BY **DOING**

1. Your state's governor is considering a moratorium on all executions because of DNA and death row exonerations. Knowing you are a criminal justice student, you are asked by a state senator to prepare a pro-con paper concerning the benefits and issues involved with doing so, and of DNA in general. How would you respond? Include in your response an assessment of the deterrent effects of capital punishment laws.

2. Assume your criminal justice instructor has assigned you to go to http://www.uwsp.edu/psych/s/389/landy69.pdf. There you will find a journal article by Landy and Aronson titled "The Influence of the Character of the Criminal and His Victim on the Decisions of Simulated Jurors," published in the *Journal of Experimental Social Psychology* 5 (1969), pages 141–152. Read Experiment II, including the instructions and case study (involving an incident with both an attractive victim and an unattractive victim) as given to university sophomores, as well as the experiment's results and discussion, on pages 146–151. Summarize and explain the above in written form.

3. Your criminal justice class is to debate the following: "RESOLVED: Deterrence is lost for the general public when an inmate remains on death row a dozen or more years." Plan how you would respond on both the pro and con sides of the debate.

4. Assume you are a court administrator and your chief judge has tasked you to "bring the courtrooms into the new decade" by making recommendations concerning technologies that should be acquired. Using information and descriptions of the technologies presented in this chapter, select and prioritize which new technologies you would recommend be obtained, and why.

PART IV

CORRECTIONS

This part includes three chapters and examines many aspects of correctional organizations and operations.

Chapter 12 examines federal and state prisons and local jails in terms of their evolution and organization, inmate population trends and classification, and some technologies.

Chapter 13 considers the "lives inside the walls" of both the corrections personnel and the inmates; included are selected court decisions concerning inmates' legal rights; administrative challenges with overseeing executions, inmate litigation, drugs, and gangs; and the work of personnel in local jails.

Chapter 14 reviews community corrections and alternatives to incarceration: probation, parole, and several other diversionary approaches. Included are discussions of the origins of probation and parole, functions of probation and parole offices, and several intermediate sanctions (e.g., house arrest, electronic monitoring), and community corrections at the federal level.

PRISONS AND JAILS:
Structure and Function

LEARNING OBJECTIVES

As a result of reading this chapter, the student will be able to:

1 Describe why, for many members of our society, the threat of being incarcerated is not a deterrent or a punishment, but rather a "step up"—an improved lifestyle

2 Review the general mission and features of a correctional organization

3 Explain correctional organizations in terms of the number of inmates they oversee and the resources they require (e.g., employment and expenditures)

4 Describe the different factors that affect prison and jail populations

5 Explain the purposes of inmate classification

6 Review how jails are organized and constructed, including the "new generation" jail

7 Discuss how prisons have evolved, and the major reform efforts that occurred during their evolution

8 Explain the basic structure and function of the federal prison system

9 Describe how supermax prisons function, how they differ from other prisons, and critics' views concerning their effects on inmates and constitutionality

10 Describe some of the technologies now in use in corrections

CHAPTER 12

The founders of a new colony . . . recognized it among their earliest practical necessities to allot a portion of the virgin soil as a cemetery, and another portion as the site of a prison.

—Nathaniel Hawthorne

I can think of nothing, not even war, that has brought so much misery to the human race as prisons.

—Clarence Darrow, 1936

INTRODUCTION

Author Introduction:
Chapter 12

What are the differences in definitions, missions, structures, and functions of prisons and jails and in the duties of persons working in them? How are decisions made concerning which type of institution one is sent to? Are more people being incarcerated today due to the downturn in the economy? Certainly these are valid questions to ask, particularly given the differences in costs of institutionalizing someone versus his or her remaining in the community.

In his classic 1961 book, *Asylums*, Erving Goffman described life inside what he termed "total institutions," or those places "organized to protect the community against what are felt to be intentional dangers to it: jail, penitentiaries, POW camps, and concentration camps."[1] Goffman said that total institutions share the following features:

1. All aspects of life are conducted in the same place and under the same single authority.

2. Each phase of the member's daily activity is carried on in the immediate company of a large batch of others.

3. All phases of the day's activities are tightly scheduled.

4. The various enforced activities are brought together in a single rational plan . . . to fulfill the official aims of the institution.[2]

ASSESS YOUR AWARENESS:

Test your basic knowledge of prisons and jails by first reading and responding to the following seven true-false items; check your answers after reading this chapter's materials.

1. Factors influencing prison and jail populations include the nation's drug problem, violence on film and television, and a general deterioration of family and morals.

2. If one is convicted of committing a murder, he or she will likely be forced to serve a lengthy sentence in a local jail.

3. The general mission of correctional institutions is generally to securely hold criminals while providing them with opportunities to become productive and law-abiding citizens.

4. There are basically two custody levels of prisons: maximum and minimum.

5. "Supermax prisons" are so named because they offer the maximum amount of freedom and programming permitted by the courts.

6. Today, very few prison inmates, and no jail inmates, are involved in productive work programs.

7. To this point, use of robots and devices to quell riots are not in use in prisons.

Answers can be found on page 401.

Goffman appears to have captured the essence of our corrections organizations, which are typically viewed as the end result of one's movement through the criminal justice system (as described and graphically depicted in Chapter 1). However, it might well be argued that the corrections process actually begins at the point of one's *arrest*, when he or she is incarcerated in jail awaiting trial and official attempts are initiated to identify and change his or her criminal tendencies.

In any case, corrections is composed of agencies and programs that are responsible for carrying out the sentences and punishment that the courts have administered to our fellow citizens who have been accused, tried, and convicted for their criminal acts. But it should be borne in mind that most of the work of corrections is accomplished not by locking people away, but in the community, serving a term of probation or parole (the subject of Chapter 14).

Unfortunately, most of what the public "knows" about prisons and jails was probably obtained through Hollywood's fictional prism—movies such as *The Shawshank Redemption*, *The Green Mile*, *Escape From Alcatraz*, and classics like *Cool Hand Luke* and *The Longest Yard* being a few examples in our popular culture. These and other such portrayals of prison and jail life typically show the administrators and their staff being cruel, bigoted, corrupt, and morally base.

The truth, however, is probably far different from Hollywood's depictions. In fact, the point is made early in this chapter that for many members of our society, being incarcerated is not only anything but punishing but is in fact a reward and lifestyle improvement.

Although correctional populations began to decline slightly in 2011, with more than 1.6 million prisoners being held in federal or state prisons[3] and 735,000 in local jails,[4] corrections remains a boom industry. First some considerations are presented regarding reasons for these substantial corrections populations, and then the focus shifts to correctional agencies as organizations, including some demographic and cost information, their mission, and purposes of inmate classification systems. After examining local jails, next is a look at the state prison organization, supermax prisons, and the federal prison system. The chapter concludes with a summary, key terms and concepts, review questions, and some "learn by doing" exercises.

CORRECTIONAL FACILITIES AS ORGANIZATIONS

Like police and courts organizations, the correctional component of the U.S. criminal justice system also represents organizations—agencies composed of elements that are made up of collective functions and contribute to their overall mission. Discussed next are definitions, resources, and mission/goals of prisons and jails.

 Jails

Defining Jails and Prisons
The words *jail* and *prison* are often used interchangeably, but there are major differences and implications between the two—whether one is said to have been held in jail or prison says something about the crime committed. The major difference between whether someone is sentenced to jail or prison concerns the nature of the crime and the length of the sentence to be served. A **jail** is a short-term, often temporary holding facility for persons recently arrested and awaiting trial, and who often are unable to pay bond or bail for their release; or they might be serving short misdemeanor sentences, generally one year's duration or less.

Conversely, prisons are designed for longer confinement. The majority of convicted felons serve their sentences in a prison. People convicted

Jail: a facility that holds persons who have been arrested for crimes and are awaiting trial, persons who have been convicted for misdemeanors and are serving a sentence (up to a year in jail), federal offenders, and others.

Inmates in the Knox County Jail in Knoxville, Tennessee. Jails differ from prisons in that they are typically used as a short-term, temporary holding facility for persons recently arrested and awaiting trial.

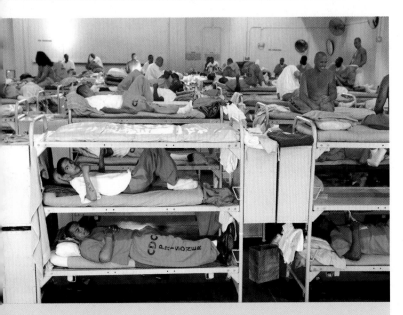

In May 2011, the U.S. Supreme Court upheld a lower-court ruling mandating that within two years the State of California reduce its prison population to alleviate overcrowding.

Corrections
Populations

of committing federal crimes are typically sentenced to federal prisons, and those who break state laws go to state prisons.

Another important distinction concerns who administers the facility. Jails are generally run by a county sheriff's department, whereas prisons are operated by state or federal governments.[5]

Inmates, Employment, Expenditures

As indicated above, more than 2.3 million Americans are now held in federal and state prisons and in local jails.[6] Furthermore, prisons hold about 3,150 persons on death rows in the 36 states and the federal government having capital punishment statutes.[7] Nearly $50 billion is spent per year by the states on corrections alone—as much as 3 percent of total state budgets, which may not appear to be significant, but which also includes expenditures for education, public welfare, highways, and health/hospitals.[8]

It would not be inaccurate to say "as California goes, so too goes the nation" with respect to U.S. prison populations. In May 2011, the U.S. Supreme Court upheld a lower-court ruling mandating that within two years the state reduce its prison population to alleviate overcrowding (built to house approximately 85,000 inmates, at that time the prison system housed nearly twice that number, approximately 156,000 inmates).[9] Known as the Public Safety Realignment (PSR) policy, this approach should reduce the state's prison population through normal attrition of the existing population, releasing many nonviolent, nonserious, nonsexual offenders. Because California incarcerates more individuals than any other state except Texas (10.8 percent of the U.S. state prison population), these changes will have national implications.[10] Figures 12.1 and 12.2 show the number of U.S. prison and jail inmates, respectively.

Factors Contributing to Corrections Populations

Several factors affect prison and jail populations. First is the nation's drug problem. Indeed, nearly half (48 percent) of the 216,000 inmates in federal prison are incarcerated for drug offenses, while only 17 percent of state prisoners are serving time for such offenses.[11] Other commonly cited factors include truth-in-sentencing laws, violence on television and in the movies, and a general deterioration of morals and of the family. In sum, the nation has become more punitive in nature.

Truth in sentencing for prison inmates began in 1984 in Washington State. The concept, which involves restriction or elimination of parole eligibility and good-time credits, quickly spread to other states after a determination

FIGURE 12.1

Prisoners Under State and Federal Jurisdiction at Year End, 2000–2011

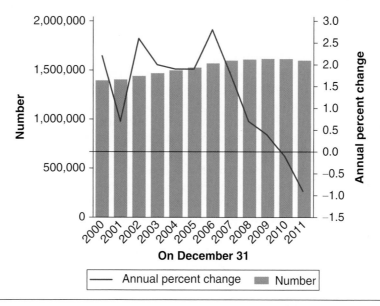

Source: Bureau of Justice Statistics, National Prisoner Statistics Program, 2000–2011.

Note: Jurisdiction refers to the legal authority of state or federal correctional officials over a prisoner regardless of where the prisoner is held.

in 1996 that prisoners were serving on average about 44 percent of their court sentence. To ensure that offenders serve larger portions of their sentence, Congress authorized funding for additional state prisons and jails if states met eligibility criteria for truth-in-sentencing programs.[12] To qualify, states must require violent offenders to serve at least 85 percent of their prison sentence. By 1998, 27 states and the District of Columbia qualified; 14 states have abolished early parole board release for all offenders.[13]

A philosophical shift about the purpose of incarceration also contributed to prison crowding. In response to the apparent failure of **rehabilitation** policies, the now-prevailing philosophy sees prisons as places to incarcerate and punish inmates in an effort to deter crime. This philosophy has resulted in get-tough sentencing practices (including mandatory sentencing laws), which contribute to rising prison populations. Legislators have essentially removed the word *rehabilitation* from the penal code while focusing on fixed sentences. This shift from rehabilitating inmates to "just deserts" is based on the view that offenders make "free will" decisions to commit crimes and, therefore, no longer deserve compassion and "correction."

FIGURE 12.2

Annual Counts of the Midyear Custody Population, Average Daily Population, and Rated Capacity in Local Jails

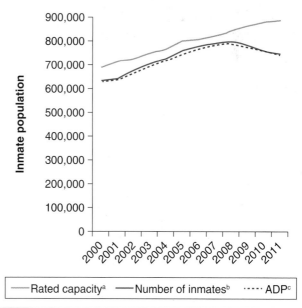

Source: Bureau of Justice Statistics, Annual Survey of Jails and the 2005 Census of Jail Inmates

[a]Number of beds or inmates assigned by rating official to facilities with in each jurisdiction.

[b]Midyear count is the number held to the last weekday in June.

[c]Sum of all inmates in jail each for a year, divided by the number of days in the year.

U.S. citizens, however, may be leaning more toward rehabilitative efforts. One survey found that about 72 percent of Americans "completely agree" or "mostly agree" that it is more important to try to rehabilitate people who are in prison than merely to punish them.[14]

Robert Martinson, who studied more than 200 correctional treatment programs and reported in 1973 that "almost nothing works," served to ignite a firestorm of debate that lasted nearly two decades.[15] Although Martinson's methodology was brought into serious question and he later attempted to recant his findings, his assessment clearly had a major impact. Legislators and corrections administrators became unwilling to fund treatment programs from dwindling budgets, whereas academics and policy makers claimed that the medical model of correctional treatment programs failed to accomplish its goals. Paul Louis and Jerry Sparger noted that "perhaps the most lasting effect of the **'nothing works' philosophy** is the spread of cynicism and hopelessness" among prison administrators and staff members.[16]

An even greater widening between the rehabilitation and "just deserts" approaches occurred in the 1980s. Ted Palmer[17] identified these modified positions as the "skeptical" and "sanguine" camps. The skeptics believed that relatively few prison programs work and that successful ones account for only negligible reductions in recidivism. Furthermore, they believed that rehabilitation programs had not been given an adequate chance in correctional settings because they were either poorly designed or badly implemented. The sanguine perspective is that although the existing rehabilitation programs have not been very effective to date, evidence indicates that many programs provide positive treatment for selected portions of the offender population. A reassessment of Martinson's "nothing works" statement by Palmer and others has given new hope for rehabilitation. Palmer rejected Martinson's critical finding, and demonstrated that many of the programs initially reviewed by Martinson were actually quite successful.[18] Other research has supported Palmer's position.[19] Still, the rehabilitative philosophy is not expected to see a resurgence in the foreseeable future.

Some observers, however, also believe that the "just deserts" logic is defeated by a combination of demography and justice system inefficiency. Each year, a new crop of youths in their upper teens constitutes the majority of those arrested for serious crimes. As these offenders are arrested and removed from the crime scene, a new crop replaces them: "The justice system is eating its young. It imprisons them, paroles them, and rearrests them with no rehabilitation in between," according to Dale Secrest.[20] Still, large-scale, long-term imprisonment unquestionably keeps truly serious offenders behind bars, preventing them from committing more crimes.

General Mission and Features

Correctional organizations are complex, hybrid organizations that utilize two distinct yet related management subsystems to achieve their goals: One is concerned primarily with managing correctional employees, and the other is concerned primarily with delivering correctional services to a designated offender population. The correctional organization, therefore, employs one group of people—correctional personnel—to work with and control another group—offenders.

Rehabilitation: attempts to reform an offender through vocational and educational programming, counseling, and so forth, so he is not a recidivist and does not return to crime/prison.

"Nothing works" philosophy: Robert Martinson's belief, published in the 1970s, that correctional treatment programs generally do not rehabilitate offenders or significantly reduce recidivism.

Many people believe that rather than using punishment alone, it is also important to try to rehabilitate offenders—that is, providing treatment programs to help them to recover from a criminal lifestyle or personality, substance abuse or addiction, and so on, in order to become productive citizens.

The mission of corrections agencies has changed little over time. It is as follows: to protect the citizens from crime by safely and securely handling criminal offenders while providing offenders some opportunities for self-improvement and increasing the chance that they will become productive and law-abiding citizens.[21]

An interesting feature of the correctional organization is that *every* correctional employee who exercises legal authority over offenders is a supervisor, even if the person is the lowest-ranking member in the agency or institution. Another feature of the correctional organization is that—as with the police—everything a correctional supervisor does may have civil or criminal ramifications, both for himself or herself and for the agency or institution. Therefore, the legal and ethical responsibility for the correctional (and police) supervisor is greater than it is for supervisors in other types of organizations.

Increased Prison Population

Finally, it is probably fair to say there are two different philosophies concerning what a correctional organization should be: (1) a custodial organization, which emphasizes the caretaker functions of controlling and observing inmates, and (2) a treatment organization, which emphasizes rehabilitation of inmates. These different philosophies contain potential conflict for correctional personnel.

"Just Deserts"

Punishment for Some, a "Step Up" for Others

Most Americans probably assume that sending offenders to prisons and jails—depriving them of their freedom of movement and many amenities while living under a very oppressive set of rules—serves a useful purpose, will bring them to the "good life," and instill in them a desire to obey the laws and avoid returning to prison after their release. In fact, experts have said that such punishments will work if they meet two conditions: (1) injure "the social standing by the punishment," and (2) make "the individual feel a danger of being excluded from the group."[22]

Unfortunately, however, this view overlooks two very important facts—facts that are perhaps a sad commentary on the kinds of lives being led by many people in the United States:

1. Most serious offenders neither accept nor abide by those norms; and

2. Most incarcerated people today come from communities where conditions fall far below the living standards that most Americans would accept.[23]

As stated by corrections researcher Joan Petersilia, the grim fact and national shame is that for many people who go to prison, the conditions inside are not all that different from (and might even be better than) the conditions outside.[24] For some members of our society, going to prison or jail—and obtaining "three hots and a cot" (three meals and a bed)—may actually represent an *increased* standard of living. Obviously, for those individuals, the threat of imprisonment no longer represents a horrible punishment and therefore has lost much of its deterrent power. When a person goes to prison, he or she seldom feels isolated but is likely to find friends, if not family, already there.[25]

Furthermore, it appears that prison life is not perceived as being as difficult as it once was. Inmates' actions speak loudly in this respect: More than 50 percent of today's inmates have served a prior prison term—and evidently believe the "benefits" of committing a new crime outweigh the costs of being in prison.[26]

Punishment

Classification
of Inmates

Classification (of inmates):
inmate security and treatment
plan based on one's security,
social, vocational, psychological,
and educational needs while
incarcerated.

Although there are safety and security concerns, several factors argue in favor of allowing inmates to engage in physical exercise: to teach them discipline and goal-setting, reduce boredom, bum off tension, and improve their overall health and self-esteem.

Finally, the stigma of having a prison record is not the same as in the past, because so many of the offenders' peers and family members also have done time. Imprisonment also confers status in some neighborhoods. To many people, serving a prison term is a badge of courage. It also is their source of food, clothing, and shelter.[27]

And so any discussion of jails and prisons should be prefaced with these facts in mind concerning the inmates' world.

Classification of Inmates: A Cornerstone of Corrections

If the prison or jail experience is to carry any benefit, classifying inmates into the proper levels of housing, programming, and other aspects of their incarceration must be accomplished so as to have an influence on their behavior, treatment, and progress while in custody—as well as for the general safety of inmates and staff.

Corrections staff must make **classification** decisions in at least two areas: the inmate's level of *physical restraint* or "security level," and the inmate's level of supervision or *custody grade*. These two concepts are not well understood and are often confused, but they significantly impact a prisoner's housing and program assignments[28] as well as an institution's overall security level.

The most recent development in classification is unit management, in which a large prison population is subdivided into several mini-institutions analogous to a city and its neighborhoods. Each unit has specified decision-making authority and is run by a staff of six, whose offices are on the living unit; this enables classification decision to be made by personnel who are in daily contact with their inmates and know them fairly well.[29]

Robert Levinson delineated four categories into which corrections officials classify new inmates: security, custody, housing, and program[30]:

1. *Security* needs are classified in terms of the number and types of architectural barriers that must be placed between the inmates and the outside world to ensure they will not escape and can be controlled. Most correctional systems have four security levels: supermax (highest), maximum (high), medium (low), and minimum (lowest).

2. *Custody* assignments determine the level of supervision and types of privileges an inmate will have. A basic consideration is whether or not an inmate will be allowed to go outside the facility's secure perimeter, so some systems have adopted a fourfold array of custody grades—two inside the fence (one more restrictive than the other) and two outside the fence (one more closely supervised than the other).

3. *Housing* needs were historically determined by an "assign to the next empty bed" system, which could place the new, weak inmate in the same cell with the most hardened inmate; a more sophisticated approach is known as internal classification, in which inmates are assigned to live with prisoners who are similar to themselves. This approach can involve the grouping of inmates into three broad categories: heavy—victimizers; light—victims; and moderate—neither intimidated by the first group nor abusers of the second.

4. *Program* classification involves using interview and testing data to determine where the newly arrived inmate should be placed in work, training, and treatment programs; these are designed to help the prisoner make a successful return to society.

In the past, most prison systems used a highly subjective system of classifying inmates that involved a review of records pertaining to the inmate's prior social and criminal history, test scores, school and work performance, and staff impressions developed from interviews. Today, however, administrators employ a much-preferred objective system that is more rational, efficient, and equitable. Factors used in making classification decisions are measurable and valid, and are applied to all inmates in the same way. Criteria most often used are escape history, detainers, prior commitments, criminal history, prior institutional adjustment, history of violence, and length of sentence.[31]

JAILS AS ORGANIZATIONS

Across the United States, approximately 3,316 jails are locally administered.[32] Their primary purpose is to hold accused law violators who cannot post bond to ensure their appearance at trial, and to hold those persons convicted of lesser offenses until they complete their court-ordered sentence. Occasionally local jails also house felony inmates for the federal government or other jurisdictions until they can be transferred to a prison. Jail organization and hierarchical levels are determined by several factors: size, budget, level of crowding, local views toward punishment and treatment, and even the levels of training and education of the jail administrator. An organizational structure for a jail serving a population of about 250,000 is suggested in Figure 12.3.

The New Generation/ Direct Supervision Jail

As noted previously, in the past the federal courts have at times abandoned their traditional hands-off doctrine toward prison and jail administration, largely in response to the deplorable conditions and inappropriate treatment of inmates. The courts became more willing to hear inmate allegations of constitutional violations ranging from inadequate heating, lighting, and ventilation to the censorship of mail.[33]

In response to lawsuits and to improve conditions, many local jurisdictions explored new ideas and designed new jail facilities. The first **new generation/direct supervision jail** opened in the 1970s in Contra Costa County, California. This facility quickly became a success, was deemed cost-effective to build and safer for inmates and staff, and carried several advantages: Officers "live" with the inmates and are encouraged to mingle

New generation/direct supervision jail: jails that, by their architecture and design, eliminate many of the traditional features of a jail, such as allowing staff members greater interaction and control.

● ● **FIGURE 12.3**

Organization Structure for Jail Serving County of 250,000 Population

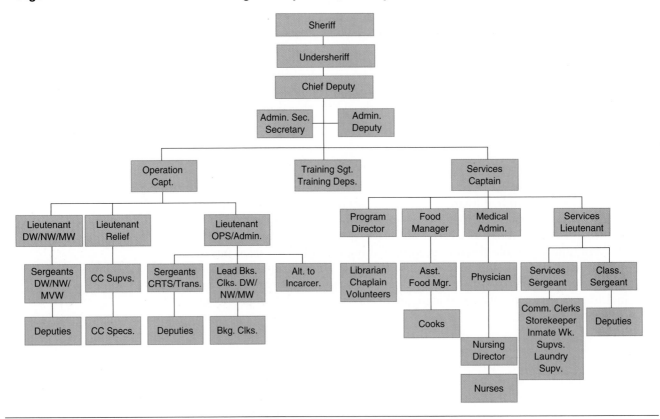

Note: DW = day watch; NW = night watch; MW = mid watch; CC = conservation camps; CRTS/Trans = court transportation; OPS/Admin = operation/administration; Comm. Clerks = commissary clerks

Mid-Chapter Quiz:
Prisons and Jails

with them and to provide them privileges and activities (thus increasing good behavior and reducing idleness) while being better able to control inmate movement; as a result, there is a low level of tension in the unit, as fights are quickly broken up, weapons are not involved, and sexual assaults are almost nonexistent. Bathroom and shower areas are closely monitored, and noise levels are low due to the architecture and close supervision.[34] To the extent possible, symbols of incarceration are removed in these new jails, which have no bars in the living units; windows are generally provided in every prisoner's room, and padded carpets, movable furniture, and colorful wall coverings are used to reduce the facility's institutional atmosphere. Inmates are to be divided into small groups of approximately 40 to 50 for housing purposes. All of these features of the facility were designed to reduce the "trauma" of incarceration.[35]

Figure 12.4 provides three views of how new generation/direct supervision jails are configured.

FIGURE 12.4

Direct Supervision Jails

Jails can have a combination of design styles – Jails that are not predominantly direct supervision in design or management can have an addition or section of inmate housing that uses direct supervision.

- **Podular/direct supervision jails** – Inmates' cells are arranged around a common area, usually called a "dayroom." An officer is stationed in the pod with the inmates. The officer moves about the pod and interacts with the inmates to manage their behavior. There is no secure control booth for the supervising officer, and there are no physical barriers between the officer and the inmates. The officer may have a desk or table for paperwork, but it is in the open dayroom area.

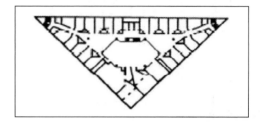

- **Linear/intermittent supervision jails** – Includes jails with cells arranged along the sides of a cell block. Officers come into the housing unit on scheduled rounds or as needed to interact with the inmates.

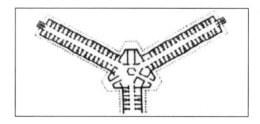

- **Podular/remote supervision jails** – Includes jails that have a podular design with cells around a dayroom, but no officer is permanently stationed inside the pod. Indirect supervision is provided through remote monitoring at a console.

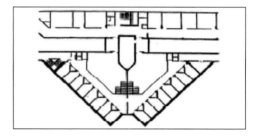

Source: U.S. Department of Justice, National Institute of Corrections, *Direct Supervision Jails: 2006 Yearbook*, p. vii, http://nicic.org/Downloads/PDF/Library/021968.pdf .

Making Jails Productive

The 1984 Justice Assistance Act removed some of the long-standing restrictions on interstate commerce of prisoner-made goods. By 1987, private sector work programs were under way in 14 state correctional institutions and two county jails.[36] Today, many inmates in U.S. jails are involved in productive work. Some simply work to earn privileges, and others earn wages applied to their custodial costs and compensation to crime victims. Some hone new

Jail and prison inmate work programs can afford several benefits, such as earning privileges and wages (including restitution to their victims), honing new job skills, and improving their chances for success following release. These Washington State inmates make mini frozen pizzas.

Author Video: Prisons and Jails as Productive Places

State prison: a correctional facility that houses convicted felons.

Warden: the chief administrator of a federal penitentiary or state prison.

job skills, improving their chances for success following release. At one end of the continuum is the trusty (an inmate requiring a low security level) who mows the grass in front of the jail and thereby earns privileges; at the other end are jail inmates working for private industry for real dollars.[37] Some jails have work programs involving training in dog grooming, auto detailing, food service, book mending, mailing service, painting, printing, carpet installation, and upholstering.

STATE PRISONS AS ORGANIZATIONS

As noted earlier in this chapter, the mission of most prisons is to provide a safe and secure environment for staff and inmates, as well as programs for offenders that can assist them after release.[38] This section describes how **state prisons** are organized to accomplish this mission. First is a look at the larger picture—the typical organization of the central office within the state government that oversees *all* prisons within its jurisdiction—and then a look at the characteristic organization of an individual prison.

Over time, prison organizational structures (see Figure 12.5) have changed considerably. Until the beginning of the 20th century, prisons were administered by state boards of charities, boards composed of citizens, boards of inspectors, state prison commissions, or individual prison keepers. Most prisons were individual provinces; wardens, who were given absolute control over their domain, were appointed by governors through a system of political patronage. Individuals were attracted to the position of **warden** because it carried many fringe benefits, such as a lavish residence, unlimited inmate servants, food and supplies from institutional farms and warehouses, furnishings, and a personal automobile. Now most wardens or superintendents are civil service employees who have earned their position through seniority and merit.[39] We discuss the warden's position more below.

Reporting to the warden are deputy or associate wardens, each of whom supervises a department within the prison. The deputy warden for operations will normally oversee correctional security, unit management, the inmate disciplinary committee, and recreation. The deputy warden for special services will typically be responsible for the library, mental health services, drug and alcohol recovery services, education, prison job assignments, religious services, and prison industries. The deputy warden for administration will manage the business office, prison maintenance, laundry, food service, medical services, prison farms, and the issuance of clothing.[40]

We now discuss correctional security, unit management, education, and penal industries in greater detail:

- The correctional security department is normally the largest department in a prison, with 50 to 70 percent of all staff. It supervises all of the security activities within a prison, including any special housing units, inmate transportation, and the inmate disciplinary process. Security staff wears military-style uniforms; a captain normally runs each 8-hour shift, and lieutenants often are responsible for an area of the prison; sergeants oversee the rank-and-file correctional staff.

• The unit management concept was originated by the federal prison system in the 1970s and now is used in nearly every state to control prisons by providing a "small, self-contained, inmate living and staff office area that operates semi-autonomously within the larger institution."[41] The purpose of unit management is twofold: to decentralize the administration of the prison and to enhance communication among staff and between staff and inmates. Unit management breaks the prison into more manageable sections based on housing assignments; assignment of staff to a particular unit; and staff authority to make decisions, manage the unit, and deal directly with inmates. Units are usually composed of 200 to 300 inmates; staff members are not only assigned to units, but their offices are also located in the housing area, making them more accessible to inmates and better able to monitor inmate activities and behavior. Directly reporting to the unit manager are "case managers," or social workers, who develop the program of work and rehabilitation for each inmate and write progress reports for parole authorities, classification, or transfer to another prison. Correctional counselors also work with inmates in the units on daily issues, such as finding a prison job, working with their prison finances, and creating a visiting and telephone list.[42]

State Prison
Productivity

• Education departments operate the academic teaching, vocational training, library services, and sometimes recreation programs for inmates. An education department is managed in similar fashion to a conventional elementary or high school, with certified teachers for all subjects that are required by the state department of education or are part of the General Educational Development (GED) test. Vocational training can include carpentry, landscaping or horticulture, food service, and office skills.

Education
Programs

• **Prison industries** are legislatively chartered as separate government corporations and report directly to the warden because there is often a requirement that the industry be self-supporting or operate from funds generated from the sale of products. Generally, no tax dollars are used to run the programs, and there is strict accountability of funds.

Prison industries: use of prison and jail inmates to produce goods or provide services for a public agency or private corporation.

FEDERAL PRISONS[43]

The Federal Bureau of Prisons (BOP) was established in 1930 to provide care for federal inmates. Today, the BOP has more than 36,000 employees and consists of 119 institutions and nearly 220,000 federal offenders. Approximately 80 percent of these inmates are confined in BOP-operated facilities, while the remainder are confined in privately managed or community-based facilities and local jails.[44]

Prison Types and General Information

The BOP operates institutions at five different security levels in order to confine offenders in an appropriate manner. Security levels are based on such features as the presence of external patrols, towers, security barriers, or detection devices; the type of housing within the institution; internal security features; and the staff-to-inmate

Prison housing units vary, but usually consist of 200-300 inmates and place staff members in the housing area, to be more accessible to inmates and better able to monitor their activities and behavior.

FIGURE 12.5

Organizational Structure for a Maximum-Security Prison

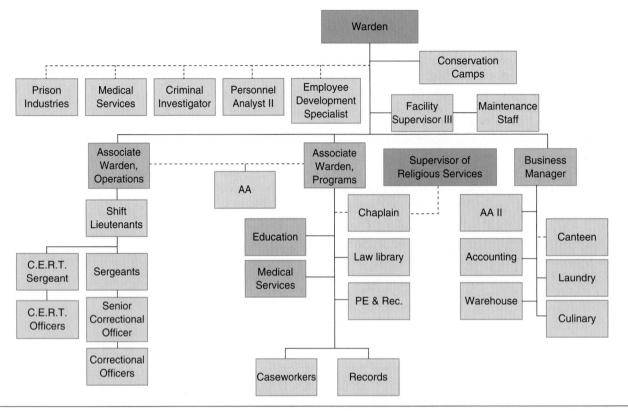

Notes: AA = administrative aide; C.E.R.T. = correctional emergency response team; PE & Rec. = physical education and recreation.

ratio. Each facility is designated as either minimum, low, medium, high, or administrative. Following are the five types:

Minimum Security

Minimum-security institutions, also known as federal prison camps, have dormitory housing, a relatively low staff-to-inmate ratio, and limited or no perimeter fencing. These institutions are work and program oriented, and many are located adjacent to larger institutions or on military bases, where inmates help serve the labor needs of the larger institution or base.

Low Security

Low-Security Prison

Low-security federal correctional institutions have double-fenced perimeters, mostly dormitory or cubicle housing, and strong work and program components. The staff-to-inmate ratio in these institutions is higher than in minimum-security facilities.

Medium Security

Medium-security correctional institutions and penitentiaries designated to house medium-security inmates have strengthened perimeters (often double fences with electronic detection systems), mostly cell-type housing, a wide variety of work and treatment programs, an even higher staff-to-inmate ratio than low-security federal correctional institutions, and even greater internal controls.

High Security

High-security institutions, also known as U.S. penitentiaries, have highly secured perimeters (featuring walls or reinforced fences), multiple- and single-occupant cell housing, the highest staff-to-inmate ratio, and close control of inmate movement.

Correctional Complexes

A number of BOP institutions belong to federal correctional complexes, where institutions with different missions and security levels are located in close proximity to one another. Examples would include administrative facilities such as for the detention of pretrial offenders; the treatment of inmates with serious or chronic medical problems; or the containment of extremely dangerous, violent, or escape-prone inmates.

In addition, a number of BOP institutions have a small, minimum-security camp adjacent to the main facility. These camps, often referred to as satellite camps, provide inmate labor to the main institution and to off-site work programs.

Community Corrections in the Federal System

Parole was abolished in the federal prison system in 1987, when the federal sentencing guidelines went into effect (discussed in Chapter 11); since then, the only time an inmate can have subtracted from a federal sentence has been 54 days a year, commencing after the person has served 12 months; this policy was upheld in 2010 by the U.S. Supreme Court.[45] Nonetheless, the BOP is actively supporting and using community-corrections techniques.

SUPERMAX PRISONS

Super-maximum—or "supermax"—prisons represent the most secure form of incarceration now in existence in the United States and abroad (although they are given different names in other countries). As will be seen below, they began to proliferate in the United States in the mid-1980s as a means of holding extremely disruptive or violent inmates. Such prisons have not been without controversy, however, and this chapter section provides a brief history, some research findings on effects on inmates, and some constitutional questions that have been raised.

 Supermax Prisons

Origin and Operation

Supermax prisons exist in both state and federal prison systems and effectively originated in 1983 in Marion, Illinois, when two correctional officers were murdered by inmates on the same day and the warden put the prison in "permanent lockdown." Thus began 23-hour-a-day cell isolation and no communal yard time for inmates, who were also not permitted to work, attend educational programs, or eat in a cafeteria.[46]

Today there are now 40 states operating supermax prisons in the United States.[47] To understand what supermax prisons are and how they operate, one can look at the "Administrative Maximum" prison, or ADX, located in Florence, Colorado, 90 miles south of Denver.

ADX is the only federal supermax in the country (the others are state prisons). It is home to a "who's who" of criminals: "Unabomber" Ted Kaczynski; "Shoe Bomber" Richard Reid; Ramzi Yousef, who plotted the 1993 World Trade Center attack; Oklahoma City bomber Terry Nichols; and Olympic Park bomber Eric Rudolph. Ninety-five percent of the prisoners at ADX,

Supermax prison: a penal institution that, for security purposes, affords inmates very few if any amenities and a great amount of isolation.

The "Administrative Maximum" prison, or ADX, located in Florence, Colorado, is the only federal supermax in the nation.

known as the "Alcatraz of the Rockies," are the most violent, disruptive, and escape-prone inmates from other federal prisons. Upon viewing its external aspect for the first time, one immediately sees that this is not the usual prison: Large cables are strung above the basketball courts and track; they are helicopter deterrents.[48]

Supermax inmates rarely leave their cells; in most, an hour a day of out-of-cell time is the norm. They eat all of their meals alone in the cells, and typically no group or social activity of any kind is permitted; they are typically denied access to vocational or educational training programs. Inmates can exist for many years separated from the natural world around them.[49]

Clearly, as shown in Table 12.1, wardens themselves believe that supermax prisons provide a high degree of safety for staff and inmates.

Effects on Inmates

Given the high degree of isolation and lack of activities, a major concern voiced by critics of supermax facilities is their "social pathology" and potential effect on inmates' mental health. Although there is very little research to date concerning the effects of supermax confinement,[50] some authors point to previous isolation research that shows greater levels of deprivation lead to psychological, emotional, and physical problems. For example, studies show that as inmates face greater restrictions and social deprivations, their levels of social withdrawal increase; limiting human contact, autonomy, goods, or services is detrimental to inmates' health and rehabilitative prognoses, and tends to result in depression, hostility, severe anger, sleep disturbances, and anxiety. Women living in a high-security unit have been found to experience claustrophobia, chronic rage reactions, depression, hallucinatory symptoms, withdrawal, and apathy.[51]

TABLE 12.1

Wardens' Views of Supermax Prisons

	SOUTH (%)	NORTHEAST (%)	WEST (%)	MIDWEST (%)	TOTAL (%)
Increase safely throughout prison system	99.1	97.7	97.7	97.5	98.4
Increase order throughout prison system	98.1	100.0	96.6	96.7	97.7
Increase control over prison system	97.5	100.0	98.9	95.9	97.6
Incapacitate violent/disruptive inmates	95.3	100.0	94.2	95.0	95.4
Improve inmate behavior in prison system	86.2	86.4	77.9	80.3	83.7
Decrease prison riots	86.1	81.4	79.3	75.2	82.4
Decrease influence of gangs In prisons	80.4	90.9	84.9	68.6	79.4
Reduce prison escapes	81.1	74.4	57.5	55.7	71.6
Punish violent and disruptive inmates	49.7	54.5	42.5	52.1	49.5
Reduce recidivism of violent/disruptive inmates	47.2	38.6	48.8	42.1	45.7
Rehabilitate violent/disruptive inmates	37.0	36.4	38.4	34.7	36.7
Deter crime In society	28.3	18.6	24.7	15.6	24.3

Note: Ns for each question ranged from 567 to 575. In the total sample (n = 601), the distribution of wardens across regions was as follows: 45 in the Northeast, 130 in the Midwest, 335 in the South, and 91 in the West.

Source: From Daniel P. Mears, "A Critical Look at Supermax Prisons," *Corrections Compendium* (published by the American Corrections Assn.), September/October 2005, p. 46. Reprinted with permission of the American Correctional Association, Alexandria, VA.

Some researchers argue that supermax facilities are not effective management tools for controlling violence and disturbances within prisons, nor are they effective in reducing violence or disturbances within the general population; they conclude that supermax prisons should not be used for their current purpose.[52]

Constitutionality

Because of their relatively recent origin, the constitutionality of supermax prisons has been tested in only a few cases. The first, *Madrid v. Gomez*,[53] in 1995, addressed conditions of confinement in California's Pelican Bay Security Housing Unit. The judge observed that its image was "hauntingly similar to that of caged felines pacing in a zoo"; however, the judge concluded that he lacked any constitutional basis to close the prison. In the most recent case,

THE WORLD'S WORST PRISONS

Certainly any attempt to catalog the worst prisons in the world will be open to serious debate, and the list provided below of five such prisons is no exception. However, as will be seen, these are included (in no particular order) for very good reasons:

• La Santé, France: This, the last remaining prison in Paris, was established in 1867. Its mattresses are infested with lice; because prisoners can only take two cold showers per week, skin diseases are common. Overcrowded cells, infestation of vermin, and inmate rape are also common. Its rate of suicide attempts each year is estimated to be almost five times higher than that of California's prison system. Its conditions have been condemned by the United Nations Human Rights Committee and the country's own minister of justice.

• Black Beach, Equatorial Guinea: Amnesty International has described life in this prison as a slow, lingering death sentence. Torture, burning, beatings, and rape are systematic and brutal. Because food rations are minimal, with prisoners sometimes going up to six days without food, starving to death is common. Amnesty also reports that inmates are routinely denied access to medical treatment.

• Vladimir Central Prison, Russia: Constructed by Catherine the Great to house political prisoners, during the Soviet era the prison became synonymous with persecution of political dissidents. Today the prison also functions as a museum for the public. Visitors are not allowed into the penitentiary, where cells often contain six prisoners and reports of abuse by guards are common. HIV and tuberculosis are also rampant.

• Camp 1391, Israel: Officially, this prison does not exist, but descriptions of its conditions have been validated. Even the Red Cross is banned from visiting, and prisoners typically have no idea where they are being kept or when they might be released—a fact that former inmates say is the worst torture of all. Sexual humiliation and even rape are reportedly used as interrogation techniques.

• The North Korean Gulag: Up to 200,000 prisoners are held in these detention centers, and one houses more than 50,000 inmates. Entire families and even neighborhoods are sent here as punishment for the infraction of one member. In some camps, up to 25 percent of the prisoners die every year, only to be replaced by new inmates. Most of the camps are located along the North Korean border with China and Russia, and thus prisoners are forced to endure harsh weather conditions as well as inhumane treatment.

Again, any such list is debatable given harsh prison conditions in many places around the world; prisons and/or labor camps in China, Thailand, Cuba, Venezuela, Syria, Africa, and other foreign venues could easily have been included.[54]

Source: Greg Shtraks, "The List: The World's Most Notorious Prisons," *Foreign Policy*, January 21, 2009, http://www.foreignpolicy.com/articles/2009/01/20/the_list_the_worlds_most_notorious_prisons (accessed March 10, 2013).

Jones 'El v. Berge,[55] in 2004, a federal district court in Wisconsin concluded that "extremely isolating conditions . . . cause SHU [Security Housing Unit] syndrome in relatively healthy prisoners . . . Supermax is not appropriate for seriously mentally ill inmates." The judge ordered several prisoners to be removed from the supermax facility.

TECHNOLOGIES

As with police and court systems, technologies are used in jails and prisons to provide a greater degree of safety for both officers and inmates, and thus improve efficiency and effectiveness of correctional practices. Some of the technologies are discussed next.

Coping With Riots

Since the beginning of institutional confinement there has been a need for correctional officers (COs) to possess tactics and equipment to handle outbreaks of violence among inmates. Although full-scale riots are rare in American prisons, potentially violent situations (such as inmates' refusing to leave their cells) can occur almost daily.

Today there are wall-climbing reconnaissance robots and "sound cannons" designed to sweep rioters into a corner or stun them with a blast of noise. Also in use are a Hydro-Force fogger (a cross between a fire extinguisher and a can of Mace); a rolling barrier with wheels and side shields that prevents officers from being struck by thrown objects[56]; and a "stinger" grenade that explodes and emits dozens of hard rubber pellets and is particularly useful in a cafeteria or yard riot.

COs often train with such devices in full view of the inmates to demonstrate the kinds of tools that can be employed. According to one prison administrator, what separates prison professionals from inmates is constant training as well as measured, unflappable control.[57]

Offender Programming and Management

Chapter Quiz: Prisons and Jails

Technology is changing the methods of offender management through the use of web-based systems that provide educational programs to prisoners, treat prisoners who are addicted to drugs or are sex offenders, and provide vocational training. Prison administrators now keep accurate records of inmates' purchases for items in the prison store, payments to victims and

---

FOCUS ON ▸ PUTTING DOWN JAIL DISTURBANCES

If a fight breaks out inside a local jail, inmates might soon get shot with a tiny wave from a device that penetrates the skin to heat up nerves. The Assault Intervention Device (AID) is a 7.5-foot-tall nonlethal weapon that transmits a focused, invisible beam at a specified target, causing an unbearable burning sensation. Using a joystick and computer monitor, deputies operate the apparatus, which emits an invisible beam with a range of about 80 to 100 feet. The millimeter wave travels at light speed and penetrates the skin up to 1/64 of an inch and warms up the nervous system's heat receptors. The inmate who is hit by the heat wave instinctively moves out of the beam, which makes the pain go away. The sensation is described as being similar to touching a hot stove or feeling a sudden blast of heat from the oven.

The device is not intended to become the weapon of choice in the jail. Rather, it is one of many less-lethal jail tools, including tear gas, rubber bullets, and batons.

Source: Adapted from Russell Nichols, "Los Angeles County Jail to Heat Up Misbehaving Inmates with Target Wave Technology," *Government Technology*, August 25, 2010, http://www.govtech.com/public-safety/102484474.html (accessed March 9, 2013).

their families, and other reasons for which money flows in and out of prisoners' bank accounts.[58] Automated systems also control access gates and doors, individual cell doors, and the climate in cells and other areas of the prison. Corrections agencies have also used computers to conduct presentence investigations, supervise offenders in the community, and train correctional personnel. With computer assistance, jail administrators receive daily reports on court schedules, inmate rosters, time served, statistical reports, maintenance costs, and other data.

The "You Be the Warden" box below describes how offenders are now being tracked using GPS bracelets.

"Virtual Visits" to Hospitals and Courtrooms

Prison and jail inmates make frequent visits to hospitals and courtrooms, which creates public safety concerns. In Ohio alone, 40,000 inmate trips to and from medical facilities were eliminated because videoconferencing technology—virtual visits—made medical consultations available from within the institution. An onsite prison physician or nurse assists with the physical part of the examination, taking cues from the offsite specialist via video and relaying information such as electrocardiogram and blood pressure data.[59]

Retinal eye scanners are being used in prisons to ensure that inmates do not swap identities in order to escape.

you be the... WARDEN

USING GPS BRACELETS TO TRACK PRISON INMATES

Both adults and juvenile offenders in correctional institutions in several states are required to wear global positioning devices on their wrists to track their locations at all times. Following are some of the anticipated benefits:

- An alarm will sound if an inmate enters an off-limits area or tries to escape.
- In the case of a prison brawl, the devices will show the corrections staff who was in the area where the fight occurred.
- If an inmate claims to have been assaulted by a prison guard, there will be a record of whether the inmate was at the correctional officer's post.

It is also expected that the devices will substantially increase the level of control without increasing staff.

Some civil libertarians and youth advocates have concerns about the bracelets, however, because the technology is far from flawless. In many jurisdictions, false alarms have strained personnel and called the effectiveness of the tracking tool into question. One state found more than 35,000 false alerts by 140 subjects wearing the GPS monitoring devices. Another concern is that the tool could be used as evidence against persons who are not involved in crimes. However, supporters say the program represents one piece of a broader crime-prevention strategy that includes a bike patrol to monitor gang hot spots and funding to support people who want to escape gang life.

1. What do you believe? Does the need for security justify adults and youths in prisons being monitored so closely via these bracelets?

2. Or, conversely, do privacy issues—and the technical problems involved—override the institutions' security interests?

Source: Adapted from Associated Press, "Prison Inmates to Wear GPS Tracking Bracelets," *Reno Gazette Journal,* June 13, 2006, p. C6.

FOCUS ON　CELL PHONES IN THE WRONG HANDS IN PRISONS

Although prisons are now more high-tech than ever before—able to employ video monitoring, GPS devices worn on wrists, biometric entry points that scan an inmate's iris or fingerprints, and even remote medical tools so inmates receive virtual checkups from doctors—the benefits provided by these enhancements can be overcome when technologies get in the hands of inmates. For example, there has been an increase in the number of cell phones being smuggled into prisons, which allow inmates to contact people outside of prison to organize crimes, commit illegal acts, and harass lawmakers and their victims' families.[60] In South Carolina, a prisoner ordered a hit on a prison guard (he was shot at his home but survived).[61] The problem is not insignificant: A sweep in a Vacaville, California, prison resulted in more than 2,000 cell phones being confiscated.[62] In some prisons, cell phones are even more valuable than drugs, with undercover officers

being offered much more money to bring in phones than for heroin.

Prisons are trying to fight back with full body scanners to detect cell phones carried on inmates' bodies. However, their bigger goal—using equipment to jam the wireless cell phone signals—has been frustrated by legal impediments. In 2009 the U.S. Senate passed the Safe Prisons Communications Act, which would have allowed prison officials to jam wireless telephone communication signals; however, the bill died in the House. Although the Federal Communications Commission has finally agreed to consider changing its rules to address the serious problem, the wireless industry and some public safety groups have opposed jamming for fear it would interfere with commercial and public safety wireless services.[63] So for the present time, the legality of prisons being able to jam prisoner cell phones remains in doubt.

IN A NUTSHELL

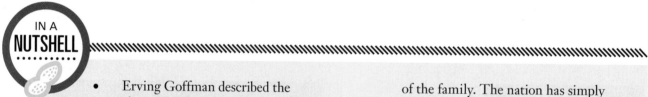

- Erving Goffman described the characteristics of "total institutions"; certainly his definition seems to capture the essence of corrections organizations. Unfortunately, most of what the public "knows" about prisons and jails is probably obtained through Hollywood's fictional versions.

- Most law-abiding Americans—and prison reformers of many years ago—probably tend to assume that sending people to serve time in prisons and jails serves a useful purpose. However, one prison expert states that for many people who go to prison, the conditions inside are not all that different from (and might even be better than) the conditions outside; indeed, for some members of our society, going to prison or jail may actually represent an increased standard of living.

- Several factors affect prison and jail populations. First is the nation's drug problem. Other commonly cited factors include truth-in-sentencing laws, violence on television and in the movies, and a general deterioration of morals and

of the family. The nation has simply become more punitive in nature. Robert Martinson's well-publicized finding in 1973 that "almost nothing works" in correctional treatment programs also served to spell the demise of the rehabilitative era.

- Correctional organizations are complex, hybrid organizations that utilize two related management subsystems to achieve their goals: One is managing correctional employees, and the other is concerned primarily with delivering correctional services to a designated offender population.

- The mission of corrections agencies has changed little over time. It is to protect the citizens from crime by safely and securely handling criminal offenders while providing offenders some opportunities for self-improvement and increasing the chance that they will become productive and law-abiding citizens.

- The primary purpose of jails is to hold accused law violators who cannot post bond to ensure their appearance at trial, and to hold those persons convicted of lesser offenses until they complete their court-ordered sentence. The term *new generation jail* refers to a style of architecture and inmate management that is totally new and unique to local detention facilities. There is a greater level of personal safety for both staff and inmates, greater staff satisfaction, more orderly and relaxed inmate housing areas, and a better maintained physical plant; these facilities are also cost-effective to construct and to operate.

- Today, many inmates in U.S. jails are involved in productive work. Some simply work to earn privileges, and others earn wages applied to their custodial costs and compensation to crime victims. Some hone new job skills, improving their chances for success following release.

- The correctional security department is normally the largest department in a prison, with 50 to 70 percent of all staff. It supervises all of the security activities within a prison.

- The unit management concept was originated by the federal prison system in the 1970s, to control prisons by providing a "small, self-contained, inmate living and staff office area that operates semi-autonomously within the larger institution." Unit management breaks the prison into more manageable sections based on housing assignments.

- Education departments operate the academic teaching, vocational training, library services, and sometimes recreation programs for inmates.

- Prison industries are separate government corporations that provide meaningful, productive employment that helps to reduce inmate idleness and supplies companies with a readily available and dependable source of labor.

- Corrections staff must make classification decisions in at least two areas: the inmate's level of *physical restraint* or "security level," and the inmate's level of supervision or *custody grade*.

- The Federal Bureau of Prisons operates institutions at five different security levels in order to confine offenders in an appropriate manner. Security levels are based on such features as the presence of external patrols, towers, security barriers, or detection devices; the type of housing within the institution; internal security features; and the staff-to-inmate ratio. Each facility is designated as either minimum, low, medium, high, or administrative.

- Supermax prison operations are quite different from traditional prisons, in that inmates rarely leave their cells; they eat all of their meals alone in the cells, and typically no group or social activity of any kind is permitted; they are typically denied access to vocational or educational training programs. Although there is very little research to date concerning the effects of supermax confinement, some authors point to previous isolation research that shows greater levels of deprivation lead to psychological, emotional, and physical problems.

- Technological developments have served to improve the operations and safety of correctional institutions, while also raising some privacy concerns.

KEY
TERMS
···· & ····
CONCEPTS

STUDY SITE

$SAGE edge™

Sharpen your skills with **SAGE edge** at **edge.sagepub.com/peak. SAGE edge for students** provides a personalized approach to help you accomplish your coursework goals in an easy-to-use learning environment. Access the videos, audio clips, quizzes, cases and SAGE journal and reference articles that are noted in this chapter.

REVIEW QUESTIONS

1. How is it that, for many members of our society, being incarcerated is not "punishment" but rather an improved lifestyle?

2. What is the general mission of a correctional organization?

3. What factors affect prison and jail populations?

4. How do jails differ in structure and functions from prisons, and how does the "new generation" jail differ from the traditional model?

5. What prison reform efforts have occurred over history?

6. What are the basic elements of the federal prison system?

7. What is the basic purpose underlying prison inmate classification?

8. How would you describe supermax prisons and how they differ from conventional prisons?

LEARN BY DOING

1. Assume you are on a high school recruiting trip for your university's criminal justice department, and a student mentions that he wishes to major in criminal justice, and that he has a friend whose uncle is "serving a three- to five-year *jail* sentence for *robbing* people's homes while they were away at work." Because of his interest in the field, you wish to tactfully correct his misunderstanding of the terms *jail* and *robbery*. What will you say?

2. You are assigned as part of a "Current Correctional Practices" class project to explain the differences between supermax prisons and traditional prisons. What will be your response?

3. Your criminal justice professor assigns the class to prepare a paper on the major differences between state prisons and local jails, including their structure and function. How will you delineate the differences between them?

THE INMATES' WORLD:
The "Keepers" and the "Kept"

LEARNING OBJECTIVES

As a result of reading this chapter, the student will be able to:

1 Describe how prisons and jails are perilous places, and some tips for determining when trouble is brewing

2 Review the general duties of prison corrections officers and jail employees

3 Explain how jails are different from prisons in terms of purpose and environment

4 List the deprivations of prison life that constitute the "pains" of imprisonment

5 Explain what is meant by prisonization

6 Review what is meant by the "hands off" era of prison administration

7 Explain several major federal court decisions that greatly expanded prisoners' rights

8 Discuss the unique challenges posed by women, gang members, senior citizens, and mentally ill persons who are in prison

9 Review the basic responsibilities in carrying out executions

10 Discuss the nature and extent of litigation by prison and jail inmates

11 Describe the general problem of drug abuse in prisons, and methods of interdiction

CHAPTER

13

Whitley v. Albers

[Correctional administrators] undoubtedly must take into account the very real threat unrest presents to inmates and officials alike, in addition to the possible harm to inmates. To resolve a disturbance . . . we think the question whether the measure taken inflicted unnecessary and wanton pain and suffering ultimately turns on whether force was applied in a good-faith effort to maintain or restore discipline or maliciously and sadistically for the very purpose of causing harm.

—Whitley v. Albers *(1986)[1]*

Boredom is beautiful.

—Former Nevada prison warden

INTRODUCTION

Author Introduction: Chapter 13

What is it like to live and work in a prison? How are gangs, drugs, and capital punishment dealt with administratively? What constitutional rights do inmates possess? This chapter will address those questions as it attempts to "lay bare" the lives of those Americans who spend their time in what might be termed a very restrictive environment.

Presented first is a look at the perilous nature of these jails and prisons, which can be "mean and brutish" places. Next is a look at the local jails: their purpose, environment, and personnel. Following that is a discussion of the role of prison correctional officers, and next are reviews of several challenges to prison administrators, including inmate litigation and drug use, special needs inmates—women, mentally ill, gangs—and administering capital punishment. Then an examination of prison life is presented, followed by a review of prisoners' constitutional rights based on selected federal court decisions. The chapter concludes with a summary, key terms and concepts, review questions, and several scenarios and activities that provide opportunities for you to "learn by doing."

ASSESS YOUR AWARENESS:

Test your knowledge of prison inmates and employees by first reading and responding to the following seven true-false items; check your answers after reading this chapter's materials.

1. Under our system of justice, it may be said that incarcerated persons are not to suffer pains beyond the deprivation of liberty; confinement itself is the punishment.

2. The warden's philosophies regarding security and treatment will have a major impact on both the prison inmates and staff.

3. Today the courts generally follow a "hands off" policy regarding prison and jail administration, allowing them to run their institutions as they see fit.

4. Supreme Court decisions support the notion that there exists an "iron curtain" between the U.S.

Constitution and the prisons—that is, inmates have no rights.

5. Federal legislation has greatly reduced litigation by inmates.

6. "Prisonization," a process whereby an inmate takes on the value system of the prison and its culture, actually helps toward rehabilitating the offender.

7. As with the police, prisons subscribe to the paramilitary system, having ranks, division of labor, and so on.

Answers can be found on page 401.

When examining what corrections personnel do, it would be good to remember two basic principles put forth by prison expert John DiIulio Jr.: First, incarcerated persons are not to suffer pains beyond the deprivation of liberty; confinement itself is the punishment. Second, regardless of the crime, even the most heinous offender is to be treated with respect and dignity.[2] The analysis of correctional institutions that follows is predicated on these two principles.

PLACES OF PERIL

It is probably a tribute and great credit to both prison and jail administrators and staff across the nation that so few institutional riots and other serious incidents occur in the United States, especially when one considers that staff are so outnumbered. Following are some noteworthy incidents where inmates have taken control of their institutions:

- At the Morey Unit of the Lewis Prison Complex in Buckeye, Arizona, two inmates took two correctional officers hostage and seized the unit's tower, triggering a 15-day standoff that remains the longest prison hostage situation in this nation's history.[3]

- Approximately 450 prisoners at the Southern Ohio Correctional Facility in Lucasville engaged in a riot, resulting in the deaths of nine inmates and one officer during the 10-day siege.[4]

- Federal detainees in a Louisiana parish jail held hostage the warden and two correctional officers, demanding a helicopter to escape.[5]

- A sheriff's negotiator won the release of three employees before a SWAT team stormed the Bay County Jail in Florida. Inmates had threatened to rape and cut off the body parts of a fourth hostage, a nurse. They had taken over the jail's infirmary, and one was holding a scalpel to the nurse's neck when the SWAT team and armed correctional officers ended the 11-hour standoff.[6]

- At the U.S. Penitentiary in Atlanta, Georgia, the U.S. Department of State reinstated an accord that permitted the repatriation of about 2,500 Cuban nationals. Three days later, the detainees seized control of the penitentiary, demanding that they not be repatriated. The uprising lasted 11 days and involved more than 100 hostages.[7]

- Permanently seared in the annals of corrections rioting are the horrific incidents at the Attica Correctional Facility in New York in 1971 (39 inmates and employees killed) and at the New Mexico State Prison in Santa Fe in 1980 (33 inmates dead).[8]

As may be seen with these tragic events, jail and prison rioting and hostage taking are potentially explosive and perilous situations from beginning to end. Hostages always are directly in harm's way, and their jeopardy is continuous and uninterrupted until they are released and safely in the hands of authorities.[9] Some inmate-involved riots and hostage situations come as a complete surprise, whereas others flow from a precipitating event or some type of a "spark."

Prisons and jails must have a coordinated plan to address riot and hostage incidents, not only to keep a small disturbance from escalating into a full-fledged riot but also to protect staff and inmates from harm. This Emergency Response Team from the Indiana Department of Corrections at New Castle Correctional facility stands down following a riot.

Corrections hostage-taking events can involve any individuals, employees, visitors, or prisoners held against their will by an inmate seeking to escape, gain concessions, or achieve other goals, such as publicizing a particular cause. They can be planned or impulsive acts[10] and can involve one hostage or hundreds.[11]

It is critical that both prisons and jails have a coordinated plan to address such incidents, not only to hopefully keep a small disturbance from escalating into a full-fledged riot but more importantly to determine whether someone lives or dies.[12]

JAIL PERSONNEL

Overcrowding

Ongoing Training

Jail employees, like other public servants, have serious responsibilities and must conduct themselves in an exemplary manner at all times while ensuring the care, custody, and control of inmates as per agency policies and procedures.

Today about 750,000 adults are incarcerated in city and county jails in the United States, either awaiting trial or serving a sentence.[13] Whereas **prisons** hold persons who have committed felonies and have been sentenced to at least one year of incarceration, as noted earlier, jails hold persons who are arrested and are waiting for a court appearance if they cannot arrange bail, as well as inmates who are serving sentences of up to one year for misdemeanors.

Jail administrators and employees need to be thoroughly trained in all aspects of their job. Jail workers have been criticized for being untrained and apathetic, although most are highly effective and dedicated. One observer wrote that

> personnel is still the number one problem of jails. Start paying decent salaries and developing decent training and you can start to attract bright young people to jobs in jails. If you don't do this, you'll continue to see the issue of personnel as the number one problem for the next 100 years.[14]

Training should be provided on the booking process, inmate management and security, general liability issues, policies related to AIDS, problems of inmates addicted to alcohol and other drugs, communication and security technology, and issues concerning suicide, mental health problems, and medication.

PRISON CORRECTIONAL OFFICERS

Job Satisfaction

As with employees of local jails, prison correctional officers have serious responsibilities, must conduct themselves in an exemplary manner at all times, and ensure the care, custody, and control of inmates as per agency policies and procedures. Next is a description of their role, functions, and training.

A Job Description

Subordinate to the prison administrators and other supervisors are the correctional staff members—those who, in the words of Gordon Hawkins, are "the other prisoners."[15] Their role is particularly important, given that they provide the front-line supervision and control of inmates and constitute the level from which correctional administrators may be chosen. Prison expert Jess Maghan described the task of the **correctional officers** as follows:

Correctional officer: one who works in a jail or prison and supervises correctional inmates.

Correctional officers are generally charged with overseeing individuals who have been arrested, are awaiting trial or other hearing, or who have been convicted of a crime and sentenced to serve time in a jail, reformatory, or penitentiary. They maintain security and observe inmate conduct and behavior to prevent disturbances and escapes. They manage and communicate with inmates, peers and supervisors, direct inmate movement, maintain key, tool, and equipment control, distribute authorized items to inmates, as well as maintain health, safety, and sanitation.[16]

Clearly the job of the prisons' correctional officers is challenging and stressful. In many if not most assignments correctional officers experience stimulus overload, assailed with the sounds of "doors clanging, inmates talking or shouting, radios and televisions playing, and food trays banging . . . [and odors] representing an institutional blend of food, urine, paint, disinfectant, and sweat."[17] According to a federal report, sources of stress for correctional officers include organization-related conditions, such as understaffing, overtime, shift work, and unreasonable supervisor demands; work-related sources of stress, including the threat of inmate violence, actual inmate violence, inmate demands and manipulation, and problems with coworkers; and a poor public image and low pay.[18] Due process rights for prisoners and the constant threat of lawsuits have also made corrections jobs even more difficult,[19] leading to what Richard Hawkins and Geoffrey Alpert referred to as "the big bitch" of correctional officers: They are losing power and influence while inmates are gaining them.[20] This frustration can be vented in physical ways.[21]

Author Video:
Prison Administrators

Chaos Control

Changes Wrought by the Attica Revolt

The core responsibilities of the correctional officer have remained essentially the same for the past 150 years: care, custody, and control. The preferred ways of performing this job, however, have undergone considerable change over time.

Attica

The civil rights movement, which began in the 1960s and continued into the 1970s, also led to more prison uprisings—an impetus to the prisoners' rights movement. With that came a point where correctional officers became the focus of considerable scholarly research and discussion, including David Fogel's *We Are the Living Proof*; Leo Carroll's *Hacks, Blacks and Cons*; James B. Jacobs's *Stateville: The Penitentiary in Mass Society*; Lucien Lombardo's *Guards Imprisoned: Correctional Officers at Work*; Robert Johnson and Shelley Price's *The Complete Correctional Officer, Human Service and the Human Environment of Prison*; and Lynn Zimmer's *Women Guarding Men*.[22]

The aforementioned brutal prison uprising in Attica, New York, in September 1971, made clear that the correctional officers and staff of the nation's state and local correctional facilities were not being appropriately selected and trained[23] and that relations between the correctional officers and inmates of those facilities were akin to a lit powder keg. Over half the town of Attica's nearly 2,800 residents worked at the facility, with white rural guards watching over a largely black and Latino urban population. This situation was an incubator of resentment and fear. As one person stated, for at least four years it was a "seething cauldron of discontent that was about to erupt."[24] Indeed, following the uprising, in which 43 hostages were held for four days and 39 people lay dead after state troopers stormed the institution, the revenge the prisoners feared was meted out as the guards retook the prison, forcing inmates to strip, beating them, and threatening to castrate them. Only a few wounded prisoners were allowed out; the others were treated in an 8- by 10-foot cell soaked in blood. A physician told the press, "It was the worst thing I've ever seen."[25]

Evolving Roles, Selection, and Training

As a result of the above examination of their roles, today prison correctional officers are viewed and used much differently than in pre-Attica times. First, the term *correctional officer* was adopted during the 1970s (replacing *guard*) as the official occupational reference term utilized by the U.S. Department of Labor. The position of correctional officer became available to both men and women, as well as closer screening and hiring by civil service exams. Likewise, the entry-level salary, overtime and hazardous duty pay, pension plans, and recognition as public safety "peace officer" status by state law also served to enhance the recruitment pool and long-term retention of corrections personnel. Staff training programs were also improved, to include such topics as constitutional law and cultural awareness, inmate behavior, contraband control, custody and security procedures, fire and safety, inmate legal rights, written and oral communication, use of force, first aid including cardiopulmonary resuscitation (CPR), and physical fitness training.[26]

Custodial staff members at most prisons are typically divided into four ranks: captain, lieutenant, sergeant, and officer. Captains typically work closely with the prison administration in policy-making and disciplinary matters; lieutenants are even more closely involved with the security and disciplinary aspects of the institution; and sergeants oversee a specified number of rank-and-file correctional officers who work in their assigned cell blocks or workplaces.

Perhaps the most difficult position of all within this hierarchy is that of the front-line officer, who is in close contact each day (and greatly outnumbered, as a rule) with the prison population. Following is a more specific listing of duties of the correctional officers:

1. Cell block officers: Officers supervise the daily activities and the general "well-being" of the inmates in the cell blocks, to ensure that inmates follow institutional rules and routines, to ensure that inmates do not harm themselves or others, and to assist inmates who are experiencing problems of a personal nature.

2. Work detail supervisors: Many prisons have inmates working in various positions, such as the prison cafeteria, laundry, and other such locations; officers must supervise them during such activities.

3. Industrial shop and educational programs: Prison industries have inmates producing everything from license plates, state-use paint, and mattresses to computer parts; correctional officers ensure that inmates do not create any problems during their work day and do not misappropriate any related tools that may be fashioned into weapons.

4. Yard officers: While inmates are outdoors and engaged in physical exercise and socialization, there is the potential for problems, such as fights between different racial or ethnic groups; officers must be alert for breaches of security and order.

5. Tower guards: Officers observe inmates who are in the prison yard while encased in an isolated, silent post high above the prison property and being vigilant for any outbreaks of violence or attempts to escape while inmates are outdoors.

6. Administrative building assignments: Officers are responsible for providing security at all prison gates, places where inmates' families come to visit, clerical work that involves inmate transfer, and so on.[27]

Direct Supervision

The Warden

Amenities

ISSUES OF PRISON GOVERNANCE

Ultimately, all topics discussed in this chapter are the responsibility of those who govern the prisons—directors and wardens. However, their challenges also include such daunting responsibilities as addressing prison litigation, administering capital punishment, attempting to prevent institutional problems relating to drugs and gangs, and addressing all manner of staffing needs and problems.

A Warden's Wisdom

Prison administration is now more challenging than ever—made much more so because of the recent fiscal crises that have faced all states as well as the federal government. Two former prison wardens from a western state have provided solid advice for administering prisons in general, and specifically in times of fiscal exigency.

First, the wise prison warden will recognize that there is simply never enough money to accomplish all four purposes of punishment: to *incapacitate* and *rehabilitate* offenders, and to provide *deterrence* to crime and *retribution*. Different states have different correctional philosophies, and that will affect how they budget and spend their prison monies. One must make choices—bearing in mind that the warden must, first and foremost, provide for incapacitation—while providing society, staff, and inmates a safe facility. Therefore, it is very important to focus on operations, programs, and finances.[28]

The warden's philosophies regarding security and treatment will have a major impact on both the prison inmates and staff. In addition to providing inmates with a variety of vocational training programs (including manufacturing such items as limousines and outdoor furniture, and training wild horses) and to a wide variety of physical fitness equipment, some prisons have allowed inmates to ride and repair their motorcycles inside the walls,[29] have an inmate band, and engage in unlimited planting of gardens, sunflowers, and fruit trees to occupy their time.

Other wardens take a more hard-line approach, and even discontinue those amenities that were initiated by their predecessors. For example, one recently halted the planting of sunflowers because inmates were planting them close to the fence line, and when the night breeze caused the sunflowers to stir from side to side, officers in the gun towers were lulled into a state of complacency—becoming conditioned to ignore the movement in the area, therefore posing a security risk. Another prison director recently disallowed inmate bands and the planting of gardens and flowers in the prison yard on grounds of institutional security (inmates were concealing weapons and other contraband in the gardens and flowers).[30] Note also that once such privileges are given to inmates, it is very difficult to take them away without generating considerable angst.

Today's prison wardens and other corrections staff members (and jail personnel as well) need to be as aware as possible of their surroundings and the general goings-on within the institution. As with police officers, whose academy training was discussed in Chapter 6, these corrections workers must also nurture a "sixth sense": a suspicion that something may be wrong.

A former western prison warden[31] termed this ability **JDLR**—knowing when things "just don't look right." In order to maintain a sense of what's going on with the inmates—"reading the yard"—some wardens recommend

Warden Esther Torres walks through one of the dormitories at the Willard-Cybulski Correctional Institution in Connecticut; Torres oversees a staff of 234 people and 1,160 prisoners.

JDLR: in prison jargon, the sense that things "just don't look right."

PRACTITIONER'S PERSPECTIVE

PRISON WARDEN

Name: Robert Bayer
   Current position: Former Director of Corrections and Prison Warden; currently an adjunct professor and prison consultant
   City, State: Reno, Nevada
   College attended/ academic major: University of New York, College at Oswego/BA, liberal arts; MA, English literature; University of Nevada, Reno/Master of Public Administration; PhD, political science, public administration

How long have you been a practitioner in this criminal justice position?

39 years

The primary duties and responsibilities of a prison warden are:

First, being responsible for one facility in a much larger network of facilities. To some degree a warden can be considered as the mayor of a city and the director/commissioner as the governor of the state in which the city resides, ensuring that facility policies, procedures, and general orders are fine-tuned for that specific facility within the guidelines of the department. Additionally, the warden is usually responsible for the human resources, safety and security operations, budget development and implementation, and the institution's physical plant. He or she must manage critical incidents that arise, and has the overall responsibility to ensure a positive work and living culture exists within that facility. To accomplish all of these tasks, the warden typically will bring extensive experience to the job. A warden is one of the highest-level management positions in a prison system and represents the "boots on the ground" administrator for the entire system.

The qualities/characteristics that are most helpful for one in this career include:

The ability to be both an administrator and a leader, with a very thorough knowledge of how a prison functions and the laws, policies, and procedures promulgated by the system; the ability to see the overall big picture of corrections and how the facility functions within that picture; a comprehension of the budget process and calendar; and the ability to be politically sensitive, personable, approachable, intelligent, hardworking, and decisive, yet thoughtful. As a leader, the warden's actions must reflect the best traditions of the agency, and the warden must be completely ethical in his or her decisions and actions. The warden should reflect all of the attributes prized in the front-line employee—loyalty, dedication, honesty, and reliability—and should instill confidence in all levels of staff and inmates. Staff want a warden who is steady under pressure and not prone to swings in mood or behavior. Ultimately, though staff may perform an infinite variety of jobs in the facility itself, they look to the warden to ensure they have the proper orders and resources needed to keep them safe day in and day out. Finally, the warden must be a skilled communicator at all levels, with good writing and verbal skills as well as being an effective listener.

In general, a *typical day* for a practitioner in this career would include:

Various functions, but the day should cover all three shifts to foster good communication. One should be at the facility during each shift change to ensure access to staff as they leave and enter the next shift, personally greeting or chatting with the support staff before the workday begins. An early morning staff meeting with the associate wardens and the maintenance supervisor is essential, to review the last 24 hours of shift activities and develop a priority list of operational issues that need resolution. Next, items in the in-basket are reviewed, delegated, or responded to, and it is important to physically "walk the yard" (for about two hours) on a daily basis to make upper management accessible to staff and inmates and to provide the opportunity for personal observation of any issues. This is also a time to obtain firsthand feedback as to the morale, conditions, and security of the yard. Next are formally scheduled meetings with inmate families, employee group representatives, other agency representatives, and so on. Time is also spent reviewing new policies, reading inmate appeals and requests, responding to correspondence, and conducting any necessary interviews of staff. Work continues after 5:00 p.m., to complete paperwork, prepare court testimony, work on difficult personnel issues, and conduct budget execution and construction. Once a week, do a facility inspection, looking at sanitation and security compliance, while focusing on a different aspect of facility operations each week (such as fire suppression readiness).

My advice to someone either wishing to study, or now studying, criminal justice to become a practitioner in this career field would be:

To become a "triple threat" in the field, which includes a solid understanding of operations, programs, and budget; to know where you are going; and to study leadership and become a leader. Try to find a competent mentor in the field who will take an interest in your career and guide you on a path of experience and education that will facilitate achieving your goals. The best administrators become leaders in our field, and to succeed one needs experience, training, and education.

that they and their staff walk the yard at least two times each day. Following are some aspects of the yard that should be noted and may portend trouble:

- Inmates banding together in groups—in political associations (i.e., by race, ethnicity, gang affiliation, and so forth)

- Loud music playing (possibly to cover up their conversations and activities from the staff)

- Unusually high canteen spending, with inmates purchasing long-term items, such as canned goods (which might indicate that a riot is being planned)[32]

Dealing With Inmate Litigation: The Prison Litigation Reform Act

As was discussed in Chapter 11, prison inmates not only can appeal their criminal conviction but may also attempt to obtain postconviction remedies through civil lawsuits; many of these are challenges to their conditions of confinement and list the prison warden as the defendant.

The volume of **inmate litigation** increased significantly following the *Cooper v. Pate* decision in 1964, discussed later in the chapter. In 1980, inmates in state and federal correctional institutions filed 23,287 petitions alleging both civil and criminal violations and seeking compensatory damages, injunctions, and property claims.[33] By 1996, the number of such petitions had grown to more than 64,000.[34]

Then, in April 1996, the Prison Litigation Reform Act (PLRA) of 1995 was enacted[35] "to provide for appropriate remedies for prison condition lawsuits, to discourage frivolous and abusive prison lawsuits, and for other purposes."[36] The PLRA requires that inmates must try to resolve their complaint through the prison's grievance procedure, pay court filing fees in full (indigent prisoners pay less), and show physical injury prior to filing a lawsuit for mental or emotional injury. Clearly PLRA served its purpose: In 1997, the first year following implementation of the act, there were 62,966 inmate petitions; by 2009 there were 10,566—an 83 percent decrease.[37]

Drug Interdiction and Treatment

Every adult in our society is aware of the problems wrought by drug abuse. Certainly that problem is reflected within the state prison populations,

Mid-Chapter Quiz: The Inmates' World

Drug Abuse

Inmate litigation: lawsuits filed by prison and jail inmates challenging their conditions of confinement.

FOCUS ON INMATE LITIGATION

Of course, there are legitimate lawsuits filed by inmates against prison administrators concerning living conditions and treatment. However, many such petitions are clearly questionable if not outright frivolous, such as the following:

- A prisoner sued 66 defendants alleging that unidentified physicians implanted mind control devices in his head.

- A prisoner suit demanded L.A. Gear or Reebok "Pumps" instead of Converse shoes.

- An inmate claimed his rights were violated because he was forced to send packages via UPS rather than U.S. mail.

- An inmate sued because he was served chunky instead of smooth peanut butter.

- An inmate claimed it was cruel and unusual punishment that he was forced to listen to his unit manager's country and western music.

- An inmate claimed $1 million in damages because his ice cream melted (the judge ruled that the "right to eat ice cream . . . was clearly not within the contemplation" of our nation's forefathers).

Source: Jennifer A. Puplava, "Peanut Butter and the Prison Litigation Reform Act," http://www.law.indiana.edu/ilj/volumes/v73/no1/puplava.html (accessed February 23, 2013).

Prison administrators often conduct surprise inspections (shakedowns) of inmates' cells to search for weapons and other contraband items.

where 17 percent of male inmates and 25 percent of female inmates are incarcerated for drug crimes.[38] Furthermore, offenders still manage to obtain illicit drugs during their incarceration, threatening the safety of inmates and staff while undermining the authority of correctional administrators, contradicting rehabilitative goals, and reducing public confidence.[39]

What can be done with drug abuse in prisons and jails? The state of Pennsylvania realized that drug use was pervasive in several of its prisons. Six inmates had died from overdoses in a 2-year period, and assaults on corrections officers and inmates had increased. To combat the problem, the state first adopted a zero-tolerance drug policy, the so-called Pennsylvania plan: Inmates caught with drugs were to be criminally prosecuted, and those testing positive (using hair testing) were to serve disciplinary custody time. Highly sensitive drug detection equipment was employed to detect drugs that visitors might try to smuggle into the prison, to inspect packages arriving in the mail, and to detect drugs that correctional staff might try to bring in. New policies were issued for inmate movement and visitation, and a new phone system was installed to randomly monitor inmates' calls.[40] The results were impressive. The state's 24 prisons became 99 percent drug free, the number of drug finds during cell searches dropped 41 percent, assaults on staff decreased 57 percent, inmate-on-inmate assaults declined 70 percent, and weapons seized during searches dropped from 220 to 76.[41]

Women in Prison: "Pains" and Adjustment

Chapter 3 discussed theories of how and why the role of women in crime has expanded since the 1970s. Here, it might be said, the punitive *effects* of their increased criminality are discussed.

Certainly the numbers speak to how large a role women now occupy in the nation's crime picture: About 2.1 million are arrested each year in the United States[42], about 200,000 women are in jails or prison, and more than 1 million are on probation or parole.[43] In many respects, female inmates resemble their male counterparts, tending to represent minorities who are relatively young and unmarried, although they are less likely to have been employed at the time of their arrest, and more likely to have been on welfare; they are also more likely to have suffered physical and sexual abuse as children.[44]

The major area of difference between male inmates and female inmates concerns their children, because child rearing is largely a mother's responsibility. Added to the "pains" of imprisonment for women, therefore, is the further frustration, conflict, and guilt that arises when women are removed from their home and are unable to care for their children.[45] Only seven states allow women who are pregnant at the time of sentencing to keep their infants with them inside a correctional facility after the baby's birth, and in most prisons the length of the child's stay with the mother depends on the length of the mother's sentence.[46]

There are also differences in how women adjust to institutional life. Women tend to value privacy more than men and, consequently, have more difficulty adjusting to communal living, prison rules, and the degrading

Female Correctional Officers at Angola

Prison Families

Specialized Populations at Angola

nature of body searches.[47] Therefore, they are more likely than male inmates to substitute emotional intimacy with other inmates for the loss of family and social ties. And, instead of forming gangs, women establish power and authority relationships through mock families; women play the role of men, cutting their hair short, wearing slacks, and walking and talking in a masculine way, while other women play the role of mother or wife; such relationships ease the pressures of incarceration.[48] Therefore, homosexuality in women's prisons is characterized more by mutual affection and caring relationships than by domination and violence that is more often found in male prisons. This does not mean, however, that women's prisons are places of safety and tranquility; in fact, it is quite the opposite, and male correctional staff typically prefer to work in men's institutions rather than in women's, because they perceive that male inmates are more cooperative and respectful than female inmates, who are more manipulative and emotional; they also tend to challenge authority and staff decisions more than their male counterparts.[49]

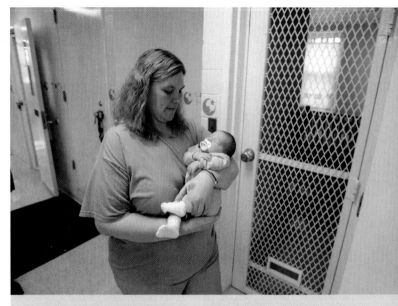

Few states allow women who are pregnant at the time of sentencing to keep their infants with them inside a correctional facility after the baby's birth.

The next "Focus On" box briefly describes another unique and growing population of prison inmates—those who are older, or "geriatric"—and a unique prison program that is dedicated to that age cohort.

Mentally Ill Inmates

It is estimated that about 13 percent of all state prison inmates are receiving therapy and/or counseling, and about 10 percent of them are also taking psychotropic medications.[50] Clearly many inmates have mental health issues. As

Mental Health

FOCUS ON GERIATRIC INMATES

As the general population is aging due to improved medical care, and criminals receive longer prison terms—due to mandatory sentencing, life without parole, and "three strikes" laws—the number of inmates who are geriatric (defined as over 60 or even over 50) is increasing. Such inmates have chronic health problems (e.g., arthritis, diabetes, cardiovascular diseases, failing eyesight and hearing, and other problems), memory and cognitive problems, mental health issues, and substance abuse and other criminal histories. A unique program at the Northern Nevada Correctional Center in Carson City, called the Senior Structured Living Program (SSLP), is designed to work with such inmates. The program provides physical fitness, diversion therapy (arts, crafts, games, reading, poetry), music (a choir and band), wellness and life skills training, individual and group therapy, and community involvement

(involving area social services, veterans', Alcoholics Anonymous, and other groups). Volunteers also provide psychological, spiritual, and social support to the men. To enter the program, inmates must sign a contract obligating them to maintain certain standards of conduct, be at least 60 years of age (one inmate in the program is 90), and not be engaged in a full-time job or educational program. Today 120 men are enrolled in the program; although an extensive evaluation of the program is under way, it is known that the prison medical department has witnessed a significant reduction in the men's overall medical complaints, overutilization of medical care, and use of psychotropic medications.

Source: Mary Harrison, *True Grit Notes* 5, no. 3 (Summer 2009); Terence P. Hubert, Mary T. Harrison, and William O. Harrison, *"True Grit": An Innovative Humanistic Living Program for a Geriatric Population* (Carson City, Nev.: Nevada Department of Corrections, n.d.).

Potentially violent, mentally ill prisoners pose a dangerous and challenging situation. Here a warden shows cages used to house mentally ill inmates during therapy sessions.

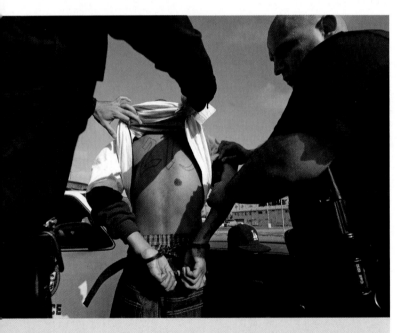

Prison gang members who return to the community may soon engage in violence and drug trafficking. These Los Angeles police officers are detaining a recently released "Street Villains" gang member.

an example, while in solitary confinement in a Massachusetts prison, an inmate cut his legs and arms, tried to hang himself with tubing from a breathing machine, smashed the machine to get a sharp fragment to slice his neck, and ate pieces of it, hoping to cause internal bleeding; he eventually hanged himself.[51] In prison, such individuals pose a dual dilemma for administrators. They are often violent and may be serving a long sentence. Therefore, they require a high level of security and are housed with other offenders who have committed equally serious offenses and who are serving equally long sentences. The presence of potentially violent, mentally ill prisoners in high-security and probably overcrowded institutions is a dangerous situation. The challenge for correctional administrators is to maintain a viable program to treat and control a difficult group of offenders. The treatment of this group requires resources, trained staff, and appropriate facilities.

Coping With Prison Gangs

Certainly an element of prisonization and a highly negative aspect of prison life is the widespread existence of prison gangs, which develop in prison for several reasons: solidarity, protection, and power. They often continue their operations outside of the penal system.

Typically, a prison gang consists of a select group of inmates who have an organized hierarchy and who are governed by an established code of conduct. They vary from highly structured to loosely structured associations, generally have fewer members than street gangs, are structured along racial or ethnic lines, and typically are more powerful in state correctional facilities than in the federal penal system.[52]

Furthermore, gang members returning to the community from prison often adversely affect neighborhoods and foment notable increases in crime, violence, and drug trafficking.[53] Prison gangs have also increased difficulty of prison officials to maintain order and discipline[54] and have wrought a rapid increase in inmate violence— often related to increases in drug trafficking, extortion, prostitution, protection, gambling, and contract inmate murders.[55] One study of prison gangs reported that they account for half or more of all prison problems.[56]

Gang members have a belligerent attitude toward all authority and its institutions when they enter prison; members are preoccupied with status and gang rivalry. They plan boycotts, strikes, and even riots. Despite administrative attempts to accommodate gangs in some prisons, they continue to pursue "loot, sex, respect, revenge, [and] will attack any outsider."[57]

Wardens and superintendents have been brought into gang-ridden prison systems specifically to "do something" with the gang problem; by transferring gang leaders and using other methods to segregate and isolate members, some have managed to greatly diminish the gangs' power.

Death Work: Administering Capital Punishment

One of the major responsibilities of prison administrators, currently in 36 states and in federal prisons,[58] is to carry out the death penalty, or capital punishment. By law, the warden or a representative presides over the execution.

To minimize the possibility of error, executions are carried out by highly trained teams. The mechanics of the process have been broken down into several discrete tasks and are practiced repeatedly. During the actual death watch—the 24-hour period that ends with the prisoner's execution—a member of the execution team is with the prisoner at all times. During the last 5 or 6 hours, two officers are assigned to guard the prisoner. The prisoner then showers, dons a fresh set of clothes, and is placed in an empty, tomb-like death cell. The warden reads the court order, or death warrant. Meanwhile, official witnesses—normally 6 to 12 citizens—are prepared for their role. The steps that are taken from this point to perform the execution depend on the method of execution that is used.[59]

Approximately 3,150 prisoners are now under sentence of death in the United States; 55 percent are white, 42 percent are black, and 2 percent are of other races; 47 (about 1.4 percent) are women.[60] As shown in Chapter 11, when executions are performed, lethal injection is the predominant method of execution in all 36 states and in federal prisons; 9 states still authorize electrocution; 3 states, lethal gas; 3 states, hanging; and 2 states, firing squad (16 states authorizing more than one method).[61] During the early 2000s the U.S. Supreme Court

Death Watch

Preparing for Execution

going GLOBAL

WORLDWIDE EXECUTIONS

Although 58 countries now have death penalty laws, only about 20 countries actually perform executions in a given year—executing about 700 people, however. Of the nations where death penalty data are released, four—Iraq (at least 68 executions), Iran (at least 360), Saudi Arabia (at least 82), and Yemen (at least 41)—accounted for 99 percent of all recorded executions in the Middle East and North Africa[62] (the United States, meanwhile, has executed an average of 56 persons per year since 2000—the highest number being 85 in 2000).[63]

In the majority of countries where people were sentenced to death or executed, Amnesty International asserts that the trials of the accused did not meet international fair trial standards—specifically, that many people were executed after supposedly "confessing" through torture or other forms of duress, particularly in China, Iran, Iraq, North Korea, and Saudi Arabia.[64]

But these figures do not include the thousands of executions that Amnesty International believes were carried out in China, where the numbers are suppressed. Thousands of people were executed in China in 2011, more than the rest of the world put together. Figures on the death penalty are a state secret. Amnesty International has stopped publishing figures it collects from public sources in China as these are likely to grossly underestimate the true number.[65]

Each year Amnesty renews its challenge to the Chinese authorities to publish data on those executed and sentenced to death, in order to confirm their claims that various changes in law and practice have led to a significant reduction in the use of the death penalty in the country since 2000.[66]

Atkins v. Virginia

rendered two significant decisions concerning the death penalty: First, in *Roper v. Simmons* (2005),[67] the Supreme Court abolished the death penalty for convicted murderers who were less than 18 years of age when they committed their crimes (affecting about 70 such persons); and second, in *Atkins v. Virginia* (2002),[68] the Court held that the execution of mentally retarded persons—which was permissible in 20 states—constituted cruel and unusual punishment.

Figure 13.1 depicts executions performed in the United States since 1976.

FIGURE 13.1

Executions by Year Since 1976

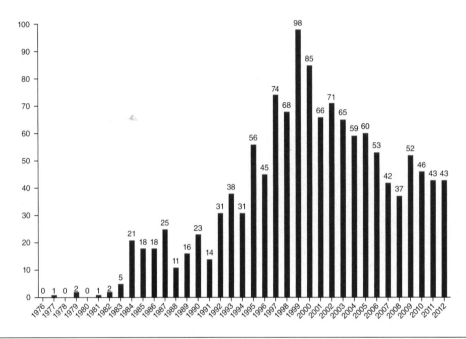

Source: Reprinted with permission of the Death Penalty Information Center.

"Hands off" doctrine: the notion by courts that prison administrators should be given free rein to run their prisons as they deem best.

Prisoners' rights: the collective body of rights given to inmates by the courts, in such areas as conditions of confinement, communications (mail and letters), access to law library and medical facilities, and so o

"Hands on" doctrine: the belief by courts that inmates have certain constitutional rights that the courts must see are upheld and also be obeyed by prison administrators.

PRISONERS' CONSTITUTIONAL RIGHTS

As will be seen in the following discussion, the rights and remedies available to prisoners have been greatly expanded over the past 150 years. Certainly prison and jail administrators must know—and apply—the law in order to be in compliance with the Constitution and federal court decisions.

Demise of the "Hands Off" Doctrine

Historically the courts followed a **"hands off" doctrine** regarding prison administration and **prisoners' rights**, deeming prisoners to be "slaves of the state." The judiciary, recognizing that it was not trained or knowledgeable in penology, allowed wardens the freedom and discretion to operate their institutions without outside interference, while being fearful of undermining the structure and discipline of the prison.

All that has changed, and the era of the **"hands on" doctrine**, beginning in the mid-1960s, brought about a change of philosophy in the courts regarding prisoners' rights; prison inmates now retain all the rights of free citizens except those restrictions necessary for their orderly confinement or to provide safety in the prison community.

Selected Court Decisions

Following is a brief discussion of selected major U.S. Supreme Court decisions that spelled the demise of the hands-off era, while also vastly improving the everyday lives of prison and jail inmates and reforming correctional administration.

A "Slave of the State"

The 1871 case of Woody Ruffin serves as an excellent beginning point for an overview of significant court decisions concerning inmates' rights. Ruffin, an inmate in Virginia, killed a correctional officer while attempting to escape, and later challenged his conviction; the Virginia Supreme Court stated that Ruffin, like other prisoners, had "not only forfeited his liberty, but all his personal rights." The court added that inmates were **"slaves of the state,"** losing all their citizenship rights, including the right to complain about living conditions (*Ruffin v. Commonwealth*, 1871).[69]

Legal Remedy and Access to the Courts

In *Cooper v. Pate* (1964),[70] the Supreme Court first recognized the use of Title 42 of U.S. Code Section 1983 (discussed in Chapter 7) as a legal remedy for inmates. An Illinois state penitentiary inmate sued prison officials claiming that he was unconstitutionally punished by being placed in solitary confinement and being denied permission to purchase certain religious materials. The Supreme Court decided that he was entitled to purchase the articles—and that he could use Section 1983 to sue the prison administration.

Another significant case involved the right of access to the courts. Here, a Tennessee prisoner was disciplined for assisting other prisoners in preparing their legal writs, which violated a prison regulation. The Court acknowledged that "writ writers" are sometimes a menace to prison discipline, and their petitions are often a burden on the courts. However, because the state provided no "reasonable alternative" for illiterate or poorly educated inmates to prepare appeals, the Supreme Court said inmates could not be prevented from giving such assistance to other prisoners (*Johnson v. Avery*, 1969).[71]

In 1977, in another court-access decision, the Court said prisoners have a constitutional right to adequate law libraries or assistance from persons trained in the law. Alternative methods for providing such access included training inmates as paralegals; using paraprofessionals and law students to advise inmates; hiring lawyers on a part-time consultant basis; and having voluntary programs through bar associations, where lawyers make visits to the prisons to consult with inmates (*Bounds v. Smith*, 1977).[72]

First Amendment: Freedom of Religion

A landmark 1972 case clarified the right of inmates to exercise their religious beliefs. The plaintiff, a Buddhist, was not allowed to use the prison chapel and was placed in solitary confinement on a diet of bread and water for sharing his religious material with other prisoners. The Supreme Court held that inmates with unconventional religious beliefs must be given a reasonable opportunity to exercise those beliefs (*Cruz v. Beto*, 1972).[73]

 Access to Courts

 Johnson v. Avery

 Bounds v. Smith

"Slave of the state": an early philosophy toward prison inmates essentially stating that inmates had no legal rights that had to be observed by prison administrators.

The U.S. Supreme Court has held that prisoners have a constitutional right to adequate law libraries or assistance from persons trained in the law.

The U.S. Supreme Court has required that inmates must be given a reasonable opportunity to exercise their religious beliefs.

The Supreme Court has also looked at prison mail censorship regulations that permitted authorities to hold back or to censor mail to and from prisoners. The Court based its ruling not on the rights of the prisoner, but instead on the *free-world* recipient's right to communicate with the prisoner, either by sending or by receiving mail. The court said mail censorship, if it is to be done, must be shown to enhance security, order, and rehabilitation; it must not be used simply to censor opinions or other expressions (*Procunier v. Martinez*, 1974).[74]

Fourth Amendment: Search and Seizure

Estelle v. Gamble (1976)[75] was the first major prison medical treatment case decided by the Supreme Court. Here, the Court coined the phrase "deliberate indifference," which is where the serious medical needs of prisoners involve the unnecessary and wanton infliction of pain. A Texas inmate claimed that he received cruel and unusual punishment due to inadequate treatment of a back injury sustained while he was engaged in prison work. The Court found that, because medical personnel saw him on 17 occasions during a three-month period, and failed to treat his injury and related problems, such deliberate indifference to his medical needs constituted the "unnecessary and wanton infliction of pain."

Religion in Prison

Fourteenth Amendment: Due Process

The Supreme Court's decision in *Wolff v. McDonnell* (1974)[76] is significant because for the first time, the court acknowledged that inmates are entitled to certain due process rights during prison disciplinary proceedings. McDonnell and other inmates at a Nebraska prison alleged, among other things, that disciplinary proceedings at the prison violated due process. The Court said that "there is no iron curtain drawn between the Constitution and the prisons of this country," that "a prisoner is not wholly stripped of constitutional protections." This statement has become known as the Court's **"iron curtain" speech**. Prisoners were given several due process rights:

Procunier v. Martinez

- Advance written notice of charges

- A written statement as to the evidence being relied on for the disciplinary action

- Ability to call witnesses and to present documentary evidence in the inmate's defense

- Use of counsel substitutes (e.g., a friend or staff member) if the inmate is illiterate or when complex issues require such assistance

- An impartial prison disciplinary board

"Iron curtain" speech: in *Wolff v. McDonnell* (1973), the Supreme Court stated that there is no iron curtain between the Constitution and the prisons of the United States; in sum, inmates have rights.

LIFE IN PRISON

As mentioned in Chapter 12, there are now approximately 2.3 million Americans living in federal and state prisons and in local jails. What was not mentioned, however, is that since 2002 the United States has had the highest imprisonment rate in the world[77] (see Table 13.1)—which has a total

TABLE 13.1

World Prison Populations

COUNTRY	PRISON POPULATION	POPULATION PER 100,000	JAIL OCCUPANCY LEVEL %	UN-SENTENCED PRISONERS %	WOMEN PRISONERS %
US	2,193,798	737	107.6	21.2	8.9
China	1,548,498	118	N/A	N/A	4.6
Russia	874,161	615	79.5	16.9	6.8
Brazil	371,482	193	150.9	33.1	5.4
India	332,112	30	139	70.1	3.7
Mexico	214,450	196	133.9	43.2	5
Ukraine	162,602	350	101.3	19.5	6.1
South Africa	158,501	334	138.6	27.5	2.1
Poland	89,546	235	124.4	16.8	3
England/Wales	80,002	148	112.7	16.4	5.5
Japan	79,052	62	105.9	14.7	5.9
Kenya	47,036	130	284.3	45.6	4.2
Turkey	65,458	91	77.4	47.7	3.3
Nigeria	40,444	30	101.5	64.3	1.9
Australia	25,790	125	105.9	21.6	7.1
Scotland	6,872	134	107.5	21	4.4
Northern Ireland	1,375	79	91.5	37.4	2.2

Source: BBC News, "World Prison Populations," http://news.bbc.co.uk/2/shared/spl/hi/uk/06/prisons/html/nn2page1.stm. Data compiled from International Centre for Prison Studies website.

prison population of more than 10.1 million people.[78] Next we describe the general lifestyle and deprivations of those individuals.

Deprivations

Jack Henry Abbott, a violent convict who spent more than 30 years in prison, gained literary celebrity from his book, *In the Belly of the Beast: Letters from Prison*, and was once supported for parole by Norman Mailer, wrote that

Estelle v. Gamble

> Men who had been in prison as much as five years still knew next to nothing on the subject. It probably took a decade behind bars for any real perception on the matter to permeate your psychology and your flesh.[79]

Research has made it possible to understand the lives led by inmates without our having to actually live in a prison for 10 years.

Although many people—and certainly many crime victims—would argue that prison life today is too "soft" for inmates, Gresham Sykes described the following "pains of imprisonment":

Wolff v. McDonnell

1. Deprivation of liberty: The inmate's loss of freedom is the most obvious aspect of incarceration; however, not only does this restriction of movement include living in a small space such as a prison cell, but it also includes doing so involuntarily. Friends and family are prohibited from visiting except at limited times, causing relationships to fray. Sykes said this pain of imprisonment is the most acute, because it represents a "deliberate, moral rejection of the criminal by free society."[80]

Among the deprivations of incarceration are those involving goods and services; inmates do not have access to the wide array of food, entertainment, and services that free people enjoy.

2. Deprivation of goods and services: Inmates do not have access to the wide array of food, entertainment, and services that free people enjoy. For some, this is a relative loss, because (as discussed in Chapter 12) for some inmates prison life is a "step up," and having room and board provided to them each day is an improvement in lifestyle. Sykes, however, felt that some inmates view this impoverishment as the prison's acting as a tyrant to deprive them of the kinds of goods and services they deserve.[81]

3. Deprivation of heterosexual relationships: Inmates do not leave their sexuality at the front gate while incarcerated. This is certainly an area of prison life that represents a source of major stress and violence. In men's prisons, Sykes contended, where one's self-concept is tied to his sexuality, by depriving men of female company their "self-image is in danger of becoming half complete, fractured," and, as seen below, with often violent results.[82]

4. Deprivation of autonomy: Inmates cannot make decisions for themselves about the most basic tasks, such as walking from one room to another, when they will eat and sleep, and so forth, and they must ask for everything. Bureaucratic rules and staff control their lives, and finding ways to cope with this deprivation can lead to stress.

5. Deprivation of security: Perhaps the most stressful pain of imprisonment, there are few places in the institution where the inmate can feel secure, and he or she is confined with people who are brutish and violent. Having to "watch one's back" and cope with people who constantly test each other and seek out weaknesses in others will lead to internal power struggles, development of gangs, and other forms of "protection."

Prisonization

Angola
Inmate Interview

Once in prison, there is a process by which inmates internalize and deem as legitimate the prison subculture—the inmates' attitudes, values, and norms. This process is known as prisonization, and it certainly overrides the conventional value systems of law-abiding Americans, transforming the inmate into a full initiate and quite likely militating against the ability of the institution to have any ability to reform or rehabilitate the inmate.[83]

In prison, everyone is subjected to strict regulation for the safety and security of the institution. Inmates are taught to line up for meals and frequent head counts, move in unison, and live a highly structured life; aggression may well be met with aggression, and thus wise inmates will simply attempt to "get along" in a highly regimented society.[84] According to prison expert Jeanne Stinchcomb, inmates conform to the norms and values considered socially acceptable by other inmates—"for example, disdain for the system and those in authority, use of vulgar language, name calling, distrust of fellow prisoners and staff, and acceptance of the status quo."[85] Stinchcomb compares the institutional adaptation of an inmate to

breaking the spirit of a wild horse to shape its response to the commands of the rider. Like horse and rider—who develop a working accommodation with each other—the subsequent relationship is characterized by routines of dominance, surrender, and behavior on cue. Among inmates, this conformity creates a façade of courtesy toward authority figures and promotes flat, non-committal responses to others, which are devoid of any emotional investment.[86]

Furthermore, every correctional institution has a subculture, with its unique system of norms that influence inmates' behavior. These norms are informal and unwritten, but the violation can quickly bring down the wrath of other inmates, ranging from ostracism to physical violence or death.

These informal rules, as originally set down by Gresham Sykes and Sheldon Messinger, are as follows[87]:

1. Don't interfere with the interests of other inmates. This means that inmates "never rat on an inmate" or betray each other; don't be nosy, don't have loose lips, and never put an inmate on the spot. There is no justification for not complying with these rules.

2. Don't quarrel or feud with fellow inmates: This is expressed in the directives "Play it cool" and "Do your own time."

3. Don't exploit other inmates: In inmate culture, this means "don't break your word," "don't steal from other inmates," and "don't go back on bets."

4. Don't weaken; withstand frustration or threat without complaint: This means "Be tough," and "Be a man."

5. Don't trust the custodians or the things they stand for: This translates to "Don't be a sucker" and "The officials are wrong and the prisoners are right."

As part of this process, Figure 13.2 provides a sampling of the kinds of arcane words and phrases that are a part of the prison culture—a sort of **prison vocabulary** with which the inmate identifies and that has secret meaning.

Chapter Quiz: The Inmates' World

Prison vocabulary: a language that is adopted by inmates with particularized meaning and must be learned by prison staff to keep abreast of prison activities; for example, a *shiv* or *shank* is a prison knife.

FIGURE 13.2

Prison Vocabulary: A Partial Listing of Words, Terms, Phrases, and Usage

AD SEG Administrative segregation: a secure cell location for inmates who have been significantly or continuously disruptive.

BOW-LEGGED A consecutive sentence structure.

DIME A 10-year sentence, or a piece of information given by an informant.

DO YOUR OWN NUMBER To be concerned with oneself and to avoid being involved with others.

DOG EYE To stare at someone, usually a prison official, with contempt and disrespect.

DOING IT ALL Serving a life sentence with or without the possibility of parole.

DUCK/MALLARD Someone who is easily taken advantage of.

FISH A reference to any new inmate or staff member.

GATE JITTERS The state of nervousness prior to being released from prison.

GIT BACKS Acts of revenge.

GET DOWN FIRST To tell one's version of an incident before anyone else does, usually to direct suspicion away from oneself.

GREEN A reference to street money, which is contraband within prisons.

HOLDING Someone in possession of a weapon, narcotics, or another item prohibited within the prison.

(Continued)

FIGURE 13.2

(Continued)

HOLE TIME A period of time spent in disciplinary detention.

JACKET One's reputation.

STASH The location or quantity of a valuable, hidden commodity.

KICK ROCKS Doing nothing or having nothing interesting to do.

KID A term usually referring to the submissive partner in a homosexual relationship.

KNOCK-KNEED A concurrent sentence structure.

LOCKUP A high-security section of the prison, to the prison itself, or to a routine security activity.

LOP A derogatory reference to a person thought to have little ability or respect.

MULE Someone who carries or smuggles contraband items, or the act of doing so.

NICKLE A five-year sentence.

NUT UP A reference to becoming psychologically disturbed or unstable.

PACKIN' Possessing a weapon, narcotics, or another item prohibited within the prison.

PC Protective custody. It is also used as a derogatory reference to inmates who are unable to live in the general prison population.

POP A CAP To fire a shot into or to get the attention of a group of prisoners.

PRIOR A reference to one or more prior felony convictions.

PRUNO Any of a variety of prison-made alcoholic beverages; it may have prunes as a base.

PUMP SUNLIGHT A reference to a highly restrictive security or housing classification.

RABBIT An inmate with an escape history on his record or a reference to escaping.

ROAD DOG A close friend or running mate.

ROLL OVER To testify against another or to inform on another, particularly on a crime partner.

SELLING WOLF TICKETS Spreading rumors of impending violence or extraordinary occurrences; it originated with the phrase "crying wolf."

SHANK A prison-made knife.

SHU Security Housing Unit, or the Hole.

SNITCH An informant.

SNITCH KITE A written statement by one inmate anonymously informing on another.

STICK To stab another inmate with a shank or other sharp weapon.

VELVEETA VILLAGE A disparaging reference to protective custody housing for informants, derived from cheese and rats.

Source: John Slansky, personal communication.

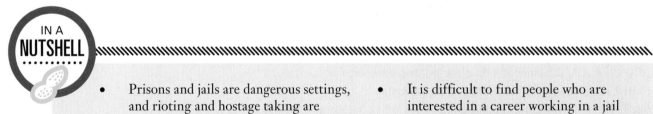

IN A NUTSHELL

- Prisons and jails are dangerous settings, and rioting and hostage taking are potentially explosive and perilous situations. It is critical that both prisons and jails have a coordinated plan to address such incidents.

- It is difficult to find people who are interested in a career working in a jail because after being initially hired to work in detention, they often want to do "real police work" and transfer to the patrol division as soon as possible.

- Prison expert John DiIulio Jr. stated that incarcerated persons are not to suffer pains beyond the deprivation of liberty; confinement itself is the punishment. Furthermore, regardless of the crime, even the most heinous offender is to be treated with respect and dignity.

- Some wardens believe there is simply never enough money to accomplish all four purposes of punishment: to *incapacitate* and *rehabilitate* offenders, and to provide *deterrence* to crime and *retribution*. One must make choices—bearing in mind that the warden must, first and foremost, provide for incapacitation.

- Astute prison leadership will develop a JDLR mentality—knowing when things "just don't look right." It is having a sense of what's going on with the inmates— "reading the yard"—and thus knowing when problems are about to erupt.

- Gresham Sykes described the "pains of imprisonment" as deprivations of liberty, goods and services, heterosexual relationships, autonomy, and security.

- Once in prison, there is a process by which inmates internalize and deem as legitimate the prison subculture—the inmates' attitudes, values, and norms. This process is known as prisonization; it quite likely militates against the ability of the institution to have any ability to reform or rehabilitate the inmate.

- Historically the courts followed a "hands off" policy regarding prisons and prisoners' rights; that has changed, and the "hands on" era, beginning in the mid-1960s, brought about a change of philosophy in the courts regarding prisoners' rights; prison inmates now retain all the rights of free citizens except those restrictions necessary for their orderly confinement or to provide safety in the prison community.

- Although in many respects female inmates resemble their male counterparts, tending to represent minorities who are relatively young and unmarried, the major area of difference concerns their children; child rearing is largely a mother's responsibility. Women's prisons are not safe and tranquil; in fact, it is quite the opposite, and male correctional staff typically prefer to work in men's institutions rather than in women's because they perceive male inmates as more cooperative and respectful; women also tend to challenge authority and staff decisions more than their male counterparts.

- Prison administrators must also address prison litigation, administer capital punishment, and deal with problems relating to litigation, drugs, mental illness, and gangs.

- The role of correctional officers is particularly important given that they provide the front-line supervision and control of inmates. But due process rights for prisoners have made their jobs even more difficult, and many believe they are losing power and influence while inmates are gaining them.

KEY
TERMS
···· & ····
CONCEPTS

Capital punishment	Inmate litigation	Prison vocabulary
Correctional officer	"Iron curtain" speech	Prisoners' rights
"Hands off" doctrine	Jails	Prisons
"Hands on" doctrine	"JDLR"	"Slave of the state"

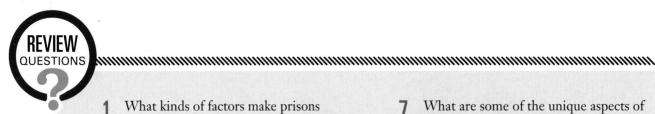
1. What kinds of factors make prisons and jails dangerous in nature, and what indicators or conditions might exist that would foreshadow a riot or another major incident?

2. How do jails differ from prisons in terms of purpose and environment?

3. What are the deprivations of prison life that constitute the "pains" of imprisonment?

4. What are the duties of correctional officers?

5. How would you describe the administrative duties involved in carrying out executions?

6. What is meant by prisonization?

7. What are some of the unique aspects of women being in prison in terms of their deprivations and adjustment? Of older (geriatric) and mentally ill inmates?

8. What major federal court decisions have been rendered concerning prisoners' rights?

9. What is the nature and extent of litigation by prison and jail inmates?

10. What are some good examples of frivolous prisoners' lawsuits?

11. What is the extent of—and some possible solutions to—the problem of drug abuse in prisons? How do illegal drugs enter the prisons?

12. What, from the inmates' point of view, is the benefit of joining a prison gang?

STUDY SITE

⑤SAGE edge™

LEARN BY DOING

1. Running a "take back the streets" anticrime campaign, a newly elected governor sends all prison wardens a letter stating in effect that prisons should not be a "Hotel Ritz" operation and that he is considering a new policy that would end all "useless educational programs beyond a GED," and "end all weight-lifting and such programs as Alcoholics Anonymous, the prison band, and gardening." The governor asks you as a warden for your viewpoint concerning these changes, particularly the following:

   a. Do such prison programs have positive benefits for the inmates? Negative aspects for the institution?

   b. Where might you try to negotiate with the governor?

2. The prison warden's associate director for security has been directed to prepare an immediate plan for dealing with the following situation:

Inmates in the local prison are stocking up on long-term items (e.g., canned goods) in the commissary and banding together more throughout the institution by racial groupings; furthermore, inmates tend to be seen standing in or near doorways, as if preparing for a quick exit. Over the last several months the inmates have become increasingly unhappy with their conditions of confinement—not only concerning the food, but also with the increasing numbers of assaults and gang attacks. The staff members, for their part, have also become increasingly unhappy, particularly with their low salaries and benefits, perceived unsafe working conditions and attacks on officers, prison overcrowding, and a trend toward greater amounts of contraband being found in the cell blocks. They demand that the prison administration ask the parole board to grant more early releases and the courts to give more consideration to house arrest and electronic monitoring to ease the situation.

What sort of plan will the associate warden prepare? Include in your response the critical issues that should be dealt with immediately, what steps you would take to defuse the potential for a riot, and measures that might be adopted later, in the long term, concerning staff morale and demands.

CORRECTIONS IN THE COMMUNITY:
Probation, Parole, and Other
Alternatives to Incarceration

LEARNING OBJECTIVES

As a result of reading this chapter, the student will be able to:

1 Describe what is meant by community corrections

2 Describe the definitions, origins, and differences between probation and parole, as well as the rights accorded people who are serving terms of probation and parole

3 Explain why the criminal justice system uses alternatives to incarceration

4 Explain the functions of probation and parole officers— and the impact of high caseloads

5 Review the process used when the state wishes to remove a probationer's or parolee's freedom

6 Delineate several reasons for and against probation and parole officers being armed

7 Explain the purposes and functions of intermediate sanctions, including intensive supervision, house arrest, electronic monitoring, shock incarceration/boot camps, and day reporting centers

8 Explain the rationale that underlies the use of restorative justice

CHAPTER

14

The mood and temper of the public in regard to the treatment of crime and criminals is one of the most unfailing tests of the civilization of any country.

—Winston Churchill

INTRODUCTION

Author Introduction: Chapter 14

"I would like to use my college degree to help people who have gotten into trouble. Should I work in probation or parole? Should I work with adults or juveniles? And what kind of work would I be doing?" These questions have a ring of familiarity to most if not all criminal justice professors, as many students today seek to make their contributions to society by working with and trying to reform criminal offenders.

The word *probation* is probably familiar to most college and university students. If not "making the grades," they can be placed on academic probation; if their athletic programs fail to adhere to the rules of the National Collegiate Athletic Association (NCAA), the institution and its athletic program(s) can be placed on probationary status. The common thread here is that each group or individual is served warning that it had better change its behavior, or there will be more severe penalties.

And so it is with our criminal offenders—most of whom are sentenced to serve a *community-based* form of punishment, with probation being one form that is quite often used. This chapter examines **community corrections**—probation, parole, and a variety of other measures that constitute a broad array of alternatives to incarceration. It begins by considering the rationales for punishment—why we punish, and the four purposes or goals we hope to achieve because of it. Following is a look at another fundamental aspect of sentencing and punishment: the impact of determinate and indeterminate sentencing.

Next is a look at arguments for having alternatives to incarcerations, both philosophical and economical in nature, and following that are discussions of the origins and contemporary aspects of probation and parole. Included here are the rights that probationers and parolees have when the state wishes

Community corrections: locally operated services that offer minimum-security, work-release alternatives to prisoners about to be paroled.

ASSESS YOUR AWARENESS:

Test your knowledge of probation and parole by first reading and responding to the following seven true-false items; check your answers after reading this chapter's materials.

1. Probation began with the voluntary work of a simple Boston shoe cobbler.

2. Probation, because it is more costly than prison, is used very sparingly in the United States.

3. Being placed on parole allows the offender to remain in the community and thus avoid the "pains" of imprisonment.

4. A person may have his or her probation revoked and then be sent to prison for such behaviors as use of alcohol, curfew violations, and associating with other known criminals.

5. Persons whose probation or parole status might be revoked and who thus might be sent to prison enjoy no legal rights or benefits.

6. In addition to probation and parole, other alternatives to prison that have been attempted include house arrest, electronic monitoring, and boot camps.

7. Restorative justice places stronger emphasis on involving the community and focusing on the victim.

Answers can be found on page 401.

to remove their freedom and send them to prison, as well as the functions of probation and parole officers—including the impact of high caseloads and the debate concerning whether or not these officers should be armed.

Then intermediate sanctions are discussed. These are other alternatives to incarceration that are lesser known, perhaps, but still quite beneficial to offenders and for decreasing prison and jail populations; they include intensive supervision (of probation), house arrest, electronic monitoring, shock incarceration/boot camps, and day reporting centers. Following that is a review of a relatively new movement in criminal justice: restorative justice. The chapter concludes with a chapter summary, key terms and concepts, review questions, and several scenarios and activities that provide opportunities for you to "learn by doing."

WHY ALTERNATIVES TO INCARCERATION

The leading alternative to incarceration is probation, which was discussed briefly in Chapter 1 and is defined as the court's allowing a convicted person to remain at liberty in the community, while being subject to certain conditions and restrictions on his or her activities. The United States is not soft on crime, but there are several valid reasons in support of using **alternatives to incarceration**:

 Recidivism

- It allows the offender to remain in the community, which has a greater rehabilitative effect than incarceration, thereby reducing recidivism.

- It allows the offender to take greater advantage of treatment or counseling options.

- It allows the offender to avoid the "pains" of imprisonment (as discussed in Chapter 13).

- It is far less expensive.

- It permits ongoing ties with family, employment, and other social networks.

However, to be effective, a real alternative to incarceration needs to have three elements: It must incapacitate offenders enough so that it is possible to interfere with their lives and activities to make committing a new offense extremely difficult; it must be unpleasant enough to deter offenders from wanting to commit new crimes; and it has to provide real and credible protection for the community.[1]

Nearly a half-century ago, the President's Commission on Law Enforcement and Administration of Justice (1967) endorsed community-based corrections—the use of probation and parole—as a humane, logical, and effective approach for working with and changing criminal offenders; the commission said that includes

> building or rebuilding solid ties between the offender and the community, obtaining employment and education, securing in the large sense a place for the offender in the routine functioning of society. This requires . . . efforts directed towards changing the individual offender (and) mobilization and change of the community and its institutions.[2]

The demand for prison space has created a reaction throughout corrections.[3] With the cost of prison construction now exceeding a quarter of a

Alternatives to incarceration: a sentence imposed by a judge other than incarceration, such as probation, parole, shock probation, or house arrest.

Intermediate
Sanctions

million dollars per cell in maximum-security institutions, cost-saving alternatives are becoming more attractive if not essential.

The realities of prison construction and overcrowding have led to a search for intermediate punishments.[4] This in turn has brought about the emergence of a new generation of programs, making community-based corrections, according to Barry Nidorf, a "strong, full partner in the fight against crime and a leader in confronting the crowding crisis."[5] Economic reality dictates that cost-effective measures be developed, and this is motivating the development of intermediate sanctions.[6]

ORIGINS OF PROBATION AND PAROLE

The concepts of probation and parole have long and interesting histories. Next is a brief discussion of how both of them came into being and their eventual use in the United States.

Probation Begins: The Humble Shoe Cobbler

Although contemporary **probation** has roots dating back to biblical times,[7] its history in the United States dates back to the 19th century. "Judicial reprieve" was used in English courts to serve as a temporary suspension of sentence to allow the defendant to appeal to the Crown for a pardon. In the United States the suspended sentence was used as early as 1830 in Boston and became widespread in American courts, even though there was no statutory provision for it. By the mid-19th century, though, many courts were using a judicial reprieve to suspend sentences.[8] This posed a legal question: Could judges suspend sentences wholesale, after trials that were scrupulously fair, simply to give the defendant a second chance?[9]

In 1916 the U.S. Supreme Court, in a decision affecting only the federal courts, held that judges did not have the discretionary authority to suspend sentences. However, the Court ruled that Congress could authorize the temporary or indefinite suspension of sentences; this led to the development of probation statutes.[10]

> John Augustus, a Boston shoe cobbler, is credited as being the "father of probation." In 1841 Augustus appeared in court on behalf of a drunkard; as Augustus later explained, "I was in court one morning . . . in which the man was charged with being a common drunkard. He told me that if he could be saved from the House of Correction, he never again would taste intoxicating liquors; I bailed him, by permission of the court."[11] During his first year of service as an unpaid, volunteer probation officer, Augustus assisted 10 drunkards. By Augustus' own account, he eventually bailed "eleven hundred persons, both male and female."

Augustus performed several tasks that are reminiscent of modern probation. He investigated each case—inquiring into the offender's character, age, and influences—and kept careful records of each person's progress. His probation work soon caused him to fall into financial difficulties, however, requiring his friends' monetary assistance. Augustus died in 1859.

By 1869, the Massachusetts legislature had required that a state agent be present if court actions might result in the placement of a child in a reformatory (the forerunner of today's caseworkers). Then, in 1878, Massachusetts passed the first probation statute, mandating an official state probation system with salaried probation officers. Other states quickly followed suit:

Probation: an alternative to incarceration where the convict remains out of jail or prison and in the community and thus on the job, with family, and so on, while subject to conditions and supervision of the probation authority; if violating those conditions, probation may be revoked and the probationer may be sent to prison.

- By 1900, Vermont, Rhode Island, New Jersey, New York, Minnesota, and Illinois passed probation laws.

- By 1910, 32 more states passed legislation establishing juvenile probation.

- By 1930, juvenile probation was legislated in every state except Wyoming.[12]

Parole Origins: Alexander Maconochie

The word *parole* stems from the French *parol*, or "word of honor," which was a means of releasing prisoners of war who promised not to resume arms in a current conflict.[13] One writer cited the year 1840 as one in which "one of the most remarkable experiments in the history of penology was initiated."[14]

In that year, Alexander Maconochie (1787–1860) became superintendent of the British penal colony on Norfolk Island, about 930 miles northeast of Sydney, Australia. He began a philosophy of **punishment** based on reforming offenders: The convict was to be punished for the past while being trained for the future. Maconochie advocated open-ended ("indeterminate") sentences. His system worked, although it was harshly ridiculed by some Australians as "coddling criminals."

Returning to England in 1844, Maconochie began writing and speaking of his experiment. One of those impressed by Maconochie was Walter Crofton, who in 1854 became director of the renowned Irish system of penal management. Crofton implemented, among many other things, a "ticket of leave" system, allowing inmates to be conditionally released from prison, to be supervised by the police. Crofton recommended a similar system for the United States.

Crofton System

In 1876, when Zebulon Brockway was appointed superintendent of the Elmira Reformatory in New York, he drafted a statute providing for indeterminate sentences. Continued good behavior by inmates resulted in early release—America's first parole system. Paroled inmates remained under the jurisdiction of reformatory authorities for an additional 6 months, during which the parolee was required to report on the first day of every month to his appointed guardian and provide an account of his or her conduct and situation. This system was copied by other states; it was further expanded by the Great Depression, which abolished economic exploitation of convict labor.[15]

Once introduced in the United States, parole spread fairly rapidly. In doing so, it survived an early series of constitutional challenges.[16] A 1939 survey reported that, by 1922, parole existed in 44 states, the federal system, and Hawaii.[17] Mississippi adopted a parole law in 1944, becoming the last state to do so.

Many reasons have been offered for the relatively rapid spread of parole legislation.

- There was general dissatisfaction with the determinate sentencing provisions of the time, and parole was seen as a response to some of the criticisms: Parole would promote reformation of prisoners by providing an incentive to change; at the same time, it would serve as a means of equalizing disparate judicial sentences.[18]

- Release before sentence expiration was already an aspect of most prison systems—through "good time" deductions, which began in New York in 1817, and through gubernatorial clemency, which was used far more extensively than today.

- Parole was believed useful for enforcing prison discipline and for controlling prison population levels.[19]

Parole: early release of a prisoner, who must then comply with certain terms and conditions for a specified period of time.

PROBATION AND PAROLE TODAY

Probation Programs

Revocation

Probation and parole—together termed "community corrections"—is the status of a majority of persons who are under correctional supervision. Today there are about 4.8 million adults under correctional supervision in the community in the United States; about 4 million of these adults are on probation, and the remainder are serving parole.[20] Regarding offenses, about half (53 percent) of the persons on *probation* were convicted for committing a felony; furthermore, about one-fourth of them committed a drug offense, while another one-fourth committed a property offense.[21]

Probation: Eligibility and Rights

Judges consider a number of factors when evaluating the eligibility of an offender for probation:

1. The nature and seriousness of the current offense

2. Whether a weapon was used and the degree of physical or emotional injury, if any, to the victim

3. Whether the victim was an active or a passive participant in the crime

4. The length and seriousness of the offender's prior record

5. The offender's previous success or failure on probation

6. The offender's prior incarcerations and success or failure on parole[22]

Although a decision is made for the offender to remain free and avoid incarceration, the probationer must still abide by certain conditions that the court and probation officers will put in place to govern his or her behavior.

you be the... JUDGE

PROBATION DECISION MAKING FOR CASEY ANTHONY

After a jury acquitted 25-year-old Casey Anthony in July 2011 on charges of first-degree murder, aggravated child abuse, and aggravated manslaughter of her 2-year-old daughter Caylee, the only convictions that remained were for lying to detectives seeking to find out what happened to the child. The task then facing Orlando, Florida, Judge Belvin Perry was to determine whether and how Anthony would serve a term of probation. Complicating Judge Perry's decision was a survey that found Anthony was the most hated person in America—and a high probability that many people would like to do her harm. Anthony's attorneys argued that she had already served her probation while in jail awaiting the murder trial. On the other side, prosecutors maintained that probation should be continued, because the purpose of

probation is to help offenders after they are released back into the community. Meanwhile, Anthony's parents stated that she would not be returning to their home (wishing to avoid media and traffic problems there). Other possibilities included having her serve probation out of state or giving her administrative probation—being able to travel anywhere but contacting her probation officer each month.

1. Should the judge order Casey Anthony to serve probation?

2. If so, where, how, and for what length of time would you recommend it be served?

The judge's decision is provided in the Notes section at the end of the book.[23]

If the probationer does not comply with those conditions, there are two possible types of violations that might be committed:

1. **Technical violations**: These may include failure to pay court costs or fines, missing a probation meeting, use of alcohol, curfew violations, associating with other known criminals, failing to submit to a mandatory drug test, failing a drug test, failing to complete community service, and out-of-state travel or change of address without permission.

2. **Substantive violations**: These occur when the probationer commits a new criminal offense.

Following are several factors that the judge and prosecutor may take into account when considering a probation violation:

- The seriousness and nature of the probation violation
- The history of previous probation violations
- New criminal activity surrounding the probation violation
- Aggravating and mitigating circumstances of the probation violation
- The probation officer and/or probation department's view of the probation violation
- The probation violation with respect to the probation term (whether it occurred at the beginning, middle, or end of the probationary term)

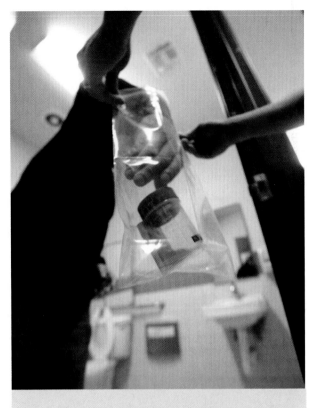

One of the typical conditions placed on a probationer is that he or she submit to mandatory drug tests.

About 30 percent of probationers exit probation supervision each year because they are incarcerated for a new crime, violate a condition of supervision, or abscond, or for some other reason (see Table 14.1).[24] The violation of probation is a serious offense, can be a felony, and can result in a judge revoking probation. As soon as a probation violation occurs, an arrest may soon follow, and the defendant may be ordered to appear in court for a probation violation hearing. If a judge revokes probation, state laws often allow the judge to impose the maximum penalty for the charge.

Mempa v. Rhay

Certain rights have been afforded probationers who are about to undergo a probation **revocation** hearing. First, in *Mempa v. Rhay* (1967),[25] the U.S. Supreme Court held that such hearings are a "critical stage" where substantive rights could be lost, and that the Sixth Amendment therefore required the presence of counsel to help in "marshaling facts." Later, in 1973, the Supreme Court decided *Gagnon v. Scarpelli*,[26] in which a probationer had his probation revoked without a hearing; the court determined that probationers had certain due process rights, including the following:

Gagnon v. Scarpelli

- Notice of the alleged violation
- A preliminary hearing to determine probable cause
- The right to present evidence
- The right to confront adverse witnesses
- A written report of the hearing
- A final revocation hearing

TABLE 14.1

Probationers Who Exited Supervision, by Type of Exit, 2008–2011

TYPE OF EXIT	2008	2009	2010	2011
Total	100%	100%	100%	100%
Completion	63%	65%	65%	66%
Incarceration[a]	17	16	16	16
Absconder	4	3	3	2
Discharged to custody, detainer, or warrant	1	1	1	1
Other unsatisfactory[b]	10	10	11	9
Transferred to another probation agency	1	*	1	1
Death	1	1	1	1
Other[c]	4	4	4	4
Estimated number[d]	2,320,100	2,327,800	2,261,300	2,189,100

Source: Laura M. Maruschak and Erika Parks, "Probationers Who Exited Supervision, by Type of Exit, 2008–2011," *Probation and Parole in the United States, 2011* (Washington, D.C.: Bureau of Justice Statistics U.S. Department of Justice, November 2012), p. 6, http://www.bjs.gov/content/pub/pdf/ppus11.pdf.

Note: Details may not sum to total due to rounding. Distributions are based on probationers for which type of exit was known.

* = Less than 0.5%

[a]Includes probationers who were incarcerated for a new offense for those who had their current probation sentence revoked (e.g., violating a condition of their supervision).

[b]Includes probationers discharged from supervision who did not meet all conditions of supervision, including some with financial conditions remaining, some who had their probation sentence invoked but were not incarcerated because their sentence was immediately reinstated, and another type of unstatisfactory exits. May include some early terminations and expirations of sentence reported as unstatisfactory exits.

[c]Includes probationers discharged from supervision through legislative mandate because they were deported or transferred to the jurisdiction of Immigrations and Customs Enforcement (ICE); transferred to another state through an interstate compact agreement; had their sentence dismissed or turned by the court through an appeal; had their sentence closed administratively, defferd, or terminated by the court; we are awaiting a hearing; we released on bond; and other type of exits.

[d]Estimates rounded to the nearest hundred.Includes estimated for nonreporting agencies.Estimates are based on most recent data available and may differ from published BJS reports.

Parole: Eligibility and Rights

Morrissey v. Brewer

About one-third of all *parolees* were incarcerated for a drug offense and one-fourth had committed a property offense.[27]

Similar to probation decision making, the following general criteria will be taken into account when considering whether or not an inmate should be granted parole:

- The nature and seriousness of the current offense, including aggravating and mitigating circumstances
- Statements made in court concerning the sentence
- The length and seriousness of the offender's prior record
- The inmate's attitude toward the offense, family members, the victim, and authority in general
- The attitude of the victim or victim's family regarding the inmate's release
- The inmate's insight into causes of past criminal conduct
- The inmate's adjustment to previous probation, parole, or incarceration

- The inmate's participation in institutional programs
- The adequacy of the inmate's parole plan, including residence and employment[28]

As with probationers, the parolee must still abide by certain conditions that the court and parole officers will put in place. If the parolee does not comply with those conditions, there are two possible types of violations that might be committed:

 Parolee Rights

1. **Technical violations**: These may include failing to regularly report to the parole officer (PO), not keeping the PO advised of changes in address, not providing notice of change in employment, not reporting any new arrest, associating with other felons, travel in violation of time or distance constraints, possession of weapons, use of alcohol or drugs, improper wearing of electronic monitoring device, and contact with a domestic violence partner.

2. **Substantive violations**: These occur when the parolee commits a new criminal offense.

If either or a combination of these conditions occurs, charges of parole violation may be initiated by a parole officer.

Until 1972, decisions to revoke one's parole and return him to prison could be arbitrarily made by individual parole officers. However, the U.S. Supreme Court, in *Morrissey v. Brewer*,[29] held in that year that parolees who faced the possibility of losing their freedom possessed certain rights under the Fourteenth Amendment:

A condition of one's parole status might be that he or she wear an electronic monitoring device.

- Written notice of the alleged violation(s)
- A preliminary hearing to establish whether there is probable cause that the parolee violated the conditions of his parole
- Disclosure of the evidence against the parolee
- The opportunity to be heard in person and to present witnesses and documentary evidence
- The right to confront and cross-examine adverse witnesses
- A neutral and detached body to hear the evidence
- A written statement by the fact-finders concerning the evidence relied upon for any revocation decision

If the hearing officer (not necessarily a judge) makes a finding that probable cause exists to believe that a violation has occurred, the hearing will move to the adjustment phase, which is where the information is introduced about why the individual should or should not be continued on supervision.

One of the most important groups of individuals that parole board members come in contact with is victims of crime. While at one time victims were not typically involved with the parole process in this country, that has

Technical violation: in probation and parole, where one violates certain conditions that must be obeyed to remain out of prison, such as curfew violation, drug or alcohol use, or not maintaining a job.

Probation Officer
Functions

Author Video: Probation
Officers and Challenges

changed. Through strong victim advocacy, crime victims have begun to be recognized as key stakeholders in the criminal justice process. Today, it is typical that paroling authorities provide victims with information concerning any activity in their offender's case, provide opportunities for input to the board—in person and/or in writing—and take into account the needs and dangers to victims as part of their decision-making procedures. A number of states now appoint victims of crime or victim advocates as members of their paroling authorities.[30]

Figure 14.1 shows the parole decision-making guidelines employed by the Pennsylvania Board of Probation and Parole.

PRACTITIONER'S PERSPECTIVE

PROBATION AND PAROLE OFFICER

Name: Dori Ege

Current Position: Arizona Deputy Compact Administrator for Adult Probation; Arizona Compact Commissioner for Parole and Probation

City, State: Phoenix, Arizona

College attended/ academic major: St. Cloud State University/BA, criminal justice

How long have you been a practitioner in a career relating to probation and parole? 13 years, 3 months

The primary duties and responsibilities of a probation and parole officer are:

To ensure offender compliance of the conditions of supervision imposed by the court or paroling authority through required face-to-face contacts, reports from treatment providers, drug testing, residence searches, and providing or referring the offender to other resources as needed (e.g., employment skills training). In addition, officers must update the court or paroling authority regarding the offender's compliance of the conditions of supervision through official memos, e-mails, or petitions to either modify the term of supervision for compliant behavior or revoke the offender's supervision and return him or her to a custody status. Probation and parole officers are often required to testify at status or official hearings regarding the offender's compliance with conditions and terms. These can range from hearings to determine early termination of supervision or hearings to revoke supervision and return the offender to custody. In many, officers are

also required to update victims who are associated with an offender's case in accordance with local victim notification requirements.

The qualities/characteristics that are most helpful for one in a probation or parole career are, succinctly:

- Resilience
- Integrity
- Confidence
- Reliability
- Excellent writing skills
- Excellent communication skills
- Leadership skills
- Fairness and consistency

In general, a *typical day* for a probation or parole practitioner would include:

Office and field visits with offenders to monitor compliance with conditions imposed by a court or paroling authority; writing reports regarding compliance or noncompliance of conditions; testifying at or attending court hearings regarding assigned offenders; and fielding phone calls and e-mail correspondence from offenders, their families, employers, treatment providers, attorneys, and other members of the criminal justice system regarding cases assigned to the officer's caseload.

My advice to someone either wishing to study, or now studying, criminal justice to become a practitioner in this career field would be:

If you possess a passion for working in the criminal justice system, remember that passion and always remain fair and consistent. Complacency has no place in this field, and it can be detrimental. This is a rewarding field of study and an incredible field for a career for those who want to affect change in others, while also promoting public safety.

FIGURE 14.1

Pennsylvania Board of Probation and Parole, Parole Decision-Making Guidelines

PENNSYLVANIA BOARD
OF PROBATION AND PAROLE

PAROLE DECISION MAKING GUIDELINES

Name _____

Parole No. _____ SID No. _____ Institution No. _____

Date of Interview _____ Institution _____

Interview Type ___ Minimum ___ Review ___ Reparole Review ___ Parole Application

---

Violence Indicator

1. Instant Offense

Violent ☐ +3

Non-Violent ☐ +1

(1) Murder, Voluntary Manslaughter, Aggravated Assault, Robbery, Arson, Burglary (Residential), Assault by Prisoner, Assault by Life Prisoner, Kidnapping, Extortion Accompanied by Threats of Violence, all Sex Crimes, and criminal attempt, criminal conspiracy, and/or criminal solicitation to commit any of the above-noted offenses.

Risk/Needs Assessment

2. Level of Service Inventory - Revised   **Sex Offender Risk Assessment (Static 99)**

Raw Score: _____   Raw Score: _____

High Risk ☐ +3   High Risk ☐ +3

Medium Risk ☐ +2   Medium Risk ☐ +2

Low Risk ☐ +1   Low Risk ☐ +1

(All offenders considered for parole shall be assessed using the Level of Service Inventory - Revised ("LSI-R"). Offenders convicted of a sex offense shall be assessed using the LSI-R as well as the Sex Offender Risk Assessment Instrument. The higher level of risk shall be used for all sex offenders.

Institution Adjustment

3. Institutional Programming

Unacceptable Program Compliance   ☐ +3

Reasonable Efforts (2)   ☐ +2

Currently Involved   ☐ +1

Completion of Required Programs (3)   ☐ +0

(2) No access or on waiting list.

(3) Includes offenders who are currently involved and will complete prior to release

---

(Continued)

FIGURE 14.1

(Continued)

4. Institutional Behavior

Any of the following acts which occurred: while incarcerated on the instant offense; and, within one year of the parole interview date or since the date of last review.

1. Crimes Code Violation - *Criminal charges pending in which probable cause has been established or a conviction has occurred from an offense that was committed while serving sentence currently under consideration for parole; and/or*

☐ +5

2. Drug/alcohol offense - *Determined to be in possession of any controlled substance and/or positive test result of drugs or alcohol; and/or*

3. Assaultive behavior - *Verbal or physical aggression which is documented by the Department of Corrections or the Board of Probation and Parole; and/or*

4. CCC failure - *Return to institution as a result of inappropriate behavior occurring while in prerelease status; and/or*

5. Pattern of institutional misconducts - *Three or more class II, two class II and one class I, or two or more class I misconducts.*

No occurrence within one year of the parole interview date or since date of last review.

☐ +0

Notate cumulative score from first four components _____

Likely to Parole
Unlikely to Parole

☐ 2 to 6
☐ 7 or greater

Source: Peggy B. Burke, *A Handbook for New Parole Board Members* (Washington, D.C.: U.S. Department of Justice, National Institute of Corrections, and Association of Paroling Authorities International, April 2003), pp. 41–42, http://www.apaintl.org/documents/CEPPParoleHandbook.pdf (accessed August 17, 2013).

Note: The Level of Service Inventory—Revised (LSI-R) mentioned in Figure 14.1 includes both criminal history items and measures of offender needs, such as substance abuse, employment, and special needs accommodations. The tool is administered during a standardized, one-hour interview, and it evaluates indicators of program success (e.g., residence, family ties, employment) and predictors of program failure (e.g., prior convictions, prior failures to appear, prior violations of sentence). It includes 54 items, and responses are totaled to give a risk-needs score. Source: Joan Petersilia, *When Prisoners Come Home* (New York: Oxford University Press, 2003), pp. 72–73.

you be the... PAROLE BOARD

PAROLE DECISION MAKING FOR A NOTORIOUS KILLER

Assume you are serving on the state parole board in the following matter: Charles Manson, age 77, is serving a life sentence for a 1969 killing spree in Los Angeles (his "family" brutally murdered seven people). Manson has not been a model inmate, recently possessing a weapon, threatening a peace officer, and being caught twice with contraband cell phones. Given his age, this could be Manson's final appearance before the state parole board. Debra Tate, a victim's sister (murdered actress Sharon Tate), is attending the hearing, and attorneys from both sides are prepared to give presentations, read documents by victims' relatives or other interested parties, and examine Manson's prison records. Manson, as is his custom, is not attending the parole hearing.

- Will you vote to grant or deny Manson's parole at this time?
- If not, do you believe there are programs or redeeming actions or qualities Manson might undertake or possess to secure his freedom in the future?

The outcome of his 2012 parole hearing is provided in the Notes section at the end of the book.[31]

DO PROBATION AND PAROLE WORK?

Do probation and parole work by reducing arrests? An ambitious 2013 study by California's Council of State Governments (CSG) Justice Center attempted to learn the answer, examining more than 2.5 million adult arrest, probation, and parole supervision records from 11 agencies in four cities—Los Angeles, Redlands, Sacramento, and San Francisco—over a 42-month period.[32] The CSG wanted to determine (1) the extent to which people on probation and parole contribute to crime, as measured by arrests, and (2) the types of crimes these people are most likely to commit.[33]

The findings were a bit surprising. First, people under probation or parole supervision accounted for 22 percent of total arrests—which means that nearly 8 of 10 arrestees were not supervised, certainly a respectable finding. However, one in three arrests for *drug* crimes involved someone who was on probation or parole—in fact, people under supervision were more likely to be arrested on drug offenses than for violent, property, or other types of crimes.[34] However, during the study period the number of total arrests declined by 18 percent, while the number of arrests of people who were under supervision declined by *40 percent*—61 percent for persons on parole and 26 percent for individuals under probation supervision.[35] It seems, therefore, that supervision generally works, but that there remains work to do in terms of keeping parolees and probationers from reoffending for drug abuse. Figure 14.2 displays some of the findings.

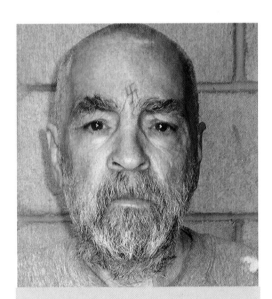

Charles Manson, born in 1934, is serving a life sentence for leading a 1969 killing spree in Los Angeles that ended the lives of seven people. Manson has not been a model inmate. Should he ever be paroled?

FUNCTIONS OF PROBATION AND PAROLE OFFICERS

Both probation and parole officers perform similar functions; in fact, in some states, the jobs of parole and probation officers are combined. Both must possess important skills, such as good interpersonal communication, decision-making, and writing skills. They operate very independently, with

Parole Officers

FIGURE 14.2

Do Probation and Parole Work?

RESEARCH FINDINGS

Approximately one in five arrests involved an individual under probation or parole supervision; the majority of total arrests involved people who were not under supervision.

A key objective of this study was to determine to what extent people under correctional supervision drove arrest activity. To make that determination, researchers matched arrest data with parole and probation supervision data.

Supervision Status among All Adult Arrestees:

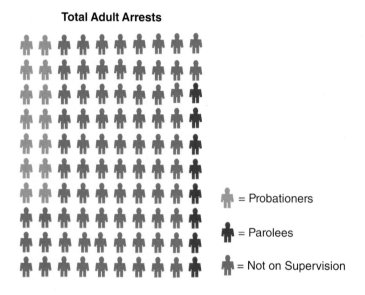

Total Adult Arrests

= Probationers
= Parolees
= Not on Supervision

DESIGNATION	ADULT ARRESTS	% OF TOTAL
Total	**476,054**	**100%**
Paroles	40,476	8.5%
Probationers	66,251	13.9%
Not Supervised	369,327	77.6%

Source: Council of State Governments Justice Center, *The Impact of Probation and Parole Populations on Arrests in Four California Cities* (January 2013), p. 14, http://www.cdcr.ca.gov/Reports/docs/External-Reports/CAL-CHIEFS-REPORT.pdf.

less supervision than most prison staff experience. Both are trained in the techniques for supervising offenders and then assigned a caseload. They may be on call 24 hours a day to supervise and assist offenders at any time.[36]

Following is a breakdown of their duties.

Probation and "Front End" Duties

Probation officers supervise offenders at the *front* end of the sentencing continuum—those offenders with a suspended prison sentence—monitoring their behavior in the community and their compliance with the conditions of their probation. Probation officers usually work with either adults or juveniles exclusively. Only in small, usually rural, jurisdictions do probation officers counsel both adults and juveniles.

Probation officer: one who supervises the activities of persons on probation.

Probation officers have a number of duties, including

- report to the court any violations of probation;

- as officers of the courts, perform presentence investigations and prepare reports concerning the clients on their caseload;

- enforce court orders, such as arresting those who violate the terms of their probation;

- perform searches, seize evidence, and arrange for drug testing;

- attend hearings to update the court on offenders' efforts at rehabilitation and compliance with the terms of their sentences;

- utilize technologies as required, including electronic monitoring devices and drug screening; and

- seek the assistance of community organizations, such as religious institutions, neighborhood groups, and local residents, to monitor the behavior of many offenders.[37]

Probation officers monitor offenders' behavior in order to check their compliance with the conditions of their probation. These probation officers are performing a compliance sweep at a probationer's home.

Probation officers—as well as parole officers—often experience role conflict, which is brought about by what they perceive as a discrepancy between their two main functions: On the one hand, their job is to "enforce" lawful behavior of their clients, and sometimes revoke their probation and parole, which is obviously more law enforcement oriented in nature; on the other hand, they must also be empathetic and understanding, and provide guidance and counseling to their clients, which is more of a social worker role.[38] These seemingly contradictory roles can contribute to job stress.

Training and Education

Parole and "Back End" Duties

Parole officers perform *back*-end duties of the sentencing continuum, supervising offenders who have been released from prison. Parole officers are most often employed by the state department of corrections, the state criminal justice department, or a youth authority/juvenile corrections, county, or federal justice department. Like probation officers, parole officers supervise offenders through personal contact with the offenders and their families; this can be quite dangerous (and lead to role conflict, discussed above), as parole officers work with paroled convicts, their friends, and their family. As with probationers, some parolees are required to wear an electronic device so that probation officers can monitor their location and movements. Parole officers

Mid-Chapter Quiz: Corrections in the Community

- help parolees adjust back into society, as well as avert any actions that would jeopardize their parole status;

- develop a plan for the parolee before he or she is released from prison;

- plan the employment, housing, health care, education, drug screening, and other activities that help the parolee's rehabilitation and function in a community environment;

Parole officer: one who supervises those who are on parole.

- arrange for offenders to get substance abuse rehabilitation or job training; and

- attend parole hearings and make recommendations based on their interviews with and surveillance of parolees.[39]

The Burden of Large Caseloads

Caseload refers to the average number of cases supervised by a probation or parole officer in a given period. Each case represents an offender on probation and parole supervised by an individual officer. As John Conrad observed:

> There is much that a good probation/parole officer can do for the people on his or her caseload. A parole officer who makes it clear that, "fellow, if you don't watch your step I'm gonna run your ass right back to the joint," is not in a position to be helpful as a counselor or facilitator. With the best intentions, a[n] officer struggling with the standard unwieldy caseload of 100 or more will deal with emergencies only, and sometime will not be able to do that very well.[40]

As noted above, today there are about 4.8 million persons either on probation or parole in the United States. Is there a precise number of offenders that can effectively be supervised by an officer? The answer is no, because the number of offenders an officer can effectively supervise is a function of the type of offenders being supervised by certain officers; all offenders and officers are unique and bring different knowledge, skills, capacities, and competencies. The American Probation and Parole Association (APPA) asks the question, rhetorically,

> How many patients can a surgeon operate on in a given day? How many cars can a mechanic fix each week? How many haircuts can a barber complete in a month? It does not take an expert in any of these fields to realize the answer normally is that *it depends*.[41]

Of course, caseload size can affect the quality of supervision that an officer is able to provide—and can also bring the glare of the media when something goes horribly wrong. An example is where a newspaper in Detroit published an exposé titled "Felons on Probation Often Go Unwatched." This county had roughly 30,000 probationers and approximately 250 officers to supervise them—an average of nearly 120 offenders per officer. In one case, an officer was fired after a probationer was arrested for attempted murder and engaging in a shoot-out with police. The probationer was a fugitive, missing several office visits, but he was never reported as an absconder, nor was he listed as a fugitive at the time of the shooting. According to the article, the probation officer "was so overworked that she failed to get an arrest warrant for [the probationer] when he became a fugitive for missing his monthly probation office appointment. [The officer] still hadn't done so by March 28 when he was arrested."[42]

The APPA points out that caseload sizes have long been too large, and for several identifiable reasons:

> For at least the past four decades it has been well-known to professional insiders that probation and parole officer workloads exceed realistic potential for accomplishing the numerous tasks required to supervise offenders. The point here is that many departments are increasing caseloads to well over 200 offenders per officer, making it virtually impossible for offenders to receive adequate attention and

Caseload: the number of cases awaiting disposition by a court, or the number of active cases or clients maintained by a probation or parole officer.

interaction from officers to have any substantial rehabilitative effect. Compounding these issues is the current trend of concentrating on sex-offenders, the infusion of electronic monitoring technologies, and increasing the use of probation for higher-risk offenders as well as widening the justice net to low risk offenders.[43]

To Arm or Not to Arm

Whether probation and parole officers should be armed has also been debated. Traditionalists believe that carrying a firearm contributes to an atmosphere of distrust between the client and the officer; they argue that if officers carry weapons they are perceived differently than as counselors or advisors, whose purpose is to guide offenders into treatment and self-help programs. Conversely, some people view a firearm for these officers as an essential for protecting them from the risks associated with confronting violent, serious, or high-risk offenders.[44] Officers must make visits to the homes and places of employment in the neighborhoods in which offenders live; some of these areas are not safe. Equally or more dangerous is when officers must revoke their parole or probation, which could result in the offender's imprisonment.

 Arming Parole Officers

There is no national or standard policy regarding weapons, and officers themselves are not in agreement about being armed. Some states classify probation and parole officers as peace officers and grant them the authority to carry a firearm both on and off duty.[45] In sum, it would seem the prudent decision concerning arming should be placed on the need, officer safety, and local laws and policies.

OTHER ALTERNATIVES: INTERMEDIATE SANCTIONS

There are additional corrections programs—**intermediate sanctions**—that are less restrictive than total confinement but more restrictive than probation. A survey by the federal Bureau of Justice Statistics found that, of about 63,000 persons being supervised outside a jail facility, about 19 percent were under electronic monitoring, 19 percent were involved in some form of community service, and about 28 percent were undergoing home detention without electronic monitoring.[46] These and other forms of supervision are discussed below.

Intensive Supervision Probation and Parole

Since their beginning, **intensive supervision probation and parole** have been based on the premise that increased client contact would enhance rehabilitation while affording greater client control. Current programs are largely a means of easing the burden of prison overcrowding.[47]

Intensive supervision can be classified into two types: those stressing diversion and those stressing enhancement. A diversion program is commonly known as a "front door" program because its goal is to limit the number of generally low-risk offenders who enter prison. Enhancement programs generally select already sentenced probationers and parolees and subject them to closer supervision in the community than they receive under regular probation or parole.[48]

As of 1990, jurisdictions in all 50 states had instituted *intensive supervision probation* (ISP). Persons placed on ISP are supposed to be those offenders who, in the absence of intensive supervision, would have been sentenced to imprisonment. Although ISP is invariably more costly than regular supervision, the costs "are compared not with the costs of normal supervision but rather with the costs of incarceration."[49]

Intermediate sanction: a form of punishment that is between freedom and prison, such as home confinement and day reporting.

Intensive supervision probation and parole: ISP usually includes much closer and stricter supervision, more contact with offenders, more frequent drug tests, and other such measures.

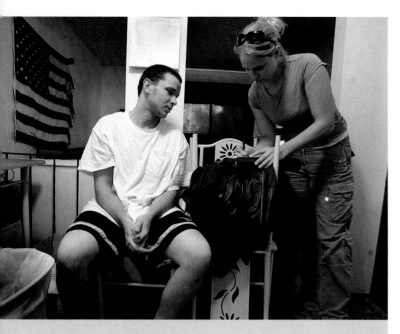

Intensive supervision probation and parole are premised on the idea that increased client contact enhances rehabilitation while affording greater client control.

ISP is demanding for probationers and parolees and does not represent freedom; in fact, it may stress and isolate repeat offenders more than imprisonment does. Given the option of serving prison terms or participating in ISPs, many offenders have chosen prison.[50] Consider the alternatives now facing offenders in one western state:

ISP. The offender serves 2 years under this alternative. During that time, a probation officer visits the offender two or three times per week and phones on the other days. The offender is subject to unannounced searches of his or her home for drugs and has his or her urine tested regularly for alcohol and drugs. The offender must strictly abide by other conditions as set by the court: not carrying a weapon, not socializing with certain persons, performing community service, and being employed or participating in training or education. In addition, he or she will be strongly encouraged to attend counseling and/or other treatment, particularly if he or she is a drug offender.

Prison. The alternative is a sentence of 2 to 4 years of which the offender will serve only about 3 to 6 months. During this term, the offender is not required to work or to participate in any training or treatment but may do so voluntarily. Once released, the offender is placed on a 2-year routine parole supervision and must visit his or her parole officer about once a month.[51]

Although evidence of the effectiveness of this program is lacking, it has been deemed a public relations success.[52] Intensive supervision is usually accomplished by severely reducing caseload size per probation or parole officer, leading to increased contact between officers and clients or their significant others (such as spouse or parents).[53]

House Arrest

House Arrest

Electronic Monitoring

Since the late 1980s, house arrest (also known as home confinement) has become increasingly common. With house arrest, offenders receive a "sentence" of detention in their own homes, and their compliance is often monitored electronically. The primary motivation for using this intermediate sanction is a financial one: the conservation of scarce resources.

Many people apparently feel that house arrest is not effective or punitive enough for offenders. Indeed, one study reported that nearly half (44 percent) of the public feels that house arrest is not very effective or not effective at all.[54]

Does house arrest work? Looking at a sample of 528 adult felony offenders who had been released from house arrest, Jeffery Ulmer[55] found that the sentence combination associated with the least likelihood of rearrest was house arrest/probation. The combinations of house arrest/work release and house arrest/incarceration were also significantly associated with decreased chances of rearrest compared to traditional probation. Furthermore, whenever any other sentence option was paired with house arrest, that sentence combination significantly reduced chances and severity of rearrest.[56] House arrest puts the offender in touch with opportunities and resources for rehabilitative services (substance abuse or sex offender counseling, anger management classes, and so on), which supports the contention that for intermediate sanctions of any type to reduce recidivism, they must include a rehabilitative emphasis.[57]

Electronic Monitoring

Electronic monitoring or supervision can be used for a variety of offenders, but it is particularly useful for high-risk offenders, especially sex offenders for whom use of a global positioning system (GPS) is desirable.[58] And, because it is often used in conjunction with house arrest, it is often employed with offenders convicted of driving under the influence (in fact, Scottsdale, Arizona [population 210,000] recently announced plans to save at least $500,000 in annual jail costs by implementing a house arrest/electronic monitoring program for DUI offenders).[59]

Two basic types of electronic monitoring devices are available: active and passive. Active forms are continuous signaling devices attached to the offender that constantly monitor his or her presence at a particular location. A central computer accepts reports from the receiver–dialer over telephone lines, compares them with the offender's curfew schedule, and alerts corrections officials to unauthorized absences.[60] Simpler systems consist of only two basic components: a transmitter and a portable receiver. The transmitter, which is strapped to the offender's ankle or wrist or worn around the neck, emits a radio signal that travels about one city block. By driving past the offender's residence, his or her place of employment, or wherever he or she is supposed to be, the officer can verify his or her presence with the handheld portable receiver.[61]

The passive type of electronic monitoring involves the use of programmed contact devices that contact the offender periodically to verify his or her presence. One system uses voice verification technology. Another system uses satellite technology; the subject wears an ankle bracelet and carries or wears a portable tracking device about the size of a small lunchbox and weighing 3.5 pounds. A GPS satellite constellation is able to establish an offender's whereabouts within 150 feet of his or her location 24 hours a day.[62]

Shock Probation/Parole

Shock probation/parole is another less costly intermediate alternative to incarceration that is supported by many correctional administrators. This form of corrections combines a brief exposure to incarceration with subsequent release. It allows sentencing judges to reconsider the original sentence to prison and, upon motion, to recall the inmate after a few months in prison and place him or her on probation, under conditions deemed appropriate. The idea is that the "shock" of a short stay in prison will give the offender a taste of institutional life and will make such an indelible impression that he or she will be deterred from future crime and will avoid the negative effects of lengthy confinement.[63]

Boot Camps/Shock Incarceration

Correctional **boot camps,** also called shock incarceration, were first implemented as an intermediate sanction in 1983.[64] Early versions of boot camps placed offenders in a quasi-military program of 3 to 6 months' duration similar to a military basic training program. The goal was to reduce

Electronic monitoring: use of electronic devices (bracelets or anklets) to emit signals when a convicted offender (usually on house arrest) leaves the environment in which he or she is to remain.

Shock probation/parole: a situation where individuals are sentenced to jail or prison for a brief period, to give them a taste or "shock" of incarceration and hopefully turn them into more law-abiding citizens.

Boot camp: a short-term jail or prison program that puts offenders through a rigorous physical and mental regimen designed to instill discipline and respect for authority.

Electronic monitoring systems are particularly useful for high-risk offenders, especially sex offenders for whom use of a global positioning system (GPS) is desirable.

Correctional boot camps, also called shock incarceration, have been used in jails and prisons to place offenders in a quasi-military program to instill discipline and thus reduce recidivism, prison and jail populations, and operating costs.

recidivism, prison and jail populations, and operating costs. Offenders generally served a short institutional sentence and then were put through a rigorous regimen of drills, strenuous workouts, marching, and hard physical labor. To be eligible, inmates generally had to be young, nonviolent offenders.

Unfortunately, early evaluations of boot camps generally found that participants did no better than other offenders without this experience.[65] Only boot camps that were carefully designed, targeted the right offenders, and provided rehabilitative services and aftercare were deemed likely to save the state money and reduce recidivism.[66] As a result of these findings, the number of boot camps declined; by the year 2000, only 51 prison boot camps remained.[67] Boot camps have evolved over time, however, and have added such components as alcohol and drug treatment and social skills training (some even including postrelease electronic monitoring, house arrest, and random urine tests); some boot camps have substituted an emphasis on educational and vocational skills for the military components.[68]

Day Reporting Centers

Boot Camps

Another intermediate sanction that has gained recent popularity among correctional administrators and policy makers is the **day reporting center** (DRC). DRCs are places where offenders report with some frequency (usually once or twice a day), and treatment services (job training and placement, counseling, and education) are usually provided either by the agency running the program or by other human services agencies.[69]

Day Reporting Centers

The purposes of DRCs are to heighten control and surveillance of offenders placed on community supervision, increase offender access to treatment programs, give officials more proportional and certain sanctions, and reduce prison or jail crowding. One study of the effect of day reporting centers on recidivism, however, found no significant reduction in the rate of rearrest.[70]

RESTORATIVE JUSTICE

For some time, many people who have experienced the criminal justice system have grown dissatisfied—specifically, that as participants they feel disconnected; as victims, dissatisfied; and as people working in the system, frustrated. Policy makers are increasingly concerned about the burgeoning cost of justice in the face of this discontent and the high rates of recidivism that exist.

Over the past decades, there has been growing interest in new approaches to justice, which involve the community and focus on the victim. The current system, in which crime is considered an act against the state, works on a premise that largely ignores the victim and the community that is hurt most by crime. Instead, it focuses on punishing offenders without forcing them to face the impact of their crimes.

Restorative justice has been finding a receptive audience, along with its guiding principles:

Day reporting center: a structured corrections program requiring offenders to check in at a community site on a regular basis for supervision, sanctions, and services.

Restorative justice: the view that crime affects the entire community, which must be healed and made whole again through the offender's remorse, community service, restitution to the victim, and other such activities.

1. Crime is an offense against human relationships.

2. Victims and the community are central to justice processes.

3. The first priority of justice processes is to assist victims.

4. The second priority is to restore the community, to the degree possible.

5. The offender has personal responsibility to victims and to the community for crimes committed.

6. The offender will develop improved competency and understanding as a result of the restorative justice experience.[71]

A fundamental precept of restorative justice is as follows:

- Violations create obligations and liabilities.
  - ○ *Offenders' obligations are to make things right as much as possible.*
  - ○ *The community's obligations are to victims and to offenders and for the general welfare of its members.*
  - ○ *The community has a responsibility to support and help victims of crime to meet their needs.*[72]

Restorative justice maintains that crime affects not only the victim but the entire community as well, so it involves meetings between the offender, the victim, and members of the community in order to devise a rehabilitative plan to make them whole again.

The next "Focus On" box shows a model experience of restorative justice in Minnesota.

Chapter Quiz: Corrections in the Community

FOCUS ON THE MINNESOTA RESTORATIVE JUSTICE INITIATIVE

The Minnesota Department of Corrections (DOC) has as its purpose repairing the harm of crime and strengthening communities in all jurisdictions around the state.

The Minnesota initiative has been implemented in numerous schools, law enforcement agencies, community corrections departments, juvenile facilities, adult institutions, and neighborhoods.

In the Schools: Restorative practices are used in response to discipline problems, particularly as an alternative to expulsion. Practices include peer mediation, classroom circles to resolve problems, and family group conferencing—all of which involve face-to-face resolution in which the multiple impacts of the offending behavior are identified and addressed.

In Law Enforcement: The major new restorative practice in law enforcement, piloted by about a dozen police departments in Minnesota, is the use of family group conferencing as a diversion process for juveniles.

In Community Corrections: Community corrections departments and DOC offices have implemented victim-offender meeting programs, family group conferencing, a crime repair crew of supervised offenders, increased emphasis on paying restitution, community panels that meet with offenders, multidisciplinary case management with juveniles and their families, and victim awareness education for staff.

In Prisons: Several adult institutions have begun to apply restorative principles, implementing a victim empathy curriculum for all new inmates entering the facility and encouraging community volunteer involvement in the facility.

Source: Adapted from Kay Pranis, in "The Minnesota Restorative Justice Initiative: A Model Experience," *The Crime Victims Report* (U.S. Department of Justice, National Institute of Justice, May/June 1997), http://www.ojp.usdoj.gov/nij/topics/courts/restorative-justice/perspectives/The%20Minnesota%20Restorative%20Justice%20Initiative:%20A%20Model%20Experience.htm (accessed February 16, 2013).

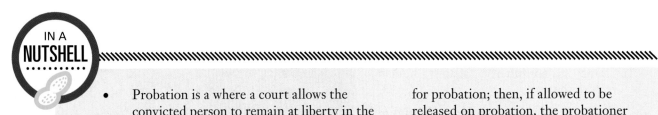

- Probation is a where a court allows the convicted person to remain at liberty in the community while being subject to certain conditions and restrictions on his or her activities; parole is the conditional release of a prisoner before the prisoner's full sentence has been served.

- Alternatives to incarceration—probation and parole—allow the offender to remain in the community, providing a greater rehabilitative effect than incarceration, thereby reducing recidivism; allow the offender to take greater advantage of treatment or counseling options; are less expensive; and permit ongoing ties with family, employment, and other social networks.

- To be effective, an alternative to incarceration must incapacitate offenders enough so that it makes committing a new offense extremely difficult, and be unpleasant enough to deter offenders from wanting to commit new crimes.

- Although contemporary probation has roots dating back to biblical times, its history in the United States dates back to the 19th century. "Judicial reprieve" was used in English courts to serve as a temporary suspension of a sentence to allow the defendant to appeal for a pardon; John Augustus, a Boston shoe cobbler, is credited as being the "father of probation." He bailed people out by permission of the court, serving as the first unpaid, volunteer probation officer.

- The roots of parole reach back to 1840, when Alexander Maconochie became superintendent of the British penal colony on Norfolk Island, near Sydney, Australia. He began a philosophy whereby the convict was to be punished for the past while being trained for the future and advocating open-ended ("indeterminate") sentences. Returning to England in 1844, his writing and speaking of his experiment led to a "ticket of leave" system, allowing inmates to be conditionally released from prison. Later reformers expanded the concept.

- Judges consider a number of factors when evaluating the eligibility of an offender for probation; then, if allowed to be released on probation, the probationer must still abide by certain conditions. A *technical violation* is where, for example, the probationer fails to pay court costs or fines, misses a probation meeting, uses alcohol, or violates curfew. A *substantive* violation is where a new crime is committed by the probationer.

- Because they may lose their freedom if found in violation of the conditions of probation, probationers are allowed to have counsel present at the probation revocation hearing, as well as a notice of the alleged violation, a preliminary hearing to determine probable cause, the right to present evidence and confront adverse witnesses, and other rights.

- Parolees must also abide by certain conditions that the court and parole officers put in place; if not complying, parole may be revoked and the parolee returned to prison. Parolees also have certain rights prior to revocation, such as written notice of the alleged violation(s), a preliminary hearing to establish whether there is probable cause that the parolee violated the conditions of his parole, disclosure of the evidence against the parolee, and the opportunity to be heard in person and to present witnesses.

- Probation officers perform such duties as report to the court any violations of probation, perform presentence investigations, arrest those who violate the terms of their probation, perform searches, seize evidence, and arrange for drug testing.

- Parole officers supervise offenders who have been released from prison through personal contact with the offenders and their families. They help parolees adjust back into society; develop a plan for the parolee before he or she is released from prison; plan the employment, housing, health care, education, drug screening, and other activities that help the parolee's rehabilitation and function in a community environment; arrange for offenders to get substance abuse rehabilitation or job training;

and attend parole hearings and make recommendations based on their interviews and surveillance of parolees.

- Caseload size can affect the quality of supervision that an officer is able to provide—which is a function of the type of offenders being supervised by certain officers; all offenders and officers are unique and bring different knowledge, skills, capacities, and competencies.

- Whether probation and parole officers should be armed has been a debated topic in corrections, and whether having armed corrections personnel will affect whether they can effectively perform traditional—rehabilitative and helpful in orientation—kinds of duties. There is no national or standard policy for these personnel regarding weapons, and officers themselves are not in agreement about being armed.

- Intensive supervision probation/parole can be classified into two types: those stressing diversion and those stressing enhancement. ISP is demanding for probationers and parolees and does not represent freedom; in fact, it may stress and isolate repeat offenders more than imprisonment does.

- With house arrest, offenders receive a "sentence" of detention in their own homes, and their compliance is often monitored electronically.

- Two basic types of electronic monitoring devices are available: active and passive. Active are continuous signaling devices attached to the offender that constantly monitor his or her presence at a particular location. Passive involve the use of programmed contact devices that contact the offender periodically to verify his or her presence.

- Shock probation combines a brief exposure to incarceration with subsequent release. It allows sentencing judges to reconsider the original sentence to prison and, upon motion, to recall the inmate after a few months in prison and place him or her on probation, under conditions.

- Early evaluations of boot camps generally found that participants did no better than other offenders without this experience. Only boot camps that were carefully designed, targeted the right offenders, and provided rehabilitative services and aftercare were deemed likely to save the state money and reduce recidivism.

- Offenders report to day centers frequently (usually once or twice a day), and treatment services (job training and placement, counseling, and education) are usually provided on-site either by the agency running the program or by other human services agencies.

- Restorative justice maintains that crime is an offense against human relationships, that victims and the community are central to justice processes, and that the first priority of justice processes is to assist victims while the second priority is to restore the community; the offender has personal responsibility to victims and to the community for crimes committed.

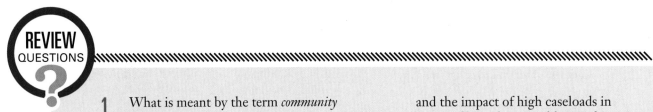

REVIEW QUESTIONS

1. What is meant by the term *community corrections*?

2. What historical events led to modern-day probation? Parole?

3. What are the rights granted by the U.S. Supreme Court to people who are on probation and parole in general? When the state wishes to revoke their probation/parole status and send them to prison?

4. Why does the criminal justice system utilize alternatives to incarceration?

5. How would you describe the primary functions of probation and parole officers, and the impact of high caseloads in terms of how they are able to achieve their goals?

6. How would you describe the arguments for and against arming probation and parole officers?

7. What are the purposes and functions of intermediate sanctions, including intensive supervision, house arrest, electronic monitoring, shock incarceration/boot camps, and day reporting centers?

8. What is restorative justice, and what are the rationales underlying it?

LEARN BY DOING

1. You recently graduated with a criminal justice major and are now employed as a state probation and parole officer; you are asked by a criminal justice professor at a nearby college to guest lecture in an introduction to criminal justice course concerning the primary challenges of working in probation and parole. Develop what would be your presentation for the class.

2. Assume it is your first day working as a state probation and parole officer, and your new training officer says the following:

"Hi, nice to meet you. I'm Chuck, the training advisor. Here's what I tell everyone on their first day. First, the real world is different from what you've been told in college classes. Politicians promise the public that they will get tough on crime, so first off they spend money for more police officers. No one gets elected by promising to build more courts, or add more probation and parole officers. Eventually having more police means the courts get backlogged, which in turn crowds the prisons and the jails, puts more people on probation, and forces the parole board to grant more early releases. Meanwhile, our average caseload increases by 50 percent. We also have more drug and sex offenders than we know what to do with. We spend too much time bailing water out of the boat, with no one steering, so we are just drifting in circles. To vent the frustrations, about once a week the gang and I hold 'choir practice' at a bar down the street. After about five or six beers and some carousing and loud singing, then this job looks a lot better."

a. Should Chuck be retained as a training officer? Why or why not?

b. How would changes in politics affect the corrections system directly and indirectly?

c. Do you believe Chuck's comments are accurate concerning the police getting so much new funding—and the subsequent impacts on courts and corrections?

d. Why do crowded jails and prisons make the job of parole officers more difficult?

e. If you were Chuck's supervisor and heard others discussing their frequent "choir practices" at the bar, would you attempt to discontinue such gatherings or leave the situation alone?

3. Your criminal justice instructor has assigned a class debate concerning the use of incarceration versus alternatives to incarceration (e.g., intensive probation and parole, house arrest, shock probation). What will be your argument?

PART V

SPANNING THE SYSTEM: METHODS AND ISSUES

This part is composed of two chapters. **Chapter 15** examines juvenile justice—an area where the legal and criminal justice processes are quite different from those of adults. Included are the history and extent of juvenile crime, the case flow of juvenile courts, and juvenile rights.

Chapter 16 provides an in-depth view of three selected problems that—because of their nature and/or extent—plague society and pose serious questions for the future concerning criminal justice policy and practices.

JUVENILE JUSTICE:
Philosophy, Law, and Practices

LEARNING OBJECTIVES

As a result of reading this chapter, the student will be able to:

1 Describe the early treatment of juveniles and history of our juvenile justice system, which includes the houses of refuge, reformatories, and Illinois's creating the first juvenile court

2 Review which kinds of behaviors by juveniles constitute status offenses

3 Discuss the extent of, and theories underlying, juvenile criminality

4 Explain the unique philosophy, principles, and goals underlying the treatment of youthful offenders by the juvenile court system

5 Review the process and flow of cases through the juvenile justice system

6 Relate when and why a juvenile offender may be transferred to the jurisdiction of an adult criminal court

7 Delineate the due process and other major rights of juveniles as set forth by the U.S. Supreme Court

CHAPTER

15

There are three ways of trying to win the young. You can preach at them, that is a hook without a worm. You can say, "You must volunteer," that is the devil; and you can tell them, "You are needed." That appeal hardly ever fails.

—Kurt Hahn

INTRODUCTION

Author Introduction:
Chapter 15

What rights does one possess as a juvenile? What are the differences in law and criminal justice treatment of juveniles? These are important questions, because as an old adage states, crime is primarily a "young person's game." Indeed, of about 9.5 million persons arrested in a recent year in the United States, about 1.1 million (or about 12 percent) of them were under age 18; furthermore, persons under age 18 represent about 13 percent of all persons arrested for violent crimes (see Table 15.1).[1]

As indicated in Chapter 1, the criminal justice system's philosophy toward juveniles is very different from its philosophy toward adults. Consequently, police officers and others whose occupations put them in frequent contact with juvenile offenders must know and apply a different standard of treatment in these situations. The philosophical approach toward juvenile offenders overall is that *society*—through poor parenting, poverty, environment, and so forth—is primarily responsible for their criminal behavior.

As will also be emphasized in this chapter, the juvenile justice system seeks to protect the child—to rehabilitate, not punish; therefore, the juvenile justice process is generally amiable, not adversarial. However, many of today's juvenile offenders are also quite violent. At such times, this protective shroud extended by the juvenile justice process can disappear—when a juvenile commits an act that is so heinous and violent that the juvenile court philosophy is not tenable in the matter; as we shall see, in such cases the youthful offender may be transferred to the jurisdiction of the adult court to be processed as an adult.

This chapter begins with a discussion of the origins of juvenile justice, beginning with the houses of refuge and on to the creation of the juvenile court.

ASSESS YOUR AWARENESS:

Test your knowledge of juvenile rights and the justice system by first reading and responding to the following seven true-false items; check your answers after reading this chapter's materials.

1. The prevailing philosophy toward all juveniles is that there should be as much involvement as possible by the state, through the juvenile justice system.

2. The overall juvenile justice philosophy, process, and terminology are essentially the same as those of adult offenders.

3. A juvenile who commits a heinous crime and is thus not felt to be suited to the philosophy of the juvenile court may be transferred to the jurisdiction of an adult court.

4. Procedural safeguards in the juvenile court system include the right to counsel, the right to confront and cross-examine witnesses, and the privilege against self-incrimination.

5. Juvenile offenders who are under the age of 18 when committing a murder may be executed.

6. Juveniles being questioned by police while in custody do not have to have the *Miranda* warning read to them.

7. Juveniles may be sentenced to life without parole.

Answers can be found on page 401.

Next is a profile of the nature and speculative causes of juvenile crime, followed by a look at the unique philosophy, principles, and goals that underlie today's juvenile justice system. Following is a review of the general flow of juvenile cases through the juvenile justice process, and then is an examination of the major U.S. Supreme Court decisions granting juveniles legal rights. The chapter concludes with a summary, key terms and concepts, review questions, and several scenarios and activities that provide opportunities for you to "learn by doing."

HISTORY OF JUVENILE JUSTICE

Reformatories

As indicated above, the United States' juvenile justice system has a rich and, at times, painful history. Next is a brief discussion of the early treatment of juveniles, and how this system developed from one that was very harsh and dangerous to that of today, which is much more protective and rehabilitative in philosophy and practice.

Early Treatment: Houses of Refuge, Reformatories

In the early part of the 19th century, to the chagrin of prosecutors and many citizens, many juries were acquitting children who were charged with crimes—not wishing to see children incarcerated with adults in ramshackle facilities. Quakers in New York City sought to establish a balance between those two camps—people wanting to see justice done with child offenders, and those not wanting them to be incarcerated— and founded the first **house of refuge** in 1825 to "receive and take . . . all such children as shall be taken up or committed as vagrants, or convicted of criminal offenses." The children worked an 8-hour day at various trades in addition to attending school for another 4 hours. Many of them had not committed any criminal act, and a number were probably status offenders.[2]

At about the middle of the 19th century, the house of refuge movement evolved into the slightly more punitive reform school, or **reformatory**, approach,[3] to segregate young offenders from adult criminals; imprison the young and remove them from adverse home environments until the youth was reformed; help youth avoid idleness through military drills, physical exercise, and supervision; focus on education— preferably vocational and religious; and teach sobriety, thrift, industry, and prudence.

Later in the 19th century, an occasional legal attack on the incarceration of children in such youth prisons was successful. In an 1870 case, the Illinois Supreme Court held it unconstitutional to confine in a Chicago reform school a youth who had not been convicted of criminal conduct or afforded legal due process.[4] It was against this backdrop in the last quarter of the 19th century that the juvenile court movement began.

A Movement Begins: Illinois Legislation

In 1899, the Illinois legislature enacted the **Illinois Juvenile Court Act**,[5] creating the first

Houses of refuge: workhouses established in the early 1800s as a means of separating juvenile offenders from adult offenders.

Reformatory: a detention facility designed to reform individuals— historically juveniles.

Quakers in New York City founded the House of Refuge in 1825 to provide an alternative to children being housed with adult offenders. This picture depicts some of the work- and school-related daily activities at the House.

An 8-year-old boy charged with stealing a bicycle appears in juvenile court in 1910.

separate **juvenile court**. At that time in the United States, juveniles were tried along with adults in criminal courts and sometimes sentenced to prison and occasionally to death. Prior to 1900, at least 10 children were executed in the United States for crimes committed before their 14th birthdays.[6]

Other children died in adult prisons. Virginia penitentiary records from 1876 reflect that a 10-year-old prisoner died from being scalded accidentally in a tub of boiling coffee. These deaths shocked the public conscience. Accordingly, Americans in the 19th century sought more pervasive reform than the infancy defense to address the distinctive nature of children and youth.[7]

While the Illinois act did not fundamentally change procedures in the existing courts that now were sitting as juvenile courts to adjudicate cases involving children, it did emphasize the *parens patriae* philosophy (discussed below) to govern such cases. In addition to giving the courts jurisdiction over children charged with crimes, the act gave them jurisdiction over a variety of behaviors and conditions, including

any child who for any reason is destitute or homeless or abandoned; or dependent on the public for support; or has not proper parental care or guardianship; or who habitually begs or receives alms; or who is living in any house of ill fame or with any vicious or disreputable person; or whose home, by reason of neglect, cruelty or depravity on the part of its parents, guardian or other person in whose care it may be, is an unfit place for such a child; and any child under the age of 8 who is found peddling or selling any article or singing or playing a musical instrument upon the street or giving any public entertainment.[8]

Author Video: Juvenile Offenders

The act was unique in that it created a special court for neglected, dependent, or delinquent children under age 16; defined a rehabilitative rather than punishment purpose for that court; established the confidentiality of juveniles' court records to minimize stigma; required that juveniles be separated from adults when placed in the same institution in addition to barring altogether the detention of children under age 12 in jails; and provided for the informality of procedures within the court.[9]

In its initial year, the Chicago judge presiding over the first juvenile court, the Honorable Richard S. Tuthill, sent 37 boys to the grand jury for adult handling, deeming them unsuitable for the juvenile court's treatment orientation. His successor, Judge Julian Mack, described the court's goals as follows:

Illinois Juvenile Court Act (1899): legislation that established the first juvenile court in the United States.

Juvenile court: a court that has original jurisdiction to hear juvenile crime matters.

The child who must be brought into court should, of course, be made to know that he is face to face with the power of the state, but he should at the same time, and more emphatically, be made to feel that he is the object of its care and solicitude. The ordinary trappings of the courtroom are out of place in such hearings. The judge on a bench, looking down upon the boy standing at the bar, can never evoke a proper sympathetic spirit. Seated at a desk, with the child at his side, where he can on occasion put his arm around his shoulder and draw the lad to him, the judge, while losing none of his judicial dignity, will gain immensely in the effectiveness of his work.[10]

Status Offenses

The post–World War II period witnessed further development, as the **status offense** became a separate category. New York created a new jurisdictional category for persons in need of supervision (**PINS**): runaways, truants, and other youth who committed acts that would not be criminal if committed by an adult. Other states followed New York's lead. Then came the enactment of the very powerful and far-reaching Juvenile Justice and Delinquency Prevention Act of 1974,[11] which

Status Offenses

- removed status offenders from secure detention and correctional facilities; and more significantly, perhaps,

- prevented the placement of any juveniles in any institutions where they would have regular contact with adults convicted of criminal charges.

JUVENILE OFFENDING TODAY

Although the total number of arrests of persons under age 18 has decreased somewhat in recent years, this nation still should not take solace in that fact: As indicated above there are still more than 1 million such arrests each year; furthermore, as seen in Table 15.1, nearly 2.5 million people under age 21 are arrested each year—representing about one-fourth of all arrests for violent crimes and about 37 percent of all property crimes. Also consider the following, from the federal Office of Juvenile Justice and Delinquency Prevention (OJJDP):

Juvenile Offending

- Juveniles were involved in 1 in 10 arrests for murder; about 1 in 4 arrests for robbery, burglary, larceny-theft, and disorderly conduct; and about 1 in 5 arrests for larceny-theft and motor vehicle theft. Substantially above the juvenile proportion of arrests in other violent offenses are forcible rape (14 percent), aggravated assault (11 percent), and murder (9 percent).

- Overall from 1980 to 2010, the drug abuse violation arrest rates for youth ages 15–17 increased 44 percent.[12]

Many theories have been offered by experts to explain juvenile crime; however, no single theory has been universally accepted. However, experts agree that there is a correlation between juvenile crime and the following:

- *Family dysfunction*: Family background is one of the most potent influences on juvenile development. Dysfunctional families transfer dysfunctional norms to their children. Juveniles who live in unstable homes and social environments are deemed to be *at-risk* children because of their vulnerability to detrimental influences. Such environments can contribute to antisocial behavior in children, often resulting in criminally deviant behavior later in life.

- *Drug use and deviance*: Alcohol and tobacco are the drugs of choice for many juveniles.

Status offense: a crime committed by a juvenile that would not be a crime if committed by an adult; examples would be purchasing alcohol and tobacco products, truancy, and violating curfew.

PINS (person in need of supervision): usually a juvenile thought to be on the verge of becoming a delinquent.

TABLE 15.1

Arrests: Persons Under 15, 18, 21, and 25 Years of Age, 2011

OFFENSE CHARGED	TOTAL ALL AGES	NUMBER OF PERSONS ARRESTED				PERCENT OF TOTAL ALL AGES			
		UNDER 15	UNDER 18	UNDER 21	UNDER 25	UNDER 15	UNDER 18	UNDER 21	UNDER 25
TOTAL	9,537,673	307,864	1,129,456	2,446,645	3,921,051	3.2	11.8	25.7	41.1
Murder and non-negligent manslaughter	8,359	72	651	2,171	3,836	0.9	7.8	26.0	45.9
Forcible rape	14,679	736	2,071	4,005	6,053	5.0	14.1	27.3	41.2
Robbery	82,557	3,417	18,377	37,072	51,578	4.1	22.3	44.9	62.5
Aggravated assault	305,939	10,036	31,265	63,392	109,962	3.3	10.2	20.7	35.9
Burglary	228,401	12,962	47,654	90,957	126,592	5.7	20.9	39.8	55.4
Larceny-theft	981,116	55,599	197,159	355,872	491,894	5.7	20.1	36.3	50.1
Motor vehicle theft	51,027	2,150	10,786	19,088	26,541	4.2	21.1	37.4	52.0
Arson	8,994	2,117	3,714	4,763	5,570	23.5	41.3	53.0	61.9
Violent crime	411,534	14,261	52,364	106,640	171,429	3.5	12.7	25.9	41.7
Property crime	1,269,538	72,828	259,313	470,680	650,597	5.7	20.4	37.1	51.2
Other assaults	955,620	55,684	145,424	237,597	374,182	5.8	15.2	24.9	39.2

Source: Federal Bureau of Investigation, "Table 41," *Crime in the United States 2011*, http://www.fbi.gov/about-us/cjis/ucr/crime-in-the-u.s/2011/crime-in-the-u.s.-2011/tables/table-41.

- *Socioeconomic class.* Children from poor and working-class backgrounds are much more likely to engage in delinquent behavior. Studies of the inner-city underclass have found that large numbers of the urban poor are caught in a chronic generational cycle of poverty, low educational achievement, teenage parenthood, unemployment, and welfare dependence.

- *Educational experiences.* Academic achievement is considered to be one of the principal stepping-stones toward success in American society. Ideally, opportunities for education, mentoring, and encouragement to excel would be equally available for all children. Unfortunately, that is not the situation. Socioeconomic and demographic factors can also have an impact on educational opportunities and performance so that poor children often experience a very different educational environment in comparison to middle-class children, such as in inner-city, underclass environments, where educational achievement is frequently not commonly encouraged—or achieved.[13]

UNIQUE PHILOSOPHY, PRINCIPLES, AND GOALS

This chapter section examines the general philosophy underpinnings of the juvenile justice system as well as a number of contrasts (in both terminology and court proceedings) between these and the adult criminal courts.

Parens Patriae and *In Loco Parentis*

The prevailing doctrine or philosophy guiding our treatment of juveniles is ***parens patriae***, meaning that the "state is the ultimate parent" of the child. In effect, this means that as long as we as parents adequately care for and provide at least the basic amenities for our children as required under the law, they are ours

Parens patriae: a doctrine in which the state is the ultimate parent of the child (and will step in to provide and care for the child if parents neglect those duties).

to keep. But when our children are physically or emotionally neglected or abused, the juvenile court and police may intervene and remove the children from that environment. Then the doctrine of *in loco parentis* takes hold, meaning that the state will act in place of the parent.

For police and other criminal justice personnel, there is probably no greater or more awe-inspiring duty than having to testify under subpoena in juvenile court that a woman is an unfit mother (and that her parental ties should be legally severed). However, when a parent or guardian's actions indicate a pattern of neglect and/or abuse toward a child(ren), it is clearly better that the state assume responsibility for the child(ren)'s care and custody.

Table 15.2 shows the **idealistic contrast** between the juvenile court process and adults' criminal procedure. Note that this is the *ideal* process for juveniles, in keeping with the more nurturing and forgiving juvenile justice philosophy; however, that can easily go away when a juvenile commits a crime(s) that is so heinous that he or she is deemed to not be amenable to the more lenient philosophy and jurisdiction of the juvenile courts, and will thus be remanded to the custody of the appropriate adult court. Also note that much of the difference between the philosophies of juvenile and adult courts is found in the terminology used.

Underlying Principles of the Juvenile Court

Most states' juvenile court acts contain three underlying principles[14]:

1. The presumption of innocence

2. The presumption of the least amount of involvement with the system

3. The presumption of the best interest of the minor

The decision maker—whether the police deciding to take a minor into custody, an intake worker deciding to detain a child, or a juvenile court judge presiding at a hearing—must apply these three principles unless evidence exists to the contrary. The amount of evidence may vary depending on the decision maker; for example, although police or detention intake may hold a minor if reasonable or probable cause exists to believe that the minor has committed an offense, a judge must be satisfied beyond a reasonable doubt that an offense has been committed.

Children from poor, disadvantaged backgrounds are much more likely to engage in delinquent behavior.

● ● **TABLE 15.2**

The Idealistic Contrast Between Juvenile and Adult Criminal Justice Processes

ADULT	JUVENILE
Adversarial procedure	Relatively amiable procedure
Individual responsibility for crime	Societal/family factors involved
Punishment is typically the goal	Rehabilitation is the goal
Arrest process	Petition
Trial—public	Hearing—private
Guilt or innocence	Guilt not the sole issue
Public record	Confidential record
Verdict	Decision
Sentence	Disposition

Female Juvenile
Offenders

In loco parentis: a doctrine in
which the state will act in place
of the parents if they fail in their
duties to protect and provide for
the child.

Idealistic contrast: the
differences between juvenile and
adult criminal justice processes,
to include treatment and
terminology.

Presumption of innocence:
the premise that a defendant is
assumed to be innocent until
guilt is established beyond a
reasonable doubt.

Presumption of Innocence

The **presumption of innocence** is one of the hallmarks of our criminal
justice system. It places the burden on the state to prove that the accused
has committed an offense. The state cannot force accused persons to testify
against themselves, cannot use illegally seized evidence, and must use a process consistent with due process standards to establish guilt.

Least Involvement With the System

The principle of least involvement assumes that minors, like adults, have liberty interests that include the right to be left alone or the right to live in a
family situation without state interference. The state has the burden of showing that intervention is necessary for the protection of either the minor or
society. Diversion should be considered before a formal petition is filed and
probation before commitment to an institution. In the detention situation,
many codes require that a child not be held unless a probable cause exists to
believe that a minor has committed a crime and an immediate and urgent
necessity exists to admit the child. Detention is discussed more below.

Best Interest of the Child

The primary purpose of juvenile justice is to operate in the best interest of the
child; this interest must be balanced against the interests of society. Society
benefits by programs that help minors mature into law-abiding citizens, and
children benefit by being held accountable and developing responsibility.

Goals of the Juvenile Justice System

The three primary goals of the juvenile justice system are as follows:

1. *Separation from adults.* This is clearly the most important goal of the
juvenile justice system. Reformers argued that children and families needed
(a) a different form of justice, (b) separate courtrooms, (c) separate detention centers and institutions to avoid corruption
of juveniles by adult criminals, and (d) separate
sentencing guidelines to avoid the harsh penalties of adult sentencing. Furthermore, there is a
separate group of professionals, judges, probation officers, and detention staff with specialized training who are dedicated to working with
youth and their families.

2. *Youth confidentiality.* Confidentiality of
court proceedings and services for youth rein-
forces the belief that youth will mature beyond
a criminal lifestyle if given proper guidance and
alternatives. Because of their immaturity, youth
lack sound judgment and should not be held
fully accountable. Consequently, no criminal
record should hinder adult advancement. From a
developmental standpoint, confidentiality minimizes stigma and labeling, thereby reducing the
likelihood that the young person will perceive
himself as a criminal and maintaining a positive
self-image.

3. *Community-based corrections.* Reformers
strongly believed that young people should learn

Society benefits by programs that help young offenders mature into
law-abiding citizens, be held accountable, and develop responsibility.
These youths are attending a juvenile corrections math class.

and grow in their own communities. Offering probation as a method for monitoring youth behavior in the community, while providing services that allow the youth to grow to adulthood, is seen as the primary dispositional alternative.

4. *Individualized justice of minors.* Finally, each case is to be viewed separately. A social history that explores the total social circumstances of the youth and his or her family, and a casework plan that encourages appropriate development and reduced future criminality, is developed. Probation staff members are to look into the social situation early in the process and be involved in the decision to file a case. Whenever possible, the case is not formally filed, and an informal outcome is encouraged.[15]

Juvenile Detention Centers

Individualized Justice

CASE FLOW OF THE JUVENILE JUSTICE PROCESS

Next is a description of the youthful offender's flow through the juvenile justice process, using as a guide the diagram shown in Figure 15.1.[16]

Note that each state's processing of law violators is unique, depending on local practice and tradition; therefore, any description of juvenile justice processing must be general, outlining a common series of decision points.

Mid-Chapter Quiz: Juvenile Justice

1. Law enforcement diverts many juvenile offenders out of the justice system:

Young law violators generally enter the juvenile justice system through police contacts, but school officials, social services agencies, neighbors, and even parents provide information about a juvenile's crime that commences the process. At arrest, a decision is made either to send the matter further into the justice system or to divert the case out of the system, often into alternative programs. Usually the police make this decision after talking to the victim, the juvenile, and the parents, and after reviewing the juvenile's prior contacts

you be the... PROSECUTOR

SHOULD JUVENILES BE TRIED AS ADULTS?

Should juveniles be prosecuted as adults? A number of states have said yes, responding to public perceptions that violent juvenile crime is a growing menace by making it easier to transfer juveniles from the relatively "protective shroud" of juvenile court to the jurisdiction of adult courts, thus trying juveniles as adults (also known as "certification" or "waiver"). States are also lowering the age and increasing the list of crimes for which juveniles can be transferred. Today, at least 24 states have laws sending violent juveniles to adult courts. Concerns regarding due process include the worry that this

approach carries the possibility of juveniles being incarcerated with adult offenders and possibly being raped or assaulted by the older inmates. Advocates of restorative justice emphasize that juveniles are the prime example of where efforts at reconciliation are likely to yield more positive results than punitive measures.

Source: Adapted from R. E. Redding and J. C. Howell, "Blended Sentencing in American Juvenile Courts," *The Changing Borders of Juvenile Justice: Waiver of Adolescents to the Criminal Court,* eds. J. Fagan and F. E. Zimring (Chicago: University of Chicago Press, 2002), pp. 145–180; also see David Neubauer, *America's Courts and the Criminal Justice System,* 9th ed. (Belmont, Calif.: Thomson Wadsworth, 2010), pp. 449–453.

FIGURE 15.1

Case Flow Diagram of the Juvenile Justice Process

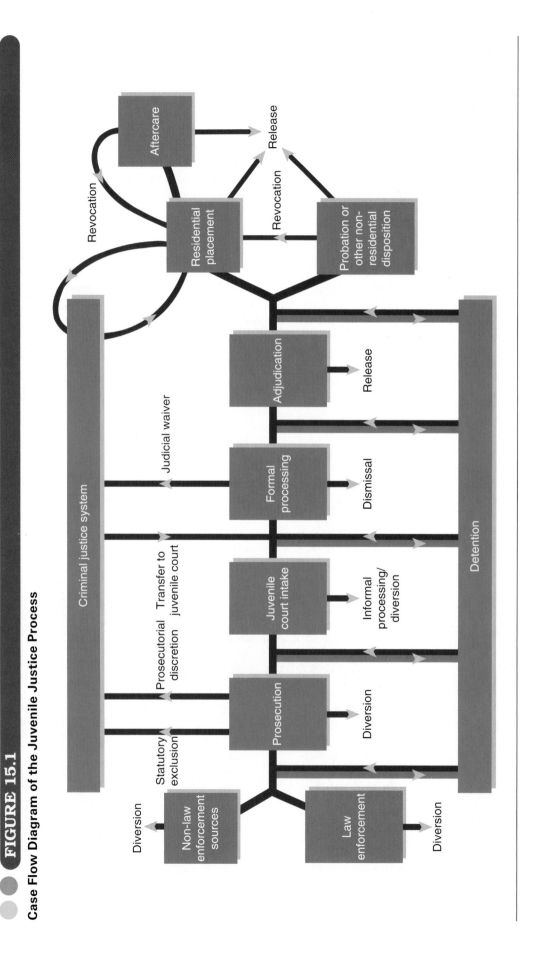

with the juvenile justice system. Examples of alternative programs include drug treatment, individual or group counseling, or referral to educational and recreational programs.

2. A non–law enforcement agency may divert juvenile offenders out of the justice system:

The court intake function is generally the responsibility of the juvenile probation department and/or the prosecutor's office. At this point intake must decide to either dismiss the case, handle the matter informally, or request formal intervention by the juvenile court. To make this decision, an intake officer first reviews the facts of the case to determine if there is sufficient evidence to prove the allegation. If there is not, the case is dismissed. If there is sufficient evidence, intake will then determine if formal intervention is necessary. About half of all cases referred to juvenile court intake are handled informally. Most informally processed cases are dismissed. In the other informally processed cases, the juvenile voluntarily agrees to specific conditions for a specific time period. Conditions may include victim restitution, school attendance, drug counseling, or a curfew. If the juvenile successfully complies with the informal disposition, the case is dismissed. If, however, the juvenile fails to meet the conditions, the intake decision may be to formally prosecute the case.

Adjudication

3. During the processing of a case, a juvenile may be held in a secure detention facility:

Juvenile courts may hold delinquents in a secure detention facility if the court believes it is in the best interest of the community or the child. After arrest a youth is often brought to the local juvenile detention facility by the police. Juvenile probation officers or detention workers review the case and decide if the juvenile should be held pending a hearing by a judge. In all states, a detention hearing must be held within a time period defined by statute, generally within 24 hours. At the detention hearing a judge reviews the case and determines if continued detention is warranted. As a result of the detention hearing the youth may be released or detention continued. Detention may extend beyond further hearings.

4. Filing cases in either juvenile or criminal court:

In many states, the legislature excludes certain (usually serious) offenses from the jurisdiction of the juvenile court regardless of the age of the accused. In other states and at the federal level under certain circumstances, prosecutors have the discretion to either file criminal charges against juveniles directly in criminal courts or proceed through the juvenile justice process. The juvenile court's intake department or the prosecutor may petition the juvenile court to transfer jurisdiction to criminal court. The juvenile court also may order referral to criminal court for trial as adults. In some jurisdictions, juveniles processed as adults may upon conviction be sentenced to either an adult or a juvenile facility.

Case Disposition

5. A **disposition** is reached in the case:

At the disposition hearing, recommendations are presented to the judge. The prosecutor and the youth (usually through his or her *guardian ad litem*) may also present dispositional recommendations. After considering options presented, the judge orders a disposition in the case. Most juvenile dispositions are multifaceted. In disposing of cases, juvenile courts usually have

Disposition: an outcome of a criminal or juvenile court process signifying that the matter is completed.

Residential commitment may provide juveniles with either a secure prison-like environment or a more open, even home-like setting. This teen lives in a small, home-like setting that stresses group therapy and personal development over isolation and punishment.

Court Decisions

far more discretion than adult courts. In addition to such options as probation, commitment to a residential facility, restitution, and fines, state laws grant juvenile courts the power to order removal of children from their homes to foster homes or treatment facilities. Juvenile courts also may order participation in special programs aimed at shoplifting prevention, drug counseling, or driver education. Once a juvenile is under juvenile court disposition, the court may retain jurisdiction until the juvenile legally becomes an adult (at age 21 in most states). In some jurisdictions, juvenile offenders may be classified as youthful offenders, which can lead to extended sentences.

6. The judge may order the juvenile committed to a residential placement:

Residential commitment may be for a specific or indeterminate ordered time period. The facility may be publicly or privately operated and may have a secure prison-like environment or a more open, even home-like setting. In many states, when the judge commits a juvenile to the state department of juvenile corrections, the department determines where the juvenile will be placed and when the juvenile will be released. In other instances the judge controls the type and length of stay. In these situations review hearings are held to assess the progress of the juvenile.

7. Juvenile aftercare, similar to adult parole:

Following release from an institution, the juvenile is often ordered to a period of aftercare or parole. During this period the juvenile is under

FOCUS ON JUVENILE DETENTION ALTERNATIVES INITIATIVE (JDAI)

A very ambitious national strategy now at nearly 200 sites in 39 states and the District of Columbia is the Juvenile Detention Alternatives Initiative (JDAI), which was designed to support the vision that all youth involved in the juvenile justice system have opportunities to develop into healthy, productive adults. JDAI believes juveniles are often unnecessarily or inappropriately detained, and at great expense, with long-lasting negative consequences for both public safety and youth development. JDAI promotes changes to policies, practices, and programs to reduce reliance on secure confinement; improve public safety; reduce racial disparities and bias; save taxpayers' dollars (and avoid having to build new juvenile facilities); and stimulate overall juvenile

justice reforms. One of its hallmarks is that it relies on objective data on detention population, utilization, and operations to provide a portrait of who is being detained and why, and to monitor the impacts of its policies and practices.[17]

In addition to drastically reducing the number of juveniles in detention, JDAI has tremendous cost benefits: The price of detaining a young person can range from $32,000 to $65,000 annually; and including construction, finance, and operating costs, a single detention bed can cost $1.5 million over a 20-year period. JDAI cuts these costs by safely reducing detention populations, allowing states to completely close detention units, and avoiding the expense of new construction.[18]

supervision of the court or the juvenile corrections department. If the juvenile does not follow the conditions of aftercare, he or she may be recommitted to the same facility or to another facility.[19]

SIGNIFICANT COURT DECISIONS

Between 1960 and 1970, several important decisions by the U.S. Supreme Court addressed and expanded the legal rights of juveniles; then, from 2010 to 2012, there was another such spate of decisions; these cases are discussed next.

Kent v. United States

Right to Counsel

Kent v. United States (1966)[20] involved a 16-year-old boy who was arrested in the District of Columbia for robbery, rape, and burglary. The juvenile court, without conducting a formal hearing, transferred the matter to a criminal court, and Kent was tried and convicted as an adult. Kent appealed, arguing that the **transfer** (known as **remand**) to adult court without a hearing violated his right to due process. The Supreme Court agreed, and also decided that there must be a meaningful right to representation by counsel—who must be given access to the documents being considered by the juvenile court in making its decision—and that the court must also provide reasons for transfer.[21]

In Re Winship

The Centerpiece: *In Re Gault*

Gerald Gault, age 15, was accused of making an obscene call to a neighbor. The police picked up Gerald and took him to the juvenile detention center while his parents were at work. His parents were told later that a hearing would be held the next day, but the charges against Gerald were not explained. The complaining neighbor did not show up at the hearing; rather,

Death Penalty

Transfer (remand): the movement or assigning of a juvenile offender to an adult court, because his behavior is such that he is not amenable to the juvenile court's rehabilitative philosophy.

a police officer testified to what the neighbor had said. Gerald, who had no attorney present, denied making the obscene calls. No record was made of the court testimony, and there was no jury present; only a judge heard the case, who declared Gault to be a delinquent and ordered him to be sent to a state reform school—until he was released or turned 21 years old,[22] whichever came first. Ultimately Gault filed a *writ of habeas corpus* (discussed in Chapter 9), claiming that he had been denied due process rights at his hearing; this writ was denied, and state courts offered him no relief; the case was eventually taken up by the U.S. Supreme Court.[23] The Court noted the historically different treatment of juveniles, including their often being committed to an institution for several years, where "his world is peopled by guards, custodians, state employees, and 'delinquents' confined with him for anything from waywardness to rape and homicide." Finding that the Fourteenth Amendment is not "for adults alone,"[24] the Court held that juveniles were entitled to the same basic procedural safeguards afforded therein, including advance notice of charges; right to counsel and to confront and cross-examine witnesses; and the privilege against self-incrimination.

The U.S. Supreme Court has decided that juveniles have the right to be represented by counsel as well as several other procedural rights prior to and during their involvement with the juvenile justice process.

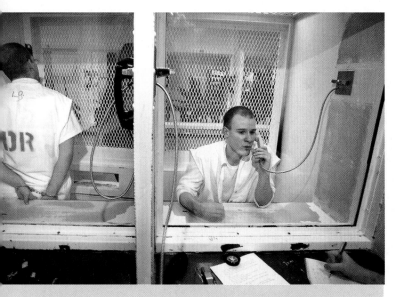

The U.S. Supreme Court has held that the Constitution forbids the execution of offenders who were under the age of 18 when their crimes were committed. Leo Little, being age 17 when sentenced to death, was removed from death row following the Court's decision.

Burden of Proof Standard

In 1970, *In re Winship* involved a 12-year-old boy convicted of larceny in New York.[25] At trial, the court relied on the "preponderance of the evidence" standard of proof against him rather than the more demanding "beyond a reasonable doubt" standard used in adult courts. The U.S. Supreme Court reversed Winship's conviction on grounds that the "beyond a reasonable doubt" standard had not been used.

Trial by Jury, Double Jeopardy, Executions

In *McKeiver v. Pennsylvania* (1971),[26] the Supreme Court said that juveniles do not have an absolute right to trial by jury; whether or not a juvenile receives a trial by jury is left to the discretion of state and local authorities. Then, in *Breed v. Jones* (1975),[27] the Court concluded that the Fifth Amendment protected juveniles from double jeopardy, or being tried twice for the same offense. (Breed had been tried both in California Juvenile Court and later in Superior Court for the same offenses.) Finally, as noted in Chapter 11, in 2005 the U.S. Supreme Court held that the Eighth and Fourteenth Amendments forbid the execution of offenders who were under the age of 18 when their crimes were committed.[28]

McKeiver v. Pennsylvania

Breed v. Jones

J.D.B. v. North Carolina

Chapter Quiz: Juvenile Justice

Right to the *Miranda* Warning

In 2011 the U.S. Supreme Court expanded the *Miranda* warning for suspects to include children questioned by police in school. In *J. D. B. v. North Carolina*,[29] a 13-year-old North Carolina boy was taken from his classroom by a police officer and questioned, without an attorney or guardian present, in a conference room (where a police investigator and three school officials were present) concerning a string of burglaries. The boy eventually confessed, and his attorney lost his state appeal in trying to have the confession tossed due to his age and lack of *Miranda* warning (the state had argued that the boy should have felt free to leave the room, and therefore was not in custody). The Supreme Court agreed, saying for the first time that age must be considered in determining whether a suspect is aware of his rights. This decision tells police they cannot avoid giving a youth the *Miranda* warning simply by questioning him at school, away from his parents or guardians; it is thus expected to force police to adopt a "when in doubt, give the *Miranda* warnings" approach with juveniles.

Serving Sentences of Life Without Parole

In 2012, the U.S. Supreme Court, combining two cases, ruled that the Eighth Amendment's ban on cruel and unusual punishment prohibits sentencing any juvenile offender who commits a murder to serve a term of **life without parole** (LWOP) (see *Miller v. Alabama* and *Jackson v. Hobbs*).[30] The court had already (in 2010) rejected life sentences for juveniles who had committed a *nonhomicidal* offense (see *Graham v. Florida*, 130 S. Ct. [2011]), noting that such sentences had been "rejected the world over." The Court's reasoning was that such sentences do not take into account the possibility that an adolescent's personality and judgment are still developing, and that criminal tendencies can be outgrown.

Life without parole: a penalty or sentence imposed where the inmate is to serve a life sentence without parole eligibility.

you be the... OFFICER

JUVENILE LAW AND JUSTICE

It is about 10:00 on a warm summer's night. A municipal police officer is dispatched to a residence to take a theft report. Upon arrival, she is informed by the residents that a very expensive bicycle has been stolen from their front porch. The victims further inform the officer that earlier that afternoon they observed a juvenile—whom they know by name, because he lives a few blocks up the street—walking on the sidewalk across the street and looking furtively at the bicycle. The officer recognizes the youth's name by reputation (i.e., prior involvement with police).

She drives her patrol car by the youth's home and, through the open front door, observes that the living room is dark but the television is turned on. She goes to the front door, and the juvenile is alone watching television; he comes to the door and tells the officer that his parents are sleeping. The officer knows that if she wakes the parents and (in their presence) asks the boy if he knows anything about the stolen bicycle, he will deny any such knowledge.

1. How should the officer proceed?

Note: This relatively simple case study actually represents police work as it often occurs on the streets, where there is little opportunity for patrol officers to immediately seek a search warrant; it also involves the Fourth Amendment (probable cause, arrest, search and seizure); the police being aware of someone's history with and reputation for committing certain types of offenses; police policy and procedures (re: treatment of juveniles); and, of course, police ethics. Also implicated are the informal nature of police work, use of discretion, and Packer's crime control/due process dichotomy (discussed in Chapter 1).

IN A NUTSHELL

- Quakers in New York City in 1825 sought to establish a balance between two camps—people wanting to see justice done with child offenders, and those not wanting them to be incarcerated; they founded the first house of refuge.

- At about the middle of the 19th century, the house of refuge movement evolved into the slightly more punitive reform school, or reformatory, approach, to segregate young offenders from adult criminals, remove the young from adverse home environments, minimize court proceedings, and provide indeterminate sentences.

- In 1870, the Illinois Supreme Court held it unconstitutional to confine in a Chicago reform school a youth who had not been convicted of criminal conduct or afforded legal due process; thus, the juvenile court movement began.

- In 1899, the Illinois legislature enacted the Illinois Juvenile Court Act, creating the first separate juvenile court.

- In the post–World War II period, *status offenses* became a separate category: acts that would not be criminal if committed by an adult.

- Experts agree that there is a correlation between juvenile crime and family dysfunction, drug use and deviance, socioeconomic class, and educational experiences.

- The prevailing philosophy with the treatment of juveniles is *parens patriae*, meaning that the "state is the ultimate parent" of the child; the doctrine of *in loco parentis* means the state will act in place of the parent.

- There is an idealistic contrast between the juvenile court process and adults' criminal procedure, involving different terminology and court processes.

- Most states' juvenile court acts contain three underlying principles: the presumption of innocence, the presumption of the least amount of involvement with the system, and the presumption of the best interest of the minor.

- The primary goals of the juvenile justice system are separation from adults,

- youth confidentiality, community-based corrections, and individualized justice of minors.
- Each state's processing of law violators is unique, depending on local practice and tradition.

- Several important rights have been granted to juveniles by the courts, in the areas of due process, representation by counsel, advance notice of charges, confronting and cross-examining witnesses, the privilege against self-incrimination, burden of proof standard, having *Miranda* warnings given, and serving sentences of life without parole.

KEY TERMS & CONCEPTS

Disposition
Houses of refuge
Idealistic contrast
Illinois Juvenile
  Court Act (1899)
In loco parentis

Juvenile court
Life without parole
Parens patriae
PINS (person in need of
  supervision)

Presumption
  of innocence
Reformatory
Status offenses
Transfer (remand)

STUDY SITE

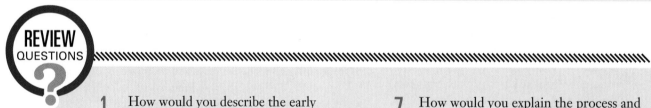

Sharpen your skills with **SAGE edge** at **edge.sagepub.com/peak. SAGE edge for students** provides a personalized approach to help you accomplish your coursework goals in an easy-to-use learning environment. Access the videos, audio clips, quizzes, cases and SAGE journal and reference articles that are noted in this chapter.

REVIEW QUESTIONS

1. How would you describe the early treatment of juveniles, including houses of refuge and reformatories?

2. What contributions were made by the Illinois legislation creating the first juvenile justice/court system?

3. What are the major differences in philosophy and treatment between juvenile and adult offenders?

4. What is the definition of a status offense?

5. What are the prevailing theories underlying juvenile criminality causation?

6. What is the "idealistic contrast" between the juvenile and adult justice systems?

7. How would you explain the process and flow of cases through the juvenile justice system?

8. For what reason(s) might a juvenile offender be transferred to the jurisdiction of an adult criminal court?

9. How would you describe the Juvenile Detention Alternatives Initiative?

10. What due process rights were given to juveniles in *In re Gault?*

11. Aside from *Gault,* what other rights do juveniles now enjoy in their justice system?

12. What suggestions were made in a report by the Office of the Surgeon General for dealing with juvenile delinquency?

1. Your criminal justice class has been assigned a group project, with each group citing what it believes are the major factors contributing to juvenile delinquency and related policy implications. Develop your argument using the following: Terence P. Thornberry, David Huizinga, and Rolf Loeber, "The Causes and Correlates Studies: Findings and Policy Implications," *Juvenile Justice* 9, no. 1 (September 2004), http://www.ncjrs.gov/html/ojjdp/203555/jj2.html (accessed August 17, 2013).

2. Assume you are a juvenile probation officer and have been tasked by your supervisor to prepare a position paper on the use of detention for juveniles. Use the January 2004 article by Jill Young for the National Juvenile Defender Center titled "The Use and Abuse of Juvenile Detention: Understanding Detention and Its Uses," available from http://www.njdc.info/pdf/factsheetdetention.pdf (accessed August 17, 2013).

ON THE CRIME POLICY AND PREVENTION AGENDA:

Terrorism, Gun Control, and Marijuana

LEARNING OBJECTIVES

As a result of reading this chapter, the student will be able to:

1 Delineate the types of terrorism, the cybercrime threat posed by China, bioterrorism, and some law enforcement and legislative approaches enacted for combating it (to include several accompanying issues regarding police use of unmanned aerial vehicles)

2 Describe the primary policy issues involved in gun control

3 Explain the movement to legalize marijuana use and some legal, political, and technical questions involved

CHAPTER
16

INTRODUCTION

Author Introduction:
Chapter 16

What should be done about terrorists who now attack by using little help and inexpensive, widely available weapons and explosives from everyday ingredients—and, increasingly, computers?[1] Do you believe existing gun laws should be tightened or loosened? Should marijuana be legalized?

The U.S. criminal justice system is affected, directly or indirectly, by nearly every public crime and policy issue that is raised (such as those mentioned above), because the system reflects the broader society and its changing times. And, like any other academic discipline or occupational environment, the system's priorities and trends are constantly in flux as to what is considered a crime and what methods of punishment are appropriate.

Certainly there is no shortage of additional policy challenges on today's radar screen: How should Congress and the nation deal with human trafficking? What should be done with repeat sex offenders, and those who abuse children in particular? What should be done about prison and jail overcrowding? Nonviolent drug offenders? Repeat offenders? These are all issues that have been, or must be, confronted in our nation and the international community.

This chapter briefly examines three such "hot button" issues—specifically, the nature of terrorism, gun control, and marijuana in our society. Each has been at the forefront of our collective consciousness—and media reports—to some extent in recent times, and gives no sign of abating in the foreseeable future. The chapter includes several boxed exhibits that challenge you to air (and defend) your viewpoints after studying each of these three policy issues. A summary, key terms and concepts, review questions, and "learn by doing" exercises conclude the chapter.

Terrorism: acts that are intended to intimidate or coerce a civilian population or government, usually for some political purpose or objective.

TERRORISM

The Federal Bureau of Investigation (FBI) defines **terrorism** as the "unlawful use of force against persons or property to intimidate or coerce a government, the civilian population, or any segment thereof, in furtherance of political or

ASSESS YOUR AWARENESS:

Test your knowledge of selected criminal justice policy issues by first reading and responding to the following seven true-false items; check your answers after reading this chapter's materials.

1. Currently, terrorist attacks in the United States and abroad involve well-organized groups and sophisticated weaponry.

2. The greatest threat of cyberterrorism against U.S. military and business establishments is now posed by Iran.

3. Unquestionably, the U.S. Constitution supports our government's use of drones against its citizens, both here and abroad, who fit the profile of a terrorist.

4. The United States leads the world in gun ownership and gun-related crimes.

5. Public colleges and universities have now become a major front in the nation's debate over guns.

6. There have been no changes in traditional U.S. marijuana laws, in terms of either its recreational use or its medical use.

7. Federal law currently prohibits the use (except for medical purposes)—and legalization—of marijuana.

Answers can be found on page 401.

social objectives."[2] Terrorism can take many forms, however, and does not always involve bombs and guns; as examples, environmental and animal activists seek to further their agendas by burning greenhouses, tree farms, logging sites, ski resorts, and mink farms.[3]

Several attacks on American soil have demonstrated this nation's vulnerability to both foreign and domestic terrorists: that which occurred in September 2001 with hijacked jetliners against the World Trade Center complex in New York City and the Pentagon in Virginia (almost 3,000 people killed or missing)[4]; the bombing of the World Trade Center in New York City in February 1993 (killing 6 and injuring 1,000)[5]; the April 1995 bombing of the Alfred P. Murrah Building in Oklahoma City (killing 168 and injuring more than 500)[6]; and, more recently, the bombing of the Boston Marathon in April 2013 (killing 3 and injuring 264).[7] Also demonstrated was the need for the nation's law enforcement agencies to become much more knowledgeable about terrorists' methods and how to respond in the event of an attack, adopting a long-term view of protecting the homeland (the organization and functions of the Department of Homeland Security were discussed in Chapter 5). This chapter section defines types of terrorism, law enforcement and legislative responses, and a related issue: the use of unmanned aerial vehicles (or drones).

Table 16.1 delineates terrorist attacks in the United States since 9/11; note that at least three dozen additional attempts to attack targets were thwarted by law enforcement agencies before they could be carried out.

Cyberterrorism—and the Asian Threat

Cybercrime or **cyberterrorism** includes such activities as identity theft, attacks against computer data and systems, the distribution of child sexual abuse images, Internet auction fraud, and the penetration of online financial services, as well as the deployment of viruses, botnets, and various e-mail scams such as phishing.[8] According to Interpol, cybercrime is one of the fastest growing areas of crime, with increasing numbers of criminals now exploiting the anonymity, speed, and convenience that modern technologies provide. The Internet also allows such criminals to commit almost any illegal activity anywhere in the world, making it essential for all countries to adapt their domestic offline controls to cover crimes carried out in cyberspace.

Without question the most challenging and potentially disastrous type of cybercrime—actually, cyberespionage—now being perpetrated against the United States is by Chinese hackers, who are estimated to be responsible for the theft of 50 to 80 percent of all American intellectual property and have compromised many of the nation's most sensitive advanced weapons systems, including missile defense technology and combat aircraft.[9] It is believed that Chinese hackers have accessed designs for more than two dozen of the U.S. military's most important and expensive weapon systems (the cost to develop plans for one aircraft alone—the F-35 Joint Strike Fighter—was $1.4 trillion). Doing so enables China to understand those systems and be able to jam or otherwise disable them. The Pentagon recently concluded that another country's computer sabotage can constitute an act of war, which could eventually lead to U.S. use of military force.[10]

Of course, China's computer hacking does not stop with the U.S. military complex; corporate and business secrets are also prime targets of hackers. Estimates are that hundreds of private companies, research institutions, and Internet service providers have already been hacked, and there are also concerns

Several attacks on American soil have demonstrated this nation's vulnerability to terrorism. But perhaps the most shocking were those occurring in September 2001 when hijacked jetliners crashed into the World Trade Center complex in New York City and the Pentagon in Virginia.

Cybercrime/cyberterrorism: computer uses to commit crimes, such as embezzlement, diversion of bank monies to other accounts, and so on; making use of high technology, normally the Internet, to plan and carry out acts of terrorism.

TABLE 16.1

Terrorist Attacks in the United States, 2001 to Present

DATE	LOCATION	KILLED	INJURED	DESCRIPTION
11 Sep 2001	New York City, New York	2759	8700	Two hijacked planes crash into World Trade Center towers
11 Sep 2001	Alexandria, Virginia	189	200	Crashing of hijacked plane into Pentagon
11 Sep 2001	Somerset County, Pennsylvania	45	0	Crashing of hijacked plane into rural area of Pennsylvania
18 Sep 2001	West Palm Beach, Florida	1	10	Anthrax-laced letters mailed to West Palm Beach, Florida, and New York City
9 Oct 2001	Washington, D.C.	4	7	Anthrax-laced letters mailed to Washington, DC
4 Jul 2002	Los Angeles, California	2	4	Egyptian gunman kills two Israelis at Los Angeles International Airport
2–23 Oct, 2002	Maryland, Virginia, D.C.	0	1	Two Beltway snipers kill at least 10 people, aiming to extort money and recruit more shooters*
29 Nov 2005	Santa Cruz, California	0	4	Four injured via incendiary attacks by suspected animal rights activists
5 Mar 2006	Chapel Hill, North Carolina	0	9	Man drives vehicle into pedestrians at the University of North Carolina
28 Jul 2006	Seattle, Washington	1	5	Gunman fires on women at the Jewish Federation of Greater Seattle
24 Feb 2008	Los Angeles, California	0	1	Animal rights activists attempt home invasion of biomedical researcher, injuring the researcher's husband
27 Jul 2008	Knoxville, Tennessee	2	7	Gunman fires on congregation at a church
31 May 2009	Wichita, Kansas	1	0	One doctor killed in shooting attack at Reformation Lutheran Church
1 Jun 2009	Little Rock, Arkansas	1	1	One Army private killed, another injured in shooting attack at Army Navy Career Center
10 Jun 2009	Washington, D.C.	1	1	One guard killed in shooting attack at the Holocaust Museum
11 Sep 2009	Owosso, Michigan	2	0	Abortion protester shot and killed outside a school; shooter also killed an area businessman
5 Nov 2009	Foot Hood, Texas	13	44	Shooting attack at Soldier Readiness Center at Foot Hood
25 Dec 2009	Michigan	0	3	Yemeni terrorist attempts to detonate bomb on flight from Amsterdam to Detroit; passengers and crew subdue the terrorist
18 Feb 2010	Austin, Texas	2	13	Suicide crash of small plane into federal office building
4 Mar 2010	Alexandria, Virginia	1	2	Shooting at gate outside Pentagon; gunman killed
1 Sep 2010	Silver Spring, Maryland	1	0	Three hostages held by gunman at Discovery Communications headquarters
8 Jan 2011	Tucson, Arizona	6	13	Shooting attack at political event at a supermarket; a federal judge is killed, Congresswoman injured
5 Aug 2012	Oak Creek, Wisconsin	7	4	Seven killed, four injured in shooting attack at a Sikh temple

DATE	LOCATION	KILLED	INJURED	DESCRIPTION
14 Aug 2012	LaPlace, Louisiana	2	4	Two police officers killed, four injured while investigating attack; shooters had ties to the sovereign citizen movement
15 Aug 2012	Washington, D.C.	0	1	One guard shot and injured while subduing gunman at Family Research Council offices
15 Apr 2013	Boston, Massachusetts	3	264	Two bombings at Boston Marathon kill three, injure 264
17 Apr 2013	Washington, D.C.	0	0	Two letters testing positive for ricin mailed to Mississippi state senator and President Obama are found at mail screening facilities
18–19 Apr 2013	Watertown, Massachusetts	2	2	One police officer killed, one injured during manhunt for the Boston Marathon bombers; one terrorist killed and one injured and captured

Source: Adapted from Wm. Robert Johnston, "Terrorist Attacks and Related Incidents in the United States," http://www.johnstonsarchive.net/terrorism/wrjp255a.html

*Regarding the Beltway Snipers case, see Crime Museum, "The DC Sniper: *The Beltway Sniper Attacks*," http://www.crimemuseum.org/Washington_DC_Sniper

about threats posed to U.S. nuclear reactors, banks, subways, and pipeline companies.[11] The specter of electricity going out for days and perhaps weeks, the gates of a major dam opening suddenly and flooding complete cities, or pipes in a chemical plant rupturing and releasing deadly gas are nightmare scenarios that keep homeland security professionals awake at night.

Cyberterrorism

Bioterrorism

Another means of attack by terrorists involves the use of chemical/biological agents, or **bioterrorism**. We know that poisons have been used for several millennia; recent attacks using chemical/biological agents including toxins, viruses, or bacteria such as anthrax, ricin, and sarin have underscored their potential dangers and uses by terrorists today. Chemical weapons—including several types of gases—suffocate the victim immediately or cause massive burning. Biological weapons are slower acting, spreading a disease such as anthrax or smallpox through a population before the first signs are noticed. Many experts believe it is only a matter of time before chemical/biological weapons are used like explosives have been to date.[12] All that is required is for a toxin to be cultured and put into a spray form that can be weaponized and disseminated into the population. Fortunately, such dissemination is extremely difficult for all but specially trained individuals to make in large quantities and in the correct dosage; they are also difficult to transport because live organisms are delicate.

Bioterrorism

Law Enforcement Measures

Police have several possible means of addressing terrorism. On a broad level, there are four major aspects involved in dealing with terrorist organizations[13]:

1. Gathering raw intelligence on the organization's structure, its members, and its plans (or potential for the use of violence)

2. Determining what measures can be taken to counter or thwart terrorist activities

3. Assessing how the damage caused by terrorists can be minimized through rapid response and containment of the damage

Many experts believe it is only a matter of time before chemical/biological weapons are used by terrorists. Here, several regional agencies participate in a bioterrorism response drill

4. Apprehending and convicting individual terrorists and dismantling their organizations

Another means of addressing domestic terrorism is military support of law enforcement. The Posse Comitatus Act of 1878 prohibits using the military to execute the laws domestically; the military may be called on, however, to provide personnel and equipment for certain special support activities, such as domestic terrorist events involving weapons of mass destruction.[14]

Furthermore, President George W. Bush directed the Department of Homeland Security secretary to develop and administer a National Incident Management System (NIMS). This system provides a consistent nationwide approach for federal, state, and local governments to work effectively together to prepare for, prevent, respond to, and recover from domestic incidents. This directive required all federal departments and agencies to adopt the NIMS and to use it—and to make its adoption and use by state and local agencies a condition for federal preparedness assistance beginning in fiscal year 2005.[15]

Finally, each FBI field office has established a Field Intelligence Group (FIG), composed of agents, analysts, linguists, and surveillance specialists. Their mantra is "Know Your Domain." As the FIGs have evolved, each office has developed its own model for intelligence gathering and operations. Furthermore, the FBI developed a Strategic Execution Team (SET) to help in assessing the intelligence program, evaluate best practices, and decide what works and what does not work. This intelligence is regularly shared with police around the nation.[16]

The FBI and Terrorism

Legislative Measures

Legislation

A number of new investigative measures were provided to federal law enforcement agencies through the enactment of the Uniting and Strengthening America by Providing Appropriate Tools Required to Intercept and Obstruct Terrorism Act of 2001 (known as the USA PATRIOT Act) shortly after the 9/11 attacks. The act dramatically expanded the federal government's ability to investigate Americans without establishing probable cause for "intelligence purposes" and to conduct searches if there are "reasonable grounds to believe" there may be national security threats. Federal agencies such as the FBI and others are given access to financial, mental health, medical, library, and other records.[17] The act was reauthorized in March 2006, providing additional tools for protecting mass transportation systems and seaports from attack, the "roving wiretap" portion and the "sneak and peek" section. The first allows the government to get a wiretap on every phone a suspect uses, while the second allows federal investigators to get access to library, business, and medical records without a court order.[18]

The fight against terrorism was also aided and expanded in October 2006 when President George W. Bush signed Public Law 109-366, the

Military Commissions Act (MCA).[19] Under the MCA, the president is authorized to establish military commissions to try unlawful enemy combatants, the commissions are authorized to sentence defendants to death, and defendants are prevented from invoking the Geneva Conventions as a source of rights during commission proceedings. The law contains a provision stripping detainees of the right to file *habeas corpus* petitions in federal court and also allows hearsay evidence to be admitted during proceedings, so long as the presiding officer determines it to be reliable. This law allows the Central Intelligence Agency (CIA) to continue its program for questioning key terrorist leaders and operatives—a program felt by many to be one of the most successful intelligence efforts in U.S. history. The MCA excludes all statements obtained by use of torture, makes U.S. interrogators subject to only a limited range of "grave breaches," and clarifies what actions would subject interrogators to liability under the existing federal War Crimes Act.[20]

Balancing Security and Privacy: Use of Unmanned Aerial Vehicles

Americans have been willing to give up much of their privacy since 9/11, but when will they begin to balk given the aforementioned legislation—and the fact that government also has access to their telephone, computer, travel, financial, and other personal information (now available through social media, smartphones, the automatic license plate recognition system, and other technologies)? There is a delicate balance between security and privacy, and every U.S. president has had to face the question of where the line should be drawn between the two; to this point, there has been no clear answer. President John Adams signed into law the Alien and Sedition Acts (empowering him to restrict speech and detain or deport immigrants) following the French Revolution; President Abraham Lincoln suspended the writ of *habeas corpus* during the Civil War; President Franklin Roosevelt allowed the government to put Japanese Americans in internment camps; following the 9/11 attacks President George W. Bush signed into law the USA Patriot Act; the administration of Barack Obama killed four U.S. citizens in drone strikes overseas and helped to fund the New York Police Department's controversial surveillance program against Muslim Americans.[21]

Unmanned aerial vehicles (UAVs), or drones, are powered aerial vehicles that are directed by a ground or airborne controller, do not carry human operators, and are designed to carry nonlethal payloads for reconnaissance, command and control, and deception. UAVs have rapidly become available in a variety of shapes, sizes, and capabilities, from one that is about the size and appearance of a hummingbird and carrying a tiny camera, to another the size of a jumbo airplane.[22]

Drones would seem to be tailor-made for seeking out and surveilling persons who are planning or involved in terroristic activities. However, the issue concerning use of drones came to the forefront in early 2013 during Senate confirmation hearings for President Obama's nominee to head the CIA, John Brennan. A U.S. Department of Justice (DOJ) memo came

UAVs

//

Unmanned aerial vehicles: also termed "drones," aircraft without a human pilot that are controlled by computers and used for a variety of purposes by military and civilian police agencies.

Unmanned aerial vehicles (UAVs), or drones, are powered aerial vehicles that have many capabilities and beneficial uses. However, their increasing use has raised security and privacy concerns as well.

you be the... JUDGE

POLICE USE OF DRONES

Assume you are an advisor to a presidential panel that is to make recommendations for *police* use of UAVs/drones, and respond to the following questions:

- Would you support police use of drones for surveillance purposes involving serious offenses? If so, for what crime-related purposes?
- Would you allow the police to use drones for Fourth Amendment (searches and seizures)

types of operations, if legal conditions have been met?

- Do you endorse using drones for lower-level functions, such as catching traffic speeders?
- Would your panel be in favor of arming the drones with bullets or tear gas?
- Do you believe drones should be used, without prior consent from any courts or other oversight body, for killing persons whose "profile" indicates they are a dangerous threat to security?

to light in which the DOJ supported Obama's legal authority to use drones as mentioned above—to target American citizens whose behavior conforms to a particular profile and are working with al-Qaeda—but with little or no oversight by Congress or the judicial system.[23] What is evident from the hearings is that Americans are very suspicious of—and may demand that legal criteria be established for—the overflights of drones in this country as we have deployed them over Pakistan and other countries. Clearly these are vexing security and privacy issues that our government and society must resolve, and each day the U.S. criminal justice system is closer and closer to the day when it will likewise be embroiled in those same issues.

GUN CONTROL: THE "RIGHT" TO BE WELL-ARMED

Gun Control

The United States is well supplied with guns (see Figure 16.1); however, in the aftermath of the tragic deaths of 26 children and teachers in Newtown, Connecticut, in December 2012,[24] many citizens and politicians issued calls for action—including, among other things, new gun laws, giving arms to teachers, and gun prepurchase background checks for mental illness. Cries for new gun controls were also raised, as were demands that no new restrictions be placed on gun ownership and types of guns (i.e., so-called assault weapons) and magazines (or "clips") that can be sold.[25]

● ● ● FIGURE 16.1

Civilian Gun Ownership in the United States

Number of Privately Owned Firearms: between 270,000,000 and 310,000,000

Rate of Civilian Firearm Possession per 100 Population: 101.05 firearms per 100 people

Number of Privately Owned Firearms: compared with 178 other countries, the United States ranks first

Rate of Privately Owned Firearms per 100 Population: compared with 178 other countries, the United States ranks first

Number of Privately Owned Rifles: estimated to be 110,000,000

Number of Privately Owned Shotguns: estimated to be 86,000,000

Number of Privately Owned Handguns: estimated to be 114,000,000

Source: Alpers, Philip, Amélie Rossetti, Marcus Wilson and Quentin Royet. 2013. *Guns in the United States: Facts, Figures and Firearm Law.* Sydney School of Public Health, The University of Sydney. GunPolicy.org, 9 July. Accessed 30 July 2013 at: http://www.gunpolicy.org/firearms/region/united-states.

The question of **gun control** has become, more than ever before, a virtual standoff. Predictably, in the aftermath of Newtown and as the president of the United States began talking about the need for such controls, weapons sales soared even higher.

At the crux of the matter is the meaning of the **Second Amendment**: *A well regulated Militia, being necessary to the security of a free state, the right of people to keep and bear Arms, shall not be infringed.* Many people argue that the amendment's purpose was for a young America to resist aggression from European powers or hostile Indian tribes—and then only as part of a "well-organized militia," to put down rebellions. These gun control advocates do not believe the Founding Fathers would have permitted citizens to own the powerful weapons with high-capacity magazines that are quite accessible today. On the other side are those who consider it their constitutional right to own any form of gun or ammunition.

One thing is certain: Something must be done about mass killings (defined as incidents in which four or more people are killed by the attacker), which only account for about 1 percent of all murders but occur on average about every two weeks.[26]

Gun ownership, use, and sales are all controversial subjects in the United States. Here, the father of a shooting victim testifies in favor of increased gun control.

going GLOBAL

WORLD GUN LAWS

After the tragic mass shooting at Sandy Hook Elementary School in Newtown, Connecticut, in December 2012, gun laws in other countries were given greater scrutiny—particularly those nations having far fewer than the more than 11,000 gun-related killings each year in the United States.

For example, in Japan, guns and gun violence are virtually nonexistent compared to the United States. With 130 million people, guns are used in fewer than 10 murders per year. Why so little gun violence? It comes down to public perception of guns: in the United States, people believe they have a right to own a gun, while people in Japan do not hold such a view. Therefore, gun ownership is treated as a privilege rather than a right, which leads to some important policy differences. First, anyone who wants to get a gun must demonstrate a valid reason why they should be allowed to do so. Public policy is that no civilian needs to own a handgun, so these guns are nearly completely banned. Guns can still be bought on the black market, but gun crimes are extremely rare. Rifles may be owned by the general public, but they are tightly controlled. Applicants will receive a lecture and a written test, train on a shooting range, and be subjected to a background check—which includes their temper, financial troubles, and stability of the household. A doctor must attest to their mental health, and applicants must tell the police where in the home the gun will be stored—to be under lock and key and kept separate from ammunition.[27]

Researchers at Harvard's School of Public Health, using data from 26 developed countries, argue that wherever there are more firearms, there are more homicides. They found the U.S. murder rate to be roughly 15 times the rate for other wealthy countries that have much tougher gun laws. Another important difference is that other nations often react quickly to gun-related problems; as examples, in both Australia (where a gunman killed 35 people with a semiautomatic weapon in 1996) and Scotland (where 16 children and their teacher were killed by a gunman, also in 1996), the governments moved quickly to enact laws banning all private ownership of automatic weapons and virtually all handguns.[28]

FOCUS ON   GUN USE IN THE UNITED STATES

• Today the United States has the highest murder rate involving guns of any industrialized country in the world. The United States, with about 5 times the population of Britain, has about 200 times as many gun murders per year,[29] as well as the highest number of guns per capita and the highest rate of deaths due to assault. In fact, the United States has more homicides by guns than the next 20 developed countries combined.[30]

• Gunshot wounds and deaths cost Americans about $12 billion a year in lost work, court proceedings, insurance costs, and hospitalizations. Medical care alone costs $3.2 billion for 105,000 shooting deaths and injuries, but $5.4 billion is lost in tax revenue because of lost work.[31]

• Adding to concerns about Americans being heavily armed is the fact that there are about 50 million mentally ill Americans—and mental illness is a common condition of armed mass killers, such as those in the recent mass shootings at Virginia Tech and in Tucson, Arizona; Newtown, Connecticut; and Aurora, Colorado. This, added to the fact that the United States is teeming with violent movies and video games, makes the situation a highly volatile one. Although firearms laws generally prohibit the possession or purchase of guns by persons who are deemed to be mentally defective, such provisions in gun laws obviously have not stopped the mass killings. Indeed, many of the shooters involved in such acts of violence were taking prescribed psychoactive drugs at the time of the shootings.[32]

• Some cities now "require" their citizens to own guns (although the laws are generally considered unenforceable). Communities from Idaho to Georgia require or recommend their residents arm themselves to preemptively block gun control laws.[33]

Gun Control

Gun Violence Prevention

Gun control: a broad term representing attempts to regulate the sale, transfer, manufacture, and use of firearms.

Second Amendment: the portion of the Bill of Rights that allows citizens to keep and bear arms.

Attempts to Prevent Gun Violence

Immediately following the Newtown shootings, President Obama formed a commission to study gun violence and make recommendations; such presidential commissions mean well but are often ineffectual and notoriously slow to make recommendations or have any impact. The gun lobby would oppose *any* recommendations including limitations on weapons or ammunition. Meanwhile, one is left to wonder how, even if new laws prevent the sales of clips that hold more than 10 rounds, the thousands of clips that hold up to 40 rounds of ammunition can ever be confiscated. In similar fashion, when looking at tightening the requirement for background checks, we are also left to wonder how the current 40 percent of all gun transfers that take place without background checks (primarily at gun shows) will ever be stopped.

Even a flurry of new gun laws on the books and proposals to cover criminals or the mentally deranged would seem to fall short in preventing such people from obtaining their weapons of mass killing. Nor do such proposals as requiring gun locks appear to hold much promise, due to lack of enforcement. And allowing more groups to be armed—such as teachers or other school personnel (as has been suggested by the gun lobby)—would certainly appear to be ineffectual as well (given that such armed personnel probably cannot react quickly enough to stop an active shooter, even if they were to choose to engage in such a shoot-out).[34]

Therefore, today the United States finds itself still mired in a gun control policy quandary. There will no doubt be new laws enacted to place at least some restrictions on gun sales and their "accoutrements." (Indeed, almost as soon as the biennial legislature convened in Nevada in January 2013, both pro and con gun control bills were introduced that would allow people with concealed-carry permits to be armed on college campuses; make it a "constitutional carry" state, eliminating the need for a concealed weapon permit; ban the sale of assault weapons and magazine clips of more than 10 rounds; compel the state's attorney general to "protect Nevadans" if a presidential order infringes on Second Amendment rights; tax firearm and ammunition sales, with revenues earmarked for mental health; and require anyone previously recommended for commit-tal to a state psychiatric hospital be listed on a national background check system and barred from such purchases.[35]) There may also be calls for controls over the levels of violence in video games and movies, and demands for more thor-ough background checks, greater restrictions on private guns sales, and possibly subjecting the mentally ill to government oversight.

One thing, however, is virtually certain: Americans will continue to witness more mass killing incidents, bringing about more calls for action to control certain types of guns, others' plaintive cries to leave their guns alone, and on and on it goes.

Public colleges and universities have now become a major front in the nation's debate over guns, and such legal disputes as that recently occurring in Colorado could also arise in other states. There, the state's flagship university in Boulder had a long-standing firearms ban. But the state's supreme court ruled in March 2012 that the university had to allow those persons with a con-cealed weapon permit to carry their guns on cam-pus because such a ban had never been approved

Gun protesters display signs leaving no doubt as to their beliefs concerning the Second Amendment.

you be the... JUDGE

HOW (AND WHETHER) TO BRING ABOUT GUN CONTROL

Assume you are an advisor to a presidential commission that has been convened to study and recommend national gun control policy, and respond to the following questions:

- Would you recommend that limits be placed on the types of rifles, bullet clips, and ammunition that can be sold?
- Would you compel persons wishing to purchase firearms be first subjected to more strenuous

background checks as well as some form of "mental fitness" criteria?

- Do you propose that teachers be armed on campuses? Other people, such as judges?
- Would you make recommendations for enforcement of such laws, as well as bringing in guns and ammunition that are already owned but are now outlawed under your president's new policy?

FOCUS ON MASS MURDERERS

Since 2006 there have been 29 massacres where the shooters' victims were killed totally at random. Of those 29 shootings, only 5 (17 percent) of the shooters eventually went to trial; 15 (52 percent) committed suicide at or near the scene, and 3 (10 percent) were killed by the police. In most cases, the shooter's motive is never established, and many were suffering from mental illness—believing

themselves victims of conspiracies or persecution. Two (7 percent) of the cases ended with the suspects being declared mentally incompetent to stand trial, and four (14 percent) had mental health issues but were deemed able to go to trial.

Source: Adapted from Gary Strauss, Meghan Hoyer, and Paul Overberg, "Aurora Mass Shooting Suspect's Expected Plea a Rarity," *Reno Gazette Journal*, March 12, 2013, http://www.rgj.com/usatoday/article/1973839 (accessed March 12, 2013).

by the legislature. Colorado's legislature reacted swiftly in early 2013, with a number of bills being introduced that would ban concealed weapons on all public college campuses in the state.[36]

THE MARIJUANA CONUNDRUM

Mid-Chapter Quiz: On the Crime Policy and Prevention Agenda

A social issue that has long been heavily debated concerns the legalization of marijuana. No matter whether one is pro or con with respect to **marijuana laws**, however, there is no question that the enforcement of U.S. marijuana laws consumes tremendous criminal justice resources: A Harvard University economist estimated that legalizing marijuana would save $13.7 billion per year in government expenditures on enforcement of prohibition by eliminating arrests for trafficking and possession as well as costs for related courts and jail/prison activities. There are, of course, others who believe the enforcement of marijuana laws has been successful and balanced, and has contributed to reductions in the rate of marijuana use in the nation.[37] Next is a discussion of the marijuana legalization question, looking at two states that have decided to do so: Colorado and Washington.

A Sea Change in State Laws

Medical Marijuana

Marijuana use for recreational purposes was approved by voters in November 2012 in the states of Colorado and Washington. Such enactments represent a significant "chink in the armor" of the nation's marijuana laws. Furthermore, 18 states and the District of Columbia have enacted laws to legalize use of marijuana for medical purposes.[38] This sea change in marijuana laws is gaining more support than ever before (see below).

First, as indicated above, proponents of legalization point to the fact that the enforcement of marijuana laws in the United States exerts a financial strain on societal as well as criminal justice system resources. About half of all drug arrests are for marijuana, which equates to one marijuana arrest every 42 seconds.[39] Proponents also argue that legalizing marijuana would result in reduced prices and better quality control, reductions in related street crimes, benefits for cancer patients, additional tax revenues, and freeing up criminal justice resources for more serious crimes.[40]

Table 16.2 shows annual marijuana arrests as a percentage of total drug arrests for manufacturing, sale, and possession. It is seen that such arrests have typically represented more than half of all drug arrests, particularly since 2008.

Indeed, public support for legalizing adult use of marijuana has been increasing since the early 1990s.[41] Even some law enforcement officials—few of whom spoke out against marijuana laws in past decades—are now banding together in a national (and rapidly growing) organization whose name defines its purpose: Law Enforcement Against Prohibition (LEAP). This organization, launched in 2002, now boasts as members more than a thousand police, judges,

Eighteen states and the District of Columbia have enacted laws legalizing the use of marijuana for medical purposes. Shown here is a medical marijuana dispensary.

TABLE 16.2

Marijuana Arrests as a Percentage of Total Drug Arrests for Manufacturing, Sale, and Possession

	U.S. MARIJUANA ARRESTS PERCENTAGE SHARE OF TOTAL DRUG ARRESTS		
YEAR	% TOTAL DRUG ARRESTS	% TOTAL MANUFACTURING AND SALE ARRESTS	% TOTAL POSSESSION ARRESTS
2011	49.5	6.2	43.3
2010	52.1	6.3	45.8
2009	51.6	6.0	45.6
2008	49.8	5.5	44.3
2007	47.4	5.3	42.1
2006	43.9	4.8	39.1
2005	42.6	4.9	37.7
2004	44.3	5.0	39.3
2003	45.0	5.5	39.5
2002	45.3	5.4	39.9
2001	45.6	5.2	40.4
2000	46.5	5.6	40.9
1999	46.0	5.5	40.5
1998	43.8	5.4	38.4
1997	43.9	5.6	38.3
1996	42.6	6.3	36.3
1995	39.9	5.8	34.1

Source: U.S. Marijuana Arrests, Percentage Share of Total Drug Arrests, from DrugWarFacts.org, "Marijuana," http://www.drugwarfacts.org/cms/Marijuana#Share. Data from *FBI Uniform Crime Reports 1970–2011.*

prosecutors, prison wardens, and FBI and DEA agents, as well as about 70,000 civilian supporters.[42] LEAP, through its website, bemoans that

> for four decades the US has fueled its policy of a "war on drugs" with over a trillion tax dollars and increasingly punitive policies. More than 39 million arrests for nonviolent drug offenses have been made. The incarcerated population quadrupled over a 20-year period, making building prisons the nation's fastest growing industry. Each year this war costs the US another 70 billion dollars. Despite all the lives destroyed and all the money so ill spent, today illicit drugs are cheaper, more potent, and much easier to access than they were at the beginning of the war on drugs, 40 years ago.[43]

Opponents, conversely, argue that marijuana legalization can serve as a stepping-stone to harder drugs, result in people driving while

Possession, sale, and use of marijuana remains a crime in most of the United States. This police officer is carrying bundles of marijuana plants found in a remote valley.

Marijuana
Conundrum

Marijuana
Gateway

"stoned" and thus pose a danger, increase the chances of the drug being used by kids, cause physical damage to users, and lead to the possible legalization of harder drugs.[44]

But these new state laws will not offer future marijuana aficionados unfettered use of or access to pot. As an example, in May 2013 Colorado Governor John Hickenlooper, while acknowledging that the state is in "uncharted territory" in this area of law, signed bills that

- require markings on labels stating the potency of the marijuana sold, as well as childproof packaging;

- place blood limits for driving under the influence of marijuana, placed at 5 nanograms per milliliter;

- require placing of marijuana-related magazines behind the counters of stores, sold only to customers 21 or older;

- require that no more than six plants be grown, and no more than an ounce of marijuana be possessed, by adults 21 and older[45]; and

- prohibit smoking of marijuana outdoors in public, in public parks, on sidewalks, in schools or on school grounds, or in privately owned buildings and apartments where the owner prohibits its use.[46]

Conflicting Federal Law

A glaring aspect of legalization, which could soon result in challenges to the aforementioned Washington and Colorado laws, is that they are wholly in violation of federal law. Specifically, since 1970 the Code of Federal Regulations, Title 21, Section 1308.11, has listed marijuana as a Schedule I controlled substance,[47] meaning that it has no medical value and that the potential for

FOREIGN VENUES SUPPORT MARIJUANA LEGALIZATION

Following are recent actions taken in five selected foreign venues regarding the enforcement, legalization, and/or possession of marijuana under their laws.

- In August 2013, Uruguay became the world's first nation to legalize marijuana; the new law allows the government to control the cultivation, trade, and sale of the crop.[48]

- In Colombia, President Juan Manuel Santos called drugs a "matter of national security" due to the related cartels and their heinous crimes; he supports legalization, and in July 2012, the country's highest court ruled that minor possession of the drug was not a jailable offense.[49]

- The Czech Republic decriminalized minor possession of marijuana for private use in 2010 and enacted a law legalizing medical use (however, local growth is restricted to registered firms).[50]

- Argentina's Supreme Court deemed it unconstitutional in 2009 to punish people for private marijuana use as long as no one else was harmed, thus effectively authorizing personal use of pot.[51]

- In Mexico, where marijuana users can possess up to 5 grams legally, two former presidents have advocated for decriminalization in order to curb cartel violence; the current president, Enrique Peña Nieto, is open to debate.[52]

abuse is high.[53] Furthermore, for more than four decades, prohibitions on marijuana possession and use have been a major prop in the so-called war on drugs, initiated by President Richard Nixon in 1971. Indeed, following the Washington and Colorado votes to legalize marijuana, the *New York Times* reported that the Obama administration was holding "high-level meetings" to debate the response of federal law enforcement agencies.[54]

One option the federal government would have is the obvious one: to sue the states on the grounds that any effort to regulate marijuana is preempted by federal law. Or a suit could be brought to block parts of the states' laws, and even send cease-and-desist letters to marijuana outlets in those states, followed by focused enforcement measures.[55] Additionally, the federal government could admonish the governors of Colorado and Washington against regulating and taxing marijuana that is sold at their marijuana dispensaries.[56]

Author Video: Legalizing Marijuana

However, public opinion does not seem to favor the federal government's taking a hard-line approach: A recent survey found that 51 percent of Americans support these two states' efforts to legalize marijuana use for adults, and that those persons should be exempted from federal drug law enforcement. Only 30 percent of the respondents believed the federal government should enforce its drug laws in those states as it does in other states.[57]

Chapter Quiz: On the Crime Policy and Prevention Agenda

you be the... JUDGE

MARIJUANA LEGALIZATION

It may be ironic that both sides of the marijuana controversy actually have the same goal: putting an end to the U.S. drug problem. However, each side makes arguments that should be examined prior to making public policy.

First, those who are opposed to marijuana legalization argue that punishing its users with fines and jail time will decrease the number of persons who wish to indulge in such behavior (however, that has not been the case throughout marijuana's history). Furthermore, many if not most such users are nonviolent, petty offenders who are expensive to incarcerate and may well come out of jail or prison more dangerous and hardened than before.

In the other camp are those who believe marijuana is a part of our culture, has medical value, and should be legalized and its users go unpunished. Potential problems with this latter view are that legalization may well substantially increase the use of marijuana (including by motor vehicle operators), and that there is no evidence to support the notions that legalization will result in close regulation and the cessation of illegal sales.

1. More arguments can certainly be made on both sides (see this chapter section), but which faction's arguments, in your opinion, wins your support? Why?

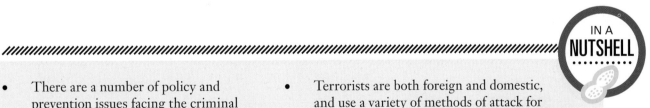

IN A NUTSHELL

- There are a number of policy and prevention issues facing the criminal justice system today, including terrorism, state legalization of marijuana sales and use, human trafficking, and treating and punishing sex offenders.

- Terrorists are both foreign and domestic, and use a variety of methods of attack for making their political and social objectives.

- Today China appears to pose the greatest threat to U.S. security through its cybercrimes.

- A number of law enforcement and legislative approaches have been developed for addressing terrorism and preventing such attacks.

- The expanding use of unmanned aerial vehicles or drones poses significant issues from both the legal and political perspectives. As the technology—size, safety, capability, expanded use—changes with the use of UAVs, so do problems and policy issues involved—one being the use of drones by the federal government against U.S. citizens here and abroad who fit the profile of a terrorist, and striking at them without oversight or approval.

- The United States leads the world in gun ownership and gun-related crimes.

- Today's gun control debate is between people who believe the right to bear arms is not to be infringed, and those who believe as strongly (in light of recent mass killings) that restrictions are needed in terms of the types of guns and ammunition that can be owned (the latter also favoring greater restrictions on background checks for criminal records and mental illness, to keep guns out of the wrong hands).

- A virtual "flurry" of proposed gun laws has occurred since the recent school mass killings, including the aforementioned background criminal history and mental illness checks, allowing more groups to be armed (including teachers), greater allowance of people with concealed-carry permits, banning the sale of assault weapons, reducing sizes of magazine clips, and a national background check system; there may also be calls for greater controls over the levels of violence in video games and movies, and demands for greater restrictions on private gun sales.

- A "sea change" in long-standing marijuana laws may be occurring, in terms of both its recreational and its medical use.

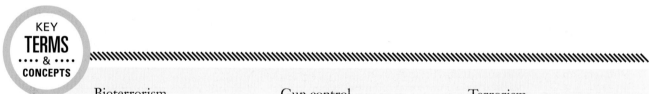

KEY TERMS & CONCEPTS

Bioterrorism	Gun control	Terrorism
Cybercrime/cyberterrorism	Second Amendment	Unmanned aerial vehicles

STUDY SITE

⑤SAGE edge™

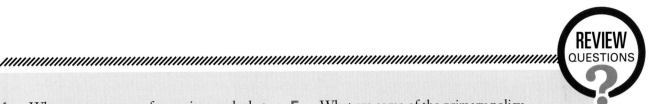

1. What are two types of terrorism, and what are examples of each?

2. What law enforcement and legislative approaches to combating terrorism have taken place?

3. What kinds of threats do cyberterrorists—particularly hackers in China—pose to our security?

4. How do unmanned aerial vehicles fit into the overall discussion of terrorism, and what are some attendant legal considerations?

5. What are some of the primary policy issues involving the question of gun control, and how does mental illness appear to fit into America's gun violence problem?

6. What kinds of laws are being proposed to help gain control of the gun problem?

7. What are some legal, technical, and policy issues that are at the heart of the marijuana-legalization question?

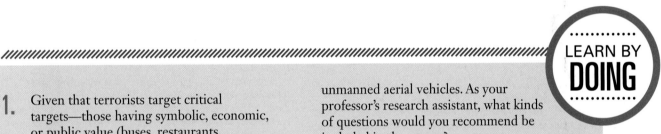

1. Given that terrorists target critical targets—those having symbolic, economic, or public value (buses, restaurants, etc.)—to get public attention and change public behavior, you are to assume the role of someone working in a local police organization or disaster planning agency and then identify all such locations in your area. Then, consider for each the priority responses (i.e., measures taken by police, fire, medical, media, and so on) that would need to occur in the event such an attack took place.

2. A state legislative subcommittee contacts your criminal justice professor seeking input concerning privacy concerns with unmanned aerial vehicles. As your professor's research assistant, what kinds of questions would you recommend be included in the survey?

3. The editorial board for a local newspaper has contacted your criminal justice professor seeking a "Guest Editorial" mapping out the central issues surrounding gun control. She asks you, her independent-study student, to prepare an outline describing the issues to use as a beginning point. What would your outline contain?

4. Assume you are contacted by your state legislator asking to have lunch and discuss the status of marijuana legalization in the United States. What will you say?

APPENDIX

//

CONSTITUTION OF THE UNITED STATES

The United States Constitution was written at a convention that Congress called on February 21, 1787, for the purpose of recommending amendments to the Articles of Confederation. Every state but Rhode Island sent delegates to Philadelphia, where the convention met that summer. The delegates decided to write an entirely new constitution, completing their labors on September 17. Nine states (the number the Constitution itself stipulated as sufficient) ratified by June 21, 1788.

The framers of the Constitution included only six paragraphs on the Supreme Court. Article III, Section 1, created the Supreme Court and the federal system of courts. It provided that "[t]he judicial power of the United States, shall be vested in one supreme Court," and whatever inferior courts Congress "from time to time" saw fit to establish. Article III, Section 2, delineated the types of cases and controversies that should be considered by a federal—rather than a state—court. But beyond this, the Constitution left many of the particulars of the Supreme Court and the federal court system for Congress to decide in later years in judiciary acts.

We the People of the United States, in Order to form a more perfect Union, establish Justice, insure domestic Tranquility, provide for the common defence, promote the general Welfare, and secure the Blessings of Liberty to ourselves and our Posterity, do ordain and establish this Constitution for the United States of America.

ARTICLE I

Section 1. All legislative Powers herein granted shall be vested in a Congress of the United States, which shall consist of a Senate and House of Representatives.

Section 2. The House of Representatives shall be composed of Members chosen every second Year by the People of the several States, and the Electors in each State shall have the Qualifications requisite for Electors of the most numerous Branch of the State Legislature.

No Person shall be a Representative who shall not have attained to the age of twenty five Years, and been seven Years a Citizen of the United States, and who shall not, when elected, be an Inhabitant of that State in which he shall be chosen.

[Representatives and direct Taxes shall be apportioned among the several States which may be included within this Union, according to their respective Numbers, which shall be determined by adding to the whole Number of free Persons, including those bound to Service for a Term of Years, and excluding Indians not taxed, three fifths of all other Persons.][1] The actual Enumeration shall be made within three Years after the first Meeting of the Congress of the United States, and within every subsequent Term of ten Years, in such Manner as they shall by Law direct. The Number of Representatives shall not exceed one for every thirty Thousand, but each State shall have at Least one Representative; and until such enumeration shall be made, the State of New Hampshire shall be entitled to chuse three, Massachusetts eight, Rhode-Island and Providence Plantations one, Connecticut five, New-York six, New Jersey four, Pennsylvania eight, Delaware one, Maryland six, Virginia ten, North Carolina five, South Carolina five, and Georgia three.

When vacancies happen in the Representation from any State, the Executive Authority thereof shall issue Writs of Election to fill such Vacancies.

The House of Representatives shall chuse their Speaker and other Officers; and shall have the sole Power of Impeachment.

Section 3. The Senate of the United States shall be composed of two Senators from each State, [chosen by the Legislature thereof,][2] for six Years; and each Senator shall have one Vote.

Immediately after they shall be assembled in Consequence of the first Election, they shall be divided as equally as may be into three Classes. The Seats of the Senators of the first Class shall be vacated at the Expiration of the second Year, of the second Class at the Expiration of the fourth Year, and of the third Class at the Expiration of the sixth Year, so that one third may be chosen every second Year; [and if Vacancies happen by Resignation, or otherwise, during the Recess of the Legislature of any State, the Executive thereof may make temporary Appointments until the next Meeting of the Legislature, which shall then fill such Vacancies.][3]

No Person shall be a Senator who shall not have attained to the Age of thirty Years, and been nine Years a Citizen of the United States, and who shall not, when elected, be an Inhabitant of that State for which he shall be chosen.

The Vice President of the United States shall be President of the Senate, but shall have no Vote, unless they be equally divided.

The Senate shall chuse their other Officers, and also a President pro tempore, in the Absence of the Vice President, or when he shall exercise the Office of President of the United States.

The Senate shall have the sole Power to try all Impeachments. When sitting for that Purpose, they shall be on Oath or Affirmation. When the President of the United States is tried, the Chief Justice shall preside: And no Person shall be convicted without the Concurrence of two thirds of the Members present.

Judgment in Cases of Impeachment shall not extend further than to removal from Office, and disqualification to hold and enjoy any Office of honor, Trust or Profit under the United States: but the Party convicted shall nevertheless be liable and subject to Indictment, Trial, Judgment and Punishment, according to Law.

Section 4. The Times, Places and Manner of holding Elections for Senators and Representatives, shall be prescribed in each State by the Legislature thereof; but the Congress may at any time by Law make or alter such Regulations, except as to the Places of chusing Senators.

The Congress shall assemble at least once in every Year, and such Meeting shall [be on the first Monday in December],[4] unless they shall by Law appoint a different Day.

Section 5. Each House shall be the Judge of the Elections, Returns and Qualifications of its own Members, and a Majority of each shall constitute a Quorum to do Business; but a smaller Number may adjourn from day to day, and may be authorized to compel the Attendance of absent Members, in such Manner, and under such Penalties as each House may provide.

Each House may determine the Rules of its Proceedings, punish its Members for disorderly Behaviour, and, with the Concurrence of two thirds, expel a Member.

Each House shall keep a Journal of its Proceedings, and from time to time publish the same, excepting such Parts as may in their Judgment require Secrecy; and the Yeas and Nays of the Members of either House on any question shall, at the Desire of one fifth of those Present, be entered on the Journal.

Neither House, during the Session of Congress, shall, without the Consent of the other, adjourn for more than three days, nor to any other Place than that in which the two Houses shall be sitting.

Section 6. The Senators and Representatives shall receive a Compensation for their Services, to be ascertained by Law, and paid out of the Treasury of the United States. They shall in all Cases, except Treason, Felony and Breach of the Peace, be privileged from Arrest during their Attendance at the Session of their respective Houses, and in going to and returning from the same; and for any Speech or Debate in either House, they shall not be questioned in any other Place.

No Senator or Representative shall, during the Time for which he was elected, be appointed to any civil Office under the Authority of the United States, which shall have been created, or the Emoluments whereof shall have been encreased during such time; and no Person holding any Office under the United States, shall be a Member of either House during his Continuance in Office.

Section 7. All Bills for raising Revenue shall originate in the House of Representatives; but the Senate may propose or concur with Amendments as on other Bills.

Every Bill which shall have passed the House of Representatives and the Senate, shall, before it become a Law, be presented to the President of the United States; If he approve he shall sign it, but if not he shall return it, with his Objections to that House in which it shall have originated, who shall enter the Objections at large on their Journal, and proceed to reconsider it. If after such Reconsideration two thirds of that House shall agree to pass the Bill, it shall be sent, together with the Objections, to the other House, by which it shall likewise be reconsidered, and if approved by two thirds of that House, it shall become a Law. But in all such Cases the Votes of both Houses shall be determined by yeas and Nays, and the Names of the Persons voting for and against the Bill shall be entered on the Journal of each House respectively. If any Bill shall not be returned by the President within ten Days (Sundays excepted) after it shall have been presented to him, the Same shall be a Law, in like Manner as if he had signed it, unless the Congress by their Adjournment prevent its Return, in which Case it shall not be a Law.

Every Order, Resolution, or Vote to which the Concurrence of the Senate and House of Representatives may be necessary (except on a question of Adjournment) shall be presented to the President of the United States; and before the Same shall take Effect, shall be approved by him, or being disapproved by him, shall be repassed by two thirds of the Senate and House of Representatives, according to the Rules and Limitations prescribed in the Case of a Bill.

Section 8. The Congress shall have Power To lay and collect Taxes, Duties, Imposts and Excises, to pay the Debts and provide for the common Defence and general Welfare of the United States; but all Duties, Imposts and Excises shall be uniform throughout the United States;

To borrow Money on the credit of the United States;

To regulate Commerce with foreign Nations, and among the several States, and with the Indian Tribes;

To establish an uniform Rule of Naturalization, and uniform Laws on the subject of Bankruptcies throughout the United States;

To coin Money, regulate the Value thereof, and of foreign Coin, and fix the Standard of Weights and Measures;

To provide for the Punishment of counterfeiting the Securities and current Coin of the United States;

To establish Post Offices and post Roads;

To promote the Progress of Science and useful Arts, by securing for limited Times to Authors and Inventors the exclusive Right to their respective Writings and Discoveries;

To constitute Tribunals inferior to the supreme Court;

To define and punish Piracies and Felonies committed on the high Seas, and Offences against the Law of Nations;

To declare War, grant Letters of Marque and Reprisal, and make Rules concerning Captures on Land and Water;

To raise and support Armies, but no Appropriation of Money to that Use shall be for a longer Term than two Years;

To provide and maintain a Navy;

To make Rules for the Government and Regulation of the land and naval Forces;

To provide for calling forth the Militia to execute the Laws of the Union, suppress Insurrections and repel Invasions;

To provide for organizing, arming, and disciplining, the Militia, and for governing such Part of them as may be employed in the Service of the United States, reserving to the States respectively, the Appointment of the Officers, and the Authority of training the Militia according to the discipline prescribed by Congress;

To exercise exclusive Legislation in all Cases whatsoever, over such District (not exceeding ten Miles square) as may, by Cession of particular States, and the Acceptance of Congress, become the Seat of the Government of the United States, and to exercise like Authority over all Places purchased by the Consent of the Legislature of the State in which the Same shall be, for the Erection of Forts, Magazines, Arsenals, dock-Yards, and other needful Buildings;—And

To make all Laws which shall be necessary and proper for carrying into Execution the foregoing Powers, and all other Powers vested by this Constitution in the Government of the United States, or in any Department or Officer thereof.

Section 9. The Migration or Importation of such Persons as any of the States now existing shall think proper to admit, shall not be prohibited by the Congress prior to the Year one thousand eight hundred and eight, but a Tax or duty may be imposed on such Importation, not exceeding ten dollars for each Person.

The Privilege of the Writ of Habeas Corpus shall not be suspended, unless when in Cases of Rebellion or Invasion the public Safety may require it.

No Bill of Attainder or ex post facto Law shall be passed.

No Capitation, or other direct, Tax shall be laid, unless in Proportion to the Census or Enumeration herein before directed to be taken.[5]

No Tax or Duty shall be laid on Articles exported from any State.

No Preference shall be given by any Regulation of Commerce or Revenue to the Ports of one State over those of another; nor shall Vessels bound to, or from, one State, be obliged to enter, clear, or pay Duties in another.

No Money shall be drawn from the Treasury, but in Consequence of Appropriations made by Law; and a regular Statement and Account of the Receipts and Expenditures of all public Money shall be published from time to time.

No Title of Nobility shall be granted by the United States: And no Person holding any Office of Profit or Trust under them, shall, without the Consent of the Congress, accept of any present, Emolument, Office, or Title, of any kind whatever, from any King, Prince, or foreign State.

Section 10. No State shall enter into any Treaty, Alliance, or Confederation; grant Letters of Marque and Reprisal; coin Money; emit Bills of Credit; make any Thing but gold and silver Coin a Tender in Payment of Debts; pass any Bill of Attainder, ex post facto Law, or Law impairing the Obligation of Contracts, or grant any Title of Nobility.

No State shall, without the Consent of the Congress, lay any Imposts or Duties on Imports or Exports, except what may be absolutely necessary for executing its inspection Laws: and the net Produce of all Duties and Imposts, laid by any State on Imports or Exports, shall be for the Use of the Treasury of the United States; and all such Laws shall be subject to the Revision and Controul of the Congress.

No State shall, without the Consent of Congress, lay any Duty of Tonnage, keep Troops, or Ships of War in time of Peace, enter into any Agreement or Compact with another State, or with a foreign Power, or engage in War, unless actually invaded, or in such imminent Danger as will not admit of delay.

ARTICLE II

Section 1. The executive Power shall be vested in a President of the United States of America. He shall hold his Office during the Term of four Years, and, together with the Vice President, chosen for the same Term, be elected, as follows:

Each State shall appoint, in such Manner as the Legislature thereof may direct, a Number of Electors, equal to the whole Number of Senators and Representatives to which the State may be entitled in the Congress: but no Senator or Representative, or Person holding an Office of Trust or Profit under the United States, shall be appointed an Elector.

[The Electors shall meet in their respective States, and vote by Ballot for two Persons, of whom one at least shall not be an Inhabitant of the same State with themselves. And they shall make a List of all the Persons voted for, and of the Number of Votes for each; which List they shall sign and certify, and transmit sealed to the Seat of the Government of the United States, directed to the President of the Senate. The President of the Senate shall, in the Presence of the Senate and House of Representatives, open all the Certificates, and the Votes shall then be counted. The Person having the greatest Number of Votes shall be the President, if such Number be a Majority of the whole Number of Electors appointed; and if there be more than one who have such Majority, and have an equal Number of Votes, then the House of Representatives shall immediately chuse by Ballot one of them for President; and if no Person have a Majority, then from the five highest on the list the said House shall in like Manner chuse the President. But in chusing the President, the Votes shall be taken by States, the Representation from each State having one Vote; A quorum for this Purpose shall consist of a Member or Members from two thirds of the States, and a Majority of all the States shall be necessary to a Choice. In every Case, after the Choice of the President, the Person having the greatest Number of Votes of the Electors shall be the Vice President. But if there should remain two or more who have equal Votes, the Senate shall chuse from them by Ballot the Vice President.][6]

The Congress may determine the Time of chusing the Electors, and the Day on which they shall give their Votes; which Day shall be the same throughout the United States.

No Person except a natural born Citizen, or a Citizen of the United States, at the time of the Adoption of this Constitution, shall be eligible to the Office of President; neither shall any Person be eligible to that Office who shall not have attained to the Age of thirty five Years, and been fourteen Years a Resident within the United States.

In Case of the Removal of the President from Office, or of his Death, Resignation, or Inability to discharge the Powers and Duties of the said Office,[7] the Same shall devolve on the Vice President, and the Congress may by Law provide for the Case of Removal, Death, Resignation or Inability, both of the President and Vice President, declaring what Officer shall then act as President, and such Officer shall act accordingly, until the Disability be removed, or a President shall be elected.

The President shall, at stated Times, receive for his Services, a Compensation, which shall neither be encreased nor diminished during the Period for which he shall have been elected, and he shall not receive within that Period any other Emolument from the United States, or any of them.

Before he enter on the Execution of his Office, he shall take the following Oath or Affirmation:—"I do solemnly swear (or affirm) that I will faithfully execute the Office of President of the United States, and will to the best of my Ability, preserve, protect and defend the Constitution of the United States."

Section 2. The President shall be Commander in Chief of the Army and Navy of the United States, and of the Militia of the several States, when called into the actual Service of the United States; he may require the Opinion, in writing, of the principal Officer in each of the executive Departments, upon any Subject relating to the Duties of their respective Offices, and he shall have Power to grant Reprieves and Pardons for Offences against the United States, except in Cases of Impeachment.

He shall have Power, by and with the Advice and Consent of the Senate, to make Treaties, provided two thirds of the Senators present concur; and he shall nominate, and by and with the Advice and Consent of the Senate, shall appoint Ambassadors, other public Ministers and Consuls, Judges of the supreme Court, and all other Officers of the United States, whose Appointments are not herein otherwise provided for, and which shall be established by Law: but the Congress may by Law vest the Appointment of such inferior Officers, as they think proper, in the President alone, in the Courts of Law, or in the Heads of Departments.

The President shall have Power to fill up all Vacancies that may happen during the Recess of the Senate, by granting Commissions which shall expire at the End of their next Session.

Section 3. He shall from time to time give to the Congress Information of the State of the Union, and recommend to their Consideration such Measures as he shall judge necessary and expedient; he may, on extraordinary Occasions, convene both Houses, or either of them, and in Case of Disagreement between them, with Respect to the Time of Adjournment, he may adjourn them to such Time as he shall think proper; he shall receive Ambassadors and other public Ministers; he shall take Care that the Laws be faithfully executed, and shall Commission all the Officers of the United States.

Section 4. The President, Vice President and all civil Officers of the United States, shall be removed from Office on Impeachment for, and Conviction of, Treason, Bribery, or other high Crimes and Misdemeanors.

ARTICLE III

Section 1. The judicial Power of the United States, shall be vested in one supreme Court, and in such inferior Courts as the Congress may from time to time ordain and establish. The Judges, both of the supreme and inferior Courts, shall hold their Offices during good Behaviour, and shall, at stated Times, receive for their Services, a Compensation, which shall not be diminished during their Continuance in Office.

Section 2. The judicial Power shall extend to all Cases, in Law and Equity, arising under this Constitution, the Laws of the United States, and Treaties made, or which shall be made, under their Authority; —to all Cases affecting Ambassadors, other public Ministers and Consuls; —to all Cases of admiralty and maritime Jurisdiction; —to Controversies to which the United States shall be a Party; —to Controversies between two or more States; —between a State and Citizens of another State;[8] —between Citizens of different States; —between Citizens of the same State claiming Lands under Grants of different States, and between a State, or the Citizens thereof, and foreign States, Citizens or Subjects.

In all Cases affecting Ambassadors, other public Ministers and Consuls, and those in which a State shall be Party, the supreme Court shall have original Jurisdiction. In all the other Cases before mentioned, the supreme Court shall have appellate Jurisdiction, both as to Law and Fact, with such Exceptions, and under such Regulations as the Congress shall make.

The Trial of all Crimes, except in Cases of Impeachment, shall be by Jury; and such Trial shall be held in the State where the said Crimes shall have been committed; but when not committed within any State, the Trial shall be at such Place or Places as the Congress may by Law have directed.

Section 3. Treason against the United States, shall consist only in levying War against them, or in adhering to their Enemies, giving them Aid and Comfort. No Person shall be convicted of Treason unless on the Testimony of two Witnesses to the same overt Act, or on Confession in open Court.

The Congress shall have Power to declare the Punishment of Treason, but no Attainder of Treason shall work Corruption of Blood, or Forfeiture except during the Life of the Person attainted.

ARTICLE IV

Section 1. Full Faith and Credit shall be given in each State to the public Acts, Records, and judicial Proceedings of every other State. And the Congress may by general Laws prescribe the Manner in which such Acts, Records and Proceedings shall be proved, and the Effect thereof.

Section 2. The Citizens of each State shall be entitled to all Privileges and Immunities of Citizens in the several States.

A Person charged in any State with Treason, Felony, or other Crime, who shall flee from Justice, and be found in another State, shall on Demand of the executive Authority of the State from which he fled, be delivered up, to be removed to the State having Jurisdiction of the Crime.

[No Person held to Service or Labour in one State, under the Laws thereof, escaping into another, shall, in Consequence of any Law or Regulation therein, be discharged from such Service or Labour, but shall be delivered up on Claim of the Party to whom such Service or Labour may be due.][9]

Section 3. New States may be admitted by the Congress into this Union; but no new State shall be formed or erected within the Jurisdiction of any other State; nor any State be formed by the Junction of two or more States, or Parts of States, without the Consent of the Legislatures of the States concerned as well as of the Congress.

The Congress shall have Power to dispose of and make all needful Rules and Regulations respecting the Territory or other Property belonging to the United States; and nothing in this Constitution shall be so construed as to Prejudice any Claims of the United States, or of any particular State.

Section 4. The United States shall guarantee to every State in this Union a Republican Form of Government, and shall protect each of them against Invasion; and on Application of the Legislature, or of the Executive (when the Legislature cannot be convened) against domestic Violence.

ARTICLE V

The Congress, whenever two thirds of both Houses shall deem it necessary, shall propose Amendments to this Constitution, or, on the Application of the Legislatures of two thirds of the several States, shall call a Convention for proposing Amendments, which, in either Case, shall be valid to all Intents and Purposes, as Part of this Constitution, when ratified by the Legislatures of three fourths of the several States, or by Conventions in three fourths thereof, as the one or the other Mode of Ratification may be proposed by the Congress; Provided [that no Amendment which may be made prior to the Year One thousand eight hundred and eight shall in any Manner affect the first and fourth Clauses in the Ninth Section of the first Article; and][10] that no State, without its Consent, shall be deprived of its equal Suffrage in the Senate.

ARTICLE VI

All Debts contracted and Engagements entered into, before the Adoption of this Constitution, shall be as valid against the United States under this Constitution, as under the Confederation.

This Constitution, and the Laws of the United States which shall be made in Pursuance thereof; and all Treaties made, or which shall be made, under the Authority of the United States, shall be the supreme Law of the Land; and the Judges in every State shall be bound thereby, any Thing in the Constitution or Laws of any State to the Contrary notwithstanding.

The Senators and Representatives before mentioned, and the Members of the several State Legislatures, and all executive and judicial Officers, both of the United States and of the several States, shall be bound by Oath or Affirmation, to support this Constitution; but no religious Test shall ever be required as a Qualification to any Office or public Trust under the United States.

ARTICLE VII

The Ratification of the Conventions of nine States, shall be sufficient for the Establishment of this Constitution between the States so ratifying the Same.

Done in Convention by the Unanimous Consent of the States present the Seventeenth Day of September in the Year of our Lord one thousand seven hundred and Eighty seven and of the Independence of the United States of America the Twelfth. IN WITNESS whereof We have hereunto subscribed our Names,

George Washington, President and deputy from Virginia, and thirty-eight other delegates.

[The language of the original Constitution, not including the Amendments, was adopted by a convention of the states on September 17, 1787, and was subsequently ratified by the states on the following dates: Delaware, December 7, 1787; Pennsylvania, December 12, 1787; New Jersey, December 18, 1787; Georgia, January 2, 1788; Connecticut, January 9, 1788; Massachusetts, February 6, 1788; Maryland, April 28, 1788; South Carolina, May 23, 1788; New Hampshire, June 21, 1788.

Ratification was completed on June 21, 1788.

The Constitution subsequently was ratified by Virginia, June 25, 1788; New York, July 26, 1788; North Carolina, November 21, 1789; Rhode Island, May 29, 1790; and Vermont, January 10, 1791.]

AMENDMENTS

Amendment I

(First ten amendments ratified December 15, 1791.)

Congress shall make no law respecting an establishment of religion, or prohibiting the free exercise thereof; or abridging the freedom of speech, or of the press; or the right of the people peaceably to assemble, and to petition the Government for a redress of grievances.

Amendment II

A well regulated Militia, being necessary to the security of a free State, the right of the people to keep and bear Arms, shall not be infringed.

Amendment III

No Soldier shall, in time of peace be quartered in any house, without the consent of the Owner, nor in time of war, but in a manner to be prescribed by law.

Amendment IV

The right of the people to be secure in their persons, houses, papers, and effects, against unreasonable searches and seizures, shall not be violated, and no Warrants shall issue, but upon probable cause, supported by Oath or affirmation, and particularly describing the place to be searched, and the persons or things to be seized.

Amendment V

No person shall be held to answer for a capital, or otherwise infamous crime, unless on a presentment or indictment of a Grand Jury, except in cases arising in the land or naval forces, or in the Militia, when in actual service in time of War or public danger; nor shall any person be subject for the same offence to be twice put in jeopardy of life or limb; nor shall be compelled in any criminal case to be a witness against himself, nor be deprived of life, liberty, or property, without due process of law; nor shall private property be taken for public use, without just compensation.

Amendment VI

In all criminal prosecutions, the accused shall enjoy the right to a speedy and public trial, by an impartial jury of the State and district wherein the crime shall have been committed, which district shall have been previously ascertained by law, and to be informed of the nature and cause of the accusation; to be confronted with the witnesses against him; to have compulsory process for obtaining witnesses in his favor, and to have the Assistance of Counsel for his defence.

Amendment VII

In Suits at common law, where the value in controversy shall exceed twenty dollars, the right of trial by jury shall be preserved, and no fact tried by a jury, shall be otherwise re-examined in any Court of the United States, than according to the rules of the common law.

Amendment VIII

Excessive bail shall not be required, nor excessive fines imposed, nor cruel and unusual punishments inflicted.

Amendment IX

The enumeration in the Constitution, of certain rights, shall not be construed to deny or disparage others retained by the people.

Amendment X

The powers not delegated to the United States by the Constitution, nor prohibited by it to the States, are reserved to the States respectively, or to the people.

Amendment XI *(Ratified February 7, 1795)*

The Judicial power of the United States shall not be construed to extend to any suit in law or equity, commenced or prosecuted against one of the United States by Citizens of another State, or by Citizens or Subjects of any Foreign State.

Amendment XII *(Ratified June 15, 1804)*

The Electors shall meet in their respective states and vote by ballot for President and Vice-President, one of whom, at least, shall not be an inhabitant of the same state with themselves; they shall name in their ballots the person voted for as President, and in distinct ballots the person voted for as Vice-President, and they shall make distinct lists of all persons voted for as President, and of all persons voted for as Vice-President, and of the number of votes for each, which lists they shall sign and certify, and transmit sealed to the seat of the government of the United States, directed to the President of the Senate; — The President of the Senate shall, in the presence of the Senate and House of Representatives, open all the certificates and the votes shall then be counted; — The person having the greatest number of votes for President, shall be the President, if such number be a majority of the whole number of Electors appointed; and if no person have such majority, then from the persons having the highest numbers not exceeding three on the list of those voted for as President, the House of Representatives shall choose immediately, by ballot, the President. But in choosing the President, the votes shall be taken by states, the representation from each state having one vote; a quorum for this purpose shall consist of a member or members from two-thirds of the states, and a majority of all the states shall be necessary to a choice. [And if the House of Representatives shall not choose a President whenever the right of choice shall devolve upon them, before the fourth day of March next following, then the Vice-President shall act as President, as in the case of the death or other constitutional disability of the President. —][11] The person having the greatest number of votes as Vice-President, shall be the Vice-President, if such number be a majority of the whole number of Electors appointed, and if no person have a majority, then from the two highest numbers on the list, the Senate shall choose the Vice-President; a quorum for the purpose shall consist of two-thirds of the whole number of Senators, and a majority of the whole number shall be necessary to a choice. But no person constitutionally ineligible to the office of President shall be eligible to that of Vice-President of the United States.

Amendment XIII *(Ratified December 6, 1865)*

Section 1. Neither slavery nor involuntary servitude, except as a punishment for crime whereof the party shall have been duly convicted, shall exist within the United States, or any place subject to their jurisdiction.

Section 2. Congress shall have power to enforce this article by appropriate legislation.

Amendment XIV *(Ratified July 9, 1868)*

Section 1. All persons born or naturalized in the United States, and subject to the jurisdiction thereof, are citizens of the United States and of the State wherein they reside. No State shall make or enforce any law which shall abridge the privileges or immunities of citizens of the United States; nor shall any State deprive any person of life, liberty, or property, without due process of law; nor deny to any person within its jurisdiction the equal protection of the laws.

Section 2. Representatives shall be apportioned among the several States according to their respective numbers, counting the whole number of persons in each State, excluding Indians not taxed. But when the right to vote at any election for the choice of electors for President and Vice President of the United States, Representatives in Congress, the Executive and Judicial officers of a State, or the members of the Legislature thereof, is denied to any of the male inhabitants of such State, being twenty-one years of age,[12] and citizens of the United States, or in any way abridged, except for participation in rebellion, or other crime, the basis of representation therein shall be reduced in the proportion which the number of such male citizens shall bear to the whole number of male citizens twenty-one years of age in such State.

Section 3. No person shall be a Senator or Representative in Congress, or elector of President and Vice President, or hold any Office, civil or military, under the United States, or under any State, who, having previously taken an oath, as a member of Congress, or as an officer of the United States, or as a member of any State legislature, or as an executive or judicial officer of any State, to support the Constitution of the United States, shall have engaged in insurrection or rebellion against the same, or given aid or comfort to the enemies thereof. But Congress may by a vote of two-thirds of each House, remove such disability.

Section 4. The validity of the public debt of the United States, authorized by law, including debts incurred for payment of pensions and bounties for services in suppressing insurrection or rebellion, shall not be questioned. But neither the United States nor any State shall assume or pay any debt or obligation incurred in aid of insurrection or rebellion against the United States, or any claim for the loss or emancipation of any slave; but all such debts, obligations and claims shall be held illegal and void.

Section 5. The Congress shall have power to enforce, by appropriate legislation, the provisions of this article.

Amendment XV *(Ratified February 3, 1870)*

Section 1. The right of citizens of the United States to vote shall not be denied or abridged by the United States or by any State on account of race, color, or previous condition of servitude.

Section 2. The Congress shall have power to enforce this article by appropriate legislation.

Amendment XVI *(Ratified February 3, 1913)*

The Congress shall have power to lay and collect taxes on incomes, from whatever source derived, without apportionment among the several States, and without regard to any census or enumeration.

Amendment XVII *(Ratified April 8, 1913)*

The Senate of the United States shall be composed of two Senators from each State, elected by the people thereof, for six years; and each Senator shall have one vote. The electors in each State shall have the qualifications requisite for electors of the most numerous branch of the State legislatures.

When vacancies happen in the representation of any State in the Senate, the executive authority of such State shall issue writs of election to fill such vacancies: Provided, That the legislature of any State may empower the executive thereof to make temporary appointments until the people fill the vacancies by election as the legislature may direct.

This amendment shall not be so construed as to affect the election or term of any Senator chosen before it becomes valid as part of the Constitution.

Amendment XVIII *(Ratified January 16, 1919)*

Section 1. After one year from the ratification of this article the manufacture, sale, or transportation of intoxicating liquors within, the importation thereof into, or the exportation thereof from the United States and all territory subject to the jurisdiction thereof for beverage purposes is hereby prohibited.

Section 2. The Congress and the several States shall have concurrent power to enforce this article by appropriate legislation.

Section 3. This article shall be inoperative unless it shall have been ratified as an amendment to the Constitution by the legislatures of the several States, as provided in the Constitution, within seven years from the date of the submission hereof to the States by the Congress.[13]

Amendment XIX *(Ratified August 18, 1920)*

The right of citizens of the United States to vote shall not be denied or abridged by the United States or by any State on account of sex.

Congress shall have power to enforce this article by appropriate legislation.

Amendment XX *(Ratified January 23, 1933)*

Section 1. The terms of the President and Vice President shall end at noon on the 20th day of January, and the terms of Senators and Representatives at noon on the 3d day of January, of the years in which such terms would have ended if this article had not been ratified; and the terms of their successors shall then begin.

Section 2. The Congress shall assemble at least once in every year, and such meeting shall begin at noon on the 3d day of January, unless they shall by law appoint a different day.

Section 3.[14] If, at the time fixed for the beginning of the term of the President, the President elect shall have died, the Vice President elect shall become President. If a President shall not have been chosen before the time fixed for the beginning of his term, or if the President elect shall have failed to qualify, then the Vice President elect shall act as President until a President shall have qualified; and the Congress may by law provide for the case wherein neither a President elect nor a Vice President elect shall have qualified, declaring who shall then act as President, or the manner in which one who is to act shall be selected, and such person shall act accordingly until a President or Vice President shall have qualified.

Section 4. The Congress may by law provide for the case of the death of any of the persons from whom the House of Representatives may choose a President whenever the right of choice shall have devolved upon them, and for the case of the death of any of the persons from whom the Senate may choose a Vice President whenever the right of choice shall have devolved upon them.

Section 5. Sections 1 and 2 shall take effect on the 15th day of October following the ratification of this article.

Section 6. This article shall be inoperative unless it shall have been ratified as an amendment to the Constitution by the legislatures of three-fourths of the several States within seven years from the date of its submission.

Amendment XXI *(Ratified December 5, 1933)*

Section 1. The eighteenth article of amendment to the Constitution of the United States is hereby repealed.

Section 2. The transportation or importation into any State, Territory, or possession of the United States for delivery or use therein of intoxicating liquors, in violation of the laws thereof, is hereby prohibited.

Section 3. This article shall be inoperative unless it shall have been ratified as an amendment to the Constitution by conventions in the several States, as provided in the Constitution, within seven years from the date of the submission hereof to the States by the Congress.

Amendment XXII *(Ratified February 27, 1951)*

Section 1. No person shall be elected to the office of the President more than twice, and no person who has held the office of President, or acted as President, for more than two years of a term to which some other person was elected President shall be elected to the office of the President more than once. But this Article shall not apply to any person holding the office of President when this Article was proposed by the Congress, and shall not prevent any person who may be holding the office of President, or acting as President, during the term within which this Article becomes operative from holding the office of President or acting as President during the remainder of such term.

Section 2. This article shall be inoperative unless it shall have been ratified as an amendment to the Constitution by the legislatures of three-fourths of the several States within seven years from the date of its submission to the States by the Congress.

Amendment XXIII *(Ratified March 29, 1961)*

Section 1. The District constituting the seat of Government of the United States shall appoint in such manner as the Congress may direct:

A number of electors of President and Vice President equal to the whole number of Senators and Representatives in Congress to which the District would be entitled if it were a State, but in no event more than the least populous State; they shall be in addition to those appointed by the States, but they shall be considered, for the purposes of the election of President and Vice President, to be electors appointed by a State; and they shall meet in the District and perform such duties as provided by the twelfth article of amendment.

Section 2. The Congress shall have power to enforce this article by appropriate legislation.

Amendment XXIV *(Ratified January 23, 1964)*

Section 1. The right of citizens of the United States to vote in any primary or other election for President or Vice President, for electors for President or Vice President, or for Senator or Representative in Congress, shall not be denied or abridged by the United States or any State by reason of failure to pay any poll tax or other tax.

Section 2. The Congress shall have power to enforce this article by appropriate legislation.

Amendment XXV *(Ratified February 10, 1967)*

Section 1. In case of the removal of the President from office or of his death or resignation, the Vice President shall become President.

Section 2. Whenever there is a vacancy in the office of the Vice President, the President shall nominate a Vice President who shall take office upon confirmation by a majority vote of both Houses of Congress.

Section 3. Whenever the President transmits to the President pro tempore of the Senate and the Speaker of the House of Representatives his written declaration that he is unable to discharge the powers and duties of his office, and until he transmits to them a written declaration to the contrary, such powers and duties shall be discharged by the Vice President as Acting President.

Section 4. Whenever the Vice President and a majority of either the principal officers of the executive departments or of such other body as Congress may by law provide, transmit to the President pro tempore of the Senate and the Speaker of the House of Representatives their written declaration that the President is unable to discharge the powers and duties of his office, the Vice President shall immediately assume the powers and duties of the office as Acting President.

Thereafter, when the President transmits to the President pro tempore of the Senate and the Speaker of the House of Representatives his written declaration that no inability exists, he shall resume the powers and duties of his office unless the Vice President and a majority of either the principal officers of the executive departments or of such other body as Congress may by law provide, transmit within four days to the President pro tempore of the Senate and the Speaker of the House of Representatives their written declaration that the President is unable to discharge the powers and duties of his office. Thereupon Congress shall decide the issue, assembling within forty-eight hours for that purpose if not in session. If the Congress, within twenty-one days after receipt of the latter written declaration, or, if Congress is not in session, within twenty-one days after Congress is required to assemble, determines by two-thirds vote of both Houses that the President is unable to discharge the powers and duties of his office, the Vice President shall continue to discharge the same as Acting President; otherwise, the President shall resume the powers and duties of his office.

Amendment XXVI *(Ratified July 1, 1971)*

Section 1. The right of citizens of the United States, who are eighteen years of age or older, to vote shall not be denied or abridged by the United States or by any State on account of age.

Section 2. The Congress shall have power to enforce this article by appropriate legislation.

Amendment XXVII *(Ratified May 7, 1992)*

No law varying the compensation for the services of the Senators and Representatives shall take effect, until an election of Representatives shall have intervened.

Source: U.S. Congress, House, Committee on the Judiciary, The Constitution of the United States of America, as Amended, 100th Cong., 1st sess., 1987, H Doc 100–94.

Notes:

1. The part in brackets was changed by section 2 of the Fourteenth Amendment.
2. The part in brackets was changed by the first paragraph of the Seventeenth Amendment.
3. The part in brackets was changed by the second paragraph of the Seventeenth Amendment.
4. The part in brackets was changed by section 2 of the Twentieth Amendment.
5. The Sixteenth Amendment gave Congress the power to tax incomes.
6. The material in brackets was superseded by the Twelfth Amendment.
7. This provision was affected by the Twenty-fifth Amendment.
8. These clauses were affected by the Eleventh Amendment.
9. This paragraph was superseded by the Thirteenth Amendment.
10. Obsolete.
11. The part in brackets was superseded by Section 3 of the Twentieth Amendment.
12. See the Nineteenth and Twenty-sixth Amendments.
13. This amendment was repealed by Section 1 of the Twenty-first Amendment.
14. See the Twenty-fifth Amendment.

ANSWERS

Chapter 1	1. t; 2. f; 3. t; 4. f; 5. f; 6. t; 7. f	**Chapter 9**	1. t; 2. t; 3. t; 4. f; 5. f; 6. t; 7. f
Chapter 2	1. t; 2. f; 3. f; 4. t; 5. t; 6. t; 7. f	**Chapter 10**	1. f; 2. t; 3. t; 4. t; 5. t; 6. f; 7. f
Chapter 3	1. f; 2. f; 3. t; 4. t; 5. f; 6. t; 7. t; 8. f	**Chapter 11**	1. f; 2. t; 3. f; 4. t; 5. t; 6. f; 7. t
Chapter 4	1. t; 2. f; 3. t; 4. f; 5. f; 6. f; 7. f	**Chapter 12**	1. t; 2. f; 3. t; 4. f; 5. f; 6. f; 7. f
Chapter 5	1. t; 2. t.; 3. f; 4. t; 5. f; 6. t; 7. f	**Chapter 13**	1. t; 2. t; 3. f; 4. f; 5. t; 6. f; 7. t
Chapter 6	1. f; 2. t; 3. f; 4. f; 5. f; 6. t; 7. f	**Chapter 14**	1. t; 2. f; 3. f; 4. t; 5. f; 6. t; 7. t
Chapter 7	1. f; 2. f; 3. f; 4. t; 5. t; 6. f; 7. t	**Chapter 15**	1. f; 2. f; 3. t; 4. t; 5. f; 6. f; 7; f
Chapter 8	1. t; 2. t; 3. t; 4. t; 5. f; 6. t; 7. t	**Chapter 16**	1. f; 2. f; 3. f; 4. t; 5. t; 6. f; 7. t

GLOSSARY

This glossary contains key terms and concepts relating to the U.S. criminal justice system. Omitted are criminal justice organizations and associations as well as many crime definitions (only Part I offenses are included).

Absolute ethics: the type of ethics where there are only two sides—good or bad, black or white; some examples would be unethical behaviors such as bribery, extortion, excessive force, and perjury, which nearly everyone would agree are unacceptable for criminal justice personnel.

Absolute immunity: government officials enjoy complete immunity from lawsuits from probationers, parolees, or inmates for their actions.

Academy training: police and corrections personnel are trained in the basic functions, laws, and skills required for their positions.

Accepted lying: police activities intended to apprehend or entrap suspects. This type of lying is generally considered to be trickery.

Accessory: a person who assists another person in planning, committing, or concealing a crime.

Accused: one who is alleged to have committed a crime; the defendant in a criminal action.

Acquittal: a court or jury's judgment or verdict of not guilty of the offenses charged.

Actus reus: "guilty deed" (Latin)—an act that accompanies one's intent to commit a crime, such as pulling out a knife and then stabbing someone.

Adjudication: the legal resolution of a dispute—for example, when one is declared guilty, or a juvenile is declared to be dependent and neglected—by a judge or jury.

Adoption studies: research examining people who have been adopted from their natural parents and raised by a different set of parents to determine if a strong genetic influence over criminal behavior exists.

Adversarial system: a legal system wherein there is a contest between two opposing sides, with a judge (and possibly jury) sitting as an impartial arbiter, seeking truth.

Affiant: one who makes a statement under oath claiming to possess certain facts concerning a crime.

Affidavit: any written document in which the signer swears under oath before a notary public or someone authorized to take oaths (like a county clerk) that the statements in the document are true.

Affirm: in court, to uphold or validate an earlier decision or ruling.

Affirmative defense: a situation where the defendant admits he or she committed the act charged, but for some mitigating reason (self-defense, mental illness, duress, mistake, intoxication) should be treated more lightly (or excused) under the law; he or she thus has the burden of proof to establish the claim.

Aggravated assault: an unlawful attack against another for the purpose of inflicting serious bodily harm or injury.

Aggravating circumstances: elements of a crime that enhance its seriousness, such as the infliction of torture, killing of a police or corrections officer, and so on.

Alford plea: a *nolo contendere* ("no contest") plea where the defendant does not wish to fully admit guilt, but does admit to certain facts as charged by the prosecution.

Allocution: the right of a convicted defendant to address the court prior to imposition of a sentence.

Alternative dispute resolution: where a civil or criminal matter is decided by an impartial arbiter, with both parties agreeing to a settlement; usually followed only in minor offenses.

Alternatives to incarceration: a sentence imposed by a judge other than incarceration, such as probation, parole, shock probation, or house arrest.

AMBER alert: a system used by police and news agencies to broadcast an urgent message in serious child-abduction cases.

Amicus curiae: "friend of the court" (Latin)—one who is allowed to file a brief or opinion with a court and present legal arguments or facts on behalf of someone else.

Appeal: a written petition to a higher court to modify or reverse a decision of a lower court.

Appellant: one who initiates an appeal.

Appellate review: a rehearing of a case in a court other than that in which the trial was conducted.

Appointed (assigned) counsel: a private attorney appointed by the court to represent an indigent defendant.

Arraignment: an official proceeding in which a criminal defendant is formally charged.

Arrest: the taking into custody or detaining of one who is suspected of committing a crime, to answer the charges against him or her.

Arrest warrant (see *Warrant, arrest*).

Arson: criminal intent to burn, or attempt to burn, a home, a building, an automobile, or other property.

Assault: any unlawful attempt to use force or violence and to harm or frighten another person.

Assault and battery: the assault is put into effect by the unlawful application of violence to another person.

Assault with a deadly weapon: intentionally inflicting, or attempting to inflict, serious bodily harm, injury, or death with the use of a weapon.

Attempt (criminal): an overt action where the offender intentionally goes beyond preparation but does not necessarily complete the criminal act.

Attorney-client privilege: confidentiality that exists between lawyers and their criminal clients or defendants, to prevent disclosure of incriminating evidence.

Automobile exception: an exception to the prohibition of warrantless searches, where probable cause to conduct a search is present, and there is a likelihood that incriminating evidence may be removed or destroyed.

Bail: surety (e.g., cash or paper bond) provided by a defendant to guarantee his or her return to court to answer to criminal charges; also see *bond*.

Bailiff: a court officer who maintains order in the court, oversees the jury during trial, and at times escorts prisoners while in the courtroom.

Ballistics: the study of the action of bullets as they are acted upon by wind, gravity, temperature, and so on.

Battery: the intentional touch or striking of another person.

Beat: a geographical area assigned to a patrol, correctional, or other officer.

Bench: the place where judges sit while conducting a trial.

Bench trial: a trial in which the guilt or innocence of a defendant will be decided by the judge rather than a jury.

Bench warrant: a document issued by a judge demanding that person be brought before the court without delay.

Beyond a reasonable doubt: the standard used in criminal courts to establish a defendant's guilt.

Bifurcated trial: in a capital case, where the jury first decides guilt or innocence and, if finding guilt, then reconvenes to determine the punishment (to include the death penalty).

Bill of Rights: the first 10 amendments to the U.S. Constitution that set forth basic freedoms and guarantees.

Biological determinism: a view in criminology stating that criminality is caused for physiological reasons, such as genes, foods, hormones, and inheritance.

Bioterrorism: the use of biological material, such as anthrax or botulin, to commit an act of terrorism.

Blood-alcohol content: the amount of alcohol that is contained in one's blood; used to determine intoxication for motorists.

Blue curtain: the term for the reluctance among police to punish one of their own; the wall of police silence that prevents police from being accountable.

Body type studies: 19th- and 20th-century theorists argued that body types led to patterns of criminal behavior; currently outmoded.

Bond: a document indicating that a defendant's sureties will guarantee his or her appearance for trial; if the defendant does not appear, the bond is forfeited.

Booking: basically a clerical procedure for when an arrestee is taken to jail and a record is made of his or her name, address, charge(s), arresting officers, time and place of arrest, and so on.

Boot camp: a short-term jail or prison program that puts offenders through a rigorous physical and mental regimen designed to instill discipline and respect for authority.

Brady Bill: named for Jim Brady, President Ronald Reagan's press secretary who was shot by John Hinckley in 1981, the bill is a piece of legislation designed to reduce opportunities for criminals to purchase firearms through background checks, waiting periods, and so on.

"Broken windows" theory: the theory that states when a neighborhood begins to deteriorate (e.g., debris, neglected buildings, and abandoned cars and homes), the "signal" goes out to offenders that no one cares, and thus a downward spiral of neglect and crime will soon follow.

Burden of proof: the requirement that the state must meet to introduce evidence or establish facts.

Bureaucracy: an organizational model that often includes division of labor, clearly defined responsibilities, lines of communication, and chain of command (such as in prisons and police agencies).

Bureaus of criminal identification: similar to the FBI, these are state agencies that perform routine identification and investigation functions.

Burglary: the unlawful entry of a home or business with the intent of committing an offense therein.

Capital punishment: a sentence of death, or carrying out same via execution of the offender.

Career criminal: one who habitually and chronically commits crimes and has a lengthy criminal record.

Caseload: the number of cases awaiting disposition by a court, or the number of active cases or clients maintained by a probation or parole officer.

Castle doctrine: the common law doctrine that states, "A man's home is his castle." One could use whatever force was necessary to protect his home.

Causation: a link between one's act and the injurious act or crime, such as one tossing a match in a forest and igniting a deadly fire.

Chain of command: vertical and horizontal power relations within an organization, showing how one position relates to others.

Change of venue: a change in the location of trial, so as to hopefully have a more fair trial where there has been less publicity and emotion tied to the case.

Chief justice: the presiding or principal judge of a court, particularly the U.S. Supreme Court or a state court of last resort.

Chief of police: a police officer who is appointed or elected as head of a police agency.

Child abuse: any form of cruelty to the physical, moral, or mental well-being of a child, to include such behaviors as violence, neglect, endangerment, sex trafficking, and molestation.

Circuit courts: originally courts wherein judges traveled a circuit to hear appeals, now courts with several counties or districts in their jurisdiction; the federal court system contains 11 circuit courts of appeals (plus the District of Columbia and territories), which hear appeals from district courts.

Circumstantial evidence: material information provided by a witness from which a jury might infer a fact.

Citation: a document issued by a police officer and ordering someone to appear in court (or pay a fine) to answer to a specific charge.

Citizen complaint: a grievance filed by a citizen with the police or the prosecutor alleging he or she was injured or harmed in some way.

Civil law: a generic term for all noncriminal law, usually relating to settling disputes between private citizens.

Civil liability: in tort law, the basis for which a cause of action (e.g., fine) is made to recover damages; in criminal justice, where a police or corrections officer, for example, violates someone's civil rights.

Civil liberties: rights guaranteed by the U.S. Constitution and Bill of Rights.

Civil rights: liberties possessed by citizens and guaranteed by the government.

Classical school (of criminology): a perspective indicating that people have free will to choose between criminal and lawful behavior, and that crime can be controlled by sanctions and should be proportionate to the offense.

Classification (of inmates): inmate security and treatment plan based on one's security, social, vocational, psychological, and educational needs while incarcerated.

Clearance rate: the percentage of crimes known to police that are cleared by an arrest or some other means.

Clemency: a grant of mercy by an executive official to a convicted offender, to include commuting or pardoning a criminal sentence.

Code of ethics: rules of behavior developed by an organization to guide the actions of its workers.

Code of Hammurabi: Babylon's first written criminal code, in about 1770 B.C.

Code of silence or secrecy (see *Blue curtain*).

CODIS: a "Combined DNA Index System" that contains federal, state, and local databases and uses DNA to solve a variety of crimes.

Color of law (*see Section 1983*).

Comity: a judicial courtesy whereby the federal courts first defer to the state courts to try their criminal cases, or where states recognize the laws of other jurisdictions.

Community corrections: the supervision of criminal offenders in the community, primarily through probation and parole status.

Community era: beginning in about 1980, a time when the police retrained to work with the community to solve problems by looking at their underlying causes and developing tailored responses to them.

Community policing and problem solving (see *Community era*).

Competency hearing: a court hearing to determine whether a defendant is mentally fit to stand trial.

Complainant: one who swears out a criminal complaint against another person.

CompStat: a crime analysis and management process begun by the New York Police Department that includes collecting, analyzing, and mapping of crime data and deploying resources accordingly—with performance measures and accountability placed on police managers to reduce crime.

Concurrent sentence: a situation where two or more criminal sentences are served simultaneously.

Conditional pardon: an action by a governor or pardons board to grant a pardon to a convicted offender, with conditions or requirements articulated.

Conflict theory: said to exist in societies where the worker class is exploited by the ruling class, which owns and controls the means of production and thus maintains the constant state of conflict between the two classes.

Conjugal visits: in jails or prisons, visits where inmates showing good behavior are permitted to spend time and have contact with their spouses or significant others; sexual contact is often allowed between inmates and their spouses.

Consecutive sentences: a situation where one's criminal sentences are to be served one after another (as opposed to concurrently).

Consensus theory: said to exist where a society functions as a result of a group's common interests and values, which have been developed largely because the people have experienced similar socialization.

Constable: in England, favored noblemen who were forerunners of modern-day U.S. criminal justice functionaries; largely disappearing in the United States by the 1970s.

Constitution, U.S.: the basis of law in the United States, written in 1787 and ratified by the states in 1788, and amended subsequently to afford greater rights as new Supreme Court decisions and congressional interpretations are issued.

Control theories (of crime): explanations of crime that include cohesiveness of social ties and interpersonal obligations.

Convict: an adult who has been found guilty of perpetrating a crime; also an inmate of a jail or prison.

Coroner: an early English court officer; today one (usually a physician) in the United States whose duty it is to determine cause of death.

Corporate crime: crimes committed by wealthy or powerful individuals in the course of their professions or occupations; includes price-fixing, insider trading, and other "white collar" crimes.

Correctional facility: a building or set of buildings intended to house convicted offenders or adjudicated delinquents.

Correctional officer: one who works in a jail or prison and supervises correctional inmates.

Corrections: a broad term that includes facilities, programs, and organizations responsible for the management of people who have been accused or convicted of a crime(s).

Court: a public, judicial body that applies the law to criminal and civil matters and oversees the administration of justice and jurisprudence.

Court delay: the unnecessary prolonging or continuing of a judicial proceeding.

Courthouse violence: acts ranging from physical attacks against the courtroom work group, victims, or witnesses to attempts to maim or kill same.

Court of last resort: the last court that may hear a case at the state or federal level.

Courtroom work group: all parties involved in the adversarial process: judges, defense and prosecuting attorneys, court clerks, bailiffs, and court reporters.

Court unification: a proposal that seeks to centralize, unify, or otherwise simplify a state's court system.

CPTED: crime prevention through environmental design—a concept of crime prevention that maintains that crimes may be reduced or eliminated by changing certain characteristics of the physical environment.

Crime against persons: a violent crime, to include murder, rape, robbery, and assault.

Crime against property: a crime where no violence is perpetrated, such as burglary, theft, auto theft, and arson.

Crime Clock: a graph published by the FBI that depicts how many crimes are committed by hour, minute, or second.

Crime control model: a model by Packer that emphasizes law and order and argues that every effort must be made to suppress crime, and to try, convict, and incarcerate offenders.

Crime mapping: plotting of crimes on maps so as to show patterns of location, time, day, and so on.

Crime of passion: a crime that is prompted by intense anger and emotion, often between spouses or lovers.

Crime rate: the number of reported crimes divided by the population of the jurisdiction, and multiplied by 100,000 persons; developed and used by the FBI *Uniform Crime Reports*.

Criminal: anyone who has committed a crime, whether convicted of the offense or not.

Criminal atavism: the idea that offenders possess anomalies that make them biologically and physiologically similar to our ancestors—savage throwbacks to an earlier time.

Criminal intent: a necessary element of a crime; the evil intent, or *mens rea*.

Criminalist: a police crime scene analyst or laboratory examiner skilled in criminalistics or forensics aspects of investigation.

Criminalistics: the use of chemical, biological, physics, or other techniques to solve crimes by evaluating evidence.

Criminal justice flow and process: the horizontal movement of defendants and cases

through the criminal justice process, beginning with the commission of a crime, investigation, arrest, initial appearance, arraignment, trial, verdict, sentencing, and appeal (to include vertical movement, as when a case is dropped or for some other reason one leaves the system).

Criminal law: the body of law that defines criminal offenses and prescribes punishments for their infractions.

Criminal procedure: rules of law governing the manner in which cases are investigated, prosecuted, adjudicated, and punished.

Criminal responsibility: any personal liability incurred as the result of one's committing a crime.

Criminal sanction: the right of a state or federal jurisdiction to punish offenders as set forth in criminal codes, or the punishment connected to the commission of a crime.

Criminal trial: an adversarial proceeding in which a judicial determination of issues can be made and a defendant's guilt or innocence decided.

Criminal typologies: categories by which criminologists classify offenders.

Criminological theory: any systematic attempt to explain the causes or roots of crime.

Criminologist: a professional, usually a scholar, who studies crime, criminal law, criminals, and criminal behavior and trends.

Criminology: the study of crime and behavior (see *criminological theory*).

Critical theory: a school of thought in criminology arguing that crime is largely a product of capitalism, that laws are created to separate haves and have-nots and are wielded by those in power.

Cruel and unusual punishment: punishment prohibited by the Eighth Amendment, sometimes said to "shock the conscience."

"CSI effect": a phenomenon reported by prosecutors who claim that television shows based on scientific crime solving have made actual jurors reluctant to vote to convict when, as is typically true, forensic evidence is neither necessary nor available.

Culpability: sufficiently responsible for criminal acts or negligence to be at fault and liable for the conduct.

Custodial interrogation: questions posed by police while the suspect is held in custody, pretrial.

Custodial officer: any official with the responsibility for ensuring the care, custody, and safety of incarcerated persons.

Custody: restraint of a person who is held on suspicion of committing a crime.

Custody, maximum: holding inmates or patients in jails or prisons with few amenities or freedom.

Custody, medium: a situation where inmates are given more amenities than in maximum security, such as freedom to go to the prison yard.

Custody, minimum: the least restrictive form of custody, where inmates have more extensive freedoms of movement and amenities.

Cybercrime/cyberterrorism: computer uses to commit crimes, such as embezzlement, diversion of bank monies to other accounts, and so on; making use of high technology, normally the Internet, to plan and carry out acts of terrorism.

Cyberstalking: using computers or the Internet to harass or invade privacy of another person.

Damages: sums of money awarded to prevailing litigants.

Day reporting center: a structured corrections program requiring offenders to check in at a community site on a regular basis for supervision, sanctions, and services.

Deadly force: lethal force used by law enforcement officers or other persons to apprehend an offender or protect one's own life.

Deadly weapon: an instrument designed to inflict serious bodily harm or injury.

Death penalty (see *Capital punishment*).

Death row: a place within a prison setting in which condemned inmates are housed while awaiting execution for committing a capital offense.

Decor, court: The physical aspects of courtroom facilities, which are to convey an image of dignity and solemnity in a facility is which justice is rendered.

Decorum: the manner in which one must conduct his or her behavior in a courtroom—for example, obtaining permission to speak to the judge or to approach the bench.

Defendant: a person against whom a criminal charge is pending; one charged with a crime.

Defense: the response by a defendant to a criminal charge, to include denial of the criminal allegations in an attempt to negate or overcome the charges.

Defense attorney: one whose responsibility is to see that the rights of the accused are upheld prior to, during, and after trial; the Sixth Amendment provides for "effective" counsel, among other constitutionally enumerated rights that defense attorneys must see are upheld.

Deinstitutionalization: providing programs in a community setting rather than placing one in jail or prison.

Delay (trial): an attempt (usually by defense counsel) to have a criminal trial continued until a later date.

Deontological ethics: one's duty to act.

Detective/investigator: a police officer who is assigned to investigate reported crimes, to include gathering evidence, completing case reports, testifying in court, and so on.

Detention: a period of custody—usually of juveniles—prior to their case disposition.

Determinate sentence: a specific, fixed-period sentence ordered by a court.

Determinism: a concept holding that people do not have free will but are instead subjected to the influence of various forces over which they have little or no control.

Deterrence, general/specific: actions that are designed to prevent crimes from occurring;

Deviance: conduct that departs from what is considered to be accepted and lawful by society or a group.

Deviant lying: occasions when officers commit perjury to convict suspects or are deceptive about some activity that is illegal or unacceptable to the department or public in general

Differential association: a crime theory by Sutherland that through interactions with others, one learns the values, attitudes, techniques, and motives for criminal behavior.

Diminished capacity: a defense based on the claim of a mental condition that negates or reduces one's level of guilt.

Direct evidence: evidence that is offered by an eyewitness who testifies to what he or she actually saw.

Direct examination: questioning by an attorney of one's own (defense or prosecution) witness during a trial.

Directed patrol: a patrol strategy designed to direct police resources to the high-crime areas in a proactive manner.

Directed verdict: an order by a court declaring that the prosecution has failed to provide its case with sufficient evidence, or prove guilt beyond a reasonable doubt.

Discovery: a procedure wherein both the prosecution and the defense exchange and share information as to witnesses to be used, results of tests, recorded statements by defendants, psychiatric reports, and so on, so that there are no major surprises at trial; known as "Brady material," based on *Brady v. Maryland* (1963).

Discretion: authority to make decisions in enforcing the law based on one's observations and judgment ("spirit of the law") rather than the letter of the law.

Disorder: behavior that disturbs the public peace.

Displacement: the relocation of crimes to another geographical area, often due to enhanced police presence or practices.

Disposition: an outcome of a criminal or juvenile court process signifying that the matter is completed.

District attorney: a federal, state, or local prosecutor who represents the people, particularly victims.

District courts: trial courts at the county, state, or federal level with general and original jurisdiction.

Diversion program: removing a case from the criminal justice system, normally to move a defendant into another treatment program or modality.

DNA: deoxyribonucleic acid, or the acids found in all cells; used in forensics to match evidence (e.g., hair, semen) left at a crime scene with a particular perpetrator.

Domestic terrorism: terroristic acts committed on domestic soil by a nation's own citizens.

Domestic violence: an altercation or conflict of such nature as to justify police intervention; spousal abuse is common, as is parent-child abuse.

Double jeopardy: subjecting an accused person to be tried twice for the same offense; prohibited by the Fifth Amendment.

Driving while black or brown: also known as biased policing, a phrase used to describe a police practice whereby minority citizens are stopped in their vehicles or on the streets and questioned when there is no legal justification for such a stop.

Dual court system: a term basically meaning there are both state and federal court systems.

Due process: essentially, giving one his or her process that is due: presumption of innocence, right to be heard and present witnesses, right to burden of proof beyond reasonable doubt, right to appeal, and so on.

Due process model: articulated by Packer (see *Crime control model*), it assumes that freedom is so important that all acts and processes of the justice system must be right and proper, with no restriction or abridgment of individual rights, and that police must act accordingly.

Duress: an affirmative defense where one argues he or she lacked criminal intent but committed the offense because of the psychological or physical force or threat posed by someone else.

Durham rule: an insanity test that says one has a mental disease or defect that caused him or her to commit a crime, and thus he or she did not possess the requisite intent or *mens rea.*

Duty of care: a legal obligation imposed on someone; in the case of the police, they have a legal responsibility to see that persons in their custody are free from harm, given necessary medical assistance when necessary, and treated humanely.

Economic crime: a crime that is committed to bring financial gain to the offender.

Eighth Amendment: an amendment to the U.S. Constitution that prohibits excessive bail and cruel and unusual punishment.

Electronic monitoring: use of electronic devices (bracelets or anklets) to emit signals when a convicted offender (usually on house arrest) leaves the environment in which he or she is to remain.

Entrapment: police tactics that overly encourage or entice individuals to commit crimes they normally would not commit.

Equal protection: in the Fourteenth Amendment, a guarantee to all citizens of equal treatment under the law without regard to race, gender, class, religion, or ethnicity.

Estoppel (also termed *Collateral estoppel*): a legal term for preventing someone from doing something.

Ethics: a set of rules or values that spell out appropriate human conduct.

Etiology of crime: the study of the causes of crime.

Evidence: materials that are admissible in court that indicate the guilt or innocence of a defendant.

Excessive force: physical force that is used beyond that which is allowed or necessary under the circumstances.

Exclusionary rule: the rule (see *Mapp v. Ohio*, 1961) providing that evidence obtained improperly cannot be used against the accused at trial.

Exculpatory evidence: evidence that tends to establish or indicate innocence of the accused.

Excusable homicide: a death resulting from some act that involves an accident or from misfortune.

Execution: the legal enforcement of the death penalty.

Executioner: one who actually puts condemned persons to death.

Exigent circumstance: an instance where quick, emergency action is required, such as searching for drugs before they are removed or destroyed.

Exoneration: to absolve someone of criminal blame, or find someone not guilty.

Expert witness: one with expertise and special knowledge in a given field who is qualified to appear at trial and render an opinion about reports or actions involved in a criminal case.

***Ex post facto* laws:** laws that make an act illegal retroactively; such laws are not constitutional.

Expunge: to delete one's arrest record, or remove an arrest from the record.

Extenuating circumstances: conditions under which an offender might be excused from being blameworthy, such as one arguing he was provoked into killing someone and is thus not guilty of murder.

Extradition: the taking of a person from one jurisdiction to another (the site of the offense, usually) for purpose of a criminal prosecution.

Eyewitness testimony: information given in court by someone who saw a crime occur.

Failure to appear: when a defendant fails to appear for trial or some other formal proceeding.

Failure to protect: a situation where police place someone in jeopardy, such as giving out the location of a battered spouse or names of victims or witnesses.

False arrest: unlawful physical restraint by a police officer, for no valid reason.

False imprisonment: unlawfully detaining or restraining a person.

Family court: a court of original jurisdiction that handles family problems, from juvenile crimes to divorces.

Federal court system: the four-tiered federal system that includes supreme courts, circuit courts of appeal, district courts, and magistrate courts.

Federal district courts: basic trial courts for the federal government, for federal offenses; there are 94 of them.

Federal law enforcement agencies: federal organizations that, for example, are charged with protecting the homeland (DHS); investigating crimes (DOJ, FBI) and enforcing particular laws, such as those pertaining to drugs (DEA) or alcohol/tobacco/firearms/ explosives (ATF); and guarding the courts and transporting prisoners (USMS).

Federal prison: a correctional facility operated by the Federal Bureau of Prisons for confining and punishing those who commit federal crimes.

Federal rules of evidence: procedures spelled out that guide the presentation of evidence in federal courts or bodies.

Federal Witness Security Program: an organization that exists to protect persons giving evidence against criminal in

federal trials, giving them new names and identifications, places of residence, and so forth so as to protect them from retribution.

Felon: one who has committed a crime defined as a felony.

Felony: a crime that is viewed as being more serious in nature and punishable by at least one year in prison.

Felony-murder rule: the legal doctrine that says if a death occurs during the commission of a felony, the perpetrator of the crime may be charged with murder in the first degree.

Feminist theory: a theory that emphasizes gender involvement in crime.

Field training officer (FTO): one who is to oversee and evaluate the new police officer's performance as he or she transitions from the training academy to patrolling the streets.

Fifth Amendment: in the Constitution, among other protections, it guards against self-incrimination and double jeopardy.

Fine: a financial penalty for committing a crime(s).

Fingerprint: the residual, individual pattern left on a surface by one's hands and fingers.

Fingerprint classification: a system of classifying and identifying one's unique whorls, loops, and so on, for police use.

Firearms identification: matching known bullet samples to unknown ones.

Firing squad: a method of carrying out executions, usually with rifles.

Fleeing-felon rule: now outlawed (see *Tennessee v. Garner,* 1985), it allowed police to use deadly force to stop and apprehend a fleeing felon.

Foot patrol: a policing method whereby police officers patrol communities on foot, thus being closer to citizens.

Force, reasonable: using the amount or degree of force that is appropriate for a given situation when confronted with an aggressive suspect.

Forced entry: entry where a burglar unlawfully enters a home or business with intent to commit a crime therein.

Forcible rape: unlawful sexual intercourse with a person that is forcible and without his or her consent.

Forensic entomology: the use of insects (i.e., their stages of development) with decomposing bodies or in some other evidentiary manner to learn about a particular crime.

Forensic pathologist: one who is medically trained to expertly determine cause of death.

Forensic science: the study of causes of crimes, deaths, and crime scenes.

Fourteenth Amendment: in the Constitution, it contains the equal protection and due process clauses.

Fourth Amendment: in the Constitution, it contains the protection against unreasonable searches and seizures and protects people's homes, property, and effects.

Fraud: an act of deceit, usually involving some form of misrepresentation.

Frisk: patting down or running one's hands over the body to search for weapons (see *Terry v. Ohio,* 1968)

"Fruits of the poisonous tree" doctrine: a legal doctrine saying that evidence derived by police through illegal means is inadmissible against a defendant because of its original taint.

Fugitive warrant: a judicial order authorizing police to capture and return a particular person.

Full pardon: a pardon that frees the criminal without any conditions; usually by a governor or the president.

Funnel effect: viewed as a funnel, it is the reduction of the number of committed crimes reduced down to the number of actual convictions; in other words, only a fraction of all arrests result in a conviction.

Gallows: a structure used to hang a condemned person.

Gang: a group that forms, with common identity, for the purpose of engaging in criminal activity; can be in free society or in prison, and adult or youth in its composition.

Gang Resistance Education and Training (GREAT): a program designed to assist youth in resisting the allure of gang membership.

Gaols: early English jails.

Gas chamber: a type of legal execution whereby the condemned person is placed in an airtight chamber and poisonous gasses are released, which causes death.

Gateway drugs: a term for less-serious substances that are believed to lead to abuse of more serious drugs.

General deterrence: the belief that punishment of offenders will deter others from lawbreaking.

Global positioning system (GPS): a network of satellites used to locate people and objects.

Good-faith exception: an exclusionary-rule exception where police act with good or honest beliefs and conduct a search or seizure based on faulty or flawed information, and thus their conduct is excused.

Good-time credits: an amount of time that is deducted from period of incarceration due to an offender's good behavior.

Grand jury: a body that hears evidence and determines probable cause regarding crimes and can return formal charges against suspects; use, size, and functions vary among the states.

Grand larceny/theft: the taking of property that is valued in excess of a certain amount, and thus usually results in a felony.

Grand theft auto: stealing an automobile, which is a felony.

Grass-eaters: a term used to describe police officers who engage in improper activities that are considered to be less serious in nature (see *Meat-eaters*).

Gratuities: the receipt of some benefit (a meal, gift, or some other favor) either for free or for a reduced price.

Gross misdemeanor: an offense classification that is more serious than a lesser misdemeanor, usually calling for a more severe penalty of up to a year in jail.

Gross negligence: a situation where someone fails to use a level of care that is due in a given situation.

Group home: a custodial facility for juveniles that provides limited supervision and counseling and other programs.

Guardian *ad litem*: legal representation for a juvenile, appointed by a court and seeing that the youth's rights and well-being are addressed during litigation.

Guilt: the state of one's having committed a crime; being blameworthy or culpable.

Guilty: a situation where one is legally responsible for having committed a crime.

Guilty but mentally ill: a legal verdict where the suspect has performed the criminal act but was acting under diminished mental capacity or state at the time of the offense.

Guilty plea: a defendant's formal admission of guilt to charges contained in the complaint.

Gulag: a term, originally Russian, used to describe prisons and camps, normally very oppressive and cruel to inmates, particularly political prisoners.

Gun control: a broad term representing attempts to regulate the sale, transfer, manufacture, and use of firearms.

Habeas corpus: "You have the body" (Latin)—a writ used by prisoners to ask a court to hear their allegations concerning the nature and length of confinement.

Habitual offender: one who has been convicted of multiple offenses; often identified and tracked by repeat offender program police officers who surveil and attempt to catch such offenders in the act.

Halfway house: a community center or home staffed by professionals or volunteers designed to provide counseling to ex-prisoners as they transition from prison to the community.

Hallucinogen: a natural or synthetic substance that produces distorted effects of the senses.

"Hands off" doctrine: the notion by courts that prison administrators should be given free rein to run their prisons as they deem best.

"Hands on" doctrine: the belief by courts that inmates have certain constitutional rights that the courts must see are upheld and also be obeyed by prison administrators.

Hanging: a form of punishment wherein the condemned is placed on a scaffold, has a rope looped around the neck, and then is dropped and thus experiences a broken neck due to the tightened rope.

Hard labor: a form of punishment whereby convicted offenders are forced to engage in vigorous physical work.

Harmful error: an error by a judge that may have prejudiced the defendant's right to a fair trial, and may lead to a reversal of a conviction.

Harmless error: an error by a judge that is relatively minor in nature and is not perceived on appeal to a higher court to have prejudiced the defendant's right to a fair trial.

Hate crime: a crime committed based on and motivated by the victim's race, religion, sexual preference, or other status.

Hearing: a formal proceeding in which a court hears evidence from prosecutors and defense attorneys and renders a decision as to the dispute or matter at issue.

Hearsay evidence: evidence that is not heard firsthand, but rather is based on information from another person; normally not permitted at trial.

Hereditary theory: a theory of crime that maintains that crime is a product of genetically transmitted characteristics—for example, inherited genes from parents or ancestors who were criminals.

Hierarchy rule: in the FBI *Uniform Crime Reports* reporting scheme, the practice whereby only the most serious offense of several that are committed during a criminal act is reported by the police.

High-speed pursuit: a motor-vehicle chase by police of suspects at high rates of speed in their vehicles in an attempt to capture them.

Holding cell: a small area designed to confine suspects temporarily.

Homicide: the umbrella term used to include all taking of human life, both the criminal and noncriminal (e.g., that which involves an accident, is justified, or occurs during wartime or by a public executioner).

Hostile witness: a person in a criminal case who gives evidence but also fails to cooperate with the side (prosecution or defense) that subpoenaed him or her.

Hot pursuit (see *High-speed pursuit*).

House arrest/home confinement (see *Electronic monitoring*).

Houses of refuge: workhouses established in the early 1800s as a means of separating juvenile offenders from adult offenders.

Hue and cry: in the 1500s, a system whereby volunteer watchmen were to shout out for help if a crime was observed.

Hung jury: a situation where a jury cannot reach a verdict.

Idealistic contrast: the differences between juvenile and adult criminal justice processes, to include treatment and terminology.

Identity theft: a theft where one fraudulently assumes the identity of another, such as by using his or her credit card, driver's license, or other personal data, to obtain the victim's funds or for some other purpose.

Ignorance (of law): a legal doctrine (weak) where the defendant argues he or she was not aware that the act committed was in fact criminal in nature.

Illegal alien: one who enters and remains in a country without legal authorization to do so; now often termed "undocumented alien."

Illegal detention: similar to false arrest.

Illegal search and seizure (see *Exclusionary rule*).

Illinois Juvenile Court Act (1899): legislation that established the first juvenile court in the United States.

Immigration laws: statutes governing foreign nationals and their coming to the United States as well as their being prevented to do so.

Immunity: exemption from civil suit or criminal prosecution, or an agreement with a prosecutor to testify for special considerations in return.

Impeach: attempts by prosecutors and defense attorneys to challenge the credibility of a witness and thus have his or her statement struck from the record or prevented from otherwise being used for their case.

Imprisonment: the incarceration of a convicted offender.

Impulse, irresistible: a test for insanity that maintains the accused acted out of a compulsion over which he or she had no control.

Inadmissible: evidence that cannot be admitted as evidence at trial.

Incapacitation: rendering someone as unable to act or move about, either through incarceration or by court order.

Incarceration: imprisonment in a jail or prison.

Inchoate offenses: acts that are preparatory to or related to a crime, such as conspiracy or attempt.

Incident: a criminal act involving one or more victims.

Incorrigible: a term usually applied to juveniles, meaning their behavior is such that they must be supervised and controlled.

Inculpatory evidence: evidentiary information that would show or tend to establish guilt.

Indeterminate sentence/ing: a scheme whereby one is sentenced for a flexible time period (e.g., 5–10 years) so as to be released when rehabilitated or the opportunity for rehabilitation is presented.

Index crimes: eight crimes for which the FBI's *Uniform Crime Reports* provide various forms of analyses: murder, forcible rape, robbery, aggravated assault, burglary, theft, auto theft, and arson.

Indigent: one who is poor; in criminal justice, one who cannot afford the services of an attorney.

Inevitability of discovery exception: a legal doctrine providing that evidence would have most likely been discovered anyway, and can thus be used at trial if obtained in violation of the Fourth Amendment.

Inferior courts: lower courts.

In flagrante delicto: in the act; one who is caught in the act of committing a crime.

Informant: one who provides information to police concerning a crime.

In forma pauperis: finding that someone is indigent; the waiving of formal filing fees and other costs associated with a judicial proceeding (often an appeal).

Information: a formal charge by a prosecutor asserting that an individual committed a crime(s) charged.

Informed consent: an agreement that one has made a willing decision to do something with full knowledge of what will take place.

Initial appearance: a formal proceeding during which the accused is read his or her rights and informed of the charges and the amount of bail required to secure pretrial release.

Injunction: a court order prohibiting someone from doing something.

In loco parentis: a doctrine in which the state will act in place of the parents if they fail in their duties to protect and provide for the child.

Inmate: a prisoner in a jail or prison.

Inmate classification (see *Classification*).

Inmate code/subculture (see *Institutionalization*).

Inmate litigation: lawsuits filed by prison and jail inmates challenging their conditions of confinement.

In re: "concerning" or "in the matter of."

Insanity defense: an affirmative defense that seeks to exonerate an individual for a crime, asserting that he or she was acting under some form of mental defect or deficiency.

Institutionalization: a process that occurs with long-term inmates, whereby they take on the values and mores of the inmate culture and thus are more likely unable to succeed in the free world.

Intake: a process of screening juveniles who are charged with crimes and determine whether to release to parents, detain in a facility, or provide some other disposition.

Intensive supervision probation and parole: ISP usually includes much closer and stricter supervision, more contact with offenders, more frequent drug tests, and other such measures.

Intent, specific: a purposeful act or state of mind to commit a crime.

Intermediate courts of appeal: a level of courts in state courts that stand between trial courts and courts of last resort; they typically have appellate jurisdiction only.

Intermediate sanction: a form of punishment that is between freedom and prison, such as home confinement and day reporting.

Internal affairs: a division of a police or corrections agency that investigates reports of officer misconduct and possible criminal behavior.

International Court of Justice: the main judicial organ of the United Nations (UN), established in June 1945, it settles legal disputes submitted to it by states and renders advisory opinions on legal questions posed by UN members.

Interpol: the only international crime-fighting organization, it collects intelligence information, issues alerts, and assists in capturing world criminals; it has nearly 200 member countries.

Interrogation: police questioning of a suspect about a particular crime(s); the suspect may have an attorney present if he or she desires (see *Escobedo v. Illinois,* 1964).

Intoxication: being in a state of inebriation, through consumption of alcohol or drugs.

Inventory exception: a legal doctrine allowing police to take an inventory of an automobile that has been towed to a police station following the arrest of its owner or driver; to protect the police against unfounded charges that they stole articles of value from the vehicle.

Investigation: an inquiry into suspected criminal behavior, involving a number of police questioning and deductive techniques as well as forensic tests and examinations.

Involuntary manslaughter: a lesser type of murder in which the perpetrator was negligent or reckless in the taking of a human life.

"Iron curtain" speech: in *Wolff v. McDonnell* (1973), the Supreme Court stated that there is no iron curtain between the Constitution and the prisons of the United States; in sum, inmates have rights.

Jail: a facility that holds persons who have been arrested for crimes and are awaiting trial, persons who have been convicted for misdemeanors and are serving a sentence (up to a year in jail), federal offenders, and others.

Joinder: combining two or more criminal prosecutions into a single trial proceeding, where two or more defendants are charged with participating in the crime(s) together.

Judge: a political officer who is elected or appointed to preside over a court of law, to include its trials and other proceedings.

Judgment: the final determination of a case, which might be guilt, innocence, a fine, probation, or some other outcome.

Judicial misconduct: inappropriate behavior by a judge (see *Model Code of Judicial Conduct*).

Judicial selection (methods of): means by which judges are selected for the bench, to include election, a nominating commission, or a hybrid of these methods.

Jurisdiction, court: the power of a court to hear a particular type of case; also, the territory where a court may conduct its work—city, county, state, or federal.

Jurisdiction, original: the authority of a court to hear or act on a case from its beginning to conclusion.

Jurisprudence: the application of law in a jurisdiction.

Jurist: a person who acts as a judge.

Juror: a person serving on a jury, sitting to determine guilt or innocence of a defendant.

Jury instructions: verbal advice given by a judge before the jury members begin their deliberations; usually pertaining to the law and the elements of the crimes for which the defendant is charged.

Jury nullification: a situation where a jury refuses to accept the evidence presented at trial and acquits or convicts for a lesser offense.

Jury poll: a poll conducted of the jury to determine whether or not the verdict it rendered truly represents each juror's own belief or verdict.

Jury tampering: an attempt to threaten, intimidate, bribe, or otherwise influence a witness.

Jury trial: a trial in which guilt or innocence will be determined by a jury rather than a judge alone.

"Just deserts" model: a model whereby the punishment for the crime is equated with the seriousness of the offense committed.

Justice: a judge, usually a Supreme Court justice; also, the ideal concerning the doing of what is right and the punishing of acts that are wrong.

Justice of the peace (JP): a minor justice official who oversees lesser criminal trials; one of the early English judicial functionaries.

Justifiable homicide: a killing of another person that is considered to be nonblameworthy given the circumstances (e.g., police shooting a bank robber who is armed and about to kill a hostage; a citizen acting in self-defense).

Juvenile: one who is under the age of consent, and of minor age, usually under 18 or 21 for legal purposes.

Juvenile court: a court that has original jurisdiction to hear juvenile crime matters.

Juvenile justice system: a broad term including the whole of justice processes and proceedings concerning juveniles who commit crimes.

Kansas City Preventive Patrol Experiment: in the early 1970s, a study of the effects of different types of patrolling on crime—patrolling as usual in one area, saturated patrol in another, and very limited patrol in a third area; the results showed no significant differences.

Kefauver Committee: a special committee convened by the U.S. Senate in the 1950s to study organized crime in the United States.

Kitty Genovese syndrome: a syndrome that basically says people don't wish to get involved in reporting or combating crime; based on the attacks and killing of a woman in New York where nearby residents refused to call police or intervene.

Knapp Commission: a body created in the early 1970s to investigate police corruption in the New York Police Department.

Labeling theory (of crime): a theory holding that persons acquire labels or defined characteristics that are deviant or criminal; thus,

perceiving themselves as criminals, they follow through and commit crimes.

La Cosa Nostra: "this thing of ours"; a reference to the Mafia, a secret criminal organization.

Latent prints: fingerprints lifted from surfaces due to the natural oils on hands and fingers.

Law enforcement: a term used to signify efforts or persons appointed to uphold the law; most often used in connection with federal agents.

Learning theory (of crime): any school of thought that suggests criminal behaviors are learned from associating with others and from social interactions and social experiences.

Less lethal force: a broad term that includes all less lethal tools used by police, to include batons, gases, dogs, nets, electronic control devices, and so on.

Lethal force: force employed by police, prison, or other personnel that results in the death of a suspect, a citizen, or an inmate.

Level of custody: the security level in which a prisoner is placed—maximum, medium, or minimum—depending on nature of the crime and other factors.

Lex talionis: "eye for eye, tooth for tooth"; retaliation or revenge that dates back to the Bible and Middle Ages.

Life without parole: a penalty or sentence imposed where the inmate is to serve a life sentence without parole eligibility.

Limited jurisdiction: the restriction of a court to hear certain types of cases.

Linear design: a type of prison architecture in which inmates' cells are aligned along corridors.

Lineup: a procedure in which police ask suspects to submit to a viewing by witnesses to determine the guilty party, based on personal and physical characteristics; information obtained may be used later in court.

Litigation: a lawsuit, either criminal or civil.

Locard's exchange principle: the notion that when one commits a crime, he leaves a part of himself at the crime scene wherever he steps, whatever he touches, and so on; the crime scene analyst or investigator's job is to locate that evidence and use it in the investigation.

Lockdown: complete locking up of inmates, usually following a jail or prison riot.

Lockup: a facility used to house inmates; usually referring to local jails.

Mafia: organized crime syndicates.

Magistrate: a judge who handles cases; an officer of the lower courts.

Mala in se **crimes:** acts that are inherently wrong—murder, rape.

Mala prohibita crimes: acts that are not wrong in and of themselves, but have been codified as crimes—embezzlement, drunkenness, and so on.

Malfeasance: misconduct by a public official or officer.

Malice aforethought: intent to commit a wrongful act, or the actual commission of such an act; sometimes said to be the "evil heart"—the part of the crime involving stabbing, shooting, and so on.

Management by walking around: a principle usually applied to prisons whereby the administrators go out into the yard to observe firsthand the inmates' activities.

Mandatory sentencing: sentencing in which a court is required to impose a specific length of incarceration, as in those states that require a lengthier sentence where offenders use a weapon.

Manslaughter: homicide that is without malice, committed intentionally after provocation or recklessly.

Mass murder: the killing of more than a single person as part of a single act.

Maximum security: a prison where inmates are kept under the highest degree of custody and control, with fewer privileges and amenities.

Meat-eaters: slang for police officers who accept large payoffs and engage in egregious activities that are designed to benefit them financially or in some other manner (see *Grass-eaters*).

Medical marijuana: marijuana that is legally prescribed to alleviate symptoms of a disease, usually cancer.

Mens rea (see *Criminal intent*).

Mental illness (see *Insanity defense*).

Merit selection: a means of selecting judges whereby names of interested candidates are considered by a committee and recommendations are then made to the governor, who then makes the appointment; known also as the Missouri Plan.

Mesomorph: a body type by Sheldon characterized by muscularity and once believed to indicate a criminal type.

Methamphetamine: a synthetic drug that produces euphoria and other effects.

Military justice (see *Uniform Code of Military Justice*).

Minimum custody: a level of confinement that allows inmates who do not pose a risk to others the ability to have little supervision and greater amenities and freedom of movement.

Minor (see *Juvenile*).

Miranda rights/warning: the landmark 1966 Supreme Court ruling that suspects must be advised by police before questioning of their right to remain silent, to have an attorney, to refuse to answer questions, and other privileges.

Misdemeanor: a lesser offense, normally punishable by a fine or up to one year in a local jail.

Misfeasance: the improper performance of official duties.

Misprision: concealment of a crime.

Missouri Plan (see *Merit selection*).

Mistake of fact: ignorance of a fact involving crime; for example, a person innocently removes a laptop from a library believing it is his, but it is not; he would have a defense.

Mistake of law: ignorance of the law; for example, a person steals an item worth $100 from his roommate in the mistaken belief that, because the roommate owes him that amount and refuses to pay, he can settle the debt by taking the item; he can be charged with the theft of the item.

Mistrial: a trial that is invalid, because of errors on the part of the prosecutor, defense attorney, juror, witness, and so on.

Mitigating circumstances: circumstances that would tend to lessen the severity of the sentence, such as one's youthfulness, mental instability, not having a prior criminal record, and so on.

M'Naghten Rule: an insanity defense in which the defendant is said to have committed a crime while not understanding the nature and quality of the act or its consequences; often termed the "right-wrong test."

Model Code of Judicial Conduct: adopted by the House of Delegates of the American Bar Association in 1990, it provides a set of ethical principles and guidelines for judges.

Model Penal Code: a set of recommendations developed by the American Law Institute for clarifying crimes and punishment; voluntary in nature, jurisdictions are free to adopt all or part of the recommendations.

Modus operandi: the characteristic method(s) used by a person to commit a crime.

Molestation: making improper sexual advances.

Money laundering: a situation where ill-gotten money is funneled through a series of steps to banks (or such places as gambling casinos) and subsequently "cleaned" so as to conceal its illegal nature.

Moot question: a question that is no longer relevant.

Motion: an oral or written request to a judge that he or she make a specific ruling, finding, or order.

Motive: the reason for committing a crime.

Mug shot: a photograph of a criminal suspect taken by the police at time of booking, after an arrest.

Municipal courts: courts of special jurisdiction that hear cases within a specified city or municipality.

Municipal police department: a police force that enforces laws and maintains peace within a specified city or municipality.

Murder: the taking of a human life through criminal means; can be in first or second degree, or manslaughter.

National Crime Victimization Survey: a random survey of households that measures crimes committed against victims; includes crimes not reported to police.

National Incident-Based Reporting System: a crime reporting system in which police describe each offense in a crime as well as describing the offender.

Natural law: principles and rules imposed by a higher power than man-made law, considered to be fitting for and binding on society.

Necessity: a situation where one is forced to act; for example, one's car breaks down in a winter storm so he is forced to take shelter in a log cabin; he would have a defense against burglary for acting out of necessity.

Neglect: passive or active failure to protect or give care to someone.

Negligence: failure to perform a duty owed.

Neighborhood watch: an organization of residents to maintain surveillance over a given area and thus hopefully prevent and discover crimes.

Neoclassical criminology: a perspective in which the accused is viewed as exempted from conviction if circumstances prevented the exercise of free will.

New generation/direct supervision jail: jails that, by their architecture and design, eliminate many of the traditional features of a jail, such as allowing staff members greater interaction and control.

Noble cause corruption: a situation where one commits an unethical act but for the greater good; for example, a police officer violates the Constitution in order to capture a serious offender.

No-knock law: a law where the police may execute a search or arrest warrant without first announcing their presence; usually employed where there is known to be armed and dangerous suspects.

Nolle prosequi: an instance where a prosecutor declines to prosecute.

Nolo contendere: a plea of no contest to charges; the defendant does not dispute the facts.

Not guilty by reason of insanity: an instance where the defendant is not criminally responsible because at the time the crime was committed he or she was under the influence and acting as a result of a mental defect or deficiency.

"Nothing works" philosophy: Robert Martinson's belief, published in the 1970s, that correctional treatment programs generally do not rehabilitate offenders or significantly reduce recidivism.

Notorious/celebrated case: a case where a celebrity is the defendant; usually requiring special treatment of the jury members to remove them from news items and other adaptations.

Oath: an affirmation of statements about to be given as true.

Offender: one who has been convicted of committing one or more crimes.

Omission: the failure to perform an act as required by law (such as paying income taxes).

Order maintenance: police preventing behavior that disturbs the public peace.

Ordinance: a law enacted by a local governing board, such as a city council.

Organization: an entity of two or more people who cooperate to achieve an objective(s).

Organizational structure/chart: a diagram of the vertical and horizontal parts of an organization, showing its chain of command, lines of communication, division of labor, and so on.

Organized crime: a self-perpetuating crime group, such as teen gangs, Mafia, biker gangs, and so on.

Overcrowding: when the number of prisoners exceeds the rated capacity of a jail or prison.

Overt act: an action by a person that is to further the commission of a crime.

Pardon: unconditional release of an inmate, usually by the governor.

Parens patriae: a doctrine in which the state is the ultimate parent of the child (and will step in to provide and care for the child if parents neglect those duties).

Parole: early release from prison, with conditions attached and under supervision of a parole agency.

Parolee: one who is on parole.

Parole officer: one who supervises those who are on parole.

Parole revocation: the removal of one's parole status for the purpose of returning him or her to prison (usually for not following the conditions of parole or for committing a new offense).

Part I offenses (see *Index crimes*).

Part II offenses: crimes designated by the FBI as "less serious," as compared with Part I offenses; only arrest data are provided for them.

Pat-down search (see *Frisk*).

PATRIOT Act: prompted by the 9/11 attacks, the act provides expanded law enforcement authority to combat terrorism.

Patrol beat/district: a geographical area to which police officers are assigned for patrol.

Patrol officer: a police officer whose duties normally include keeping the peace, service, and patrolling by vehicle, foot, air, bicycle, or some other method.

Peacekeeping role: police seeing that their communities are maintained in a peaceable manner.

Peace officer: a broad term applied to those who enforce the laws and preserve public peace.

Pedophile: a molester of children.

Penitentiary: a prison, usually federal in nature.

Peremptory challenge: a member of a jury pool being rejected, and for which no reason need be given by the prosecutor or defense attorney.

Perjury: lying under oath in a court of law.

Perpetrator: one who commits or attempts to commit a crime.

Petit jury: the trier of fact in a criminal matter; the jury of one's peers. Size varies by state.

PINS (person in need of supervision): usually a juvenile thought to be on the verge of becoming a delinquent.

Plaintiff: the party who is bringing a lawsuit or initiating a legal action against someone else.

Plain view/sight: a doctrine in which officers who are searching may seize contraband that is in plain view, provided the officers have a legal right to be on the premises.

Plea: an answer to a criminal charge by a defendant; can be guilty, not guilty, *nolo contendere*, or not guilty by reason of insanity.

Plea negotiation (or bargaining): a preconviction process between the prosecutor and the accused in which a plea of guilty is given by the defendant, with certain specified considerations in return—having several

charges or counts tossed out, a plea by the prosecutor to the court for leniency or shorter sentence, and so on.

Police: persons whose responsibility is to enforce the laws; usually the term used for city or municipal officers, as opposed to county deputies.

Police advisory board: a board composed of citizens who oversee police policies and procedures.

Police brutality: unnecessary use of force by police against citizens, resulting in injury.

Police citizen/civilian review board: a body of citizens that investigates citizen complaints of police misconduct and brutality, and recommends sanctions against officers where guilt is established.

Police corruption: misconduct by police officers that can involve but is not limited to illegal activities for economic gain, gratuities, favors, and so on.

Police discretion: the ability of police to use their authority selectively, so as to "marry" the law with the facts at hand; full enforcement of the laws is neither desirable nor plausible.

Police ethics: responsibilities of the police to act in moral, upright, and value-laden ways in the conduct of their duties.

Police misconduct: a broad term that includes any illegal or improper behaviors by police in violation of state or local laws or agency policies or procedures.

Police officer (see *Peace officer*).

Police pursuit (see *High-speed pursuit*).

Policing styles: James Q. Wilson argued that there are three styles of policing: watchman, legalistic, and service.

Police subculture: through socialization to their roles, academy training, and interactions with other officers, police develop job-related norms and values, means of behavior, a certain language, and so on.

Political era (of policing): from the 1840s to the 1930s, the period of time when police were tied closely to politics and politicians, dependent on them for being hired, promoted, and assignments—all of which raised the potential for corruption.

Policy making: the act of creating laws or setting standards to govern the activities of government; the Supreme Court, for example, has engaged in policy making in several areas, such as affirmative action, voting, freedom of communication and expression, and so on.

Political influence: matters taken into account for developing public policies, allocating funds and other resources, and choosing among preferred alternatives.

Polling the jury (see *Jury poll*).

Positivist School: a school of thought arguing that science can be used to discover the true causes of crime, which are a result of social, biological, psychological, and economic factors.

***Posse Comitatus* Act of 1878:** a prohibition against the police using military personnel in civil law enforcement (but a state's National Guard may be activated in times of emergencies).

Possession: the charge for having a quantity of prohibited drugs or stolen property.

***Post facto*:** after the fact.

Posthumous/*post mortem*: after death.

Preliminary hearing: a stage in the criminal process conducted by a magistrate to determine whether a person charged with a crime should be held for trial based on probable cause; does not determine guilt or innocence.

Presentence investigation: an analysis of a convicted offender's personal and criminal background, performed by a probation officer, usually ordered by a court, to assist in assigning an appropriate sentence.

Presumption of innocence: the premise that a defendant is assumed to be innocent until guilt is established beyond a reasonable doubt.

Pretrial motions/processes: any number of motions filed by prosecutors and defense attorneys prior to trial, to include quashing of evidence, change of venue, discovery, to challenge a search or seizure, to raise doubts about expert witnesses, to exclude a defendant's confession, and so on.

***Prima facie*:** "on its face" (Latin)—a matter appears to be evident on its face, or when taken at face value.

Prison: a state or federal facility housing long-term offenders, normally felons, for a period greater than one year.

Prisoners' rights: the collective body of rights given to inmates by the courts, in such areas as conditions of confinement, communications (mail and letters), access to law library and medical facilities, and so on.

Prison industries: use of prison and jail inmates to produce goods or provide services for a public agency or private corporation.

Prisonization (see *Institutionalization*).

Prison/jail riot: an attempt by inmates to gain control over all or a portion of the facility, often to show displeasure with living conditions, and to take hostages.

Prison labor (see *Prison industries*).

Prison subculture: the norms, values, beliefs, traditions, customs, and even language adopted by inmates over time, which tends to solidify as people are isolated from the larger culture for an extended period of time.

Prison vocabulary: a language that is adopted by inmates with particularized meaning and must be learned by prison staff to keep abreast of prison activities; for example, a *shiv* or *shank* is a prison knife.

Private police/security: all nonpublic officers, including guards, watchmen, private detectives, and investigators; they have limited powers and only the same arrest powers as regular citizens.

Private prisons: for-profit prisons that are constructed and operated by private corporations for state and local governments.

Proactive policing: an approach that emphasizes preventing crimes from occurring, such as directed patrol, problem solving, and looking at causes and general trends of crime.

Probable cause: reasonable suspicion or belief that a crime has been, or is about to be, committed by a particular person.

Probation: an alternative to incarceration where the convict remains out of jail or prison and in the community and thus on the job, with family, and so on, while subject to conditions and supervision of the probation authority; if violating those conditions, probation may be revoked and the probationer may be sent to prison.

Probation officer: one who supervises the activities of persons on probation.

Probation revocation (see *Probation*).

Problem-oriented policing: a strategy whereby police and citizens combine to learn about and successfully address neighborhood crime and disorder, using a problem-solving approach.

Problem solving: a process in which police use scanning, analysis, response, and assessment (the SARA problem-solving model) to identify and address crime and disorder.

Procedural law: rules that set forth how substantive laws are to be enforced, such as those covering arrest, search, and seizure.

Professional model (of policing) (see *Reform era*).

Property bond: providing bail in the form of land, homes, stocks, or other property; if the defendant fails to come to trial, the items in the bond become the property of the court.

Property crime: a crime against property, nonviolent in nature; includes but is not limited to burglary, theft, and arson.

Prosecuting attorney: one who brings prosecutions, representing the people of the jurisdiction.

Prosecution: the bringing of charges against an individual, based on probable cause, so as to cause the matter to go to court.

Protective custody: booking into jail a person who poses a danger to himself or others; also, the segregation of inmates who might be in danger of harm.

Proximate cause: a factor that contributed heavily to an event, such as an auto crash or death.

Psychological rationales for crime: explanations of crime that link it to mental states or antisocial personality.

Public defender: an attorney whose full-time job is to represent indigent defendants.

Public safety exception: the doctrine that states police can legally question an arrested suspect without *Mirandizing* him if the public's safety is in jeopardy.

Punishment (and its purposes): penalties imposed for committing criminal acts, to accomplish deterrence, retribution, incapacitation, and/or rehabilitation.

Racial profiling (see *Driving while black or brown*).

Racketeer Influenced and Corrupt Organizations Act (RICO): a federal statute permitting officers to investigate and arrest members of criminal enterprises, and to force offenders to forfeit any related assets (houses, cars, boats, guns, cash, etc.).

Racketeering: any organized crime—prostitution, gambling, drugs.

Rational choice theory: a theory that states that crime is the result of a decision-making process where the offender weighs the pros (rewards) and cons (possibility of being caught) of committing a crime.

Reactive patrol: police basically reacting to calls for police service after a crime or problem has surfaced, as opposed to being proactive and taking measures to prevent crime.

Reasonable doubt: the standard used by jurors to arrive at a verdict—whether or not the government (prosecutor) has established guilt beyond a reasonable doubt.

Reasonableness test: a judicial concept that states prison rules and restrictions on inmates' rights must be reasonably related to some legitimate purpose—institutional security, primarily.

Reasonable suspicion: suspicion that is less than probable cause but more than a mere hunch that a person may be involved in criminal activity.

Recidivism: one's committing crimes more than once; repeat offending.

Recognizance: personal responsibility to return to court at a specified time; normally people released from jail "on recognizance" do not have to post bail or bond.

Record: one's criminal history; prior offenses.

Reformatory: a detention facility designed to reform individuals—historically juveniles.

Reform era (police): also the professional era, from the 1930s to 1980s, when police sought to extricate themselves from the shackles of politicians, and leading to the crime-fighter era—with greater emphases being placed on *numbers* of arrests, citations, response times, and so on.

Rehabilitation: attempts to reform an offender through vocational and educational programming, counseling, and so forth, so he is not a recidivist and does not return to crime/prison.

Relative ethics: the "gray" area of ethics that is not so clear-cut, such as releasing a serious offender in order to use him later as an informant.

Release on recognizance (ROR) (see *Recognizance*).

Repeat offender (see *Recidivism*).

Residential community center: a facility for juveniles whose behavior does not justify a strict form of incarceration (as in a training school) and that thus allows for greater community contact and privileges.

***Respondeat superior*:** "let the master answer" (Latin)—a doctrine in liability that establishes a duty of supervisors to control their employees and be considered liable for their actions.

Response time: the time interval between when a call for service is made and the police respond to the call or arrive at the scene.

Restoration: the goal of the justice system that strives to make the victim "whole" again.

Retribution: a goal of punishment that states the offender ought to be made to experience revenge for his actions.

Restorative justice: the view that crime affects the entire community, which must be healed and made whole again through the offender's remorse, community service, restitution to the offender, and other such activities.

Revocation (see *Parole revocation*).

Reversible error: an error committed by a judge during trial that may result in a retrial of the defendant.

Right to counsel (see *Defense attorney*).

Right-wrong test (see *M'Naghten Rule*).

Routine activities theory: a theory by Cohen and Felson that argues crime is a product of everyday habits of potential victims—a crime will occur where there is a suitable victim, a motivated offender, and the absence of a capable guardian (police, security officers, parents, etc.).

Rule of law: the totality of the system of law that guides behaviors of citizens and punishes wrongdoers, as set forth by political bodies.

Rules of criminal procedure: rules by which a criminal case is conducted.

Sanction: a penalty or punishment.

Sanity hearing: a formal proceeding to determine the mental health of the defendant—for example, sane or insane.

SARA model (see *Problem solving*).

Scared Straight: a delinquency deterrence program that seeks to scare young offenders away from a life of crime by subjecting them to the realities of prison life.

School resource officer: a police officer assigned to a school(s) to prevent delinquency, protect safety of students and staff, solve problems, and protect school property.

Scientific jury selection: using social science techniques during the jury selection phase of the trial, when lawyers question jurors, to gauge the disposition of jurors and better guide the selection of jurors and the use of peremptory challenges. Research concerning its usefulness is mixed.

Search and seizure: in the Fourth Amendment, the term refers to an officer's searching for and taking away evidence of a crime.

Search incidental to arrest: an arresting officer is allowed to search the immediate area within control of the arrestee, to search for weapons and avoid the destruction of evidence.

Search warrant (see *Warrant, search*).

Second Amendment: the portion of the Bill of Rights that allows citizens to keep and bear arms.

Second-degree murder: an intentional, often spontaneous and impulsive killing that is not premeditated, as when two men begin arguing in a bar and one pulls out a knife and stabs the other.

Second-generation jail: jails that began to be seen in the 1980s having a linear construction, with multiple-occupancy cells and dormitories aligned along corridors.

Section 1983: a portion of the U.S. Code that allows a legal action to be brought against a police officer or other person in position of authority who, it is believed, used his position ("acted under color of law") to violate one's civil rights.

Security officer/guard: a privately employed person who protects persons and property. Either employed by a proprietary (in-house) firm or a contracted firm that can be hired.

Seizure (see *Search and seizure*).

Selective enforcement: when police officers or their agencies prioritize particular offenses to be enforced.

Self-defense: an instance where a person defends himself against an aggressor; usually a defense if done in a reasonable manner.

Self-incrimination: the act of giving evidence against oneself; coerced self-incrimination is prohibited by the Fifth Amendment.

Sentence: a penalty imposed on a convicted person, which may include a period of incarceration, a fine, community service, or some other alternative.

Sentence, suspended: a situation where a judge elects to withhold incarceration while a convicted person serves a period of time on probation.

Sentencing disparity: inconsistency in the sentencing of convicted offenders, as when some judges sentence more harshly than others for the same offense.

Sentencing guidelines: an instrument developed by the federal government that uses a grid system to chart the seriousness of offense, criminal history, and so forth and thus allow the court to arrive at a more consistent sentence for everyone.

Sentencing hearing: a hearing in which defendants and victims can hear the contents of presentence investigations as prepared by probation officers; defendants and victims may be invited to comment publicly prior to the judge rendering a sentence.

Sequestration: the isolation of jurors from the outside world—particularly communications about the trial in which they are sitting—to avoid being tainted or affected by same.

Serial murder: the killing of a number of people over time by a single offender.

Service style (of policing): a style that is marked by concern with helping people rather than strict enforcement of the laws.

Severance: an instance where criminal cases are separated so they may be tried separately in different courts.

Sex/human trafficking: a form of modern-day slavery where people profit by controlling and exploiting others and that normally involves the sex trade.

Sex offense: one of several offenses that involve sexual misconduct, to include rape, child sexual abuse and molestation, and prostitution.

Sex slave: a person who is forced by her captor to engage in acts of prostitution.

Sexual deviance: any abnormal sexual practice.

Sexual harassment: unequal treatment in the workplace that often involves sexual coercion, or the unwelcome or inappropriate promise of rewards in exchange for sexual favors.

Sexual predator: a sex offender who preys on others and chronically commits sex offenses.

Shakedown: an intensive search of an inmate's cell or property to see if he possesses contraband; also, a form of police corruption where officers "look the other way" while criminals ply their trade.

Sheriff: the chief law enforcement officer of a county, normally elected and frequently operating the jail as well as law enforcement functions.

Shire-reeve: in early England, the law enforcement figure (reeve) who watched over the land (shire); the forerunner of today's sheriff.

Shock probation/parole: a situation where individuals are sentenced to jail or prison for a brief period, to give them a taste or "shock" of incarceration and hopefully turn them into more law-abiding citizens.

Situational crime prevention: a technique that focuses on preventing crime rather than apprehending and punishing offenders; it considers aspects of the environment, increasing the effort required to commit a crime, making crime commission less attractive, increasing the risk of being caught, reducing the potential rewards of crime, and so on.

Sixth Amendment: in the Bill of Rights, it guarantees the right to a speedy and public trial by an impartial jury, the right to effective counsel at trial, and other protections.

"Sixth sense": in policing, the notion that an officer can "sense" or feel when something is not right, as in the way a person acts, talks, and so on.

"Slave of the state": an early philosophy toward prison inmates essentially stating that inmates had no legal rights that had to be observed by prison administrators.

"Slippery slope": the idea that a small first step can lead to more serious behaviors, such as the receipt of minor gratuities by police officers believed to eventually cause them to desire or demand receipt of items of greater value.

Social control theory: a theory arguing that deviant behavior results when social controls are weakened or break down, so that people are not motivated to conform to them.

Social process theory: argues that criminality is a normal behavior and that everyone has the potential to commit crime, depending on the influences that compel them toward or away from crime and in view of how they are viewed by others.

Social structure theory: generally attempts to explain criminality as a result of the creation of a lower-class culture based on poverty and deprivations, and the subsequent response of the poor to the situation.

Speedy Trial Act of 1974: later amended, it originally was enacted to ensure compliance with the Sixth Amendment's provision for a speedy trial by requiring that a federal case be brought to trial no more than 100 days following the arrest (with additional time limits within, for the preliminary hearing and arraignment).

Standard of proof: the criminal standard at criminal trial is "beyond a reasonable doubt," whereas the standard in a civil matter is "a preponderance of evidence."

Standing: a legal doctrine requiring that one must not be a party to a lawsuit unless he has a personal stake in its outcome.

Star Chamber: an early English court that secretly tried to mete out justice and punishment.

Stare decisis: "to stand by a decision" (Latin)—a doctrine referring to court precedent, whereby lower courts must follow (and render the same) decisions of higher courts when the same legal issues and questions come before them, thereby not disturbing settled points of law.

State bureau of investigation: a state agency that is responsible for enforcing state highway laws and investigating crimes involving state statutes; they may also be called in to assist police agencies in serious criminal matters, and often publish state crime reports.

State court reform (see *Court unification*).

State court system: civil or criminal courts in which cases are decided through an adversarial process; normally including a court of last resort, an appellate court, trial courts, and lower courts.

State police: a state agency responsible for highway patrol and other duties as delineated in the state's statutes; some states require their police to investigate crimes against persons and property.

State prison: a correctional facility that houses convicted felons.

State's evidence: testimony given by persons involved in crimes that incriminates others, usually in exchange for leniency or some other concession.

Status offense: a crime committed by a juvenile that would not be a crime if committed by an adult; examples would be purchasing alcohol and tobacco products, truancy, and violating curfew.

Statute of limitations: the period of time within which the government must prosecute a criminal matter after the crime has committed; this allows people to not be concerned about crimes committed long ago. There is no statute of limitations for capital crimes, however.

Statutes: laws enacted by state legislatures and codified in state statutes.

Stay of execution: the temporary stoppage of a capital sentence for one who is sentenced to death; it is commonly issued by a governor until issues involved in the death sentence can be resolved.

"Stop and frisk" (see *Frisk*).

Stored Communications Act: a federal law requiring voluntary and compelled disclosure of "stored wire and electronic communications and transactional records" held by third-party Internet service providers.

Strain theory: a theory arguing that the gap between culturally accepted goals and the legitimate means of achieving them causes frustration (strain) leading to criminal behavior.

Stressors: factors that can cause stress; for police and corrections workers, they can include poor supervision, dangers of the job, lack of public approval, excessive paperwork, and so on.

Strict liability: illegal acts whose elements do not require that proof be offered of *mens rea*; examples include an adult having sexual relations with a minor, or selling alcohol to a minor.

Substantive law: the body of law that spells out the elements of criminal acts.

Supermax prison: a penal institution that, for security purposes, affords inmates very few if any amenities and a great amount of isolation.

Superpredator: a term usually for juveniles describing one who is coming of age and who is turning to a violent lifestyle.

Suspicion: a reasonable belief that a crime has been or is about to be committed by a particular person.

Sworn officer: one who has full law enforcement power to investigate crimes, make arrests, and use force as necessary in the course of his duties.

Syndicate: an organized crime organization.

Tactical response team: found in police, prison, and jail organizations, they respond to emergency incidents (e.g., hostage situations, removing people from their cells) and their members are highly trained in use of lethal weapons and other tools to confront the situations they are called on the address.

Target-hardening: making a business or residence less susceptible to being invaded by a burglar or other criminal, by such means as installing heavy-duty locks on doors and windows.

Tasks of policing (four basic): enforce the law, prevent crime, protect the innocent, and perform welfare tasks.

Team policing: the use of teams of patrol officers and investigators to a specific geographical area to solve crimes therein.

Technical violation: in probation and parole, a situation where one violates certain conditions that must be obeyed to remain out of prison, such as curfew violation, drug or alcohol use, or not maintaining a job.

Temporary restraining order: an injunction prohibiting one party from seeing, harassing, offending against, or being in the area of another person.

Termination of parental rights: a situation where a court determines that a parent is unfit to raise his or her child and severs the legal ties between them, due to the parental neglect of the child, criminal activity, and so on.

Terrorism: acts that are intended to intimidate or coerce a civilian population or government, usually for some political purpose or objective.

Therapeutic community: a residential treatment unit that emphasizes inmate participation in decision making and group responsibility.

"Third degree": an old interrogation technique that used sleep deprivation, bright lights, and even physical abuse to obtain confessions; prohibited by federal court decisions.

Third-generation jail: beginning construction in the 1970s, and also termed a direct-supervision jail, it involves a style where inmates are housed in pods, officers' interaction with inmates is high, and bars and metal doors are omitted.

Three-strikes law: a crime control strategy whereby an offender who commits three or more violent offenses will be sentenced to a lengthy term in prison, usually 25 years to life.

Tier system: the early architectural style of prisons and jails begun in the early 1800s where inmates lived on levels that were linear and correctional officers walked the halls to check on inmates in cells.

Tithing: under Anglo-Saxon law, an association of 10 families bound together for the purpose of crime control.

Tort: a civil wrong or infraction; the remedy will be damages awarded in civil trial.

Total institution: Erving Goffman's term for a place that totally isolates the lives of persons living within it.

Totality of conditions: a standard used by the courts to determine if conditions in a jail or prison, taken together, constitute cruel and unusual treatment.

Toxicology: the study of poisons and other lethal substances.

Trace evidence: any physical evidence left by the offender at the crime scene.

Traffic function: the aggregate of motor vehicles, pedestrians, streets, and highways, for which police must investigate and apply laws to provide safe travels for citizens in their jurisdiction.

Trait theory: a theory holding that youths engage in criminal activities due to physical or psychological traits that govern their behavioral choices—which are normally believed to be impulsive rather than rational.

Transfer (remand): the movement or assigning of a juvenile offender to an adult court, because his behavior is such that he is not amenable to the juvenile court's rehabilitative philosophy.

Trial: an adversarial proceeding in a court where the determination of guilt or innocence is to be made, and including specified rules of criminal evidence and processes.

Trial *de novo*: a new hearing or trial, usually granted to defendants where errors are found to have been committed at an earlier trial.

Trial process: all of the steps in the adjudicatory process, from indictment or charge to conviction or acquittal.

True bill: a grand jury decision that sufficient probable cause exists to charge a specific person with having committed a particular crime(s); an indictment.

Trusty: a prisoner who is granted special work privileges for good behavior.

Truth in sentencing laws: laws where the sentence imposed and that which is actually served closely agree.

Turnkey: a term for inmates who are responsible for opening and closing certain gates or doors.

Twinkie defense: a defense used by Dan White, who killed San Francisco politician Harvey Milk; White argued that he killed because of an addiction to sugar-laden foods, which led to biochemical changes that caused his conduct.

Twin studies: criminological research that uses identical twins to look for possible genetic transmission of criminal traits or tendencies.

Unconditional release: the final release of an offender from supervision and jurisdiction of a corrections agency.

Underboss: in a crime organization or syndicate, the second highest ranking official.

Under color of law (see *Section 1983*).

Undercover officer: a sworn police officer who poses as a criminal in the underworld as part of an investigation, such as a drug ring or gang.

Uniform Code of Military Justice (UCMJ): the system of laws and punishments enacted by the armed forces to govern the behavior of its personnel.

***Uniform Crime Reports*:** published annually by the FBI, each UCR describes the nature of crime as reported by law enforcement agencies; includes analyses of Part I crimes.

Unit management: teams of prison workers who assist inmates in their educational, vocational, and counseling needs.

Unlawful entry: illegally entering a residence or commercial building for the purpose of committing a crime therein.

Unmanned aerial vehicles: also termed *drones*, aircraft without a human pilot that are controlled by computers and used for a variety of purposes by military and civilian police agencies.

Unreported crime: the so-called shadow of crime, or those crimes that, for a variety of reasons, are not reported by victims to the police.

Unsecured bail: a form of release where bail is not secured by real property, a bail bondsman, or cash; one type allows a defendant to go free on his word that he will return to face charges on time, and the other is often termed a signature bond, where the defendant merely signs a bond guaranteeing appearance at a later date; if he defaults, he must pay the amount of the bond, however.

USA PATRIOT Act (see *PATRIOT Act*).

U.S. attorneys: officials who are responsible for prosecuting crimes that violate the U.S. Code.

U.S. Code: a comprehensive body of laws in which are codified all federal laws and statutes as well as punishments.

U.S. courts of appeals (see *Circuit courts*).

U.S. district courts (see *District courts*).

Use of force continuum: a guide for deciding which level of force is appropriate for a police officer to deploy based on the actions of the suspect.

U.S. magistrates: lower-court federal judges who perform pretrial obligations of the federal judiciary.

U.S. Supreme Court: the court of last resort in the United States; also the highest appellate court; it consists of nine justices who are appointed for life.

Utilitarianism: in ethics, as articulated by John Stuart Mill, a belief that the proper course of action is that which maximizes utility—usually defined as that which maximizes happiness and minimizes suffering.

Vacated sentence: a criminal sentence that has been nullified by action of a court.

Venire: a list of prospective jurors composed of registered voters, drivers, taxpayers, and so on, who will potentially serve as a jury in a criminal proceeding.

Venue, change of: relocation of a criminal trial to an area where less is known and emotions are perhaps less high toward the defendant and the crime, thus hopefully affording a more fair trial and unbiased jurors.

Verdict: the decision by a judge or jury as to one's guilt or innocence as proven at trial.

Vicarious liability: a legal doctrine whereby responsibility rests upon one person for the actions of another and is to exercise reasonable and prudent care in supervising that person; for example, under certain circumstances a police supervisor is held civilly responsible for the misdeeds of his patrol officers.

Vice: any moral violation, including gambling, prostitution, or drugs.

Victim: one who has suffered through the actions of an offender, through either personal injury or property loss.

Victim impact statements: information provided prior to sentencing by the victims of a crime (or, in cases of murder, the surviving family members) about the impact the crime had on their lives; allowed by the U.S. Supreme Court.

Victimization: a measure of the occurrence of crime, or a specific criminal act against a specific victim.

Victimless crime: a crime committed in which there are said to be no apparent victims, or the participants are willingly involved, such as gambling and prostitution.

Victimology: the study of crime victimization.

Victim-precipitated crime: a situation where one is said to have played a part in—facilitate—his or her victimization, such as when a person attempts to rob a drug dealer and is shot in the process.

Vigilante: one who takes the law into his hands, in an effort to apprehend and punish criminals; historically, it included members of lynch mobs.

Such people often overstep their bounds and are themselves arrested or subject to arrest.

Violation: a criminal offense.

Violence: force used by one person against another person or object that produces some injury; it may include person-to-person crime or as when someone bombs an unoccupied building or residence.

Voice identification/analysis: the unique pattern associated with a person's speaking voice that is, like fingerprints, unique to that person. One school of thought holds that one's lies can be detected by his voice pattern.

Voir dire: "to see and to say," or to "speak truly" (French)—the process whereby prospective jurors are questioned by prosecution and defense attorneys as to their fitness for jury duty (looking for any biases, prejudices, etc.).

Voluntary manslaughter: an intentional taking of a human life, without malice and often in the heat of passion or when provoked.

Walnut Street Jail: deemed the first American prison for correcting offenders, it was built in 1776 by Philadelphia Quakers who sought to reform through penitence; it was first to segregate female and male offenders and children from adults.

Warden: the chief administrator of a federal penitentiary or state prison.

War on drugs: a federal and state initiative to control the distribution and use of illegal drugs in the United States.

Warrant, arrest: a document issued by a judge directing police to immediately arrest a person accused of a crime.

Warrant, search: a document issued by a judge, based on probable cause, directing police to immediately search a person, a premises, an automobile, or a building for the purpose of finding illegal contraband felt to be located therein and as stated in the warrant.

Weapon: any tool, firearm, or other instrument that can be used for fighting or defense and is capable of inflicting injury upon another person.

Weapons offenses: the unlawful sale, manufacturing, alteration, transportation, use, or possession of deadly or dangerous weapons as restricted under the laws.

"Wedding cake" model of criminal justice: a model of the criminal justice process whereby a four-tiered hierarchy exists, with a few celebrated cases at the top, and lower tiers increasing in size as the severity of cases become less (serious felonies, felonies, and misdemeanors).

Weed and Seed operations: a joint federal, state, and local law enforcement and community initiative launched in 1992 to prevent, control, and reduce violent crime, drug abuse, and gang activity in targeted high-crime neighborhoods in the United States.

Welfare tasks: those functions performed by the police that do not involve law enforcement, to include looking for lost or missing persons, assisting at fire calls, providing first aid, checking the well-being of citizens, watching homes while residents are away, and so on.

Whistleblower Protection Act: a federal law prohibiting reprisal against employees who reveal information concerning a violation of law, rule or regulation, gross mismanagement or waste of funds, an abuse of authority, and so on.

White-collar crime (see *Corporate crime*).

Wickersham Commission: a 1929 body established by President Herbert Hoover to investigate crimes related to national prohibition (alcohol laws) and also make recommendations for police training and professionalism.

Wiretapping: police interception of telephone transmissions, generally via court order and based on probable cause, to gather evidence for criminal prosecution.

Without prejudice: an instance where charges are dismissed but can later be brought again against the same defendant.

With prejudice: an instance where charges are dismissed and cannot later be brought again against the same defendant.

Working personality (see *Police subculture*).

Workplace violence: any physical action resulting in death or injury in the workplace, by a current or former employee.

Writ: a document issued by a judicial officer that either orders or forbids a particular act.

XYY chromosome: the so-called criminal chromosome, where criminal behavior is felt to be caused in some offenders who possess an extra Y chromosome—believed to cause agitation, aggression, and greater criminal tendencies—as opposed to the "passive" X chromosome.

Zero tolerance: a policy whereby police officials do not tolerate any crime or disorder, particularly as concerns public order offenses such as disorderly conduct, prostitution, and so on; also a federal program against drugs that permitted confiscated of planes, boats, or vehicles believed to be carrying large quantities of drugs or other contraband.

NOTES

CHAPTER 1

1. Federal Bureau of Investigation, "Table 2. Crime in the United States by Community Type, 2011," *Crime in the United States—2011* (Washington, D.C.: Uniform Crime Reporting Program), http://www.fbi.gov/about-us/cjis/ucr/crime-in-the-u.s/2011/crime-in-the-u.s.-2011/tables/table-2 (accessed January 18, 2013).
2. Tracey Kyckelhahn, "Justice Expenditures and Employment, FY 1982–2007," *Statistical Tables* (Washington, D.C.: U.S. Department of Justice, Office of Justice Systems, Bureau of Justice Statistics, December 2011), p. 1, http://bjs.ojp.usdoj.gov/content/pub/pdf/jee8207st.pdf (accessed January 18, 2013).
3. YourDictionary, "Justice Quotes," *Webster's New World Dictionary of Quotations* (Hoboken, N.J.: Wiley, 2010), http://www.yourdictionary.com/quotes/justice (accessed March 4, 2013).
4. See, for example, Joe Domanick, *Cruel Justice: Three Strikes and the Politics of Crime in America's Golden State* (Berkeley: University of California Press, 2004).
5. James Austin, "'Three Strikes and You're Out': The Likely Consequences on the Courts, Prisons, and Crime in California and Washington State," *St. Louis University Public Law Review* 14, no. 1 (1994), pp. 239–257.
6. Ibid.
7. Scott Ehlers, Vincent Schiraldi and Jason Ziedenberg, *Still Striking Out: Ten Years of California's Three Strikes* (Washington, D.C.: Justice Policy Institute, 2004), http://www.justicepolicy.org/research/2028 (accessed February 15, 2013).
8. Brent Staples, "California Horror Stories and the 3-Strikes Law," *New York Times,* November 24, 2012, http://www.nytimes.com/2012/11/25/opinion/sunday/california-horror-stories-and-the-3-strikes-law.html (accessed March 4, 2013).
9. Ehlers et al., *Still Striking Out.*
10. Ibid.
11. Staples, "California Horror Stories and the 3-Strikes Law."
12. Ibid.
13. Alexander B. Smith and Harriet Pollack, *Criminal Justice: An Overview* (New York: Holt, Rinehart and Winston, 1980), p. 9.
14. Ibid., p. 10.
15. Ibid., p. 366.
16. Thomas J. Bernard, *The Consensus–Conflict Debate: Form and Content in Social Theories* (New York: Columbia University Press, 1983), p. 78.
17. William D'Urso, "'Sovereign Citizen' Gets 8 Years in Money Laundering Case," *Las Vegas Sun,* March 20, 2013, http://www.lasvegassun.com/news/2013/mar/20/sovereign-citizen-gets-8-years-money-laundering-ca/ (accessed March 26, 2013).
18. Nadine Maeser, "Special Report: A Closer Look at Sovereign Citizens," *WECT 6,* February 22, 2013, http://www.wect.com/story/21237082/special-report-sovereign-citizens (accessed March 26, 2013).
19. Ibid.
20. See Federal Bureau of Investigation's Counterterrorism Analysis Section, "Sovereign Citizens: A Growing Domestic Threat to Law Enforcement," *Law Enforcement Bulletin* (September 2011), http://www.fbi.gov/stats-services/publications/law-enforcement-bulletin/september-2011/sovereign-citizens (accessed March 26, 2013).
21. Thomas Hobbes, *Leviathan* (New York: E. P. Dutton, 1950), pp. 290–291.
22. Jean-Jacques Rousseau, "A Discourse on the Origin of Inequality," in G. D. H. Cole (ed.), *The Social Contract and Discourses* (New York: E. P. Dutton, 1946), p. 240.
23. Bernard, *Consensus–Conflict Debate,* pp. 83, 85.
24. Frank Schmalleger, *Criminal Justice Today,* 8th ed. (Upper Saddle River, N.J.: Prentice Hall, 2005), p. 18.
25. One of the first publications to express the nonsystems approach was the American Bar Association, *New Perspective on Urban Crime* (Washington, D.C.: ABA Special Committee on Crime Prevention and Control, 1972).
26. Herbert L. Packer, *The Limits of the Criminal Sanction* (Stanford, Calif.: Stanford University Press, 1968).
27. Herbert L. Packer, *Two Models of the Criminal Process,* 113 U. PA. L. REV. 1, 2 (1964).
28. Norm Stamper, *Breaking Rank: A Top Cop's Exposé of the Dark Side of American Policing* (New York: Nation Books, 2005), p. 185.
29. See Office of Juvenile Justice and Delinquency Prevention, "Upper Age of Original Juvenile Court Jurisdiction," *Statistical Briefing Book: Juvenile Justice System Structure and Process* (Washington, D.C.: U.S. Department of Justice, 2012), http://www.ojjdp.gov/ojstatbb/structure_process/qa04101.asp (accessed March 4, 2013).
30. Samuel Walker, *Sense and Nonsense about Crime and Drugs,* 4th ed. (Belmont, Calif.: Wadsworth, 1997), p. 15.
31. Adapted from Mike Broemmel, *The Wedding Cake Model Theory of Criminal Justice* (Bellevue, Wash.: eHow, n.d.), http://www.ehow.com/about_5143074_wedding-model-theory-criminal-justice.html (accessed February 15, 2013).
32. The President's Commission on Law Enforcement and Administration of Justice, *The Challenge of Crime in a Free Society* (Washington, D.C.: U.S. Government Printing Office, 1967), p. 5.
33. Robert F. Kennedy, *The Enemy Within: The McClellan Committee's Crusade against Jimmy Hoffa and Corrupt Labor Unions* (Jackson, Tenn.: Perseus Books, 1994), p. 324.
34. Benjamin S. Bloom (ed.), Max D. Englehart, Edward J. Furst, Walker H. Hill, and David R. Krathwohl, *Taxonomy of Educational Objectives: The Classification of Educational Goals. Handbook I: Cognitive Domain* (New York: Longman, 1956).

CHAPTER 2

1. Brian P. Block and John Hostettler, *Famous Cases: Nine Trials that Changed the Law* (Hook, Hampshire: Waterside Press, 2002), pp. 9–12.
2. Henry Campbell Black, *Black's Law Dictionary,* 4th ed. (St. Paul, Minn.: West, 1951).
3. Law Library of Congress, "Case Law (or Common Law)," *American Memory,* http://memory.loc.gov/ammem/awhhtml/awlaw3/common_law.html (accessed February 17, 2013).
4. Texas Politics, "State Constitutions," *The Texas Constitution Today,* http://texaspolitics.laits.utexas.edu/7_3_1.html (accessed February 15, 2013).
5. Carissa Byrne Hessick, "Motive's Role in Criminal Punishment," *Southern California Law Review* 80, no. 89 (2006), p. 89.
6. See Arizona Criminal Code, generally, at http://www.azleg.gov/arizonarevisedstatutes.asp?title=13 (accessed February 15, 2013).
7. Ibid.
8. Federal Bureau of Investigation, "Table 1. Crime in the United States by Volume and Rate per 100,000 Inhabitants, 1992–2011," *Crime in the United States—2011* (Washington, D.C.: Uniform Crime Reporting Program), http://www.fbi.gov/about-us/cjis/ucr/crime-in-the-u.s/2011/crime-in-the-u.s.-2011/tables/table-1 (accessed February 15, 2013).
9. *People v. Anderson,* 70 Cal.2d 15 (1968).
10. *U.S. v. Brown,* 518 F.2d 821 (1975).
11. See, for example, James R. Elkins, "Depraved Heart Murder," *West Virginia Homicide Jury Instructions Project* (Morgantown: West Virginia University College of Law, Spring 2006), http://myweb.wvnet.edu/~jelkins/adcrimlaw/depraved_heart_murder.html (accessed May 28, 2013).

12. Federal Bureau of Investigation, "Murder," *Crime in the United States—2011* (Washington, D.C.: Uniform Crime Reporting Program), http://www.fbi.gov/about-us/cjis/ucr/crime-in-the-u.s/2011/crime-in-the-u.s.-2011/violent-crime/murder (accessed February 15, 2013).

13. Ibid.

14. Ibid.

15. Ibid.

16. Ibid.

17. For Nevada's larceny-theft statute, see *Nevada Revised Statutes*, Chapter 205.220; for Iowa's larceny statutes, see *Iowa Code*, Chapter 714.2, "Degrees of Theft," http://coolice.legis.iowa.gov/cool-ice/default.asp?category=billinfo&service=iowacode&ga=83&input=714#714.2 (accessed February 15, 2013).

18. Federal Bureau of Investigation, "Property Crime," *Crime in the United States—2011* (Washington, D.C.: Uniform Crime Reporting Program), http://www.fbi.gov/about-us/cjis/ucr/crime-in-the-u.s/2011/crime-in-the-u.s.-2011/property-crime/property-crime (accessed February 15, 2013).

19. Ibid.

20. Federal Bureau of Investigation, "Arson," *Crime in the United States—2011* (Washington, D.C.: Uniform Crime Reporting Program), http://www.fbi.gov/about-us/cjis/ucr/crime-in-the-u.s/2011/crime-in-the-u.s.-2011/property-crime/arson (accessed March 28, 2013).

21. *Sherman v. U.S.*, 356 U.S. 369 (1958).

22. *U.S. v. Russell*, 411 U.S. 423 (1973).

23. Leo Katz, "Excuse: Duress—The Nature of the Threat, the Nature of the Crime, the Mistaken Defendant, the Semiculpable Defendant—Superior Orders: Husbands and Wives," *Law Library: American Law and Legal Information—Crime and Criminal Law*, http://law.jrank.org/pages/1128/Excuse-Duress.html (accessed February 15, 2013).

24. *Spakes v. State*, 913 S.W.2d 597 (Tex. Crim. App. 1996).

25. PBS, "Biography: John Hinckley, Jr." *American Experience*, http://www.pbs.org/wgbh/americanexperience/features/biography/reagan-hinckley/ (accessed March 4, 2013).

26. David Gates, "Everybody Has Scars," *Newsweek*, October 13, 1986, p. 10; also see "Man Given 5-to-15-Year Term in Model's Slashing," *New York Times*, May 12, 1987, http://www.nytimes.com/1987/05/12/nyregion/man-given-5-to-15-year-term-in-model-s-slashing.html (accessed February 15, 2013).

27. Carol Pogash, "Myth of the 'Twinkie Defense': The Verdict in the Dan White Case Wasn't Based on His Ingestion of Junk Food," *San Francisco Chronicle*, November 23, 2003, http://www.sfgate.com/health/article/Myth-of-the-Twinkie-defense-The-verdict-in-2511152.php (accessed February 15, 2013).

28. Michael Perlin, *The Jurisprudence of the Insanity Defense* (Durham, N.C.: Carolina Academic Press, 1994), p. 108.

29. M'Naghten's Case, 8 Eng. Rep. 718 (H.L. 1843).

30. Dirk Johnson, "Milwaukee Jury Says Dahmer Was Sane," *New York Times*, February 16, 1992, http://www.nytimes.com/1992/02/16/us/milwaukee-jury-says-dahmer-was-sane.html (accessed February 15, 2013).

31. PBS, "Other Notorious Insanity Cases," *Frontline*, http://www.pbs.org/wgbh/pages/frontline/shows/crime/trial/other.html (accessed February 15, 2013).

32. Ibid.

33. See, generally, James F. Hooper and Alix M. McLearen, "Does the Insanity Defense Have a Legitimate Role?" *Psychiatric Times*, April 1, 2002, http://www.psychiatrictimes.com/display/article/10168/54196 (accessed February 15, 2013).

34. This is a double-jeopardy case, with the prosecutor apparently intending to continue going around the table, prosecuting Ashe for the robbery of each individual card player until he finally got a conviction. Ashe was convicted, and eventually his appeal went to the U.S. Supreme Court, which reversed the conviction on the grounds of *collateral estoppel*—which means that the government is prohibited from going in a different direction (e.g., here, on to subsequent poker players) and reprosecuting the defendant in hopes of obtaining a conviction. In other words, the *Ashe* case involved *one* robbery event, with six *counts*, so Ashe could only be tried once. *Ashe v. Swenson*, 397 U.S. 436 (1970).

35. Defendant Peterson was charged with manslaughter. At trial, the judge instructed the jury that self-defense is *not* available as a defense where someone acts as the aggressor; stands one's ground when other options are available; and actually provokes a conflict. Peterson was convicted, and appealed on the ground that his shooting the driver should be excused because he acted in self-defense. The appellate court agreed with the trial judge: One cannot claim he acted in "self-defense" by a *self-generated necessity to kill* another person. The evidence demonstrated that Peterson instigated the confrontation, and his failure to retreat was also a factor that could be taken into account by the jury. *U.S. v. Peterson*, 483 F. 2d 1222 (D.C. Cir. 1973).

36. The defendant, Blaue, was acquitted of murder—only on grounds of his "diminished responsibility" due to his having a mental impairment—but convicted of manslaughter. In such cases, courts like to consider whether or not the "chain of causation" was broken; in other words, the links in the chain of events here would be the girl's being stabbed (the act), her refusal to accept blood, and her death. The prosecution would argue that the links in the chain were *not* broken—that Blaue's actions directly caused her death. The defense, conversely, would argue that the links in the chain *were* broken—that all that the victim had to do was to accept a blood transfusion, and she would still be alive today. The appellate court ruled that the chain of causation was *not* broken by her failure to receive blood. Significantly, the court wrote that those who use violence "must take their victims as they find them"; this means the *whole* person (including her religious beliefs), not just the physical person. The stab wound caused her death, and "the fact that the victim refused to stop this end coming about did not break the causal connection between the act and death." See *Regina v. Blaue*, 1 W.L.R. 1411 (1975).

CHAPTER 3

1. Meghan Hoyer and Brad Heath, "Mass Killings Occur in USA Once Every Two Weeks," *USA TODAY*, December 19, 2012, http://www.usatoday.com/story/news/nation/2012/12/18/mass-killings-common/1778303/ (accessed June 10, 2013).

2. E. A. Wallis Budge, *Rosetta Stone in the British Museum* (London: Harrison and Sons, 1929).

3. Cesare Beccaria, *On Crimes and Punishments,* trans. H. Paolucci (Indianapolis, Ind.: Bobbs-Merrill, 1963; original work published 1764).

4. Frank E. Hagan, *Introduction to Criminology: Theories, Methods, and Criminal Behavior*, 8th ed. (Los Angeles, Calif.: Sage. Publications, 2013), p. 115.

5. Adapted from George F. Cole and Christopher E. Smith, *Criminal Justice in America*, 6th ed. (Belmont, Calif.: Wadsworth, 2011), p. 56.

6. Hagan, *Introduction to Criminology*, p. 129.

7. Ibid.

8. Ibid.

9. Mary Gibson, *Born to Crime: Cesare Lombroso and the Origins of Biological Criminology* (Westport, Conn.: Praeger, 2002); David G. Horn, *The Criminal Body: Lombroso and the Anatomy of Deviance* (New York: Routledge, 2003).

10. Ibid.

11. Hagan, *Introduction to Criminology*, pp. 132–133.

12. R. G. Fox, "The XYY Offender: A Modern Myth?" *Journal of Criminal Law, Criminology, and Police Science* 62 (March 1971), pp. 59–73.

13. Ibid.

14. William H. Sheldon, *Varieties of Delinquent Youth: An Introduction to Constitutional Psychiatry* (New York: Harper, 1949); William H. Sheldon, *The Varieties of Human Physique: An Introduction to Constitutional Psychology* (New York: Harper, 1940).

15. John Glatt, *Evil Twins: Chilling True Stories of Twins, Killing and Insanity* (New York: St. Martin's, 1999).

16. Ibid.

17. Hagan, *Introduction to Criminology*, p. 143.

18. Sigmund Freud, *The Complete Works of Sigmund Freud,* Vol. 19 (London: Hogarth, 1961).

19. Edwin H. Sutherland, "Mental Deficiency and Crime," in *Social Attitudes,* ed. Kimball Young (New York: Holt, Rinehart and Wilson, 1931), pp. 357–375.

20. Robert Gordon, "Prevalence: The Rare Datum in Delinquency Measurement and Its Implications for the Theory of Delinquency," in *The Juvenile Justice System,* ed. Malcolm W. Klein, (Beverly Hills, Calif.: Sage, 1976); Travis Hirschi and Michael J. Hindelang, "Intelligence and Delinquency: A Revisionist Review," *American Sociological Review* 42 (1977), pp. 572–587.

21. Robert K. Merton, "Social Structure and Anomie," *American Sociological Review* 3, no. 5 (October 1938), pp. 672–682.

22. Ibid.

23. Ibid., pp. 675–676.

24. E. D. Sutherland, D. Cressey and D. Luckenbill, *Principles of Criminology* (New York: General Hall, 1992).

25. Travis Hirschi, *Causes of Delinquency* (Berkeley: University of California Press, 1969).

26. Howard S. Becker, *Outsiders: Studies in the Sociology of Deviance* (New York: Free Press, 1963), p. 9.

27. Bald Eagle Protection Act of 1940, as amended, P.L. 95-616 (92 Stat. 3114), November 8, 1978.

28. Otwin Marenin, "Parking Tickets and Class Repression: The Concept of Policing in Critical Theories of Criminal Justice," *Contemporary Crises* 6 (1982), pp. 241–266.

29. George Vold, *Theoretical Criminology* (New York: Oxford University Press, 1958).

30. Thorsten Sellin, *Culture and Conflict in Crime* (New York: Social Science Research Council, 1938); Austin Turk, *Criminality and Legal Order* (Chicago: Rand McNally, 1969); also see Vold, *Theoretical Criminology.*

31. See, for example, Mark Kleiman, "Smart on Crime," *Democracy: A Journal of Ideas* 28 (Spring 2013), http://www.democracyjournal.org/28/smart-on-crime.php?page=all (accessed May 29, 2013).

32. Freda Adler, *Sisters in Crime: The Rise of the New Female Criminal* (New York: McGraw-Hill, 1975), p. 12.

33. Equal Employment Opportunity Act, Public Law 92–261.

34. Pregnancy Discrimination Act of 1978, 42 U.S.C. Sec. 2000e (k).

35. Family and Medical Leave Act (FMLA Public Law 103-3, 5 U.S.C. 6381-6387, 5 CFR part 630.

36. Robert Witt and Ann Dryden Witte, "Crime, Imprisonment, and Female Labor Force Participation: A Time-Series Approach," *Social Science Research Network,* November 1998, http://papers.ssrn.com/sol3/papers.cfm?abstract_id=226386 (accessed September 30, 2013).

37. Adler, *Sisters in Crime*, p. 3.

38. B. Brown, "Women and Crime: The Dark Figures of Criminology," *Economy and Society* 15, no. 3 (1986), p. 355.

39. Adler, *Sisters in Crime*, pp. 83–84.

40. B. Brown, "Women and Crime," p. 355.

41. Rita Simon, *Women and Crime* (Lexington, Mass.: Lexington Books, 1975).

42. M. Chesney-Lind and L. Pasko, *The Female Offender,* 2nd ed. (Thousand Oaks, Calif.: Sage, 2004).

43. See, for example, Sandra Walklate, *Gender, Crime, and Criminal Justice,* 2nd ed. (Cullompton, Devon, England: Willan Publishing, 2004); Drew Humphries, ed., *Women, Violence, and the Media: Readings in Feminist Criminology,* Northeastern Series on Gender, Crime, and Law (Lebanon, N.H.: Northeastern University Press, 2009); Lynne M. Vieraitis, Tomislav V. Kovandzic, and Sarah Britto, "Women's Status and Risk of Homicide Victimization: An Analysis with Data Disaggregated by Victim-Offender Relationship," *Homicide Studies* 12, no. 2 (2008), pp. 163–176; Matthew Makarios and Andrew Myer, "Gender, Race, and Marijuana Use: Testing the Generality of Traditional and Feminist Theories of Crime," paper presented at the ASC Annual Meeting, St. Louis Adam's Mark, St. Louis, Missouri, November 11, 2008.

44. Frank E. Hagan, *Introduction to Criminology: Theories, Methods, and Criminal Behavior,* 8th ed. (Los Angeles, Calif.: Sage. Publications, 2013), p. 320.

45. Quoted in ibid., p. 284.

46. Edwin H. Sutherland, "White Collar Criminality," *American Sociological Review* 5 (February 1940), pp. 1–12.

47. Hagan, *Introduction to Criminology*, p. 281.

48. Ibid., p. 288.

49. Robert Lenzner, "Bernie Madoff's $50 Billion Ponzi Scheme," *Forbes,* December 12, 2008, http://www.forbes.com/2008/12/12/madoff-ponzi-hedge-pf-ii-in_rl_1212croesus_inl.html (accessed June 7, 2013).

50. "Martha Stewart's Conviction Upheld," February 11, 2009, http://www.cbsnews.com/2100-207_162-1183526.html (accessed June 7, 2013).

51. Charles B. Fleddermann, "The Ford Pinto Exploding Gas Tank," in *Engineering Ethics,* 2nd ed. (Upper Saddle River, N.J.: Prentice Hall, 2004), pp. 72–73.

52. Hagan, *Introduction to Criminology*, p. 258.

53. See, for example, Steven Pizzo, Mary Fricker, and Paul Muolo, *Inside Job: The Looting of America's Savings and Loans* (New York: McGraw-Hill, 1989); P. J. Benekos and Frank E. Hagan, "The Great Savings and Loan Scandal," *Journal of Security Administration* (July 14, 1991), pp. 41–64.

54. Richard T. Wright and Scott H. Decker, "Creating the Illusion of Impending Death," in Paul Cromwell, *In Their Own Words: Criminals on Crime*, 5th ed. (Cary, N.C.: Oxford University Press, 2009), pp. 159–164.

55. Ibid., pp. 161–162.

56. Ibid., p. 162.

57. Ibid., p. 164.

58. Richard T. Wright and Scott H. Decker, "Deciding to Commit a Burglary," in Paul Cromwell, *In Their Own Words: Criminals on Crime*, 5th ed. (Cary, N.C.: Oxford University Press, 2009), pp. 90–101.

59. Ibid., p. 100.

60. Volkan Topalli and Richard T. Wright, "Dubs and Dees, Beats and Rims," in Paul Cromwell, *In Their Own Words: Criminals on Crime*, 5th ed. (Cary, N.C.: Oxford University Press, 2009), pp. 129–141.

61. See the Anti Car Theft Act of 1992, Public Law 102-519; the full text of the act may be viewed at http://www.ojp.usdoj.gov/BJA/pdf/Anti_Car_Theft_Act.pdf (accessed February 2, 2013).

62. Topalli and Wright, "Dubs and Dees, Beats and Rims," p. 129.

63. Ibid., pp. 131, 140.

64. See "Statistics," http://www.twainquotes.com/Statistics.html (accessed February 17, 2013).

65. Federal Bureau of Investigation, "Hate Crimes Accounting," *Hate Crime Statistics—2011,* December 10, 2012, http://www.fbi.gov/news/stories/2012/december/annual-hate-crimes-report-released/annual-hate-crimes-report-released (accessed February 9, 2013).

66. Lynn Langton and Michael Planty, *Hate Crime, 2003–2009* (Washington, D.C.: U.S. Department of Justice, Office of Justice Programs, Bureau of Justice Statistics, June 2011), p. 2, http://bjs.ojp.usdoj.gov/content/pub/pdf/hc0309.pdf (accessed December 19, 2012).

67. For access to the publications, see Federal Bureau of Investigation, *Uniform Crime Reports,* http://www.fbi.gov/ucr/ucr.htm (accessed January 28, 2013).

68. Federal Bureau of Investigation, "Caution Against Ranking: Variables Affecting Crime," *Crime in the United States 2011* (Washington, D.C.: U.S. Department of

Justice), http://www.fbi.gov/about-us/cjis/ucr/crime-in-the-u.s/2011/crime-in-the-u.s.-2011/caution-against-ranking (accessed February 17, 2013).

69. See, for example, Nathan James and Logan Rishard Council, "How Crime in the United States Is Measured," *Congressional Research Service Report for Congress* (January 3, 2008), pp. 17–20, http://www.policyarchive.org/handle/10207/bitstreams/18912.pdf (accessed June 5, 2013).

70. See Federal Bureau of Investigation, *Uniform Crime Reporting Handbook* (Washington, D.C.: U.S. Department of Justice), http://www.fbi.gov/about-us/cjis/ucr/additional-ucr-publications/ucr_handbook.pdf/view (accessed February 17, 2013), p. 10.

71. Federal Bureau of Investigation, "Table 1," *Crime in the United States—2011* (Washington, D.C.: U.S. Department of Justice), http://www.fbi.gov/about-us/cjis/ucr/crime-in-the-u.s/2011/crime-in-the-u.s.-2011/tables/table-1 (accessed February 18, 2013).

72. Federal Bureau of Investigation, "NIBRS General Frequently Asked Questions," *Uniform Crime Reports* (Washington, D.C.: U.S. Department of Justice), http://www.fbi.gov/ucr/nibrs_general.html#basics (accessed January 28, 2013).

73. Bureau of Justice Statistics, "Data Collection: National Crime Victimization Survey (NCVS)," http://bjs.ojp.usdoj.gov/index.cfm?ty=dcdetail&iid=245 (accessed February 17, 2013).

74. National Archive of Criminal Justice Data, "National Crime Victimization Survey Resource Guide," http://www.icpsr.umich.edu/icpsrweb/NACJD/NCVS/ (accessed February 17, 2013).

75. National Archive of Criminal Justice Data, "Accuracy of NCVS Estimates," http://www.icpsr.umich.edu/NACJD/NCVS/accuracy.html (accessed January 15, 2013).

CHAPTER 4

1. Adapted from John R. Jones and Daniel P. Carlson, *Reputable Conduct: Ethical Issues in Policing and Corrections,* 2nd ed. (Upper Saddle River, N.J.: Prentice Hall, 2001), p. 14.

2. This scenario is loosely based on David Gelman, Susan Miller, and Bob Cohn, "The Strange Case of Judge Wachtler," *Newsweek* (November 23, 1992), pp. 34–35. Wachtler was later arraigned on charges of attempting to extort money from the woman and threatening her 14-year-old daughter (it was later determined that the judge had been having an affair with the woman, who had recently ended the relationship). After being placed under house arrest with an electronic monitoring bracelet, the judge resigned from the court, which he had served with distinction for two decades.

3. Adapted from Jones and Carlson, *Reputable Conduct,* pp. 162–163.

4. Immanuel Kant, "Foundations of the Metaphysics of Morals," *The German Library* 13 (New York: Continuum, 2006).

5. Richard Kania, "Police Acceptance of Gratuities," *Criminal Justice Ethics* 7 (1988), pp. 37–49.

6. John Kleinig, *The Ethics of Policing* (New York: Cambridge University Press, 1996).

7. T. J. O'Malley, "Managing for Ethics: A Mandate for Administrators," *FBI Law Enforcement Bulletin* (April 1997), pp. 20–25.

8. Thomas J. Martinelli, "Unconstitutional Policing: The Ethical Challenges in Dealing with Noble Cause Corruption," *The Police Chief* (October 2006), p. 150.

9. John P. Crank and Michael A. Caldero, *Police Ethics: The Corruption of Noble Cause* (Cincinnati: Anderson, 2000), p. 75.

10. U.S. Department of Justice, National Institute of Justice, Office of Community Oriented Policing Services, *Police Integrity: Public Service with Honor* (Washington, D.C.: U.S. Government Printing Office, 1997), p. 62.

11. Ibid.

12. Lawrence W. Sherman, ed., *Police Corruption: A Sociological Perspective* (Garden City, N.Y.: Anchor, 1974), p. 1.

13. Herman Goldstein, *Policing a Free Society* (Cambridge, Mass.: Ballinger, 1977), p. 188.

14. Ibid.

15. "Police Aides Told to Rid Commands of All Dishonesty," *New York Times*, October 29, 1970.

16. William A. Westley, *Violence and the Police* (Cambridge, Mass.: MIT Press, 1970), pp. 113–114.

17. International Association of Chiefs of Police, "What Is the Law Enforcement Oath of Honor?" http://www.theiacp.org/PoliceServices/ExecutiveServices/ProfessionalAssistance/Ethics/WhatistheLawEnforcementOathofHonor/tabid/150/Default.aspx (accessed March 10, 2013).

18. David Carter, "Theoretical Dimensions in the Abuse of Authority," in *Police Deviance,* ed. Thomas Barker and David Carter (Cincinnati: Anderson, 1994), pp. 269–290; also see Thomas Barker and David Carter, "Fluffing Up the Evidence and 'Covering Your Ass': Some Conceptual Notes on Police Lying," *Deviant Behavior* 11 (1990), pp. 61–73.

19. "More Than 3,000 Mexican Federal Police Fired, Commissioner Says," *CNN World*, March 10, 2010, http://articles.cnn.com/2010-08-30/world/mexico.federal. police.fired_1_federal-police-officers-police-headquarters?_s=PM:WORLD (accessed March 10, 2013).

20. Anne Barrowclough, "Hundreds of Mexican Police Officers Sacked over Corruption," *The Times: U.S. & Americas*, November 3, 2012, http://www.thetimes.co.uk/tto/news/world/americas/article3589373.ece (accessed March 10, 2013).

21. Dudley Althaus, "Despite Millions in U.S. Aid, Police Corruption Plagues Mexico," *Houston Chronicle*, October 18, 2010, http://www.chron.com/news/houston-texas/article/Despite-millions-in-U-S-aid-police-corruption-1710872.php (accessed March 10, 2013).

22. Gary T. Marx, "Who Really Gets Stung? Some Issues Raised by the New Police Undercover Work," *Crime & Delinquency* (1982), pp. 165–193.

23. *Illinois v. Perkins,* 110 S. Ct. 2394 (1990).

24. Barker and Carter, *Police Deviance.*

25. Thomas Barker, "An Empirical Study of Police Deviance Other than Corruption," *Police Deviance,* ed. Thomas Barker and David Carter (Cincinnati: Anderson, 1994), pp. 123–138.

26. For an excellent analysis of how the acceptance of gratuities can become endemic to an organization and pose ethical dilemmas for new officers within, see Jim Ruiz and Christine Bono, "At What Price a 'Freebie'? The Real Cost of Police Gratuities," *Criminal Justice Ethics* (Winter/Spring 2004), pp. 44–54. The authors also demonstrate through detailed calculations how the amount of gratuities accepted can reach up to 40 percent of an annual officer's income—and is therefore no minor or inconsequential infraction of rules that can be left ignored or unenforced.

27. Edward Tully, "Misconduct, Corruption, Abuse of Power: What Can the Chief Do?" http://www.neiassociates.org/mis2.htm (Part I) and http://www.neiassociates.org/misconductII.htm (Part II) (accessed January 18, 2013).

28. Roscoe Pound, "The Causes of Popular Dissatisfaction with the Administration of Justice," address before the annual convention of the American Bar Association, August 29, 1906, in 14 AM. LAW. 445 (1996).

29. John P. MacKenzie, *The Appearance of Justice* (New York: Scribner, 1974).

30. Pierro Calamandrei, quoted in Frank Greenberg, "The Task of Judging the Judges," *Judicature* 59 (May 1976), p. 464.

31. For thorough discussions and examples of these areas of potential ethical shortcomings, see Jeffrey M. Shaman, Steven Lubet, and James J. Alfini, *Judicial Conduct and Ethics,* 3rd ed. (San Francisco: Matthew Bender & Co., 2000).

32. Ibid.

33. Ibid., p. vi.

34. Tim Murphy, "Test Your Ethical Acumen," *Judges' Journal* 8 (1998), p. 34.

35. Walter Pavlo, "Pennsylvania Judge Gets 'Life Sentence' for Prison Kickback Scheme," http://www.forbes.com/sites/walterpavlo/2011/08/12/pennsylvania-judge-gets-life-sentence-for-prison-kickback-scheme/ (accessed March 8, 2013).

36. Ian Urbina and Sean D. Hamill, "Judges Plead Guilty in Scheme to Jail Youths for Profit," *The New York Times*, February 12, 2009, http://www.nytimes.com/2009/02/13/us/13judge.html?pagewanted=all&_r=0 (accessed March 8, 2013).

37. Ibid.

38. See *In re Gault,* 387 U.S. 1 (1967).

39. Urbina and Hamill, "Judges Plead Guilty in Scheme to Jail Youths for Profit."

40. American Judicature Society, *Judicial Conduct Reporter* 16 (1994), pp. 2–3.

41. Shaman, Lubet, and Alfini, *Judicial Conduct and Ethics,* p. viii.

42. Deut. 1:16–17.

43. *Berger v. U.S.,* 295 U.S. 78 (1935).

44. See *Dunlop v. U.S.,* 165 U.S. 486 (1897), involving a prosecutor's inflammatory statements to the jury.

45. 386 U.S. 1 (1967). In this case, the Supreme Court overturned the defendant's conviction after determining that the prosecutor "deliberately misrepresented the truth."

46. Elliot D. Cohen, "Pure Legal Advocates and Moral Agents: Two Concepts of a Lawyer in an Adversary System," in *Justice, Crime and Ethics,* 2nd ed., ed. Michael C. Braswell, Belinda R. McCarthy, and Bernard J. McCarthy (Cincinnati: Anderson, 1996), p. 168.

47. Ibid.

48. Ibid., pp. 131–167.

49. Cynthia Kelly Conlon and Lisa L. Milord, *The Ethics Fieldbook: Tools for Trainers* (Chicago: American Judicature Society, n.d.), pp. 23–25.

50. Ibid., p. 28.

51. Elizabeth L. Grossi and Bruce L. Berg, "Stress and Job Dissatisfaction among Correctional Officers: An Unexpected Finding," *International Journal of Offender Therapy and Comparative Criminology* 35 (1991), p. 79.

52. Irving L. Janis, "Group Dynamics under Conditions of External Danger," in *Group Dynamics: Research and Theory,* ed. Darwin Cartwright and Alvin Zander (New York: Harper & Row, 1968).

53. Ibid.

54. Ibid., p. 85.

55. CBS News, March 30, 1977; see Jones and Carlson, *Reputable Conduct,* p. 76.

56. Jones and Carlson, *Reputable Conduct,* p. 77.

57. Kleinig, *The Ethics of Policing.*

58. Ibid.

59. Adapted from Gail Diane Cox, "Judges Behaving Badly (Again)," *The National Law Journal* 21 (May 3, 1999), pp. 1–5.

CHAPTER 5

1. Bruce Smith, *Rural Crime Control* (New York: Columbia University, 1933), p. 40.

2. Ibid.

3. Ibid.

4. Ibid., pp. 182–184.

5. Ibid., pp. 188–189.

6. Ibid., pp. 218–222.

7. Ibid., pp. 245–246.

8. David R. Johnson, *American Law Enforcement History* (St. Louis, Mo.: Forum Press, 1981), pp. 18–19.

9. Leon Radzinowicz, *A History of English Criminal Law and Its Administration from 1750: Volume IV. Grappling for Control* (London: Stevens and Son, 1968), pp. 20–21.

10. A. C. Germann, Frank D. Day, and Robert R. J. Gallati, *Introduction to Law Enforcement and Criminal Justice* (Springfield, Ill.: Charles C. Thomas, 1962), p. 63.

11. Johnson, *American Law Enforcement History*, p. 26.

12. James F. Richardson, *Urban Police in the United States* (London: Kennikat Press, 1974), pp. 47–48.

13. Johnson, *American Law Enforcement History*, p. 26.

14. Herman Goldstein, *Policing a Free Society* (Cambridge, Mass.: Ballinger, 1977).

15. Richardson, *Urban Police in the United States,* pp. 139–143.

16. Herman Goldstein, *Policing a Free Society* (Cambridge, Mass.: Ballinger, 1977).

17. Kenneth J. Peak and Ronald W. Glensor, *Community Policing and Problem Solving: Strategies and Practices*, 5th ed. (Upper Saddle River, N.J.: Prentice Hall, 2008), pp. 15–16.

18. Elaine Cumming, Ian Cumming, and Laura Edell, "Policeman as Philosopher, Guide, and Friend," *Social Problems* 12 (1965), p. 285; T. Bercal, "Calls for Police Assistance," *American Behavioral Scientist* 13 (1970), p. 682; Albert J. Reiss Jr., *The Police and the Public* (New Haven, Conn.: Yale University Press, 1971).

19. U.S. Department of Homeland Security, "Creation of the Department of Homeland Security," http://www.dhs.gov/creation-department-homeland-security (accessed October 29, 2012).

20. National Priorities Project, "U.S. Security Spending Since 9/11," May 26, 2011, http://nationalpriorities.org/analysis/2011/us-security-spending-since-911/ (accessed October 29, 2012).

21. U.S. Customs and Border Protection, "On a Typical Day," http://www.cbp.gov/linkhandler/cgov/about/accomplish/typical_day_fy11.ctt/typical_day_fy11.pdf (accessed October 5, 2012).

22. Department of Homeland Security, "ICE: Enforcement and Removal Operations," http://www.ice.gov/about/offices/enforcement-removal-operations/ (accessed October 6, 2012).

23. Department of Homeland Security, Transportation Security Administration, "TSA Workforce," http://www.tsa.gov/about-tsa (accessed October 7, 2012).

24. See United States Coast Guard, Office of Law Enforcement, "Mission," http://www.uscg.mil/hq/cg5/cg531/ (accessed June 3, 2013).

25. United States Secret Service, "Frequently Asked Questions about the United States Secret Service," www.secretservice.gov/faq.shtml#employees (accessed July 9, 2010).

26. Michael Fooner, *Interpol: Issues in World Crime and International Criminal Justice* (New York: Plenum Press, 1989), p. 179.

27. U.S. Department of Justice, Federal Bureau of Investigation, "About Us—Quick Facts," http://www.fbi.gov/about-us/quick-facts/quickfacts (accessed October 29, 2012).

28. U.S. Department of Justice, Federal Bureau of Investigation, "What We Investigate," http://www.fbi.gov/about-us/investigate/what_we_investigate (accessed October 29, 2012).

29. "FBI Seeks Sweeping New Powers," *The Nation*, August 22, 2008, www.thenation.com/article/fbi-seeks-sweeping-new-powers (accessed July 10, 2010).

30. Bureau of Alcohol, Tobacco, Firearms and Explosives, "ATF's History," http://www.atf.gov/about/history/ (accessed October 7, 2012).

31. U.S. Department of Justice, Drug Enforcement Administration, "DEA History," http://www.justice.gov/dea/about/history.shtml (accessed October 6, 2012).

32. U.S. Marshals Service, *The FY 1993 Report to the U.S. Marshals* (Washington, D.C.: U.S. Department of Justice, 1994), pp. 188–189; also see U.S. Marshals Service, "Fact Sheets: Facts and Figures," *Office of Public Affairs*, April 15, 2011 (Washington, D.C.: U.S. Department of Justice), http://www.usmarshals.gov/duties/factsheets/facts-2011.html (accessed October 7, 2012).

33. Central Intelligence Agency, "CIA Vision, Mission, & Values," https://www.cia.gov/about-cia/cia-vision-mission-values/index.html; also see CIA, "About CIA," https://www.cia.gov/about-cia/index.html (accessed October 7, 2012).

34. Internal Revenue Service, "Financial Investigations: Criminal Investigation (CI)," http://www.irs.gov/uac/Financial-Investigations---Criminal-Investigation-(CI) (accessed October 29, 2012).

35. Brian Reaves, *Census of State and Local Law Enforcement Agencies, 2008* (Washington, D.C.: U.S. Department of Justice, Bureau of Justice Statistics, July 2011), http://bjs.ojp.usdoj.gov/content/pub/pdf/csllea08.pdf (accessed October 8, 2012).

36. Ibid., p. 1.

37. Ibid.

38. Bureau of Justice Statistics, "Census of State and Local Law Enforcement Agencies, 2008" (Washington, D.C.: U.S. Department of Justice, July 2011), p. 1, http://bjs.ojp.usdoj.gov/content/pub/pdf/csllea08.pdf (accessed November 5, 2012).

39. Bureau of Justice Statistics, *Local Police Departments, 2007* (Washington, D.C.: U.S. Department of Justice, December 2010), p. 6, http://bjs.ojp.usdoj.gov/content/pub/pdf/lpd07.pdf (accessed January 24, 2013).

40. Bureau of Justice Statistics, *Sheriff's Offices, 2003* (Washington, D.C.: U.S. Department of Justice), http://bjs.ojp.usdoj.gov/index.cfm?ty=tp&tid=72 (accessed January 24, 2013).

41. Bureau of Justice Statistics, *Local Police* (Washington, D.C.: U.S. Department of Justice), http://www.bjs.gov/index.cfm?ty=tp&tid=71 (accessed August 3, 2013).

42. Andrea M. Burch, *Sheriff's Offices, 2007* (Washington, D.C.: U.S. Department of Justice, Bureau of Justice Statistics, December 6, 2012), http://www.bjs.gov/index.cfm?ty=pbdetail&iid=4555 (accessed August 3, 2013).

43. Saul D. Astor, "A Nation of Thieves," *Security World* 15 (September 1978).

44. Bureau of Justice Statistics, *Criminal Victimization—2011* (Washington, D.C.: U.S. Department of Justice, October 2012), http://bjs.ojp.usdoj.gov/index.cfm?ty=pbdetail&iid=4494 (accessed November 1, 2012).

45. Ibid., p. 238.

46. Lawrence J. Fennelly, ed., *Handbook of Loss Prevention and Crime Prevention*, 2nd ed. (Boston: Butterworths, 1989), in foreword.

47. George F. Cole and Christopher E. Smith, *The American System of Criminal Justice*, 11th ed. (Belmont, Calif.: Thomson Wadsworth, 2007), p. 253.

48. National Advisory Commission on Criminal Justice Standards and Goals, *Private Security* (Washington, D.C.: U.S. Government Printing Office, 1976), p. 99.

CHAPTER 6

1. William A. Westley, *Violence and the Police* (Cambridge, Mass.: MIT Press, 1970).

2. Quoted in V. A. Leonard and Harry W. More, *Police Organization and Management*, 3rd ed. (Mineola, N.Y.: Foundation Press, 1971), p. 128.

3. Lawrence S. Wrightsman, *Psychology and the Legal System* (Monterey, Calif.: Brooks/Cole, 1987), pp. 85–86.

4. Roger G. Dunham and Geoffrey P. Alpert, *Critical Issues in Policing: Contemporary Readings,* 5th ed. (Long Grove, Ill.: Waveland, 2005), p. 12.

5. Ibid., p. 111.

6. Jerome Skolnick, "A Sketch of the Policeman's Working Personality," quoted in *The Police Community,* eds. Jack Goldsmith and Sharon S. Goldsmith (Pacific Palisades, Calif.: Palisades, 1974), p. 106.

7. John J. Broderick, *Police in a Time of Change* (Prospect Heights, Ill.: Waveland Press, 1987), p. 215.

8. Adapted from Dennis Nowicki, "Twelve Traits of Highly Effective Police Officers," *Law and Order* (October 1999), pp. 45–46.

9. Samuel Walker, *The Police in America: An Introduction,* 2nd ed. (New York: McGraw-Hill, 1992), p. 61.

10. Steven M. Cox, *Police: Practices, Perspectives, Problems* (Boston: Allyn and Bacon, 1996), p. 61.

11. See Albert Reiss, *The Police and the Public* (New Haven, Conn.: Yale University Press, 1971), p. 96.

12. Jerome H. Skolnick and David H. Bayley, *The New Blue Line: Police Innovation in Six American Cities* (New York: Free Press, 1986), p. 4.

13. James Q. Wilson, *Varieties of Police Behavior* (Cambridge, Mass.: Harvard University Press, 1968), pp. 140–226.

14. Sarah Korones, "The 10 Most Dangerous Jobs in America," *CBS News,* January 27, 2013, http://www.smartplanet.com/blog/bulletin/the-10-most-dangerous-jobs-in-america/11396 (accessed February 22, 2013).

15. U.S. citizen living in Saudi Arabia, personal communication, September 12, 1994.

16. Chris Hedges, "Everywhere in Saudi Arabia, Islam Is Watching," *New York Times,* January 6, 1993, p. A4(N), col. 3.

17. Federal Bureau of Investigation, "Officers Feloniously Killed," *Uniform Crime Report: Law Enforcement Officers Killed and Assaulted 2011* (Washington, D.C.: U.S. Department of Justice), http://www.fbi.gov/about-us/cjis/ucr/leoka/2011/officers-feloniously-killed/felonious-final2011.pdf (accessed August 4, 2013); also see Federal Bureau of Investigation, "Officers Accidentally Killed," *Uniform Crime Report: Law Enforcement Officers Killed and Assaulted 2011* (Washington, D.C.: U.S. Department of Justice), http://www.fbi.gov/about-us/cjis/ucr/leoka/2011/officers-accidentally-killed-1/officers-accidentally-killed; Federal Bureau of Investigation, "Officers Assaulted," *Uniform Crime Report: Law Enforcement Officers Killed and Assaulted 2011* (Washington, D.C.: U.S. Department of Justice), http://www.fbi.

gov/about-us/cjis/ucr/leoka/2011/officers-assaulted-1/officers-assaulted (accessed January 19, 2013).

18. Quoted in Kevin Krajick, "Does Patrol Prevent Crime?" *Police Magazine* 1 (September 1978), pp. 4–16.

19. Bureau of Justice Statistics, *Characteristics of Drivers Stopped by Police, 2002* (Washington, D.C.: U.S. Department of Justice, 2006), pp. 1–2, 5.

20. See, for example, Terry C. Cox and Mervin F. White, "Traffic Citations and Student Attitudes toward the Police: An Examination of Selected Interaction Dynamics," *Journal of Police Science and Administration* 16, no. 2 (Fall 1988), pp. 105–121.

21. Carl B. Klockars and Stephen D. Mastrofski, "Police Discretion: The Case of Selective Enforcement," in *Thinking about Police: Contemporary Readings,* 2nd ed., edited by Carl B. Klockars and Stephen D. Mastrofski (Boston: McGraw-Hill, 1991), p. 330.

22. David H. Bayley and Egon Bittner, "Learning the Skills of Policing," in *Critical Issues in Policing: Contemporary Readings*, edited by Roger G. Dunham and Geoffrey P. Alpert (Prospect Heights, Ill.: Waveland, 1989), pp. 87–110.

23. Kenneth Culp Davis, *Police Discretion* (St. Paul, Minn.: West, 1975), p. 73.

24. Kenneth Culp Davis, *Discretionary Justice* (Urbana: University of Illinois Press, 1969), p. 222.

25. Klockars and Mastrofski, "Police Discretion," p. 331.

26. This scenario is based on a quote by former Los Angeles Chief of Police Bernard Parks, in Randall Kennedy, "Suspect Policy," *New Republic,* September 13, 1999, pp. 30–35.

27. Quoted in Leonard Roy Frank, ed., *Random House Webster's Quotationary* (New York: Random House, 1999), p. 761.

28. Marc H. Caplan and Joe Holt Anderson, *Forensic: When Science Bears Witness* (Washington, D.C.: U.S. Government Printing Office, 1984), p. 2.

29. Charles R. Swanson, Neil C. Chamelin, Leonard Territo, and Robert W. Taylor, *Criminal Investigation,* 9th ed. (Boston: McGraw-Hill, 2006), p. 10.

30. Peter R. DeForest, R. E. Gaensslen, and Henry C. Lee, *Forensic Science: An Introduction to Criminalistics* (New York: McGraw-Hill, 1983), p. 29.

31. W. Jerry Chisum and Brent E. Turvey, "Evidence Dynamics: Locard's Exchange Principle & Crime Reconstruction," *Journal of Behavioral Profiling* 2, no. 1 (2000), p. 3.

32. President's Commission on Law Enforcement and the Administration of Justice, *Task Force Report: Science and Technology* (Washington, D.C.: U.S. Government Printing Office, 1967), pp. 7–18.

33. Paul B. Weston and Kenneth M. Wells, *Criminal Investigation: Basic Perspectives*, 4th ed. (Englewood Cliffs, N.J.: Prentice Hall, 1986), pp. 5–10.

34. Peter W. Greenwood and Joan Petersilia, *The Criminal Investigation Process: Volume 1. Summary and Policy Implications* (Santa Monica, Calif.: RAND, 1975). The entire report is found in Peter W. Greenwood, Jan M. Chaiken, and Joan Petersilia, *The Criminal Investigation Process* (Lexington, Mass.: D. C. Heath, 1977).

35. Ibid., p. 19.

36. Weston and Wells, *Criminal Investigation*, p. 5.

37. Thomas Hughes and Megan Magers, "The Perceived Impact of Crime Scene Investigation Shows on the Administration of Justice," *Journal of Criminal Justice and Popular Culture* 14, no. 3 (2007), p. 262, http://www.albany.edu/scj/jcjpc/vol14is3/HughesMagers.pdf (accessed October 28, 2012).

38. Ibid., p. 265.

39. Kit Roane, "The CSI Effect," *U.S. News & World Report*, April, 17, 2005, http://www.usnews.com/usnews/culture/articles/050425/25csi.htm (accessed February 23, 2013).

40. Solomon Moore, "Progress Is Minimal in Clearing DNA Cases," *New York Times*, October 24, 2008, http://www.nytimes.com/2008/10/25/us/25dna.html?pagewanted=all&_r=0 (accessed February 22, 2013).

41. DeForest et al., *Forensic Science*, p. 11.

42. John S. Dempsey and Linda S. Forst, *An Introduction to Policing,* 6th ed. (Independence, Ky.: Cengage, 2012), p. 470, http://books.google.com/books?id=PmUwsHp8m1wC&pg=PA470&dq= (accessed August 6, 2013).

43. Richard Willing, "DNA to Clear 200th Person," *USA Today,* April 23, 2007, http://usatoday30.usatoday.com/news/nation/2007-04-22-dna-exoneration_N.htm (accessed August 6, 2013).

CHAPTER 7

1. L. Morris, *Incredible New York* (New York: Bonanza, 1951).

2. James A. Inciardi, *Criminal Justice,* 5th ed. (Orlando, Fla.: Harcourt Brace, 1996).

3. Charles Joyner and Chad Basile, "The Dynamic Resistance Response Model," *FBI Law Enforcement Bulletin* (September 2007), p. 17.

4. *Tennessee v. Garner*, 471 U.S. 1 (1985).

5. Kenneth J. Peak, *Policing America: Challenges and Best Practices,* 6th ed. (Upper Saddle River, N.J.: Prentice Hall, 2009), p. 263.

6. A. C. Germann, Frank D. Day, and Robert R. J. Gallati, *Introduction to Law Enforcement and Criminal Justice* (Springfield, Ill.: Charles C. Thomas, 1976), p. 225.

7. H. E. Barrineau III, *Civil Liability in Criminal Justice* (Cincinnati, Ohio: Pilgrimage, 1987), p. 58.

8. Ibid., p. 5.

9. Kenneth J. Peak, *Policing America: Methods, Issues, Challenges* (Englewood Cliffs, N.J.: Regents/Prentice Hall), 1992; for a complete account of King's beating and its aftermath, see pp. 318–327.

10. Seth Mydans, "Punitive Damages Denied in Beating of Rodney King," *New York Times*, June 2, 1994, http://www.nytimes.com/1994/06/02/us/punitive-damages-denied-in-beating-of-rodney-king.html?sec=&spon=&pagewanted=all (accessed January 18, 2013).

11. See, for example, *Black v. Stephens,* 662 F.2d 181 (1991).

12. *Fielder v. Jenkins* (N.J. Super. A.D. 1993833 A.2d 906).

13. Kenneth J. Peak, Larry K. Gaines, and Ronald W. Glensor, *Police Supervision and Management: In an Era of Community Policing,* 3rd ed. (Upper Saddle River, N.J.: Prentice Hall, 2010).

14. *Thomas v. Williams,* 124 S.E.2d 409 (Ga. App. 1962).

15. *Guice v. Enfinger,* 389 So.2d 270 (Fla. App. 1980).

16. *Davis v. City of Detroit*, 386 N.W.2d 169 (Mich. App. 1986).

17. Ronald Palmer, chief of police, *Procedure Manual* (Tulsa, Okla.: Police Department, June 10, 1998), p. 1.

18. The U.S. Supreme Court said, in a 7-2 decision, that Gonzales could not sue the city and claim the police had violated her rights to due process. Furthermore, it held she had no constitutionally protected interest in the enforcement of the restraining order. The opinion also established that the holder of a restraining order is not entitled to any specific mandatory action by the police; rather, restraining orders only provide grounds for *arresting* the person restrained by order. See *Castle Rock v. Gonzales,* 545 U.S. 748 (2005).

19. See *County of Sacramento v. Lewis*, 118 S.Ct. 1708 (1998).

20. *Scott v. Harris,* 550 U.S. 372 (2007), at p. 13.

21. Bureau of Justice Statistics, *Local Police Departments, 2007* (Washington, D.C.: U.S. Department of Justice, 2010), p. 14.

22. Bureau of Justice Statistics, *Women in Law Enforcement, 1987–2008* (Washington, D.C.: U.S. Department of Justice, June 2010), p. 3; also see Bureau of Justice Assistance, *Recruiting & Retaining Women: A Self-Assessment Guide for Law Enforcement* (Washington, D.C.: U.S. Department of Justice, June 2001), https://www.ncjrs.gov/pdffiles1/bja/188157.pdf (accessed January 18, 2013).

23. Ibid., p. 2.

24. See Jon Felperin, "Women in Law Enforcement: Two Steps Forward, Three Steps Back," http://www.policeone.com/police-recruiting/articles/87017-Women-in-Law-Enforcement-Two-steps-forward-three-steps-back/ (accessed June 11, 2013).

25. National Advisory Commission on Civil Disorders, *Report Summary*, http://www.eisenhowerfoundation.org/docs/kerner.pdf (accessed June 10, 2013).

26. See, for example, Allen D. Grimshaw, *Racial Violence in the United States* (Chicago: Aldine, 1969), pp. 269–298; *Report of the National Advisory Commission on Civil Disorders* (New York: Bantam Books, 1968); Steven M. Cox and Jack D. Fitzgerald, *Police in Community Relations: Critical Issues,* 2nd ed. (Dubuque, Iowa: William C. Brown, 1992), p. 129.

27. "How to Police the Police in 'Nobody Knows My Name,'" *New York Times*, September 21, 1983, http://www.nytimes.com/1983/09/21/opinion/how-to-police-the-police-in-nobody-knows-my-name.html (accessed June 10, 2013).

28. Office of Justice Programs, *Police Stop White, Black, and Hispanic Drivers at Similar Rates According to Department of Justice Report* (Washington, D.C.: U.S. Department of Justice, 2007), www.ojp.usdoj.gov/newsroom/pressreleases/2007/BJS07020.htm (accessed March 5, 2013).

29. Samuel Walker, *The Police in America: An Introduction,* 2nd ed. (New York: McGraw-Hill, 1993), p. 224.

30. Bureau of Justice Statistics, *Local Police Departments, 2007* (Washington, D.C.: U.S. Department of Justice, December 2010), p. 14.

31. Kaveh Ghaemian, "Small-Town Cops Wield Big-City Data," *Government Technology* 9 (September 1996), p. 38.

32. Lois Pilant, "Computerized Crime Mapping," *Police Chief* (December 1997), p. 58.

33. U.S. Department of Justice, National Institute of Justice, *Crime Mapping Research Conference,* http://www.nij.gov/events/maps/ (accessed August 6, 2013); the CMRC web address is www.ojp.usdoj.gov/nij/maps/welcome.htm (accessed March 5, 2013).

34. Bill McGarigle, "Crime Profilers Gain New Weapons," *Government Technology* (December 1997), pp. 28–29.

35. Ibid.

36. Lauren Katims, "Crime Scan," *Government Technology* (April 2011), p. 38.

37. Bureau of Justice Statistics, *Local Police Departments, 2007* (Washington, D.C.: U.S. Department of Justice, 2010), p. 17; Bureau of Justice Statistics, *Sheriff's Offices, 2003* (Washington, D.C.: U.S. Department of Justice, 2006), p. 26.

38. Kyle Malone, "The Fourth Amendment and the Stored Communications Act: Why the Warrantless Gathering of Historical Cell Site Location Information Poses No Threat to Privacy," *Pepperdine Law Review* 39, no. 3 (September 8, 2012), http://digitalcommons.pepperdine.edu/cgi/viewcontent.cgi?article=1368&context=plr&sei-

redir=1&referer=http%3A%2F%2Fwww
.google.com%2Furl%3Fsa%3Dt%26rc
t%3Dj%26q%3D1986%2520stored%25
20communications%2520act%2520wa
rrantless%2520searches%26source%3D
web%26cd%3D7%26ved%3D0CFgqFjA
G%26url%3Dhttp%253A%252F%252F
digitalcommons.pepperdine.edu
%252Fcgi%252Fviewcontent.
cgi%253Farticle%253D1368%2526conte
xt%253Dplr%26ei%3D3j09UNDsOMbmi
wLDsoC4Aw%26usg%3DAFQjCNEs
KOZHRJZkkCfueOF_QKYroFrfxQ
#search=%221986%20stored%20
communications%20act%20
warrantless%20searches%22 (accessed
December 3, 2012).

39. Massimo Calabresi, "The Phone
Knows All," *Time* (August 27, 2012),
http://www.time.com/time/magazine/
article/0,9171,2122241,00.html (accessed
December 3, 2012).

40. See 18 U.S.C. Chapter 121 §§ 2701–2712.

41. 18 U.S.C. § 2703(b) (2006).

42. Brian Huber, "Wis. Police Get Robo-Cop's
Help," *PoliceOne.com*, November 14, 2006,
www.policeone.com/police-technology/
robots/articles/1190983 (accessed March
5, 2013).

43. Alison Bath, "Accident Scene Investigation
Is High Tech," *Reno Gazette-Journal*
(Sparks Today section), November 18, 2003,
p. 4.

44. Ibid., p. 46.

CHAPTER 8

1. *McCulloch v. Maryland*, 17 U.S. 316 (1819).

2. John Adams, "Novanglus Papers," in *The
Works of John Adams,* ed. Charles Francis
Adams (Boston: Little Brown and Company,
1851), p. 106.

3. David Neubauer, *America's Courts and the
Criminal Justice System*, 9th ed. (Belmont,
Calif.: Wadsworth, 2008), pp. 294–300.

4. *Draper v. United States*, 358 U.S. 307 (1959).

5. *Illinois v. Gates*, 462 U.S. 213 (1983).

6. *U.S. v. Sokolow*, 109 S.Ct. 1581 (1989).

7. *People v. Defore*, 242 N.Y. 214, 150 N.E. 585
(1926).

8. *Weeks v. United States*, 232 U.S. 383 (1914).

9. *Mapp v. Ohio*, 367 U.S. 643 (1961).

10. *Payton v. New York*, 445 U.S. 573 (1980).

11. *Delaware v. Prouse*, 440 U.S. 648 (1979).

12. *Michigan Department of State Police v. Sitz*,
110 S.Ct. 2481, 110 L.Ed.2d 412 (1990).

13. *Pennsylvania v. Muniz*, 110 S.Ct. 2638, 110
L.Ed.2d 528 (1990).

14. *Maryland v. Pringle*, 124 S.Ct. 795 (2004).

15. *Illinois v. Lidster*, 124 S.Ct. 885 (2004).

16. *Kentucky v. King*, 131 S.Ct. 1849 (2011).

17. *California v. Greenwood*, 486 U.S. 35 (1988).

18. *Florida v. Bostick*, 59 LW 4708 (June 20, 1991).

19. *California v. Hodari D.*, 59 LW 4335
(April 23, 1991).

20. *Florida v. Jardines*, 569 U.S. ___ (Docket
No. 11-564 [2013]). Justice Antonin Scalia's
opinion stated that "to find a visitor
knocking on the door is routine (even if
sometimes unwelcome); to spot that same
visitor exploring the front path with a metal
detector, or marching his bloodhound into
the garden before saying hello and asking
permission, would inspire most of us to—
well, call the police." Scalia said using the
dog was no different from using thermal
imaging technology from afar to peer inside
homes without a warrant.

21. *Florida v. Harris*, 569 U.S. ___ (Docket No.
11-817 [2013]). In a unanimous decision,
the Supreme Court gave police authority
to use dogs to uncover illegal drugs at
traffic stops, upholding a police Labrador
retriever's search of a truck that uncovered
methamphetamine ingredients inside.

22. *Chimel v. California*, 395 U.S. 752 (1969).

23. *Maryland v. Buie*, 58 LW 4281 (1990).

24. *Arizona v. Gant*, 07-542 (2009).

25. *Maryland v. King*, Docket No. 12-207 (2013).

26. *Minnesota v. Dickerson*, 113 S.Ct. 2130
(1993).

27. *Maryland v. Wilson*, 117 S.Ct. 882 (1997).

28. *Carroll v. United States*, 267 U.S. 132 (1925).

29. *Harris v. United States*, 390 U.S. 234 (1968).

30. *Florida v. Jimeno*, 59 LW 4471 (May 23,
1991).

31. *Wyoming v. Houghton*, 119 S.Ct. 1297 (1999).

32. *Illinois v. Caballes*, 543 U.S. 405 (2005).

33. World Justice Project, "Who We Are,"
http://worldjusticeproject.org/rule-law-
index-map (accessed June 6, 2013).

34. *U.S. v. Jones*, 565 U.S. ___, 132 S.Ct. 945
(2012).

35. *Oliver v. United States*, 466 U.S. 170 (1984).

36. *California v. Ciraolo*, 476 U.S. 207 (1986).

37. *New York v. Class*, 54 LW 4178 (1986).

38. *Bumper v. North Carolina*, 391 U.S. 543 (1968).

39. *Stoner v. California*, 376 U.S. 483 (1964).

40. *Georgia v. Randolph*, 126 S.Ct. 1515 (2006).

41. *Katz v. United States*, 389 U.S. 347 (1967).

42. *Berger v. New York*, 388 U.S. 41 (1967).

43. *Lee v. United States*, 343 U.S. 747 (1952).

44. "Driver Consents to Search; Drugs
Found in Car," *The Journal Times*
(Racine County, Wis.), September 29,
2012, http://journaltimes.com/news/
local/crime-and-courts/police-reports-
driver-consents-to-search----drugs/
article_30f2d086-09ed-11e2-b880-
001a4bcf887a.html (accessed March 28,
2013).

45. "NHP: Traffic Stop Turns Up Pound of
Cocaine," *Reno Gazette Journal*, December
6, 2008, p. 2b.

46. John Kaplan, Jerome H. Skolnick, and
Malcolm M. Feeley, *Criminal Justice:
Introductory Cases and Materials*, 5th ed.
(Westbury, N.Y.: Foundation Press, 1991),
pp. 220–221.

47. *Berkemer v. McCarty*, 468 U.S. 420 (1984).

48. *Arizona v. Roberson*, 486 U.S. 675 (1988).

49. *Edwards v. Arizona*, 451 U.S. 477 (1981).

50. *Michigan v. Mosley*, 423 U.S. 93 (1975).

51. *Colorado v. Spring*, 479 U.S. 564 (1987).

52. *Connecticut v. Barrett*, 479 U.S. 523 (1987).

53. *Duckworth v. Eagan*, 109 S.Ct. 2875 (1989).

54. *U.S. v. Wade*, 388 U.S. 218 (1967).

55. *Kirby v. Illinois*, 406 U.S. 682 (1972).

56. *Foster v. California*, 394 U.S. 440 (1969).

57. *Powell v. Alabama*, 287 U.S. 45 (1932).

58. *Gideon v. Wainwright*, 372 U.S. 335 (1963).

59. *Argersinger v. Hamlin*, 407 U.S. 25 (1973).

60. *Escobedo v. Illinois*, 378 U.S. 478 (1964).

CHAPTER 9

1. Erwin C. Surrency, "The Courts in the
American Colonies," *American Journal of
Legal History* 11 (1967), p. 258.

2. Kermit Hall, *The Magic Mirror: Law in
American History* (New York: Oxford
University Press, 1989).

3. Surrency, "The Courts in the American
Colonies," p. 258.

4. Freda Adler, Gerhard O. W. Mueller, and
William S. Laufer, *Criminal Justice: An
Introduction* (Boston: McGraw-Hill, 2006),
pp. 325–326.

5. Alexis de Tocqueville, *Democracy in
America*, Vol. 1, trans. H. Reeve (New York:
D. Appleton, 1904), pp. 283–284.

6. H. Ted Rubin, *The Courts: Fulcrum of the
Justice System* (Santa Monica, Calif.:
Goodyear, 1976), p. 3.

7. Stephen Whicher and R. Spiller, eds., *The
Early Lectures of Ralph Waldo Emerson*
(Philadelphia: University of Pennsylvania
Press, 1953), p. 112.

8. 382 U.S. 406 (1966), 416.

9. Howard Abadinsky, *Law and Justice: An
Introduction to the American Legal System*,
4th ed. (Chicago: Nelson-Hall, 1999), p. 174.

10. Ibid., p. 170.

11. U.S. Department of Justice, "Table 5.65:
Petitions Filed in U.S. District Courts by
Federal and State Prisoners," *Sourcebook
of Criminal Justice Statistics Online*,
http://www.albany.edu/sourcebook/pdf/
t5652010.pdf (accessed February 19, 2013).

12. Malcolm M. Feeley and Edward L. Rubin,
*Judicial Policy Making and the Modern
State: How the Courts Reformed America's
Prisons* (New York: Cambridge University
Press, 1998).

13. Stephen L. Wasby, *The Supreme Court
in the Federal System*, 3rd ed. (Chicago:
Nelson-Hall, 1989), p. 5.

14. Abadinsky, *Law and Justice*, p. 171.

15. Ibid., p. 166.

16. Ibid., pp. 81, 83.

17. Ibid., p. 82.

18. Ibid., pp. 82–83.

19. Bureau of Justice Statistics, *State Court
Organization, 1987–2004* (Washington,
D.C.: U.S. Department of Justice, October
2007), p. 3.

20. Cassie Spohn and Craig Hemmens, *Courts: A Text/Reader* (Thousand Oaks, Calif.: Sage, 2008), p. 10.

21. Denise Lavoie, "Budget Cuts Force Tough Choices on Court Security," *Associated Press*, January 11, 2010, http://www.boston.com/news/local/maine/articles/2010/01/10/budget_cuts_force_tough_choices_on_court_security/ (accessed January 18, 2013).

22. Mike Blasky and Frances McCabe, "Court Officer, Suspect Killed in Federal Courthouse Shooting," http://www.lvrj.com/news/courthouse-shooting-80624367.html (accessed February 19, 2013).

23. Gary Hengstler, "Judicial Violence: Tipping the Scales," *Case in Point* (Summer/Fall 2006), pp. 3–5.

24. Ibid., p. 3.

25. Ibid.

26. Center for Judicial and Executive Security, LLC, *Disorder in the Court: Incidents of Courthouse Violence* (January 2012), p. 6, http://www.cjesconsultants.com/assets/documents/CJES-JCVI-Disorder-in-the-Court-Incidents-IV.pdf (accessed February 19, 2013).

27. Don Hardenbergh and Neil Alan Weiner, "Preface," *The Annals of the American Academy of Political and Social Science* 576 (July 2001), p. 10.

28. Bryan Vossekuil, Randy Borum, Robert Fein, and Marisa Reddy, "Preventing Targeted Violence Against Judicial Officials and Courts," *The Annals of the American Academy of Political and Social Science* 576 (July 2001), pp. 78–90.

29. Susan Voyles, "Shooting Sparks Worries About Safety," *Reno Gazette-Journal*, June 14, 2006, p. 1C.

30. See GovTrackUS, "H.R. 1751 [109th]: Court Security Improvement Act of 2006," http://www.govtrack.us/congress/bill.xpd?bill=h109-1751 (accessed February 18, 2013).

31. David W. Neubauer, *America's Courts and the Criminal Justice System,* 8th ed. (Belmont, Calif.: Thomson Wadsworth, 2005), p. 81.

32. Ibid., pp. 402–403.

33. American Bar Association, "FAQs About the Grand Jury System," http://www.abanow.org/2010/03/faqs-about-the-grand-jury-system/ (accessed May 29, 2013).

34. Arlen Specter, book review, 76 *Yale Law Journal* 604 (1967), pp. 606–607.

35. Alvin Rubin, "How We Can Improve Judicial Treatment of Individual Cases Without Sacrificing Individual Rights: The Problems of the Criminal Law," *Federal Rules Decisions* 70 (1976), p. 176.

36. John Nisbet, *Burma Under British Rule—and Before*, Vol. I (London: Archibald Constable & Co., 1901), p. 177.

37. Cora L. Daniels and C. M. Stevans, eds., *Encyclopedia of Superstitions, Folklore, and the Occult Sciences of the World, Vol. III* (Milwaukee: J. H. Yewdale & Sons Co., 1903), p. 1243.

38. Absoluteastronomy.com, "Trial by Ordeal," http://www.absoluteastronomy.com/topics/Trial_by_ordeal (accessed February 18, 2013).

39. 399 U.S. 78, 86 (1970).

40. *Apodaca v. Oregon*, 406 U.S. 404 (1972).

41. Larry Larue, "Excuses Endless When Trying to Evade Jury Duty," *Tacoma News Tribune,* November 5, 2012, http://www.thenewstribune.com/2012/11/05/2355840/excuses-endless-when-trying-to.html (accessed February 16, 2013).

42. "Jury Duty Excuses Could Bring Charges," July 10, 2007, http://newsok.com/jury-duty-excuses-could-bring-charges/article/3080282 (accessed February 16, 2013).

43. See *Brady v. Maryland*, 373 U.S. 83 (1963).

44. Neubauer, *America's Courts and the Criminal Justice System*, p. 263.

45. See Thomas Alexander Fyfe, *Charles Dickens and the Law* (London: Chapman and Hall, 1910), pp. 28–29.

46. Charles Dickens, *Bleak House* (London: Penguin Book, 1971; first published in 1853).

47. William Shakespeare, *Hamlet*, Act 3, Scene 1.

48. *Strunk v. United States*, 412 U.S. 434 (1973).

49. Speedy Trial Act of 1974, 18 U.S.C.S. §§ 3161–3174 (as amended, 1979).

50. *Barker v. Wingo,* 407 U.S. 514 (1972).

51. Ibid.

52. Ibid., p. 522.

53. American Prosecutors Research Institute, *Basic Trial Techniques for Prosecutors* (May 2005), http://www.ndaa.org/pdf/basic_trial_techniques_05.pdf (accessed May 30, 2013).

54. Justia, "Criminal Appeals Overview," http://www.justia.com/criminal/criminal-appeals/ (accessed February 19, 2013).

55. *Douglas v. California*, 372 U.S. 353 (1963).

56. *Ross v. Moffitt*, 417 U.S. 600 (1974).

57. Neubauer, *America's Courts and the Criminal Justice System*, p. 85.

58. Ibid., p. 87

59. Bureau of Justice Statistics, *State Court Organization, 1987–2004* (Washington, D.C.: U.S. Department of Justice, October 2007), p. 3.

60. National Center for State Courts, *Examining the Work of the State Courts: An Analysis of 2010 State Court Caseloads*, p. 37, http://www.courtstatistics.org/Other-Pages/~/media/Microsites/Files/CSP/DATA%20PDF/CSP_DEC.ashx (accessed February 19, 2013).

61. Neubauer, *America's Courts and the Criminal Justice System*, p. 85.

62. Supreme Court of the United States, "A Brief Overview of the Supreme Court," http://www.supremecourt.gov/about/briefoverview.aspx (accessed February 19, 2013).

63. David W. Neubauer, *America's Courts and the Criminal Justice System,* 9th ed. (Belmont, Calif.: Thomson Wadsworth, 2008), p. 63.

64. Supreme Court of the United States, "Instructions for Admission to the Bar," http://www.supremecourtus.gov/bar/barinstructions.pdf (accessed January 12, 2013).

65. Robert H. Jackson Center, "The Flags at Nuremberg," http://www.roberthjackson.org/the-man/speeches-articles/speeches/speeches-related-to-robert-h-jackson/the-flags-at-nuremberg/ (accessed February 18, 2013).

66. Supreme Court of the United States, "The Court and its Traditions," http://www.supremecourtus.gov/about/traditions.pdf (accessed January 11, 2013).

67. COURTECHFORUM, "Cameras in the Courtrooms: Pro and Con," July 6, 2011, http://www.courtechforum.com/2011/07/06/cameras-in-the-courtroom-pros-and-cons/ (accessed February 18, 2013).

68. Zanto Peabody, "Blake Case Revives Issue of Cameras in Court," *Los Angeles Times*, May 27, 2002, p. 1A.

69. Ibid.

70. S. L. Alexander, "Cameras in the Courtroom: A Case Study," *Judicature* 74 (1991), pp. 307–313; Paul Raymond, "The Impact of a Televised Trial on Individuals' Information and Attitudes," *Judicature* 57 (1992), pp. 204–209.

71. See United States Courts, "U.S. Supreme Court Procedures," http://www.uscourts.gov/EducationalResources/ConstitutionResources/SeparationOfPowers/USSupremeCourtProcedures.aspx (accessed February 19, 2013).

72. Ibid.

73. Supreme Court of the United States, "The Justices' Caseload," http://www.supremecourt.gov/about/justicecaseload.aspx; also see, as examples of written opinions, Supreme Court of the United States, "2011 Term Opinions of the Court," http://www.supremecourt.gov/opinions/slipopinions.aspx?Term=11 (accessed February 19, 2013).

74. Ibid.; see the *Rules of the Supreme Court of the United States*, generally, at http://www.supremecourt.gov/ctrules/2010RulesoftheCourt.pdf (accessed February 19, 2013).

75. Federal Judicial Center, "The U.S. Courts of Appeals and the Federal Judiciary," http://www.fjc.gov/history/home.nsf (accessed February 19, 2013).

76. Federal Judicial Center, "The U.S. District Courts and the Federal Judiciary," http://www.fjc.gov/history/home.nsf/page/courts_district.html (accessed February 15, 2013).

77. HG.org, "Global Legal Resources," http://www.hg.org/international-law.html (accessed February 19, 2013).

78. Ibid.

79. International Court of Justice, "The Court," http://www.icj-cij.org/court/index.php?p1=1 (accessed February 19, 2013).

80. Keith Suter, *The International Court of Justice*, http://global-directions.com/Articles/Peace%20and%20Conflict/InternationalCourtof Justice.pdf (accessed February 19, 2013).

CHAPTER 10

1. Samuel J. Brakel and Alexander D. Brooks, *Law and Psychiatry in the Criminal Justice System* (Buffalo, N.Y.: William S. Hein, 2001), p. 130.

2. Quoted in David Landy and Elliott Aronson, "The Influence of the Character of the Criminal and His Victims on the Decisions of Simulated Jurors," *Journal of Experimental Social Psychology* 5 (1969), pp. 141–142.

3. Abraham Blumberg, *Criminal Justice* (Chicago: Quadrangle Books, 1967), p. 120.

4. See, for example, Pennsylvanians for Modern Courts, "Choosing Judges," http://www.pmconline.org/node/25 (May 30, 2013).

5. Bureau of Justice Statistics, *State Court Organization, 2004* (Washington, D.C.: U.S. Department of Justice, October 2006), p. 23.

6. American Judicature Society, *Judicial Selection in the States: How It Works, Why It Matters* (Des Moines, Iowa: Author, 2008), p. 4.

7. American Judicature Society, *Judicial Selection in the States*, p. 4.

8. ABA Journal, "O'Connor on Judicial Elections: 'They're Awful. I Hate Them,'" http://www.abajournal.com/news/oconnor_chemerinsky_sound_warnings_at_aba_conference_about_the_dangers_of_s/ (accessed February 24, 2013).

9. Ibid.

10. Law.com, "O'Connor Says Judges Shouldn't be Elected," http://www.law.com/jsp/law/LawArticleFriendly.jsp?id=1194429842107 (accessed February 24, 2013).

11. Martha Neil, "Top Court Hears Judicial Influence Case, Leans Toward Stricter Recusal Standard," *ABA Journal,* http://www.abajournal.com/news/top_court_hears_judicial_influence_case_leans_toward_stricter_recusal_stand (accessed February 24, 2013).

12. Jeff Cranson, *The Grand Rapids Press*, "The Price of Justice: High Court Wrestles with a Case That Should Spark Discussion in Michigan," March 3, 2009, http://blog.mlive.com/talkingpolitics/2009/03/the_price_of_justice_high_cour.html (accessed February 22, 2013).

13. American Judicature Society, *Judicial Selection in the States*, p. 4.

14. Blumberg, *Criminal Justice*, p. 120.

15. Russell R. Wheeler and Howard R. Whitcomb, *Judicial Administration: Text and Readings* (Englewood Cliffs, N.J.: Prentice-Hall, 1977), p. 370.

16. Ibid., p. 372.

17. Ibid.

18. Ibid.

19. Ibid., p. 373.

20. William A. Batlitch, "Reflections on the Art and Craft of Judging," *The Judges Journal* 43, no. 4 (Fall 2003), pp. 7–8.

21. Charles E. Patterson, "The Good Judge: A Trial Lawyer's Perspective," *The Judges Journal* 43, no. 4 (Fall 2003), pp. 14–15.

22. See, for example, Allen K. Harris, "The Professionalism Crisis—The 'Z' Words and Other Rambo Tactics: The Conference of Chief Justices' Solution," 53 S.C. L. Rev. 549, 589 (2002).

23. *In re First City Bancorp of Tex., Inc.*, 282 F.3d 864 (5th Cir. 2002).

24. Marla N. Greenstein, "The Craft of Ethics," *The Judges Journal* 43, no. 4 (Fall 2003), pp. 17–18.

25. Ty Tasker, "Sticks and Stones: Judicial Handling of Invective in Advocacy," *The Judges Journal* 43, no. 4 (Fall 2003), pp. 17–18.

26. Collins T. Fitzpatrick, "Building a Better Bench: Informally Addressing Instances of Judicial Misconduct," *The Judges' Journal* (Winter 2005), pp. 16–20.

27. Ibid., pp. 18–20.

28. Southern Poverty Law Center, "Are There Limits to Prosecutorial Discretion?" http://www.splcenter.org/get-informed/intelligence-report/browse-all-issues/2007/summer/legal-brief#.UafrguDn_cs (accessed May 30, 2013).

29. *Berger v. United States*, 295 U.S. 78 (1935).

30. *Maine v. Moulton*, 474 U.S. 159 (1985).

31. Legal Information Institute, "Effective Assistance of Counsel," http://www.law.cornell.edu/anncon/html/amdt6frag9_user.html (accessed April 29, 2013).

32. See California Innocence Project, "Ineffective Assistance of Counsel," http://californiainnocenceproject.org/issues-we-face/ineffective-assistance-of-counsel (accessed May 31, 2013).

33. Ibid.; also see *Strickland v. Washington*, 466 U.S. 668 (1984).

34. William A. Mintz, "Lawyer Wouldn't Go to 'Sleazy Bar,' Client Wins Freedom from Life Term," *National Law Journal*, November 24, 1980, p. 7.

35. FindLaw, "Plea Bargaining Pros and Cons," http://criminal.findlaw.com/criminal-procedure/plea-bargain-pros-and-cons.html (accessed May 30, 2013).

36. See, for example, Texas Fair Defense Project, "What Defense Lawyers Do," http://www.texasfairdefenseproject.org/info/right_to_counsel/defense_lawyers (accessed February 23, 2013).

37. 351 U.S. 12 (1956).

38. For more information about defense attorneys in general and indigent services in specific, see Cassia Spohn and Craig Hemmens, *Courts: A Text/Reader,* 2nd ed. (Los Angeles, Calif.: Sage, 2012), pp. 218–223.

CHAPTER 11

1. Quoted in Louis P. Carney, *Probation and Parole: Legal and Social Dimensions* (New York: McGraw-Hill, 1977), p. 75.

2. Francis T. Cullen and Paul Gendreau, "Assessing Correctional Rehabilitation: Policy, Practice, and Prospects," *Criminal Justice 2000*, p. 111, https://www.ncjrs.gov/criminal_justice2000/vol_3/03d.pdf (accessed May 31, 2013).

3. Brandon C. Welsh, "Monetary Costs and Benefits of Correctional Treatment Programs: Implications for Offender Reentry," *Federal Probation* (September 2004), p. 12, http://bcotn.org/subcommittees/csct/monetary_costs_and_benefits_of_correctional_treatment.pdf (accessed May 31, 2013).

4. Ibid., pp. 9–12.

5. Jacqueline Cohen, *Incapacitating Criminals: Recent Research Findings I* (Washington, D.C.: National Institute of Justice, Research in Brief, 1983), p. 2.

6. CBS News, "The Cost of a Nation of Incarceration," http://www.cbsnews.com/8301-3445_162-57418495/the-cost-of-a-nation-of-incarceration/ (accessed May 30, 2013). Query: Is deterrence lost when the public sees someone on death row who has not yet been executed for his or her capital offense perhaps 12, 15, or more years following the act? Is capital punishment a deterrent at all for murder?

7. John J. Dilulio Jr., "Prisons Are a Bargain, by Any Measure," *New York Times*, January 16, 1996, p. A17.

8. The discussion of the corrections models is adapted from Todd R. Clear, George F. Cole, and Michael D. Reisig, *American Corrections,* 8th ed. (Belmont, Calif.: Thomson Wadsworth, 2009), pp. 40–64; the discussion of the accompanying prison design and operation is adapted from Steven E. Schoenherr, "Prison Reforms in American History," http://history.sandiego.edu/gen/soc/prison.html (accessed February 19, 2013).

9. Quotes taken from the *Handbook of Correctional Institution Design and Construction* (U.S. Bureau of Prisons, 1949).

10. Amnesty International, "Death Sentences and Executions in 2011," http://www.amnesty.org/en/library/asset/ACT50/001/2012/en/241a8301-05b4-41c0-bfd9

-2fe72899cda4/act500012012en.pdf; also see ibid., *The Death Penalty in 2011*, http://amnesty.org/en/death-penalty/death-sentences-and-executions-in-2011 (accessed February 19, 2013).

11. Tracy L. Snell, *Capital Punishment 2010* (Washington, D.C.: U.S. Department of Justice, Bureau of Justice Statistics, December 2011), http://www.bjs.gov/index.cfm?ty=pbdetail&iid=2236 (accessed February 19, 2013).

12. "U.S. Student Tells of Pain of His Caning in Singapore," *New York Times*, June 26, 1994, http://www.nytimes.com/1994/06/26/us/us-student-tells-of-pain-of-his-caning-in-singapore.html?pagewanted=1 (accessed February 19, 2013).

13. Bureau of Justice Statistics, "Expenditures/Employment," http://www.bjs.gov/index.cfm?ty=tp&tid=16 (accessed February 19, 2013).

14. Bureau of Justice Statistics, *State Corrections Expenditures, FY 1982-2010* (Washington, D.C.: U.S. Department of Justice, December 2011), http://bjs.ojp.usdoj.gov/content/pub/pdf/scefy8210.pdf (accessed February 19, 2013).

15. Adapted from U.S. Department of Justice, National Institute of Corrections, and Association of Paroling Authorities International, *A Handbook for New Parole Board Members* (April 2003), http://www.apaintl.org/documents/CEPPParoleHandbook.pdf (accessed January 19, 2013), p. 3.

16. Quoted by Sheldon G. Glueck in his "Foreword" to John V. Barry, *Alexander Maconochie of Norfolk Island* (Melbourne: Oxford University Press, 1958).

17. Mark Allenbaugh, "The Supreme Court's New Blockbuster U.S. Sentencing Guidelines Decision," http://writ.news.findlaw.com/allenbaugh/20050114.html (accessed February 19, 2013).

18. At 18 U.S.C. Secs. 3551–3626 and 28 U.S.C. Secs. 991–998 (October 12, 1984).

19. Allenbaugh, "The Supreme Court's New Blockbuster U.S. Sentencing Guidelines Decision."

20. Lisa M. Seghetti and Alison M. Smith, *Federal Sentencing Guidelines: Background, Legal Analysis, and Policy Options* (Congressional Research Service Report for Congress, June 30, 2007), http://www.fas.org/sgp/crs/misc/RL32766.pdf (accessed February 19, 2013).

21. *Blakely v. Washington,* 542 U.S. (2004).

22. *United States v. Booker,* 543 U.S. 125 (2005).

23. Allenbaugh, "The Supreme Court's New Blockbuster U.S. Sentencing Guidelines Decision," p. 2.

24. *Gall v. United States*, 552 U.S. 38 (2007).

25. *Kimbrough v. United States*, 552 U.S. 85 (2007).

26. *2011 Washington State Sentencing Guidelines Manual*, http://www.cfc.wa.gov/PublicationSentencing/SentencingManual/Adult_Sentencing_Manual_2011.pdf (accessed January 28, 2013).

27. The National Center for Victims of Crime, "Victim Impact Statements," http://www.victimsofcrime.org/help-for-crime-victims/get-help-bulletins-for-crime-victims/victim-impact-statements (accessed February 19, 2013).

28. *Payne v. Tennessee*, 501 U.S. 808 (1991).

29. *Snyder v. Massachusetts*, 291 U.S. 97 (1934), at 122.

30. James Q. Wilson, *Thinking about Crime* (New York: Vintage Books, 1985), p. 260.

31. H. Naci Mocan and R. Kaj Gittings, "Getting Off Death Row: Commuted Sentences and the Deterrent Effect of Capital Punishment," *Journal of Law and Economics* 46 (October 2003), pp. 453–478.

32. Hashem Dezhbakhsh, Paul H. Rubin, and Joanna M. Shepherd, "Does Capital Punishment Have a Deterrent Effect? New Evidence from Postmoratorium Panel Data," *American Law and Economics Review* 5, no. 2 (2003), pp. 344–376.

33. Paul R. Zimmerman, "State Executions, Deterrence, and the Incidence of Murder," *Journal of Applied Economics* 7, no. 1 (May 2004), pp. 163–193.

34. Paul R. Zimmerman, "Estimates of the Deterrent Effect of Alternative Execution Methods in the United States: 1978–2000," *American Journal of Economics and Sociology* 65, no. 4 (October 2006), pp. 909–941.

35. Richard Berk, "New Claims about Executions and General Deterrence: Déjà Vu All Over Again?" *Journal of Empirical Legal Studies* 2 (2005), pp. 303–330.

36. Jeffrey Fagan, "Death and Deterrence Redux: Science, Law and Causal Reasoning on Capital Punishment," *Ohio State Journal of Criminal Law* 4 (2006), pp. 255–320.

37. Quoted in Amnesty International, "Death Penalty and Race," http://www.amnestyusa.org/death-penalty/death-penalty-facts/death-penalty-and-race/page.do?id=1101091 (accessed February 19, 2013).

38. Ibid.

39. Ibid.

40. *Furman v. Georgia*, 408 U.S. 238 (1972).

41. *Gregg v. Georgia*, 428 U.S. 153 (1976).

42. *Roper v. Simmons,* 543 U.S. 551 (2005).

43. *Ford v. Wainwright*, 477 U.S. 399 (1986).

44. *Kennedy v. Louisiana*, 554 U.S. ___ (2008).

45. *Strickland v. Washington*, 466 U.S. 668 (1984)

46. *Witherspoon v. Illinois*, 391 U.S. 510 (1968).

47. *Baze v. Rees*, 553 U.S. 35 (2008).

48. *Hill v. Florida*, No. SC06-2 (2006).

49. Death Penalty Information Center, "The Innocence List," http://www.deathpenaltyinfo.org/innocence-list-those-freed-death-row (accessed February 19, 2013).

50. Innocence Project, "Facts on Post-conviction DNA Exoneration," http://www.innocenceproject.org/Content/351.php (accessed February 19, 2013).

51. Pew Center on the States, "Illinois, Nebraska Study Death Penalty as Others Quicken Use," http://www.stateline.org/live/ViewPage.action?siteNodeId=136&languageId=1&contentId=13798 (accessed February 13, 2013); also see The Clark County Prosecuting Attorney, "Capital Punishment Timeline," http://www.clarkprosecutor.org/html/death/timeline.htm (accessed February 19, 2013).

52. *Roper v. Simmons*, 125 S.Ct. 1183.

53. *Ring v. Arizona*, 536 U.S. 584 (2002).

54. Adapted from *Nevada Revised Statutes* 200.033.

55. Adapted from *Nevada Revised Statutes* 200.035.

56. Justia.com, "Criminal Appeals," http://www.justia.com/criminal/criminal-appeals/ (accessed May 31, 2013).

57. *Douglas v. California*, 372 U.S. 353 (1963).

58. *Griffin v. Illinois*, 351 U.S. 12 (1956).

59. *Ross v. Moffitt*, 417 U.S. 600 (1974).

CHAPTER 12

1. Erving Goffman, *Asylums* (Garden City, N.Y.: Anchor Books, 1961), p. 5.

2. Ibid., p. 6.

3. Bureau of Justice Statistics, *Prisoners in 2011* (Washington, D.C.: U.S. Department of Justice, December 2012), p. 1, http://bjs.ojp.usdoj.gov/content/pub/pdf/p11.pdf (accessed March 12, 2013).

4. Bureau of Justice Statistics, *Jail Inmates at Midyear 2011—Statistical Tables* (Washington, D.C.: U.S. Department of Justice, April 26, 2012), http://bjs.ojp.usdoj.gov/index.cfm?ty=pbdetail&iid=4293 (accessed March 12, 2013).

5. See, for example, Deanne Katz, "What's the Difference Between Jail and Prison?" *FindLaw*, December 10, 2012, http://blogs.findlaw.com/blotter/2012/12/whats-the-difference-between-jail-and-prison.html (accessed August 15, 2013).

6. Bureau of Justice Statistics, *Jail Inmates at Midyear 2011—Statistical Tables* (Washington, D.C.: U.S. Department of Justice, April 26, 2012), http://www.bjs.gov/index.cfm?ty=pbdetail&iid=4293 (accessed May 31, 2013).

7. Bureau of Justice Statistics, *Capital Punishment, 2010—Statistical Tables* (Washington, D.C.: U.S. Department of Justice, December 20, 2011), http://bjs.ojp.usdoj.gov/index.cfm?ty=pbdetail&iid=2236 (accessed March 12, 2013).

8. Bureau of Justice Statistics, *State Corrections Expenditures, FY 1982–2010* (Washington, D.C.: U.S. Department of

Justice), p. 1, http://bjs.ojp.usdoj.gov/content/pub/pdf/scefy8210.pdf (accessed March 12, 2013).

9. See William J. Newman and Charles L. Scott, "*Brown v. Plata*: Prison Overcrowding in California," *Journal of the American Academy of Psychiatry Law* 40, no. 4 (December 2012), pp. 547–552, http://www.jaapl.org/content/40/4/547.full (accessed May 31, 2013).

10. Bureau of Justice Statistics, *Prisoners in 2011* (Washington, D.C.: U.S. Department of Justice), p. 4.

11. Ibid., pp. 1, 9.

12. See the Violent Offender Incarceration and Truth-in-Sentencing Incentive Grants program, Public Law 103–322, 108 Stat. 1796 (1994).

13. U.S. Department of Justice, *Bureau of Justice Statistics Special Report: Truth in Sentencing in State Prisons* (Washington, D.C.: Author, 1999), pp. 1–3.

14. "Attitudes Toward Whether the Criminal Justice System Should Try to Rehabilitate Criminals," *Sourcebook of Criminal Justice Statistics*, p. 139, http://www.albany.edu/sourcebook/pdf/t246.pdf (accessed March 12, 2013).

15. T. Paul Louis and Jerry R. Sparger, "Treatment Modalities within Prison," *Are Prisons Any Better? Twenty Years of Correctional Reform*, ed. John W. Murphy and Jack E. Dison (Newbury Park, Calif.: Sage, 1990), p. 148; also see Francis T. Cullen, Paula Smith, Christopher T. Lowenkamp, and Edward J. Latessa,"Nothing Works Revisited: Deconstructing Farabee's *Rethinking Rehabilitation*," *Victims and Offenders* 4 (2009), pp. 101–123, http://www.uc.edu/content/dam/uc/ccjr/docs/articles/nothing_works_revisted.pdf (accessed May 31, 2013).

16. Ibid., p. 149.

17. Ted Palmer, "The 'Effectiveness' Issue Today: An Overview," *Federal Probation* 42 (1983), pp. 3–10.

18. Ibid.

19. See D. A. Andrews, "Program Structure and Effective Correctional Practices: A Summary of the CAVIC Research," *Effective Correctional Treatment*, ed. Robert R. Ross and Paul Gendreau (Toronto, Canada: Butterworth, 1980); R. Peters, *Deviant Behavioral Contracting with Conduct Problem Youth* (Kingston, Canada: Queen's University, 1981).

20. Quoted in Andrews, "Program Structure and Effective Correctional Practices," p. 42.

21. Richard P. Seiter, *Correctional Administration: Integrating Theory and Practice* (Upper Saddle River, N.J.: Prentice Hall, 2002), p. 11.

22. Franklin E. Zimring and Gordon J. Hawkins, *Deterrence: The Legal Threat in Crime Control* (Chicago: University of Chicago Press, 1973).

23. Joan Petersilia, "When Probation Becomes More Dreaded Than Prison," *Federal Probation* 54 (March 1990), pp. 27.

24. Ibid.

25. Ibid.

26. Ibid., p. 25.

27. Ibid.

28. Robert B. Levinson, "Classification: The Cornerstone of Corrections," *Prison and Jail Administration: Practice and Theory,* ed. Peter M. Carlson and Judith Simon Garrett (Boston: Jones and Bartlett, 2006), pp. 261–267.

29. Ibid., p. 262.

30. Ibid., pp. 262–263.

31. James Austin and Patricia L. Hardyman, *Objective Prison Classification: A Guide for Correctional Agencies* (Washington, D.C.: National Institute of Corrections, July 2004); also see R. Buchanan, "National Evaluation of Objective Prison Classification Systems: The Current State of the Art," *Crime & Delinquency* 32, no. 3 (1986), pp. 272–290.

32. U.S. Department of Justice, *Bureau of Justice Statistics Bulletin, Prison and Jail Inmates at Midyear 1998* (Washington, D.C.: U.S. Government Printing Office, 1999), pp. 1, 7.

33. National Sheriffs' Association, *The State of Our Nation's Jails, 1982* (Washington, D.C.: Author, 1982), p. 55.

34. See a description of such a jail in use and its benefits, by the Corrections Center of Northwest Ohio, "The New Generation Direct Supervision Jail," http://www.ccnoregionaljail.org/newgenerationjail.htm (accessed June 5, 2013).

35. Linda L. Zupan, *Jails: Reform and the New Generation Philosophy* (Cincinnati, Ohio: Anderson, 1991), p. 67.

36. U.S. Department of Justice, *National Institute of Justice Research in Brief, Making Jails Productive* (Washington, D.C.: Author, 1987), p. 1.

37. Ibid., p. 16.

38. Ibid., p. 192.

39. James A. Inciardi, *Criminal Justice,* 7th ed. (Fort Worth, Tex.: Harcourt Brace, 2001), p. 454.

40. Ibid., p. 194.

41. United States Bureau of Prisons, *Unit Management Manual* (Washington, D.C.: Author, 1977), p. 6.

42. Seiter, *Correctional Administration*, p. 196.

43. U.S. Bureau of Prisons, "Prison Types & General Information," http://www.bop.gov/locations/institutions/index.jsp (accessed March 12, 2013).

44. U.S. Bureau of Prisons, "About the Bureau of Prisons," http://www.bop.gov/about/index.jsp (accessed March 12, 2013).

45. *Barber v. Thomas*, No. 09–5201. (9th Cir., 2010).; also see U.S. Department of Justice, United States Parole Commission, *History of the Federal Parole System*, http://www.usdoj.gov/uspc/history.pdf (accessed March 12, 2013).

46. Laura Sullivan, "Timeline: Solitary Confinement in U.S. Prisons," http://www.npr.org/templates/story/story.php?storyId=5579901 (accessed March 12, 2013).

47. Ibid.

48. Terry Frieden, "Reporters Get First Look Inside Mysterious Supermax Prison," *CNN.com/U.S.,* September 14, 2007, http://www.cnn.com/2007/US/09/13/supermax.btsc/index.html (accessed March 13, 2013).

49. Craig Haney, "Mental Health Issues in Long-Term Solitary and 'Supermax' Confinement," *Crime & Delinquency* 49, no. 1 (January 2003), pp. 124–156.

50. See ibid., however.

51. Jesenia Pizarro and Vanja M. K. Stenius, "Supermax Prisons: Their Rise, Current Practices, and Effect on Inmates," *The Prison Journal* 84, no. 2 (June 2004), pp. 248–264.

52. Ibid., p. 260.

53. *Madrid v. Gomez,* 889 F. Supp. 1146 (1995), at p. 1229.

54. "The Ten Worst Prisons in the World," http://www.thetoptenworld.com/violent_prisons.html (accessed March 10, 2013).

55. At 374 F.3d 541 (7th Cir. 2004), at p. 1118.

56. Thomas Hayden, "Putting Down a Riot," *U.S. News and World Report*, June 14, 2004, pp. 72–73.

57. Ibid.

58. Shane Peterson, "The Internet Moves Behind Bars," *Government Technology* (Supplement: *Crime and the Tech Effect*) (April 2001), p. 18.

59. Jim McKay, "Virtual Visits," *Government Technology* (October 2001), p. 46.

60. South University, "Prison Security Goes High-Tech," http://source.southuniversity.edu/prison-security-goes-hightech-24647.aspx (accessed March 30, 2013).

61. "Start Jamming Prisoner Cell Phones," *The Post and Courier*, January 22, 2013, http://www.postandcourier.com/article/20130122/PC1002/130129834/1268/start-jamming-prisoner-cell-phones&source=RSS (accessed March 30, 2013).

62. Tom McNichol, "Prison Cell-Phone Use a Growing Problem," *Time.com*, May 26, 2009, http://www.time.com/time/nation/article/0,8599,1900859,00.html (accessed March 30, 2013).

63. "Start Jamming Prisoner Cell Phones."

CHAPTER 13

1. At 475 U.S. 312.

2. John J. DiIulio Jr., *Governing Prisons: A Comparative Study of Correctional Management* (New York: Free Press, 1987), p. 167.

3. State of Arizona, Office of the Governor, *The Morey Unit Hostage Incident: Preliminary Findings and Recommendations* (Phoenix, Ariz.: Author), p. 1.

4. Ohio History Central, "Lucasville Prison Riot," http://www.ohiohistorycentral.org/entry.php?rec=1634 (accessed February 23, 2013).

5. Tribune News Services, "Meet Captors' Demands, Hostages Urge," *Chicago Tribune News*, December 17, 1999, http://articles.chicagotribune.com/1999-12-17/news/9912170075_1_warden-todd-louvierre-jolie-sonnier-female-guard (accessed February 23, 2013).

6. Associated Press, "Officials: Inmates Talked of Killing Jail Hostage," *St. Petersburg Times,* September 8, 2004, http://www.sptimes.com/2004/09/08/State/Officials__Inmates_ta.shtml (accessed February 23, 2013).

7. National Institute of Justice, *Resolution of Prison Riots* (Washington, D.C.: U.S. Department of Justice, October 1995), pp. 1–2.

8. For an examination and comparison of these two extremely violent prison riots, see Sue Mahan, "An Orgy of Brutality at Attica and the Killing Ground at Santa Fe: A Comparison of Prison Riots," in *Prison Violence in America* 2nd ed., ed. Michael C. Braswell, Reid H. Montgomery Jr., and Lucien X. Lombardo (Cincinnati, Ohio: Anderson, 1994), pp. 253–264.

9. Thomas A. Zlaket, personal communication to Hon. Janet Napolitano, Governor of Arizona, October 25, 2004.

10. Kelly Taylor and Jilian Flight, *Hostage-Taking Incidents Involving Women Inmates: A Profile and Exploratory Investigation* (Ottawa, Ontario, Canada: Correctional Service of Canada, 2003), p. 5.

11. David Ensor, "U.S. Captures Mastermind of Achille Lauro Hijacking," http://www.cnn.com/2003/WORLD/meast/04/15/sprj.irq.abbas.arrested (accessed February 23, 2013).

12. See for example, Kenneth J. Peak, Eric Radli, Cecil Pearson, and Darin Balaam, "Hostage Situations in Detention Settings: Planning and Tactical Considerations," *FBI Law Enforcement Bulletin* 77, no. 10, pp. 1–14.

13. Bureau of Justice Statistics, *Jail Inmates at Midyear 2010—Statistical Tables* (Washington, D.C.: U.S. Department of Justice, April 2011), p. 1, http://bjs.ojp.usdoj.gov/content/pub/pdf/jim10st.pdf (accessed February 23, 2013).

14. Quoted in Advisory Commission on Intergovernmental Relations, *Jails: Intergovernmental Dimensions of a Local Problem* (Washington, D.C.: Author, 1984), p. 1.

15. Gordon Hawkins, *The Prison* (Chicago: University of Chicago Press, 1976).

16. Jess Maghan, "Correctional Officers in a Changing Environment: 21st Century—USA," http://www.jmfcc.com/CorrOfficersChangingEnvirnmnt.pdf (accessed February 23, 2013).

17. Ben M. Crouch, *The Keepers: Prison Guards and Contemporary Corrections* (Springfield, Ill.: Charles C Thomas, 1980), p. 73.

18. Peter Finn, *Addressing Correctional Officer Stress: Programs and Strategies* (Washington, D.C.: U.S. Department of Justice, National Institute of Justice, December 2000), p. 2, https://www.ncjrs.gov/pdffiles1/nij/183474.pdf (accessed May 31, 2013).

19. Richard Hawkins and Geoffrey P. Alpert, *American Prison Systems: Punishment and Justice* (Upper Saddle River, N.J.: Prentice Hall, 1989), p. 340.

20. Ibid., p. 345.

21. See Lee H. Bowker, *Prison Victimization* (New York: Elsevier, 1980), Chapter 7.

22. Maghan, "Correctional Officers in a Changing Environment."

23. Ibid.

24. State Representative Bertram L. Podell, quoted in Linda Charlton, "Deaths Decried; Critics Disagree," *New York Times*, September 14, 1971, http://jfk.hood.edu/Collection/White%20%20Files/Attica/Attica%20050.pdf (accessed February 23, 2013).

25. Ibid.

26. Ibid.

27. Adapted from Lucien X. Lombardo, *Guards Imprisoned: Correctional Officers at Work* (Cincinnati, Ohio: Anderson, 1989), pp. 51–71.

28. Robert Bayer, personal communication, November 12, 2009.

29. John J. DiIulio Jr., *Governing Prisons: A Comparative Study of Correctional Management* (New York: Free Press, 1987), p. 37.

30. Bayer, personal communication.

31. John Slansky, personal communication, October 28, 1993.

32. Ibid.

33. Timothy J. Flanagan and Kathleen Maguire, eds., *Sourcebook of Criminal Justice Statistics 1991* (Washington, D.C.: U.S. Government Printing Office, 1992), p. 555.

34. Ibid.; also see Kathleen Maguire and Ann L. Pastore, eds., *Sourcebook of Criminal Justice Statistics 1995* (Washington, D.C.: U.S. Government Printing Office, 1996), p. 177.

35. Public Law No. 104-134, 110 Stat. 1321 [codified as amended in scattered sections of 18 U.S.C., 28 U.S.C., and 42 U.S.C.] (1996).

36. See 141 *Congressional Record* S14413 (daily ed., Sept. 27, 1995), Senator Robert Dole's statement in his introduction of the PLRA as a bill to the Senate. Senator Dole provided other examples of the frivolous litigation that he felt the PLRA was needed to cure: "insufficient storage locker space, a defective haircut by a prison barber, [and] the failure of prison officials to invite a prisoner to a pizza party for a departing prison employee."

37. U.S. Courts, "Caseload Statistics, 2009," Table C3, http://www.uscourts.gov/Statistics/FederalJudicialCaseloadStatistics/FederalJudicialCaseloadStatistics2009.aspx (accessed June 5, 2013).

38. Bureau of Justice Statistics, *Prisoners in 2011* (Washington, D.C.: U.S. Department of Justice, December 2012), p. 9, http://bjs.ojp.usdoj.gov/content/pub/pdf/p11.pdf (accessed February 23, 2013).

39. Thomas E. Feucht and Andrew Keyser, *Reducing Drug Use in Prisons: Pennsylvania's Approach* (Washington, D.C.: National Institute of Justice Journal, October 1999), p. 11.

40. Ibid., pp. 11–12.

41. Ibid., pp. 14–15.

42. Federal Bureau of Investigation, "Table 33. Ten-Year Arrest Trends by Sex, 2002–2011," *Crime in the United States—2011* (Washington, D.C.: U.S. Department of Justice), http://www.fbi.gov/about-us/cjis/ucr/crime-in-the-u.s/2011/crime-in-the-u.s.-2011/tables/table-33 (accessed January 12, 2013).

43. American Civil Liberties Union, "Women in Prison," http://www.aclu.org/prisoners-rights/women-prison (accessed February 23, 2013).

44. Ibid.

45. Sandra Enos, *Mothering from the Inside: Parenting in a Women's Prison* (Albany: Sate University of New York Press, 2001).

46. Institute on Women and Criminal Justice, "Mothers, Infants and Imprisonment: A National Look at Prison Nurseries and Community-Based Alternatives" (May 2009), p. 9, http://www.wpaonline.org/pdf/Mothers%20Infants%20and%20Imprisonment%202009.pdf (accessed February 23, 2013).

47. Jocelyn M. Pollock-Byrne, "Women in Prison: Why Are Their Numbers Increasing?" in *Corrections: Dilemmas and Directions*, eds. Peter J. Benekos and Alida V. Merlo (Cincinnati, Ohio: Anderson, 1992), p. 91.

48. Kathryn Watterson Burkhart, *Women in Prison* (New York: Doubleday, 1973), pp. 365–366.

49. Christine E. Rasche, *Special Needs of the Female Offender: Curriculum Guide for Correctional Officers* (Tallahassee: Florida Department of Education, n.d.), p. 68.

50. Bureau of Justice Statistics, *Sourcebook of Criminal Justice Statistics Online* (Washington, D.C.: U.S. Department of Justice), p. 53 http://www.albany.edu/sourcebook/index.html (accessed May 31, 2013).

51. Pam Belluck, "Mentally Ill Inmates Are at Risk Isolated, Suit Says," *New York Times*, March 9, 2007, p. A10.

52. U.S. Department of Justice, "About Violent Gangs," http://www.usdoj.gov/criminal/gangunit/about/prisongangs.html (accessed May 15, 2009).

53. National Gang Intelligence Center, *National Gang Threat Assessment 2011* (Washington, D.C.: U.S. Department of Justice), http://www.fbi.gov/stats-services/publications/2011-national-gang-threat-assessment/2011-national-gang-threat-assessment-emerging-trends, p. 11 (accessed February 23, 2013).

54. Joel Samaha, *Criminal Justice* (St. Paul, Minn.: West, 1988), p. 558.

55. James Jacobs, *Stateville: The Penitentiary in Mass Society* (Chicago: University of Chicago Press, 1977).

56. John Irwin, *Prisons in Turmoil* (Boston: Little, Brown, 1980).

57. George M. Camp and Camille G. Camp, *The Correctional Year Book* (South Salem, N.Y.: Criminal Justice Institute, 1987).

58. Bureau of Justice Statistics, *Capital Punishment, 2010—Statistical Tables*, (Washington, D.C.: U.S. Department of Justice, December 2011), pp. 1, 6, http://bjs.ojp.usdoj.gov/content/pub/pdf/cp10st.pdf (accessed February 23, 2013).

59. See Robert Johnson, *Death Work: A Study of the Modern Execution Process*, 2nd ed. (Belmont, Calif.: West/Wadsworth, 1998); Robert Johnson, "This Man Has Expired," *Commonweal* (January 13, 1989), pp. 9–15.

60. Ibid.

61. Bureau of Justice Statistics, *Capital Punishment, 2010—Statistical Tables*, p. 6.

62. Amnesty International, "Figures on the Death Penalty," http://www.amnesty.org/en/death-penalty/numbers (accessed March 10, 2013).

63. Death Penalty Information Center, "Executions by Year Since 1976," http://www.deathpenaltyinfo.org/executions-year (accessed May 31, 2013).

64. Amnesty International, "Death Penalty 2011: Alarming Levels of Executions in the Few Countries That Kill," http://www.amnesty.org/en/news/death-penalty-2011-alarming-levels-executions-few-countries-kill-2012-03-27 (accessed March 10, 2013).

65. Ibid.

66. Ibid.

67. *Roper v. Simmons*, 543 U.S. 551 (2005).

68. *Atkins v. Virginia*, 536 U.S. 304 (2002).

69. *Ruffin v. Commonwealth*, 62 Va. 790 (1871).

70. *Cooper v. Pate*, 378 U.S. 546, 384 S Ct 1733 (1964).

71. *Johnson v. Avery*, 393 U.S. 483, 89 S.Ct. 747 (1969).

72. *Bounds v. Smith*, 430 U.S. 817, 97 S.Ct. 1491 (1977).

73. *Cruz v. Beto*, 405 U.S. 319, 92 S. Ct. 1079 (1972).

74. *Procunier v. Martinez*, 416 U.S. 396, 94 S. Ct. 1800 (1974).

75. *Estelle v. Gamble*, 429 U.S. 974, 97 S.Ct. 285 (1976).

76. *Wolff v. McDonnell*, 418 U.S. 539, 394 S. Ct. 296 (1974).

77. Tyjen Tsai and Paola Scommegna, "U.S. Has the World's Highest Incarceration Rate," Population Reference Bureau, http://www.prb.org/Articles/2012/us-incarceration.aspx (accessed June 6, 2913)

78. International Centre for Prison Studies, "More Than Ten Million Prisoners in the World, New Report Shows," http://www.prisonstudies.org/news/all/140-more-than-ten-million-prisoners-in-the-world,-new-report-shows.html (accessed June 5, 2013).

79. Jack Henry Abbott, *In the Belly of the Beast: Letters from Prison* (New York: Vintage Books, 1981), p. x.

80. Gresham Sykes, *The Society of Captives: A Study of Maximum Security Prison* (Princeton, N.J.: Princeton University Press, 1974), p. 65.

81. John Randolph Fuller, *Criminal Justice: Mainstream and Crosscurrents*, 2nd ed. (Upper Saddle River, N.J.: Prentice Hall, 2010), p. 396.

82. Sykes, *The Society of Captives*, p. 12.

83. Donald Clemmer, *The Prison Community* (New York: Holt, Rinehart, & Winston, 1940).

84. Jeanne B. Stinchcomb, *Corrections: Past, Present, and Future* (Lanham, Md.: American Correctional Association, 2005), p. 306.

85. Ibid., p. 307.

86. Ibid.

87. Gresham Sykes and Sheldon Messinger, "The Inmate Social Code," in *The Sociology of Punishment and Corrections*, eds. Normal Johnston, Leonard Savitz, and Marvin Wolfgang (New York: Wiley, 1970), pp. 401–408.

CHAPTER 14

1. Peter J. Benekos, "Beyond Reintegration: Community Corrections in a Retributive Era," *Federal Probation* 54 (March 1990), p. 53.

2. See the President's Commission on Law Enforcement and Administration of Justice, *Task Force Report: Corrections* (Washington, D.C.: U.S. Government Printing Office, 1967), p. 7.

3. Benekos, "Beyond Reintegration," p. 53.

4. Belinda R. McCarthy, *Intermediate Punishments: Intensive Supervision, Home Confinement, and Electronic Surveillance* (Monsey, N.Y.: Criminal Justice Press, 1987), p. 3.

5. Barry J. Nidorf, "Community Corrections: Turning the Crowding Crisis into Opportunities," *Corrections Today* (October 1989), p. 85.

6. Benekos, "Beyond Reintegration," p. 54.

7. Although neither the word *probation* nor today's definition of it appear in the Bible, it was historically assumed that all mankind was under the sentence of eternal death—an endless life in misery during this life. However, humans could escape this sentence through repentance and faith in Christ; this was man's "probation," an opportunity to escape hell and secure heaven; if he failed to improve this opportunity, and died impenitent, the sentence was irrevocably executed and the man was eternally lost. See Tentmaker, "Probation," http://www.tentmaker.org/books/SpiritOfTheWord/014Probation.htm (accessed February 16, 2013).

8. Howard Abadinsky, *Probation and Parole: Theory and Practice*, 3rd ed. (Englewood Cliffs, N.J.: Prentice Hall, 1987), p. 18.

9. Lawrence M. Friedman, *A History of American Law* (New York: Simon and Schuster, 1973), p. 518.

10. Paul F. Cromwell Jr., George C. Killinger, Hazel B. Kerper, and Charles Walker, *Probation and Parole in the Criminal Justice System*, 2nd ed. (St. Paul, Minn.: West, 1985).

11. John Augustus, *John Augustus, First Probation Officer* (Montclair, N.J.: Patterson Smith, 1972), pp. 4–5.

12. John Augustus, *A Report of the Labors of John Augustus* (Boston: Wright & Hasty, 1852) (republished in 1984 by the American Probation and Parole Association, Lexington, Ky., pp. 96–97).

13. Abadinsky, *Probation and Parole*, p. 143.

14. Torsten Eriksson, *The Reformers: An Historical Survey of Pioneer Experiments in the Treatment of Criminals* (New York: Elsevier, 1976), p. 81.

15. Abadinsky, *Probation and Parole*, pp. 146–147.

16. The issues concerned whether parole (1) infringed on the power of the judiciary to sentence, the governor to pardon, or the legislature to determine penalty levels; (2) denied prisoners due process; or (3) constituted cruel and unusual punishment.

17. U.S. Attorney General's Survey of Release Procedures, *Parole*, Vol. 4 (New York: Arno Press, 1974), p. 20.

18. Sheldon L. Messinger, "Introduction," *The Question of Parole: Retention, Reform, or Abolition?* ed. Andrew von Hirsch and Kathleen J. Hanrahan (Cambridge, Mass.: Ballinger, 1970), pp. xviii–xix.

19. U.S. Attorney General's Survey of Release Procedures, *Parole*, p. 20.

20. Laura M. Maruschak and Erika Parks, *Probation and Parole in the United States, 2011* (Washington, D.C.: U.S. Department of Justice, Bureau of Justice Statistics, November 2012), pp. 1–2, http://www.bjs.

gov/content/pub/pdf/ppus11.pdf (accessed February 16, 2013).

21. Ibid., p. 7.

22. Robert M. Regoli and John D. Hewitt, *Exploring Criminal Justice: The Essentials* (Sudbury, Mass.: Jones and Bartlett, 2010), p. 316.

23. Adapted from Michael Muskal, "Two of Casey Anthony's Four Convictions Overturned by Appeals Court," *Los Angeles Times,* January 25, 2013, http://www.latimes.com/news/nation/nationnow/la-na-nn-casey-anthony-appeals-court-20130125,0,3022534.story (accessed February 16, 2013); "Judge Perry Rules on Casey Probation," *WESH Orlando,* August 12, 2011, http://www.wesh.com/news/casey-anthony-extended-coverage/Judge-Perry-Rules-On-Casey-Probation/-/13479888/13130886/-/item/0/-/po7t4vz/-/index.html (accessed February 16, 2013). Judge Perry ruled that Anthony must serve a year of supervised probation, with the Florida Department of Corrections to keep Anthony's residential information confidential. Perry said in the order he did not want any information released that could lead to the discovery of her location.

24. Laura M. Maruschak and Erika Parks, *Probation and Parole in the United States, 2011* (Washington, D.C.: U.S. Department of Justice, Bureau of Justice Statistics, November 2012), p. 6, http://www.bjs.gov/content/pub/pdf/ppus11.pdf (accessed May 31, 2013).

25. *Mempa v. Rhay,* 389 U.S. 128 (1967).

26. *Gagnon v. Scarpelli,* 411 U.S. 778 (1973).

27. Maruschak and Parks, *Probation and Parole in the United States, 2011,* p. 20.

28. Park Dietz, "Hypothetical Criteria for the Prediction of Individual Criminality," *Dangerousness: Probability and Prediction, Psychiatry, and Public Policy* ed. in Christopher Webster, Mark Ben-Aron, and Stephen Hucker (Cambridge, UK: Cambridge University Press, 1985), p. 32.

29. *Morrissey v. Brewer,* 92 S.Ct. 2593 (1972).

30. Ibid.

31. Manson was denied parole for the 12th time in April 2012. The parole board duly noted that he had recently bragged to a prison psychologist, "I'm special. I'm not like the average inmate. I have spent my life in prison. I have put five people in the grave. I am a very dangerous man." The board stated: "This panel can find nothing good as far as suitability factors go." See Christina Ng, "Charles Manson Denied Parole After Saying He Is a 'Very Dangerous Man,'" *ABC News,* April 11, 2012, http://abcnews.go.com/US/charles-manson-denied-parole-dangerous-man/story?id=16111128 (accessed February 16, 2013).

32. Council of State Governments Justice Center, *The Impact of Probation and Parole Populations on Arrests in Four California Cities* (January 2013), p. 4, http://www.cdcr.ca.gov/Reports/docs/External-Reports/CAL-CHIEFS-REPORT.pdf (accessed June 4, 2013).

33. Ibid., p. 1.

34. Ibid., p. 17.

35. Ibid., p. 6.

36. U.S. Bureau of Labor Statistics, "Occupational Outlook Handbook: Probation Officers and Correctional Treatment Specialists," http://www.bls.gov/ooh/Community-and-Social-Service/Probation-officers-and-correctional-treatment-specialists.htm#tab-2 (accessed February 16, 2013).

37. Ibid.

38. H. S. Ntuli, V. I. Khoza, J. M. Ras, and P. J. Potgieter, "Role Conflict in Correctional Supervision," *Acta Criminologica* 20, no. 4 (2007), pp. 85–95.

39. Ibid.

40. John Conrad, "The Pessimistic Reflections of a Chronic Optimist," *Federal Probation* 55 (June 1991), pp. 4–9.

41. Matthew T. DeMichele, *Probation and Parole's Growing Caseloads and Workload Allocation: Strategies for Managerial Decision Making* (Lexington, Ky.: American Probation and Parole Association), pp. 14–15, http://www.appa-net.org/eweb/docs/appa/pubs/SMDM.pdf (accessed February 16, 2013).

42. M. Claxton, N. Sinclair, and R. Hanson, "Felons on Probation Often Go Unwatched," *Detroit News*, December 10, 2002, p. 2.

43. DeMichele, *Probation and Parole's Growing Caseloads and Workload Allocation*, pp. 13, 33.

44. Shawn E. Small and Sam Torres, "Arming Probation Officers: Enhancing Public Confidence and Officer Safety," *Federal Probation* 65, no. 3 (2001), pp. 24–28.

45. Richard P. Seiter, *Correctional Administration: Integrating Theory and Practice* (Upper Saddle River, N.J.: Prentice Hall, 2002), p. 387.

46. Bureau of Justice Statistics, *U.S. Jail Population Declines for Third Consecutive Year* (Washington, D.C.: U.S. Department of Justice, April 25, 2012), http://bjs.ojp.usdoj.gov/content/pub/press/jim11stpr.cfm (accessed February 16, 2013).

47. Howard Abadinsky, *Probation and Parole: Theory and Practice,* 7th ed. (Upper Saddle River, N.J.: Prentice Hall, 2000), p. 410.

48. Joan Petersilia and Susan Turner, *Evaluating Intensive Supervision Probation/Parole: Results of a Nationwide Experiment* (Washington, D.C.: National Institute of Justice, 1993).

49. Lawrence A. Bennett, "Practice in Search of a Theory: The Case of Intensive Supervision—An Extension of an Old Practice," *American Journal of Criminal Justice* 12 (1988), pp. 293–310.

50. Ibid., p. 293.

51. This information was compiled from ISP brochures and information from the Oregon Department of Corrections by Joan Petersilia.

52. Todd R. Clear and Patricia R. Hardyman, "The New Intensive Supervision Movement," *Crime & Delinquency* 36 (January 1990), pp. 42–60.

53. Ibid., p. 44.

54. Barbara A. Sims, "Questions of Corrections: Public Attitudes Toward Prison and Community-Based Programs," *Corrections Management Quarterly* 1, no. 1 (1997), p. 54.

55. Jeffery T. Ulmer, "Intermediate Sanctions: A Comparative Analysis of the Probability and Severity of Recidivism," *Sociological Inquiry* 71, no. 2 (Spring 2001), pp. 164–193.

56. Ibid., p. 184.

57. Ibid., p. 185.

58. Bureau of Justice Assistance, *Offender Supervision with Electronic Technology: Community Corrections Resource,* 2nd ed. (U.S. Department of Justice, 2009), p. 16, http://www.appa-net.org/eweb/docs/APPA/pubs/OSET_2.pdf (accessed May 31, 2013).

59. Lynh Bui, "Electronic Monitoring OK'd for DUI Offenders," AZCentral.com, http://www.azcentral.com/community/scottsdale/articles/2010/04/28/20100428scottsdale-electronic-monitoring.html (accessed May 31, 2013).

60. Annesley K. Schmidt, "Electronic Monitors: Realistically, What Can Be Expected?" *Federal Probation* 59 (June 1991), pp. 47–53.

61. Abadinsky, *Probation and Parole,* p. 428.

62. David Brauer, "Satellite 'Big Brother' Tracks Ex-Inmates," *Chicago Tribune,* December 18, 1998, p. 31.

63. Jeanne B. Stinchcomb and Vernon B. Fox, *Introduction to Corrections*, 5th ed. (Upper Saddle River, N.J.: Prentice Hall, 1999), p. 165.

64. Gaylene Styve Armstrong, Angela R. Gover, and Doris Layton MacKenzie, "The Development and Diversity of Correctional Boot Camps," *Turnstile Justice: Issues in American Corrections,* eds. Rosemary L. Gido and Ted Alleman (Upper Saddle River, N.J.: Prentice Hall, 2002), pp. 115–130.

65. Doris Layton MacKenzie, "Boot Camp Prisons and Recidivism in Eight States," *Criminology* 33, no. 3 (1995), pp. 327–358.

66. Doris Layton MacKenzie and Alex Piquero, "The Impact of Shock Incarceration Programs on Prison Crowding," *Crime & Delinquency* 40, no. 2 (April 1994), pp. 222–249.

67. John Ashcroft, Deborah J. Daniels, and Sarah V. Hart, *Correctional Boot Camps: Lessons from a Decade of Research* (Washington, D.C.: U.S. Department of Justice, Office of Justice Programs, June 2003), p. 2.

68. Ibid.
69. Dale G. Parent, "Day Reporting Centers: An Evolving Intermediate Sanction," *Federal Probation* 60 (December 1996), pp. 51–54.
70. Liz Marie Marciniak, "The Addition of Day Reporting to Intensive Supervision Probation: A Comparison of Recidivism Rates," *Federal Probation* 64 (June 2000), pp. 34–39.
71. U.S. Department of Justice, National Institute of Justice, "Restorative Justice, http://www.ojp.usdoj.gov/nij/topics/courts/restorative-justice/welcome.htm (accessed February 16, 2013).
72. U.S. Department of Justice, National Institute of Justice, "Fundamental Concepts of Restorative Justice," http://www.ojp.usdoj.gov/nij/topics/courts/restorative-justice/fundamental-concepts.htm (accessed February 16, 2013).

CHAPTER 15

1. Federal Bureau of Investigation, "Table 41. Arrests: Persons Under 15, 18, 21, and 25 Years of Age, 2011," *Crime in the United States—2011* (Washington, D.C.: U.S. Department of Justice), http://www.fbi.gov/about-us/cjis/ucr/crime-in-the-u.s/2011/crime-in-the-u.s.-2011/tables/table-41 (accessed February 21, 2013)
2. R. Pickett, *House of Refuge: Origins of Juvenile Reform in New York State 1815–1857* (Syracuse, N.Y.: Syracuse University Press, 1969), p. 21.
3. A. M. Platt, *The Child Savers: The Invention of Delinquency,* 2nd ed. (Chicago, Ill.: University of Chicago Press, 1977).
4. *People ex rel O'Connell* v. *Turner,* 55 Ill. 280, 283-84, 287 (1870).
5. 1899 Ill. Laws 132 *et seq.*
6. Victor L. Streib, *Death Penalty for Juveniles* (Bloomington: Indiana University Press, 1987).
7. Robert E. Shepherd Jr., "The Juvenile Court at 100 Years: A Look Back," *Juvenile Justice* 6, no. 2 (December 1999), http://www.ncjrs.gov/html/ojjdp/jjjournal1299/2.html (accessed May 27, 2009).
8. Ibid.
9. Ibid.
10. Julian Mack, "The Juvenile Court," *Harvard Law Review* 23 (1909), pp. 104–122.
11. P. L. 93-415, 42 U.S.C. 5601 *et seq.*
12. Charles Puzzanchera, *Juvenile Arrests 2007* (Washington, D.C.: U.S. Department of Justice, Office of Juvenile Justice and Delinquency Prevention, April 2009), http://www.ncjrs.gov/pdffiles1/ojjdp/225344.pdf (accessed February 21, 2013).
13. Adapted from Gus Martin, *Juvenile Justice: Process and Systems* (Thousand Oaks, Calif.: Sage, 2005), pp. 64–67.
14. David W. Roush, *A Desktop Guide to Good Juvenile Detention Practice* (Washington, D.C.: Office of Juvenile Justice and Delinquency Prevention, 1996), pp. 26–27.
15. Ibid., pp. 23–24.
16. Both the text and the diagram are from U.S. Department of Justice, Office of Juvenile Justice and Delinquency Prevention Programs, "Juvenile Justice Structure and Process: Case Flow Diagram," http://www.ojjdp.gov/ojstatbb/structure_process/case.html (accessed February 21, 2013).
17. Juvenile Detention Alternatives Initiative, "About JDAI," http://www.jdaihelpdesk.org/SitePages/about.aspx (accessed June 1, 2013).
18. Annie E. Casey Foundation, *Detention Reform: A Cost-Saving Approach* (n.d.), http://www.aecf.org/upload/PublicationFiles/jdai_facts1.pdf (accessed June 3, 2013).
19. Adapted from U.S. Department of Justice, Bureau of Justice Statistics, "The Juvenile Justice System," http://www.ojp.usdoj.gov/bjs/justsys.htm#sentencing (accessed May 5, 2009).
20. *Kent v. United States*, 383 U.S. 541 (1966).
21. American Bar Association, "Still Seeking the Promise of *Gault*: Juveniles and the Right to Counsel," http://www.abanet.org/crimjust/juvjus/cjmag/18-2shep.html (accessed February 21, 2013).
22. American Bar Association, "For Schools: Lessons," http://www.abanet.org/publiced/lawday/schools/lessons/handout_gault.html (accessed February 21, 2013).
23. *Gault v. Arizona,* 387 US 1 (1967).
24. Ibid., p. 14.
25. *In Re Winship,* 397 U.S. 358 (1970).
26. *McKeiver v. Pennsylvania,* 403 U.S. 528 (1971).
27. *Breed v. Jones,* 421 U.S. 519 (1975).
28. *Roper v. Simmons,* 543 U.S. 551 (2005).
29. No. 09–11121 (2011).
30. *Miller v. Alabama*, 132 S. Ct. 2455 (2012); *Jackson v. Hobbs*, No. 10–9647 (2012).

CHAPTER 16

1. See, for example, a discussion of the "lone wolf model" of terrorism now in use here and abroad—and discussed in al-Qaeda publications—in Lori Hinnant, "Intel Dilemma in Boston, London, Paris Attacks," *Associated Press*, May 31, 2013, http://abcnews.go.com/International/wireStory/intel-dilemma-boston-london-paris-attacks-19294987#.UazbZuDn_cs (accessed June 3, 2013).
2. Quoted in M. K. Rehm and W. R. Rehm, "Terrorism Preparedness Calls for Proactive Approach," *Police Chief* (December 2000), pp. 38–43.
3. D. Westneat, "Terrorists Go Green," *U.S. News and World Report,* June 4, 2001, p. 28; also see "SUVs Torched in Pennsylvania," *Reno Gazette Journal,* January 5, 2003, p. 4A.
4. See Kenneth J. Peak, *Policing America: Challenges and Best Practices,* 8th ed. (Columbus, OH: Pearson Education, in press).
5. Ibid.
6. Ibid.
7. See, for example, "Reconstructing the Scene of the Boston Marathon Bombing," *New York Times*, April 23, 2013, http://www.nytimes.com/interactive/2013/04/17/us/caught-in-the-blast-at-the-boston-marathon.html?ref=bostonmarathon (accessed May 28, 2013).
8. Interpol, "Cybercrime," http://www.interpol.int/Crime-areas/Cybercrime/Cybercrime (accessed May 29, 2013).
9. "Admit Nothing and Deny Everything," *The Economist*, June 8, 2013, http://www.economist.com/news/china/21579044-barack-obama-says-he-ready-talk-xi-jinping-about-chinese-cyber-attacks-makes-one (accessed June 13, 2013).
10. Siobhan Gorman and Julian E. Barnes, "Cyber Combat: Act of War," *The Wall Street Journal*, May 30, 2011, http://online.wsj.com/article/SB10001424052702304563104576355623135782718.html (accessed June 13, 2013).
11. Michael Riley and John Walcott, "China-Based Hacking of 760 Companies Shows Cyber Cold War," December 14, 2011, http://www.bloomberg.com/news/2011-12-13/china-based-hacking-of-760-companies-reflects-undeclared-global-cyber-war.html (accessed June 11, 2013).
12. Dana A. Shea and Frank Gottron, *Small-Scale Terrorist Attacks Using Chemical and Biological Agents: An Assessment Framework and Preliminary Comparisons*, Congressional Research Service, Report for Congress, May 20, 2004, http://www.fas.org/irp/crs/RL32391.pdf (accessed May 28, 2013).
13. Edward J. Tully and E. L. Willoughby, "Terrorism: The Role of Local and State Police Agencies," National Executive Institute Associates, May 2002, http://www.neiassociates.org/terrorism-role-local-state-pol/ (accessed May 28, 2013).
14. D. G. Bolgiano, "Military Support of Domestic Law Enforcement Operations: Working Within Posse Comitatus," *FBI Law Enforcement Bulletin* (December 2001), pp. 16–24.
15. U.S. Department of Homeland Security, *National Incident Management System* (Washington, D.C.: Author, March 2004), pp. viii, ix.
16. Robert S. Mueller III, "Statement Before the Senate Judiciary Committee," September 17, 2008, http://www.fbi.gov/news/testimony/preparing-for-the-challenges-of-the-future (accessed May 28, 2013).

17. Gary Peck and Laura Mijanovich, "Give Us Security While Retaining Freedoms," *Reno Gazette Journal,* August 28, 2003, p. 9A.

18. "House Approves Patriot Act Renewal," http://www.cnn.com/2006/POLITICS/03/07/patriot.act/ (accessed May 28, 2013).

19. Jurist: Legal News and Research, "Bush Signs Military Commissions Act," http://jurist.law.pitt.edu/paperchase/2006/10/bush-signs-military-commissions-act.php (accessed January 2, 2007).

20. Ibid.

21. Liz Sidoti, "A Nation of Co-existing, Conflicted Values," *Associated Press*, May 28, 2013, http://www.boston.com/business/news/2013/05/28/column-nation-existing-conflicted-values/4gMny1sjdXt11AUDH5G0mK/story.html (accessed May 29, 2013).

22. Lev Grossman, "Drone Home," *Time*, February 11, 2013, pp. 26–33.

23. See "White House, Justice Officials Defend Drone Program After Release of Memo," *Associated Press* and *Fox News*, February 5, 2013, http://www.foxnews.com/politics/2013/02/05/senators-threaten-confrontation-with-obama-nominees-over-drone-concerns/ (accessed February 17, 2013).

24. Meghan Hoyer and Brad Heath, "Mass Killings Occur in USA Once Every Two Weeks," *USA Today*, December 19, 2012, http://www.usatoday.com/story/news/nation/2012/12/18/mass-killings-common/1778303/ (accessed December 21, 2012).

25. Tyrus W. Cobb, "The Debate over Gun Control," *Reno Gazette Journal*, January 13, 2013, p. 6A.

26. Hoyer and Heath, "Mass Killings Occur in USA Once Every Two Weeks."

27. Eric Talmadge, "Around World, Gun Rules, and Results, Vary Wildly," http://www.boston.com/news/world/asia/2013/01/27/around-world-gun-rules-and-results-vary-wildly/csGqz0HZFfDdLSWBadlJDN/story.html (accessed March 10, 2013).

28. "In Other Countries, Laws Are Strict and Work," *New York Times*, December 17, 2012, http://www.nytimes.com/2012/12/18/opinion/the-gun-challenge-strict-laws-work.html (accessed March 10, 2013).

29. Cobb, "The Debate over Gun Control," p. 6A.

30. Ibid.

31. Kelly Kennedy, "Gun Violence Has a High Cost," *USA Today*, March 8, 2013, http://www.usatoday.com/story/news/nation/2013/03/04/gunshot-wounds-medicaid-insurance-costs/1956445/ (accessed March 10, 2013).

32. Cobb, "The Debate over Gun Control," p. 6A.

33. Glenn Adams, "Mandatory Gun Ownership Provisions Under Consideration in Communities Across the Country," *Associated Press*, March 8, 2013, http://www.huffingtonpost.com/2013/03/08/mandatory-gun-ownership_n_2839799.html (accessed March 10, 2013).

34. Ibid.

35. Ray Hagar, "Gun Debate Comes Home," *Reno Gazette Journal*, February 17, 2013, pp. 1A, 8A.

36. "Colleges Become Major Front in Fight over Carrying Guns," *New York Times*, February 16, 2013, http://www.nytimes.com/2013/02/17/education/gun-advocates-push-for-more-access-on-campus.html?nl=todaysheadlines&emc=edit_th_20130217&_r=1& (accessed February 19, 2013).

37. Rob Reuteman, "The Cost-and-Benefit Arguments Around Enforcement," CNBC, April 20, 2010, http://www.cnbc.com/id/36600923 (accessed June 3, 2013).

38. ProCon.org, "20 Legal Medical Marijuana States and DC," *Medical Marijuana,* February 22, 2013, http://medicalmarijuana.procon.org/view.resource.php?resourceID=000881 (accessed February 28, 2013).

39. Matt Ferner, "One Marijuana Arrest Occurs Every 42 Seconds in U.S.: FBI Report," *The Huffington Post,* October 29, 2012, http://www.huffingtonpost.com/2012/10/29/one-marijuana-arrest-occu_n_2041236.html (accessed February 28, 2013).

40. BalancedPolitics.org, "Should Marijuana Be Legalized Under Any Circumstances?" http://www.balancedpolitics.org/marijuana_legalization.htm (accessed February 28, 2013).

41. Micah Cohen, "Marijuana Legalization and States Rights," *New York Times*, December 8, 2012, http://fivethirtyeight.blogs.nytimes.com/2012/12/08/marijuana-legalization-and-states-rights/?pagewanted=print (accessed February 28, 2013).

42. Law Enforcement Against Prohibition, "Who We Are," http://www.leap.cc/about/who-we-are/ (accessed February 28, 2013).

43. Ibid.

44. BalancedPolitics.org, "Should Marijuana Be Legalized Under Any Circumstances?"

45. Raven Clabough, "Colorado Governor Signs Marijuana Regulations into Law," *The New American,* May 31, 2013, http://www.thenewamerican.com/usnews/politics/item/15578-colorado-governor-signs-marijuana-regulations-into-law (accessed June 3, 2013).

46. John Ingold, "Colorado Pot Legalization: 30 Questions (and Answers)," *The Denver Post,* December 12, 2012, http://www.denverpost.com/breakingnews/ci_22184944/colorado-pot-legalization-30-questions-and-answers (accessed June 3, 2013).

47. See U.S. Department of Justice, Drug Enforcement Administration, "Title 21 CFR, Part 1300-1399," http://www.deadiversion.usdoj.gov/21cfr/cfr/index.html (accessed February 28, 2013).

48. Lizette Borelli, "Uruguay to Legalize Marijuana for Entire Country: Will the Bill Save Money and Lives?" *Medical Daily,* August 13, 2013, http://www.medicaldaily.com/uruguay-legalize-marijuana-entire-country-will-bill-save-money-and-lives-248250 (accessed August 13, 2013).

49. Natalie Dalton, "Marijuana Should Be Legalized Worldwide: Santos," *Colombia Reports*, October 25, 2011, http://colombiareports.com/marijuana-should-be-globally-legalized-santos/ (accessed August 13, 2013).

50. "Czech Republic Legalizes Medical Marijuana Use," *The Huffington Post*, February 15, 2013, http://www.huffingtonpost.com/2013/02/15/czech-republic-medical-marijuana_n_2693657.html (accessed August 13, 2013).

51. Arthur Brice, "Argentina Court Ruling Would Allow Personal Use of Pot," CNN.com/World, August 25, 2009, http://www.cnn.com/2009/WORLD/americas/08/25/argentina.drug.decriminalization/ (accessed August 13, 2013).

52. *Washington Post*, "Time to Legalize Marijuana in Mexico City" (editorial appearing in TicoTimes.net, July 27, 2013), http://www.ticotimes.net/More-news/News-Briefs/Time-to-legalize-marijuana-in-Mexico-City_Sunday-July-28-2013 (accessed August 13, 2013).

53. "Medical Marijuana: Research, Not Fear," *Los Angeles Times*, July 13, 2011, http://articles.latimes.com/2011/jul/13/opinion/la-ed-marijuana-20110713 (accessed February 28, 2013).

54. Charlie Savage, "Administration Weighs Legal Action Against States That Legalized Marijuana Use," *New York Times*, December 6, 2012, http://www.nytimes.com/2012/12/07/us/marijuana-initiatives-in-2-states-set-federal-officials-scrambling.html?_r=1& (accessed February 28, 2013).

55. Alex Dobuzinskis, "Marijuana Legalization Victories Could Be Short-Lived," *Reuters,* November 7, 2012, http://www.reuters.com/article/2012/11/08/us-usa-marijuana-votes-idUSBRE8A705E20121108 (accessed February 28, 2013).

56. Savage, "Administration Weighs Legal Action Against States That Legalized Marijuana Use."

57. Emily Swanson, "Marijuana Legalization Poll Finds Americans Want Federal Government to Leave States Alone," *The Huffington Post*, December 7, 2012, http://www.huffingtonpost.com/2012/12/07/marijuana-legalization-poll_n_2257106.html?view=print&comm_ref=false (accessed February 28, 2013).

INDEX

Page numbers in *italics* indicate illustrations, figures or tables.

PHOTO CREDITS

All images are copyright their respective owners.

About the Author
p. xxv: Tiffany Miller.

PART I

p. xx: AP Photo/Tracy Woodward

Chapter 1
p. 2: iStockphoto.com/Antonprado; p. 6: AP Photo/Damian Dovarganes; p. 7: North Wind Picture Archives via AP Images, John Michael Wright; p. 8: Maurice Quentin de La Tour; p. 11: iStockphoto.com/alptraum; p. 14: AP Photo/Julio Cortez, AP Photo/The Denver Post, RJ Sangosti, Pool, File; p. 15: AP Photo/Press of Atlantic City, Danny Drake; p. 16: ©iStockphoto.com/wsmahar.

Chapter 2
p. 24: AP Photo/Red Huber, Pool; p. 27: iStockphoto.com/jsp; p. 30: AP Photo/Pool, Myung J. Chun; p. 31: iStockphoto.com/ftwitty, U.S. National Archives and Records Administration, AP Photo/J. Scott Applewhite, Steve Petteway, Collection of the Supreme Court of the United States; p. 32: iStockphoto.com/fotograv, iStockphoto.com/Jason Lugo; p. 35: AP Photo/Joshua Polson, The Greeley Tribune; p. 36: San Quentin State Prison, California Department of Corrections and Rehabilitation, iStockphoto.com/Juanmonino; p. 38: iStockphoto.com/sturti; p. 42: AP Photo/Orlando Sentinel, Jacob Langston, Pool; p. 44: AP Photo/Judy Lineberger.

Chapter 3
p. 48: AP Photo/Jessica Hill; p. 52: AP Photo/Steve Pope; p. 53: Cesare Lombroso; p. 54: Walter Sanders/Time & Life Pictures/Getty Images; p. 55: iStockphoto.com/cgering; p. 56: Ferdinand Schmutzer; p. 57: AP Photo/Patrick Semansky; p. 61: AP Photo/Dave Martin; p. 65: AP Photo/Kathy Willens.

Chapter 4
p. 78: AP Photo/Mary Altaffer; p. 83: iStockphoto.com/dcdebs; p. 85: AP Photo/Jim Wells; p. 88: AP Photo/Felix Marquez, AP Photo/Drug Enforcement Agency; p. 92: AP Photo/The Citizen's Voice, Kristen Mullen; p. 96: AP Photo/The Salt Lake Tribune, Trent Nelson; p. 98: iStockphoto.com/terrymorris, iStockphoto.com/DNY59, iStockphoto.com/malerapaso.

PART II

p. 102: AP Photo/Milwaukee Journal-Sentinel, Mike De Sisti.

Chapter 5
p. 104: Andrew Burton/Getty Images News/Getty Images; p. 108: Hulton Archive/Getty Images; p. 109: AP Photo/Walter Zeboski; p. 111: James R. Tourtellotte, U.S. Customs and Border Protection – U.S. Department of Homeland Security, TSGT STEVE FAULISI, USAF; p. 115: Library of Congress Prints and Photographs Division, Harris & Ewing, Federal Bureau of Investigation; p. 116: United States Marshall Service; p. 122: iStockphoto.com/EdStock; p. 125: iStockphoto.com/Blend_Images.

Chapter 6
p. 130: iStockphoto.com/Anna Bryukhanova; p. 135: Najlah Feanny/CORBIS SABA, iStockphoto.com/JayLazarin; p. 137: iStockphoto.com/Imagesbybarbara; p. 139: iStockphoto.com/CribbVisuals; p. 141: iStockphoto.com/EdStock; p. 144: iStockphoto.com/Dieter Spears; p. 147: iStockphoto.com/Skyhobo; p. 149: AP Photo/Mike Groll; p. 150: AP Photo/The Tribune (of San Luis Obispo), Joe Johnston; p. 152: AP Photo/Santa Monica Daily Press, Paul Alvarez Jr.; p. 153: AP Photo/Mike Groll.

Chapter 7
p. 158: iStockphoto.com/sipkin; p. 162: AP Photo/Damian Dovarganes; p. 165: Charles Steiner/Image Works/Time Life Pictures/Getty Images, AP Photo/The Enterprise, Wayne Tilcock; p. 167: iStockphoto.com/code6d; p. 168: iStockphoto.com/JayLazarin; p. 170: Bettmann/CORBIS, iStockphoto.com/Allkindza; p. 171: AP Photo/Ross D. Franklin, Jim Rankin/Toronto Star/Getty Images; p. 173: Wikipedia User Junglecat; p. 174: AP Photo/The Gazette, Cliff Jette.

Chapter 8
p. 178: AP Photo/The Buffalo News, Derek Gee; p. 183: AP Photo/Greg Barnette/Record Searchlight; p. 184: iStockphoto.com/grandriver; p. 185: iStockphoto.com/SoCalShooter; p. 189: iStockphoto.com/Supersport; p. 190: iStockphoto.com/JayLazarin; p. 192: iStockphoto.com/kneafsey; p. 193: AP Photo/The Hutchinson News, Travis Morisse; p. 194:

Gerald L. Nino, CBP, U.S. Dept. of Homeland Security; p. 196: iStockphoto.com/Moodboard_Images.

PART III

p. 200: AP Photo/Don Heupel.

Chapter 9
p. 206: iStockphoto.com/ftwitty; p. 207: iStockphoto.com/Rich Legg; p. 216: AP Photo/Lori Shepler; p. 217: iStockphoto.com/dcdebs; p. 219: AP Photo/The Daily Reflector, Jenni Farrow; p. 222: AP Photo/Red Huber, iStockphoto.com/Moodboard_Images; p. 226: Kjetil Ree; Vince Bucci/AFP/Getty Images.

Chapter 10
p. 234: AP Photo/Eric Gay; p. 239: Steve Petteway; p. 244: iStockphoto.com/ EdStock; p. 247: John Munson/Star Ledger/Corbis; p. 249: AP Photo/Paul Buck; p. 250: Andrew Lichtenstein/Corbis.

Chapter 11
p. 254: AFP/Getty Images; p. 257: iStockphoto.com/duncan1890; p. 260: Mike Graham; p. 262: AP Photo; p. 264: AP Photo/Jessica Hill; p. 266: AP Photo/John Lovretta; p. 270: iStockphoto.com/EyeJoy; p. 271: California Department of Corrections and Rehabilitation; p. 274: AP Photo/Ron Heflin.

PART IV

p. 280: AP Photo/Don Heupel.

Chapter 12
p. 282: AP Photo/Rich Pedroncelli; p. 286: iStockphoto.com/jcarillet, AP Photo/California Department of Corrections; p. 288: AP Photo/Idaho Press-Tribune, Adam Eschbach; p. 290: AP Photo/Rich Pedroncelli; p. 294: iStockphoto.com/EdStock; p. 295: AP Photo/Rich Pedroncelli; p. 298: AP Photo/Pueblo Chieftain, Chris McLean; p. 301: AP Photo/Steve Pope.

Chapter 13
p. 306: Tony Avelar/The Christian Science Monitor/Getty Images; p. 309: AP Photo/Michael Conroy; p. 313: AP Photo/Bob Child; p. 316: AP Photo/Southern Illinoisan, Joe Jines; p. 317: AP Photo/Michael Conroy; p. 318: AP Photo/Rich Pedroncelli, Kevork Djansezian/

SAGE researchmethods

The essential online tool for researchers from the world's leading methods publisher

Find exactly what you are looking for, from basic explanations to advanced discussion

More content and new features added this year!

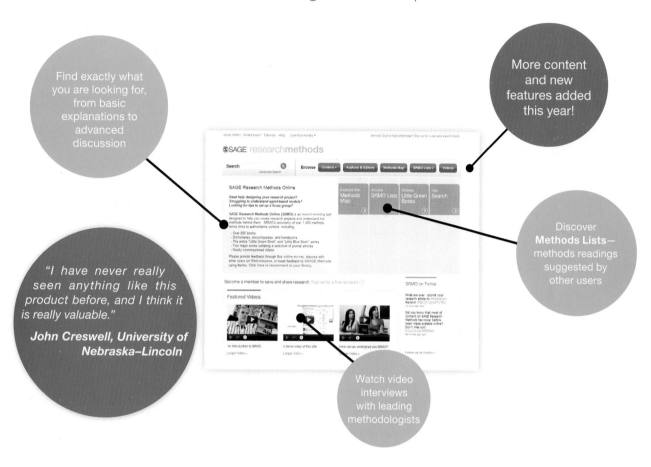

"I have never really seen anything like this product before, and I think it is really valuable."

John Creswell, University of Nebraska–Lincoln

Discover **Methods Lists**— methods readings suggested by other users

Watch video interviews with leading methodologists

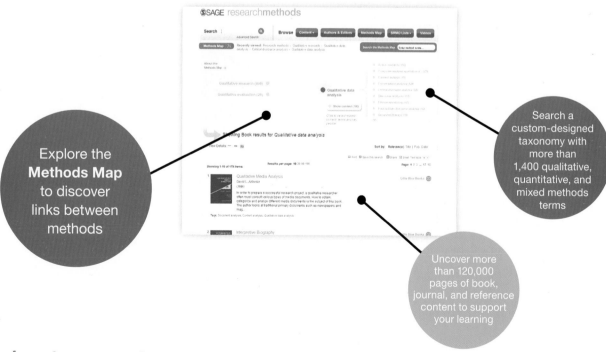

Explore the **Methods Map** to discover links between methods

Search a custom-designed taxonomy with more than 1,400 qualitative, quantitative, and mixed methods terms

Uncover more than 120,000 pages of book, journal, and reference content to support your learning

Find out more at
www.sageresearchmethods.com